D1264107

THE LOEB CLASSICAL LIBRARY

FOUNDED BY JAMES LOEB, LL.D.

MINOR LATIN POETS

MINOR LATIN POETS

WITH INTRODUCTIONS AND ENGLISH TRANSLATIONS BY

J. WIGHT DUFF

EMERITUS PROFESSOR OF CLASSICS, ARMSTRONG COLLEGE (IN THE UNIVERSITY OF DURHAM), NEWCASTLE-UPON-TYNE, FELLOW OF THE BRITISH ACADEMY

AND

ARNOLD M. DUFF

ASSISTANT LECTURER IN CLASSICS, UNIVERSITY COLLEGE OF WALES, ABERYSTWYTH

CAMBRIDGE, MASSACHUSETTS
HARVARD UNIVERSITY PRESS
LONDON
WILLIAM HEINEMANN LTD
MCMLXI

First edition 1934
Revised edition 1935
Reprinted 1954, 1961

Printed in Great Britain

CONTENTS

CONTENTS

CONTENTS

PREFACE

To select for inclusion in a single volume of the Loeb Library a series of works representing the minor poetry of Rome has been a task of much interest but of no little difficulty. The mere choice of poets and poems could hardly be thought easy by anyone acquainted with the massive volumes issued in turn by Burman senior and his nephew, the *Poetae Latini Minores* by the former (1731) and the *Anthologia Latina* by the latter (1759—1773). But a more serious difficulty confronted the editors; for, in spite of the labours of scholars since the days of Scaliger and Pithou on the minor poems collected from various sources, the text of many of them continues to present troublesome and sometimes irremediable *cruces*. This is notably true of *Aetna* and of Grattius; but even for the majority of the poems there cannot be said to be a *textus receptus* to be taken over for translation without more ado. Consequently the editors have had in most cases to decide upon their own text and to supply a fuller *apparatus criticus* than is needful for authors with a text better established. Certainly, the texts given by Baehrens in his *Poetae Latini Minores* could not be adopted wholesale; for his *scripsi* is usually ominous of alterations so arbitrary as to amount to a rewriting of the Latin.

At the same time, a great debt is due to Baehrens in his five volumes and to those who before him, like the Burmans and Wernsdorf, or after him, like

Vollmer, have devoted scholarly study to the *poetae Latini minores*. Two excellent reminders of the labours of the past in this field can be found in Burman's own elaborate account of his predecessors in the *Epistola Dedicatoria* prefixed to his *Anthologia*, and in the businesslike sketch which Baehrens' *Praefatio* contains. The editors' main obligations in connection with many problems of authorship and date may be gauged from the bibliographies prefixed to the various authors.

In making this selection it had to be borne in mind that considerable portions of Baehrens' work had been already included in earlier Loeb volumes—*e.g.* the *Appendix Vergiliana* (apart from *Aetna*) and the poems ascribed to Petronius. Also, the *Consolatio ad Liviam* and the *Nux*, both of which some scholars pronounce to be by Ovid, were translated in the Loeb volume containing *The Art of Love*. Other parts such as the *Aratea* of Germanicus were considered but rejected, inasmuch as an English translation of a Latin translation from the Greek would appear to be a scarcely suitable illustration of the genuine minor poetry of Rome. It was felt appropriate, besides accepting a few short poems from Buecheler and Riese, to add one considerable author excluded by Baehrens as dramatic, the mime-writer Publilius Syrus. He is the earliest of those here represented, so that the range in time runs from the days of Caesar's dictatorship up to the early part of the fifth century A.D., when Rutilius had realised, and can still make readers realise, the destructive powers of the Goths as levelled against Italy and Rome in their invasions. This anthology, therefore, may be regarded as one of minor imperial poetry extending over four and a half centuries. The arrangement is broadly chronological, though some poems, like the *Aetna*, remain of unsettled date and authorship.

While, then, the range in time is considerable, a correspondingly wide variety of theme lends interest to the poems. There is the didactic element—always typical of Roman genius—pervading not only the crisp moral saws of Publilius Syrus and the *Dicta Catonis*, but also the inquiry into volcanic action by the author of *Aetna* and the expositions of hunting-craft by Grattius and by Nemesianus; there is polished eulogy in the *Laus Pisonis*, and eulogy coupled with a plaintive note in the elegies on Maecenas; there is a lyric ring in such shorter pieces as those on roses ascribed to Florus. A taste for the description of nature colours the *Phoenix* and some of the brief poems by Tiberianus, while a pleasant play of fancy animates the work of Reposianus, Modestinus and Pentadius and the vignette by an unknown writer on *Cupid in Love*. Religious paganism appears in two *Precationes* and in the fourth poem of Tiberianus. Pastoral poetry under Virgil's influence is represented by Calpurnius Siculus, by the Einsiedeln Eclogues and by Nemesianus, the fable by Avianus, and autobiographic experiences on a coastal voyage by the elegiacs of Rutilius Namatianus. Although Rutilius is legitimately reckoned the last of the pagan classic poets and bears an obvious grudge against Judaism and Christianity alike, it should be noted, as symptomatic of the fourth century, that already among his predecessors traces of Christian thought and feeling tinge the sayings of the so-called "Cato" and the allegorical teaching of the *Phoenix* on immortality.

PREFACE

The English versions composed by the editors for this volume are mostly in prose; but verse translations have been written for the poems of Florus and Hadrian, for two of Tiberianus and one of Pentadius. Cato's *Disticha* have been rendered into heroic couplets and the *Monosticha* into the English iambic pentameter, while continuous blank verse has been employed for the pieces on the actor Vitalis and the two on the nine Muses, as well as for the *Cupid Asleep* of Modestinus. A lyric measure has been used for the lines by Servasius on *The Work of Time.* Some of the poems have not, so far as the editors are aware, ever before been translated into English.

The comparative unfamiliarity of certain of the contents in the miscellany ought to exercise the appeal of novelty. While *Aetna* fortunately engaged the interest of both H. A. J. Munro and Robinson Ellis, while the latter also did excellent service to the text of Avianus' *Fables*, and while there are competent editions in English of Publilius Syrus, Calpurnius Siculus and Rutilius Namatianus, there are yet left openings for scholarly work on the minor poetry of Rome. It possesses at least the merit of being unhackneyed: and the hope may be expressed that the present collection will direct closer attention towards the interesting problems involved.

Both editors are deeply grateful for the valuable help in copying and typing rendered by Mrs. Wight Duff.

July, 1934.

J. W. D.
A. M. D.

PREFATORY NOTE TO NEW EDITION

The editors are much gratified that the demand for this work has speedily made a second edition necessary. The fact has been appreciated that many of the authors represented are not easily accessible elsewhere, and that it is a convenience to have them united in a single volume. A few slight changes have been introduced and certain typographical errors corrected.

April 26, 1935.

J. W. D.
A. M. D.

PUBLILIUS SYRUS

INTRODUCTION
TO PUBLILIUS SYRUS

To the Caesarian age belonged two prominent writers of mimes with both of whom the great Julius came into contact—Decimus Laberius (105–43 B.C.) and Publilius Syrus. Publilius reached Rome, we are told by the elder Pliny,[a] in the same ship as Manilius, the astronomical poet, and Staberius Eros, the grammarian. As a dramatic performance the mime[b] had imported from the Greek cities of Southern Italy a tradition of ridiculing social life in tones of outspoken mockery; it represented or travestied domestic scandals with ribald language and coarse gestures. At times it made excursions into mythological subjects: at times it threw out allusions which bore or seemed to bear audaciously on politics. Audiences who were tiring of more regular comedy found its free-and-easy licence vastly amusing, though Cicero's critical taste made it hard for him to sit through a performance of pieces by Laberius and Publilius.[c]

[a] Plin. *N.H.* xxxv. 58 (199). The correct form of his name, instead of the erroneous "Publius," was established by Woelfflin, *Phil.* 22 (1865), 439.

[b] See Hermann Reich, *Der Mimus, ein litterarentwickelungs-geschichtlicher Versuch*, Berlin, 1903. For brief account, J. Wight Duff, *Lit. Hist. of Rome*, 1909, pp. 222–23; Klotz, *Gesch. der röm. Lit.*, 1930, p. 77.

[c] *Ad Fam.* XII. 18. 2.

INTRODUCTION

There came a day in 45 B.C. when Caesar forced the veteran knight Laberius—he was then sixty—to play in one of his own mimes as a competitor against the alien Publilius, who had thrown down a dramatic challenge to all comers. The dictator, while he awarded the prize to the foreigner, restored to the Roman, with ostentatious condescension, the ring which outwardly confirmed the equestrian rank sullied by his appearance on the stage. This eclipse of Laberius marked for Publilius an opportunity which he knew how to use. Some fresh invention, some originality in treatment capable of catching the popular favour, may be conjectured as the reason why the elder Pliny calls him "the founder of the mimic stage." Of Syrian origin, he had come to Rome as a slave, most likely from Antioch.[a] His wit secured his manumission, and the gift of understanding Roman psychology was a factor in his dramatic success. And yet, in contrast with forty-four known titles of plays by his vanquished rival Laberius, only two of Publilius' titles have come down to us in uncertain form—"The Pruners," *Putatores* (or, it has even been suggested, *Potatores*, "The Tipplers"), and one conjecturally amended to *Murmidon*.[b] Perhaps his improvisations were too precariously entrusted to actors' copies to guarantee literary immortality; and, in any case, though pieces of his were still staged under Nero, the mime gradually lost its vogue in favour of pantomime. The didactic element in him, however, was destined to survive. The elder Seneca praises him for

[a] Plin. *N.H. loc. cit. Publilium † lochium* (*Antiochium*, O. Jahn, *Phil.* 26, 11) *mimicae scenae conditorem.*

[b] Nonius, 2, p. 133; Priscian, *Gramm. Lat.* (Keil), 2, 532, 25.

putting some thoughts better than any dramatist, Greek or Roman; Petronius gives a specimen of his style in a passage sixteen lines long, and in the second century Gellius recognises the neatness and quotability of his moral maxims, of which he cites fourteen examples, all but one to be found in our extant collections.[a] Roman educators soon saw practical advantage in excerpting from his mimes, for use in school, wise saws and modern instances, the inherited experience of human conduct brought up to date in pithy Latin. Similar anthologies had already been made from Menander in Greek and very possibly from Ennius in Latin.[b] Such a text-book had been available for generations before Jerome [c] as a schoolboy learned the line "aegre reprendas quod sinas consuescere." But if the earliest collection of the maxims in the first century A.D. was purely Publilian, it is now hard to decide how much proverbial philosophy has been foisted into later collections by free paraphrase of genuine verses and by insertion of thoughts from Seneca (or Pseudo-Seneca) and others. It is equally hard to decide how much has been spoiled or lost by such misreading and distortion of genuine verses (iambic senarii or trochaic septenarii) as led copyists to mistake them for prose. There is, however, good authority for the acceptance of over 700 lines as genuine survivals of what was once a considerably larger selection.

It will be appreciated that Publilius' lines, originally

[a] Sen. *Controv.* VII. 3. 8; Petron. *Sat.* 55; Gell. *N.A.* xvii. 14.

[b] Phaedrus, III. *Epil.* 33–35.

[c] Hieron. *Epist.* 107, 8 (I. 679, Vallarsi): cited again *Epist.* 128, 4: see F. A. Wright, *Select Letters of St. Jerome* (Loeb Cl. Lib.), pp. 356, 478.

spoken by different dramatic characters, could not constitute a uniform ethical standard. In contrast, therefore, with generous sentiments we meet such self-regarding maxims as " It mayn't be right, but if it pays think it so " (quamvis non rectum quod iuvat rectum putes), or the pernicious morality of " The end justifies the means " (honesta turpitudo est pro causa bona). As in the proverbs of all nations, there are contradictory ways of looking at the same thing: while " Deliberation teaches wisdom " (deliberando discitur sapientia), it is also true that " Deliberation often loses a good chance " (deliberando saepe perit occasio); for the sagacity of the ages has always to reckon with both the impetuous and the over-cautious.

Further, if not necessarily either moral or consistent, proverbs are not necessarily profound. So if a few aphorisms dare to be paradoxical, some are the sheerest of platitudes. But, though shallow sayings take us nowhere, the reader meets with pleasure even familiar thoughts in Latin guise like " Honour among thieves " (etiam in peccato recte praestatur fides); " Least said, soonest mended " or *Qui s'excuse s'accuse* (male dictum interpretando facias acrius); " No man is a hero to his valet " (inferior rescit quicquid peccat superior); and " Touch wood ! " (irritare est calamitatem cum te felicem voces).

A few remarks on the manuscript collections are needed to indicate how the text is composed.[a] To

[a] Cf. Schanz-Hosius, *Gesch. der röm. Lit.* ed. 4, 1927, pp. 261–62; W. Meyer, *Die Sammlungen der Spruchverse des Publilius Syrus*, Leipzig, 1877, and the introd. to his edition of the *Sententiae*, Leipzig, 1880. Friedrich (ed. 1880) testifies to Woelfflin's full discussion of Publilian MSS. in the Prolegomena to his edition of 1869, II. pp. 15–23.

the so-called "Seneca Collection," of which the best manuscripts go back to the ninth or tenth century, and are classed under Σ in the Sigla, belong 265 verses arranged in sequence by their initials from A to N. Of these, 159 are preserved in that collection alone. By the ninth century the latter half of the verse-sayings from O to V had disappeared, and the collection was filled up with 149 prose *sententiae* from the so-called Senecan work *De Moribus.* The title then imposed on the collection was *Senecae sententiae* or *Senecae proverbia*: and in some manuscripts these proverbs, wherein Publilius lay embedded but unnamed, were combined with works of Augustine. This is true of the codex Dunelmensis, brought early in the fourteenth century to Durham, which has been inspected during the preparation of the present volume, and is described in a subsequent note. In the tenth century the latter half of the verse-sayings had reappeared: and the Π collection, now represented by lines A to I, in the Palatino-Vaticanus (formerly Heidelbergensis), supplied 325 additional verses. It was when Π still contained the second half of the sayings that a scribe in the eleventh century combined the texts of a Π and a Σ manuscript into Ψ, inserting any new verses from Π after the prose sentences under each alphabetical letter, so that his manuscript, F, the Frisingensis, is the most complete corpus of Publilian *sententiae* extant. To the 265 verse *sententiae* of Σ it added 384, making a total of 649. Gretser's Ingolstadt edition of 1600, four years before Gruter, made use of the Frisingensis. The Zürich Collection, Z, contains 132 sayings, including 50 not found elsewhere: it is represented by Turicensis C. 78 (tenth century), giving a set of *sententiae* C to V;

and Monacensis 6369 (eleventh century), giving a set of *sententiae* A to D. The Verona excerpts, O (fourteenth century), entitled *Flores moralium autoritatum*, give 60 verses (16 of them new), indicating their Publilian origin under the incorrect names of "Publius," "Publius Syrus" or "Publius mimus."

EDITIONS

(A full list is given in Bickford-Smith's bibliography.)

D. Erasmus. *Disticha moralia titulo Catonis . . . Mimi Publiani (cum scholiis Erasmi), . . .* London. 1514.

Jos. Scaliger. *P. Syri Sentent. et Dion. Catonis Disticha graece redd.* Leyden. 1598.

J. Gretser. Ingolstadt. 1600.

J. Gruter. *Senecae et Syri Mimi forsan etiam aliorum singulares Sententiae centum aliquot versibus ex codd. Pall. et Frising. auctae* (Ed. i. 1604). Leyden. 1708. [Contains 771 iambics and 81 "trochaici quasi."]

R. Bentley: at end of his edition of Terence and Phaedrus. Cambridge. 1726. [238 iambics and 27 trochaics.]

J. Konrad Orelli. *Publii Syri Mimi et aliorum Sententiae . . .* Leipzig. 1822. [791 iambics and 83 trochaics, with Scaliger's Greek verse renderings.]

—— *Supplementum editionis Lipsiensis . . .* Leipzig. 1824.

J. Kaspar Orelli (with *Phaedri fabulae novae*). *Publii Syri Codd. Basil. et Turic. antiquissimi.* Zürich. 1832. [216 verses from the *Basiliensis*, and others from the *Turicensis.*]

O. Ribbeck. *P. Publilius Lochius* (*sic*) *Syrus* in *Comicorum Latinorum Reliquiae*. Leipzig. 1855. [857 *sententiae*, including 269 " minus probatae " and 43 from the *Turicensis*.]

E. Woelfflin. *Publilii Syri Sententiae*. Leipzig. 1869. [693 verses, including 40 from the *Turicensis*. Woelfflin rejected many spurious verses.]

A. Spengel. *Publilii Syri Sententiae*. Berlin. 1874. [721, including 71 from Zürich and Munich MSS., some in prose.]

W. Meyer. *Publilii Syri Sententiae*. Leipzig. 1880. [733 lines.]

O. Friedrich. *Publilii Syri Mimi Sententiae*. Berlin. 1880. [761 lines besides others under the headings of " Caecilii Balbi Sententiae," " Pseudo-Seneca," " Proverbia " and 390 " Sententiae falso inter Publilianas receptae."]

R. A. H. Bickford-Smith. *Publilii Syri Sententiae*. London. 1895. [722 lines.]

SIGLA

O = Collectio Veronensis: codex Capituli Veron. 168 (155): a. 1329.

Σ = Collectio Senecae.
 P = P[a] et P[b].
 P[a]: Paris. 2676: saec. x–xi.
 P[b]: Paris. 7641: saec. x.
 R = Rheinaugiensis 95: saec. x.
 B = Basiliensis A.N. iv. 11 (K. III. 34): saec. x.
 A = Vindobonensis 969: saec. x.
 F et V: *cf. infra.*
 C = Paris. 8049: saec. xiv.
 S = Monac. 484 chart.: saec. xv.

Z = Monac. 23474: saec. xiv.
Dun. = Dunelmensis B II. 20: saec. xiv.
Inc. = editiones ante editionem Erasmi (a. 1514) impressae.

Π = Collectio Palatina.
H = Palatino-Vatic. 239 (olim Heidelbergensis): saec. x–xi. (A–I).

Ψ = Collectio Frisingensis.
F = Monac. 6292 (olim Frisingensis): saec. xi.
V = Vindobon. 299: saec. xii. (circ. cxx. versus).
ψ = Monac. 17210: saec. xiii.
Dresd. = Dresdensis J. 44: saec. xiii (contulit M. Manitius, *Hermes* xli, 1906, pp. 294–99).
Bart : = Giunta ad librum Bartholomaei da San Concordio " Ammaestramenti degli Antichi."
π = Vatic. Regin. 1896: saec. xiii.
α = Albertani Brixiensis libri.
κ = Monac. 7977: saec. xiii.
σ = Monac. 17210: saec. xiii.
par. = Paris. 8027: saec. xiv.

Z = Collectio Turicensis.
M = Monac. 6369: saec. xi. (A–D).
T = Turic. C. 78: saec. x. (C–V).

Φ = Caecilii Balbi quae vocatur collectio maior: φ minor.

A Note on the Dunelmensis

The Durham manuscript, examined in preparing the text of this work, may be briefly described as an example of the Σ group. This codex of the *Sententiae* forms, under the significant misnomer of " Proverbia Senec(a)e," part of a folio volume of

212 double-columned vellum sheets, of which the main contents are tractates, genuine or doubtful, bearing the name of Augustine. Immediately preceding the "Proverbia" there is a page given to "Sententiae quorumdam philosophorum" and over two pages to excerpts from Cicero's *De Divinatione*. In a note near the end of the volume it is described as "liber Sti. Cuthberti de Dunelm. ex procuratione fr̃is Robti. de Graystan." Robert de Graystan was "electus" as bishop of Durham in 1333, but was not admitted to the episcopate. The manuscript cannot be said to possess independent value with regard to Publilius. Though written in well-formed letters with decorated initials, it has not a few imperfections apart from unscannable lines and its mixture of prose and verse. Within the first 30 lines there occur blunders like the haplography of *aut* (6), *a deo* for *deo* (22), *actus sñ dũ* for *aetas cinaedum* (24), and *crinem* for *crimen* (29). Of its total of over 450 *sententiae*, the letters A to N have 313 sayings which are mainly verse (though of the 45 under N about four-fifths are prose). For the remainder, O to V, beginning "Omne peccatum actio est," material is drawn entirely in prose from a work of uncertain authorship, *De Moribus*. After the V *sententiae* there follows a moral poem of about 120 hexameters by a Christian poet, beginning

> Quisquis vult vere Domino per cuncta placere,
> Hunc fugiens mundum totum cor vertat ad illum.

The text of Publilius is in this volume largely based on Meyer's valuable edition of 1880: the main alterations are noted. Lines accepted by Meyer at the close of each letter-section under the formula "Publilii esse videtur" are given in brackets: also l. 145, which, though not in any manuscript of Publilius, is entitled to the same heading, because it is quoted by Gellius and Macrobius.

For the significance of the Greek letters on the left of the Latin text, readers are referred to the table of *Sigla* and to the remarks on the manuscript collections earlier in the Introduction. Meyer's obelus (†) has been retained only where the text printed remains unsatisfactory in respect of metre or meaning.

Σ ALIENUM est omne quicquid optando evenit.
Ab alio exspectes alteri quod feceris.
Animus vereri qui scit, scit tuto ingredi.
Auxilia humilia firma consensus facit.
5 Amor animi arbitrio sumitur, non ponitur.
Aut amat aut odit mulier: nihil est tertium.
Ad tristem partem strenua est suspicio.
Ames parentem si aequus est: si aliter, feras.
Adspicere oportet quicquid possis perdere.
10 Amici vitia si feras, facias tua.

Alienum aes homini ingenuo acerba est servitus.
Absentem laedit cum ebrio qui litigat.

Amans iratus multa mentitur sibi.

3 tuto *m* 2 in B et Pa : tuta PRAFVS : tutus C *Incun.*
10 *sic* M : si B *m* 1 *in rasura*, C : nisi *ceteri.* facis *plerique codd.* : facias *Ribbeck.*

PUBLILIUS SYRUS

WHAT comes by wishing is never truly ours.[a]

As you treat a neighbour, expect another to treat you.

Courage that can fear can take the road with safety.

United feeling makes strength out of humble aids.

5 Love starts but is not dropped at will.

Woman either loves or hates: there is no third thing.

Suspicion is ever active on the gloomy side.[b]

Love your parent, if he is just: if not, bear with him.

You ought to watch whatever you can lose.

10 Tolerate a friend's faults, and you make them your own.

For the freeborn, debt is bitter slavery.

Wrangling with a drunk man is hurting one who is off the scene.

The lover in anger tells himself many a lie.

[a] Quoted by Seneca, *Epist.* viii. 9.

[b] A long exegetical account is given in Gruter's *notae postumae* (1708 ed.). There is no need to change with Friedrich to *attritam in partem*.

Avarus ipse miseriae causa est suae.

15 Amans quid cupiat scit, quid sapiat non videt.

Amans quod suspicatur vigilans somniat.

Ad calamitatem quilibet rumor valet.

Amor extorqueri non pote, elabi potest.

Ab amante lacrimis redimas iracundiam.

20 Aperte mala cum est mulier, tum demum est bona

Avarum facile capias ubi non sis item.

Amare et sapere vix deo conceditur.

Avarus nisi cum moritur nihil recte facit.

Aetas cinaedum celat, aetas indicat.

25 Avarus damno potius quam sapiens dolet.

Avaro quid mali optes nisi: "vivat diu!"

Animo dolenti nihil oportet credere.

Aliena nobis, nostra plus aliis placent.

Amare iuveni fructus est, crimen seni.

[18] *sic Spengel, Meyer*: potest . . . potest *pler. codd.*: pote . . . pote V. elabi HC: sed elabi PRAFVSZ: sed labi B.

[21] item *Bothe*: idem *codd.*

[22] deo H *Erasmus*: adeo *ceteri.*

[24] aetas *Pithoeus*: aestate P[b] P[a] *corr.* BRA: aestatem P[a]: astute FVCS: astus *Woelfflin* cinae dum A: cinedum B: cenae dum P[a]: crines dum FVCS: caelat P[b]A: actus sñ dũ

The miser is himself the cause of his misery.

15 A lover knows his desire: his wisdom is out of sight.

Even when awake, the lover has dreams of his suspicions.

To accredit disaster any tale has power.

Love can't be wrested from one, but may slip away.

Tears may buy off a lover's wrath.

20 A woman is good at last, when she's openly bad.

The miser may be your easy prey, when you're not a miser too.

Wisdom with love is scarcely granted to a god.

The one right thing a miser does is to die.

Time conceals and time reveals the reprobate.

25 It's the miser, not the wise man, whom a loss pains.

What ill could you wish a miser save long life?

One must not trust at all a mind in pain.

We fancy the lot of others; others fancy ours more.

Love is the young man's enjoyment, the old man's reproach.

Dunelm. etas te celat, etas te iudicat *Dresd.* astute dum celatur aetas se indicat *Erasmus*: astu crimen celatur, aetas indicat *Zwinger cit. apud Gruterum*: astus cinaedum celat, aestus indicat *Friedrich.*

[26] *sic* M H: nisi ut *pler. codd.*

30 Anus cum ludit morti delicias facit.

Amoris vulnus idem sanat qui facit.

Ad paenitendum properat, cito qui iudicat.

Aleator quanto in arte est, tanto est nequior.

Amor otiosae causa est sollicitudinis.

Π Avidum esse oportet neminem, minime senem.

36 Animo virum pudicae, non oculo eligunt.

Amantis ius iurandum poenam non habet.

Amans ita ut fax agitando ardescit magis.

Amor ut lacrima ab oculo oritur in pectus cadit.

40 Animo imperabit sapiens, stultus serviet.

Amicum an nomen habeas aperit calamitas.

Amori finem tempus, non animus, facit.

Z Audendo virtus crescit, tardando timor.

Auxilium profligatis contumelia est.

45 Affatim aequa cui fortuna est interitum longe effugit.

[34] otioso C *Inc.*
[39] oculis H *Meyer*: ab oculis FVακ: ab oculo *Woelfflin*: amoris lacrima ab oculis in p.c. *Spengel*: ámor ut lacrima obóritur oculis, óculis in pectús cadit *Friedrich*.

30 The old woman in skittish mood is Death's darling toy.

The one who causes also cures the wound of love.

Hasty judgement means speedy repentance.

The cleverer the gamester, the greater his knavery.

Love causes worry in the leisure hour.

35 None should be greedy, least of all the old

Modest women choose a man by mind, not eye.

A lover's oath involves no penalty.

A lover is like a torch—blazes the more he's moved.

Love, like a tear, rises in the eye and falls on the breast.

40 The sage will rule his feelings, the fool will be their slave.

Misfortune reveals whether you have a friend or only one in name.

'Tis time, not the mind, that puts an end to love.

Courage grows by daring, fear by delay.

Help wounds the pride of those whose cause is lost.

45 The man whose luck is fair enough gives ruin a wide berth.

---

[45] *sic Wight Duff*: Affatim inqua fortuna longe non habet interitum M: affatim si cui fortuna *Christ* affatim si quoi fortunast *Ribbeck*: affatim aequa si fortuna *Meyer*.

Avaro acerba poena natura est sua.

Avaro non est vita sed mors longior.

Alienam qui orat causam se culpat reum.

Adsidua ei sunt tormenta qui se ipsum timet.

50 Animo imperato ne tibi animus imperet.

Animo ventrique imperare debet qui frugi esse vult.

O Aegre reprendas quod sinas consuescere.

Amico firmo nihil emi melius potest.

ϕ (Amicis ita prodesto ne noceas tibi.)

55 (Avarus animus nullo satiatur lucro.)

(Amici mores noveris non oderis.)

Σ Bis fiet gratum quod opus est si ultro offeras.

Bonarum rerum consuetudo pessima est.

Beneficium dare qui nescit iniuste petit.

60 Bonum est fugienda adspicere in alieno malo.

Beneficium accipere libertatem est vendere.

[48] *sic Meiser* : Alienam qui suscipit causam semet criminat esse rerum M.

For the miser his own nature is bitter punishment.

The miser has no life save death delayed.

The pleader of another's cause arraigns himself.

He who dreads himself has torment without end.

50 Rule your feelings lest your feelings rule you.

He who would be discreet must rule his mind and appetite.

Reproof comes ill for a habit you countenance.[a]

There's nothing better in the market than a staunch friend.

Benefit friends without hurt to yourself.

55 No gain satisfies a greedy mind.[b]

Study but do not hate a friend's character.

Twice welcome the needed gift if offered unasked.

Constant acquaintance with prosperity is a curse.

He who can't do a good turn has no right to ask one.

60 In another's misfortune it is good to observe what to avoid.

To accept a benefit is to sell one's freedom.

[a] St. Jerome records his reading this maxim when at school: *Epist.* 107, 8 (*legi quondam in scholis puer*: *aegre*, etc.). He quotes it also in *Epist.* 128, 4: see Introduction.

[b] Quoted by Seneca, *Epist.* xciv. 43.

Bona nemini hora est ut non alicui sit mala.

Bis emori est alterius arbitrio mori.

Beneficia plura recipit qui scit reddere.

65 Bis peccas cum peccanti obsequium commodas.

Bonus animus laesus gravius multo irascitur.

Bona mors est homini vitae quae exstinguit mala.

Beneficium dando accepit qui digno dedit.

Blanditia non imperio fit dulcis venus.

70 Bonus animus numquam erranti obsequium commodat.

Beneficium qui dedisse se dicit petit.

Benivoli coniunctio animi maxima est cognatio.

Beneficium saepe dare docere est reddere.

Bonitatis verba imitari maior malitia est.

75 Bona opinio hominum tutior pecunia est.

Nobody has a good time without its being bad for someone.

To die at another's bidding is to die a double death.

He receives more benefits who knows how to return them.

65 You sin doubly when you humour a sinner.[a]

When a good disposition is wounded, it is much more seriously incensed.

Good for man is death when it ends life's miseries.

The giver of a gift deserved gets benefit by giving.

Coaxing, not ordering, makes love sweet.

70 Good judgement never humours one who is going wrong.

Claiming to have done a good turn is asking for one.

The alliance of a well-wisher's mind is truest kinship.

To confer repeated kindness is tuition in repayment.

Aping the words of goodness is the greater wickedness.

75 There is more safety in men's good opinion than in money.

[a] It is difficult to grasp the meaning of some of the sayings, as the original dramatic context is unknown. The double sin here may imply a sin twice as bad: *cf.* the expression *bis emori*, 63, and the sentiment in 10.

Bonum quod est supprimitur, numquam exstinguitur.

Bis vincit qui se vincit in victoria.

Benignus etiam causam dandi cogitat.

Bis interimitur qui suis armis perit.

80 Bene dormit qui non sentit quam male dormiat.

Bonorum crimen est officiosus miser.

Bona quae veniunt nisi sustineantur opprimunt.

Bona fama in tenebris proprium splendorem tenet.

Bene cogitata si excidunt non occidunt.

85 Bene perdit nummos iudici cum dat nocens.

Bona imperante animo bono est pecunia.

Bonum ad virum cito moritur iracundia.

Brevissima esto memoria iracundiae.

82 *sic Gruter*: b.q. eminent nisi sustineantur obprimunt *Buecheler*: n. s. cadunt ut opprimant *pler. codd.*

86 *sic Bickford-Smith*: bona imperante animo est pecunia S: bono PRA: in parente anima *nonnulli codd.*: bona imperante bono animo est pecunia *Meyer in not.*

A good thing may be trampled on but never annihilated.

Twice is he conqueror who in the hour of conquest conquers himself.

Generosity seeks to invent even a cause for giving.

Doubly destroyed is he who perishes by his own arms.

80 He sleeps well who feels not how ill he sleeps.

The dutiful man reduced to misery is a reproach to the good.

Prosperity must be sensibly sustained or it crushes you.

A good name keeps its own brightness in dark days.

Good ideas may fail but are not lost.

85 When the culprit bribes the judge, he loses coin to some purpose.

When the mind issues good orders, money is a blessing.

With the good man anger is quick to die.

Let the harbouring of angry thoughts be of the briefest.

---

88 *sic Gruter in notis postumis* (*om.* Dunelmensis): breve mens BRP[b]AP[a] *corr.*: breviens P[a]: brevis mens S: breve amans FV. est ipsa FVS.

Bona turpitudo est quae periclum vindicat.

90 Bona comparat praesidia misericordia.

Beneficium dignis ubi des omnes obliges.

Π Brevis ipsa vita est sed malis fit longior.

Beneficia donari aut mali aut stulti putant.

Bene perdis gaudium ubi dolor pariter perit.

95 Bene vixit is qui potuit cum voluit mori.

† Bene audire alterum patrimonium est.

Boni est viri etiam in morte nullum fallere.

Z Bona causa nullum iudicem verebitur.

Bonus vir nemo est nisi qui bonus est omnibus.

Σ Consueta vitia ferimus, nova reprendimus.

101 Crudelis est in re adversa obiurgatio.

Cavendi nulla est dimittenda occasio.

Cui semper dederis ubi neges rapere imperes.

---

96 *sic* FVH : bene vulgo audire *Gruter* : bene e patre audire *Friedrich.*

100 nova *Bentley, Meyer* : inconsueta Z : non *ceteri codd., Woelfflin, Spengel, Friedrich.*

Foul is fair if it punishes the menace of a foe.

90 Pity provides good defences.

Whenever you benefit the deserving, you put the world in your debt.

Life, short itself, grows longer for its ills.

They are either rogues or fools who think benefits are merely gifts.

You are content to miss joy when pain is also lost.

95 Well has he lived who has been able to die when he willed.

To have a good name is a second patrimony.

It is the mark of a good man to disappoint no one even in his death.[a]

A good case will fear no judge.

No one is a good man unless he is good to all.

100 We tolerate the usual vices but blame new ones.

Rebuke is cruel in adversity.

No opportunity for caution should be let slip.

By perpetual giving you would invite robbery when you say "no."

[a] *i.e.* his manner of dying must equal the standard of his life.

Crudelem medicum intemperans aeger facit.

105 Cuius mortem amici exspectant vitam cives oderunt.

Cum inimico nemo in gratiam tuto redit.

Citius venit periclum cum contemnitur.

Casta ad virum matrona parendo imperat.

Cito ignominia fit superbi gloria.

110 Consilio melius vincas quam iracundia.

Cuivis dolori remedium est patientia.

Cotidie damnatur qui semper timet.

Cum vitia prosunt, peccat qui recte facit.

Contumeliam nec fortis pote nec ingenuus pati.

115 Conscientia animi nullas invenit linguae preces.

Comes facundus in via pro vehiculo est.

Cito improborum laeta ad perniciem cadunt.

Contemni ⟨sapienti⟩ gravius est quam stulto percuti.

Cotidie est deterior posterior dies.

115 nullas PA : nullus RB : nullius FVC : nimias *Friedrich.*
118 sapienti *addidit Gruter in notis* : contemni est * gravius quam stultitiae percuti *Meyer.*

The intemperate patient makes the doctor cruel.

105 He for whose death his friends are waiting lives a life his fellows hate.

No one is safe to be reconciled to a foe.

Danger comes more quickly when under-estimated.

The chaste matron of her husband's home rules through obedience.

The boast of arrogance soon turns to shame.

110 Policy is a better means of conquest than anger.

Endurance is the cure for any pain.

The man in constant fear is every day condemned.

When vices pay, the doer of the right is at fault.

Insult is what neither bravery nor free birth can brook.

115 A good conscience invents no glib entreaties.[a]

A chatty road-mate is as good as a carriage.

The joys of rascals soon collapse in ruin.

Contempt hurts the wise man more than a scourge does the fool.

Daily the following day is worse (*i.e.* for prompt action).

[a] Friedrich takes *conscientia* as "a bad conscience" and reads *nimias*.

120 Crimen relinquit vitae qui mortem appetit.

II Cogas amantem irasci amare si velis.

Contra imprudentem stulta est nimia ingenuitas.

Crudelis est non fortis qui infantem necat.

Consilium inveniunt multi sed docti explicant.

125 Cave quicquam incipias quod paeniteat postea.

Cui omnes bene dicunt possidet populi bona.

Cui nolis saepe irasci irascaris semel.

Crudelis lacrimis pascitur non frangitur.

Caeci sunt oculi cum animus alias res agit.

130 Caret periclo qui etiam cum est tutus cavet.

Cum ames non sapias aut cum sapias non ames.

Cicatrix conscientiae pro vulnere est.

Cunctis potest accidere quod cuivis potest.

[122] imprudentem *codd.*: impudentem *Gruter, Meyer.*
[124] consiliis iuniorum multi se docti explicant FV : *alii alia.*

120 Eagerness for death bequeaths an indictment of life

Force a lover to anger if you wish him to love.

To counter ignorance, too much breadth of mind is fatuous.

Barbarous, not brave, is he who kills a child.

Many can hit on a plan, but the experienced find the way out.

125 Beware of starting what you may later regret.

The man of whom all speak well earns the people's favours.

Lose your temper once for all with the man with whom you don't want to lose it often.

Cruelty is fed, not broken, by tears.

The eyes are blind when the mind is otherwise occupied.

130 He's free from danger who even in safety takes precaution.

Love means you can't be wise: wisdom means you can't be in love.

The scar of conscience is as bad as a wound.

What can happen to any can happen to all.

---

[133] Cunctis . . . cuivis FV: cuivis . . . cuiquam *cit. apud Senecam, de Tranq.* xi. 8: cf. *Consol. ad Marciam* ix. 5.

Cave amicum credas nisi si quem probaveris.

135 Contra felicem vix deus vires habet.

Cum das avaro praemium ut noceat rogas.

Z Cum se ipse vincit sapiens minime vincitur.

Contra hostem aut fortem oportet esse aut supplicem.

Cito culpam effugias si incurrisse paenitet.

140 Cum periclo inferior quaerit quod superior occulit.

Consilium in dubiis remedium prudentis est.

† Cum inimico ignoscis amicos gratis complures acquiris.

Contubernia sunt lacrimarum ubi misericors miserum adspicit.

O Crebro ignoscendo facies de stulto improbum.

145 (Cui plus licet quam par est plus vult quam licet.)

139 *sic Orelli* : culpa effugiri T : potest MT : si T : culpam penitet incurrisse MT : cito culpam effugere pote quem culpae paenitet *Meyer*.
141 *sic Meyer* : in adversis medicinae remedium MT.
142 *alii alia*.

Mind you think no man a friend save him you have tried.

135 Against the lucky one scarcely a god has strength.

In rewarding the avaricious you ask for harm.

When the sage conquers himself, he is least conquered.

Facing a foe, one must be either brave or suppliant.

You could soon avoid a fault, if you repent having run into it.

140 At his peril does an inferior search for what a superior hides.

The prudent man's remedy at a crisis is counsel.

When you forgive an enemy, you win several friends at no cost.

When pity sees misery, there comes the comradeship of tears.

Frequent pardons will turn a fool into a knave.

145 He who is allowed more than is right wants more than is allowed.[a]

[a] This *sententia* (*cf.* "give an inch and he takes an ell") is quoted by Gellius, *N.A.* xvii. 14, and Macrob. *Saturn.* ii. 7, but omitted by MSS. of Publilius.

Σ Discipulus est prioris posterior dies.

Damnare est obiurgare cum auxilio est opus.

Diu apparandum est bellum ut vincas celerius.

Dixeris male dicta cuncta cum ingratum hominem dixeris.

150 De inimico non loquaris male sed cogites.

Deliberare utilia mora tutissima est.

Dolor decrescit ubi quo crescat non habet.

Didicere flere feminae in mendacium.

Discordia fit carior concordia.

155 Deliberandum est saepe: statuendum est semel.

Difficilem habere oportet aurem ad crimina.

Dum est vita grata, mortis conditio optima est.

Damnum appellandum est cum mala fama lucrum.

Ducis in consilio posita est virtus militum.

160 Dies quod donat timeas: cito raptum venit.

155 quicquid PBRA: diu quicquid CSZ: saepe quicquid F: saepe *Woelfflin*: diu del. st. est semel *Bothe*: del. est decies *Friedrich*.

Next day is pupil of the day before.

When there's need of help, reproach is to make things worse.

War needs long preparation to make you win the sooner.

Call a man ungrateful and you have no words of abuse left.

150 Devise evil against your enemy, but speak none of him.

To think out useful plans is the safest delay.

Pain lessens when it has no means of growth.

Woman has learned the use of tears to deceive.

Harmony is the sweeter for a quarrel.

155 Think things out often: decide once.

One should not lend a ready ear to accusations.

When life is pleasant, the state of death is best.[a]

Ill-famed gain should be called loss.

Soldiers' valour hangs on their general's strategy.

160 Fear what a day gives: soon it comes to rob.

[a] The *sententia* means that the best time for death is while (*dum* temporal) life is pleasant: *i.e.* before sorrows come, one might die, in Tacitus' words, *felix opportunitate mortis.* Joseph Scaliger's translation of the line is εὐημεροῦσιν αἵρεσις θανάτου καλή.

Dimissum quod nescitur non amittitur.

Π Deliberando discitur sapientia.

Deliberando saepe perit occasio.

Duplex fit bonitas simul accessit celeritas.

165 Damnati lingua vocem habet, vim non habet.

Dolor animi ⟨nimio⟩ gravior est quam corporis.

Dulce etiam fugias fieri quod amarum potest.

Difficile est dolori convenire cum patientia.

Deos ridere credo cum felix vovet.

Z Durum est negare superior cum supplicat.

171 Dissolvitur lex cum fit iudex misericors.

Dominari ex parte est cum superior supplicat.

Decima hora amicos plures quam prima invenit.

Σ Etiam innocentes cogit mentiri dolor.

175 Etiam in peccato recte praestatur fides.

[166] nimio *add. Bothe*: quam corporis dolor *Gruter, Orelli.* [168] difficilius cum dolore convenit sapientiae *Friedrich.* [169] fovet H: vocet F: infelix vovet *Meyer in notis*: deo se credere credit cum felix vovet *Friedrich.*

The loss that is not known is no loss.

Deliberation teaches wisdom.

Deliberation often means a chance is lost.

Bounty is doubled so soon as speed is added.[a]

165 The condemned man's tongue has utterance, not force.

Pain of mind is far more severe than bodily pain.

Shun even a sweet that can grow bitter.

'Tis hard for pain to agree with patience.

I trow the gods smile when the lucky man makes his vow.[b]

170 Refusal is difficult when your better entreats.[c]

Law is weakened when a judge yields to compassion.

One is half master when one's better entreats.

Evening discovers more friends than the dawn does.[d]

Pain forces even the innocent to lie.

175 Even in crime loyalty is rightly displayed.

[a] *Cf. bis dat qui cito dat* and l. 274.

[b] If the reading is right, it implies that the gods rejoice in their prospect of gain: the lucky man's vow is a sure debt.

[c] *Cf.* use of *superior* in 172.

[d] It is a cynical thought that friends are more likely to gather round a man late in the day. They can then be social and convivial without any need to help him in his daily task. There might even be a hint that morning tempers are often unsociable.

Etiam celeritas in desiderio mora est.

Ex vitio alterius sapiens emendat suum.

Et deest et superest miseris cogitatio.

Etiam oblivisci quid sis interdum expedit.

180 Ex hominum questu facta Fortuna est dea.

Effugere cupiditatem regnum est vincere.

Exsul ubi ei nusquam domus est sine sepulcro est mortuus.

Etiam qui faciunt oderunt iniuriam.

Eripere telum non dare irato decet.

185 Exsilium patitur patriae qui se denegat.

Etiam capillus unus habet umbram suam.

Eheu quam miserum est fieri metuendo senem!

Etiam hosti est aequus qui habet in consilio fidem.

Excelsis multo facilius casus nocet.

Π Extrema semper de ante factis iudicant.

191 Ex lite multa gratia fit formosior.

Etiam bonis malum saepe est adsuescere.

Desire finds even quickness slow.

From a neighbour's fault a wise man corrects his own.

The wretched have too little and too much of thought.

Sometimes 'tis fitting even to forget what you are.

180 The grumbling of men made Fortune a goddess.

To shun desire is to conquer a kingdom.

The exile with no home anywhere is a corpse without a grave.

Even those who do an injustice hate it.

Anger is rightly robbed of a weapon, not given one.

185 He suffers exile who denies himself to his country.

Even one hair has a shadow of its own.

Alas, how wretched to be aged by fear!

He who has confidence in his policy is fair even to an enemy.

The exalted are much more readily hurt by misfortune.

190 The end always passes judgement on what has preceded.

After much strife reconciliation becomes more beautiful.

It is often bad to grow used even to good things.

Z † Est utique profunda ignorantia nescire quod pecces.

194 Etiam sine lege poena est conscientia.

O Errat datum qui sibi quod extortum est putat.

Σ Fidem qui perdit quo rem servat relicuam?

Fortuna cum blanditur captatum venit.

Fortunam citius reperias quam retineas.

Formosa facies muta commendatio est.

200 Frustra rogatur qui misereri non potest.

Fortuna unde aliquid fregit cassumst ⟨reficere⟩.

Fraus est accipere quod non possis reddere.

Fortuna nimium quem fovet stultum facit.

Fatetur facinus is qui iudicium fugit.

205 Felix improbitas optimorum est calamitas.

Feras non culpes quod mutari non potest.

Futura pugnant ne se superari sinant.

Furor fit laesa saepius patientia.

Fidem qui perdit nihil pote ultra perdere.

196 *sic Friedrich*: se servet FB*m*l : se servat PBAC : reservat R. reliquum PBRA : relicuo *Bentley, Meyer*.

201 *sic Spengel* : cassum est F : quassum est PBRACS : cassum est non perit *Ribbeck* : quassat omnia *Friedrich*.

It is surely the depth of ignorance not to know your fault.

Even without a law conscience works as punishment.

195 It is a mistake to think one is given what has been extorted.

With credit lost, what means are there of saving what remains?

When Fortune flatters, she comes to ensnare.

It is easier to strike luck than to keep it.

A handsome appearance is an unspoken testimonial.

200 Vain is the appeal to him who cannot pity.

That from which Fortune breaks off something, 'tis vain to repair.

It's cheating to take what you could not restore.

Fortune turns her spoiled darling into a fool.

A man owns guilt by avoiding trial.

205 Successful wickedness means good folk's disaster.

What can't be changed you should bear, not blame.

The future struggles not to let itself be mastered.

Patience too often wounded turns to frenzy.

Lose credit and one can lose no more.[a]

[a] *Cf.* 196.

210 Facilitas animi ad partem stultitiae rapit.

Fides in animum unde abiit ⟨vix⟩ umquam redit.

Fidem nemo umquam perdit nisi qui non habet.

Fortuna obesse nulli contenta est semel.

Fulmen est ubi cum potestate habitat iracundia.

215 Frustra, cum ad senectam ventum est, repetas adulescentiam.

Falsum maledictum malevolum mendacium est.

Feminae naturam regere desperare est otium.

Feras difficilia ut facilia perferas.

Fortuna vitrea est: tum cum splendet frangitur.

220 Feras quod laedit ut quod prodest perferas.

Facit gradum Fortuna quem nemo videt.

Fortuna plus homini quam consilium valet.

Π Frugalitas miseria est rumoris boni.

Z Famulatur dominus ubi timet quibus imperat.

[210] animi *codd.*: nimia *Woelfflin*: ad partem *codd.*: sapit PBRA: rapit FCS: f. nimia partem stultitiae sapit *Spengel, Meyer.*

[211] *sic Spengel.*

[221] gratum *codd.* (gatum R): gradum *Nauck*: Facit Fortuna quem non remoreris gradum *Friedrich, cuius praefationem vide.*

[222] homini PᵃRFCZ: in homine *Spengel, Meyer.*

210 Complaisance is a rapid road in the direction of folly.

Honour scarce ever revisits the mind it has quitted.

None ever loses honour save him who has it not.

Fortune is not content with hurting anyone once.

'Tis thunder and lightning when anger dwells with power.

215 It is no good asking for youth again when age is reached.

The ill-grounded curse is an ill-intentioned lie.[a]

To control woman's nature is to abandon the hope of a quiet life.

Endure what's hard so as to stand the test of the easy.

Luck is like glass—just when it glitters, it smashes.

220 Bear what hurts so as to stand the test of success.

Luck takes the step that no one sees.

Luck avails a man more than policy.

Frugality is wretchedness with a good name.

The master is valet when he fears those he orders.

[a] " Frigida omnino sententia " is Orelli's criticism. " Sententia nimium quantum languet," Ribbeck.

225 Facile invenies qui bene faciant cum qui fecerunt coles.

Frenos imponit linguae conscientia.

O Felicitatem in dubiis virtus impetrat.

Falsum etiam est verum quod constituit superior.

Σ Grave praeiudicium est quod iudicium non habet.

230 Gravissima est probi hominis iracundia.

Gravis animi poena est quem post facti paenitet.

Gravis animus dubiam non habet sententiam.

Gravius malum omne est quod sub adspectu latet.

Gravius nocet quodcumque inexpertum accidit.

235 Gravis est inimicus is qui latet in pectore.

Gravissimum est imperium consuetudinis.

Grave crimen, etiam leviter cum est dictum, nocet.

Z Grave est quod laetus dederis tristem recipere.

ϕ (Geminat peccatum quem delicti non pudet.)

[227] *sic Baehrens*: facilitatem . . . imperat *codd.*
[238] *sic Woelfflin in notis*, p. 115: quod fronte laeta des tristi accipi *Meyer.*

225 You'll easily find folk to do kindnesses by cultivating those who have done them.

Conscience sets a bridle on the tongue.

Valour secures success in hazards.

Even false becomes true when a superior so decides.

Where there is no judgement, there is grave prejudging.[a]

230 Most potent is the anger of an upright man.

Heavy the penalty on the mind which afterwards regrets a deed.

The steadfast mind admits no halting opinion.

It is always a more serious evil that lurks out of sight.

A novel disaster always works the graver mischief.

235 The foe that lurks in the heart is one to be reckoned with.

Most tyrannous is the sway of custom.

A serious charge, even lightly made, does harm.

'Tis hard getting back in sadness what you gave in joy.

He who is unashamed of his offence doubles his sin.

[a] *E.g.* hanging without trial might be called the worst "prejudice."

Σ Heu quam difficilis gloriae custodia est!

241 Homo extra corpus est suum cum irascitur.

Heu quam est timendus qui mori tutum putat!

Homo qui in homine calamitoso est misericors meminit sui.

Honesta turpitudo est pro causa bona.

245 Habet in adversis auxilia qui in secundis commodat.

Heu quam miserum est ab eo laedi de quo non possis queri!

Hominem experiri multa paupertas iubet.

Heu dolor quam miser est qui in tormento vocem non habet!

Heu quam multa paenitenda incurrunt vivendo diu!

250 Heu quam miserum est discere servire † ubi sis doctus dominari!

Habet suum venenum blanda oratio.

Homo totiens moritur quotiens amittit suos.

Homo semper aliud, Fortuna aliud cogitat.

Honestus rumor alterum est patrimonium.

255 Homo ne sit sine dolore fortunam invenit.

240 Alas, how hard the maintenance of fame!

A man when angry is outside himself.

Ah, how formidable is he who thinks it safe to die!

Pity for a stricken fellow-man is to remember one's own lot.

Foul is fair when the cause is good.

245 Aid lent in weal brings aid in woe.

Ah, how ghastly is a hurt from one of whom you daren't complain!

Poverty orders many an experiment.

How pitiful the pain that has no voice amid torture!

Ah, how many regrets does length of life incur!

250 Ah, how wretched to learn to be a servant when you have been trained to be master!

The wheedling speech contains its special poison.

One dies as often as one loses loved ones.

Man's plans and Fortune's are ever at variance.

An honourable reputation is a second patrimony.[a]

255 Man meets with fortune that pain may dog him still.[b]

[a] *Cf.* the sentiment in 96.

[b] Nisard's rendering is "L'homme serait sans douleur s'il ne trouvait la fortune."

Honeste servit qui succumbit tempori.

Homo vitae commodatus non donatus est.

Heredis fletus sub persona risus est.

Heredem ferre utilius est quam quaerere.

260 Habent locum maledicti crebrae nuptiae.

Π Honeste parcas improbo ut parcas probo.

Humanitatis optima est certatio.

Honos honestum decorat, inhonestum notat.

Heu, conscientia animi gravis est servitus!

265 Hominem etiam frugi flectit saepe occasio.

Homini tum deest consilium cum multa invenit.

Z Humilis nec alte cadere nec graviter potest.

Honestum laedis cum pro indigno intervenis.

Σ Inferior rescit quicquid peccat superior.

270 Inimicum ulcisci vitam accipere est alteram.

[264] haec (c *in rasura*) F: heu quam *Gruter*: heu *Woelfflin*, *Meyer*.

[269] rescit PA: nestit R: orrescit B: horrescit FCSZ: reus est *Ribbeck*.

To yield to the need of the time is honourable service.

Man is only lent to life, not given.

Beneath the mask an heir's weeping is a smile.

It's of more use to tolerate an heir than seek one out.

260 Frequent re-marriage gives room for the evil tongue.

To spare the good you may fairly spare the bad.

The finest rivalry is in humanity.

Honour adorns the honourable; the dishonourable it brands.

Ah, conscience doth make bondsmen of us all!

265 Opportunity often sways even an honest man.

When you discover many openings, you are gravelled for a plan.

The humble can fall neither far nor heavily.

You hurt the honourable by intervening for the unworthy.

Any fault in a superior is found out by his inferior.[a]

270 Revenge on an enemy is to get a new lease of life.

[a] The usual form is *resciscere*, but for the simple verb *rescire* see Gell. *N. A.* ii. 19. 2.

Invitum cum retineas, exire incites.

Ingenuitatem laedas cum indignum roges.

In nullum avarus bonus est, in se pessimus.

Inopi beneficium bis dat qui dat celeriter.

275 Inopiae desunt multa, avaritiae omnia.

Instructa inopia est in divitiis cupiditas.

Invitat culpam qui peccatum praeterit.

Iucundum nihil est nisi quod reficit varietas.

Ingenuitas non recipit contumeliam.

280 Irritare est calamitatem cum te felicem voces.

Impune pecces in eum qui peccat prior.

Ingratus unus omnibus miseris nocet.

In miseria vita etiam contumelia est.

Ita amicum habeas, posse ut facile fieri hunc inimicum putes.

285 Invidiam ferre aut fortis aut felix potest.

In amore semper mendax iracundia est.

Hold back a man against his will, and you might as well urge him to go.

An appeal to the unworthy is an insult to the noble mind.

The miser treats none well—himself the worst.

To do a kindness to the needy at once is to give twice.

75 Beggary lacks much, but greed lacks everything.

In riches greed is but poverty well furnished.

He who passes over a sin invites wrong-doing.

There's nothing pleasant save what variety freshens.

The noble mind does not take an insult.

280 To call yourself "happy" is to provoke disaster.

You may safely offend against him who offends first.

One ungrateful person does harm to all the unfortunate.

In misery even life is an insult.

Treat a friend without forgetting that he may easily become a foe.

285 It's either the brave man or the lucky that can stand unpopularity.

In love anger is always untruthful.

Invidia tacite sed inimice irascitur.
Iratum breviter vites, inimicum diu.

Iniuriarum remedium est oblivio.
290 Iracundiam qui vincit hostem superat maximum.
Iactum tacendo crimen facias acrius.

In malis sperare bene nisi innocens nemo solet.
In iudicando criminosa est celeritas.
Inimicum quamvis humilem docti est metuere.
295 In calamitoso risus etiam iniuria est.
Iudex damnatur cum nocens absolvitur.
Ignoscere hominum est nisi pudet cui ignoscitur.

In rebus dubiis plurimi est audacia.
Illo nocens se damnat quo peccat die.

300 Ita crede amico ne sit inimico locus.
Iratus etiam facinus consilium putat.

[291] iáctum in te tacéndo acumen crímen facias ácrius (*trochaicus*) *Friedrich.*
[293] *sic* HBCF : vindicando PRAS.
[297] nisi *codd.* : ubi *Incun.*, *Meyer.*

Silent but unfriendly is the anger of envy.

Avoid an angry man for a little, but an enemy for long.

For wrongs the cure lies in forgetfulness.[a]

290 Who quells his wrath o'ercomes the mightiest foe.

You aggravate a charge thrown at you, if you meet it with silence.

None but the guiltless can nurse bright hopes in woe.

In judgement rapidity is criminal.

Experience dreads an enemy however humble.

295 When a man is ruined, even a laugh is a wrong.

Acquittal of the guilty damns the judge.[b]

It is for men to pardon, unless the pardoned puts one to the blush.

In a tight corner boldness counts for most.

The culprit condemns himself on the day of his offence.

300 So trust a friend as to give no room for an enemy.

The angry man takes (hostile) intention as an actual deed.

[a] Quoted by Seneca, *Epist.* xciv. 28.

[b] This line, chosen as the motto for *The Edinburgh Review*, founded 1802, marked its tendency to severity in criticism.

Invidia id loquitur quod videt non quod subest.

II Iniuriam aures facilius quam oculi ferunt.

Iacet omnis virtus fama nisi late patet.

305 Ignis calorem suum etiam in ferro tenet.

In venere semper certat dolor et gaudium.

In amore forma plus valet quam auctoritas.

Ingrata sunt beneficia quibus comes est metus.

Imprudens peccat quem peccati paenitet.

310 Inertia indicatur cum fugitur labor.

Iratus cum ad se rediit sibi tum irascitur.

In amore saepe causa damni quaeritur.

Iucunda macula est ex inimici sanguine.

In venere semper dulcis est dementia.

315 In misero facile fit potens iniuria.

Interdum habet stultitiae partem facilitas.

306 certant ψ *Spengel.*

Envy speaks of what she sees, not of what is beneath the surface.

The ear tolerates a wrong more readily than the eye.

Every virtue is depressed unless it gains wide recognition.

305 Fire keeps its own heat even in steel.

In love, pain is ever at war with joy.

In love, beauty counts for more than advice does.

Unwelcome are the favours whose attendant is fear.

He who regrets his offence offends without foresight.

310 Work shunned is an index of laziness.

It is on returning to his senses that the angry man is angry with himself.

In love, an opportunity for suffering loss is often sought.[a]

It's a pleasant stain that comes from an enemy's blood.

To lose your wits in love is always sweet.

315 Over the wretched unfairness easily gets power.

Compliance is sometimes half folly.

[a] Possibly of a lover's lavish expenditure on a lady-love which may eventually be a serious loss to him; but it probably means that lovers are so foolish that they are continually devising something which really does them harm.

Inertia est laboris excusatio.

Iniuriam facilius facias quam feras.

Iratus nihil non criminis loquitur loco.

320 Incertus animus dimidium est sapientiae.

In turpi re peccare bis delinquere est.

Ingenuus animus non fert vocis verbera.

Iniuriam ipse facias ubi non vindices.

Is minimum eget mortalis qui minimum cupit.

325 Inimici ad animum nullae conveniunt preces.

Inimico exstincto exitium lacrimae non habent.

Ibi semper est victoria ubi concordia est.

Iter est quacumque dat prior vestigium.

Ibi pote valere populus ubi leges valent.

Z Insanae vocis numquam libertas tacet.

331 Improbe Neptunum accusat qui iterum naufragium facit.

Σ Loco ignominiae est apud indignum dignitas.

[320] remedium *codd.*: dimidium *Bothe*: incertis animis r. e. sapientia *Meyer in appar. crit.*

[324] minimo *Seneca, Epist.* cviii. 11.

[326] exitum H ψ: exitium (*antiquo sensu usurpatum*) *celeri codd.*

[330] † invectibe T: insanae *Friedrich*: invectae *Bickford-Smith.*

Excusing oneself from work is laziness.

A wrong is easier done than stood.

An angry man has nothing but accusations to utter.

320 The hesitant mind is the half of wisdom.[a]

An offence in base circumstances is a double fault.

A noble mind brooks not the lashes of the tongue.

You yourself do wrong when you do not punish.

The man with least desires is least in want.

325 No entreaties are fitted to reach an unfriendly mind.

When an enemy is destroyed, tears have no outlet.

Victory is ever there where union of hearts is.[b]

The road runs wheresoever a predecessor leaves his footprint.

Where laws prevail, there can the people prevail.

330 The outspokenness of wild invective is never hushed.

It is an outrage in a man twice shipwrecked to blame the God of Sea.

To stand high with the unworthy is tantamount to shame.

[a] *Cf.* 162.
[b] The saying means that victory in a conflict lies with the thoroughly united side.

Laus nova nisi oritur, etiam vetus amittitur.

Laeso doloris remedium inimici est dolor.

335 Levis est Fortuna: cito reposcit quod dedit.

Lex universa est quae iubet nasci et mori.

Lucrum sine damno alterius fieri non potest.

Lascivia et laus numquam habent concordiam.

Legem nocens veretur, Fortunam innocens.

340 Libido, non iudicium est, quod levitas sapit.

Libido cunctos etiam sub vultu domat.

Π Longum est quodcumque flagitavit cupiditas.

Ψ Lapsus ubi semel sis, sit tua culpa, si iterum cecideris.

Lex videt iratum, iratus legem non videt.

345 Legem solet obliviscier iracundia.

Locis remotis qui latet lex est sibi.

Late ignis lucere, ut nihil urat, non potest.

[341] cunctos *codd.*: cinctos (= strenuos) *Salmasius.*
[342] *sic Friedrich*: † longum est quod flagitat cup. FH, *Meyer*: longinquum est omne quod cup. fl. *Gruter.*
[345] oblivisci *codd.*: obliviscier *Gruter.*
[347] *alii alia.*

Unless fresh praise is won, even the old is lost.

The injured man's cure for pain is his enemy's pain.

335 Fickle is Fortune: she soon demands back what she gave.

'Tis a universal law that ordains birth and death.

Gain cannot be made without another's loss.

Wantonness and honour are never in harmony.

The guilty fear the law, the guiltless Fortune.

340 Flippancy's taste is caprice, not judgement.

The wanton will subdues all under its very glance.[a]

Tedious the tale of greed's demands.

When you've slipped once, be it your fault if you fall again.

The law sees the angry man, the angry man doesn't see the law.

345 Anger usually forgets the law.

He who lurks in remote places is a law unto himself.

Fire cannot throw its light afar without burning anything.

[a] Gruter explains "eam esse vim libidinis ut homines superet ipso aspectu": according to his second explanation *sub vultu* implies "beneath their apparently grave countenance."

Licentiam des linguae cum verum petas.

Z Lucrum est dolorem posse damno exstinguere.

Σ Malignos fieri maxime ingrati docent.

351 Multis minatur qui uni facit iniuriam.

Mora omnis odio est sed facit sapientiam.

Mala causa est quae requirit misericordiam.

Mori est felicis antequam mortem invoces.

355 Miserum est tacere cogi quod cupias loqui.

Miserrima est fortuna quae inimico caret.

Malus est vocandus qui sua est causa bonus.

Malus bonum ubi se simulat tunc est pessimus.

Metus cum venit, rarum habet somnus locum.

360 Mori necesse est, sed non quotiens volueris.

Male geritur quicquid geritur fortunae fide.

You must give licence to the tongue when you ask for the truth.

It is gain to be able to extinguish pain at the cost of a loss.

350 It is especially the ungrateful who teach folk to become niggardly.

A wrong done to one means a threat to many.

All delay is hateful, but it makes wisdom.

It's a poor case that seeks pity.

Lucky to die before having to invoke death.

355 It's wretched to be forced to conceal what you'd like to reveal.

It's a very poor fortune that has no enemy.

He must be called bad who is good only in his own interest.

When the villain pretends to be good, he is most villain.

When fear has come, sleep has scanty place.

360 You needs must die, but not as often as you have wished.[a]

The business that trusts to luck is a bad business.

[a] *Cf.* "Cowards die many times before their death: The valiant never taste of death but once" (*Jul. Caes.* ii. 2).

Mortuo qui mittit munus, nil dat illi, adimit sibi.

Minus est quam servus dominus qui servos timet.
Magis fidus heres nascitur quam scribitur.

365 Malo in consilio feminae vincunt viros.
Mala est voluntas ad alienam adsuescere.

Maximo periclo custoditur quod multis placet.
Mala est medicina, ubi aliquid naturae perit.
Malae naturae numquam doctore indigent.
† Misereri scire sine periclo est vivere.
371 Male vivunt qui se semper victuros putant.
Male dictum interpretando facias acrius.
Male secum agit aeger medicum qui heredem facit.

Minus decipitur cui negatur celeriter.
375 Mutat se bonitas irritata iniuria.
Mulier cum sola cogitat male cogitat.
Male facere qui vult numquam non causam invenit.

366 ad alienum consuescere *codd.*: adsuescere *Erasmus*: alienam ads. *Meyer* (*in apparatu*).
370 misereri R *Dresd.*: miseri PA: miseriam FS *Inc.*

A gift sent to a dead man is nothing to him, but means less for oneself.

A master who fears his slaves is lower than a slave.

One can trust the heir by birth more than the heir by will.[a]

365 In an ill design woman beats man.

'Tis poor will-power to get used to another's beck and call.

What many like is very perilous to guard.

It's a bad cure when a bit of nature is lost.

Bad natures never lack an instructor.

370 To know how to pity is to live without danger.[b]

Theirs is a bad life who think they are to live for ever.

Explain an ill saying and you make it worse.

The patient who makes an heir of his doctor treats himself badly.

There is less mistake when one says " no " at once.

375 Kindness alters when provoked by wrong.

A woman when she thinks alone thinks ill.

The intention to injure can always find a reason.

[a] *Cf.* 259.
[b] The Dresdensis alone shares with R the likeliest reading.

Malivolus semper sua natura vescitur.
Multos timere debet quem multi timent.
380 Male imperando summum imperium amittitur.
Mulier quae multis nubit multis non placet.
Ψ Malivolus animus abditos dentes habet.
Medicina calamitatis est aequanimitas.
Muliebris lacrima condimentum est malitiae.
385 Metum respicere non solet quicquid iuvat.
Malo etiam parcas, si una periturus bonus.

Magnum secum affert crimen indignatio.
Malus etsi obesse non potest tamen cogitat.

Mage valet qui nescit quod calamitas valet.

390 Mora cogitationis diligentia est.
Multa ignoscendo fit potens potentior.
Multis placere quae cupit culpam cupit.
Minimum eripit Fortuna cum minimum dedit.
Meretrix est instrumentum contumeliae.

389 † magis F, *Meyer* : mage *Gruter, J. C. Orelli, Woelfflin.*
393 cum F : cui σ, *Bentley, Meyer.*

The spiteful man ever battens on his own nature.

Many must he fear whom many fear.[a]

380 By bad ruling the most exalted rule is lost.

The woman who marries many is disliked by many.

The spiteful mind has hidden teeth.

The medicine for disaster is equanimity.

A woman's tear is the sauce of mischief.

385 It's pleasure's way to take but small account of fear.

You may spare even the bad, if the good is to perish along with him.[b]

Indignation brings with her some serious charge.

A villain, even though he cannot do a hurt, yet thinks of it.

He has the more power who knows not the power of calamity.

390 Slow deliberation is but carefulness.

By forgiving much, power grows more powerful.

She who would fain please many would fain be frail.

Fortune robs least when she has given least.

A harlot is an instrument of shame.

[a] *Cf.* Laberius' *Necesse est multos timeat quem multi timent.* For Laberius see Introduction.

[b] *Cf.* 261.

395 Malus bonum ad se numquam consilium refert.
Manifesta causa secum habet sententiam.
Multorum calamitate vir moritur bonus.
Metus improbos compescit non clementia.
Muneribus est, non lacrimis, meretrix misericors.
400 Metuendum est semper, esse cum tutus velis.
Mors infanti felix, iuveni acerba, nimis sera est seni.

Malam rem cum velis honestare improbes.

Malum est consilium quod mutari non potest.
Malitia unius cito fit male dictum omnium.
405 Mortem ubi contemnas viceris omnes metus.
Misera est voluptas ubi pericli memoria est.
Male vincit ⟨is⟩ quem paenitet victoriae.
Misericors civis patriae est consolatio.
Malitia ut peior veniat se simulat bonam.
410 Malus animus in secreto peius cogitat.
Mutare quod non possis, ut natum est, feras.
Multa ante temptes quam virum invenias bonum.

402 honestatem F ψ : honestare *Meyer*.

395 The villain never lays a good plan before his mind.

A clear case brings the right verdict with it.

The affliction of many is death for the good man.

Fear, not clemency, restrains the wicked.

Not tears but gifts can touch a courtesan.

400 You must always fear when you would be safe.

Death is luck for childhood, bitter for youth, too late for age.

In wishing to give fair colour to a bad case, you condemn it.

It's an ill plan that can't be changed.

The malice of one soon becomes the curse of all.

405 Despise death and you've conquered every fear.

It's but sorry pleasure when danger is remembered.

He's a poor victor who regrets his victory.

A merciful citizen is the solace of his country.

To make her onset worse, malice pretends to be good.

410 The evil mind thinks worse evil in secret.

What you cannot change, you should bear as it comes.

You may make many attempts before finding a good man.

Miserrimum est arbitrio alterius vivere.

Mansueta tutiora sunt sed serviunt.

415 Mala mors necessitatis contumelia est.

Minus saepe pecces si scias quid nescias.

Malus quicumque in poena est praesidium est bonis.

Z Mala est inopia ex copia quae nascitur.

O Monere non punire stultitiam decet.

420 Multo turpius damnatur cui in delicto ignoscitur.

ϕ (Malum ne alienum feceris tuum gaudium.)

Σ Nihil agere semper infelici est optimum.

Nihil peccant oculi, si animus oculis imperat.

Nihil proprium ducas quicquid mutari potest.

425 Non cito ruina obteritur qui rimam timet.

416 quod F ψ : quid *Gruter, Meyer.*

420 *sic* O, *Meyer* : cuius delictum (*vel* delicto) agnoscitur ϕ : cui delictum ignoscitur *Friedrich, Bickford-Smith.*

425 perit ruina *a Meyer* : ruina perit CS : r. peritur P^b : r. perituir P^aRAF : r. opteritur *Woelfflin* : rimam P^b : ruinam TFCSZ *Dunelm.*

The height of misery is life at another's will.

The tame way is safer, but it's the way of slaves.

415 A dishonourable death is fate's insolence.

You'd go wrong less often if you knew your ignorance.

Any evil-doer under punishment is a protection to the good.

It's an ill want that springs from plenty.

Advice, not punishment, is what fits folly.

420 He who is pardoned in his wrong-doing is far more shamefully condemned.[a]

Make not another's misfortune your joy.

For the unlucky it's always best to do nothing.

The eyes commit no wrong, if the mind controls the eyes.

Think nothing your own that can change.

425 It's long before the downfall overwhelms him who fears a crack.

[a] *i.e.* a man who has such a bad character that no one pays attention to his misdeed is, in fact, wholly out of court. To treat his misdeed so lightly shows what is thought of the offender.

Nullus est tam tutus quaestus quam quod habeas parcere.

Nescias quid optes aut quid fugias: ita ludit dies.

Numquam periclum sine periclo vincitur.

Nulla tam bona est fortuna de qua nihil possis queri.

430 Nusquam melius morimur homines quam ubi libenter viximus.

Negandi causa avaro numquam deficit.

Ψ Naturam abscondit cum improbus recte facit.

Non turpis est cicatrix quam virtus parit.

Numquam ubi diu fuit ignis defecit vapor.

435 Necesse est minima maximorum esse initia.

Non corrigit, sed laedit, qui invitum regit.

Nimia concedendo interdum fit stultitia ⟨stultior⟩.

Nihil magis amat cupiditas quam quod non licet.

[426] tantus *codd.*: tam tutus *Woelfflin*: parcere *Ingolst.*: carcere R: arcere PFC *Dunelm.*: carere A *Inc.*
[437] stultior *supplevit Meyer.*

There's no gain so safe as saving what you've got.

You never can tell what to wish for or what to avoid: such is the day's jest.

A risk is never mastered save by risk.

There's no luck so good but you could make some complaint about it.

430 Nowhere do we men die better than where we have lived to our liking.

The miser never lacks a reason for saying "no."[a]

When a rascal does right, he is concealing his character.

Never ugly is the scar which bravery begets.

Where there has been fire for long, there's never a lack of smoke.

435 Very big things must have very small beginnings.

He who controls the unwilling hurts rather than corrects.

By excessive yielding, folly sometimes grows more foolish still.

Greed likes nothing better than what is not allowed.

[a] This is the last of the verses in Σ, the rest of whose *sententiae* are in prose.

Nisi vindices delicta, improbitatem adiuves.

440 Nulli facilius quam malo invenies parem.

Nihil non acerbum prius quam maturum fuit.

Nocere posse et nolle laus amplissima est.

Non vincitur, sed vincit, qui cedit suis.

Necessitas dat legem, non ipsa accipit.

445 Nescio quid agitat, cum bonum imitatur malus.

Nulla hominum maior poena est quam infelicitas.

Non novit virtus calamitati cedere.

Necessitas ab homine quae vult impetrat.

Necessitati quodlibet telum utile est.

450 Nocere casus non solet constantiae.

Non pote non sapere qui se stultum intellegit.

Necessitas egentem mendacem facit.

Non facile solus serves quod multis placet.

Necessitas quod poscit nisi des eripit.

455 Nocens precatur, innocens irascitur.

If you didn't punish offences, you'd help roguery.

440 It's the bad man whose like you'll find most easily.

Everything ripe was once sour.

Power to harm without the will is the most ample fame.

He who yields to his own people is conqueror, not conquered.

Necessity prescribes law: she does not bow to it herself.

445 When the rogue copies good folk, he has something in mind.

Man meets no worse punishment than misfortune.

Bravery knows no yielding to calamity.

Necessity wins what she wants from man.

Necessity finds any weapon serviceable.

450 Misfortune seldom hurts steadfastness.

He must have wit who understands he is a fool.

Necessity makes beggars liars.

Single-handed, you'd find it hard to keep what many want.

Necessity snatches what she asks, unless you give it.

455 Guilt entreats where innocence feels indignant.

Nec vita nec fortuna hominibus perpes est.

Non semper aurem facilem habet felicitas.

Numquam non miser est qui quod timeat cogitat.

Ni qui scit facere insidias nescit metuere.

460 Negat sibi ipse qui quod difficile est petit.

Nimium altercando veritas amittitur.

Nullo in loco male audit misericordia.

Necessitas quod celat frustra quaeritur.

Necessitas quam pertinax regnum tenet!

465 Nemo immature moritur qui moritur miser.

Nocentem qui defendit sibi crimen parit.

Nihil non aut lenit aut domat diuturnitas.

Nihil turpe ducas pro salutis remedio.

Noli contemnere ea quae summos sublevant.

470 Nihil aliud scit necessitas quam vincere.

Nemo timendo ad summum pervenit locum.

456 *sic Gruter*: propria est hominibus *Spengel, Meyer*: perpetua est F *a*.

Neither life nor luck is lasting[a] for man.

Success has not always the ready ear.

Misery never quits him whose thoughts run on something to dread.

Everyone fails to fear an ambush except him who can set one.

460 He who begs for what is difficult says " no " to himself.

In excessive wrangling truth gets lost.

Pity gets a bad name nowhere.

What necessity hides is sought for in vain.

How firm the hold of Necessity upon her throne!

465 None dies untimely who dies in misery.

The champion of the guilty begets a charge against himself.

There's naught that time does not either soothe or quell.

To cure bad health, think nothing unclean.

Do not despise the steps which raise to greatness.

470 Necessity knows naught else but victory.

Fear never brought one to the top.

[a] *perpes* is a Plautine as well as a late Latin word: *perpetem pro perpetuo dixerunt poetae*, Fest. 217, Müll.

Nisi per te sapias, frustra sapientem audias.

Necessitati sapiens nihil umquam negat.

Non facile de innocente crimen fingitur.

475 Nimium boni est in morte cum nihil est mali.

Ni gradus servetur, nulli tutus est summus locus.

Nihil est miserius quam ubi pudet quod feceris.

Nec mortem effugere quisquam nec amorem potest.

Necessitatem ferre non flere addecet.

480 Nusquam facilius culpa quam in turba latet.

Z Non leve beneficium praestat qui breviter negat.

(Non est beatus esse se qui non putat.)

Ψ Omnis voluptas quemcumque arrisit nocet.

Officium benivoli animi finem non habet.

485 O vita misero longa, felici brevis!

Obiurgari in calamitate gravius est quam calamitas.

480 numquam F ψ: nusquam *Woelfflin.*
483 *sic* F: qu(a)ecunque ψ.
484 officium F: obsequium a ψ, *Meyer.*
485 *sic citat. apud Senecam, Contr.* vii. 18.

Without mother-wit of your own, it's no good listening to the wise.

A wise man never refuses anything to necessity.

A charge is not easily framed against the guiltless.

475 Death is too much a boon when it has no bane.

Unless one's step be guarded, the summit is safe for none.[a]

There's nothing more wretched than being ashamed of what you've done.

There's no one can escape either death or love.

'Tis fitting to bear and not bemoan necessity.

480 Crime is nowhere more easily hidden than in a crowd.

To say "no" at once is to confer no slight kindness.

He's not happy who does not think himself so.[b]

All pleasure harms whomso it charms.

The services of a benevolent mind have no end.

485 O life, long for woe but brief for joy!

To be scolded in misfortune is harder than misfortune's self.

[a] *i.e.* a slip in the highest positions is ruin.
[b] The Latin comes from Sen. *Ep.* ix. 21.

O dulce tormentum ubi reprimitur gaudium!

Omnes aequo animo parent ubi digni imperant.

Occidi est pulchrum, ignominiose ubi servias.

490 O tacitum tormentum animi conscientia!

Optime positum est beneficium ⟨bene⟩ ubi meminit qui accipit.

Obsequio nuptae cito fit odium paelicis.

Occasio receptus difficiles habet.

O pessimum periclum quod opertum latet!

495 Omnes cum occulte peccant, peccant ocius.

Occasio aegre offertur, facile amittitur.

O Oculi ⟨occulte⟩ amorem incipiunt, consuetudo perficit.

Ψ Probus libertus sine natura est filius.

Prodesse qui vult nec potest, aeque est miser.

500 Pericla timidus etiam quae non sunt videt.

Pudor doceri non potest, nasci potest.

[491] *sic Spengel*: ubi eius *Gruter*.
[495] *sic Woelfflin*: o. c. peccant occulte pacantur citius F.

'Tis sweet torture when joy is held in.

When worth holds sway, all cheerfully obey.

It is noble to be slain, when your servitude is shameful.

590 O conscience, silent torture of the mind!

A benefit is best bestowed when the recipient has a good memory.

The bride's complaisance soon brings loathing for a harlot.

The favourable moment is hard to recover.

O worst of dangers that lurks unseen!

595 Sinners in secret are always quicker to sin.

Opportunity is slow to offer, easy to miss.

The eyes start love secretly: intimacy perfects it.

An upright freedman is a son without the tie of blood.

The wish to help without the power means sharing misery.[a]

600 Cravens see even dangers which do not exist.

Modesty is born, not taught.

[a] Meyer punctuates "nec potest aeque, est miser."

Plus est quam poena sinere miserum vivere.

Pudorem alienum qui eripit perdit suum.

Patientia animi occultas divitias habet.

505 Peiora multo cogitat mutus dolor.

Pecunia ⟨una⟩ regimen est rerum omnium.

Pudor dimissus numquam redit in gratiam.

Perdendi finem nemo nisi egestas facit.

Poena ad malum serpens iam cum properat venit.

510 Plus est quam poena iniuriae succumbere.

Pro medicina est dolor dolorem qui necat.

Patiens et fortis se ipsum felicem facit.

Prospicere in pace oportet quod bellum iuvet.

Parens iratus in se est crudelissimus.

515 Perdit non donat qui dat nisi sit memoria.

Probi delicta neglegens, leges teras.

[502] sine rem F : sinere *Spengel* : sine spe *Woelfflin* (*in not.*), *Meyer*.
[505] multa *codd.* : multo *Tzschucke, Meyer*.
[509] serpentia F : serpendo *Bothe* : serpens, iam *Bickford Smith*.

It is more than punishment to let one live in misery.

Who steals another's modesty loses his own.

Patience of mind has secret wealth.

505 Dumb grief thinks of much worse to come.

Money alone is the ruling principle of the world.

Modesty, once dismissed, never returns to favour.

Only want sets a limit to waste.

Punishment with creeping pace comes on the offender in the moment of his haste.

510 'Tis more than punishment to yield to wrong.

The pain that kills pain acts as medicine.

The man who unites patience and courage secures his own happiness.

In peace one must forecast the sinews of war.

The parent enraged is most cruel to himself.

515 A gift is lost, not presented, unless there be recollection of it.

In overlooking even a good man's offences, you would impair the laws.

---

516 † probe delicta cum legas deteras *codd.*, *Meyer*: probi *Ingol.*: cum tegas *Spengel*: cum neglegas (? nĕglĕgās), leges teras *Woelfflin.*

Pars benefici est quod petitur si belle neges.

Properare in iudicando est crimen quaerere.

Populi est mancipium quisquis patriae est utilis.

520 Per quae sis tutus illa semper cogites.

Perfugere ad inferiorem se ipsum est tradere.

Peccatum amici veluti tuum recte putes.

Potens misericors publica est felicitas.

Praesens est semper absens qui se ulciscitur.

525 Perfacile quod vota imperant felix facit.

Poenam moratur improbus, non praeterit.

Perdidisse ad assem mallem quam accepisse turpiter.

Paucorum est intellegere quid donet deus.

Perenne coniugium animus, non corpus, facit.

530 Pereundi scire tempus adsidue est mori.

[527] ad assem *add. Friedrich*: honeste *Woelfflin*: *om. codd.*
[528] † det F, *Meyer*: celet *Ribbeck*: dicat *Buecheler*: donet dies *Woelfflin*: doceat dies *Meiser*.

A nice refusal of a request is half a kindness done.

Haste in judgement is to look for guilt.

Whoever is useful to his country is the nation's slave.

520 Always bethink yourself of means of safety.

To take refuge with an inferior is self-betrayal.

You would do right to consider your friend's fault as if it were your own.

Mercy in power is good fortune for a people.

He who avenges himself though absent is ever present.[a]

525 It's very easy for the lucky man to do what his wishes command.

The villain delays his punishment—he does not escape it.

I'd rather lose to the last farthing than get dishonourably.

It is granted to few to comprehend what God gives.

Mind, not body, makes lasting wedlock.

530 To know the hour of doom is continual death.

[a] *E.g.* a tyrant through a system of espionage might be called ubiquitous: *cf.* the "eyes and ears" of the Persian king, Xen. *Cyrop.* viii. 2, 9–10 (τίς δ' ἄλλος ἐδυνάσθη ἐχθροὺς ἀπέχοντας πολλῶν μηνῶν ὁδὸν τιμωρεῖσθαι ὡς Περσῶν βασιλεύς;)

Potenti irasci sibi periclum est quaerere.

Peccare pauci nolunt, nulli nesciunt.

Paucorum improbitas est multorum calamitas.

Pro dominis peccare etiam virtutis loco est.

535 Patiendo multa venient quae nequeas pati.

Paratae lacrimae insidias non fletum indicant.

Peccatum extenuat qui celeriter corrigit.

Pudorem habere servitus quodammodo est.

Potest uti adversis numquam felicitas.

540 Prudentis vultus etiam sermonis loco est.

Probo beneficium qui dat ex parte accipit.

Pudor si quem non flectit, non frangit timor.

Poena allevatur ubi relaxatur dolor.

Plures tegit Fortuna quam tutos facit.

545 Post calamitatem memoria alia est calamitas.

Probo bona fama maxima est hereditas.

533 est multorum *Buecheler* : universis est F.
539 *sic Bickford-Smith* : potest ultus in F.

To be angry with the powerful is seeking danger for oneself.

Few are unwilling to sin—none but know the way.

The wickedness of a few is widespread calamity.

To do wrong for one's master even passes for merit.

535 Sufferance will bring much you could not suffer.

The ready tear means treachery, not grief.

The quick corrector weakens sin.

To feel qualms is in a measure slavery.

The lucky man never knows how to deal with adversity.

540 The wise man's looks are as good as a discourse.

The giver of a benefit to the good is in part the receiver.

If honour sways one not, fear cannot quell.

The punishment is lightened when the pain slackens.

Fortune shields more people than she makes safe.

545 After misfortune, remembrance is misfortune renewed.

For the upright a good name is the greatest inheritance.

Pericla qui audet ante vincit quam accipit.

Perpetuo vincit qui utitur clementia.

Z Plures amicos mensa quam mens concipit.

O Prudentis est irascier sero et semel.

551 Per quem sis clarus illi quod sis imputes.

Poenae sat est qui laesit cum supplex venit.

Ψ Quamvis non rectum quod iuvat rectum putes.

Quisquis nocere didicit meminit cum potest.

555 Qui metuit calamitatem rarius accipit.

Quam miserum est mortem cupere nec posse emori!

Qui pro innocente dicit satis est eloquens.

Qui cum dolet blanditur post tempus sapit.

Quod timeas citius quam quod speres evenit.

560 Quod vult cupiditas cogitat, non quod decet.

550 *sic Friedrich*: irasci et sero et semel O: nec sero et semel *Halm, Meyer*.

The bold defeat danger before meeting it.

He is for ever victor who employs clemency.

One's table receives more friends than one's heart does.

550 It is wisdom to lose one's temper late and then once for all.

To the man who made you famous give the credit of what you are.

'Tis penalty enough when the offender comes on his knees.

Think right what helps, though right it may not be.

Power to harm once learned is remembered when the chance comes.

555 He who dreads disaster rarely meets it.

How wretched to long for death yet fail to die!

The pleader for innocence is eloquent enough.

If a man takes to coaxing when he feels the smart, it is wisdom learned too late.

The dreaded thing happens sooner than you might expect

560 Greed contemplates what it wishes, not what befits.

---

554 quicquid *Meyer.*
555 contumeliam raro *Spengel, Meyer.*

Quicquid conaris, quo pervenias cogites.

Qui bene dissimulat citius inimico nocet.

Quod semper est paratum non semper iuvat.

Quodcumque celes ipse tibi fias timor.

565 Qui ius iurandum servat quovis pervenit.

Quod aetas vitium posuit aetas auferet.

Quemcumque quaerit calamitas facile invenit.

Quod periit quaeri pote, reprendi non potest.

Quam miserum officium est quod successum non habet!

570 Quam miser est cui est ingrata misericordia!

Quam miserum est cogi opprimere quem salvum velis!

Quem fama semel oppressit vix restituitur.

Quod vix contingit ut voluptatem parit!

Quam miserum est id quod pauci habent amittere!

573 vix . . . vix *Gruter*: vi . . . vix *Woelfflin*: quidvis . . . ut (*velut sententia ex Epicureorum disciplina profecta*) *Friedrich.*

In your every endeavour contemplate your goal.

An apt dissembler sooner hurts his foe.

What is always at hand does not always help.

Your guarded secret means you grow a terror to yourself.

565 He who observes his oath reaches any goal.

The fault which time has set up time will take away.

Disaster easily finds whomsoever it seeks.

What is destroyed can be looked for but never recovered.

How sorry the service that has no success!

570 How wretched he to whom pity is against the grain!

How wretched to be forced to crush him you fain would save!

It is hard restoring him whom ill report has once crushed.

What pleasure is produced by what is won with difficulty!

How pitiable it is to lose what few possess!

575 Qui in vero dubitat male agit cum deliberat.

Qui timet amicum, amicus ut timeat, docet.

Quicquid vindicandum est, ⟨omnis⟩ optima est occasio.

Quam miserum auxilium est ubi nocet quod sustinet!

Qui pote consilium fugere sapere idem potest.

580 Qui ulcisci dubitat improbos plures facit.

Qui obesse cum potest non vult prodest ⟨tibi⟩.

Quicquid bono concedas, des partem tibi.

Quod nescias cui serves stultum est parcere.

Quae vult videri bella nimis, nulli negat.

585 Qui debet limen creditoris non amat.

Qui pote transferre amorem pote deponere.

Qui culpae ignoscit uni suadet pluribus.

579 potest F: pote *Gruter*. capere *Gruter* (*in not. post.*), *Spengel*: rapere *Woelfflin*.
581 tibi *add. Halm*.
584 † nimium illi negat F, *Meyer*: nimis, nulli negat *Gruter, Orelli*: nimium litigat *Spengel*.

575 He who hesitates in the case of truth acts ill when he deliberates.[a]

Who fears a friend teaches a friend to fear.

When aught has to be punished, every opportunity is best.

A sorry help when support hurts!

The man who can shun advice may yet be wise.[b]

580 A hesitating avenger makes rascals increase.

He who will not hurt when he may is your benefactor.

Whatever you may grant to the good, you give partly to yourself.

It's silly to be sparing, if you don't know for whom you're saving.

She who is over fain to be thought pretty, refuses none.

585 The debtor loves not his creditor's threshold.

If one can transfer affection, one can put it aside.

To pardon one offence is to prompt more offenders.

[a] *i.e.* he who hesitates when facts are plain commits a crime by his very deliberation.

[b] *i.e.* there is advice which it is wise not to take. This is pithier than the truism involved in the change to *capere.*

Quod improbis eripitur donatur probis.

Qui sibi non vivit aliis merito est mortuus.

590 Quicquid fit cum virtute fit cum gloria.

Qui exspectat ut rogetur officium levat.

Qui timet amicum vim non novit nominis.

Qui ⟨non⟩ potest celare vitium non facit.

Qui omnes insidias timet in nullas incidit.

595 Quam malus est culpam qui suam alterius facit!

Qui docte servit partem dominatus tenet.

Qui se ipse laudat cito derisorem invenit.

[589] sibi non **F**: sibi minime **T**: sibimet *Ribbeck, Spengel*: sibi modo *Gruter* (*not. post.*), *Bothe*.

[593] *sic Meyer in not*: qui potest zelare non facit vitium *ψ*: qui pote celare vitium, vitium non facit *Gruter* (fugit *Ribbeck*).

What is snatched from the bad is a gift to the good.

He who does not live a busy life of his own is as good as dead for others.[a]

590 A deed of valour is a deed of fame.

He who waits to be asked lessens his service.

He who fears a friend doesn't know the meaning of the word.

He who cannot conceal a vicious act does not commit it.[b]

He who fears every ambush falls into none.[c]

595 What a rascal he is who throws his own guilt upon another!

The skilled servant holds part of his master's power.

The self-praiser soon finds a mocker.

[a] The man who cannot attend to his own affairs with competence is no good to others. *Sibi vivere* is not here "to live only for oneself": it does not, as Orelli takes it, imply a miser who spends neither on himself nor on others. Friedrich aptly illustrates the sense from Sen. *Ep.* lv. 4–5, where the phrase is used of one who rises above slothful retirement or an animal-like existence of self-indulgence to a strenuous and full life in which through serving others he will serve his highest self (cf. *ibid. non continuo sibi vivit, qui nemini*).

[b] A criminal is usually inspired with the hope of eluding detection: so a character in a mime might be imagined to say, "He who can't get away with it, doesn't do it." The text is, however, uncertain (see appar. crit.).

[c] *Cf.* sentiment in 400.

Quam miserum est bene quod feceris factum queri!

Quam est felix vita quae sine odiis transiit!

600 Quicquid futurum est summum ab imo nascitur.

Quam miserum est ubi consilium casu vincitur!

Quicquid fortuna exornat cito contemnitur.

Quicquid plus quam necesse est possideas premit.

Qui pote nocere timetur cum etiam non adest.

605 Quem bono tenere non potueris, contineas malo.

Quod senior loquitur omnes consilium putant.

Quam miserum est, ubi te captant, qui defenderent!

Quod quisque amat laudando commendat sibi.

Quem diligas etiam † queri de ipso malum est.

610 Qui venit ut noceat semper meditatus venit.

Quis miserum sciret, verba nisi haberet dolor?

Quam miserum est cum se renovat consumptum malum!

A sorry thing to complain of a good deed you've done!

How happy the life which has passed without strife!

600 Whatever is to be top springs from the bottom.

A pity when chance beats design!

Whatever fortune bedizens is soon despised.

Any possession beyond the needful overburdens you.

He who can hurt is dreaded even when not upon the scene.

605 Him you have failed to control by fair means, you must restrain by foul.

What a senior says all take for advice.

Pity it is when your supposed defenders take you prisoner!

Everyone commends his hobby to himself by praising it.

It's ill complaining even about the very friend you love.

610 Who comes to injure always comes with mind made up.

Who would know the wretched, if pain had no words?

What a pity when an outworn evil is renewed!

Quanto serius peccatur tanto incipitur turpius.

Quam miser est qui excusare sibi se non potest!

615 Quo caveas, cum animus aliud verba aliud petunt?

Qui invitus servit, fit miser, servit tamen.

Quod est timendum decipit si neglegas.

Quid tibi pecunia opus est, si uti non potes?

Quod fugere credas saepe solet occurrere.

620 Quamvis acerbus qui monet nulli nocet.

Z Qui numerosis studet amicis is etiam inimicos ferat.

† Qui semet accusat ab alio non potest criminari.

Qui dormientem necat absentem ulciscitur.

Quod est venturum sapiens ut praesens cavet.

[615] cavetis F: caveas *Bothe, Woelfflin, Spengel, Meyer*: cavet is *Orelli*.

[621] *sic Haupt.*: qui numerosis s. a. et inimicos necesse est ferat T: q. studet multis a. multos i. f. *Meyer*.

[622] qui se ipse accusat, accusari non potest *Ribbeck*: *alii alia*.

The later the sin in coming, the more disgraceful its start.

How wretched the man who cannot make his excuses to himself!

615 How take precautions when heart seeks one thing and words another?

The unwilling slave grows wretched, but is still a slave.

The object of your fear tricks you, if you overlook it.

Why do you need money, if you can't use it?

What you suppose to be in flight is often wont to face you.

620 The warning voice, however sharp, hurts none.

He who is devoted to numerous friends should likewise put up with foes.

He who accuses himself cannot be accused by another.[a]

The slayer of a sleeping man is taking vengeance on the absent.

The wise man guards against what is to come, as if it were present.

[a] *criminari* is deponent in classical Latin.

O Quem diligas, ni recte moneas, oderis.

626 (Quod vult habet qui velle quod satis est potest.)

Ψ Ratione non vi vincenda adulescentia est.

Rei nulli prodest mora nisi iracundiae.

Reus innocens fortunam non testem timet.

630 Rarum esse oportet quod diu carum velis.

Rapere est accipere quod non possis reddere.

Regnat non regitur qui nihil nisi quod vult facit.

Rivalitatem non amat victoria.

Ruborem amico excutere amicum est perdere.

635 Rex esse nolim ut esse crudelis velim.

Res quanto est maior tanto est insidiosior.

Roganti melius quam imperanti pareas.

Respicere nihil consuevit iracundia.

Rapere est, non petere, quicquid invito auferas.

640 Remedium frustra est contra fulmen quaerere.

640 remedium fraus F : remigium frustra *Gruter in notis postumis.* flumen F : fulmen *Bentley.*

25 You will hate the man you love, unless you admonish him aright.

He who can wish for what is enough has his wish.[a]

Youth must be mastered not by force but by reason.

Anger is the one thing benefited by delay.

The innocent man on trial fears fortune, but not a witness.

30 Rare must be that which you would long hold dear.

It is robbery to take what you could never return.

He is a king and no subject who does only what he likes.

Victory loves not rivalry.

Wring a blush from a friend and you lose him.

35 I'd fain have no kingly power with its promptings to cruelty.

The bigger the affair, the greater the snare.

A request is better to comply with than an order.

Anger's way is to regard nothing.

It's no request, it's robbery, to take from the unwilling.

40 It's no good to seek an antidote for a thunderbolt.

[a] The Latin is from Sen. *Ep.* cviii. 11.

Rogare officium servitus quodammodo est.

Z Reddit non perdit cui quod alienum est perit.

Ψ † Semper iratus plus se posse putat quam possit.

Spes est salutis ubi hominem obiurgat pudor.

645 Suadere primum dein corrigere benivoli est.

Sapiens contra omnes arma fert cum cogitat.

Sanctissimum est meminisse cui te debeas.

Stulti timent fortunam, sapientes ferunt.

Sensus, non aetas, invenit sapientiam.

650 Semper beatam se putat benignitas.

Sapiens locum dat requiescendi iniuriae.

Solet esse in dubiis pro consilio temeritas.

Semper consilium tunc deest cum opus est maxime.

Sapiens quod petitur, ubi tacet, breviter negat.

655 Semper plus metuit animus ignotum malum.

642 *sic Haupt* : qui quod alienum erat persolvit T.
643 se posse plus iratus quam possit putat *Pithoeus* : *fortasse trochaicus* semper iratus plus sese posse quam possit putat *A. M. Duff.*

To ask a favour is slavery of a sort.

To lose what is not your own is not to lose but to give back.

Anger always thinks it has power beyond its power.

When shame rebukes a man, there's hope for his soul's health.

645 It's the well-wisher's way to advise before he corrects.

The sage bears arms against the world when he thinks.

'Tis most just to remember to whom you owe yourself.

Fools fear fortune, wise men bear it.

Wisdom is found by sense, not years.

650 Bounty holds herself ever rich.

The wise man gives an injury room to settle down.

In a hazard venturesomeness replaces deliberation.

Counsel is ever lacking when most needed.

It's a curt refusal when the wise man meets a request with silence.

655 The mind always fears the unknown evil more.

---

651 *sic Spengel*: † sapiens semper quiescendi dat locum iniuriae F, *Meyer*: saepe ignoscendo das iniuriae locum *Gruter*: semper quiescens des iniuriae locum *Meyer in not.*

654 *sic* F: cum . . . si . . . graviter O, *Meyer*.

Secunda in paupertate fortuna est fides.

Si nihil velis timere, metuas omnia.

Summissum imperium non tenet vires suas.

Secundus est a matre nutricis dolor.

660 Sibi supplicium ipse dat quem admissi paenitet.

Suum sequitur lumen semper innocentia.

Stultum est ulcisci velle alium poena sua.

Sibi primum auxilium eripere est leges tollere.

Suis qui nescit parcere inimicis favet.

665 Sine dolore est vulnus quod ferendum est cum vic toria.

Semper metuendo sapiens evitat malum.

Stultum est queri de adversis, ubi culpa est tua.

Solet hora quod multi anni abstulerunt reddere.

Spina etiam grata est ex qua spectatur rosa.

In poverty faith is fortune renewed.[a]

If you want to fear nothing, you should dread all.

Diminished power keeps not its strength.

The nurse's pangs are second to the mother's.

660 He who repents his deed inflicts punishment on himself.

Innocence ever follows her own light.

It's folly to want vengeance on another by punishing oneself.

To destroy the laws is to rob oneself of one's first support.

He who cannot spare his own folk befriends his foes.

665 It's a painless wound that the victor must bear.

By constant fear the wise man escapes harm.

Silly to grumble about misfortune when the fault's your own.

An hour often restores what many years have taken away.

Pleasant even the thorn which yields a rose to view.

[a] *i.e.* if a man reduced to poverty retains a faith in better times to come, that is in some degree a restoration of fortune.

670 Stultum est vicinum velle ulcisci incendio.

Stultum facit Fortuna quem vult perdere.

Spes inopem, res avarum, mors miserum levat.

Se damnat iudex innocentem qui opprimit.

Sibi ipsa improbitas cogit fieri iniuriam.

675 Satis est beatus qui potest cum vult mori.

Solet sequi laus, cum viam fecit labor.

Socius fit culpae qui nocentem sublevat.

Suspicio sibi ipsa rivales parit.

Semper metuendum quicquid irasci potest.

680 Seditio civium hostium est occasio.

Salutis causa bene fit homini iniuria.

Stultitia est insectari quem di diligunt.

Sat magna usura est pro beneficio memoria.

Sero in periclis est consilium quaerere.

Z Sua servat qui salva esse vult communia.

686 Satis est superare inimicum, nimium est perdere.

Suspiciosus omnium damnat fidem.

670 It's silly to want vengeance on a neighbour by firing the house.

Fortune makes a fool of him whom she would ruin.[a]

Hope eases the beggar, wealth the miser, death the wretched.

A judge who crushes the guiltless is self-condemned.

Villainy compels injury to be done to itself.

675 Happy enough he who can die when he wills!

Praise ever follows when toil has made the way.

To help the guilty is to share his crime.

Suspicion doth breed rivals for herself.

What can show anger must ever be dreaded.

680 Discord mid citizens is the foeman's chance.

Injury may well be done a man for safety's sake.

'Tis folly to upbraid the favourite of heaven.

'Tis high enough interest for a benefit to remember it.

'Tis too late in perils to search for advice.

685 He who wishes safety for the common property is the guardian of his own.

It is enough to beat a foe, too much to ruin him.

The suspicious man condemns the good faith of all.

[a] A more familiar form of this idea is *quem Iuppiter vult perdere dementat prius.*

Suspicio probatis tacita iniuria est.

Superari a superiore pars est gloriae.

690 Supplicem hominem opprimere virtus non est sed crudelitas.

Sat est disertus e quo loquitur veritas.

Ψ Thesaurum in sepulcro ponit qui senem heredem facit.

Taciturnitas stulto homini pro sapientia est.

Tam deest avaro quod habet quam quod non habet.

Z Tarde sed graviter sapiens ⟨mens⟩ irascitur.

696 Tuti sunt omnes unus ubi defenditur.

O Temptando cuncta caeci quoque tuto ambulant.

Tam de se iudex iudicat quam de reo.

Ψ Ubi fata peccant, hominum consilia excidunt.

700 Voluptas e difficili data dulcissima est.

Ubi omnis vitae metus est, mors est optima.

Unus deus poenam affert, multi cogitant.

[691] de quo T : pro quo O : e quo *Casp. Orelli in not.*
[695] *alii alia* : mens *Bickford-Smith.*
[702] u. deus poenam affert quam m. cogitant F : dies (*delevit* quam) *Gruter* : citant *Buecheler* : irrogant *Meyer* : coquunt *Friedrich.*

Suspicion is an unspoken wrong to tested worth.

To be bested by a better means a share in the glory.

90 To crush the suppliant is not valour but barbarity.

Eloquent enough is he who has the accent of truth.

He stows treasure in the tomb who makes an old man his heir.

For a fool it is wisdom to hold his tongue.

The miser lacks what he has as much as what he hasn't.[a]

95 A wise mind grows angry slowly but seriously.[b]

All are safe when one is defended.

By testing everything even the blind walk safely.

A judge passes judgement on himself as much as on the accused.

When fate goes awry, human counsels fail.

00 Out of difficulty comes the sweetest pleasure.

When life is all one terror, death is best.

God alone brings punishment, though many intend it.

[a] One of the best known lines of Publilius: it is quoted by Seneca, *Controv.* vii. 3 (18) 8; Quintilian, viii. 5, 6 and ix. 3, 64; Hieronymus, *Epist.* liii, 10 *sub fin.* Jerome's order is *avaro tam deest* . . .

[b] *Cf.* 550.

Ubi peccat aetas maior, male discit minor.

Ubi nihil timetur, quod timeatur nascitur.

705 Ubi sis cum tuis et absis, patriam non desideres.

Verum est quod pro salute fit mendacium.

Ubicumque pudor est, semper ibi sancta est fides.

Utilius ferrum est in sulco quam orichalcum est in proelio.

Ubi innocens formidat damnat iudicem.

710 Voluntas impudicum non corpus facit.

Virtuti melius quam fortunae creditur.

Verbum omne refert in quam partem intellegas.

Virum bonum natura non ordo facit.

Ubi coepit ditem pauper imitari, perit.

715 Veterem ferendo iniuriam invites novam.

Virtutis spolia cum videt, gaudet labor.

Virtutis vultus partem habet victoriae.

Virtute quod non possis blanditia auferas.

Utrumque casum adspicere debet qui imperat.

705 absis patria *Meyer*: patriam desideres F: non *add. Orelli.*

708 *om. Meyer*: Utilius est vero in sulco quam gravis galea in proelio *Par.* 8027 *servat solus*: veru est *Woelfflin*: ferrum est *alii*: quam orichalcum *Friedrich.*

When seniors blunder, juniors learn but ill.

When nothing is feared, something arises to fear.

)05 When far away with your own folk, you would not miss your fatherland.

Falsehood for safety's sake is true.

Where scruples are, there faith is ever revered.

Steel in the furrow is more useful than yellow copper in battle.

Innocence in terror condemns the judge.

10 The will, not the body, makes impurity.

It's better trusting to valour than to luck.

For any word it matters how you understand it.

Nature, not rank, makes the gentleman.

When the poor man starts to ape the rich, he's lost.

15 Tolerate an old wrong and you may invite a new one.

The sight of valour's spoil makes the delight of toil.[a]

Bravery's countenance has a share in the victory.

Coaxing may win what the stout heart could not.

A ruler should look at both the sides of chance.

[a] *Labor* is personified: hard-wrought soldiers, after the fight, look with joy on the spoil which proves their victorious bravery.

720 Voluptas tacita metus est mage quam gaudium.

Viri boni est nescire facere iniuriam.

Vultu an natura sapiens sis, multum interest.

Virtuti amorem nemo honeste denegat.

Z Ubi libertas cecidit, audet libere nemo loqui.

725 Vita otiosa regnum est et curae minus.

Ubi omnes peccant, spes querelae tollitur.

Ut plures corrigantur, † rite pauci eliduntur.

Virtutis omnis impedimentum est timor.

Ubi iudicat qui accusat, vis non lex valet.

730 Ubi emas aliena, caveas ne vendas tua.

O Ubi peccatum cito corrigitur, fama solet ignoscere.

Ubi innocens damnatur, pars patriae exsulat.

Vincere est honestum, opprimere acerbum, pulchrum ignoscere.

ϕ (Velox consilium sequitur paenitentia.)

720 magis F, *Spengel*, *Meyer*: mage metus *Gruter*.

727 *sic* T: rite unus perit *Casp. Orelli in not.*: ut plures sanes recte paucos amputes *Friedrich*.

20 Dumb pleasure is rather fear than joy.

Goodness means inability to do a wrong.

It makes a wide difference whether you were born wise or only look it.

From virtue no man honourably withholds his love.

Where freedom has fallen, none dare freely speak.

25 The life of ease is a kingdom without the worry.

Where all go wrong, the hope of remonstrance is removed.

A few are justly destroyed that more may be reformed.

All virtue finds an obstacle in fear.

When the accuser is judge, force, not law, has power.

0 In buying others' goods, see you don't have to sell your own.

When an offence is soon corrected, scandal commonly overlooks it.

When the innocent is found guilty, part of his native land is exiled.

It is honourable to conquer, bitter to crush, handsome to forgive.

Repentance follows on a hasty plan.

---

730 *sic Meyer in apparatu* : invenies necesse est tua T.

Dumb pleasure is rather fear than joy. 10

Goodness means inability to do a wrong.

It makes a wide difference whether you were born wise or only look it.

From virtue no man honourably withholds his love.

Where freedom has fallen, none dare freely speak.

The life of ease is a kingdom without the worry. 15

Where all go wrong, the hope of remonstrance is removed.

A few are justly destroyed that more may be reformed.

All virtue finds an obstacle in fear.

When the accuser is judge, force, not law, has power.

In buying others' goods, see you don't have to sell your own. 20

When an offence is seen corrected, scandal commonly overlooks it.

When the innocent is found guilty, part of his native land is exiled.

It is honourable to conquer, bitter to crush, handsome to forgive.

Repentance follows on a hasty plan.

---

78 sic Meyer in apparatu: servi enim necesse est tua B.

ELEGIAE IN MAECENATEM

INTRODUCTION
TO THE ELEGIES

THESE two elegies are transmitted as a single continuous poem in manuscripts of the minor "Virgilian" works (*Culex*, *Dirae*, *Copa*, *Moretum*). The ascription to Virgil is chronologically impossible; for Maecenas died in 8 B.C., eleven years after Virgil. Scaliger first separated the longer poem from the thirty-four lines which give the "Dying Words of Maecenas," and he propounded the guess (once considered attractive) that both elegies, as well as the *Consolatio ad Liviam*, might be the work of Albinovanus Pedo. To some extent modern opinion inclines to accept as genuine the claim of the author (*Eleg.* I. 1–2: *cf.* II. 3–4) to have already written the consolatory lament addressed to Livia on the death of Drusus.[a] The repetition of the phrases *Caesaris illud opus* and *illa rapit iuvenes* [b] as well as the noteworthy parallelism between two other passages [c] strengthens the case, though it is conceded that the *Elegiae* are artistically inferior to the *Consolatio*. They have, however, a similar rhetorical ring; and the metrical technique of the elegies, while it shows fewer elisions than does the *Consolatio*, is in keeping with that of the Augustan

[a] The *Consolatio* is translated in the Loeb Library: Ovid, *Art of Love and other Poems*, pp. 325 sqq.
[b] *Cons.* 39, *Eleg.* II. 6; *Cons.* 372, *Eleg.* I. 7.
[c] *Cons.* 47–48, *Eleg.* I. 15–16.

period. Haupt's endeavour to regard the first elegy as a defence of Maecenas against a charge of *tunicae solutae* in Seneca's 114th letter has been successfully rebutted by Skutsch:[a] Seneca's letter contains other censures which the poet could not have left unanswered, if he had ever seen them. In this elaborate letter on decadence, and in particular on speech as a mirror of morals, emphasis is laid upon Maecenas' undisciplined style as a parallel to the dishabille which he notoriously affected. There are no convincing allusions to prove that the poem followed the letter, and we should not expect a reply to it to ignore the instances adduced.[b]

The contents and tone of the poems give the impression that the author stood close to the facts introduced.[c] This direct contact with reality, which appears to underlie the allusions to Maecenas' war-service, to his *cura urbis* and intellectual interests,

[a] P. W. *Realencyclopädie*, IV. 1901: art. on 'Consolatio ad Liviam.'

[b] Th. Birt, like Haupt, considers the *Elegiae* post-Senecan, and holds that the passage about the beryl (I. 19–20) refers to the wide difference between Maecenas' style and the common level of expression (*Ad hist. hexam. latini symb.*, Bonn, 1876, p. 66).

[c] Prof. R. S. Radford in *The Culex and Ovid, Philologus*, 1930, 86, 1, defends the Ovidian authorship of both *Consolatio* and the *Elegiae*. Dealing with *The Order of Ovid's Works* (*Trans. Amer. Philol. Assoc.*, 1923) he assigns the former to 9 B.C., the latter to 8 B.C. In E. Wagner's *De Martiale Poetarum Augusteae aetatis imitatore*, Regimonti (=Königsberg), 1880, similarities of phraseology between Elegy I and Martial were unduly stressed as suggestive of a difference in style between Elegy I and Elegy II. A few years earlier M. Hertz in *Analecta ad carm. Horat. historiam*, Breslau, 1876, had discovered echoes of Horace in I, but none in II. This sort of internal "evidence" amounts to very little.

makes a pleasant contrast to the occasional declamatory or mythological passages. There is something agreeably personal in the tenderness of the farewell to Terentia (II. 7–10) and in the poet's confession that, though he had not himself belonged to Maecenas' intimate circle, Lollius had put him in a position to compose this memorial poem (I. 10). The Lollius here meant had been consul in 20 B.C., and died in 1 B.C.

EDITIONS

Th. Gorallus (Clericus). *C. Pedonis Albinovani Elegiae III.* Amsterdam, 1703 (assigning both elegies and the *Consolatio ad Liviam* to Albinovanus).

P. Burman. *Anthologia Veterum Latinorum Epigrammatum et Poematum* (ascribing the Elegiae to an "incertus auctor"), I. pp. 251–287. Amsterdam, 1759.

C. Wernsdorf. *Poetae Latini Minores,* III. p. 155 sqq. Altenburg, 1782.

J. Plumtre. *The Elegies of C. Pedo Albinovanus with an English version* (heroic couplets). Kidderminster, 1807.

J. H. F. Meineke. *Drei dem C. Pedo Albinovanus zugeschriebene Elegien . . . mit einer metrischen Uebersetzung.* Quedlinburg, 1819.

H. Meyer. *Anthologia vet. Lat. epigram. et poematum* (based on Burman), Nos. 109 and 110. Leipzig, 1835.

O. Ribbeck. *Appendix Vergiliana,* pp. 193–204. Leipzig, 1868.

E. Baehrens. *Poetae Latini Minores,* I. pp. 122–136. Leipzig, 1879.

F. Bücheler, and A. Riese. *Anthologia Latina*, I. 2, ed. 2. Leipzig, 1906.
R. Ellis. *Appendix Vergiliana*. Oxford, 1907.
J. Middendorf. *Elegiae in Maecenatem* (text and notes). Marburg, 1912.
F. Vollmer. *Poetae Latini Minores*, I. pp. 143–155. Leipzig, 1927.

Relevant Works

E. Hübner. In *Hermes*. 13 (1878), p. 239.
E. Wagner. *De Martiale poetarum Augusteae aetatis imitatore* (pp. 42–46 on points of style in *Elegiae* and *Consolatio*).
F. Skutsch. P. W. *Realencyclopädie*, IV. col. 944 sqq. 1901.
F. Lillge. *De Elegiis in Maecen. quaestiones*, diss. Breslau, 1901.
B. Axelson. In *Eranos*, xxviii. (1930), 1 sqq. (Contention that the *Elegiae* and the *Consolatio ad Liviam* belong to a date not earlier than that of Statius and Martial.)
R. B. Steele. *The Nux, Maecenas, and Consolatio ad Liviam*. Nashville, Tennessee, U.S.A., 1933. (One of the contentions here is that similarities of diction in the works of Seneca to the *Consolatio* and to the Maecenas poems fix their publication within or later than the reign of Nero.)

SIGLA

Ω = archetype of all the codices.
S = Scaliger's lost manuscript whose readings are preserved in his " Virgilii Appendix. . . ." pp. 528–541. Leyden, 1573.

F = codex Fiechtianus, now Mellicensis, 11th cent. (contains lines 1–25).
B = codex Bruxellensis 10676, 12th cent.
P = codex Parisinus lat. 16236, 10th cent. (contains lines 1–43).
Z = a lost codex represented by three 15th century MSS.:
H = Helmstadiensis 332.
A = Arundelianus, Brit. Mus. 133.
R = Rehdigeranus, Breslau Public Library.
M = Monacenses (manuscripts in Munich), including:
m = Mon. lat. 305, 11th–12th cent.
n = Mon. lat. 18059, 11th cent.
V = Vossianus lat. oct. 81 (Leyden), 15th cent.
ς = any correction by Italian scholars in the later MSS. or early editions.

Considerable departures have been made from Vollmer's text in readings and in punctuation.

ELEGIAE IN MAECENATEM

I

Defleram iuvenis tristi modo carmine fata,
sunt etiam merito carmina danda seni.
ut iuvenis deflendus enim tam candidus et tam
longius annoso vivere dignus avo.
irreligata ratis, numquam defessa carina,
it, redit in vastos semper onusta lacus:
illa rapit iuvenes prima florente iuventa,
non oblita tamen sed † repetitque senes.
nec mihi, Maecenas, tecum fuit usus amici,
Lollius hoc ergo conciliavit opus;
foedus erat vobis nam propter Caesaris arma
Caesaris et similem propter in arma fidem.
regis eras, Etrusce, genus; tu Caesaris almi
dextera, Romanae tu vigil urbis eras.
omnia cum posses tanto tam carus amico,
te sensit nemo posse nocere tamen.

[6] et Ω (= *codd.*), *Vollmer*: it *ed. Ascens.* 1507.
[11] fidus Ω: foedus *Heinsius*.
[13] almi Ω: alti *Heinsius*.

TWO ELEGIES ON MAECENAS

I

My saddened muse of late had mourned a young man's [a] death: now to one ripe in years also let songs be duly offered. As youth is mourned, so must we mourn for one so white-souled, so worthy to live beyond the span of an age-laden grandsire. The barque that knows no fastening, the never-wearied keel, goes and returns for ever with its load across the vasty pools: it carries off the young in the first bloom of their youth, yet unforgetful claims the old as well. At one time, my Maecenas, I lacked converse with thee as a friend: my present task, then, 'twas Lollius [b] won for me. For between you two was a bond because of your war-service for Caesar and your equal loyalty to Caesar's service. Thou wert of royal race, O Tuscan-born, thou wert the right hand of bounteous Caesar, thou wert the guardian of the Roman city. All-powerful though thou wert in such favour with so exalted a friend, yet no man ever felt thou hadst the power to hurt.

[a] *i.e.* Drusus, who died in 9 B.C., the year before Maecenas' death.

[b] M. Lollius, consul 20 B.C., died 1 B.C. Gorallus and Meineke take *opus* of gaining Maecenas' friendship for the author. *Opus*, however, seems odd in this connexion, and here Wernsdorf's view is followed that the *opus* is the present elegy.

Pallade cum docta Phoebus donaverat artes:
  tu decus et laudes huius et huius eras,
vincit vulgares veluti beryllus harenas,
  litore in extremo quas simul unda movet. 20
quod discinctus eras, animo quoque, carpitur unum:
  diluitur nimia simplicitate tua.
sic illi vixere, quibus fuit aurea Virgo,
  quae bene praecinctos postmodo pulsa fugit.
livide, quid tandem tunicae nocuere solutae 25
  aut tibi ventosi quid nocuere sinus?
num minus urbis erat custos et Caesaris opses?
  num tibi non tutas fecit in urbe vias?
nocte sub obscura quis te spoliavit amantem,
  quis tetigit ferro, durior ipse, latus? 30
maius erat potuisse tamen nec velle triumphos,
  maior res magnis abstinuisse fuit.

19 *sic Birt*: vincit vulgares vincit FBPHMV, *Vollmer*: vicit vulgares vicit AR: sicut volgares vincit *Riese, Middendorf*. beritus FBPH *m*: berithus AR: peritus *n* V: berillus *Ald.* 1517: Berytus *Ellis.*

22 diluvii hoc Ω (ac V): diluis hoc *Oudendorp, Baehrens, Vollmer*: diluitur *Ald.* 1517, *Riese.*

27 obses (op- B) Ω: hospes A[1].

Apollo with learned Minerva had conferred their arts on thee: thou wert the ornament and glory of both—even as the beryl[a] surpasses the common sands which the wave tosses about along with it on the shore's edge. That thou wert luxurious in mind as in dress is the one slander urged against thee: it is dispelled by thine exceeding plainness of life. So did they live among whom dwelt the golden Maid[b] who soon fled into exile from the bustle of mankind. Backbiter, say what harm his loosened tunic did you, or dress through which the air could play? Was he a whit less guardian of the city, and less a hostage for our absent emperor? Did he make the streets of Rome unsafe for you? 'Neath the murk of night who could rob you in an amour, or who in excess of heartlessness drive steel into your side? Greater it was to have had the power, yet not to wish for triumphs: a greater thing it was to refrain from mighty deeds.

[a] With an allusion to Maecenas' fondness for jewels. Among terms applied to Maecenas in a jocular letter from Augustus were *Cibriorum smaragde . . . berylle Porsennae* (Macrob. *Saturn.* II. iv. 12). The beryl (βήρυλλος) is a transparent gem, usually sea-green, and, though now found in many parts of the Old World and the New, was mainly known to the ancients as coming from India (Plin. *N.H.* XXXVII. 5, 20, *India eos gignit raro alibi repertos,* a passage which tempts one to take *extremo in litore* as " on a distant shore " : cf. *extremos equos,* 56). Pliny rightly associates it with the emerald. Since one species was the aquamarine, some knowledge of this may have prompted the reference to the sea-shore in 20. It is difficult, however, to imagine that this product of granitic rocks can have been often washed up among the sands of the sea, though Gorallus quotes Greek hexameters from Dionysius Periegetes, of which one interpretation supports the view.

[b] Astraea, or Justice, sojourned among men in the Golden Age, but was driven from earth by the growth of depravity.

maluit umbrosam quercum lymphasque cadentes
paucaque pomosi iugera certa soli:
Pieridas Phoebumque colens in mollibus hortis 35
sederat argutas garrulus inter avis.
marmorea Aonii vincent monumenta libelli:
vivitur ingenio, cetera mortis erunt.
quid faceret? defunctus erat comes integer, idem
miles et Augusti fortis et usque pius: 40
illum piscosi viderunt saxa Pelori
ignibus hostilis reddere ligna ratis;
pulvere in Emathio fortem videre Philippi;
quam nunc ille tener, tam gravis hostis erat.
cum freta Niliacae texerunt lata carinae, 45
fortis erat circa, fortis et ante ducem,
militis Eoi fugientis terga secutus,
territus ad Nili dum fugit ille caput.
pax erat: haec illos laxarunt otia cultus:
omnia victores Marte sedente decent. 50
Actius ipse lyram plectro percussit eburno,
postquam victrices conticuere tubae.

33 nymphas Ω: lymphas *Wernsdorf*. cadentes BP: canentes ZMV.
37 marmora m(a)eonii ARMV: marmora minei SPH: marmorea Aonii *vel* marmora Smyrnaei *Scaliger*.
44 tam . . . tam B, *Vollmer*.
45 l(a)eta BZ, *Vollmer*: lata MV, *Ellis*.

He chose rather the shady oak, the falling waters, the few sure acres of fruit-bearing soil. Honouring the Muses and Apollo in luxurious gardens, he reclined babbling verse among the tuneful birds. Aonian writings[a] will eclipse marble monuments: genius means life, all else will belong to death. What was he to do? He had filled his part as blameless comrade, yea, as Augustus' warrior, gallant and devoted throughout. The rocks of Pelorus abounding in fish saw him give the enemy's craft for fuel to the flames:[b] Philippi[c] saw his bravery amid Emathian dust: as tender of heart as he is to-day, so dread a foe was he then. When (Antony's) Egyptian ships covered the waters wide, Maecenas showed bravery around and bravery in front of his leader,[d] following in the wake of the fugitive Oriental warrior, while he flees panic-stricken to the mouth of the Nile. Peace came: its leisure brought a slackening of those ways: when the War-god sits idle, everything beseems the conquerors.

The very god of Actium[e] smote the lyre with ivory quill after the bugles of victory were hushed. He

[a] *i.e.* poetic: "Aonian" is an epithet of the Muses.

[b] The reference is to the fighting against Sextus Pompeius in Sicilian waters, 38–35 B.C.

[c] Philippi, on the borders of Thrace, is here called "Emathian" (*i.e.* Macedonian). The allusion is to the defeat of Brutus and Cassius by Octavian Caesar and Antony, 42 B.C.

[d] *i.e.* at Actium in 31 B.C. Most authorities accept the testimony of Dio, li. 3. 5, that Maecenas was in Rome when Actium was fought. See E. Groag, art. "Maecenas," P. W. *Realencl.* XIV. i. col. 210, and Gardthausen, *Augustus und seine Zeit*, I. i. p. 365. This *Elegia* is the one ancient source which suggests the contrary view.

[e] Apollo. In the games instituted at Actium by Augustus in honour of his victory, musical performances were included.

hic modo miles erat, ne posset femina Romam
  dotalem stupri turpis habere sui;
hic tela in profugos—tantum curvaverat arcum— 55
  misit ad extremos exorientis equos:
Bacche, coloratos postquam devicimus Indos,
  potasti galea dulce iuvante merum,
et tibi securo tunicae fluxere solutae,
  te puto purpureas tunc habuisse duas. 60
sum memor et certe memini sic ducere thyrsos
  bracchia purpurea candidiora nive,
et tibi thyrsus erat gemmis ornatus et auro,
  serpentes hederae vix habuere locum;
argentata tuos etiam sandalia talos 65
  vinxerunt certe nec, puto, Bacche negas.
mollius es solito mecum tum multa locutus
  et tibi consulto verba fuere nova.
impiger Alcide, multo defuncte labore,
  sic memorant curas te posuisse tuas, 70
sic te cum tenera laetum lusisse puella
  oblitum Nemeae, iamque, Erymanthe, tui.

61 thyrsos Ω: tigres *Burman, Vollmer.*
62 Bacchea RMV: bracchia *Ald.* 1517. purpurea Ω: hyperborea *Vollmer.*
65 talaria Ω, *Vollmer*: sandalia V.
71 multum BHM, *Vollmer*: laetum *Ascens.* 1507.

was of late a warrior to prevent a woman[a] from having Rome as a marriage-gift for her foul lewdness : he sped his arrows after the runaways—so mighty the bow he had bent—far as the furthest steeds of the rising sun.

O Bacchus,[b] after we subdued the dark-skinned Orientals, thou didst drink sweet wine with thy helmet's aid, and in thy care-free hour loose flowed thy tunics—'twas the time, I fancy, when thou didst wear two[c] of brilliant colour. My memory works, and certes I remember that thus arms whiter than the gleaming snow led the Bacchic wands, and thy wand was adorned with gems and gold—the trailing ivy scarce had room thereon; silvern surely were the slippers which bound thy feet: this I trow, Bacchus, thou dost not deny. Softer e'en than thy wont was much that thou saidst then in converse with me : 'twas of set design that thy words were new to the ear.

O Hercules unwearied, after mighty toil performed, 'twas even so, they relate, thou didst lay aside thy cares, and even so didst hold joyous sport with tender damsel, forgetful of Nemea, forgetful now of Erymanthus.[d]

[a] Apollo is fancied to have fought for Octavian against Cleopatra of Egypt and her lover Antony.

[b] Vollmer takes ll. 57–68 as a " dithyramb " addressed by Apollo to Bacchus. Antony's historic posing as Bacchus gives point to the passage.

[c] To wear two was a sign of luxury.

[d] Hercules' twelve labours included the slaying of the Nemean lion and of the Erymanthian boar. An oracle having ordered Hercules to undergo for penance a period of menial service, he placed himself under the charge of Omphale, princess of Lydia, and found favour with her by spinning and dressing like a woman, while she donned his lion's skin. The tale of the strong hero relaxing into effeminacy is adduced here as an apology for Maecenas' luxury after he had accomplished great tasks.

ultra numquid erat? torsisti pollice fusos,
  lenisti morsu levia fila parum.
percussit crebros te propter Lydia nodos, 75
  te propter dura stamina rupta manu.
Lydia te tunicas iussit lasciva fluentis
  inter lanificas ducere saepe suas.
clava torosa tua pariter cum pelle iacebat,
  quam pede suspenso percutiebat Amor. 80
quis fore credebat, premeret cum iam impiger infans
  hydros ingentes vix capiente manu,
cumve renascentem meteret velociter Hydram,
  frangeret immanes vel Diomedis equos,
vel tribus adversis communem fratribus alvom 85
  et sex adversas solus in arma manus?
fudit Aloidas postquam dominator Olympi,
  dicitur in nitidum percubuisse diem,
atque aquilam misisse suam, quae quaereret, ecqui
  posset amaturo digna referre Iovi, 90
valle sub Idaea dum te, formose sacerdos,
  invenit et presso molliter ungue rapit.
sic est: victor amet, victor potiatur in umbra,
  victor odorata dormiat inque rosa;
victus aret victusque metat; metus imperet illi, 95
  membra nec in strata sternere discat humo.
tempora dispensant usus et tempora cultus,
  haec homines, pecudes, haec moderantur avis.
lux est; taurus arat: nox est; requiescit arator,
  liberat et merito fervida colla bovi. 100

[83] terret Ω: tereret *Ald.* 1517: meteret *Struchtmeyer*, *Vollmer*.
[89] ecquid BAR, *Vollmer*: et quid HM: et qui V: ecquis *s*: ecqui *Baehrens*, *Ellis*.
[90] signa Ω: digna *Heinsius*: vina *edd. var.*
[91] sacerdos Ω: iacentem *Heinsius*: *fortasse* satelles *Ellis*.

Could aught exceed this?—twirling spindles with the thumb, and biting the rough threads smooth with the mouth! Lydian Omphale beat thee for leaving too many knots or for breaking the threads with that hard hand. The sportive Lydian bade thee often wear loose-flowing robes among her spinning-maids. The knotty club was thrown down along with thy lion-skin, and on it the Love-god danced with light-poised toe. That this would come who was like to believe in the hour when the active babe strangled monstrous serpents which his hand could hardly grasp? or when he nimbly lopped each Hydra-head as it grew again? or conquered the savage steeds of Diomede or the body common to three confronting brothers, and the six confronting hands,[a] which he fought unaided? After the Ruler of Olympus routed the sons of Aloeus,[b] they say he lay asleep till the bright dawn, and sent his eagle in quest of one who could render fitting service to Jove bent on love, until in Ida's vale he found thee, fair priest,[c] and carried thee off in talons softly closed.

Such is the world's way: the victor must love, the victor have the mastery in the shade, the victor must sleep on scented rose-leaves: the vanquished must plough, the vanquished must reap: fear must be his lord: never must he learn to rest his limbs on the cushioned ground. The seasons regulate different habits and ways in life: the seasons rule mankind and cattle and birds. 'Tis dawn—the bull ploughs: 'tis night—the ploughman rests; he frees the steaming neck of the ox which has

[a] *i.e.* of the three-headed monster Geryon.
[b] Giants who had warred against the Gods.
[c] Ganymede is thereafter to minister to Jove.

conglaciantur aquae; scopulis se condit hirundo:
verberat egelidos garrula vere lacus.
Caesar amicus erat: poterat vixisse solute,
cum iam Caesar idem quod cupiebat erat.
indulsit merito: non est temerarius ille: 105
vicimus: Augusto iudice dignus erat.
Argo saxa pavens postquam Scylleia legit
Cyaneosque metus, iam religanda ratis,
viscera dissecti mutaverat arietis agno
Aeetis sucis omniperita suis: 110
his te, Maecenas, iuvenescere posse decebat,
haec utinam nobis Colchidos herba foret!
redditur arboribus florens revirentibus aetas:
ergo non homini quod fuit ante redit?
vivacesque magis cervos decet esse paventis 115
si quorum in torva cornua fronte rigent?
vivere cornices multos dicuntur in annos:
cur nos angusta condicione sumus?
pascitur Aurorae Tithonus nectare coniunx
atque ita iam tremulo nulla senecta nocet: 120

[107] Scilleia BHA: Scylleia R. legit Ω: Scyllaea relegit *Salmasius.*
[109] disiecti BARV: directi SH[1]: dissecti *Vat.* 3269. agni Ω: agno *Ald.* 1517.

done its work. The streams are frozen—then the swallow shelters 'mid the crags: in spring loud-twittering she skims the genial meres.

The Emperor was Maecenas' friend: so he was free to live a life of ease when the Emperor was now all he longed to be. He granted indulgence to Maecenas' merits: nor is Maecenas reckless: we have won our victory [a]: 'twas the judgement of Augustus that counted him deserving.[b] After the Argo had skirted in affright the reefs of Scylla [c] and the peril of the Clashing Rocks, when the barque had now to be moored, the daughter [d] of Aeetes, all-skilled in her magic juices, had changed into a lamb the body of the ram she had cut up. 'Twas right, Maecenas, that by such means thou shouldst have power to grow young again: would that we had the herb of the Colchian (sorceress)!

Trees reclothed in green have the bloom of their life restored: and to man then does not that which was his before come again? Is it meet that the timid deer with stiff horns on their wild foreheads should have longer life? Crows, 'tis said, live for many a year: why do we men exist on narrow terms? Tithonus, as Aurora's consort, feeds on nectar, and so, though he be palsied now, no length of age can work him harm. That thy life, Maecenas, might

[a] As Antony has been overthrown, easy-going relaxation is no longer a danger.

[b] *i.e.* to indulge in a more luxurious life after Antony's defeat.

[c] The Argo would not naturally pass by Scylla and Charybdis on the outward voyage to Colchis.

[d] Medea, princess of Colchis, famous for her powers in sorcery.

ut tibi vita foret semper medicamine sacro,
 te vellem Aurorae complacuisse virum.
illius aptus eras croceo recubare cubili
 et, modo puniceum rore lavante torum,
illius aptus eras roseas adiungere bigas,   125
 tu dare purpurea lora regenda manu,
tu mulcere iubam, cum iam torsisset habenas
 procedente die, respicientis equi.
quaesivere chori iuvenum sic Hesperon illum,
 quem nexum medio solvit in igne Venus,   130
quem nunc in fuscis placida sub nocte nitentem
 Luciferum contra currere cernis equis.
hic tibi Corycium, casias hic donat olentis,
 hic et palmiferis balsama missa iugis.
nunc pretium candoris habes, nunc redditus umbris:
 te sumus obliti decubuisse senem.   135
ter Pylium flevere sui, ter Nestora canum,
 dicebantque tamen non satis esse senem:

129 chori SBHAM : thori V. iuvenem Ω : iuvenum *Scaliger.*
131 infusci BM : infusi Z : in fluscis *corr. in* fuscis V : infusa *Vollmer.* placida Ω : placide *Baehrens* : placidus *Vollmer.*

---

[a] *i.e.* caused Hesperos to set; in myth, Hesperos was a fair youth elevated by Venus into the "Evening-star," which was by the ancients correctly identified with Phosphoros (Lucifer),

last for ever in virtue of a holy drug, I could wish thou hadst found favour with Aurora as husband. Worthy wert thou to recline on her saffron bed, and, as the morning-dew was just moistening the purple couch, worthy wert thou to yoke the two steeds to her rosy car, worthy to give the reins for guidance by the bright-hued hand, worthy to stroke the mane of the horse as it looked back (on its nightly course), now that Aurora had turned the reins at the advance of day.

In such a way did the bands of his youthful comrades feel the loss of Hesperos, whom Venus attached to herself and released in the midst of his fiery course:[a] thou canst see him now as Lucifer gleaming in the dark 'neath the stilly night and charioting his steeds on an opposite course.[b] He it is that presents to thee the Corycian saffron-flower, he presents the aromatic cinnamon, he too the balsams sent from palm-growing hills.

Now hast thou, Maecenas, the guerdon of sincerity, now that thou art given to the shades: we have forgotten that thou didst die an old man.[c] His people mourned the King of Pylos, Nestor, hoary after three generations of life; and yet they said he had not fully reached old age. Thou wouldst

the "Morning-star." Actually it is the planet Venus. The allusion is to the fact that, after a cycle of brilliancy, the planet's apparent height above the horizon at sunset gradually diminishes and it sinks into invisibility.

[b] Lucifer, particularly associated with the East, appropriately offers, in honour of Maecenas, fragrant Oriental plants, *crocus* from Corycus in Cilicia (Plin. *N.H.* XXI. 6. 17), *casia* from Arabia Felix (*ib.* XII. 18, 41), and balsam from Judaea (Joseph. *Ant. Jud.* XIV. 4 (7)).

[c] *i.e.* we do not realise that you were old when you died, because in life you always seemed young, and in our thoughts you still retain the charm of perpetual youth.

Nestoris annosi vicisses saecula, si me
  dispensata tibi stamina nente forent. 140
nunc ego, quod possum: "Tellus, levis ossa teneto,
  pendula librato pondus et ipsa tuom.
semper serta tibi dabimus, tibi semper odores,
  non umquam sitiens, florida semper eris."

II

Sic est Maecenas fato veniente locutus,
  frigidus et iam iam cum moriturus erat:
"mene," inquit, "iuvenis primaevi, Iuppiter, ante
  angustam Drusi non cecidisse diem!
pectore maturo fuerat puer, integer aevo 5
  et magnum magni Caesaris illud opus.
discidio vellemque prius"—non omnia dixit
  inciditque pudor quae prope dixit amor,

[140] nempe Ω: nente *Ald.* 1517.
[4] augustam AR, *Vollmer*: angustam BHMV, *Heinsius.* bruti Ω: Drusi *Francius et I.F. Gronovius.* fidem Ω, *Vollmer*: diem *Heinsius.*

have surpassed the generations of long-lived Nestor, if I had been spinner to assign thee the threads of destiny. But as things are, all that I can, I pray: "O Goddess Earth, light be thy touch on his bones; o'erhanging keep thine own weight as in a balance suspended: so shall we ever give thee wreaths, and ever fragrances: never shalt thou feel thirst, but ever be decked with flowers."

II

[Scaliger was the first to distinguish this as a separate poem: in the MSS. it runs on after Elegia I without break.]

Thus spoke Maecenas at the coming of fate, chill on the very brink of death. "Why," said he, "did I not sink in death, O Jupiter, before young Drusus' narrow day of life? He had shown himself a youth of ripe judgement, a stalwart for his years—the mighty achievement of mighty Caesar's training.[a] Would that before our civil strife . . ."[b] The rest he never spoke: scruples cut short what affection nearly said—yet was he clearly understood:[c] dying,

[a] *Caesaris illud opus* is used similarly, *Consol. ad Liviam*, 39.

[b] Maecenas recalls the hostilities between Octavian Caesar and Mark Antony.

[c] *Manifestus erat moriens* might be taken, with Scaliger, as a Graecism, δῆλος ἦν ἀποθνήσκων, "it was clear he was dying."

sed manifestus erat: moriens quaerebat amatae
 coniugis amplexus oscula verba manus. 1
"sed tamen hoc satis est: vixi te, Caesar, amico
 et morior" dixit, "dum moriorque, satis.
mollibus ex oculis aliquis tibi procidet umor,
 cum dicar subita voce fuisse tibi.
hoc mihi contingat: iaceam tellure sub aequa. 1
 nec tamen hoc ultra te doluisse velim.
sed meminisse velim: vivam sermonibus illic;
 semper ero, semper si meminisse voles.
et decet et certe vivam tibi semper amore
 nec tibi qui moritur desinit esse tuus. 2
ipse ego quicquid ero cineres interque favillas,
 tunc quoque non potero non memor esse tui.
exemplum vixi te propter molle beati,
 unus Maecenas teque ego propter eram.
arbiter ipse fui; volui, quod contigit esse; 2
 pectus eram vere pectoris ipse tui.
vive diu, mi care senex, pete sidera sero:
 est opus hoc terris, te quoque velle decet.
et tibi succrescant iuvenes bis Caesare digni
 et tradant porro Caesaris usque genus. 3

[16] potuisse Ω: doluisse *Heinsius*.
[23] beate Ω: beati *Salmasius*.
[24] unus Ω: unctus *Maehly*.
[25] voluit, q.c. esse, pectus eram *Vollmer*: voluit Ω: volui *Ald*. 1517.

he sought for his beloved wife's embraces, her kisses, words and hands:

"Yet after all this is enough," he said, "I have lived and I die in thy friendship, Caesar; and, as I die, it is enough. From thy kindly eyes some drop will fall, when thou art told the sudden news that I am gone. This be my lot, to lie 'neath the impartial earth: nor yet would I have thee longer grieve for this. But I would wish for remembrance: there in thy talk would I live; for I shall always exist, if thou wilt always remember me. 'Tis fitting so, and I shall surely live for thee in affection ever; thy dying friend ceases not to be thine own. Myself, whatever I shall be among the ashes and the embers, e'en then I shall not be able to forget Caesar. 'Tis thanks to thee I have lived the luxurious pattern of bliss, thanks to thee that I was the one Maecenas of the day. I was my own controller: I willed to be what fell to my lot:[a] I was truly the heart of thine own heart.

Long mayest thou live, old friend I love so well; late mayest thou pass to heaven: the earth hath need of this: this should be thy will too. May the youths doubly worthy of Caesar[b] grow up to thy support and thenceforward hand on to the future the house

[a] As captain of his fate, Maecenas did not aim at rising above his equestrian rank.

[b] Gaius and Lucius, the sons of Agrippa by Julia, were adopted by Augustus in 17 B.C. as "Caesares." "Doubly" is variously explained: it may refer to their paternity by blood and by adoption; or to their personal qualities added to adoption; or, as Gorallus thought, simply to the fact that they were two. Lucius died A.D. 2, and Gaius A.D. 4.

sit secura tibi quam primum Livia coniunx,
  expleat amissi munera rupta gener.
cum deus intereris divis insignis avitis,
  te Venus in patrio collocet ipsa sinu." 34

[31] sit secura tibi Ω : set tibi securo V : sed tibi sit curae *Ellis*.
[33] cum Ω : tum *Wernsdorf* : tu *Baehrens*. in terris Ω : intersis *Ribbeck* : intereris *Vollmer* : cur deus in terris ? *Ellis*.
[34] patrio Ω : proprio *Ribbeck, Riese, Baehrens*. ipsa BHM : alma AR.

of Caesar. Right soon may thine Empress Livia be free from anxiety: let a son-in-law fulfil the broken duties of him who is lost.[a] When thou hast taken thy place, a god distinguished among a line of deities, let Venus' own hand set thee in the paternal bosom."[b]

[a] Tiberius is the *gener*: Agrippa, the *gener amissus*. In 11 B.C. Augustus had forced Tiberius to divorce Vipsania Agrippina and marry his daughter Julia, the widow of Agrippa. This marriage, it is hoped in the couplet 31–32, will both assure Livia of descendants through her own son Tiberius and, at the same time, strengthen dynastic prospects by adding to the number of Augustus' grandchildren, now that Agrippa is dead.

[b] *i.e.* the bosom of Julius Caesar, Augustus' adoptive father. The reference to Venus is appropriate, as the Julian *gens* claimed descent from her (Suet. *Jul.* 6).

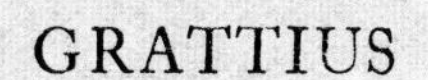

GRATTIUS

INTRODUCTION

TO GRATTIUS

THE period of Grattius is fixed as Augustan by one of Ovid's pentameters, *Ep. ex Ponto*, IV. 16. 34, "aptaque *venanti* Grattius arma daret." This is a specific reference to Grattius' twenty-third line, whether the reading there be *venanti* or *venandi*, and it places him in a list of Ovid's contemporaries before A.D. 8. It is possible, though not certain, that his work was known to Manilius : otherwise, antiquity is silent about him. If it were as certain that he borrowed from the *Aeneid* as it is that he borrowed from the *Georgics*, then his work could be placed between the limits 19 B.C. and A.D. 8. His title to the epithet *Faliscus*, reported to have been in a manuscript now vanished, is not admitted by all. *Nostris Faliscis* of l. 40 does not necessarily imply that he was a native of Falerii :[a] any Italian or even Sicilian might have used the phrase; and indeed there is a possibility that he was connected with Sicily; for he mentions (435–36) that he had frequently seen ailing dogs dipped in the bituminous pools of Sicily. *Silvis nostris* of 137, though taken by Curcio to mean "our Roman woods," may not imply more than "our western woods" in contrast

[a] Among recent writers Vollmer and P. J. Enk are convinced that he was Faliscan.

with the East which Grattius had just mentioned. There is more of the Roman note in the allusion to the simple board of ancient heroes of Rome (321); but it must always be remembered how, from Ennius onwards, Latin authors born far from the capital itself tended to speak and write as Romans. If, then, we cannot add the descriptive *Faliscus* to his name, it is left "Grattius"[a] without cognomen or praenomen.

If Grattius ever wrote lyric poetry,[b] it is long since lost. His sole surviving work is his *Cynegetica*, of which we have one book of about 540 hexameters mutilated towards its end. Here, like several other writers of antiquity, he treats of the chase and especially of the rearing and training of dogs for hunting purposes. The sources of his material are not easy to trace.[c] Some authorities affirm, while others deny, his debt to the *Cynegeticus* of Xenophon (or pseudo-Xenophon) and to Plutarch. It seems at least likely that some Greek author of the Alexandrian period lay behind his list of dogs, in which the Asiatic breeds come before the European, with the "Celtae"[d] sandwiched between "Medi" and "Geloni" (155–57). The Latin influence which is most noticeable upon Grattius is that of Virgil, especially his *Georgics*.

The debt of subsequent writers to Grattius was of the slightest; largely for the reason that a

[a] The spelling *Gratius* in Ovid is less correct. Buecheler, *Rh. Mus.* 35 (1880), p. 407: *cf. C.I.L.* vi. 19–117 *sqq.*

[b] This hypothesis is briefly discussed by Enk, *proleg.* pp. 2–3.

[c] Enk, *op. cit.* pp. 31–32.

[d] Can his Greek original have meant "Galatian" instead of "Gaulish"? Radermacher, *Rh. Mus.* 60 (1905), p. 249.

didactic poem on so restricted a subject had little chance of a great vogue. Even upon Nemesianus, who handled the same theme in the third century, his influence has been doubted. But while Schanz, Curcio and others hold that Grattius was unknown to Nemesianus, Enk has made out a good case to support the belief that the earlier author was consulted by the later.[a]

Grattius' method of treatment is, after his proem (1–23), to treat first (24–149) of the huntsman's equipment in the means of catching and killing game, and secondly (150–541) of his companions in the chase, dogs and horses, with a brief sub-section on the dress to be worn by hunters. The longest portion is that devoted to dogs (150–496) and it thus justifies the title of the poem; but, besides handling their breeds and breeding, their points and diseases, it is, on the whole fortunately, broken by episodes. These episodes, although in them rhetoric contends with poetry, are enlivening additions or insertions. They are four, and concern a renowned hunter Hagnon (213–62); the miserable effects of luxury on human beings (310–25), somewhat quaintly appended to the prescription of plain fare for dogs; a grotto in Sicily (430–66); and a sacrifice to Diana (480–96). The earlier part on nets, devices for frightening game, on snares, springes, spears and arrows, is also diversified with episodes, namely, a eulogy of the chase (61–74) and of the ingenious hunter Dercylus (95–110). Many readers will welcome these digressions as pleasant side-paths; for it is not everyone to whom the methods of the ancient hunter can make appeal. At the same time

[a] *Mnemos.* 1917, pp. 53–68.

the subject has decidedly antiquarian interest, and it is only fair to remember that great scholars of the past, including Julius Caesar Scaliger and Nicolaus Heinsius, awarded high praise to Grattius' elegance.

His well-turned hexameters show that he was an apt student of Virgil; and his alliteration may indicate admiration for still older poets of Rome. There is also an independent turn in him which shows itself in his employment of words in unusual senses, e.g. *nodus*, 32, of a mesh; *vellera*, 77, of feathers; *verutus*, 110, of a weapon's teeth; *caesaries*, 273, of a dog's hair; *populari*, 376, of spoiling; *dulcedo*, 408, of scratching. There are several ἅπαξ εἰρημένα in his poem: *plagium*, 24; *cannabius*, 47 (? *cannabinus*, Vollmer); *praedexter*, 68; *apprensat*, 239; *perpensare*, 299; *delecta* from *delicio*, 303 (if that be the reading and not *dilecta* or even *de lacte*); *nardifer*, 314; *offectus*, 406; *termiteus*, 447.

EDITIONS

G. Logus (de Logau): Editio princeps (with Ovid's *Halieutica*, Nemesianus and Calpurnius). Venice, 1534.

J. Ulitius (van Vliet): In *Venatio Novantiqua.* Leyden, 1645, 1655.

Thos. Johnson: *Gratii Falisci Cynegeticon* (cum poematio Nemesiani). London, 1699.

R. Bruce and S. Havercamp: In *Poetae latini rei venaticae scriptores et bucolici antiqui* (cum notis Barthii, Ulitii, Johnsonii). [Elaborate commentary at end.] Leyden, 1728.

P. Burman: In *Poetae latini minores* I. Leyden, 1731.

C. A. Küttner: *Gratii Cynegeticon et Nemesiani Cyneg.* (cum notis selectis Titii, Barthii, Ulitii, Johnsonii et Burmanni integris). Mitaviae (= Mitau), 1775.

J. C. Wernsdorf: In *Poetae latini minores* I. Altenburg, 1780.

R. Stern: *Gratii et Nemesiani carmina venatica* . . . Halle, 1832.

M. Haupt: *Ovidii Halieutica, Gratii et Nemesiani Cynegetica.* [Important as a critical edition.] Leipzig, 1838.

E. Baehrens: In *Poetae latini minores* I. Leipzig, 1879.

G. Curcio: In *Poeti latini minori* I. Acireale, 1902.

J. P. Postgate: In *Corpus poetarum latinorum* II. London, 1905.

F. Vollmer: In *Poetae latini minores* II. 1. Leipzig, 1911.

P. J. Enk: *Gratti Cynegeticon quae supersunt* (cum proleg., not. crit., comm. exeget.). [A learned edition showing genuine appreciation of Grattius.] Zutphen, 1918.

TRANSLATION

Grati Falisci Cynegeticon, or a poem on hunting by Gratius the Faliscian, Englished and illustrated by Chris. Wase, w. commendatory poem by Edmund Waller. London, 1654.

RELEVANT WORKS

Th. Birt: *Ad historiam hexametri latini symbola*, diss. Bonn, 1876.

Fr. Buecheler: *Coniectanea* in *Rhein. Mus.* 35 (1880), p. 407 [defends spelling "Grattius"].

Robinson Ellis: *Ad Grattii Cyneg.* in *Philolog.* 52 (1894).

H. Schenkl: *Zur Kritik und Ueberlief. des Grattius u. anderen lateinischen Dichtern*, Teubner (= Fleck. Jahrb. Suppl. xxiv. 1898 pp. 387–480).

L. Radermacher: *Interpretationes latinae* in *Rhein. Mus.* 60 (1905), pp. 246–49.

G. Pierleoni: *Fu poeta Grattius?* in *Riv. fil.* 1906, pp. 580–97. [A depreciatory criticism on Grattius' style, answered by P. J. Enk in the *Prolegomena* to his edition.]

F. Vollmer: art. *Grattius* in Pauly-Wissowa, *Real-encycl.*

J. Herter: *Grattianum* in *Rhein. Mus.* (N. F. 78), 1929, pp. 361–70.

A. J. Butler: *Sport in Classic Times.* London, 1930. [A fuller list is given in P. J. Enk's edn., 1918.]

SIGLA

A = codex Vindobonensis lat. 277 : saec. ix.

B = ex A descriptus :[a] Parisinus lat. 8071 : saec. ix.

Sann. = emendationes factae a Giacomo Sannazaro in apographis quae extant in codice Vindob. lat. 277 fol. 74-83 et in codice Vindob. lat. 3261 fol. 43-72.

Ald. = editio princeps, anno 1534 a Georgio de Logau curata.

[a] L. Traube, in *Berlin. philol. Wochenschrift*, 1896, p. 1050. As a copy of A, B does not give independent evidence. It contains lines 1–159.

GRATTI CYNEGETICON

DONA cano divom, laetas venantibus artes,
auspicio, Diana, tuo. prius omnis in armis
spes fuit et nuda silvas virtute movebant
inconsulti homines vitaque erat error in omni.
post alia propiore via meliusque profecti
te sociam, Ratio, rebus sumpsere gerendis.
hinc omne auxilium vitae rectusque reluxit
ordo et contiguas didicere ex artibus artes
proserere, hinc demens cecidit violentia retro.
sed primum auspicium deus artibus altaque circa
firmamenta dedit; tum partes quisque secutus
exegere suas tetigitque industria finem.

[2] inermis *Barth* (*in not.* "forte legend."): in armis A.

GRATTIUS

THE CHASE

Under thine auspices, Diana, do I chant the gifts of the gods[a]—the skill that has made the hunters glad. Erstwhile their sole hope lay in their weapons:[b] men untrained stirred the woods with prowess unaided by skill:[c] mistakes beset life everywhere. Afterwards, by another and a more fitting way,[d] with better schooling they took thee, Reason, to aid their enterprises. From Reason came all their help in life: the true order of things shone forth: men learned out of arts to produce kindred arts: from Reason came the undoing of mad violence. But 'twas a divinity who gave the first favouring impulse to the arts, putting around them their deep-set props: then did every man work out the portions of his choice, and industry

[a] Like Xenophon or the pseudo-Xenophon, *Cyn.* ad init. τὸ μὲν εὕρημα θεῶν κ.τ.λ., Grattius claims a divine origin for hunting.

[b] Good sense is got without taking *armis* from *armi*, "members," as Vollmer does with Barth, Burman and others. A. E. Housman, *Cl. Rev.* 14 (1900), 465–66, and P. J. Enk, in his edn. 1918, take *armis* from *arma*.

[c] *Nuda virtute*: *cf.* 153 *nudo marte* contrasted with *ex arte*.

[d] *i.e.* by training they attained to a more convenient and suitable method (*via*) than the old haphazard hunting. For sense of *propior cf.* Cic. *ad Att.* XIV. xix., *nos alium portum propiorem huic aetati videbamus.*

tu trepidam bello vitam, Diana, ferino,
qua primam quaerebat opem, dignata repertis
protegere auxiliis orbemque hac solvere noxa. 15
adscivere tuo comites sub nomine divae
centum: omnes nemorum, umentes de fontibus
omnes
Naides, et Latii ⟨satyri⟩ Faunus⟨que subibant⟩
Maenaliusque puer domitrixque Idaea leonum
mater et inculto Silvanus termite gaudens. 20
his ego praesidibus nostram defendere sortem
contra mille feras et non sine carmine iussus,
carmine et arma dabo et venandi persequar artes.
armorum casses plagiique exordia restes.
prima iubent tenui nascentem iungere filo 25
limbum et quadruplices tormento adstringere limbos:

[17] gentem *Radermacher, Schenkl, Vollmer*: centem A: mentem *Haupt*: centum B *ex. corr., Postgate, Enk.*
[18] *sic Enk*: Faunusque subibat *Vollmer in not.*: iuvabant *vel* favebant *Herter*: Latii cultor qui Faunus amoeni *Ald.*
[22] lusus A: nisus *Ulitius*: iussus *Graevius. post v.* 23 *videntur Vollmero restituendi vv.* 61–74.
[23] et venandi A: venanti et *Ulitius. cf. Ov. ex Ponto* IV. xvi. 34 cum . . . aptaque venanti Grattius arma daret.
[24] plagii *sic* A (*vocabulum a* plaga *formatum*). exordia restes *Vollmer*: exordiar estis A: exordiar astus *Ald. et vulgo.*

attained its goal. The life that was imperilled by warfare against wild beasts, where most it needed help, thou, Diana, didst deign to shield with aids of thy discovery, and to free the world from harm so great. Under thy name the goddesses joined to them a hundred comrades:[a] all the nymphs of the groves, all the Naiads dripping from the springs, and Latium's satyrs and the Faun-god came in support; Pan, too, the youth of the Arcadian mount, and the Idaean Mother, Cybele, who tames the lions, and Silvanus rejoicing in the wilding bough. I by these guardians ordained—and not without song—to defend our human lot against a thousand beasts, with song too will furnish weapons and pursue the arts of the chase.

The beginning of hunting equipment consists in nets and the ropes of the snare.[b] First of all, experts prescribe that the rope along the edge of the net be twined, at the start, of thin thread and then fourfold strands be drawn tight to form the twist;[c]

[a] Herter, *Rhein. Mus.*, 78 (1929), p. 366, takes *centum* with *divae*.

[b] With lines 24–60, 75–94, on hunting-nets, *cf.* Xen. *Cyn.* ii. 3–8; Arrian, *Cyn.* 1; Pollux, *Onomast.* V. 26–32; Oppian, *Cyn.* I. 150–51; Nemes. *Cyn.* 299 *sqq.* The Latin *rete* (δίκτυον) means net in general, or specifically a large "hay"; *plaga* (ἐνόδιον) means a net placed in the known run or track of the game; *cassis* (ἄρκυς) means a funnel-shaped net resembling, according to Pollux, a κεκρύφαλος (*reticulum*)—which may be applied either to a network cap for the hair or to the bag-shaped reticule, pouch or belly of a hunting-net.

[c] *Limbus*, the rope along the edge of the net, corresponds to the τόνος in Xen. *Cyn.* x. 2, Pollux V. 27. Grattius uses *limbi*, the plural, for the *fila linea* out of which the *limbus* is made (*Limbus grandis et capitalis linea illa est cui minores limbi quadrangulo sinuamine circumstringuntur*, Barth).

illa operum patiens, illa usus linea longi.
tunc ipsum e medio cassem quo nascitur ore
per senos circum usque sinus laqueabis, ut omni
concipiat tergo, si quisquam est plurimus, hostem. 30
at bis vicenos spatium praetendere passus
rete velim plenisque decem consurgere nodis;
ingrati maiora sinus impendia sument.

optima Cinyphiae, ne quid cunctere, paludes
lina dabunt; bonus Aeolia de valle Sibyllae 35
fetus et aprico Tuscorum stuppea campo
messis contiguum sorbens de flumine rorem,
qua cultor Latii per opaca silentia Thybris
labitur inque sinus magno venit ore marinos.
at contra nostris imbellia lina Faliscis 40
Hispanique alio spectantur Saetabes usu.
vix operata suo sacra ad Bubastia lino
velatur sonipes aestivi turba Canopi:
ipse in materia damnosus candor inerti
ostendit longe fraudem atque exterruit hostes. 45
at pauper rigui custos Alabandius horti
cannabi⟨n⟩as nutrit silvas, quam commoda nostro
armamenta operi. gravis ⟨est⟩ tutela, sed illis
tu licet Haemonios includas retibus ursos.
tantum ne subeat vitiorum pessimus umor 50

---

[a] *Ingrati* is predicative: "Thankless (*i.e.* profitless) will be the nets that demand greater expense."

that makes a length to stand its work; that will serve many a day. The snare itself, at the central mouth which it has when being made, you must entangle all round with six pouches so that in the whole cavity it may catch the savage quarry, however big he is. But I should have the whole net extend forty paces in length and rise ten full meshes in height from the ground. Nets likely to cost more outlay are unremunerative.[a]

The Cinyphian marshes,[b] doubt it not, will yield excellent thread-material; there is fine produce from the Aeolian valley[c] of the Sibyl, and there is the flax harvest on the sunny Tuscan meadow drinking in the neighbouring moisture from the river, where Tiber that fertilises Latium glides through the shady silences and meets with mighty mouth the gulfs of the sea. But on the other hand our Falerians have flax-crops unfit for conflict, and (those of) the Spanish Saetabes are tested by a different use.[d] The dancing crowds of sultry Canopus[e] are scarcely veiled by their transparent native linen when sacrificing in the ritual at Bubastis: its very whiteness, ruinous in a material useless for nets, reveals the deceit afar off and frightens away the beasts. Yet the poor guardian of a well-watered estate at Alabanda[f] can rear a growth of hemp, right fitting equipment for this task of ours. Burdensome is the care needed, but you may entrap within such toils the bears of Thessaly. Only, first take pains that no moisture, worst of plagues, steal thereon:

[b] In North Africa between the two Syrtes.
[c] At Cumae on the Bay of Naples.
[d] *i.e.* are unsuitable for nets.
[e] In Egypt. [f] In Caria, Asia Minor.

ante cave: non est umentibus usus in armis,
nulla fides. ergo seu pressa flumina valle
inter opus crassaeque malum fecere paludes
sive improvisus caelo perfuderit imber,
illa vel ad flatus Helices oppande serenae 55
vel caligineo laxanda reponite fumo.
idcirco et primas linorum tangere messes
ante vetant quam maturis accenderit annum
ignibus et claro Plias se prompserit ortu.
imbiberint: tanto respondet longior usus. 60

magnum opus et tangi, nisi cura vincitur, impar.
nonne vides veterum quos prodit fabula rerum
semideos—illi aggeribus temptare superbis
caeli iter et matres ausi ⟨a⟩ttrectare deorum—
quam magna mercede meo sine munere silvas 65
impulerint? flet adhuc et porro flebit Adonin
victa Venus ceciditque suis Ancaeus in armis
(et praedexter erat geminisque securibus ingens).
ipse deus cultorque feri Tirynthius orbis,

[53] clausaeque *Barth*: causaeque A: crassaeque *Sann.*[2], *Ald.*
[59] prompserit *Sann.*: promiserit A.
[60] imbiberit A: -int *Burman.*
[64] Jr& fr&a (*sic* = iret freta *contra metrum*) A: ire freta et *Ulitius, Johnson, Stern et alii*: aethera tum *Heinsius*: aethera et ad *Haupt*: sidera et ad (ad *cum* trectare *per tmesin*) *Vollmer*: caeli iter et *Enk.*: ausi *Heinsius*: ausit A. trectare A: tractare *Sann.*: ⟨a⟩ttrectare *Heinsius.*

in damp equipment there is no use, no dependence. Therefore, whether streams in a narrow valley and sluggish swamps have wrought harm amid the hunter's task, or unforeseen rain from heaven shall have drenched the nets, either unfold them to face the northern breezes of serene Helice [a] or set them in murky smoke to slacken. For such reasons too it is forbidden to touch the first crops of flax before the Pleiad [b] has kindled the year with ripening fires and appeared in its brilliant rising. If nets drink in breeze or smoke,[c] their longer service answers accordingly.

The chase is a mighty task, unfit to be handled, save it is mastered by pains.[d] Do you not see the demigods whom old mythic lore records (they dared on proud-piled mountains to essay the way to heaven [e] and assault the mothers of the gods) —at what mighty cost they hunted the woodlands without the boon of my teaching? Venus, baffled, still weeps and long will weep Adonis: Ancaeus [f] fell, arms in hand (yet was he right skilful and imposing with the double axe). The god himself, he of Tiryns, who civilised a barbarous world,

[a] Ursa Major.

[b] Summer began with the rising of the constellation of the Seven Pleiades (Lat. *Vergiliae*), and winter with their setting.

[c] *i.e. si lina imbiberint flatus vel fumum* : *cf.* 55–56.

[d] Lines 61–74 are by some editors transposed to follow either 23 or 24.

[e] Unsatisfying attempts have been made to read *ire freta* and explain it as applicable either to the giants traversing the ocean of the sky in their attack on heaven or even to the Argonauts crossing the sea, which is Curcio's strange suggestion.

[f] A son of Neptune and an Argonaut, who, like Adonis, was killed by a boar.

quem mare, quem tellus, quem praeceps ianua Ditis 70
omnia temptantem, qua laus erat obvia, passa est,
hinc decus et famae primum impetravit honorem.
exige, si qua meis respondet ab artibus, ergo,
gratia quae vires fallat collata ferinas.

sunt quibus immundo decerptae vulture plumae 75
instrumentum operis fuit et non parva facultas.
tantum inter nivei iungantur vellera cygni,
et satis armorum est. haec clara luce coruscant
terribiles species, at vulture dirus ab atro
turbat odor silvas meliusque alterna valet res. 80
sed quam clara tuis et pinguis pluma sub armis,
tam mollis tactu et non sit creberrima nexu,
ne reprensa suis properantem linea pennis
implicet atque ipso mendosa coarguat usu.
hic magis in cervos valuit metus; ast ubi lentae 85
interdum Libyco fucantur sandyce pennae
linteaque expositis lucent anconibus arma,
rarum si qua metus eludet belua falsos.
nam fuit et laqueis aliquis curracibus usus:

[71] obvia *Sann.*: obula A. passi A, *Vollmer*: passa est *Haupt.*

to whom sea and earth and the sheer gateway of Pluto yielded as he essayed all things where glory's path lay open, even he (Hercules) won from the chase the chiefest ornament and honour of his fame. Consider, then, what benefit, derived from the arts I treat, can trick the strong beasts when matched against them.

Some hunters have found in plumes plucked from the filthy vulture a handy means of working and no slight help. Only, at intervals along the line there must be added the down of the snow-white swan, and that is implement enough: the white feathers glitter in clear sunlight, formidable appearances for game,[a] whereas the dread stench from the black vulture disturbs the forest-creatures; and the contrast of colour works the better effect. But, while the plumage hanging from your device has its bright gleam or heavy scent, let it be at the same time soft to handle and not very closely entwined, so that the cord when pulled in will not entangle you with its feathers in your hurry and by its faultiness convict you in the very using. This device of terror has more use against stags; but when the pliant feathers are sometimes dyed with African vermilion and the flaxen cord gleams from its projecting forks,[b] it is rare for any beast to escape the counterfeit terrors. Yes, and there is also some use in "running"

[a] The *linea pinnis distincta* intended to drive game into snares was called a "formido" (*cf. metus*, 85); Sen. *Dial.* iv. 11. 5; *Phaedra* 46–48; Virg. *G.* III. 372; Lucan IV. 437–38.

[b] The *ancon* (ἀγκών) was a forked pole on which to spread nets. A pure Latin term for a similar trestle was the *ames* of Hor. *Epod.* ii. 33: *cf. varae*, Lucan, *Phars.* IV. 439; and in Greek στάλικες, σταλίδες, or σχαλίδες; Xen. *Cyn.* ii. 7, Oppian, *Cyn.* I. 151.

cervino iussere magis contexere nervo; 90
fraus teget insidias habitu mentita ferino.
quid qui dentatas iligno robore clausit
venator pedicas? quam dissimulantibus armis
saepe habet imprudens alieni lucra laboris!
o felix, tantis quem primum industria rebus 95
prodidit auctorem! deus ille an proxima divos
mens fuit, in caecas aciem quae magna tenebras
egit et ignarum perfudit lumine vulgus?
dic age Pierio, fas est, Diana, ministro.
Arcadium stat fama senem, quem Maenalus auctor
et Lacedaemoniae primum vidistis Amyclae 101
per non adsuetas metantem retia valles
Dercylon. haut illo quisquam se iustior egit,
haut fuit in terris divom observantior alter:
ergo illum primis nemorum dea finxit in arvis 105
auctoremque operi digna⟨ta⟩ inscribere magno
iussit adire suas et pandere gentibus artes.
ille etiam valido primus venabula dente
induit et proni moderatus vulneris iram
omne moris excepit onus; tum stricta verutis 110

100 auctor A: altor *Turnebus, Postgate.*
103 haud *Sann.*: aut A.
104 hau fuit *Baehrens*: au fuit A: auṭ (t *deleta*) fuit *Paris.* 8071.

nooses:[a] it is recommended to compose these of deer's leather preferably: the deceit will cloak the snare through falsely suggesting a creature of the wild.[b] What of the hunter who to his toothed springe adds an oaken stake? How often, thanks to these tricksome devices, does one unexpectedly reap the fruit of another's toil![c]

Fortunate the man whose industry made him first inventor of arts so great! Was he a god or was that mind close kin to the gods which mightily sped its clear gaze into blind darkness and flooded the uninstructed crowd with light? Come speak, Diana, for 'tis heaven's will, unto a servant of the Muses. The story stands secure that it was an old Arcadian whom you, Maenalus, his witness, and you, Lacedaemonian Amyclae, first saw laying out hunting-nets in unaccustomed vales—Dercylos his name. Never did man bear himself more justly than he: on earth there was no other more regardful of the gods. He then it was whom the goddess fashioned in primeval fields,[d] and deigning to inscribe him as author of a mighty work, she enjoined him to go and unfold her own arts to the nations. He was the first also to dress hunting-spears with a strong tooth, and, controlling the angry onslaught of a forward thrust, to receive all the (boar's) weight on projecting spear-guards.[e]

[a] Enk, pp. 36–38, has a full note on different interpretations of *laquei curraces*.

[b] *i.e.* the *cervinus nervus* will have the smell of the *cervus*.

[c] An animal partly lamed or dragging with it the *robur* would be easily caught.

[d] Arcadia.

[e] The term *morae* is applied to projecting metal *alae* or *orbes* fixed behind the spear-head so as to hinder the spear from going too deeply into the beast.

dentibus et gemina subiere hastilia furca
et quidam totis clauserunt ensibus ⟨hastas⟩,
ne cessaret iners in vulnere massa ferino.
blandimenta vagae fugies novitatis: ibidem
exiguo nimiove nocent. sed lubricus errat 115
mos et ab expertis festinant usibus omnes.
quid, Macetum immensos libeat si dicere contos?
quam longa exigui spicant hastilia dentes!
aut contra ut tenero destrictas cortice virgas
praegravat ingenti pernix Lucania cultro! 120
omnia tela modi melius finxere salubres.
quocirca et iaculis habilem perpendimus usum,
ne leve vulnus eat neu sit brevis impetus illi.
ipsa arcu Lyciaque suos Diana pharetra
armavit comites: ne tela relinquite divae: 125
magnum opus et volucres quondam fecere sagittae.

disce agedum et validis dilectum hastilibus omnem.
plurima Threiciis nutritur vallibus Hebri
cornus et umbrosae Veneris per litora myrtus
taxique pinusque Altinatesque genestae 130

112 *post* ensibus *nihil in* A: orbes *male add. Ald.*: tortis . . . hastas *H. Schenkl.*
117 dicere A: ducere *Baehrens.*
120 praegravat *Ald.*: -av& A.
123 neu leve A: ne leve *Sann.*

Later, there succeeded to them weapons furnished with spit-like teeth and twofold fork, and some gave their spear-ends a ring of sharp points to prevent the thick steel remaining inactive in the wounded quarry.[a] You are to shun the allurements of fleeting novelty: in this same field of hunting they do harm by a small or excessive size of spear. But slippery fashion goes its wandering round, and all men are in haste to discard usages which have been tried. What if I choose to speak of the enormous Macedonian pikes? How long are the shafts and how small the teeth which furnish their spikes! Or, on the other hand, how does nimble Lucania overload with a huge point thin rods stripped of their tender bark! All weapons have been the better fashioned by healthy moderation. Wherefore for javelins too we weigh thoroughly their manageable handling, lest their wounding power speed lightly or the weapon's force fall short.[b] Diana herself armed her own comrades with bow and Lycian quiver: abandon ye not the weapons of the goddess: once on a day great work was wrought by swift arrows.

Now, moreover, learn the whole range of choice for strong spears. The cornel tree grows abundantly in the Thracian valleys of the Hebrus; there are shady myrtles along the shores of Venus;[c] there are yew trees and pines and the broom-plants of Altinum,[d] and the lopped bough more likely to help

[a] The sharp points would make the wound worse.
[b] *Vulnus* is used of the weapon which wounds in Virg. *Aen.* IX. 745, X. 140; Sil. Ital. I. 397; Val. Flacc. III. 197. *Illi* sc. *vulneri* i.e. *iaculo.*
[c] *i.e.* in Cyprus.
[d] On the Adriatic shore, not far from Venice.

et magis incomptos opera iuturus agrestes
termes. ab Eois descendit virga Sabaeis
mater odorati multum pulcherrima turis:
illa suos usus intractatumque decorem
(sic nemorum iussere deae) natalibus hausit 13
arbitriis; at enim multo sunt ficta labore
cetera quae silvis errant hastilia nostris:
numquam sponte sua procerus ad aera termes
exiit inque ipsa curvantur stirpe genestae.
ergo age luxuriam primo fetusque nocentes 14
detrahe: frondosas gravat indulgentia silvas.
post ubi proceris generosa⟨m⟩ stirpibus arbor
se dederit teretesque ferent ad sidera virgae,
stringe notas circum et gemmantes exige versus.
his, si quis vitium nociturus sufficit umor, 14
ulceribus fluet et venas durabit inertes.
in quinos sublata pedes hastilia plena
caede manu, dum pomiferis advertitur annus
frondibus et tepidos autumnus continet imbres.

sed cur exiguis tantos in partibus orbes 15
lustramus? prima illa canum, non ulla per artes
cura prior, sive indomitos vehementior hostes
nudo marte premas seu bellum ex arte ministres.

131 in comptos A: in contos *Johnson*. opera A: superat *Stern*. lutores A: lotaster *Johnson*: iuturus *Sudhaus*. agstis (-st- *ex* -rt- *corr.*) A: agrestis *Sann*.
148 avertitur *Vollmer*: advertitur A.

with its service the uncouth country-folk. From the Arabians in the East comes the branch that is far the fairest mother of fragrant frankincense: it draws from the laws of its birth (so have the goddesses of the groves ordained) its own uses and its natural shapeliness; but it is only with much toil that the other stems widely grown in our western woods are fashioned into spear-shafts. Never did bough of its own accord rise tall into the air; and the broom curves even in its lower stem. Come, then, strip off at once the excessive growth and harmful branches: indulgence overloads trees with leaves. Later, when the tree proves its goodliness in its tall stems and the shapely branches tend starwards, cut round the places where suckers start and remove the rows of sprouting branches. If any sap of an injurious sort causes harm, it will flow out of these wounds and so harden the weak veins. When the shafts have risen to a height of five feet, cut them with full grasp, while the year approaches the season of fruit-laden leafage and autumn holds back the warm showers.

But why do we traverse these wide rounds amidst small details? The foremost care is that of dogs;[a] no other care comes before that throughout the whole system of hunting, whether you energetically pursue the untamed quarry with bare force or use skill to manage the conflict. Dogs belong to a

[a] On dogs generally see Xen. *Cyn.* iii–iv, vii; Aristotle, *Hist. An.* 574a 16 *sqq.* and *passim*; Arr. *Cyn.* 2 *sqq.*; Poll. *Onom.* V. 37 *sqq.*; *Geoponica* (10th cent.) xix. 1 *sqq.*; Virg. *G.* III. 404 *sqq.*; Varro, *R.R.* II. 9; Plin. *N.H.* VIII. 142 *sqq.*; Colum. *R.R.* VII. 12–13; Nemes. *Cyn.* 103 *sqq.*; Oppian, *Cyn.* I. 368–588; Claud. *Stil.* III. 298–301.

mille canum patriae ductique ab origine mores
quoique sua. magna indocilis dat proelia Medus 15
magnaque diversos extollit gloria Celtas.
arma negant contra martemque odere Geloni,
sed natura sagax: Perses in utroque paratus.
sunt qui Seras alant, genus intractabilis irae;
at contra faciles magnique Lycaones armis. 16
sed non Hyrcano satis est vehementia gentis
tanta suae: petiere ultro fera semina silvis;
dat Venus accessus et blando foedere iungit.
tunc et mansuetis tuto ferus errat adulter
in stabulis ultroque gravem succedere tigrin 16
ausa canis maiore tulit de sanguine fetum.
sed praeceps virtus: ipsa venabitur aula
ille tibi et pecudum multo cum sanguine crescet.
pasce tamen: quaecumque domi sibi crimina fecit,
excutiet silva magnus pugnator adepta. 17
at fugit adversos idem quos repperit hostes
Umber: quanta fides utinam et sollertia naris,
tanta foret virtus et tantum vellet in armis!
quid, freta si Morinum dubio refluentia pont⟨o⟩
veneris atque ipsos libeat penetrare Britanno⟨s⟩? 17

---

[a] *i.e.* the breeds are innumerable: *cf.* Oppian, *Cyn.* I. 400, τὰ δὲ μυρία φῦλα πέλονται.
[b] A Sarmatian tribe in the region of the modern Ukraine.
[c] In pugnacity and sagacity.
[d] Or, possibly, Tibetan.
[e] British dogs were, Strabo tells us, IV. v. 2 (C 199), exported as εὐφυεῖς πρὸς τὰς κυνηγεσίας. *Cf.* Nemes. 225, *divisa*

thousand lands [a] and they each have characteristics derived from their origin. The Median dog, though undisciplined, is a great fighter, and great glory exalts the far-distant Celtic dogs. Those of the Geloni,[b] on the other hand, shirk a combat and dislike fighting, but they have wise instincts: the Persian is quick in both respects.[c] Some rear Chinese [d] dogs, a breed of unmanageable ferocity; but the Lycaonians, on the other hand, are easy-tempered and big in limb. The Hyrcanian dog, however, is not content with all the energy belonging to his stock: the females of their own will seek unions with wild beasts in the woods: Venus grants them meetings and joins them in the alliance of love. Then the savage paramour wanders safely amid the pens of tame cattle, and the bitch, freely daring to approach the formidable tiger, produces offspring of nobler blood. The whelp, however, has headlong courage: you will find him a-hunting in the very yard and growing at the expense of much of the cattle's blood. Still you should rear him: whatever enormities he has placed to his charge at home, he will obliterate them as a mighty combatant on gaining the forest. But that same Umbrian dog which has tracked wild beasts flees from facing them. Would that with his fidelity and shrewdness in scent he could have corresponding courage and corresponding will-power in the conflict! What if you visit the straits of the Morini, tide-swept by a wayward sea, and choose to penetrate even among the Britons? [e]

Britannia mittit Veloces nostrique orbis venatibus aptos: Claud. *Stil.* III. 301, *magnaque taurorum fracturae colla Britannae.* The Morini were northern Gauls whose chief town Gesoriacum became Bononia (Boulogne).

o quanta est merces et quantum impendia supra!
si non ad speciem mentiturosque decores
pronus es (haec una est catulis iactura Britannis),
at magnum cum venit opus promendaque virtus
et vocat extremo praeceps discrimine Mavors:
non tunc egregios tantum admirere Mol⟨os⟩s⟨os⟩.
comparat his versuta suas Athamania ⟨gentes⟩
Azorusque Pheraeque et clandestinus Acar⟨nan⟩:
sicut Acarnanes subierunt proelia furto,
sic canis illa suos taciturna supervenit hostes.
at clangore citat quos nondum conspicit apros
Aetola quaecumque canis de stirpe: malignum
officium, sive illa metus convicia rupit
seu frustra nimius properat favor. et tamen ill⟨ud⟩
ne vanum totas genus aspernere per artes:
mirum quam celeres et quantum nare merentur,
tum non est victi quoi concessere labori.
idcirco variis miscebo gentibus usum:
quondam inconsultis mater dabit Umbrica Gallis

178 pronis (*ut sit principium parenthesi*) *Vollmer*: pronuis A, *Postgate*, ἅπαξ εἰρημένον: pronus es *H. Schenkl*: protinus *Sann. et vulgo, extra parenthesin.*

182 *finis versus periit in* A: fraudes *add. Ald.*: gentes *Vollmer.*

183 Azorusque *Wernsdorf*: Acirusque A.

189 furor A, *Burm.*, *Wernsdorf*, *Stern*: favor *Gronov*, *Johnson*: cf. 230 favore, 240 faventem.

O how great your reward, how great your gain beyond any outlays! If you are not bent on looks and deceptive graces (this is the one defect of the British whelps), at any rate when serious work has come, when bravery must be shown, and the impetuous War-god calls in the utmost hazard, then you could not admire the renowned Molossians[a] so much. With these last[b] cunning Athamania compares her breeds; as also do Azorus, Pherae and the furtive Acarnanian: just as the men of Acarnania steal secretly into battle, so does the bitch surprise her foes without a sound. But any bitch of Aetolian pedigree rouses with her yelps the boars which she does not yet see—a mischievous service, whether it is that fear makes these savage sounds break out or excessive eagerness speeds on uselessly. And yet you must not despise that breed as useless in all the accomplishments of the chase; they are marvellously quick, marvellously efficient in scent; besides, there is no toil to which they yield defeated. Consequently, I shall cross the advantages of different breeds:—one day an Umbrian mother will give to the unskilled Gallic pups[c] a smart disposition;

[a] Molossian dogs are frequently mentioned in ancient literature: *e.g.* Aristoph. *Thesm.* 416; Poll. V. 37; Opp. *Cyn.* I. 375; Plaut. *Capt.* 86; Lucr. V. 1063; Virg. *G.* III. 405; Hor. *Epod.* vi. 5; *Sat.* II. vi. 114; Lucan IV. 440; Sen. *Phaedra*, 33; Stat. *Theb.* III. 203, *Silv.* II. vi. 19; *Ach.* I. 747; Mart. XII. i. 1; Claud. *Stil.* II. 215, III. 293; Nem. *Cyn.* 107.

[b] It seems appropriate to take *his* of Molossian dogs rather than of British, as the proper names refer to neighbouring districts of Epirus, Thessaly, Aetolia and Acarnania. Athamania is a district in Epirus near the Pindus range.

[c] *Cf.* the qualities suggested in 171–73, and 156. "Gallic" in 194 may mean "Galatian": see Introduction.

sensum agilem, traxere animos de patre Gelonae 19
Hyrcano et vanae tantum Calydonia linguae
exibit vitium patre emendata Molosso.
scilicet ex omni florem virtute capessunt
et sequitur natura favens. at te leve si qua
ta⟨n⟩git opus pavidosque iuvat compellere dorcas 20
aut versuta sequi leporis vestigia parvi,
Petronios (haec fama) canes volucresque Sycambros
et pictam macula Vertraham delige flava:
ocior affectu mentis pennaque cucurrit,
sed premit inventas, non inventura latentes 20
illa feras, quae Petroniis bene gloria constat.
quod si maturo pressantes gaudia lusu
dissimulare feras tacitique accedere possent,
illis omne decus, quod nunc, metagontes, habetis,
constaret: silva sed virtus irrita damno est. 21
at vestrum non vile genus, non patria. vulgo

[196] tantum A: natum *Stern.*
[202] cani *Haupt*: cana A: Petroniost haec fama cani *Vollmer.*
[203] vertraham *sic* A: *cf. Mart.* XIV. cc. falsa A: flava *vel* fulva *Johnson.*
[210] *ante* silva *primus distinxit Baehrens.*

puppies of a Gelonian mother have drawn spirit from a Hyrcanian sire;[a] and Calydonia,[b] good only at pointless barking, will lose the defect when improved by a sire from Molossis. In truth, the offspring cull the best from all the excellence of the parents, and kindly nature attends them. But if in any wise a light sort of hunting captivates you, if your taste is to hunt the timid antelope or to follow the intricate tracks of the smaller hare, then you should choose Petronian[c] dogs (such is their reputation) and swift Sycambrians[d] and the Vertraha[e] coloured with yellow spots—swifter than thought or a winged bird it runs, pressing hard on the beasts it has found, though less likely to find them when they lie hidden; this last is the well-assured glory of the Petronians. If only the latter could restrain their transports until the completion of their sport, if they could affect not to be aware of their prey and approach without barking, they would be assured all the honour which you dogs of the *metagon*[f] breed now hold: as it is, in the forest ineffectual spirit means loss. But you *metagontes* have no ignoble pedigree or home.

[a] *Cf.* 157–58 and 161–63.
[b] *i.e.* Aetolia: *cf.* 186–92.
[c] *Petroni*: possibly dogs workable on stony ground (*petra*).
[d] *Sycambri*, a tribe of Western Germany near the Rhine.
[e] Perhaps *Vertagra*: *cf.* Italian *veltro*, a greyhound. MSS. of Martial, XIV. cc. 1 give the forms *vertrăcus, vertăgus, vetrăgus.* The word seems to be Celtic: Arrian, *Cyneg.* 3. 6, αἱ δὲ ποδώκεις κύνες αἱ Κελτικαὶ καλοῦνται μὲν οὐέρτραγοι φωνῇ τῇ Κελτῶν . . . It has sometimes been explained as a "tumbler" dog that inveigled game by rolling himself into a heap to disguise his appearance.
[f] The μετάγων is mentioned only by Grattius. Burman suggested the word implied the tracking of game: Ulitius and Curcio take it of the cross-breeding of the dog.

Sparta suos et Creta suos promittit alumnos:
sed primum celsa lorum cervice ferentem,
Glympice, te silvis egit Boeotius Hagnon,
Hagnon Astylides, Hagnon, quem plurima semper 21
gratia per nostros unum testabitur usus.
hic trepidas artes et vix novitate sedentes
vidit qua propior peteret via nec sibi turbam
contraxit comitem nec vasa tenentia longe:
unus praesidium atque operi spes magna petito 22
adsumptus metagon lustrat per nota ferarum
pascua, per fontes, per quas trivere latebras.
primae lucis opus: tum signa vapore ferino
intemerata legens si qua est qua fallitur eius
turba loci, maiore secat spatia extera gyro; 22
atque hic egressu iam tum sine fraude reperto
incubuit, spatiis qualis permissa Lechaeis
Thessalium quadriga decus, quam gloria patrum
excitat et primae spes ambitiosa coronae.
sed ne qua ex nimio redeat iactura favore, 23

[212] Sparta suos A: Sparte vos *Baehrens*: Sparte quos *H. Schenkl.*
[218] peteret viam A: patuit via *Ald.*: ferret via *Baehrens.*

Sparta,[a] by common report, and Crete[b] alike claim you as their own nurslings. But, Glympic[c] hound, you were the first to wear leash on high-poised neck and he that followed you in the forest was the Boeotian Hagnon, Hagnon son of Astylos, Hagnon, to whom our abundant gratitude shall bear witness as pre-eminent in our practice of the chase. He saw where the easier road lay to a calling as yet nervously timorous and owing to its newness scarce established: he brought together no band of followers or implements in long array: his single *metagon* was taken as his guard, as the high promise of the longed-for spoil; it roams across the fields which are the haunts of beasts, over the wells and through the lurking-places frequented by them. 'Tis the work of early dawn: then, while the dog is picking out the trail as yet unspoiled by another animal's scent, if there is any confusion of tracks in that place whereby he is thrown off, he runs an outside course in a wider circle and, at last discovering beyond mistake the footprints coming out, pounces on the track like the fourfold team, the pride of Thessaly, which is launched forth on the Corinthian race-course, stirred by ancestral glory and by hopes covetous of the first prize. But lest loss be the outcome of excessive zeal, the dog's

[a] For Spartan or Lacedaemonian dogs *cf.* Soph. *Aj.* 8; Xen. *Cyn.* iii. 1; Opp. *Cyn.* I. 372; Pollux, V. 37; Virg. *G.* III. 405; Hor. *Epod.* vi. 5; Ov. *Met.* III. 208, 223; Sen. *Phaedra,* 35; Lucan, IV. 441; Claud. *Stil.* III. 300 (*tenuesque Lacaenae*); Nemes. *Cyn.* 107, etc.

[b] For Cretan dogs *cf.* Xen. *Cyn.* x. 1; Poll. V. 37; Opp. *Cyn.* I. 373; Ov. *Met.* III. 208, 223; Sen. *Phaedra,* 34; Claud. *Stil.* III. 300 (*hirsutae Cressae*), etc.

[c] The reference is to a locality on the Argive and Laconian border.

lex dicta officiis: neu voce lacesseret hostem
neve levem praedam aut propioris pignora lucri
amplexus primos nequiquam effunderet actus;
iam vero impensum melior fortuna laborem
cum sequitur iuxtaque domus quaesita ferarum, 23
et sciat occultos et signis arguat hostes:
aut effecta levi testatur gaudia cauda
aut ipsa infodiens uncis vestigia plantis
mandit humum celsisve apprensat naribus auras.
et tamen, ut ne prima faventem pignora fallant, 24
circum omnem aspretis medius qua clauditur orbi⟨s⟩
ferre pedem accessusque abitusque notare ferarum
admonet et, si forte loco spes prima fefellit,
rusum opus incubuit spatiis; at, prospera si res,
intacto repetet prima ad vestigia gyro. 24
ergo ubi plena suo rediit victoria fine,
in partem praedae veniat comes et sua norit
praemia: sic operi iuvet inservisse benigne.
  hoc ingens meritum, haec ultima palma tropae⟨i⟩,
Hagnon magne, tibi divom concessa favore: 25

233 offenderet A, *Vollmer*: effunderet *Johnson*, *vulgo*.
236 & sciat A: ut sciat *Sann.*
240 faventem (= *studiosum*, *cf.* *v.* 230).
211 orbis *Sann.*: orbi A: orbem *Baehrens.*

duties are regulated: he must not assail his foe with barking;[a] he must not seize on some trivial prey or on signs of a nearer catch and so blindly lose the fruit of his first activities. When, however, better fortune already attends the outlay of toil, and the sought-for lair of the wild beasts is near, he must both know his enemies are hidden and prove this by signs: either he shows his new-won pleasure by lightly wagging the tail, or, digging in his own footprints with the nails of his paws, he gnaws the soil and sniffs the air with nostrils raised high. And yet to prevent the first signs from misleading the dog in his keenness, the hunter bids him run all about the inner space encircled by rough ground and nose the paths by which the beasts come and go; then, if it happens that the first expectation has failed him in the place,[b] he turns again to his task in wide coursings; but, if the scent was right, he will make for the first trail again as the quarry has not crossed the circle. Therefore, when full success has arrived with its proper issue, the dog must come as comrade to share the prey and must recognise his own reward: thus let it be a delight to have given ungrudging service to the work.

Such was the mighty benefit, such the surpassing prize of triumph granted to thee, great Hagnon, by favour of the gods: so shalt thou live for ever, as long

[a] *Cf.* Lucan, *Phars.* IV. 441, *nec creditur ulli Silva cani nisi qui presso vestigia rostro Colligit et praeda nescit latrare reperta,* and Pliny's description of the silent tracking of game, *N.H.* VIII. 147, *quam silens et occulta sed quam significans demonstratio est cauda primum deinde rostro.*

[b] *i.e.* if the animal has already escaped and is no longer lying hidden there.

ergo semper eris, dum carmina dumque manebunt
silvarum dotes atque arma Diania terris.
hic et semiferam thoum de sanguine prolem
finxit. non alio maior sub pectore virtus,
sive in lora voces seu nudi ad pignora martis. 255
thoes commissos (clarissima fama) leones
et subiere astu et parvis domuere lacertis;
nam genus exiguum et pudeat, quam informe, fateri;
vulpina species: tamen huic exacta voluntas.
at non est alius quem tanta ad munia fetus 260
exercere velis, aut te tua culpa refellet
inter opus, quo sera cadit prudentia damno.
iunge pares ergo et maiorum pignore signa
feturam prodantque tibi metagonta parentes,
qui genuere sua pecus hoc immane iuventa. 265
et primum expertos animi, quae gratia prima est,
in venerem iungam. tum sortis cura secunda,
ne renuat species aut quem detractet honorem.
sint celsi vultus, sint hirtae frontibus aures,
os magnum et patulis agitatos naribus ignes 270
spirent, adstricti succingant ilia ventres,
cauda brevis longumque latus discretaque collo

255 lora *Ellis*: ora A.
262 quom *Gronov*: quo A.
265 tenuere A: genuere *Gesner*.
268 aut quem *Baehrens*: atque A: aut quae *Ald.*: aut qua *Barth.*

as my songs shall last, as long as the woods keep their treasures and Diana's weapons abide on earth.

'Twas he too who developed a species with a wild strain from the blood of the *thoes*.[a] Beneath no other breast is there higher courage, whether you call them to the leash or to the test of open conflict. The *thoes* (their reputation is famous) can steal craftily on lions pitted against them[b] and overcome them with their short legs; for it is a small-sized breed, and one may scruple to own how ugly: it has a fox-like look: still its resolution is perfect. But there is no other breed which you could wish to train for tasks so important; or else your own mistake will find you out in the hunt when loss of game makes late-learned wisdom vain.

Now then couple well-matched mates[c] and mark the offspring with the pledge of their pedigree, letting the parents who produce this wonderful progeny in the vigour of their youth yield you a fine *metagon*. First I shall mate dogs tried in courage, the foremost quality: the next care in the apportionment is that outward appearance shall not belie descent or lower any of its merits. They should have the face high, they should have shaggy ears by their foreheads, the mouth big, and they should breathe fiery blasts from wide nostrils; a neat belly should gird their flanks below; tail should be short and sides long, hair parted on the neck, and that

[a] The θῶες of Oppian, *Cyneg.* III. 336–38, are jackals sprung from a union of wolves with leopards. The θώς of Aristotle is perhaps rather a civet than a jackal. Pliny, *N.H.* VIII. 123, mentions *thoes* as a kind of wolf.

[b] *e.g.* in the public games at Rome.

[c] For the mating of dogs, with 263 *sqq.* *cf.* Nemesianus, *Cyn.* 103 *sqq.*; Oppian, *Cyn.* I. 376 *sqq.*

caesaries neu pexa nimis neu frigoris illa
impatiens; validis tum surgat pectus ab armis,
quod magnos capiat motus magnisque supersit.
effuge qui lata pandit vestigia planta:
mollis in officio. siccis ego dura lacertis
crura velim et solidos haec in certamina calces.
 sed frustra longus properat labor, abdita si non
altas in latebras unique inclusa marito ⟨est⟩
femina: nec patres veneris sub tempore magnos
illa neque emeritae servat fastigia laudis.
primi complexus, dulcissima prima voluptas:
hunc veneri dedit impatiens natura furorem.
si tenuit custos et mater adultera non est,
da requiem gravidae solitosque remitte labores:
vix oneri super illa suo. tum deinde monebo,
ne matrem indocilis natorum turba fatiget,
percensere notis iamque inde excernere pravos.
signa dabunt ipsi. teneris vix artubus haeret
ille tuos olim non defecturus honores,
iamque illum impatiens aequae vehementia sortis
extulit: affectat materna regna sub alvo,
ubera tota tenet, a tergo liber aperto,

280 in latebras *Sann.*: illecebras A. est *add. Lachmann.*
281 patres *Sann.*: patre A.
285 custos A: castus *Ellis*: fastus *Lachmann*: renuit cunctos *Pith.*, *Burm.*
289 pravos *Burman*: parvos A.
294 tenet, a tergo ς: ten& eatergo A: tenetque a tergo *Baehrens.*

neither too shaggy nor yet unable to stand cold; and then from strong limbs[a] must rise a breast capable of drawing deep breaths, and with strength left for more. Avoid the dog that spreads his steps with a broad foot: he is weak in hunting-duty. I should want hardy legs with firm muscles and I should want solid feet for such struggles.

But zealous and prolonged trouble is all in vain unless the bitch is shut up in some deep retreat and secluded for a single male: otherwise she cannot at the time of coupling maintain unspoilt the pedigree of a fine sire or the pitch of past distinction won. The first unions, the first pleasure is sweetest: such frenzy has uncontrolled nature given to love. If the attendant has kept her shut up and the pregnant bitch has no unions with other dogs,[b] give her rest and remit her usual tasks: she is barely sufficient for her own burden. Then later I shall suggest, to prevent an unruly litter of whelps from wearing their mother out, that you examine them by their points and thereupon pick out the inferior ones. They will themselves give indications. The puppy that one day will not fail[c] your pride in him[d] is scarcely yet firm in his tender limbs, and already his vigour, impatient of equality with the rest, has raised him above them: he aims at sovereignty beneath his mother's belly, keeps her teats wholly to himself, his back unen-

[a] The shoulder-blades should be broad, as in Oppian, *Cyn.* I. 409, εὐρέες ὠμοπλάται: *cf.* Xen. *Cyn.* iv. 1; Pollux, V. 58; Arr. *Cyn.* 5. 9; Colum. *R.R.* VII. xii. 4.

[b] Vollmer's inclusion of the *si tenuit* clause in the preceding sentence, with *hunc . . . furorem* as a parenthesis, is unsatisfactory.

[c] *Cf.* note on *illum . . . mergentem*, 424–5.

[d] Or "high tasks to which you may call him."

dum tepida indulget terris clementia mundi; 29
verum ubi Caurino perstrinxit frigore vesper,
ira iacet turbaque potens operitur inerti.
illius et manibus vires sit cura futuras
perpensare: leves deducet pondere fratres:
nec me pignoribus, nec te mea carmina fallent. 30

protinus et cultus alios et debita fetae
blandimenta feres curaque sequere merentem:
illa perinde suos, ut erit † dilecta, minores
ad longam praestabit opem. tum denique, fetu
cum desunt, operis fregitque industria matres, 30
transeat in catulos omnis tutela relictos.
lacte novam pubem facilique tuebere maza,
nec luxus alios avidaeque impendia vitae
noscant: haec magno redit indulgentia damno.
nec mirum: humanos non est magis altera sensus, 31
tollit ni ratio et vitiis adeuntibus obstat.
haec illa est Pharios quae fregit noxia reges,
dum servata cavis potant Mareotica gemmis

297 ire plac& A: ira iacet *Ulitius*: irreptat *Radermacher*.
298 et *Heinsius*: e A.
299 leuis A.
303 de lacte *Sann.*, *Vollmer*: delacta A: dilecta *Stern*: suo saturat de lacte *Johnson* 1699 *ed.*: delecta (*particip. a delicere*) *Heinsius*.
304–5 fetu A: fetus cum desunt operi *Ellis*. operis *Ulitius*: operi A.
311 ni *Graevius*: se A.

cumbered and unpressed by the others so long as the genial warmth of the heavens is kind to earth;[a] but when evening has shrivelled him with north-western chilliness, his bad temper flags and this strong pup lets himself be snugly covered by the sluggish crowd (of the rest). It must be your care thoroughly to weigh his promised strength in your hands: he will humble his light brothers with his weight.[b] In these signs my poems will mislead neither myself nor you.

As soon as she has produced young, you are to offer the mother different treatment and the comforts due to her, and to attend her carefully as she deserves. Exactly as she is kindly treated, she will maintain her little ones until a long service of nurture has been rendered.[c] Then finally, when the mothers fail their offspring and their assiduity in the task of suckling has shattered them, let all your concern pass over to the deserted whelps. You must sustain the young brood with milk and a simple pap: they must not know other luxuries and the outlays of a gluttonous life: such indulgence comes home at mighty cost. Nor is this surprising: no other life eats more into the senses of mankind, unless reason banishes it and bars the way against the approach of vices. Such was the fault that ruined Egyptian kings, as they drank old Mareotic wines in goblets of precious stone, reaping the perfumes

[a] *i.e.* during the sunny day.

[b] *Cf.* Livy IX. 34 . . . *ad servorum ministerium deduxisti* (= brought down, degraded). The reference is not to exact weighing in a *trutina* or balance.

[c] The text is uncertain; but the sense required is that the greater the care lavished on the mother, the longer she will be able to give milk to her pups.

nardiferumque metunt Gangen vitiisque ministrant.
sic et Achaemenio cecidisti, Lydia, Cyro:
atqui dives eras ⟨ac⟩ fluminis aurea venis.
scilicet ad summam ne quid restaret habendi,
tu quoque luxuriae fictas dum colligis artes
et sequeris demens alienam, Graecia, culpam,
o quantum et quotiens decoris frustrata paterni!
at qualis nostris, quam simplex mensa Camillis!
qui tibi cultus erat post tot, Serrane, triumphos!
ergo illi ex habitu virtutisque indole priscae
imposuere orbi Romam caput, actaque ab illis
ad caelum virtus summosque tetendit honores.
 scilicet exiguis magna sub imagine rebus
prospicies, quae sit ratio, et quo fine regendae.
idcirco imperium catulis unusque magister
additur: ille dapes poenamque operamque ⟨moramque⟩
temperet, hunc spectet silvas domitura iuventus.
nec vile arbitrium est: quoicumque haec regna dicantur,
ille tibi egregia iuvenis de pube legendus,

329 *in fine nullum lacunae signum in* A: ministrans *add. Ald.*: peraeque *Baehrens*: moramque *H. Schenkl.*

of nard-bearing Ganges and ministering to vice. By this sin fell you too, Lydia, beneath Persian Cyrus; and yet you were rich and golden in the veins of your river.[a] In good truth, so that nothing might be left to crown the possession of wealth, how much and how often, O Greece, did you too fall short of ancestral honour by gathering together the arts which luxury fashioned and by madly following the faults of other nations! But of what sort, how simple, was the table of our Camilli![b] What was your dress, Serranus, after all your triumphs![c] These were the men who, in accord with the bearing and character of ancient virtue, set o'er the world Rome as its head; and by them was virtue exalted to heaven, and so she reached highest honours.

In truth, taught by great precedent you will be able to provide for small details, finding the right system and the limits which should govern them. Therefore rule is imposed on the whelps in the shape of a single keeper: he must control their food and punishments, their service and rest: the young pack that is to master the woods must look to him. It is no trumpery charge: whosoever has such power dedicated to him should be a youth picked by you from young folk of merit, at once prudent

[a] The river Pactolus was famous for its golden sands. Postgate's *Pactolique aurea venis* suggests that *fluminis* was a gloss on the original reading.

[b] The plural alludes rhetorically to M. Furius Camillus, the conqueror of Veii, who saved Rome after the Allian disaster: for his poverty *cf.* Hor. *Od.* I. xii. 42 *sqq.*

[c] C. Atilius Regulus Serranus was consul in 257 and in 250 B.C. He was summoned from farm-work to undertake a military command, Val. Max. IV. iv. 5; Virg. *Aen.* VI. 845.

utrumque et prudens et sumptis impiger armis.
quod nisi et accessus et agendi tempora belli
noverit et socios tutabitur hoste minores, 33
aut cedent aut illa tamen victoria damno est.
  ergo in opus vigila † factusque ades omnibus armis:
arma acuere viam; tegat imas fascia suras:
⟨sit pell⟩is vitulina, suis et tergore fulvo
i⟨re decet, niteant⟩ canaque e maele galeri, 34
ima Toletano praecingant ilia cultro
terribilemque manu vibrata falarica dextra
det sonitum et curvae rumpant non pervia falces.
  haec tua militia est. quin et Mavortia bello
vulnera et errantes per tot divertia morbos 34
causasque affectusque canum tua ⟨cura⟩ tueri est.
stat Fatum supra totumque avidissimus Orcus
pascitur et nigris orbem circumsonat alis.
scilicet ad magnum maior ducenda laborem
cura, nec expertos fallet deus: huic quoque nostrae 35

337 vigil affectusque *Vollmer*.
338 arma hacuere uitã A: arma acuere viam (virum *Johnson*) *Ald.* *versuum* 339 *et* 340 *initia perierunt in* A *praeter primam v.* 340 *litteram, quae tamen utrum* j *an* p *fuerit dubitandum* (p *legit Sann.*).
339 *ante* inulina *potest fuisse* us *vel* is: inulina A: sit famulis vitulina tuis *Ulitius, Burm., Wernsd.* suīs (*genit.*, = suīs) A.
345 divertia A: divortia *vulgo.*
350 huic *Baehrens*: hinc A.

and, when he grasps his weapons, unflagging. But unless he knows the right ways of approach and the right moments for attack and can protect his allies when unequal to their enemy, then either the dogs will run away or the victory so won is after all too dear.

So then be wakeful for your work and attend equipped[a] with weapons fully. Weapons make the way of the chase more keen[b]: let bandaging protect the lower parts of the leg: the leather should be calf's leather, and tawny pig-skin is fit for the march: the caps should gleam with the grey of the badger:[c] close under the hunter's flanks should be girt a knife of Toledo steel: a missile weapon brandished in the right hand should give a terrifying sound, while curved reaping-hooks must break through thickets which block the way.

Such is your active service in the chase. But especially is it your concern to care for the martial wounds suffered in fight, the maladies which stray along so many different paths, their causes and the symptoms shown by your dogs. Above stands Fate: the insatiable Death-god devours everything and echoes round the world on sable wings. Clearly for a great task still greater care must be employed, nor will the deity[d] play the experienced false: for this our care too there is another divinity[e] easy to

[a] *factus*, if sound, must have the force of *instructus*.

[b] *Via* is the method of the hunt, *cf*. 5. Johnson's *virum* is attractive, "make the hunter keen."

[c] The nose, chin, lower sides of the cheeks and the mid forehead of the badger (*maeles*) are white: the ends of the hairs on the body are at bottom yellowish-white, in the middle black, and at the ends ash-coloured or grey: hence the proverb "as grey as a badger." The skin dressed without removing the hair can be used for caps or pouches.

[d] Diana. [e] Paean.

est aliud, quod praestet opus, placabile numen.
nec longe auxilium, licet alti vulneris orae
abstiterint atroque cadant cum sanguine fibrae:
inde rape ex ipso qui vulnus fecerit hoste
virosam eluviem lacerique per ulceris ora
sparge manu, venas dum sucus comprimat acer:
mortis enim patuere viae. tum pura monebo
circum labra sequi tenuique includere filo.
at si pernicies angusto pascitur ore,
contra pande viam fallentesque argue causas
morborum: in vitio facilis med⟨icina recenti⟩;
sed tacta impositis mulcent p⟨ecuaria palmis⟩
(id satis) aut nigrae circum picis unguine signant;
quodsi destricto levis est in vulnere noxa,
ipse habet auxilium validae natale salivae.
illa gravis labes et curis altior illis,
cum vitium causae totis egere latentes
corporibus seraque aperitur noxia summa.
inde emissa lues et per contagia mortes
venere in vulgum iuxtaque exercitus ingens
aequali sub labe ruit, nec viribus ullis
aut merito venia est aut spes exire precanti.
quod sive a Stygia letum Proserpina nocte
extulit et Furiis commissam ulciscitur iram,
seu vitium ex alto spiratque vaporibus aether

352 orae *Barth*: ora A.
353 atroque *Sann.*: utroque A.
355 ulceris *Ald.*: viceris A.
357 pura monebo *Sann.*: purmo bebo A.
360 pande *Ald.*: prande A.
361 med⟨icina recenti⟩ *Ald.*: med⟨icina reperto⟩ *Baehrens*.
362 sed A: seu *Heinsius*. tacta A: tactu *Sann.* p⟨ecuaria palmis⟩ *Ald.*
369 morbi *Sann., Vollmer*: morbis A: mortes *Stern.*
370 fusaque *Vollmer*: Iusaque A: iuxtaque *Sann.*

be entreated who can guarantee the work of healing. Nor is aid far distant, though the lips of a deep wound have parted and the fibres are dripping with dark blood: thereupon seize from the very enemy that has dealt the wound some of his fetid urine, sprinkling it with the hand over the mouth of the torn wound, till the acid juice compresses the veins: for the avenues of death lie open. Then my advice will be to go round the lips till they are clean and sew them fast with a slender thread. But if deadly danger battens in a narrow wound, contrariwise, widen the outlet and expose the treacherous causes of corruption: the remedy is easy in a newly-found mischief; but the beasts which are infected they soothe with strokes of the hands (that is enough), or seal the sore around with an ointment of black pitch: if, however, there is merely a trivial hurt in a slight wound, the dog has the natural remedy of efficacious saliva.[a] It is a serious plague, too deep for the treatments mentioned, when hidden causes have sped the malady through all the bodies of the pack and the damage is only discovered in its final consummation. Then has pestilence been let loose, and by contagion deaths have come upon the pack at large, and the great host alike perishes beneath an infection that falls on all: neither is there indulgence granted for any strength or service, nor is there hope of escape in answer to prayer. But whether it be that Proserpina has brought death forth from Stygian darkness, satisfying her wrath for some offence entrusted to the Furies to avenge, whether the infection is from on high and ether breathes with contagious vapours, or whether earth

[a] *i.e.* he licks the wound.

pestiferis, seu terra suos populatur honores,
fontem averte mali. trans altas ducere calles
admoneo latumque fuga superabitis amnem.
hoc primum effugium leti: tunc ficta valebunt
auxilia et nostra quidam redit usus ab arte. 38
sed varii motus nec in omnibus una potestas:
disce vices et quae tutela est proxima tempta.
plurima per catulos rabies invictaque tardis
praecipitat letale malum: sit tutius ergo
antire auxiliis et primas vincere causas. 38
namque subit, nodis qua lingua tenacibus haeret,
(vermiculum dixere) mala atque incondita pestis.
ille ubi salsa siti praecepit viscera longa,
aestivos vibrans accensis febribus ignes,
moliturque fugas et sedem spernit amaram. 39
scilicet hoc motu stimulisque potentibus acti
in furias vertere canes. ergo insita ferro
iam teneris elementa mali causasque recidunt.
nec longa in facto medicina est ulcere: purum
sparge salem et tenui permulce vulnus olivo: 39
ante relata suas quam nox bene compleat umbras,
ecce aderit factique oblitus vulneris ultro
blanditur mensis cereremque efflagitat ore.

376 seu terra suos *Sann.*: si litaeras vos A.
384 praecipitat *Pithou*: pręcipiat A. sit tutius *Sann.*, *qui et* securius *coniecit*: sicutius A: sic tutius *Ald.*
388 longae A: longa *Sann.*: longe *Vollmer*, *Curcio.*
390 amarã A: amatam *Ulitius.*

is devastating her own fair products,[a] remove the source of the evil. I warn you to lead the dogs over the high mountain-paths: you are to cross the broad river in your flight. This is your first escape from destruction: thereafter the aids we have devised will avail and some service is secured from our lore. But varied are the onsets of disease, nor is there the same force in all of them: learn their phases and make trial of the medicine which is most available. Rabies, prevalent among young dogs and uncontrollable for those who delay treatment, launches a deadly evil: it must be safer then to forestall it with remedies and overcome its first causes. For the mischievous and barbarous plague—it has been described as a tiny worm—steals in where the tongue is rooted to its firm ligaments. When the worm has seized on the inwards briny with prolonged thirst, darting its sweltering fires with fevers aflame, it works its escape and spurns its bitter[b] quarters. Impelled, it is plain, by its activity and potent goads, dogs turn frantic. So, when they are quite young, it is usual to cut out with the knife the deep-seated elements and causes of disease. Prolonged treatment is not needed for the wound so made: sprinkle clean salt and soothe the affected part with a little olive-oil: before returning night can well complete her shadows, look, the dog will be on the scene, and, forgetting the wound made, is actually fawning at table and pleading for bread[c] with his mouth.

[a] *i.e.* with the result that they rot and cause disease.

[b] With the meaning of *amaram* compare *salsa* in 388.

[c] The goddess' name is put by metonymy for bread: *cf.* Nemes. *Cyn.* 154, *cererem cum lacte ministra*: so for corn, Virg. *G.* I. 297; Cic. *N.D.* II. 23. 60; *Aetna*, 10.

quid, priscas artes inventaque simplicis aevi
si referam? non illa metus solacia falsi,
tam longam traxere fidem. collaribus ergo
sunt qui lucifugae cristas inducere maelis
iussere aut sacris conserta monilia conchis
et vivum lapidem et circa Melite⟨n⟩sia nectunt
curalia et magicis adiutas cantibus herbas.
ac sic offectus oculique venena maligni
vicit tutela pax impetrata deorum.

at si deformi lacerum dulcedine corpus
persequitur scabies, longi via pessima leti:
in primo accessu tristis medicina, sed una
pernicies redimenda anima, quae prima sequaci
sparsa malo est, ne dira trahant contagia vulgus.
quodsi dat spatium clemens et promonet ortu
morbus, disce vias et qua sinit artibus exi.
tunc et odorato medicata bitumina vino

408 deformis *Ios. Wassius, Vollmer*: deformi A, *Postgate*.
413 promonet A: praemonet *Titius*.
415 vino *Johnson*: viro A. *cf. v.* 476 *et Veget. mulom.* 2. 135. 5.

[a] The omission of a punctuation mark after *falsi* would imply in Grattius an Epicurean disdain for primitive superstition: "those consolations of a groundless fear did not continue to command such a lasting belief." According to

What need to record primitive devices and the inventions of an unsophisticated age? Of no groundless fear were those the consolations: so lasting a confidence have they prolonged.[a] Thus there are some whose prescription has been to fasten cock's combs upon the dog-collars made from the light-shunning badger,[b] or they twine necklets around, strung of sacred shells,[c] and the stone of living fire[d] and red coral from Malta and herbs aided by magic incantations. And so the peace of the gods won by the protective amulet is found to vanquish baleful influences and the venom of the evil eye.

But if the mange pursues a body torn with the ugly itch for scratching, it is the cruellest road of slow death: at the first onset, the remedy is a melancholy one, but destruction must be bought off by the one life (of the dog) which has first been contaminated with the infectious disease, to prevent the whole pack from contracting the dread contagion. If, however, the ailment is slight, giving time and forewarnings at the start, learn the methods of cure and by skilled devices escape wherever feasible. Then fire is found to blend and into one whole unite

the text here accepted, Grattius seems to admit that superstitious cures soothed reasonable fears, and remained long in vogue.

[b] The badger burrows underground, confining itself to its hole during the day and feeding at night.

[c] Among prophylactic amulets the *conchae* were sacred to Venus. Pliny, *N.H.* XXXII, 2–6, mentions the shell *echeneis* or *remora*, believed to have power to stop ships by adhering to the hull. The marvellous properties of such shells, he considers, became the more credible because they were preserved and consecrated in the temple of Venus at Cnidos.

[d] *Pyrites*: *cf.* Pliny, *N.H.* XXXVI. 137, *molarem quidam pyriten vocant*: *cf. Aetna*, 454.

Hipponiasque pices neclectaeque unguen amurcae
miscuit et summam complectitur ignis in unam.
inde lavant aegros: ast ira coercita morbi
laxatusque rigor. quae te ne cura timentem
differat, et pluvias et Cauri frigora vitent; 420
duc magis, ut nudis incumbunt vallibus aestus,
a vento clarique faces ad solis, ut omne
exsudent vitium subeatque latentibus ultro
quae facta est medicina vadis. nec non tamen illum
spumosi catulos mergentem litoris aestu 425
respicit et facilis Paean adiuvit in artes.
o rerum prudens quantam Experientia vulgo
materiem largita boni, si vincere curent
desidiam et gratos agitando prendere fines!

est in Trinacria specus ingens rupe cavique 430
introsum reditus, circum atrae moenia silvae
alta premunt ruptique ambustis faucibus amnes;

416 Hippŏniasque *primus agnovit Haupt*: iponiasque A: impone atque pices, *vel* impositasque pices *vel denique* fraces *Heinsius*. neclectaeque *Haupt*: nec liceat quę A: immundaeque *Ald.*
418 ast A: est *Ald.*: atque *Barth.*
419 ne cura timentem *Sann.*: nec urat in mentem A.
421 duc *H. Schenkl*: sic A: stent *Postgate.*
426 paean adiuvit *Sann.*: paeana divint A.

doses of bitumen, mixed with fragrant wine, and portions of Bruttian[a] pitch and ointment from the unregarded dregs of olive-oil. Therewith they bathe the ailing dogs: then the anger of the malady is curbed and its severity relaxed. Let not this treatment, for all your anxiety, distract you (from further precautions): the dogs must avoid both rains and the chills of the north-west wind: rather, when sultry heats hang over the bare valleys, take them (to heights) away from the wind to meet the rays of the bright sun, so that they may sweat out all the infection and moreover that the healing which has been effected may steal into their hidden veins.[b] Besides the Healing-God, kindly disposed to our skill, fails not to regard favourably and to aid him who dips[c] his whelps in the tide of the foaming beach. O Experience, foreseeing in affairs, how much material benefit hast thou lavished on the mass of men, if they make it their care to overcome sloth and by vigorous action to get a grip of fair ideals!

There is in Sicily a grotto enormous in its rocky mass—with hollow windings which return upon themselves; high ramparts of black woodland enclose it around and streams bursting from volcanic jaws—

[a] Ἱππώνιον is Vibo Valentia on the Via Popilia in the territory of the Bruttii. Curcio thinks that Hippo in Numidia is meant.

[b] *Vadis* is also explained as (1) pores (Enk), (2) intestines (Radermacher). Vollmer imagines a contrast between *latentibus vadis*, meaning *ex aquis reconditis*, and the open sea of the next sentence.

[c] The Latin of *illum mergentem* in the sense of *illum qui mergit* is questionable; but *cf. ille . . . defecturus*, 291. Vollmer proposes tentatively *illic* or *ullum*.

Vulcano condicta domus. quam supter eunti
stagna sedent venis oleoque madentia vivo.
huc defecta mala vidi pecuaria tabe 435
saepe trahi victosque malo graviore magistros.
" te primum, Vulcane, loci, pacemque precamur,
incola sancte, tuam: da fessis ultima rebus
auxilia et, meriti si nulla est noxia tanti,
tot miserare animas liceatque attingere fontes, 440
sancte, tuos " ter quisque vocant, ter pinguia libant
tura foco, struitur ramis felicibus ara.
hic (dictu mirum atque alias ignobile monstrum)
adversis specibus ruptoque e pectore montis
venit ovans Austris et multo flumine flammae 445
emicat ipse: manu ramum pallente sacerdos
termiteum quatiens " procul hinc extorribus ire
edico praesente deo, praesentibus aris,
quis scelus aut manibus sumptum aut in pectore motum est "
inclamat: cecidere animi et trepidantia membra. 450
o quisquis misero fas umquam in supplice fregit,
quis pretio fratrum meliorisque ausus amici
sollicitare caput patriosve lacessere divos,
illum agat infandae comes huc audacia culpae:
discet commissa quantum deus ultor in ira 455
pone sequens valeat. sed cui bona pectore mens est

433 supter *Sann.*: super A.
438 fessis *Sann.*: fissis A.
439 meriti *Sann.*: meritis A.
440 miserare A: -rere *Ald.*
441 vocant ter *Sann.*: vocanter A.

---

[a] *ira commissa* (a curious condensation recalling *commissa piacula*, Virg. *Aen.* VI. 569) is here taken with Wernsdorf to

Vulcan's acknowledged haunt. As one passes beneath, the pools lie motionless oozing in veins of natural bituminous oil. I have often seen dogs dragged hither fordone from mischievous wasting, and their custodians overcome by still heavier suffering. "Thee first, O Vulcan, and thy peace, holy dweller in this place, do we entreat: grant final aid to our wearied fortunes, and, if no guilt is here deserving penalty so great, pity these many lives and suffer them, holy one, to attain to thy fountains"—thrice does each one call, thrice they offer rich incense on the fire, and the altar is piled with fruitful branches. Hereat (wondrous to tell and a portent elsewhere unknown) from the confronting caves and the mountain's riven breast there has come, exultant in southern gales and darting forth 'mid a full flood of flame, the God himself: his priest, waving in pallid hand the olive branch, proclaims aloud: "In the presence of the God, in the presence of the altars, I ordain that all go out of the land far from here, who have put their hands to crime or contemplated it in their heart": forthwith droop their spirits and their nervous limbs. Oh! whoso has ever impaired heaven's law in the case of a wretched suppliant, whoso for a price has dared to aim at the life of brothers or of faithful friend or to outrage ancestral gods—if such a man be impelled hither by audacity, the comrade of unutterable sin, he will learn how mighty is the power of the God who followeth after as the avenger in wrath for crime committed.[a] But he whose mind

mean *ira quae commissis sceleribus provocata est.* The sense is different in 374, *Furiis commissam . . . iram,* unless 455 can imply "in wrath assigned to him to vent."

obsequitur⟨que⟩ deo, deus illam molliter aram
lambit et ipse, suos ubi contigit ignis ⟨hon⟩ores,
defugit a sacris rursumque reconditur antro:
huic fas auxilium et Vulcania tangere dona. 460
nec mora, si medias exedit noxia fibras,
his lave praesidiis affectaque corpora mulce:
regnantem excuties morbum. deus auctor, et ipsa
artem aluit natura suam. quae robore pestis
acrior aut leto propior via? sed tamen illi 465
hic venit auxilium valida vementius ira.
quod primam si fallet opem dimissa facultas,
at tu praecipitem qua spes est proxima labem
aggredere: in subito subita et medicina tumultu.
stringendae nares et ⟨bi⟩na ligamina ferro 470
armorum, geminaque cruor ducendus ab aure:
hinc vitium, hinc illa est avidae vehementia pesti.
ilicet auxiliis fessum solabere corpus
subsiduasque fraces defusaque Massica prisco
sparge cado: Liber tenues e pectore curas 475
exigit, et morbo Liber medicina furenti.
quid dicam tusses, quid inertis damna veterni

[463] excuties *Barth*: -iens A.
[466] hic A: hinc *Ald.*
[468] at tu *Sann.*: ad tu A: actu *Baehrens.*
[470] &na A: et bina *Haupt*: scindenda *Burm. et alii.*
[477] inertis *Sann.*: maestis A: moesti *Ald.* veterni *Sann.*: -nis A.

is good at heart and is reverent to the God, has his altar-gift gently caressed by the Fire-god, who himself, when the flame has reached the sacrifices offered in his honour, retreats from the holy ritual and again conceals himself in his cave. For such a one 'tis right to attain relief and Vulcan's kindliness. Let there be no delay: if the malady has gnawed right into the fibres, bathe with the remedies specified[a] and soothe the suffering bodies: so will you expel the tyrannous disease. The God lends support, and nature herself nourishes her own skilful remedy.[b] What plague is sharper than "robur"[c] or what path nearer to death? But still for it there comes here assistance more active than the powerful anger of the ailment.

Yet if a lost opportunity baffles first aid, then you must attack the furious pestilence where prospects are likeliest: sudden disturbance calls for sudden relief. The nostrils must be cut slightly with the steel, as well as the two muscles of the shoulders, and blood is to be drawn off from both ears: from the blood comes the corruption, from the blood the violence of the insatiate plague. Forthwith you will comfort the wearied body with palliatives, and you must sprinkle on the wounds the sediment of oil-dregs and Massic wine outpoured from its ancient cask—Bacchus expels light cares from the heart: Bacchus also is healing for the fury of disease.

Why mention coughs, why the afflictions of a

[a] *e.g.* the oil from the bituminous lake of 434.

[b] In the form of fire and bitumen.

[c] The disease has the symptoms of tetanus according to veterinary writers: Vegetius, *Mulomedicina* 2, 88; Chiron, 315; Pelagonius, ed. Ihm, 294.

aut incurvatae si qua est tutela podagrae?
mille tenent pestes curaque potentia maior.
mitte age (non opibus tanta est fiducia nostris), 480
mitte, anime: ex alto ducendum numen Olympo,
supplicibus⟨que⟩ vocanda sacris tutela deorum.
idcirco aeriis molimur compita lucis
spicatasque faces sacrum ad nemorale Dianae
sistimus et solito catuli velantur honore, 485
ipsaque per flores medio in discrimine luci
stravere arma sacris et pace vacantia festa.
tum cadus et viridi fumantia liba feretro
praeveniunt teneraque extrudens cornua fronte
haedus et ad ramos etiamnum haerentia poma, 490
lustralis de more sacri, quo tota iuventus
lustraturque deae proque anno reddit honorem.
ergo impetrato respondet multa favore
ad partes, qua poscis opem; seu vincere silvas
seu tibi fatorum labes exire minasque 495
cura prior, tua magna fides tutelaque Virgo.
restat equos finire notis, quos arma Dianae
admittant: non omne meas genus audet in artes.

478 incurvatae *ed. Gryph.* 1537 : incuratae A.
484 nemorale *Turnebus, Postgate* : nemora alta A, *Burm.*, *Wernsd.*, *Stern*, *Curcio*, *Enk.*

---

[a] 483–96, description of an Ambarval sacrifice to Diana, with allusion to her worship near Aricia.
[b] *Multa*, nom. sing. fem., agreeing with *dea* understood: *i.e.* "in full force" (like πολὺς ῥεῖ in Greek). Enk thinks *multa* neut. plur.; Vollmer takes it for *mulcta* in the sense of "mollified."

sluggish lethargy or any prophylactic there is for gout that twists the limbs? A thousand plagues hold their victims, and their power transcends our care. Come, dismiss such cares (our confidence is not so great in our own resources)—dismiss them, my mind: the deity must be summoned from high Olympus and the protection of the gods invoked by suppliant ritual. For that reason we construct cross-road shrines in groves of soaring trees [a] and set our sharp-pointed torches hard by the woodland precinct of Diana, and the whelps are decked with the wonted wreath, and at the centre of the cross-roads in the grove the hunters fling down among the flowers the very weapons which now keep holiday in the festal peace of the sacred rites. Then the wine-cask and cakes steaming on a green-wood tray lead the procession, with a young goat thrusting horns forth from tender brow, and fruit even now clinging to the branches, after the fashion of a lustral ritual at which all the youth both purify themselves in honour of the Goddess and render sacrifice for the bounty of the year. Therefore, when her grace is won, the Goddess answers generously [b] in those directions where you sue for help: whether your greater anxiety is to master the forest or to elude the plagues and threats of destiny, the Maiden is your mighty affiance and protection.

It remains to define by their characteristics the horses which Diana's equipment can accept as useful.[c] Not every breed has the courage needed for my

[c] *Dianae arma* = the chase. For horses in general see Xen. *Cyn.* 1; Pollux, *Onom.* I. 188 *sqq.*; Virg. *G.* III. 72 *sqq.*; Varro *R. R.* II. 7; Columella, VI. 26–29; Plin. *N.H.* VIII. 154; Nemes. *Cyn.* 240 *sqq.*; Oppian, *Cyn.* I. 158–367.

est vitium ex animo, sunt quos imbellia fallant
corpora, praeveniens quondam est incommoda virtus.
consule, Penei qualis perfunditur amne 501
Thessalus aut patriae quem conspexere Mycenae
glaucum? nempe ingens, nempe ardua fundet in
auras
crura. quis Eleas potior lustravit harenas?
ne tamen hoc attingat opus: iactantior illi 505
virtus quam silvas durumque lacessere martem.
nec saevos miratur equos terrena Syene
scilicet, et Parthis inter sua mollia rura
mansit honor; veniat Caudini saxa Taburni
Garganumve trucem aut Ligurinas desuper Alpes: 510
ante opus excussis cadet unguibus. et tamen illi
est animus fingetque meas se iussus in artes:
sed iuxta vitium posuit deus. at tibi contra
Callaecis lustratur ⟨e⟩quis scruposa Pyr⟨ene⟩,
non tamen Hispano martem temptare m⟨inistro⟩ 515
ausim: ⟨in⟩ muricibus vix ora tenacia ferr⟨o⟩
concedunt. at tota levi Nasam⟨onia virga⟩
fingit equos: ipsis Numidae solver⟨e capistris⟩

507 syenae A: Sidene *Burm.*: Cyrene *Wesseling.*
515 m⟨inacem⟩ *Ald.*: m⟨inistro⟩ *H. Schenkl*: m⟨aligno⟩ *Birt.*
516 ferr⟨o⟩ *Sann.*
517 at *Ulitius*: aut A: ast *H. Schenkl.* virga *Ulitius, cf. Lucan* IV, 683.

profession. Some show deficiency on the score of spirit; some have feeble bodies to play them false; at times excessive mettle is unsuitable. Bethink you—what sort of Thessalian horse bathes in Peneus' stream, or what is the grey sort on which its native Mycenae fixes its gaze? Assuredly it is huge, assuredly it will throw its legs high in air. What better steed ever traversed the race-course in Elis?[a] Yet let it not touch our hunting-work: its vigour is too impetuous for an attack on the hard fighting of the forests. Doubtless Syene[b] on the level plain has horses to admire which are not wild, and those of Parthia have kept their reputation in their own flat country: if such a horse comes to the crags of Taburnus near the Caudine Forks or to rugged Garganus[c] or over the Ligurian Alps, he will collapse before his task with hoofs battered.[d] And yet he has spirit and will mould himself to my methods if ordered: but heaven alongside of merit imposes defects. On the other hand, you find the horses of the Callaeci[e] can traverse the jagged Pyrenees. I should not, however, venture to try the conflict with a Spanish steed to serve me: amid sharp stones they scarce yield their stubborn mouths to the steel; but all Nasamonia[f] controls her horses with light switches. The bold and hard-toiling Numidian folk free theirs even

[a] *i.e.* at the Olympic games.

[b] Syene (Assouan) in Upper Egypt below the First Cataract.

[c] Taburnus was in Samnium: Garganus in Apulia.

[d] *i.e.* owing to the stony nature of the ground.

[e] The Callaeci were a people of Hispania Tarraconensis.

[f] The Nasamonian tribe dwelt in the eastern part of the Syrtis Major in N. Africa.

audax et patiens operum g⟨enus. ille vigebit⟩
centum actus spatiis atque eluctabitur iram. 520
nec magni cultus: sterilis quodcumque remisit
terra sui tenuesque satis producere rivi.
sic et Strymonio facilis tutela Bisaltae:
possent Aetnaeas utinam se ferre per arces,
qui ludus Siculis. quid tum, si turpia colla 525
aut tenuis dorso curvatur spina? per illos
cantatus Graiis Acragas victaeque fragosum
Nebroden liquere ferae: o quantus in armis
ille meis quoius dociles pecuaria fetus
sufficient! quis Chaonios contendere contra 530
ausit, vix merita quos signat Achaia palma?
spadices vix Pellaei valuere Ceranni;
at tibi devotae magnum pecuaria Cyrrhae,
Phoebe, decus meruere, leves seu iungere currus
usus, seu nostras agere in sacraria tensas. 535

519 g⟨enus. ille vigebit⟩ *Ald.*
529 illa . . . coetus *Vollmer*: ille . . . coetus A: foetus *Ald.*
533 & A: at *Vollmer.*

[a] In Thrace. Grattius proceeds to express a wish that these Thracian horses could have the chance of showing their powers on the mountains of Sicily. The Sicilian horses are mentioned for their swiftness, Oppian, *Cyn.* I. 272. Their victories in horse-racing and chariot-racing are the themes of many of Pindar's odes: *e.g. Pyth.* i. celebrates a victory won by Hieron of Aetna (*cf.* Gratt. 524). The qualities of speed and sure-footedness requisite in Sicilian sport (*cf. qui ludus Siculis,* 525, and *fragosum Nebroden,* 527–528) explained to Grattius' mind how, though not of prepossessing appearance, these

from halters: the horse will show his vigour careering in a hundred race-courses and will work off his temper in the contest. Nor does his keep cost much: whatsoever of its own the barren earth or the small rivulet doth yield, is enough to support him. So too maintenance is easy for horses of the Bisaltae[a] near the Strymon: oh, that they could career along the highlands of Aetna, the sport which Sicilians make their own! What then, though their necks are ugly or though they have a thin spine curving along their back? Thanks to such steeds Acragas was praised in song by the Greeks,[b] thanks to such, the vanquished creatures of the wild quitted craggy Nebrodes.[c] Oh, how stalwart will he be in hunting whose herds shall yield colts that can be trained! Who could dare pit against them the horses of Epirus, which are distinguished by Greece with honour scarce deserved? The chestnut-brown horses of Macedonian[d] Ceraunus have scanty worth as hunters: but the herds of Cyrrha,[e] sacred to thee, O Apollo, have won high honour, whether the need be to yoke light vehicles or pull our (image-laden) cars in procession to

horses could be trained to win glory in the games of Greece (*cantatus Graiis Acragas*, 527).

[b] Pindar, *Olymp.* iii. 2, κλεινὰν Ἀκραγάντα (= Agrigentum in Sicily, now Girgenti). *Olympian Odes* ii. and iii. celebrate victories won by Theron of Acragas in chariot-racing; *Pyth.* vi. and *Isthm.* ii. similar victories by Xenocrates of Acragas.

[c] A Sicilian mountain. *Fragosum* indicates the serviceability of Sicilian horses as hunters on rocky ground.

[d] The fact that Pella was in Macedonia and the Ceraunian range in Epirus does not justify the epithet *Pellaei*; but, as Enk says, "poeta parum curat geographiam."

[e] Cyrrha or Cirrha, a seaport in Phocis, near Parnassus on which was the Delphic oracle of Apollo.

venanti melius pugnat color: optima nigr⟨a⟩
⟨cru⟩ra illi badiosque leg⟨a⟩nt et . . .
⟨et quo⟩rum fessas imitantur terga favillas.
⟨o quan⟩tum Italiae (sic di voluere) parentes
⟨praestant⟩ et terras omni praecepimus usu 540
⟨nostraque quam pernix⟩ collustrat prata ⟨iuventus⟩!
. . . .

536 melius A: mellis *Graevius*: vineus *Burman*: maelis *Birt*: medius *H. Schenkl.* nigr . . . A: nigri *Ald.*: nigra *Enk.*
537 ⟨cru⟩ra *Ulitius*: ⟨o⟩ra *Birt*: ⟨cu⟩ra *Vollmer.* leg⟨u⟩nt *Ald.*: leg⟨a⟩nt *Vollmer.* & avedon *videtur legi in* A: in pectore crines *edd.*: glaucosque periti *Birt.*
538 ⟨et quo⟩rum *Ald.* terda A: terga *Ald.*
539 ⟨o quan⟩tum *Ulitius.*
540 ⟨praestant⟩ et *Ulitius.*
541 ⟨nostraque quam pernix⟩ *Ulitius et post* prata *add.* ⟨iuventus⟩.

the shrines. For the hunter the horse's colour is a better ally (than its origin). His legs had best be black: let brown steeds be chosen . . . and those whose backs resemble spent embers. Oh, how much do the mares of Italy (such is heaven's will) excel in their foals; how much have we outstripped the world in every practice of life; and how active the young breed which brightens our meadows! . . .[a]

[a] A portion of the poem is lost—presumably of no great extent, as *restat* of 497 suggests that the author was drawing to a conclusion.

CALPURNIUS SICULUS

INTRODUCTION

TO CALPURNIUS SICULUS

The group of poems consisting of the pastorals by T. Calpurnius Siculus and by Nemesianus, the *Laus Pisonis* and two short Einsiedeln eclogues[a] present a bundle of interconnected and, though baffling, still not uninteresting problems. Certain questions arise at once. On separating the eclogues of Calpurnius from those of Nemesianus, to what dates should one assign their authors? Why did "Calpurnius Siculus" bear these two names? Had he a relationship with C. Calpurnius Piso, the conspirator of A.D. 65, to whom, according to most authorities, the *Laus Pisonis* was addressed?[b] If so, did Calpurnius Siculus write that panegyric in praise of Piso as his patron, and can "Meliboeus," the patron in two Calpurnian eclogues, have been the same Calpurnius Piso? If he was not, was he Seneca, or someone else? Again, can the Einsiedeln eclogues have emanated from the same hand as the Calpurnian eclogues or the *Laus Pisonis*, or are they products of a school of Neronian poets influenced by a transient passion for pastoral themes,

[a] For these other poems see pp. 289–315, pp. 319–335, and pp. 451–485 in this volume.
[b] See Introduction to the *Panegyric on Piso*, p. 289.

to which school M. Hubaux [a] has ascribed *Catalepton* IX bequeathed to us in the *Appendix Vergiliana*?

To most of these and to several related questions, the most contradictory answers have been given,[b] which cannot here be more than lightly touched upon. Since Haupt in his classic essay of 1854, *De carminibus bucolicis Calpurnii et Nemesiani*, divided,[c] on principles of style, the eleven eclogues which had often passed together under the name of Calpurnius Siculus into seven by him and the remaining four by Nemesianus, there has been no serious doubt about the gap in date between the two sets. Indeed, attention to certain *subscriptiones* and headings in the manuscripts (including a tell-tale blunder in *Riccardianus* 363, *Titi Calphurnii bucolicum carmen ad Nemesianum Karthaginiensem* [d]) ought to have led to an earlier separation of the poems by all editors. In any case, it is now generally agreed that Calpurnius Siculus belongs to the Neronian age and the

[a] In *Les thèmes bucoliques dans la poésie latine*, Brussels, 1930.

[b] For a résumé of the different hypotheses, see Groag, " C. Calpurnius Piso," P. W. *Realencycl.* III. (1899); Skutsch, " T. Calpurnius Siculus," *ibid.*; Schanz, *Gesch. der röm. Literatur*, II. 2; Clementina Chiavola, *Della vita . . . di Tito Calpurnio Siculo*, 1921.

[c] Haupt was the first to make clear the Neronian date of Calpurnius' seven eclogues; but the Aldine edition of 1534 prints the two sets separately—in fact *Nemesiani Bucolica* precede *Calpurnii Siculi Bucolica.*

[d] This confusion, which quite impossibly makes Nemesianus contemporary with Calpurnius, may be due either to a misreading of a double manuscript title, giving the names of both poets at the beginning of the eclogues, or to a corruption of words separating the two collections *finis bucolicorum Calphurnii Aurelii Nemesiani poetae Carthaginiensis egloga prima.*

eclogues of Nemesianus to the author of the *Cynegetica* in the third century A.D. Features of style and of metre, like the preservation of length in final *-o* and a paucity of elision, clearly distinguish the verse of Calpurnius from that of Nemesianus,[a] imitator of Calpurnius Siculus though he was. Some of the decisive points in favour of the Neronian date for Calpurnius consist in such allusions as those to the comet of 54 A.D. (i. 77–83), to the wooden amphitheatre of 57 A.D. (vii. 23–24) and to the young prince of golden promise, handsome, eloquent, divine,[b] who can be identified with no one so aptly as with Nero at the outset of his reign.

About the poet's name there is no means of determining whether it argues a relationship with the C. Calpurnius Piso to whom it is usually thought that the *Laus Pisonis* was addressed. One hypothesis suggests that he might have been a son of one of Piso's freedmen. Certainty is equally unattainable as to the meaning of the epithet " Siculus ": it may indicate Sicilian origin in the geographical sense, but it may just as well record the literary debt of the eclogues to Theocritus. " Meliboeus," the patron in Calpurnius Siculus' first and fourth eclogues, is drawn as an actual personage in a position enabling him to recommend the author's verses to the emperor, and skilled in poetry and weather-lore. Sarpe's contention that this fits Seneca as the writer of tragedies and of the *Naturales Quaestiones* remains, on the whole, more plausible than the theory once maintained by Haupt and Schenkl, that the patron is the versatile Calpurnius Piso him-

[a] Birt, *Ad historiam hexametri latini symbola*, Bonn, 1877, 63.
[b] See i. 42–45, 84–88; iv. 84–87, 137; vii. 6, 83–84.

self. On the foundation of this latter theory was built the guess that the *Laus Pisonis* was the work of Calpurnius Siculus. But there is no consensus of opinion about the identification of "Meliboeus." While some have supposed him to represent Seneca or Calpurnius Piso, others have seen in him Columella [a] or M. Valerius Messala Corvinus,[b] consul with Nero in 58 A.D.: others still have dismissed all such identifications as sheer caprice. There is no more certainty about the two Einsiedeln eclogues. As the conjecture that they were composed by Piso [c] is countered with equal readiness to believe that Calpurnius wrote them,[d] discretion will acknowledge that there is not enough evidence to prove more than that they belong to the same literary environment as the Calpurnian poems.

The arrangement of the eclogues of Calpurnius does not follow the chronological order of composition. The four more strictly rural poems preceded in time the three which may be called "courtly" in virtue of their praises of the emperor (i, iv, vii): some, indeed, may have been written before Nero succeeded to the purple. There is much to be said for Haupt's suggested order of writing, namely, that the earliest and least finished is iii, the quarrel with Phyllis, which Scaliger considered an unamusing piece of clownishness; next, vi, a singing-match broken off by the umpire owing to the competitors' loss of temper—a weakish imitation of Theocritus iv and v and of Virgil's third eclogue; ii, somewhat

[a] Chytil, *Der Eklogendichter T. Calp. Siculus*, Znaim, 1894.
[b] Hubaux, *op. cit.*
[c] Groag, "Calp. Piso" in P. W. *Realencycl.*
[d] Hubaux, *op. cit.*

after the manner of Virgil's seventh eclogue, the amoebean praises of the pretty Crocale by two rivals, a herd and a gardener; and v, the aged Micon's expert advice to a young rustic on the management of flocks, based on *Georgics* III. 295–456. The three "courtly" poems, i, iv, vii, were written after these four and placed at the beginning, middle and end of the collection. In eclogue i, roughly modelled on Virgil's "Messianic" eclogue, the tuneful shepherds are imagined to discover a prophecy by Faunus heralding a renewal of the Golden Age under a new "Prince Charming," and they hope their poetry may reach the imperial ears through the good offices of their patron Meliboeus; in iv, the longest of the seven, hopes are expressed that the poetic eulogies on the emperor will be recommended to his majesty by Meliboeus, and it is indicated that some success had been already gained through his patronage; finally, in vii Corydon, newly back to the country from Rome, relates to Lycotas his impressions of the amphitheatre and of the handsome emperor.

Another feature of the arrangement may be noted. Eclogues ii, iv, vi are amoebean in form, and are sandwiched between eclogues which are not verse-dialogues in structure. In thought and manner, though there are, as we have seen, contemporary allusions, the pervasive influence is that of Virgil, and in a less degree that of Theocritus. The style also owes something to Ovid. Without being in the least deeply poetic, and in spite of the artificiality inherent in pastorals, the eclogues of Calpurnius breathe a rural atmosphere which makes them pleasant to read. Historically, they pass on the Virgilian tradition to Nemesianus.

EDITIONS

(The Eclogues of Calpurnius with those of Nemesianus.)

C. Schweynheim and A. Pannartz: (with Silius Italicus) eleven *Eclogae* under name of C. Calpurnius. Rome, 1471.

A. Ugoletus. *Calpurnii Siculi et Nemesiani bucolica.* Parma, *circ.* 1490. [For this edition Angelus Ugoletus used the codex of Thadeus Ugoletus: see *infra* under A in "Sigla."]

G. Logus. In edn. containing *Poetae tres egregii.* Aldus, Venice, 1534.

P. Burman. *Poet. Lat. Minores* I. Leyden, 1731.

J. C. Wernsdorf in *Poet. Lat. Minores*, Vol. II. Altenburg, 1780. [Wernsdorf gives an introductory essay and account of earlier editions.]

C. D. Beck. Recogn. annot. et gloss. instr. Leipzig, 1803.

C. E. Glaeser. *Calp. et Nemes. . . . recensuit.* Göttingen, 1842. [Glaeser's edn. made an advance in preferring the Codex Neapolitanus to the MSS. of the second group.]

E. Baehrens. In *Poet. Lat. Minores* III. Leipzig, 1881.

H. Schenkl. *Calp. et Nemes. bucol. rec.* Leipzig, 1885.

——. Re-edited in J. P. Postgate's *Corp. Poet. Lat.*, Vol. II. London, 1905.

C. H. Keene. *The Eclogues of Calpurnius Siculus and M. Aur. Olymp. Nemesianus* (introd., comment.). London, 1887.

CALPURNIUS SICULUS

C. Giarratano. *Calpurnii et Nemesiani Bucolica.* Naples, 1910.
——. *Calpurnii et Nemesiani Bucolica.* (Paravia ed.) Turin, 1924.

ENGLISH TRANSLATION

E. J. L. Scott. *The Eclogues of Calpurnius* (the seven in octosyll. verse). London, 1890.

RELEVANT WORKS

G. Sarpe. *Quaestiones philologicae.* Rostock, 1819. [Argues that " Meliboeus " = Seneca.]
M. Haupt. *De Carminibus bucolicis Calpurnii et Nemesiani.* Berlin, 1854. [Argues that " Meliboeus " = Calpurnius Piso.]
F. Chytil. *Der Eklogendichter T. Calpurnius Siculus und seine Vorbilder.* Znaim, 1894. [Identifies " Meliboeus " with Columella.]
F. Skutsch. Art. *Calpurnius Siculus.* P. W. *Realencycl.* col. 1401 *sqq.* 1899.
G. Ferrara. *Calpurnio Siculo e il Panegirico a Calpurnio Pisone.* Pavia, 1905.
Clementina Chiavola. *Della vita e dell' opera di Tito Calpurnio Siculo.* Ragusa, 1921.
J. Wight Duff. *A Literary History of Rome in the Silver Age*, pp. 330–338. London, 1927.
J. Hubaux. *Les thèmes bucoliques dans la poésie latine.* Brussels, 1930.
E. Cesareo. *La poesia di Calpurnio Siculo.* Palermo, 1931.

INTRODUCTION TO

SIGLA

USED BY H. SCHENKL IN POSTGATE'S C. P. L.

THE BEST GROUP OF MSS.

N = Neapolitanus 380, end of 14th cent. or beginning of 15th.

G = Gaddianus 90, 12 in Laurentian Library, Florence: 15th cent. [Akin to N, but somewhat inferior.][a]

A = Nicolaus Angelius' readings from the now lost MS. brought by Thadeus Ugoletus from Germany: they were entered in the year 1492 on the margin of codex Riccardianus 363 at Florence.

H = Readings in codex Harleianus 2578, 16th cent., apparently from a manuscript of Boccaccio's or the manuscript of Ugoletus.

INFERIOR MSS.

V = " vulgaris notae libri," of 15th or 16th cent. and interpolated. [Schenkl divides them into two classes:—

v = the slightly better;
w = the worst.

Giarratano dislikes Schenkl's subdivision into *v* and *w*.]

[a] Baehrens, the first collator of G, inclined to overvalue it: Schenkl, on the other hand, perhaps overvalued N. Giarratano pleads for a fair estimate of the merits of G, even if N is on the whole the better manuscript.

CALPURNIUS SICULUS

An Intervening Group

P = Parisinus 8049, 12th cent.; only reaches *Ecl.* IV. 12.

Exc. Par. = Extracts from Calpurnius and Nemesianus in two *florilegia*, liber Parisinus 7647, 12th cent., and liber Parisinus 17903, 13th cent.

[The texts of H. Schenkl and of Giarratano have been taken into account in determining the readings adopted.]

CALPURNIUS SICULUS

I

Corydon : Ornytus

C. Nondum solis equos declinis mitigat aestas,
quamvis et madidis incumbant prela racemis
et spument rauco ferventia musta susurro.
cernis ut ecce pater quas tradidit, Ornyte, vaccae
molle sub hirsuta latus explicuere genista? 5
nos quoque vicinis cur non succedimus umbris?
torrida cur solo defendimus ora galero?
O. hoc potius, frater Corydon, nemus, antra petamus
ista patris Fauni, graciles ubi pinea denset
silva comas rapidoque caput levat obvia soli, 10
bullantes ubi fagus aquas radice sub ipsa
protegit et ramis errantibus implicat umbras.
C. quo me cumque vocas, sequor, Ornyte; nam mea Leuce,
dum negat amplexus nocturnaque gaudia nobis,
pervia cornigeri fecit sacraria Fauni. 15
prome igitur calamos et si qua recondita servas.
nec tibi defuerit mea fistula, quam mihi nuper
matura docilis compegit harundine Ladon.

[1] declinis NA : declivis GV : declivus P.

CALPURNIUS SICULUS

ECLOGUE I

Corydon : Ornytus

C. Not yet doth the waning summer tame the sun's horses, although the wine-presses are squeezing the juicy clusters and a hoarse whisper comes from the foaming must as it ferments. Look, Ornytus, do you see how comfortably the cattle our father trusted us to watch have lain down to rest in the shaggy broom? Why do not we also make for the neighbouring shade? Why only a cap to protect our sunburnt faces?

O. Rather let us seek this grove, brother Corydon,—the grottoes over there, the haunt of Father Faunus, where the pine forest thickly spreads its delicate foliage and rears its head to meet the sun's fierce rays, where the beech shields the waters that bubble 'neath its very roots, and with its straying boughs casts a tangled shade.

C. Whithersoever you call me, Ornytus, I follow. For by refusing my embraces and denying me nightly pleasures, my Leuce has left it lawful for me to enter the shrine of horned Faunus. Produce your reed-pipes then and any song you keep stored for use. My pipe, you will find, will not fail you—the pipe that Ladon's skill fashioned for me lately out of a ripely seasoned reed.

O. et iam captatae pariter successimus umbrae.
sed quaenam sacra descripta est pagina fago, 20
quam modo nescio quis properanti falce notavit?
aspicis ut virides etiam nunc littera rimas
servet et arenti nondum se laxet hiatu?
C. Ornyte, fer propius tua lumina: tu potes alto
cortice descriptos citius percurrere versus; 25
nam tibi longa satis pater internodia largus
procerumque dedit mater non invida corpus.
O. non pastor, non haec triviali more viator,
sed deus ipse canit: nihil armentale resultat,
nec montana sacros distinguunt iubila versus. 30
C. mira refers; sed rumpe moras oculoque sequaci
quamprimum nobis divinum perlege carmen.
O. "qui iuga, qui silvas tueor, satus aethere Faunus,
haec populis ventura cano: iuvat arbore sacra
laeta patefactis incidere carmina fatis. 35
vos o praecipue nemorum gaudete coloni,
vos populi gaudete mei: licet omne vagetur
securo custode pecus nocturnaque pastor
claudere fraxinea nolit praesepia crate:
non tamen insidias praedator ovilibus ullas 40
afferet aut laxis abiget iumenta capistris.
aurea secura cum pace renascitur aetas
et redit ad terras tandem squalore situque
alma Themis posito iuvenemque beata sequuntur

[25] codice GA.
[35] fatis *Ulitius*: fagis *codd.*

---

[a] Themis, the Greek goddess of justice, was driven from earth by man's deterioration after the fabled Golden Age. Poets also called her "Astraea." *Squalore situque* conveys an image of the Goddess in her broken-hearted banishment, *squalore* suggesting mourning (as in Cicero often)

•. Now we have both come beneath the shade we sought. But what legend is this inscribed upon the hallowed beech, which someone of late has scored with hasty knife? Do you notice how the letters still preserve the fresh greenness of their cutting and do not as yet gape with sapless slit?

·. Ornytus, look closer. *You* can more quickly scan the lines inscribed on the bark high up. You have length enough of limb by the bounty of your father, and tall stature ungrudgingly transmitted by your mother.

). These be no verses in wayside style by shepherd or by traveller: 'tis a very god who sings. No ring here of cattle-stall; nor do alpine yodellings make refrains for the sacred lay.

:. You tell of miracles! Away with dallying; and at once with eager eye read me through the inspired poem.

). "I, Faunus of celestial birth, guardian of hill and forest, foretell to the nations that these things shall come. Upon the sacred tree I please to carve the joyous lay in which destiny is revealed. Rejoice above all, ye denizens of the woods; rejoice, ye peoples who are mine! All the herd may stray and yet no care trouble its guardian: the shepherd may neglect to close the pens at night with wattles of ash-wood—yet no robber shall bring his crafty plot upon the fold, or loosing the halters drive the bullocks off. Amid untroubled peace, the Golden Age springs to a second birth; at last kindly Themis,[a] throwing off the gathered dust of her mourning, returns to the earth; blissful ages attend the youthful prince who

and *situ* the dust that has gathered round her in her motionless grief. Now the poet pictures her springing to life again.

saecula, maternis causam qui vicit Iulis. 45
dum populos deus ipse reget, dabit impia victas
post tergum Bellona manus spoliataque telis
in sua vesanos torquebit viscera morsus
et, modo quae toto civilia distulit orbe,
secum bella geret: nullos iam Roma Philippos 50
deflebit, nullos ducet captiva triumphos;
omnia Tartareo subigentur carcere bella
immergentque caput tenebris lucemque timebunt.
candida pax aderit; nec solum candida vultu,
qualis saepe fuit quae libera Marte professo, 55
quae domito procul hoste tamen grassantibus armis
publica diffudit tacito discordia ferro:
omne procul vitium simulatae cedere pacis
iussit et insanos Clementia contudit enses.
nulla catenati feralis pompa senatus 60
carnificum lassabit opus, nec carcere pleno
infelix raros numerabit Curia patres.
plena quies aderit, quae stricti nescia ferri
altera Saturni referet Latialia regna,
altera regna Numae, qui primus ovantia caede 65
agmina, Romuleis et adhuc ardentia castris

[45] vicit NP: vīcit G: lusit V. iulis NGPV: in ulnis A.
[55] quae *codd.*: ceu *Baehrens*.
[57] iubila *Godofr. Hermann*: vulnera *Leo*: fulmina *H. Schenkl in not.*: publica *codd.* (*quo servato* confodit t. praecordia f. *Maehly*).

pleaded a successful case for the Iuli of the mother town (of Troy).[a] While he, a very God, shall rule the nations, the unholy War-Goddess shall yield and have her vanquished hands bound behind her back, and, stripped of weapons, turn her furious teeth into her own entrails; upon herself shall she wage the civil wars which of late she spread o'er all the world: no battles like Philippi shall Rome lament henceforth: no triumph o'er her captive self shall she celebrate. All wars shall be quelled in Tartarean durance: they shall plunge the head in darkness, and dread the light. Fair peace shall come, fair not in visage alone—such as she often was when, though free from open war, and with distant foe subdued,[b] she yet 'mid the riot of arms spread national strife [c] with secret steel. Clemency has commanded every vice that wears the disguise of peace to betake itself afar: she has broken every maddened sword-blade. No more shall the funereal procession of a fettered senate weary the headsman at his task; no more will crowded prison leave only a senator here and there for the unhappy Curia to count.[d] Peace in her fullness shall come; knowing not the drawn sword, she shall renew once more the reign of Saturn in Latium, once more the reign of Numa who first taught the tasks of peace to armies that rejoiced in slaughter and still drew from Romulus' camp their fiery spirit—Numa who first

[a] The reference is to an early oration by Nero on behalf of the inhabitants of Ilium (Suet. *Nero*, 7; Tac. *Ann.* xii. 58).

[b] This is best taken as a reference to the Roman invasion of Britain in Claudius' reign.

[c] If *publica* is right, *discordia* must be plural of *discordium*, a rare neuter form.

[d] There were many arbitrary executions ordered by Claudius.

pacis opus docuit iussitque silentibus armis
inter sacra tubas, non inter bella, sonare.
iam nec adumbrati faciem mercatus honoris
nec vacuos tacitus fasces et inane tribunal 70
accipiet consul; sed legibus omne reductis
ius aderit, moremque fori vultumque priorem
reddet et afflictum melior deus auferet aevum.
exultet quaecumque notum gens ima iacentem
erectumve colit boream, quaecumque vel ortu 75
vel patet occasu mediove sub aethere fervit.
cernitis ut puro nox iam vicesima caelo
fulgeat et placida radiantem luce cometem
proferat? ut liquidum niteat sine vulnere plenus?
numquid utrumque polum, sicut solet, igne
cruento 80
spargit et ardenti scintillat sanguine lampas?
at quondam non talis erat, cum Caesare rapto
indixit miseris fatalia civibus arma.
scilicet ipse deus Romanae pondera molis
fortibus excipiet sic inconcussa lacertis, 85
ut neque translati sonitu fragor intonet orbis
nec prius ex meritis defunctos Roma penates
censeat, occasus nisi cum respexerit ortus."

[76] tepet *Postgate*: patet *codd.* fervit GP: servit NV.
[79] niteat *Ulitius*: mutat NG: mittat P: nutet V *nonnulli*: nictet *Barth.*
[87] prius a NG: pr̃ios = patrios *Diels apud Levy, Gnomon*, 1928, *pp.* 594 *sqq.*

---

[a] The comet of lines 77 *sqq.* is taken to be the comet of A.D. 54 which was believed to have heralded the death of

hushed the clash of arms and bade the trumpet sound 'mid holy rites instead of war. No more shall the consul purchase the form of a shadowy dignity or, silenced, receive worthless fasces and meaningless judgement-seat. Nay, laws shall be restored; right will come in fullest force; a kinder god will renew the former tradition and look of the Forum and displace the age of oppression. Let all the peoples rejoice, whether they dwell furthest down in the low south or in the uplifted north, whether they face the east or west or burn beneath the central zone. Do ye mark how already for a twentieth time the night is agleam in an unclouded sky, displaying a comet radiant in tranquil light? and how brightly, with no presage of bloodshed, twinkles its undiminished lustre? Is it with any trace of blood-hued flame that, as is a comet's way, it besprinkles either pole? does its torch flash with gory fire? But aforetime it was not such, when, at Caesar's taking off, it pronounced upon luckless citizens the destined wars.[a] Assuredly a very god shall take in his strong arms the burden of the massive Roman state so unshaken, that the world will pass to a new ruler without the crash of reverberating thunder, and that Rome will not regard the dead as deified in accord with merit ere the dawn of one reign can look back on the setting of the last."[b]

Claudius, Suet. *Claud.* 46. Similarly, Virgil, *Georg.* I. 487 *sqq.*, described the celestial portents accompanying the assassination of Julius Caesar.

[b] The words seem obscurely to imply a succession to imperial power without disturbance or interregnum. By one of his early acts, Nero proclaimed divine honours for his predecessor, Claudius.

C. Ornyte, iam dudum velut ipso numine plenum
me quatit et mixtus subit inter gaudia terror. 90
sed bona facundi veneremur numina Fauni.
O. carmina, quae nobis deus obtulit ipse canenda,
dicamus teretique sonum modulemur avena:
forsitan augustas feret haec Meliboeus ad aures.

II

Idas : Astacus : Thyrsis

Intactam Crocalen puer Astacus et puer Idas,
Idas lanigeri dominus gregis, Astacus horti,
dilexere diu, formosus uterque nec impar
voce sonans. hi cum terras gravis ureret aestas,
ad gelidos fontes et easdem forte sub umbras 5
conveniunt dulcique simul contendere cantu
pignoribusque parant: placet, hic ne vellera septem,
ille sui victus ne messem vindicet horti;
et magnum certamen erat sub iudice Thyrsi.
adfuit omne genus pecudum, genus omne ferarum
et quodcumque vagis altum ferit aera pennis. 11
convenit umbrosa quicumque sub ilice lentas
pascit oves, Faunusque pater Satyrique bicornes;
adfuerunt sicco Dryades pede, Naides udo,

[89] plenum NGP : plenus V.
II. [1] Crotalem N.
[5] ulmos PV : umbras NG.
[7] hic ne *Baehrens* : hic ut *codd.*
[11] quaecumque *codd.* : quodcumque *Ulitius.* altum *codd.* : avium *Barth.*

C. Ornytus, long has my very being, full of the god's own spirit, been thrilled with awe: mingling with my joy it steals upon me. Come, let us praise the kindly divinity of eloquent Faunus.

O. Let us rehearse the strains which the god himself has presented us to be sung; let us make music for it on our rounded reed-pipe. Haply these verses will be borne by Meliboeus [a] to our prince's ears.

ECLOGUE II

Idas : Astacus : Thyrsis

The virgin Crocale for long was loved by young Astacus and young Idas—Idas who owned a wool-bearing flock and Astacus a garden. Comely were both; and well-matched in tuneful song. These, upon a day when oppressive summer scorched the earth, met by a cooling spring—as it chanced, beneath the same shady tree; and made ready to contend together in sweet singing and for a stake. It was agreed that Idas, if beaten, should forfeit seven fleeces and Astacus the produce of his garden for the year. Great was the contest to which Thyrsis listened as their judge. Cattle of every kind were there, wild beasts of every kind, and every creature whose roving wing smites the air aloft. There met every shepherd who feeds his lazy flocks beneath the shady oak, and Father Faunus too and the twy-horned Satyrs. Dry-foot the wood-nymphs came; with watery feet the river-nymphs; and

[a] Meliboeus represents the poet's patron, an unidentified courtier, or Seneca according to some, or Calpurnius Piso according to others: see Introduction.

et tenuere suos properantia flumina cursus; 15
desistunt tremulis incurrere frondibus Euri
altaque per totos fecere silentia montes:
omnia cessabant, neglectaque pascua tauri
calcabant, illis etiam certantibus ausa est
daedala nectareos apis intermittere flores. 20
iamque sub annosa medius consederat umbra
Thyrsis et "o pueri me iudice pignora" dixit
"irrita sint moneo: satis hoc mercedis habeto,
si laudem victor, si fert opprobria victus.
et nunc alternos magis ut distinguere cantus 25
possitis, ter quisque manus iactate micantes."
nec mora: decernunt digitis, prior incipit Idas.

I. me Silvanus amat, dociles mihi donat avenas
et mea frondenti circumdat tempora taeda.
ille etiam parvo dixit mihi non leve carmen: 30
"iam levis obliqua crescit tibi fistula canna."

A. at mihi Flora comas pallenti gramine pingit
et matura mihi Pomona sub arbore ludit.
"accipe" dixerunt Nymphae "puer, accipe fontes:
iam potes irriguos nutrire canalibus hortos." 35

I. me docet ipsa Pales cultum gregis, ut niger albae
terga maritus ovis nascenti mutet in agna,

[23] habete *Kempfer*, *Baehrens*.
[31] crescat NGP: crescit V, *Keene*: crescet *Maehly*.
[32] et APV: at NG. pallenti *De Rooy*: parienti *codd.* pingit NGP: cingit *Haupt*.
[33] matura mihi *codd.* et mihi matura Pomona sub arbore plaudit *Haupt*: *alii alia*.

hastening torrents stayed their courses. East-winds ceased their rush upon the quivering leaves and so made deep silence over all the hills; everything stood idle; bulls trampled the pasture, which they heeded not; during that contest even the craftsman bee ventured to leave unvisited the nectar-yielding flowers. Now under the shade of an aged tree had Thyrsis taken his seat between them and said, "Lads, if I am to be judge, I urge that the stakes count for nothing. Let sufficient recompense be won herefrom, if the victor take the glory and the vanquished the reproach. Now, the better to mark off your alternate songs, raise in sudden movement each your hands three times."[a] They obey at once. The finger-trial decides, and Idas begins first.

I. I am loved of Silvanus—he gives me reeds to obey my will—he wreathes my temples with leaves of pine. To me while yet a boy he uttered this prophecy of no slender import: "Already upon the sloping reed there grows a slender pipe for thee."

A. But my locks doth Flora adorn with pale-green grasses, and for me Pomona in her ripeness sports beneath the tree. "Take, boy," said the nymphs, "take for yourself these fountains. Now with the channels you can feed your well-watered orchard."

I. Pales herself teaches me the breeding of a flock, how a black ram mated with a white ewe produces a changed colour in the fleece of the lamb born to

[a] In the Italian game of *mora*, the two players raise simultaneously any number of fingers they like, each calling out a number, which wins if it gives the correct sum of the fingers raised by both. Here the winner is the one who makes the best score out of three rounds.

quae neque diversi speciem servare parentis
possit et ambiguo testetur utrumque colore.
A. non minus arte mea mutabilis induit arbos 40
ignotas frondes et non gentilia poma:
ars mea nunc malo pira temperat et modo cogit
insita praecoquibus subrepere persica prunis.
I. me teneras salices iuvat aut oleastra putare
et gregibus portare novis, ut carpere frondes 45
condiscant primoque recidere gramina morsu,
ne depulsa vagas quaerat fetura parentes.
A. at mihi cum fulvis radicibus arida tellus
pangitur, irriguo perfunditur area fonte
et satiatur aqua, sucos ne forte priores 50
languida mutata quaerant plantaria terra.
I. o si quis Crocalen deus afferat! hunc ego terris,
hunc ego sideribus solum regnare fatebor;
secernamque nemus dicamque: "sub arbore numen
hac erit; ite procul—sacer est locus—ite profani."
A. urimur in Crocalen: si quis mea vota deorum 56
audiat, huic soli, virides qua gemmeus undas
fons agit et tremulo percurrit lilia rivo,
inter pampineas ponetur faginus ulmos.
I. ne contemne casas et pastoralia tecta: 60
rusticus est, fateor, sed non et barbarus Idas.
saepe vaporato mihi cespite palpitat agnus,
saepe cadit festis devota Parilibus agna.

[41] genitalia *vulgo*: gentilia *w*.
[47] vagos *codd.*: vagas *Scaliger*.
[48] at NG: et PV. fulvis *codd.*: vulsis (*vel* furvis) *Burman*. arida NGA: altera PV.
[49] panditur V.
[54] decernamque NGPH: dicam namque V: discernamque *Glaeser*: secernamque *Gronov*.
[55] hoc erit *codd.*: hac erit *Ulitius*: incolit *Giarratano*.
[63] parilibus P: paliribus NG: palilibus V.

it, insomuch that the lamb cannot preserve the appearance of the sire so different from its dam, and yet testifies to both by varied colour.

.. No less transformable by my cunning, the tree puts on a dress of alien leaves and fruits of a diverse species. My cunning now crosses pears with apples and anon constrains engrafted peaches to supplant the early plums.

. It is my joy to lop branches from tender willow or wild olive and carry them to the young flocks, that they may learn to nibble the leaves and crop the herbage with early bite, lest the lambs though weaned may follow their straying dams.

. But I, when I plant tawny roots in the parched ground, drench the flower-bed with a welling flood and give it water in plenty lest haply the slips droop with the change of soil and feel the need of their former moisture.

. Oh, if some god bring me Crocale here, him will I acknowledge sole ruler of earth and stars. Unto him will I hallow a grove and say, "Beneath this tree a divinity shall dwell. Begone, ye uninitiated, begone far hence, 'tis holy ground."

. I burn with love for Crocale: if any of the gods hear my prayer, to him alone shall be dedicated a beechen bowl among the vine-clad elms, where the sparkling brook speeds its waters, where it flows among the lilies with its rippling stream.

. Scorn not the cottage and a shepherd's homestead. Idas is a rustic, I allow; but he is not a savage too. Oft on the altar of smoking peat writhes the lamb offered by me, oft in death falls the ewe-lamb devoted at the festival of Pales.

A. nos quoque pomiferi laribus consuevimus horti
mittere primitias et fingere liba Priapo, 65
rorantesque favos damus et liquentia mella;
nec fore grata minus, quam si caper imbuat aras.

I. mille sub uberibus balantes pascimus agnas,
totque Tarentinae praestant mihi vellera matres;
per totum niveus premitur mihi caseus annum: 70
si venias, Crocale, totus tibi serviet hornus.

A. qui numerare velit quam multa sub arbore nostra
poma legam, tenues citius numerabit harenas.
semper holus metimus, nec bruma nec impedit aestas:
si venias, Crocale, totus tibi serviet hortus. 75

I. quamvis siccus ager languentes excoquat herbas,
sume tamen calathos nutanti lacte coactos:
vellera tunc dabimus, cum primum tempus apricum
surget et a tepidis fiet tonsura Kalendis.

A. at nos, quos etiam praetorrida munerat aestas, 80
mille renidenti dabimus tibi cortice Chias,
castaneasque nuces totidem, cum sole Decembri
maturis nucibus virides rumpentur echinni.

[65] figere NGPA: fundere V: fingere *edd. ant.*
[67] sunt NGP: fore *vel* fere V.
[71] annus *vulgo*: hornus *cod. Titii.*, *edd. ant.*

[a] Flora, Pomona and Priapus are the "Lares" of the garden.

I too have been wont to offer first-fruits to the gods [a] who protect my apple-orchard and to mould for Priapus cakes of sacrifice. Dripping combs of trickling honey I present—nor think they shall be less acceptable to heaven than a goat's blood staining the altar.

A thousand lambs I feed which bleat beneath their mother's teats; as many Tarentine ewes yield me their fleeces.[b] Throughout the year I press the snow-white cheese: if you come, Crocale, the whole produce of this year will be at your command.

He who would count what multitude of apples I gather under my trees will sooner count fine sand. Ever am I plucking the green fruits of the earth—neither midwinter nor summer stays me. If you come, Crocale, the whole garden will be at your command.

Although the parched field is withering the drooping grass, yet accept from me pails of quivering curdled milk. Fleeces will I give in the early days of spring sunshine so soon as sheep-shearing starts with the temperate kalends.[c]

But I who receive gifts even from the scorching summer will give you a thousand Chian figs of glistening skin, and as many chestnuts, when the December sun ripens the nuts and their green husks burst.

[b] Sheep from the district of Tarentum in South Italy were famed for the good quality of their wool: Varro, *R.R.*, II. ii. 18; Columella, *R.R.*, VII, ii. 3; iv. 3: *cf.* Horace's reference to the valuable fleeces of sheep pasturing near the neighbouring river, the Galaesus, *Od.* II. vi. 10.

[c] The moderately warm weather in the months between the spring equinox and midsummer is recommended for shearing by Varro, *R.R.* II. xi. 6.

I. num, precor, informis videor tibi? num gravis annis?
decipiorque miser, quotiens mollissima tango 85
ora manu primique sequor vestigia floris
nescius et gracili digitos lanugine fallo?
A. fontibus in liquidis quotiens me conspicor, ipse
admiror totiens. etenim sic flore iuventae
induimur vultus, ut in arbore saepe notavi 90
cerea sub tenui lucere cydonia lana.
I. carmina poscit amor, nec fistula cedit amori.
sed fugit ecce dies revocatque crepuscula vesper.
hinc tu, Daphni, greges, illinc agat Alphesiboeus.
A. iam resonant frondes, iam cantibus obstrepit arbos:
i procul, o Doryla, plenumque reclude canalem, 96
et sine iam dudum sitientes irriget hortos.—
vix ea finierant, senior cum talia Thyrsis:
"este pares et ob hoc concordes vivite; nam vos
et decor et cantus et amor sociavit et aetas." 100

III

Iollas: Lycidas

I. Numquid in hac, Lycida, vidisti forte iuvencam
valle meam? solet ista tuis occurrere tauris,
et iam paene duas, dum quaeritur, eximit horas;
nec tamen apparet. duris ego perdita ruscis

[96] hic procul P. o GV: y N: et P: i *Haupt*. primumque *codd.*: plenumque *Haupt*, *H. Schenkl*: rivumque *Baehrens*: pronumque *C. Schenkl*. canalem PV: canale NG: canali *Baehrens*.

Tell me, pray, you do not think me uncomely, do you? not laden with years? Is it my ill fortune to be deceived whenever my hand touches my tender cheeks and when unconsciously I trace the marks of my first bloom and beguile my fingers with the slender down?

Whenever I see my image in the clear stream I wonder at myself. For my visage clothes itself with the bloom of youth in like manner as I have oft remarked wax-like quinces glistening under the delicate down upon their tree.

Love calls for song; nor is the pipe unequal to the call of love; but lo! the day departs and evening brings the gloaming back. On this side, Daphnis, drive the flocks—on that let Alphesiboeus drive them home.

Now are the leaves a-rustling; now the forest drowns our song. Go yonder, Dorylas, go; and open full the channel. Let it water the garden-plots which have thirsted so long.

Scarce had they finished so, when Thyrsis full of years gave judgement thus: "Be equal: live therefore in amity; for beauty and song, love and youth, have made you comrades both."

ECLOGUE III

Iollas: Lycidas

Have you chanced, Lycidas, to see a heifer of mine in this vale? She is wont to go to meet your bulls. By now the search for her has wasted nearly two hours; and in spite of all she is not to be seen. For long have my legs been hurt by the rough

iam dudum nullus dubitavi crura rubetis 5
scindere, nec quicquam post tantum sanguinis egi.

L. non satis attendi: nec enim vacat. uror, Iolla,
uror, et immodice: Lycidan ingrata reliquit
Phyllis amatque novum post tot mea munera Mopsum.

I. mobilior ventis o femina! sic tua Phyllis: 10
quae sibi, nam memini, si quando solus abesses,
mella etiam sine te iurabat amara videri.

L. altius ista querar, si forte vacabis, Iolla.
has pete nunc salices et laevas flecte sub ulmos.
nam cum prata calent, illic requiescere noster 15
taurus amat gelidaque iacet spatiosus in umbra
et matutinas revocat palearibus herbas.

I. non equidem, Lycida, quamvis contemptus, abibo.
Tityre, quas dixit, salices pete solus et illinc,
si tamen invenies, deprensam verbere multo 20
huc age; sed fractum referas hastile memento.
nunc age dic, Lycida: quae noxam magna tulere
iurgia? quis vestro deus intervenit amori?

L. Phyllide contentus sola (tu testis, Iolla)
Callirhoen sprevi, quamvis cum dote rogaret: 25
en, sibi cum Mopso calamos intexere cera
incipit et puero comitata sub ilice cantat.

[5] nullus *Heinsius*: nullis *codd.*
[18] quavis NG: quamvis PV. contemptus P: contentus NG V *nonnulli*.
[22] vos tam PV: nos tam G: noxam *Baehrens*.

---

[a] *Palearia*, strictly the dewlap or skin hanging from the neck of oxen, is loosely used here for mouth and throat.

broom and yet I have nowise shrunk from letting the bramble thickets scratch them: and after so much loss of blood I have effected nothing.
I paid not enough heed; for I have not the time. I burn, I burn with love, Iollas—beyond all measure. Phyllis has left her Lycidas ungratefully, and after all my presents has found a new lover in Mopsus.
O woman more inconstant than the wind! Is it thus with your Phyllis, who, I remember, when you alone were absent, would swear that without you honey itself seemed bitter?
These troubles I will tell more fully, when you chance to have leisure, Iollas. Search now these willows, and turn beneath the elms on the left. For there, when 'tis hot in the meadows, my bull loves to rest, as he reclines his great bulk in the cool shade, and in his mouth chews the cud after his morning's grazing.[a]
No, Lycidas, I will not go away, though thus mocked by you. Tityrus,[b] by yourself make for those willows he spoke of, and if indeed you find the heifer, catch her and drive her thence with many a blow here; but remember to bring back your broken crook. Come now, Lycidas, tell me. What great quarrel has brought the mischief? What god has come to sunder the love of you two?
Content with only Phyllis (you are my witness, Iollas), I spurned Callirhoe although she asked my love with a dowry to offer. Then, lo! Phyllis begins to take Mopsus' aid in joining reeds with wax and she sings beneath the oak attended by the youth.

[b] Iollas bids his attendant search for the missing heifer, while he stays behind to hear about Lycidas' quarrel with his sweetheart. Similarly in Theocr. *Idyll.* III. 1 *sqq.* it is Tityrus who has to work while his master indulges in love and song.

haec ego cum vidi, fateor, sic intimus arsi,
ut nihil ulterius tulerim. nam protinus ambas
diduxi tunicas et pectora nuda cecidi. 30
Alcippen irata petit dixitque: "relicto,
improbe, te, Lycida, Mopsum tua Phyllis amabit."
nunc penes Alcippen manet; ac ne forte negetur,
a! vereor; nec tam nobis ego Phyllida reddi
exopto quam cum Mopso iurgetur anhelo. 35

I. a te coeperunt tua iurgia; tu prior illi
victas tende manus; decet indulgere puellae,
vel cum prima nocet. si quid mandare iuvabit,
sedulus iratae contingam nuntius aures.

L. iam dudum meditor, quo Phyllida carmine placem.
forsitan audito poterit mitescere cantu; 41
et solet illa meas ad sidera ferre Camenas.

I. dic age; nam cerasi tua cortice verba notabo
et decisa feram rutilanti carmina libro.

L. "has tibi, Phylli, preces iam pallidus, hos tibi cantus
dat Lycidas, quos nocte miser modulatur acerba, 46
dum flet et excluso disperdit lumina somno.
non sic destricta marcescit turdus oliva,
non lepus, extremas legulus cum sustulit uvas,
ut Lycidas domina sine Phyllide tabidus erro. 50
te sine, vae misero, mihi lilia nigra videntur

[30] deduxi V.
[33] negetur NGP: vagetur V.
[35] cum G: quod NPHV.
[47] excluso NGP: excusso V. disperdit NGPH: dispergit V: distergit *Scaliger*.

When I saw this, I own, such fire I felt within that I could endure no more: at once I tore open both her vests and beat her naked breast. In fury she went to Alcippe, saying as she went, "Spiteful Lycidas, your Phyllis will abandon you and give her love to Mopsus." And now in Alcippe's house she stays; and oh, I fear that entry will be refused me. But more than I desire to have Phyllis restored to me, do I pant[a] to see her quarrel with Mopsus.

It was with you that your quarrel began. You must be the first to stretch out to her your hands in surrender. It is fitting to show indulgence to a girl, even when she is the aggressor. If you please to send any word to her, I as your messenger will take care to win your angry mistress' ear.

Long have I been pondering with what song I am to pacify Phyllis. Mayhap, when she hears my lay, she can be softened: and it is her way to laud my poetry to the stars.

Come, speak—for I will carve your words upon the bark of the cherry-tree and then cut away the lines on the red rind and take them to her.

"These prayers, Phyllis, your Lycidas, now wan with grief, despatches to you, this song which in misery he plays through the painful night, weeping the while and by banishment of sleep doing despite to his eyes. No thrush grows thin so much when the olive-tree is stripped, nor hare when the gleaner has gathered the last grapes, as I, Lycidas, have pined a-wandering without Phyllis for my queen. Without you (poor wretch that I am!), lilies seem black to

[a] *anhelo* might be an adjective—"the wheezy Mopsus": *exopto* would then govern first an infinitive (*reddi*) and secondly a subjunctive (*iurgetur*).

nec sapiunt fontes et acescunt vina bibenti.
at si tu venias, et candida lilia fient
et sapient fontes et dulcia vina bibentur.
ille ego sum Lycidas, quo te cantante solebas 55
dicere felicem, cui dulcia saepe dedisti
oscula nec medios dubitasti rumpere cantus
atque inter calamos errantia labra petisti.
a dolor! et post haec placuit tibi torrida Mopsi
vox et carmen iners et acerbae stridor avenae? 60
quem sequeris? quem, Phylli, fugis? formosior illo
dicor, et hoc ipsum mihi tu iurare solebas.
sum quoque divitior: certaverit ille tot haedos
pascere quot nostri numerantur vespere tauri.
quid tibi quae nosti referam? scis, optima Phylli,
quam numerosa meis siccetur bucula mulctris 66
et quam multa suos suspendat ad ubera natos.
sed mihi nec gracilis sine te fiscella salicto
texitur et nullo tremuere coagula lacte.
quod si dura times etiam nunc verbera, Phylli, 70
tradimus ecce manus: licet illae vimine torto,
si libet, et lenta post tergum vite domentur,
ut mala nocturni religavit bracchia Mopsi
Tityrus et furem medio suspendit ovili. 74
accipe, ne dubites, meruit manus utraque poenas.
his tamen, his isdem manibus tibi saepe palumbes,
saepe etiam leporem decepta matre paventem
misimus in gremium; per me tibi lilia prima
contigerunt primaeque rosae: vixdum bene florem

[68] gracili *edd. ant.*

[72] scilicet *codd.*: si libet *Burman*: seu licet *H. Schenkl*: sic licet *Giarratano*.

[75] dubita PV.

me, fountains lose their taste and wine as I drink turns sour. But if you come, lilies will grow white again, fountains taste aright and wine be sweet to drink. I am that Lycidas at whose singing you used to declare your joy, to whom you gave many a tender kiss, whose strains half-sung you did not hesitate to interrupt by seeking my lips as they strayed o'er the reed-pipe. O sorrow! and, after that, have you been pleased by the harsh voice of Mopsus, his lifeless song and the shriek of his strident pipe? Whom do you follow? and whom, Phyllis, do you avoid? I am called more comely than he, and that is but what you were wont to say to me on oath. Besides, I am richer; let him vie in pasturing as many kids as there are bulls of mine counted at even-tide. Why should I rehearse to you what you know? You are aware, darling Phyllis, how many heifers are milked over my pails, and how many have calves clinging to their teats. But when you are gone, I can weave no slender basket-work out of willow-withes: no milk quivers in its curdled form. But if even now, Phyllis, you are afraid of cruel blows, see, I surrender my hands: let them, if you choose, be bound with twisted osier and the tough vine-twig behind my back, as Tityrus once bound the knavish arms of your night-prowler Mopsus, and strung the thief up inside his sheepfold. Take them, be not slow; both hands have earned their punishment. Yet with these, yes, these same hands, have I many a time put turtle-doves or a frightened hare into your lap, after snaring their mother; through me it was your luck to get the earliest lilies and the earliest roses; scarce had the bee well partaken of the

degustarat apis, tu cingebare coronis. 80
aurea sed forsan mendax tibi munera iactat,
qui metere occidua ferales nocte lupinos
dicitur et cocto pensare legumine panem:
qui sibi tunc felix, tunc fortunatus habetur,
vilia cum subigit manualibus hordea saxis. 85
quod si turpis amor precibus, quod abominor, istis
obstiterit, laqueum miseri nectemus ab illa
ilice, quae nostros primum violavit amores.
hi tamen ante mala figentur in arbore versus:
'credere, pastores, levibus nolite puellis; 90
Phyllida Mopsus habet, Lycidan habet ultima
rerum.' "—
nunc age, si quicquam miseris succurris, Iolla,
perfer et exora modulato Phyllida cantu.
ipse procul stabo vel acuta carice tectus
vel propius latitans vicina sepe sub horti. 95

I. ibimus: et veniet, nisi me praesagia fallunt.
nam bonus a! dextrum fecit mihi Tityrus omen,
qui redit inventa non irritus ecce iuvenca.

[80] degustabat *codd.*: degustarat *Heinsius*.
[97] a dextrum *Baehrens*: a dextro GP V *plerique*: a dextra H V *nonnulli*.

flower when you were crowned with chaplets. But perhaps he may lyingly boast to you of golden gifts—he, who, they say, gathers the funeral lupines [a] when night is far spent, and makes up for the lack of bread with a boiling of greens, who deems himself happy and blest by fate in the very hour when he grinds inferior barley with a mill his own hand works. But if (I pray, heaven forfend!) a base passion is an obstacle to these my pleadings, I will in my misery twine a noose from yonder oak-tree which first did outrage to our affection.[b] Yet, ere all is o'er, these lines shall be affixed upon the accursed tree: 'Shepherds, put not your trust in fickle maids. Phyllis is loved by Mopsus; the end of all claims Lycidas.'"—Come now, Iollas, if you have any help for misery, take this missive to Phyllis and entreat her with harmonious song. Myself I will stand apart, perhaps concealed by prickly reed-grass or hiding nearer beneath the neighbouring garden hedge.'

I will go: and Phyllis will come, unless the portents cheat me. For the good Tityrus has brought me an omen—ah! a favourable one! Look, he returns successful, my heifer found.

[a] Lupines were served at feasts in honour of the dead, and were sometimes carried off by the poorer guests: *cf.* Tibull. I. v. 53–54. Their main use was to feed cattle.

[b] See 26–27.

IV

Meliboeus : Corydon : Amyntas

M. Quid tacitus, Corydon, vultuque subinde minaci
quidve sub hac platano, quam garrulus adstrepit umor,
insueta statione sedes? iuvat algida forsan
ripa levatque diem vicini spiritus amnis?
C. carmina iam dudum, non quae nemorale resultent, 5
volvimus, o Meliboee; sed haec, quibus aurea possint
saecula cantari, quibus et deus ipse canatur,
qui populos urbesque regit pacemque togatam.
M. dulce quidem resonas, nec te diversus Apollo
despicit, o iuvenis, sed magnae numina Romae 10
non ita cantari debent, ut ovile Menalcae.
C. quicquid id est, silvestre licet videatur acutis
auribus et nostro tantum memorabile pago;
nunc mea rusticitas, si non valet arte polita
carminis, at certe valeat pietate probari. 15
rupe sub hac eadem, quam proxima pinus obumbrat,
haec eadem nobis frater meditatur Amyntas,
quem vicina meis natalibus admovet aetas.
M. iam puerum calamos et odorae vincula cerae
iungere non cohibes, levibus quem saepe cicutis 20
ludere conantem vetuisti fronte paterna?
dicentem, Corydon, te non semel ista notavi:

[3] insueta NGH : inseta P : infesta *cod. Vat. Urb.* 353. humida *codd.* : algida *Baehrens* : herbida *H. Schenkl.*
[8] urbemque V.
[12] *in hoc versu desinit* P.
[14] nunc NG, *Exc. Par.* : dum V : nam *Baehrens* : non *C. Schenkl.*

ECLOGUE IV

MELIBOEUS : CORYDON : AMYNTAS

I. Corydon, why sit you silent with a visage that bodes something ever and anon? Why sit you in an unwonted place, beneath this plane-tree at whose roots brawl the prattling waters? Maybe you like the watery bank, where the breeze from the neighbouring stream assuages the heat of day?

. For long, Meliboeus, have I been pondering verses, verses of no woodland ring but fit to celebrate the golden age, to praise even that very god who is sovereign over nations and cities and toga-clad peace.[a]

I. Sweet of sound are your lays and 'tis not with cold disdain that Apollo looks upon you, young Corydon: but the divinities of mighty Rome are not to be extolled in the same style as the sheepfold of Menalcas.

. Whate'er my song, though it seem boorish to a critic's ears and worthy of record only in my own village, yet, as things are, my awkwardness, even if lacking in poetry's polish and skill, must surely win approval for its loyalty. Beneath this same rock shaded by the nearest pine-tree, kindred strains to mine are composed by my brother Amyntas, whose neighbouring years bring his time of birth near to mine.

I. Ah! do you not now stop the lad from joining his reeds in bonds of fragrant wax, as with a father-like frown you often checked him when he tried to play on slender hemlock-stems? Not once alone, Corydon, have I remarked you giving advice like this:

[a] *Cf.* I. 42 *sqq.*

" frange, puer, calamos et inanes desere Musas;
i, potius glandes rubicundaque collige corna,
duc ad mulctra greges et lac venale per urbem 25
non tacitus porta. quid enim tibi fistula reddet,
quo tutere famem? certe mea carmina nemo
praeter ab his scopulis ventosa remurmurat echo."

C. haec ego, confiteor, dixi, Meliboee, sed olim:
non eadem nobis sunt tempora, non deus idem. 30
spes magis arridet: certe ne fraga rubosque
colligerem viridique famem solarer hibisco,
tu facis et tua nos alit indulgentia farre;
tu nostras miseratus opes docilemque iuventam
hiberna prohibes ieiunia solvere fago. 35
ecce nihil querulum per te, Meliboee, sonamus;
per te secura saturi recubamus in umbra
et fruimur silvis Amaryllidos, ultima nuper
litora terrarum, nisi tu, Meliboee, fuisses,
ultima visuri trucibusque obnoxia Mauris 40
pascua Geryonis, liquidis ubi cursibus ingens
dicitur occiduas impellere Baetis harenas.
scilicet extremo nunc vilis in orbe iacerem,
a dolor! et pecudes inter conductus Iberas
irrita septena modularer sibila canna; 45
nec quisquam nostras inter dumeta Camenas
respiceret; non ipse daret mihi forsitan aurem,
ipse deus vacuam, longeque sonantia vota

39–40 *vocabula* litora *et* ultima *traiecit Haupt* (*opusc.* I. 362).

"Boy, break your pipes, forsake the beggarly Muses. Go, gather acorns instead and red cornel-cherries; lead herds to the milking-pails; loud in your cry through the city carry your milk for sale. What will the pipe bring you to ward off famine? Of a truth, no one repeats my lay save the wind-sped echo from yonder crags."
This, I confess, I did say, Meliboeus; but it was long ago; our times are not the same now, our god is changed.[a] Hope wears a more radiant smile; in sooth, it is your doing that I no more gather strawberries and brambles, or assuage hunger with green mallow. Your kindness feeds us with grain. You, in pity for our means and quick-taught youth, stop us from dispelling hunger-pangs with beech-nuts in winter. Lo! 'tis thanks to you, Meliboeus, that no complaint passes our lips: thanks to you we recline well-fed in care-free shade, and enjoy the woodland of Amaryllis.[b] But for thee, Meliboeus, we should of late have looked upon the furthest, yea, the furthest shores of earth, Geryon's meadows exposed to the Moor's fury, where mighty Baetis,[c] they say, with flowing currents strikes upon the western sands. Doubtless should I now lie an out-cast at the world's end, oh, woe! and, but an hire-ling, among Iberian flocks should be playing on sevenfold pipe my unavailing scrannel tunes: no one would give a glance at my muses among the thorn-bushes: he himself, our divine sovereign himself, may-hap would never lend a leisured ear to me, nor hear,

[a] *i.e.* an emperor has come to the throne, who favours poetry with his patronage.
[b] The reference is to Virgil's *formosam resonare doces Amaryllida silvas, Ecl.* i. 5.
[c] The Guadalquivir in Spain.

scilicet extremo non exaudiret in orbe.
sed nisi forte tuas melior sonus advocat aures 50
et nostris aliena magis tibi carmina rident,
vis, hodierna tua subigatur pagina lima?
nam tibi non tantum venturos dicere nimbos
agricolis qualemque ferat sol aureus ortum
attribuere dei, sed dulcia carmina saepe 55
concinis, et modo te Baccheis Musa corymbis
munerat et lauro modo pulcher obumbrat Apollo.
quod si tu faveas trepido mihi, forsitan illos
experiar calamos, here quos mihi doctus Iollas
donavit dixitque: "truces haec fistula tauros 60
conciliat: nostroque sonat dulcissima Fauno.
Tityrus hanc habuit, cecinit qui primus in istis
montibus Hyblaea modulabile carmen avena."

M. magna petis, Corydon, si Tityrus esse laboras.
ille fuit vates sacer et qui posset avena 65
praesonuisse chelyn, blandae cui saepe canenti
allusere ferae, cui substitit advena quercus.
quem modo cantantem rutilo spargebat acantho
Nais et implicitos comebat pectine crines.

53 dicere ventos N: discere ventos GH: dicere nimbos N[2]: noscere nimbos V *plerique*.

63 modulabile carmen V: carmen mulamine (modulabile m^2) N: carmen modulavit G: carmen modulatus *H. Schenkl.*

---

[a] For theories identifying Meliboeus see Introduction. It has been pointed out there that some take this passage as a reference to Seneca.

[b] The reference is to tragedy (the ivy being sacred to Bacchus) and to lyric poetry (the laurel being sacred to Apollo).

in sooth, the distant sound of my prayers at earth's furthest ends. But if perchance no sweeter melody attract your ear, if the songs of others fail to charm you more than mine, will you let the page I compose to-day be corrected by your critical file? For not only have the gods given to you to tell husbandmen of coming rain-storms and of the kind of sunrise a golden sunset offers, but you are often the singer of sweet poetry,[a] and now the Muse rewards you with Bacchic ivy-clusters, now fair Apollo shades your brow with laurel.[b] But if you would show favour to my nervous attempts, perhaps I might make trial of those reeds which skilful Iollas [c] presented to me yesterday with the words, "This pipe wins over savage bulls, and makes sweetest melody to our own Faunus. It once was owned by Tityrus, who among these hills of yours was the first to sing his tuneful lay on the Hyblaean pipe." [d]

M. You aim high, Corydon, if you strive to be Tityrus. He was a bard inspired, one who could on the reed-pipe outplay the lyre. Often, while he sang, beasts of the wild fawned in frolic near, and the oak came close and halted there: did he but sing, a Naiad would adorn him with red acanthus and dress with a comb his tangled locks.

[c] *Iollas,* according to Wernsdorf, stands for a scholar or poet who had prompted the writing of the Eclogues. Some have suggested one of Calpurnius' teachers, or even Theocritus—which conflicts with the idea that Tityrus is Virgil. Cesareo wisely refuses to identify Iollas, *La Poesia di Calp. Sic.*, p. 174.

[d] Ancient authority regarded the Tityrus of Virgil's *Eclogues* as representing the poet himself. The allusion in *Hyblaea* is to the pastoral poetry of the Sicilian Theocritus, which Virgil imitated: Virg. *Ecl.* X. 51, *carmina pastoris Siculi modulabor avena.*

C. est—fateor, Meliboee,—deus: sed nec mihi Phoebus
forsitan abnuerit; tu tantum commodus audi: 71
scimus enim, quam te non aspernetur Apollo.
M. incipe, nam faveo; sed prospice, ne tibi forte
tinnula tam fragili respiret fistula buxo,
quam resonare solet, si quando laudat Alexin. 75
hos potius, magis hos calamos sectare: canales
exprime qui dignas cecinerunt consule silvas.
incipe, ne dubita. venit en et frater Amyntas:
cantibus iste tuis alterno succinet ore. 79
ducite, nec mora sit, vicibusque reducite carmen;
tuque prior, Corydon, tu proximus ibis, Amynta.
C. ab Iove principium, si quis canit aethera, sumat,
si quis Atlantiaci pondus molitur Olympi:
at mihi, qui nostras praesenti numine terras
perpetuamque regit iuvenili robore pacem, 85
laetus et augusto felix arrideat ore.
A. me quoque facundo comitatus Apolline Caesar
respiciat, montes neu dedignetur adire,
quos et Phoebus amat, quos Iuppiter ipse tuetur:
in quibus Augustos visuraque saepe triumphos 90
laurus fructificat vicinaque nascitur arbos.

76 hos potius V: hospicius NG. magnos calamos *Leo*: magis hos calamos NG: calamos magis hos V: magis hos calamo *Baehrens*.

77 exprime *Leo*: et preme NG: prome *vel* pro me V: per me A, *Wernsdorf*: primi *Bursian*.

80 dicite *codd.* (*fortasse recte, cf. V.* 81 *audiat aut dicat*): ducite *Barth.*

82 canit V: canat N (*corr. m*²) G.

90 visuraque NG: visurus V: visurae *Barth.*

---

[a] Virg. *Ecl.* IV. 3, *si canimus silvas, silvae sint consule dignae.* The contrast is between the amatory poetry of Virgil's second eclogue entitled "Alexis," and the loftier tone of the fourth entitled "Pollio" after the consul of

He is, I own, a poet divine, Meliboeus, but mayhap Phoebus will not say me nay either: do you but favourably hear me; for we know how far Apollo is from slighting you.

Begin, my favour is with you; but take heed lest perchance your tinkling pipe breathe from boxwood as frail as is its usual sound whene'er the praise of Alexis is the theme. Rather these reeds, these far more you must pursue: press the pipes which sang of woods worthy a consul.[a] Begin; have no doubt. See, your brother Amyntas comes too. In alternate refrain his voice will answer your verses. Draw out your lay: dally not: in turns resume the song. You first, Corydon, and you will come next, Amyntas.

From Jove let every bard begin,[b] whoso sings of the sky, whoso essays to describe the Olympian burden which Atlas bears. For myself, may I win a glad propitious smile from the imperial lips of him whose incarnate godhead rules our lands and whose youthful prowess rules the eternal peace.

On me too may Caesar, with eloquent Apollo for comrade, look with favour: nor let him disdain to approach my hills which even Phoebus loves, which Jove himself protects; where blooms the laurel, destined to see many an imperial triumph, where rises too the laurel's companion-tree.[c]

40 B.C. and prophesying a golden age of peace. Here in Calpurnius the praises of Nero as "Caesar" correspond to the higher theme of the "Pollio."

[b] A quotation from Virg. *Ecl.* III. 60, which is in turn an echo of Theocr. XVII. 1.

[c] The oak, sacred to Jupiter, especially at the oracle of Dodona. With the laurel of victory there may be associated in the poet's mind the oak garland given for saving a citizen's life in battle.

C. ipse polos etiam qui temperat igne geluque,
Iuppiter ipse parens, cui tu iam proximus ipse,
Caesar, abes, posito paulisper fulmine saepe
Cresia rura petit viridique reclinis in antro 95
carmina Dictaeis audit Curetica silvis.

A. adspicis, ut virides audito Caesare silvae
conticeant? memini, quamvis urgente procella
sic nemus immotis subito requiescere ramis,
et dixi: "deus hinc, certe deus expulit euros." 100
nec mora; Parrhasiae sonuerunt sibila cannae.

C. adspicis, ut teneros subitus vigor excitet agnos?
utque superfuso magis ubera lacte graventur
et nuper tonsis exundent vellera fetis?
hoc ego iam, memini, semel hac in valle notavi 105
et venisse Palen pecoris dixisse magistros.

A. scilicet omnis eum tellus, gens omnis adorat,
diligiturque deis, quem sic taciturna verentur
arbuta, cuius iners audito nomine tellus
incaluit floremque dedit; cui silva vocato 110
densat odore comas, stupefacta regerminat arbos.

C. illius ut primum senserunt numina terrae,
coepit et uberior sulcis fallentibus olim
luxuriare seges tandemque legumina plenis
vix resonant siliquis; nec praefocata malignum 115
messis habet lolium nec inertibus albet avenis.

[93] *ad finem versus* ipse V: esse NG: ecce *Leo.*
[94] habes NGV: abes H: ades *Burman*: aves *D'Orville*: ovas *Baehrens.*
[101] Parrhasiae *Heinsius*: pharsalie N: farsalie G: pharsaliae AV *plerique.* sonuerunt AH: solverunt *codd. plerique.*

[a] Baehrens' allotment of stanzas is followed here. Giarratano gives 92–96 to Corydon and thinks that Amyntas' corresponding stanza has dropped out here: he also postulates transpositions later in the poem. H. Schenkl gives 87–96 to Amyntas so that he inverts Baehrens'

C. Even he, controller of the heavens in heat and cold, our father Jupiter himself, to whom you yourself, Caesar, now stand next, doth oft lay down his thunderbolt awhile to visit Cretan meads, and, in some verdant grot reclining, 'mid Dicte's forests listens to Curetic lays.[a]

A. Do you see how the green woods are hushed at the sound of Caesar's name? I remember how, despite the swoop of a storm, the grove, even as now, sank sudden into peace with boughs at rest. And I said, "A god, surely a god has driven the east winds hence." Forthwith the Parrhasian[b] reeds let their notes go free.

C. Do you see how a sudden vigour thrills the tender lambs, how the ewe's teats are more heavily laden with abundant milk, how, just after shearing, the fleeces of the dams grow in luxuriant waves? This once ere now, I mind me, I noted in this valley, and how the shepherds said, "Pales has come."

A. Yes, and him doth all the earth and every nation adore. He is beloved of the gods; as you see, the arbutus-tree pays him silent homage; at the sound of his name the sluggish earth has warmed to life and yielded flowers; invoke him, and in his honour the wood spreads thick its perfumed foliage, and the spellbound tree breaks into bud again.

C. As soon as the earth felt his divine influence, crops began to come in richer abundance, where furrows erstwhile disappointed hope; at length the beans scarce rattle in their well-filled pods: no harvest is choked with the spread of the barren tare, or whitens with unproductive oats.

allotment of stanzas from 97 to 121: he marks a missing stanza by Amyntas after verse 121.

[b] Parrhasia, in Arcadia, was one of Pan's haunts.

A. iam neque damnatos metuit iactare ligones
fossor et invento, si fors dedit, utitur auro;
nec timet, ut nuper, dum iugera versat arator,
ne sonet offenso contraria vomere massa, 120
iamque palam presso magis et magis instat
aratro.
C. ille dat, ut primas Cereri dare cultor aristas
possit et intacto Bromium perfundere vino,
ut nudus ruptas saliat calcator in uvas
utque bono plaudat paganica turba magistro, 125
qui facit egregios ad pervia compita ludos.
A. ille meis pacem dat montibus: ecce per illum,
seu cantare iuvat seu ter pede lenta ferire
gramina, nullus obest: licet et cantare choreis
et cantus viridante licet mihi condere libro, 130
turbida nec calamos iam surdant classica nostros.
C. numine Caesareo securior ipse Lycaeus
Pan recolit silvas et amoena Faunus in umbra
securus recubat placidoque in fonte lavatur
Nais et humanum non calcatura cruorem 135
per iuga siccato velox pede currit Oreas.

124 saliat A *v*: psal(l)at NG*w*.
129 gramina *edd. antiq.*: carmina *codd.*
132 Lycaeas *Heinsius*.
134 placitoque *Heinsius*: placido quin *Haupt*.

---

[a] Wernsdorf takes *damnatos* as "wretched," "miserable," because involving toil ("pro infelicibus, laboriosis, ut *invisam* [*sc. fossori*] *terram*, Hor. *Od.* III. xviii. 15–16"). *Cf.* "hateful nights," *damnatae noctes*, Propert. V. xi. 15. But a more likely sense is "criminal," "condemned," as a transferred epithet: *i.e.* the spade is now innocent because, even if it unearths treasure, this no longer brings a prosecution on the digger.

A. No more does the digger dread to ply the criminal spade:[a] what treasure-trove of gold chance offers him he puts to use. Nor, as of late, does the ploughman, while turning up his acres, fear that an ingot may ring against the impact of his ploughshare;[b] now openly he pushes on more and more with plough deep-driven.

C. By his favour[c] the cultivator can give to Ceres the first corn-ears and to Bromius pour libation of wine till now unbroached; thanks to him the light-clad vintager tramples the bursting clusters and the village throng applauds their good mayor, who holds magnificent games at the meeting of the highways.[d]

. He it is who bestows peace on my hills. See, it is through him that no one prevents me, if 'tis my pleasure to sing or to tread the sluggish grass in triple measure. In choral dance too may I sing, and I may preserve my songs on the green bark; and no more do boisterous trumpets drown our reed-pipes' note.

C. Emboldened by Caesar's divine protection, Lycean Pan himself revisits the groves and Faunus reclines untroubled in the lovely shade. The Naiad bathes in the unruffled stream and, free from the risk of treading on human gore, the Oread courses swiftly o'er mountain-ranges, her foot unstained.

[b] Treasure-trove had sometimes led to dangerous difficulties with the imperial authorities: see Juv. IV. 37 *sqq.*

[c] *i.e.* under the emperor's auspices, agriculture is in a position to honour the gods aright.

[d] The *Compitalia*, celebrated at the shrines where cross-roads met, were held at a date between the *Saturnalia* (Dec. 17) and Jan. 5. See W. Warde Fowler, *Roman Festivals*, 1899, pp. 279–80.

A. di, precor, hunc iuvenem, quem vos (neque fallor) ab ipso
aethere misistis, post longa reducite vitae
tempora vel potius mortale resolvite pensum
et date perpetuo caelestia fila metallo: 140
sit deus et nolit pensare palatia caelo!
C. tu quoque mutata seu Iuppiter ipse figura,
Caesar, ades seu quis superum sub imagine falsa
mortalique lates (es enim deus): hunc, precor, orbem,
hos, precor, aeternus populos rege! sit tibi caeli 145
vilis amor coeptamque, pater, ne desere pacem!
M. rustica credebam nemorales carmina vobis
concessisse deos et obesis auribus apta;
verum, quae paribus modo concinuistis avenis,
tam liquidum, tam dulce cadunt, ut non ego malim,
quod Paeligna solent examina lambere nectar. 151
C. o mihi quae tereti decurrunt carmina versu
tunc, Meliboee, sonent si quando montibus istis
dicar habere Larem, si quando nostra videre
pascua contingat! vellit nam saepius aurem 155
invida paupertas et dicit: " ovilia cura! "
at tu, si qua tamen non aspernanda putabis,
fer, Meliboee, deo mea carmina: nam tibi fas est

142 tu quoque mutata *codd.*: tu commutata *Haupt*: tu modo mutata *Baehrens*.
144 etenim NG: es enim *Glaeser*.
150 canunt *codd.*: cadunt *Burman*.
151 solent NGAH: sonant V: legunt *edd. antiq.*
152 o mihi HV: olim NG. quae teriti G: quam tenero V: quae tereti *Glaeser* (*post hunc versum H. Schenkl lacunam statuit*).
155 contingat NG: contigerit V, *Baehrens*.

O ye gods, I pray you, recall only after a long span of life this youth, whom ye, I know it well, have sent us from heaven itself: or rather untwine his allotted skein of mortality and grant him celestial threads of the metal of eternity. Let him be a god and yet loath to exchange his palace for the sky.[a]

Thou too,[b] Caesar, whether thou art Jupiter himself on earth in altered guise, or one other of the powers above concealed under an assumed mortal semblance (for thou art very God)—rule, I pray thee, this world, rule its peoples for ever! Let love of heaven count as nought with thee: abandon not, O Sire, the peace thou hast begun!

I used to think they were but rustic lays which the sylvan deities bestowed on you—lays fit for cloddish ears; but what you have even now sung on well-matched pipes has so clear, so sweet a fall that I would not liefer sip the nectarous honey which Pelignian swarms are wont to sip.[c]

Oh! the songs of mine which run in humble verse would then, my Meliboeus, resound, if ever on these hills I were called the owner of a homestead, if ever I had the fortune to see pastures of my own. Too often does malicious poverty pluck my ear and say, "The sheepfold is your task." But you, Meliboeus, if in spite of all you think that any of my poems are not to be disdained, then take them to the Emperor-God. For you have the right to visit

[a] *i.e.* let him remain a divine emperor in his residence on the Palatine Hill.

[b] *quoque* is justified, as the last stanza is addressed to all the gods and this one to Caesar, *i.e.* Nero.

[c] The allusion is to Ovid, who was born at Sulmo in the district of the Peligni.

sacra Palatini penetralia visere Phoebi.
tum mihi talis eris, qualis qui dulce sonantem 160
Tityron e silvis dominam deduxit in urbem
ostenditque deos et " spreto " dixit " ovili,
Tityre, rura prius, sed post cantabimus arma."

A. respiciat nostros utinam fortuna labores
pulchrior et meritae faveat deus ipse iuventae! 165
nos tamen interea tenerum mactabimus haedum
et pariter subitae peragemus fercula cenae.

M. nunc ad flumen oves deducite: iam fremit aestas,
iam sol contractas pedibus magis admovet umbras.

V

Micon

Forte Micon senior Canthusque, Miconis alumnus,
torrentem patula vitabant ilice solem,
cum iuveni senior praecepta daturus alumno
talia verba refert tremulis titubantia labris:
" quas errare vides inter dumeta capellas 5
canaque lascivo concidere gramina morsu,
Canthe puer, quos ecce greges a monte remotos

[162] deos *codd.*: deis *Heinsius.*
[168] fremit NV: premit *Heinsius*: furit *Maehly.* aestus *Ulitius.*
V. [6] canaque V: vanaque NG. gramina GV, *Giarratano*: germina NH (*corr.* m[2]), *Baehrens, H. Schenkl.*

the holy inner shrine of the Palatine Phoebus.[a] Then you shall be to me such as he was who brought Tityrus [b] of tuneful song from the woods to the queen of cities, showed him the divine powers, and said, "We will scorn the sheepfold, Tityrus, and sing first the countryside but, later, the weapons of war."

A. Oh, that a fairer fortune would look upon my labours and that the God in person would show favour to deserving youth! Yet meanwhile we will slay a tender kid and prepare withal the courses of a hasty meal.

M. Take forthwith the sheep to the river. Now 'tis the raging heat of summer: now the sun curtails the shadows and brings them closer to our feet.[c]

ECLOGUE V

Micon

It fell out that the aged Micon and Canthus, Micon's foster-son, were seeking shelter from the blazing sun beneath a spreading holm-oak, when to give counsel to his fosterling the old man with shaky lips uttered these faltering words:

"The she-goats you see straying among the thickets and cropping with playful bite the dew-glistening grass, the flocks, Canthus, my boy, which lo! you see have left the mountain-side and are

[a] The emperor was already associated with Apollo in verse 87. The palace was near the famous library of Apollo on the Palatine.

[b] Tityrus means Virgil: under the patronage of Maecenas he turned from the *Eclogues* (*e silvis*, 161) to the *Georgics* (*rura*, 163) and, later, to the *Aeneid* (*arma*, 163).

[c] *i.e.* it is the noontide of a summer day.

cernis in aprico decerpere gramina campo,
hos tibi do senior iuveni pater: ipse tuendos
accipe. iam certe potes insudare labori, 10
iam pro me gnavam potes exercere iuventam.
adspicis ut nobis aetas iam mille querellas
afferat et baculum premat inclinata senectus?
sed qua lege regas et amantes lustra capellas
et melius pratis errantes mollibus agnas, 15
percipe.
vere novo, cum iam tinnire volucres
incipient nidosque reversa lutabit hirundo,
protinus hiberno pecus omne movebis ovili.
tunc etenim melior vernanti germine silva
pullat et aestivas reparabilis incohat umbras, 20
tunc florent saltus viridisque renascitur annus,
tunc Venus et calidi scintillat fervor amoris
lascivumque pecus salientes accipit hircos.
sed non ante greges in pascua mitte reclusos,
quam fuerit placata Pales. tum cespite vivo 25
pone focum geniumque loci Faunumque Laresque
salso farre voca; tepidos tunc hostia cultros
imbuat: hac etiam, dum vivit, ovilia lustra.
nec mora, tunc campos ovibus, dumeta capellis
orto sole dabis, simul hunc transcendere montem 30
coeperit ac primae spatium tepefecerit horae.
at si forte vaces, dum matutina relaxat

[21] silvae *codd.*: tiliae *Maehly*: saltus *Baehrens*: segetes *C. et H. Schenkl.*
[32] relaxet G.

browsing on the herbage in the sunny meadow, these I, your aged sire, make over to you, while you are yet young. Take them into your own charge: now truly can you sweat o'er the task, now in my stead you can ply your active youth.

Do you see how the years now bring me a thousand plaints, and how the stoop of age leans on the staff? But learn the rules for your control over the she-goats which love the copses and over the lambs which stray to better purpose in the grassy meadows.

In the fresh spring-time when birds will be already starting to twitter and the returned swallow daubing its nest with mud, you are forthwith to shift the whole flock from its winter fold. For richer then sprouts the wood with fresh-growing buds, and, as it revives, makes the beginning of summer shade. Then the glades are in blossom and the green year is born again. Then is Venus' time, when sparkles the warm glow of love and the wanton herd welcomes the leaping he-goats. But do not turn loose the flocks and send them into the meadows till Pales has been propitiated. Then build an altar of fresh sods and with salted meal invoke the genius of the place and Faunus and the Lares. Then let a victim stain the knives warm with blood: with it too, while it yet lives, purify the sheepfold.[a] Thereafter, you will, without delay, let the sheep roam the meadows and the goats the thickets, when the sun has risen, as soon as he has begun to surmount the hill here and has warmed the course of the matin hour. But if you chance to have leisure, while the sun melts the frosts

[a] A lustration-ritual could be carried out by solemnly leading round the victim before it was sacrificed.

frigora sol, tumidis spumantia mulctra papillis
implebit quod mane fluet; rursusque premetur
mane quod occiduae mulsura redegerit horae. 35
parce tamen fetis: ne sint compendia tanti,
destruat ut niveos venalis caseus agnos;
nam tibi praecipuo fetura coletur amore.
te quoque non pudeat, cum serus ovilia vises,
si qua iacebit ovis partu resoluta recenti, 40
hanc umeris portare tuis natosque tepenti
ferre sinu tremulos et nondum stare paratos.
nec tu longinquas procul a praesepibus herbas
nec nimis amotae sectabere pabula silvae,
dum peragit vernum Iovis inconstantia tempus. 45
veris enim dubitanda fides: modo fronte serena
blandius arrisit, modo cum caligine nimbos
intulit et miseras torrentibus abstulit agnas.

at cum longa dies sitientes afferet aestus
nec fuerit variante deo mutabile caelum, 50
iam silvis committe greges, iam longius herbas
quaere; sed ante diem pecus exeat: umida dulces
efficit aura cibos, quotiens fugientibus euris
frigida nocturno tanguntur pascua rore
et matutinae lucent in gramine guttae. 55
at simul argutae nemus increpuere cicadae,

[33] spument tibi V *plerique*: spumantia *Barth.*
[34] implebis *codd.*: implebit *Haupt*: in tenebris *Housman.*
[38] coletur NG: colatur V, *Baehrens.*
[41] patenti V *plerique*: parenti NG: tepenti H*w.*
[49] sitientes G V *nonnulli*: sitientibus V *nonnulli.*

of dawn, the morning flow of milk will fill the pails a-frothing from the swelling dugs; and again the yield of milking at the evening hour will be pressed for cheese in the morning. Yet spare the younglings: let not thrift be of such moment that cheese for the market ruins the snow-white lambs.[a] For the young you will tend with supreme regard. And, when at night you visit the sheepfold, if any ewe lies enfeebled by recent lambing, be not ashamed to carry her on your own shoulders and to bear in your warm bosom the quivering lambs that cannot yet stand. You must not seek out grazing-ground far distant from your stalls, nor the food yielded by too remote a wood while the fickleness of the sky is carrying the spring season to its close. To be distrusted is the faith of spring: one hour she smiles coaxingly unclouded of brow; the next she brings rain-clouds with fog and bears away the luckless lambs in raging streams.

But when long days bring the thirsty summer heats, when the weather is no longer changeable under an inconstant sky, then trust your flocks to the woodland, then seek for pasture at a greater distance; yet see that the herd goes out ere daylight. The moist air sweetens their food, whenever, as the east winds fall, the chill meadows are touched with night-dew and in the morning sparkling drops are on the grass. But as soon as the chirping tree-crickets shrill through the grove, drive your

[a] *i.e.* your anxiety to sell must not divert to cheese-making the milk which the lambs need.

---

[54] tinguuntur V *nonnulli.*

ad fontem compelle greges; nec protinus herbas
et campos permitte sequi, sed protegat illos
interea veteres quae porrigit aesculus umbras.
verum ubi declini iam nona tepescere sole 60
incipiet seraeque † videbitur hora merendae,
rursus pasce greges et opacos desere lucos.
nec prius aestivo pecus includatur ovili,
quam levibus nidis somnos captare volucris
cogitet et tremulo queribunda fritinniat ore. 65
cum iam tempus erit maturas demere lanas,
sucida iam tereti constringere vellera iunco,
hircorumque iubas et olentes caedere barbas,
ante tamen secerne pecus gregibusque notatis
consimiles include comis, ne longa minutis, 70
mollia ne duris coeant, ne candida fuscis.
sed tibi cum vacuas posito velamine costas
denudavit ovis, circumspice, ne sit acuta
forpice laesa cutis, tacitum ne pustula virus
texerit occulto sub vulnere: quae nisi ferro 75
rumpitur, a! miserum fragili rubigine corpus
arrodet sanies et putria contrahet ossa.
providus (hoc moneo) viventia sulphura tecum
et scillae caput et virosa bitumina portes,
vulneribus laturus opem; nec Brutia desit 80
pix tibi: tu liquido picis unguine terga memento,

[58] sed G: sine V.
[60] declivi V: declivis NG: declini *Heinsius.* nona *codd.*: sera *Baehrens*: rura . . . incipient *Maehly.*
[61] incipiet serique v.h. premendi NG: incipiet seraeque v.h. merendae V: incipit atque sěri v.h. premendi *Baehrens.*
[65] tremulo tremebundo fruniat ore NG: tinniat ore AH: tremulo queribunda (*vel* gemibunda) fritinniat ore *Glaeser*: tremuli tremebunda coagula lactis V (cf. III. 69).
[66] maturas NGA: maternas V.
[74] forfice V. pusula N: pustula GV.
[81] pix tibi: tu *Baehrens*: pia tibi NG; dura tibi N²V.

flocks to the waters, and do not allow them to range over grass and open fields without a respite;[a] but for an interval let them be protected by the oak which spreads its ancient shade. When, however, 'neath a westering sun, the ninth hour already begins to mark a cooling of heat, when it seems to be time for a late luncheon, set your flocks grazing again and quit the shady groves. Do not pen your herd in the summer sheepfold until the birds in their fragile nests think of wooing sleep and twitter their plaints with tremulous note.

When the time is already come to shear the full-grown wool, the time to bind the greasy fleeces with swathes of rushes and cut the neck-tufts and rank beards of the he-goats, yet first separate the herd; brand your flocks and pen together the sheep of similar wool, lest long go with short, smooth with rough, or white with dark. But when you find a sheep has bare sides after losing the covering fleece, take heed lest the skin has been hurt by the sharp shears and lest an inflamed sore has covered a secret poison beneath the unnoticed wound; unless the sore is opened with the steel, alas! the corrupted blood will eat away the wretched body by reason of the tender ulcer and will shrivel the bones into a crumbling mass. Here is my counsel; have the foresight to take with you native sulphur and the head of a sea-leek and strong-smelling bitumen, so that you may bring relief to such wounds. Be not without Bruttian pitch; if the back is torn, forget not to smear it with the liquid ointment;

[a] *protinus* is here taken in a time sense, leading up to *interea* (*cf.* Juv. III. 140 *protinus ad censum, de moribus ultima fiet quaestio*): locally, it might mean "far and wide."

si sint rasa, linas. vivi quoque pondera melle
argenti coquito lentumque bitumen aheno,
impressurus ovi tua nomina; nam tibi lites
auferet ingentes lectus possessor in armo. 85
nunc etiam, dum siccus ager, dum fervida tellus,
dum rimosa palus et multo torrida limo
aestuat et fragiles nimium sol pulverat herbas,
lurida conveniet succendere galbana septis
et tua cervino lustrare mapalia fumo. 90
obfuit ille malis odor anguibus: ipse videbis
serpentum cecidisse minas: non stringere dentes
ulla potest uncos, sed inani debilis ore
marcet et obtuso iacet exarmata veneno.
nunc age vicinae circumspice tempora brumae 95
qua ratione geras. aperit cum vinea sepes
et portat lectas securus circitor uvas,
incipe falce nemus vivasque recidere frondes.
nunc opus est teneras summatim stringere virgas,
nunc hiemi servare comas, dum permanet umor, 100
dum viret et tremulas non excutit Africus umbras.
has tibi conveniet tepidis fenilibus olim
promere, cum pecudes extremus clauserit annus.
hac tibi nitendum est, labor hic in tempore noster,
gnavaque sedulitas redit et pastoria virtus. 105
ne pigeat ramos siccis miscere recentes

[82] rasa V: rara NG: scabra *vel* cruda *H. Schenkl.* durae NG: vivi (*sc.* argenti) V *nonnulli*: vini H V *nonnulli.* massae NG: melle *vel* molle V: durae . . . malthae ardenti *Giarratano.*

[83] argenti NG V *plerique* (ardenti G *in marg.*): arrhenici *H. Schenkl*: chalcanthi *Haupt, Baehrens.*

[91] obfuit *codd.*: obvius *Burman*: obficit *Maehly.*

[97] circitor NG: vinitor V.

[104] hoc . . . hic NG: hac . . . hinc *Glaeser*: hac . . . hic *H. Schenkl*: huc . . . huc *Baehrens.*

steep too a heavy mass of quicksilver in honey and sticky pitch in a cauldron, when you mean to stamp your name on your sheep, for the owner's name read on the shoulder will save you from serious law-suits.

Now also, while the field is parched and earth burning hot, while the marsh is seamed with cracks, scorched and seething in its plenteous mud, and the sun too powerfully reduces the slender herbs to dust, then it will be suitable to set on fire pale yellow gum-resin in the folds and purify your huts with the fumes of burned hart's horn.[a] Such an odour is enemy to noxious snakes; with your own eyes you will see the serpents' threatening mien collapse; not one can bare its crooked fangs, but, jaw powerless, each shrivels in weakness and, with its poison blunted, lies disarmed.

Now come, take heed how to manage the season of approaching winter. When the vineyard clears its rows, and the watchman, care-free, carries home the gathered grapes, then begin to prune the wood and its unwithered leaves. Now is there need to lop the tender twigs at the top of the tree, now to conserve leaves for the winter, while the sap remains, while the wood is green and the African wind does not yet dislodge the quivering shade. These leaves you will find it serviceable to bring out from your warm haylofts later, when the end of the year has confined your cattle to the fold. Thus must you strive amain; such is our work in due season. Vigorous industry and the shepherd's manly task ever come round again. Be not slow to mingle fresh boughs with dry and to supply new sap, lest

[a] In ancient times a chief source of ammonia.

et sucos adhibere novos, ne torrida nimbis
instet hiemps nimioque gelu nivibusque coactis
incursare vetet nemus et constringere frondes;
tu tamen aut leves hederas aut molle salictum 110
valle premes media. sitis est pensanda tuorum,
Canthe, gregum viridante cibo: nihil aridus illis,
ingenti positus quamvis strue, prosit acervus,
virgea si desint liquido turgentia suco
et quibus est aliquid plenae vitale medullae. 115
praecipue gelidum stipula cum fronde caduca
sterne solum, ne forte rigor penetrabile corpus
urat et interno vastet pecuaria morbo.
plura quidem meminisse velim, nam plura supersunt.
sed iam sera dies cadit et iam sole fugato 120
frigidus aestivas impellit Noctifer horas."

VI

ASTYLUS: LYCIDAS: MNASYLLUS

A. Serus ades, Lycida: modo Nyctilus et puer Alcon
certavere sub his alterno carmine ramis
iudice me, sed non sine pignore. Nyctilus haedos

[107] ne torrida NG V *plerique*: licet horrida *Martellius*: dum torr. *Haupt*: cum torr. *Giarratano*.
[109] incurvare velit NG: incursare vetet *Haupt*.
[112] cante G: chante N.

biting winter swoop upon you with its rain-clouds and by excessive frost and drifts of snow prevent you from raiding the forest and from making bundles of leaves;[a] but in the heart of the valley you will prune the smooth ivy or pliant willow-copse.[b] With fresh green fodder, Canthus, you must allay the thirst of your flocks. No withered heap, stacked in however huge a pile, would avail them, if you lacked fodder of sprouts which are swollen with juicy sap and have some life-giving substance of fullest pith. Above all strew the chill ground with stubble as well as fallen leaves lest frost nip the sensitive body and waste the herds with deep-set disease.

Fain would I recall more precepts; for more remain. But now the late day falls; and, now that the sun is put to flight, the chill Night-Bringer[c] drives forth the summer hours."

ECLOGUE VI

ASTYLUS: LYCIDAS: MNASYLLUS

A. You are here too late, Lycidas. Just now Nyctilus and young Alcon have been contending in alternate song beneath these branches. I was umpire: each laid a stake. Nyctilus pledged his

[a] The passage urges the need to get green stuff betimes for the flocks before winter makes it difficult to bring it in from the woods.

[b] *i.e.* if prevented by frost and snow from cutting other trees.

[c] *i.e.* Hesperus, the evening star: *cf.* note on *Eleg. in Maecen.* I. 129–132.

iuncta matre dedit; catulum dedit ille leaenae
iuravitque genus, sed sustulit omnia victor. 5
L. Nyctilon ut cantu rudis exsuperaverit Alcon,
Astyle, credibile est, si vincat acanthida cornix,
vocalem superet si dirus aedona bubo.
A. non potiar Petale, qua nunc ego maceror una,
si magis aut docili calamorum Nyctilus arte 10
aut cantu magis est quam vultu proximus illi.
L. iam non decipior: te iudice pallidus alter
venit et hirsuta spinosior hystrice barbam;
candidus alter erat levique decentior ovo
et ridens oculis crinemque simillimus auro, 15
qui posset dici, si non cantaret, Apollo.
A. o Lycida, si quis tibi carminis usus inesset,
tu quoque laudatum nosses Alcona probare.
L. vis igitur, quoniam nec nobis, improbe, par es,
ipse tuos iudex calamos committere nostris? 20
vis conferre manum? veniat licet arbiter Alcon.
A. vincere tu quemquam? vel te certamine quisquam
dignetur, qui vix stillantes, aride, voces
rumpis et expellis male singultantia verba?
L. fingas plura licet: nec enim potes, improbe, vera

[4] Laconem *vel* Lacaenae *Heinsius.*
[9] Petale *editio Ascensiana et vulgo*: Crocale GV.
[18] posses *codd.*: nosses *Haupt.*
[22] vinces NG: vincere V: vincen *Glaeser, Baehrens.*

goat-kids along with their mother; Alcon pledged a whelp from a lioness mother, affirming its breed on oath.[a] But he won and carried off all.

.. That untrained Alcon can have beaten Nyctilus in song is only believable, Astylus, if the crow can excel the goldfinch or the eerie owl surpass the tuneful nightingale.

.. May I never win Petale, for whom alone I pine, if Nyctilus can rank next him in trained skill upon the pipes or in song any more than in looks.

.. No longer am I deceived. When you were umpire, Nyctilus came pale, his beard pricklier than the bristly porcupine. But his rival was fair, sleeker than a smooth egg, with laughter in his eyes and the very gleam of gold in his hair, worthy the name "Apollo," if only he did not sing.

.. O Lycidas, if you'd any practice in song, you too would know how to applaud Alcon and award him the palm.

.. Well then, since you're not on a level even with me, you rascal, will you yourself, umpire though you've been, match your reed-pipes against mine? Will you join strife? Alcon, if you like, may come as arbiter.

. Can *you* beat anyone? or would anyone deign to compete with you?—scarce can your dry throat jerk out its dribbling notes and squirt words forth in miserable gasps.

. More lies you may tell; and yet, you rascal, you

[a] It was a cross similar to the *semifera proles* of Grattius *Cyneg.* 253. Pollux V. 38 mentions the Hyrcanian breed from dogs and lions (τὰς δὲ Ὑρκανὰς ἐκ κυνῶν καὶ λεόντων, καὶ κληθῆναι λεοντομιγεῖς). Alcon has offered a sort of sworn warranty of its pedigree.

exprobrare mihi, sicut tibi multa Lycotas. 26
sed quid opus vana consumere tempora lite?
ecce venit Mnasyllus: erit (nisi forte recusas)
arbiter inflatis non credulus, improbe, verbis.
A. malueram, fateor, vel praedamnatus abire 30
quam tibi certanti partem committere vocis.
ne tamen hoc impune feras: en adspicis illum,
candida qui medius cubat inter lilia, cervum?
quamvis hunc Petale mea diligat, accipe victor.
scit frenos et ferre iugum sequiturque vocantem 35
credulus et mensae non improba porrigit ora.
adspicis, ut fruticat late caput utque sub ipsis
cornibus et tereti pendent redimicula collo?
adspicis, ut niveo frons irretita capistro
lucet et a dorso, quae totam circuit alvum, 40
alternat vitreas lateralis cingula bullas?
cornua subtiles ramosaque tempora molles
implicuere rosae rutiloque monilia torque
extrema cervice natant, ubi pendulus apri
dens sedet et nivea distinguit pectora luna. 45
hunc, sicutque vides, pignus, Mnasylle, paciscor
pendere, dum sciat hic se non sine pignore vinci.
L. terreri, Mnasylle, suo me munere credit:
adspice, quam timeam! genus est, ut scitis, equarum

[30] praedamnatus NA: predam nactus V.
[42] subtiles *codd.*: summa vides *F. Leo*: sutilibus molles ramosa corollis *Heinsius*.
[44] natant NH: natent G: notant V: nitent *Ulitius*.

can't bring true reproaches against me like all that Lycotas brings against you. But what need to waste our time in fruitless wrangling? See, here comes Mnasyllus. He will be (unless mayhap you shirk the challenge) an umpire undeceived, you rascal, by boastful words.

A. I own I had preferred to depart, even though condemned beforehand, rather than match a bit of my voice against your rivalry. Still, that you may not go unpunished for all this—look, do you see yonder stag that reclines in the heart of the white lilies? Though my own Petale is fond of him, take him if you win. He is trained to bear reins and yoke and follows a call with trustfulness; 'tis no glutton mouth he shoots out for his food. Do you see how his head branches wide with antlers, and how the necklet hangs beneath his very horns and shapely neck? Do you see how his forehead gleams, enmeshed with snowy frontlet, and how from his back the side girth, circling his whole belly, has amulets of glass on this side and on that? Roses twine neatly round his horns and softly round his branching temples; and a collaret with red-gold chain dangles from beneath the neck, where a boar's pendent tusk is set, showing up his breast with snow-white crescent. This stag, just as you see him, is the stake whose forfeiture I risk, Mnasyllus, to secure that this fellow may know he is not worsted in a stakeless conflict.

L. He thinks, Mnasyllus, that his wager frightens me. Look how alarmed I am! You know I have

---

[46] sicumque vides G: sicutque *Baehrens, Giarratano*: hunc ego qualemcumque vides in valle V.

[47] perdere NH: prodere G: pendere N^2V.

non vulgare mihi; quarum de sanguine ponam 50
velocem Petason, qui gramina matre relicta
nunc primum teneris libavit dentibus: illi
terga sedent, micat acre caput, sine pondere cervix,
pes levis, adductum latus, excelsissima frons est,
et tornata brevi substringitur ungula cornu, 55
ungula, qua viridi sic exsultavit in arvo,
tangeret ut fragiles, sed non curvaret, aristas:
hunc dare, si vincar, silvestria numina iuro.

M. et vacat et vestros cantus audire iuvabit.
iudice me sane contendite, si libet: istic 60
protinus ecce torum fecere sub ilice Musae.

A. sed, ne vicini nobis sonus obstrepat amnis,
gramina linquamus ripamque volubilis undae.
namque sub exeso raucum mihi pumice lymphae
respondent et obest arguti glarea rivi. 65

L. si placet, antra magis vicinaque saxa petamus,
saxa, quibus viridis stillanti vellere muscus
dependet scopulisque cavum sinuantibus arcum
imminet exesa veluti testudine concha.

M. venimus et tacito sonitum mutavimus antro: 70
seu residere libet, dabit ecce sedilia tophus,
ponere seu cubitum, melior viret herba tapetis.
nunc mihi seposita reddantur carmina lite;
nam vicibus teneros malim cantetis amores:
Astyle, tu Petalen, Lycida, tu Phyllida lauda. 75

[50] vulgare NGA: iŭgale V. *Post* 52 *vel post* 53 *est vulgo insertus dubius versus* 54 (*pes levis etc.*): 53–57 *exstant in Exc. Par.*, *om.* 54.

[60] me sane NV: mascillo G: Mnasyllo *Baehrens.*

[70] mutavimus NG: mutabimus *Burman.*

some mares of no mean breed; from their stock swift-footed Petasos I will stake: now for the first time weaned from his mother, he has cropped the grass with tender teeth. His back is firmly set, head tossing keenly, neck free from over-weight, foot light, flank thin, forehead high-poised; and below, in narrow sheath of horn, is bound his shapely hoof—the hoof which takes him prancing across the green cornland so lightly as to touch, but not bend, the slender blades. By the woodland deities I swear, him I will give, if I lose.

I. I am at leisure and 'twill be a joy to hear your songs. Compete, of course, if you so wish and I will judge. Look, yonder, straight ahead, the Muses have made a couch under the ilex-tree.

. Nay, let us leave the meadow and the bank of the flowing stream, so that the sound of the neighbouring river may not drown our music. For under the worn porous rock the waters echo me hoarsely, and the gravel of the babbling brook spoils a song.

. If you wish, let us seek the caves rather and the crags which neighbour them, those crags where clings green moss with dripping fleece, and a vaulted roof, as it were of tortoise-shell scooped out, overhangs the rocks which make a curving hollow arch.

M. We have arrived; we have exchanged the noise for the silent cave. If you wish to sit down, look, the tufa will afford a seat; if you wish to recline, the green grass is better than couch-coverlets. Now, away with your wrangling and render me your songs; I would rather that in turn you sang of tender love-affairs. Astylus, sing you the praises of Petale, and you, Lycidas, of Phyllis.

L. tu modo nos illis (iam nunc, Mnasylle, precamur)
auribus accipias, quibus hunc et Acanthida nuper
diceris in silva iudex audisse Thalea.

A. non equidem possum, cum provocet iste, tacere.
rumpor enim, Mnasylle: nihil nisi iurgia quaerit. 80
audiat aut dicat, quoniam cupit; hoc mihi certe
dulce satis fuerit, Lycidam spectare trementem,
dum te teste palam sua crimina pallidus audit.

L. me, puto, vicinus Stimicon, me proximus Aegon
hos inter frutices tacite risere volentem 85
oscula cum tenero simulare virilia Mopso.

A. fortior o utinam nondum Mnasyllus adesset!
efficerem, ne te quisquam tibi turpior esset.

M. quid furitis, quo vos insania tendere iussit?
si vicibus certare placet—sed non ego vobis 90
arbiter: hoc alius possit discernere iudex!
et venit ecce Micon, venit et vicinus Iollas:
litibus hi vestris poterunt imponere finem.

[80] mnasille N: mascille G: merito V.
[83] te teste GH: te stante NV.
[86] mutare *Maehly*: miscere *Baehrens*: sociare *C. Schenkl.*
[90] sed G: sum *Baehrens*: sic *Barth.*

---

[a] Acanthis has been guessed to be either an ordinary shepherdess or a dangerous witch, like her namesake in

L. I pray you, Mnasyllus, do you but hear us this very hour with that same ear with which, 'tis said, you heard and judged Astylus and Acanthis of late in the Thalean wood.[a]

A. I cannot keep quiet when that fellow provokes me. I am ready to burst, Mnasyllus; he is only seeking a quarrel. Let him listen or recite, since so he desires. 'Twill be joy enough for me to watch Lycidas quaking, when, blenched, he hears in your presence his evil deeds made public.

L. It was at *me*, I suppose, friend Stimicon and at *me* neighbour Aegon had their secret laugh in the shrubbery here for wanting to ape the kisses of a grown man with young Mopsus.

A. Mnasyllus is stronger than I am. Oh, I wish he were still off the scene! then I'd take good care that you (Lycidas) never saw an uglier face than your own!

M. Why do you storm at each other? To what bounds has your madness urged you to go? If you want to compete in turn—— But no, I'll not be your umpire: someone else may be the judge to settle this! Look, here come both Mycon and neighbour Iollas: they will be able to put a close to your strife.

Propertius, IV. v. 63. *Thale(i)a* may imply either "Sicilian" from association with the nymph of that name in Sicily mentioned by Macrobius, *Sat.* V. xix, or simply "bucolic," since Thalia was muse of pastoral poetry as well as of comedy (*cf.* Virg. *Ecl.* VI. 1–2, where Servius gives *Thalea* as the proper Latin form). Some think it = Latin *virens*, connecting it with the root of θάλλειν and θαλλός, a young branch. Another view is to take *Thalea* as a nominative, *i.e.* "a true bucolic muse when you acted as judge," "a Thalea come to judgement." Whatever the obscurity of allusion, however, it is certain that Astylus is annoyed, and would assault Lycidas but for the presence of Mnasyllus.

VII

Lycotas : Corydon

L. Lentus ab urbe venis, Corydon; vicesima certe
nox fuit, ut nostrae cupiunt te cernere silvae,
ut tua maerentes exspectant iubila tauri.
C. o piger, o duro non mollior axe, Lycota,
qui veteres fagos nova quam spectacula mavis 5
cernere, quae patula iuvenis deus edit harena.
L. mirabar, quae tanta foret tibi causa morandi,
cur tua cessaret taciturnis fistula silvis
et solus Stimicon caneret pallente corymbo:
quem sine te maesti tenero donavimus haedo. 10
nam, dum lentus abes, lustravit ovilia Thyrsis,
iussit et arguta iuvenes certare cicuta.
C. sit licet invictus Stimicon et praemia dives
auferat, accepto nec solum gaudeat haedo,
verum tota ferat quae lustrat ovilia Thyrsis: 15
non tamen aequabit mea gaudia; nec mihi, si quis
omnia Lucanae donet pecuaria silvae,
grata magis fuerint quam quae spectavimus urbe.
L. dic age dic, Corydon, nec nostras invidus aures
despice: non aliter certe mihi dulce loquere 20
quam cantare soles, quotiens ad sacra vocatur
aut fecunda Pales aut pastoralis Apollo.

[2] fuit *codd.*: ruit *Heinsius*: subit *Baehrens.*
[13] scilicet *codd. plerique*: sit licet *V nonnulli.*
[18] spectavimus AH: spettamus in G: spectamus in NV.
[20] despice *codd.*: decipe *Baehrens.*

---

[a] The emperor Nero.
[b] The *Palilia* (*Parilia*) or festival of Pales (*cf.* 22 *infra,* II. 63, V. 25) was celebrated by shepherds in April and was accompanied by musical competitions.

ECLOGUE VII

Lycotas : Corydon

L. You are slow, Corydon, in coming back from Rome. For twenty nights past, of a truth, have our woods longed to see you, and the saddened bulls waited for your yodellings.

C. O you slow-coach, no more unbending than a tough axle, Lycotas, you prefer to see old beech-trees rather than the new sights exhibited by our youthful god [a] in the spacious arena.

L. I wondered what could be reason enough for your delay, why your pipe was idle in the silent woods, and why Stimicon, decked in pale ivy, sang alone: to him, for want of you, we have sadly awarded a tender kid. For while you tarried from home, Thyrsis purified the sheepfolds and bade the youths compete on shrill-toned reed.[b]

C. Let Stimicon be unconquered and win prizes to enrich him,—let him not only rejoice in the kid he has received, but let him carry off the whole of the folds which Thyrsis purifies, still he will not equal my joys, nor yet, if someone gave me all the herds of Lucanian forests, would they delight me more than what I have seen in Rome.

L. Tell me, come, tell me, Corydon. Be not so grudging as to disdain my ears. Truly, I shall find your words as sweet as your songs are wont to be whenever men to sacred rites invoke Pales the fertile or Apollo of the herds.[c]

[c] The Apollo of Euripides' *Alcestis* had been compelled to tend the flocks of King Admetus in Thessaly.

C. vidimus in caelum trabibus spectacula textis
surgere, Tarpeium prope despectantia culmen;
emensique gradus et clivos lene iacentes 25
venimus ad sedes, ubi pulla sordida veste
inter femineas spectabat turba cathedras.
nam quaecumque patent sub aperto libera caelo,
aut eques aut nivei loca densavere tribuni.
qualiter haec patulum concedit vallis in orbem 30
et sinuata latus resupinis undique silvis
inter continuos curvatur concava montes:
sic ibi planitiem curvae sinus ambit harenae
et geminis medium se molibus alligat ovum.
quid tibi nunc referam, quae vix suffecimus ipsi 35
per partes spectare suas? sic undique fulgor
percussit. stabam defixus et ore patenti
cunctaque mirabar necdum bona singula noram,
cum mihi iam senior, lateri qui forte sinistro
iunctus erat, "quid te stupefactum, rustice," dixit
"ad tantas miraris opes, qui nescius auri 41
sordida tecta, casas et sola mapalia nosti?
en ego iam tremulus iam vertice canus et ista
factus in urbe senex stupeo tamen omnia: certe
vilia sunt nobis, quaecumque prioribus annis 45
vidimus, et sordet quicquid spectavimus olim."

[25] immensosque *codd.*: emensique *Schrader*.
[43] iam NG: tam V. tremulus et NGV: tr. tam AH: tr. iam *Friesemann*.

---

[a] This is best taken as describing the wooden amphitheatre constructed by Nero in A.D. 57 (Suet. *Nero*, 12; Tac. *Ann.* xiii. 31).

[b] For the allotment of seats at Roman *spectacula* see Suet. *Aug.* 44. Keene's edition of Calpurnius has an appendix on the amphitheatre in relation to this eclogue.

[c] The first amphitheatre determined the oval shape, as it

I saw a theatre that rose skyward on interwoven beams and almost looked down on the summit of the Capitoline.[a] Passing up the steps and slopes of gentle incline, we came to the seats, where in dingy garments the baser sort viewed the show close to the women's benches. For the uncovered parts, exposed beneath the open sky, were thronged by knights or white-robed tribunes.[b] Just as the valley here expands into a wide circuit, and, winding at the side, with sloping forest background all around, stretches its concave curve amid the unbroken chain of hills, so there the sweep of the amphitheatre encircles the level ground, and the oval in the middle is bound by twin piles of building.[c] Why should I now relate to you things which I myself could scarcely see in their several details? So dazzling was the glitter everywhere. Rooted to the spot, I stood with mouth agape and marvelled at all, nor yet had I grasped every single attraction, when a man advanced in years, next me as it chanced on my left, said to me: "Why wonder, country-cousin, that you are spellbound in face of such magnificence? you are a stranger to gold and only know the cottages and huts which are your humble homes. Look, even I, now palsied with age, now hoary-headed, grown old in the city there, nevertheless am amazed at it all. Certes, we rate all cheap we saw in former years, and shabby every show we one day watched."

was made by C. Scribonius Curio (Plin. *N.H.* xxxvi. 15 (24), 117) of two wooden theatres revolving on pivots to face each other, and each greater than a semicircle. Pliny pictures the imperial Roman people whirled round by this invention through the air and cheering at the risk they ran (*loc. cit.* § 118).

balteus en gemmis, en illita porticus auro
certatim radiant; nec non, ubi finis harenae
proxima marmoreo praebet spectacula muro,
sternitur adiunctis ebur admirabile truncis 50
et coit in rotulum, tereti qui lubricus axe
impositos subita vertigine falleret ungues
excuteretque feras. auro quoque torta refulgent
retia, quae totis in harenam dentibus exstant,
dentibus aequatis; et erat (mihi crede, Lycota, 55
si qua fides) nostro dens longior omnis aratro.
ordine quid referam? vidi genus omne ferarum,
hic niveos lepores et non sine cornibus apros,
hic raram silvis etiam, quibus editur, alcen.
vidimus et tauros, quibus aut cervice levata 60
deformis scapulis torus eminet aut quibus hirtae
iactantur per colla iubae, quibus aspera mento
barba iacet tremulisque rigent palearia setis.
nec solum nobis silvestria cernere monstra
contigit: aequoreos ego cum certantibus ursis 65
spectavi vitulos et equorum nomine dictum,
sed deforme pecus, quod in illo nascitur amne
qui sata riparum vernantibus irrigat undis.
a! trepidi, quotiens sola discedentis harenae

[68] vernantibus NGA: venientibus V.
[69] sol discedentis N (nos *supra* sol m^2): sodiscendentis G: nos descendentis V: sola discedentis *Haupt*: se discindentis *Baehrens*: *alii alia.*

---

[a] *i.e.* the *podium* (πόδιον), a projecting parapet or balcony just above the arena for the emperor or other distinguished spectators. The *balteus* was a *praecinctio*, a wall running round the amphitheatre at intervals dividing the tiers of seats into stories.

Look, the partition-belt begemmed and the gilded arcade vie in brilliancy; and withal just where the end of the arena presents the seats closest to the marble wall,[a] wondrous ivory is inlaid on connected beams and unites into a cylinder which, gliding smoothly on well-shaped axle, could by a sudden turn balk any claws set upon it and shake off the beasts.[b] Bright too is the gleam from the nets of gold wire which project into the arena hung on solid tusks, tusks of equal size; and (believe me, Lycotas, if you have any trust in me) every tusk was longer than our plough. Why narrate each sight in order? Beasts of every kind I saw; here I saw snow-white hares and horned boars, here I saw the elk, rare even in the forests which produce it. Bulls too I saw, either those of heightened nape, with an unsightly hump rising from the shoulder-blades, or those with shaggy mane tossed across the neck, with rugged beard covering the chin, and quivering bristles upon their stiff dewlaps.[c] Nor was it my lot only to see monsters of the forest: sea calves also I beheld with bears [d] pitted against them and the unshapely herd called by the name of horses, bred in that river whose waters, with spring-like renewal, irrigate the crops upon its banks.[e] Oh, how we quaked, whenever we saw the

[b] Between the arena and the lowest tier of seats was a marble wall, in front of which the revolving cylinder was designed to keep the beasts from clambering up to the spectators.

[c] The humped bulls suggest the buffalo, and the shaggy ones the urus.

[d] This is an allusion to far northern seas, where Polar bears prey on seals.

[e] The countryman has not knowledge enough to name the Nile: the shapeless brute to which he alludes is the hippopotamus or "river-horse."

vidimus inverti, ruptaque voragine terrae 70
emersisse feras; et in isdem saepe cavernis
aurea cum subito creverunt arbuta nimbo.
L. o felix Corydon, quem non tremebunda senectus
impedit! o felix, quod in haec tibi saecula primos
indulgente deo demittere contigit annos! 75
nunc, tibi si propius venerandum cernere numen
fors dedit et praesens vultumque habitumque notasti,
dic age dic, Corydon, quae sit mihi forma deorum.
C. o utinam nobis non rustica vestis inesset:
vidissem propius mea numina! sed mihi sordes 80
pullaque paupertas et adunco fibula morsu
obfuerunt. utcumque tamen conspeximus ipsum
longius; ac, nisi me visus decepit, in uno
et Martis vultus et Apollinis esse putavi.

[70] in partes *codd.*: inverti *Haupt.*
[72] subito N: susito G: croceo V: fulvo *Baehrens.*
[77] fors NG: sors V.
[78] quae sit mihi *pler. codd.*: mihi quae sit *Burman, Baehrens.*
[79] obesset *Haupt.*
[84] putavi AH, *ed. Ven.*: putatur NGV: probatur *Burman, Baehrens*: notatur *Haupt*: putato *Leo, Giarratano.*

arena part asunder and its soil upturned and beasts plunge out from the chasm cleft in the earth;[a] yet often from those same rifts the golden arbutes sprang amid a sudden fountain spray (of saffron).[b]

L. O lucky Corydon, unhampered by palsied eld; lucky in that by the grace of heaven it was your lot to set[c] your early years in this age! Now if fortune has vouchsafed to you close sight of our worshipful Emperor-god, if there and then you marked his countenance and mien, tell me, come, tell me, Corydon, what I may deem to be the features of the gods.

C. O would that I had not been clad in peasant garb! Else should I have gained a nearer sight of my deity: but humble dress and dingy poverty and brooch with but a crooked clasp prevented me; still, in a way, I looked upon his very self some distance off, and, unless my sight played me a trick, I thought in that one face the looks of Mars and of Apollo were combined.

[a] Such arrangements for letting beasts rise from underground in the arena are well illustrated by the excavations at the Amphitheatrum Flavium (the "Colosseum").

[b] The beauty of an artificially contrived garden in the amphitheatre contrasts with the savage beasts; and the spectators are refreshed by jets of saffron water.

[c] Barth explains *demittere* as "inserere aut intro porrigere." The metaphor may be from planting.

LAUS PISONIS

INTRODUCTION

TO LAUS PISONIS

The *Panegyric on Piso*, by a young poet who pleads poverty but covets literary fame in preference to wealth, is addressed to one Calpurnius Piso, who is eulogised as eloquent in the law-courts, in the senate and in private declamation; as generous, musical, athletic, and an adept in the chess-like game of *latrunculi*. Such qualities agree with the description in Tacitus (*Ann.* XV. 48) of that Gaius Calpurnius Piso who was the ill-fated figure-head of the abortive plot in A.D. 65 against Nero: they also agree with the scholium on Juvenal's *Piso bonus* (V. 109), which mentions this particular Piso's power of drawing crowds to see him play the *ludus latrunculorum*. The identification with the noble conspirator is plausible, though we can prove neither that *Piso bonus* was the conspirator nor that Piso the conspirator had been consul, as the person addressed in *Laus Pisonis*, 70, clearly had been. This latter point decided Hubaux (*Les Thèmes Bucoliques*, p. 185) to see in the person addressed Lucius Calpurnius Piso, consul with Nero in A.D. 57.

The authorship is still more doubtful. In the now missing Lorsch manuscript the poem was erroneously assigned to Virgil. Certain similarities to Lucan's style indicate identity rather of period than of authorship, though the old ascription to Lucan has found modern support (B. L. Ullman, *C.P.* XXIV, 1929, 109 *sqq.*). The names of Ovid, Saleius Bassus and Statius have been advocated, of whom the first lived too early and the others too late to write the *Laus Pisonis*. Resemblances in style and in careful metrical technique led Haupt (*opusc.* I. 391) to argue that the work was by the pastoral poet Calpurnius Siculus. Haupt himself lost confidence in his hypothesis; and it has been opposed by G. Ferrara in *Calpurnio Siculo e il panegirico a Calpurnio Pisone*, Pavia, 1905.

EDITIONS

Editio Princeps in J. Sichard's edn. of Ovid. Vol. II. pp. 546–549. Basel, 1527.

Hadrianus Junius. *Lucani poema ad Calpurnium Pisonem ex libro Catalecton* in *Animadversorum Libri Sex*. Basel, 1556.

[Junius used a Codex Atrebatensis of which we lack subsequent record, unless Ullman is right in identifying it with the Arras *Florilegium*; see *infra* under Sigla "a."]

Jos. Scaliger. *Lucani ad Calpurn. Pisonem Paneguricum* in *Virgilii Maronis Appendix*. Lyon, 1573.

[Scaliger's text follows that of Junius, and agrees with the Paris MSS. more than with the *editio princeps*.]

J. C. Wernsdorf. *Poet. Lat. Min.* IV. pp. 236–282. *Saleii Bassi ad Calpurnium Pisonem poemation, Lucano vulgo adscriptum*. Altenburg, 1785.

J. Held. *Incerti Auctoris ad Calp. Pisonem carmen.* Breslau, 1831.

LAUS PISONIS

C. Beck. *Statii ad Pisonem poemation*. Ansbach, 1835.

C. F. Weber. *Incerti auctoris carmen panegyricum in Calpurn. Pisonem* (appar. crit. and prolegomena). Marburg, 1859.

E. Baehrens. *Poet. Lat. Min.* I. pp. 221–236, *Incerti Laus Pisonis*. Leipzig, 1879.

Gladys Martin. *Laus Pisonis* (thesis), Cornell Univ. U.S.A., 1917.
[Introduction, text, notes.]

B. L. Ullman. *The Text Tradition and Authorship of the Laus Pisonis* in *Class. Philol.* XXIV. (1929) pp. 109–132.
[As the *Florilegia* are the only existing MSS. of the *Laus*, Ullman prints a restoration of their archetype.]

RELEVANT WORKS

R. Unger. *P. Papinii Statii ad Calp. Pisonem Poemation*, Jahns Jahrb. 1836, p. 261.

M. Haupt. *De Carminibus Bucolicis Calpurnii et Nemesiani*, Berlin, 1854, and *Opusc.* i. p. 391. Leipzig, 1875.

E. Wœlfflin. *Zu dem carmen panegyricum in Calp. Pisonem*, in *Philologus* XVII. (1861) pp. 340–344.

J. Maehly. *Zur Literatur des Panegyricus in Pisonem*, Fleckeis. Jahrb. 1862, p. 286.

G. Ferrara. *Calpurnio Siculo e il panegirico a Calpurnio Pisone*. Pavia, 1905.

F. Skutsch. *T. Calpurnius Siculus*, in P. W. *Realencycl.* III. 1404.

C. Chiavola. *Della vita e dell' opera di Tito Calpurnio Siculo*, pp. 24–36. Ragusa, 1921.

J. Hubaux. *Les Thèmes Bucoliques dans la poésie latine*, esp. pp. 184–185. Bruxelles, 1930.

SIGLA

S = readings in J. Sichard's edition of Ovid, Vol. II. pp. 546 *sqq.*, Basel, 1527, representing a lost manuscript of the *Laus Pisonis* in the monastery at Lorsch (*ex bibliotheca Laurissana*).

Two MSS. of *Florilegia* containing, along with excerpts from other authors, excerpts amounting to almost 200 lines of the *Laus* (the gaps represent over 60 lines) :—

p = Parisinus-Thuaneus 7647, 12th–13th century.
n = Parisinus-Nostradamensis 17903, 13th century.
P = Consensus of p and n.

B. L. Ullman, *op. cit.*, adds evidence from three other kindred *Florilegia* :—

a = one at Arras which he believes may be Junius' Atrebatensis.
e = one in the Escorial, Q. I. 14.
b = one in Berlin (Diez. B. 60 f. 29) containing a few lines and probably descended from e.

[Ullman thinks the common ancestor-manuscript of e, p, a was "a sister or cousin of n: thus the testimony of n is worth as much as that of the other three manuscripts together."]

The main variants from Baehrens' text are noted.

LAUS PISONIS

Unde prius coepti surgat mihi carminis ordo
quosve canam titulos, dubius feror. hinc tua, Piso,
nobilitas veterisque citant sublimia Calpi
nomina, Romanas inter fulgentia gentes;
hinc tua me virtus rapit et miranda per omnes
vita modos: quae, si desset tibi forte creato
nobilitas, eadem pro nobilitate fuisset.
nam quid imaginibus, quid avitis fulta triumphis
atria, quid pleni numeroso consule fasti
profuerint, cui vita labat? perit omnis in illo
gentis honos, cuius laus est in origine sola.
at tu, qui tantis animum natalibus aequas,
et partem tituli, non summam, ponis in illis,
ipse canendus eris: nam quid memorare necesse est,
ut domus a Calpo nomen Calpurnia ducat
claraque Pisonis tulerit cognomina prima,
humida callosa cum "pinseret" hordea dextra?
nec si cuncta velim breviter decurrere possim;
et prius aethereae moles circumvaga flammae
annua bissenis revocabit mensibus astra,

[12] at tu S: felix P.
[17] fumida *Scaliger*: horrida *Maehly*.

PANEGYRIC ON PISO

Uncertain are my feelings where first should start the order of the poem which I have undertaken, or what titles of honour I should chant. On the one hand, Piso, comes the summons of your noble rank with the exalted names of ancient Calpus,[a] resplendent among the clans of Rome: on the other, I am thrilled by your own merit, your life in every phase inspiring admiration—such a life as would have been equal to nobility, if nobility had perchance not been yours at birth. For what shall halls strengthened by images and triumphs ancestral,[b] what shall archives filled with many a consulate, profit the man of unstable life? In him whose only merit is birth, the whole honour of a family is lost. But you, gifted with a mind to match your high descent in which you set a part but not the whole of your renown, you will yourself be a fit theme for song. What need to record how the Calpurnian house derives its name from Calpus and won its first famous surname of Piso for pounding (*pi(n)seret*) the moist barley with hard-skinned hand? I could not, if I would, rehearse the whole in brief; the circling mass of heavenly flame [c] will in a twelvemonth recall its yearly con-

[a] Through the Calpi the *gens Calpurnia* claimed descent from Numa Pompilius. The Pisones of Hor. *A.P.* 292 are termed "Pompilius sanguis."

[b] *fulta* suggests the columns to which triumphal ornaments were attached.

[c] The sun.

quam mihi priscorum titulos operosaque bella
contigerit memorare. manus sed bellica patrum
armorumque labor veteres decuere Quirites,
atque illos cecinere sui per carmina vates.
nos quoque pacata Pisonem laude nitentem
exaequamus avis. nec enim, si bella quierunt,
occidit et virtus: licet exercere togatae
munia militiae, licet et sine sanguinis haustu
mitia legitimo sub iudice bella movere.
hinc quoque servati contingit gloria civis,
altaque victrices intexunt limina palmae.
quin age maiorum, iuvenis facunde, tuorum
scande super titulos et avitae laudis honores,
armorumque decus praecede forensibus actis.
sic etiam magno iam tunc Cicerone vigente
laurea facundis cesserunt arma togatis.
sed quae Pisonum claros visura triumphos
olim turba vias impleverat agmine denso,
ardua nunc eadem stipat fora, cum tua maestos
defensura reos vocem facundia mittit.

[22] *sic* S: memorare manus. sed bellica fama *Baehrens.*
[23] docuere S: decuere *correxit vir doctus saec. XVI.*
[27] occidit et S: non periit P: *fortasse* interiit *in archetypo Wight Duff.*
[35] vigente *Wernsdorf*: iuventae S: iubente *Weber, Baehrens.*

stellations ere it could be mine to record the titles and toilsome wars of the men of olden days. But the warlike hand of their fathers and armed emprise well beseemed the citizens of yore, who were sung by bards of their own times in their lays.[a]

We too can praise as his grandsires' peer a Piso brilliant in the glories of peace. For, if wars have sunk to rest, courage is not dead also: there is freedom to fulfil the tasks of campaigning in the gown—freedom, with no blood drawn, to conduct mild warfare before the judge ordained by law. Hence too comes the distinction of saving a fellow-citizen: and so victorious palms enwreathe the lofty portals.[b] Come now, eloquent youth, o'er-climb the titles of your forbears and the honours of ancestral fame; outstep by forensic exploits the renown of arms. So too in great Cicero's day of vigour the laurelled arms gave way to eloquence begowned.[c] The crowd which once in close array thronged the streets to see the illustrious triumphs of the Pisos now packs the laborious law-courts, when your oratory utters its accents to set unhappy defendants

[a] This, it should be observed, indicates belief in the existence of heroic lays in ancient Rome: *cf.* Cic. *Tusc. Disp.* IV. ii.; *Brutus* xix. 75; Varro *apud* Nonium Marcellum, 76; Val. Maximus, II. i. 10. For Niebuhr's ballad-theory see J. Wight Duff, *Lit. Hist. of Rome to Golden Age*, pp. 72–73.

[b] *i.e.* the advocate can save a life in the law-court, as the soldier can on the battlefield. Successful pleadings were honoured by setting up palm-branches at the pleader's house-door: *cf.* Juv. VII. 118 *scalarum gloria palmae*; Mart. VII. xxviii. 6 *excolat et geminas plurima palma fores.*

[c] An intentional echo of Cicero's own alliterative line, *cedant arma togae, concedat laurea laudi, De Off.* I. xxii. 77: *cf. Philipp.* II. viii. 20.

seu trepidos ad iura decem citat hasta virorum
et firmare iubet centeno iudice causas,
seu capitale nefas operosa diluis arte,
laudibus ipsa tuis resonant fora. dum rapis una
iudicis affectum possessaque pectora temptas,
victus sponte sua sequitur quocumque vocasti:
flet si flere iubes, gaudet gaudere coactus
et te dante capit iudex, quam non habet, iram.
sic auriga solet ferventia Thessalus ora
mobilibus frenis in aperto flectere campo,
qui modo non solum rapido permittit habenas
quadrupedi, sed calce citat, modo succutit alte
flexibiles rictus et nunc cervice rotata
incipit effusos in gyrum carpere cursus.
quis non attonitus iudex tua respicit ora?
quis regit ipse suam, nisi per tua pondera, mentem?
nam tu, sive libet pariter cum grandine nimbos
densaque vibrata iaculari fulmina lingua,
seu iuvat adstrictas in nodum cogere voces
et dare subtili vivacia verba catenae,
vim Laertiadae, brevitatem vincis Atridae;
dulcia seu mavis liquidoque fluentia cursu
verba nec incluso sed aperto pingere flore,

[44] dura Piso: nam S: dum rapis una *Baehrens.*

[45] tentas S: ducis P (*fortasse ex versu* 138 *translatum*): frenas *Maehly.*

[51] rabido *Baehrens*: rapido PS.

[52] succutit alte (*sive* acre) *Baehrens*: succutit arce P: *om.* S: succedit a: subripit a².

free. Whether the spear of the decemviri summons the panic-stricken to trial and ordains the establishment of cases before the centumviri,[a] or whether with busy skill you refute a capital charge, the very courts resound with your praises. As you carry along with you a judge's feelings, assailing his captured heart, vanquished he follows of his own accord wherever you call—weeps if you say "weep," rejoices if so compelled; and you are the giver from whom a judge gets an anger not his own. So the Thessalian rider is wont on the open plain to guide his horse's steaming mouth with mobile bit, now spurring his rapid steed and not merely giving him rein, now jerking high the open jaws in his control, and now starting to wheel the horse's neck round and pull its wild rush into a circle. What judge fails to watch your lips in wonderment? Who orders his own mind save by your weighty arguments? For whether it be rain along with hail and repeated thunder-bolts that you choose to hurl with whirling tongue, or whether you please to condense compact expressions in a period and lend enduring words to the graceful texture of your speech, you surpass Ulysses' force and Menelaus' brevity; or whether with no concealed but with open flowers of speech you prefer to embellish sweet words as they flow on their clear course, the famous

[a] *Decemviri* and *centumviri* took cognisance of civil lawsuits. The spear, as a symbol of magisterial power, was set in the ground to mark the holding of a centumviral court: *cf.* Mart. VII. lxiii. 7 *centum gravis hasta virorum*; Stat. *Silv.* IV. iv. 43 *centeni moderatrix iudicis hasta.* Suet. *Aug.* 36 shows that *decemviri* (*stlitibus iudicandis*) were required from Augustus' time to call together the "Court of One Hundred" (*ut centumviralem hastam . . . decemviri cogerent*).

inclita Nestorei cedit tibi gratia mellis.
nec te, Piso, tamen populo sub iudice sola
mirantur fora; sed numerosa laude senatus
excipit et meritas reddit tibi curia voces.
quis digne referat, qualis tibi luce sub illa
gloria contigerit, qua tu, reticente senatu,
cum tua bissenos numeraret purpura fasces,
Caesareum grato cecinisti pectore numen?

quodsi iam validae mihi robur mentis inesset
et solidus primos impleret spiritus annos,
auderem voces per carmina nostra referre,
Piso, tuas: sed fessa labat mihi pondere cervix
et tremefacta cadunt succiso poplite membra.
sic nec olorinos audet Pandionis ales
parva referre sonos nec, si velit improba, possit;
sic et aedonia superantur voce cicadae,
stridula cum rapido faciunt convicia soli.

quare age, Calliope, posita gravitate forensi,
limina Pisonis mecum pete: plura supersunt
quae laudare velis inventa penatibus ipsis.
huc etiam tota concurrit ab urbe iuventus
auditura virum, si quando iudice fesso
turbida prolatis tacuerunt iurgia rebus.

69 retinente S: reticente *vulgo*: recinente *Unger, Baehrens.*

---

[a] *Cf.* Hom. *Il.* I. 249 τοῦ καὶ ἀπὸ γλώσσης μέλιτος γλυκίων ῥέεν αὐδή. For the eloquence of Ulysses and Menelaus *cf. Il.* III. 221–223 and 213–215.

[b] The passage 68–83 (*quis . . . ipsis*) is omitted here by P *i.e.* p + n; but 77–80 (*sic nec . . . soli*) are added at the close of the poem.

charm of Nestor's honied eloquence [a] yields place to you. 'Tis not only courts before a citizen jury that admire you, Piso: the senate welcomes you with manifold praise, and its assembly renders you well-earned plaudits. Who [b] may worthily recount the glory that befell you beneath the light of that day on which, when your purple counted its twelve fasces,[c] before a hushed senate you sang from grateful heart the praise of the imperial divinity?

Yet, if the strength of powerful intellect were now within me, and my early years were filled with solid force, then should I dare to recount your eloquence, Piso, in lays of mine; but my neck sways wearily beneath the load: hamstrung, my limbs drop palsied. Even so Pandion's little bird [d] dares not record the swan's notes, nor, had it the wanton will, would it have the power; even so the nightingale's song excels the grasshoppers a-chirping their noisy abuse at the scorching sun.

Wherefore come, Calliope,[e] passing over his forensic dignity, with me approach Piso's doors: there is still more abundance of what is found in his very home to tempt your praise. Hither also repair youths from all over Rome to listen to the man, whenever judges are weary, and in vacation [f] confused wrangles are

[c] When he entered on his consulate, Piso delivered a complimentary address to the emperor. Pliny's *Panegyricus* illustrates this kind of oration.

[d] Pandion's daughter, Philomela, was changed into a nightingale, or, in some accounts, a swallow, as here.

[e] The Muse particularly of heroic narrative poetry. For a summary of the provinces of the nine Muses see the lines in this volume, pp. 434–435 and pp. 634–635.

[f] Cases are said to be *prolatae* when there is a *iustitium* or cessation of legal business, particularly at times of harvest and vintage.

tunc etenim levibus veluti proludit in armis,
compositisque suas exercet litibus artes.
quin etiam facilis Romano profluit ore
Graecia, Cecropiaeque sonat gravis aemulus urbi.
testis, Acidalia quae condidit alite muros,
Euboicam referens facunda Neapolis artem.
qualis, io superi, qualis nitor oris amoenis
vocibus! hinc solido fulgore micantia verba
implevere locos, hinc exornata figuris
advolat excusso velox sententia torno.
magna quidem virtus erat, et si sola fuisset,
eloquio sanctum modo permulcere senatum,
exonerare pios modo, nunc onerare nocentes;
sed super ista movet plenus gravitate serena
vultus et insigni praestringit imagine visus.
talis inest habitus, qualem nec dicere maestum
nec fluidum, laeta sed tetricitate decorum
possumus: ingenitae stat nobilitatis in illo
pulcher honos et digna suis natalibus ora.
additur huc et iusta fides et plena pudoris
libertas animusque mala ferrugine purus,
ipsaque possesso mens est opulentior auro.
quis tua cultorum, iuvenis facunde, tuorum
limina pauper adit, quem non animosa beatum
excipit et subito iuvat indulgentia censu?
quodque magis dono fuerit pretiosius omni,

[92] foecunda S: facunda *Unger*. arcem PS, *Baehrens*: artem *Maehly*.

---

[a] Especially the exercise of declamation.

[b] Or, it may be, in settling the fictitious cases of the rhetorical *controversiae*.

[c] The Acidalian fountain in Boeotia, where the Graces bathed, was sacred to Venus. Her bird (*ales*) was the dove. *Euboicam* alludes to the connexion of Cumae, on the bay of Naples, with Chalcis in Euboea: *cf*. Virg. *Aen*. vi. 2.

hushed. For then his sport seems to be with light weapons,[a] as he plies his true accomplishments after lawsuits are settled.[b] Moreover, Greek culture flows forth readily from Roman lips, and Athens meets a weighty rival in his accents. Witness, eloquent Naples that founded her walls under Acidalian auspices and repeats the skill of Euboea.[c] What lustre, ye gods above, what lustre shines on the fair language of his lips! Here words sparkling in compact splendour have filled out his choice passages; here, decked out with tropes there flies to the hearer from the freed lathe a swift epigram.[d] Great merit truly it was, even if it had been the only one, now to delight the venerable senate with his style, now to clear the innocent, anon to lay the burden upon the guilty: yet more appealing still is a countenance full of serene dignity, while his look dazzles with the stamp of eminence. The mien he wears is such as we can call neither sad nor flippant, but seemly in a joyous seriousness. The fair honour of inborn nobility stands fast in him, and lineaments worthy of his birth. Thereto is joined true loyalty, frankness full of modesty, and a nature unstained by malicious envy—his mind itself is richer than the gold he owns.

Which of your clients, eloquent youth, approaches your threshold in poverty who is not welcomed and enriched by a generous indulgence with the aid of an unexpected income? And, what may well be more precious than any gift, you esteem him as

[d] *Cf.* the sense of *excusso* (*rudenti*) in 229. The lathe, metaphorically, is made to turn out the epigram which flies to the audience; (*cf.* Hor. *A.P.* 441 *male tornatos . . . versus*). The *tornus* is "shaken free" of its epigram, as the ship in Virg. *Aen.* VI. 353 is *excussa magistro.*

diligis ex aequo, nec te fortuna colentum
natalesve movent: probitas spectatur in illis.
nulla superborum patiuntur dicta iocorum,
nullius subitos affert iniuria risus:
unus amicitiae summos tenor ambit et imos.
rara domus tenuem non aspernatur amicum
raraque non humilem calcat fastosa clientem;
illi casta licet mens et sine crimine constet
vita, tamen probitas cum paupertate iacebit;
et lateri nullus comitem circumdare quaerit,
quem dat purus amor, sed quem tulit impia merces;
nec quisquam vero pretium largitur amico,
quem regat ex aequo vicibusque regatur ab illo,
sed miserum parva stipe focilat, ut pudibundos
exercere sales inter convivia possit.
ista procul labes, procul haec fortuna refugit,
Piso, tuam, venerande, domum: tu mitis et acri
asperitate carens positoque per omnia fastu
inter ut aequales unus numeraris amicos,
obsequiumque doces et amorem quaeris amando.
cuncta domus varia cultorum personat arte,
cuncta movet studium; nec enim tibi dura clientum
turba rudisve placet, misero quae freta labore
nil nisi summoto novit praecedere vulgo;

[120] illi n: illa p e a b: illic S. licet et S *contra metrum*: licet domus P (*ex interpolatione*): licet, licet et *Baehrens*: illic casta licet mens p *mgo. m. rec.* (*quod transiit in editt.*).
[126] focilat S: *om. in lacuna* P: munerat *aliquot edd.*

---

[a] *fōcĭlăt,* "revives," "cherishes," the reading of S, does not agree in quantity with the usual *fŏcĭlat* or *fŏcillat.*

an equal: neither the fortune nor the pedigree of clients influence you: uprightness is the test in them. They do not wince under any witticisms of overbearing jests: no man's grievance furnishes material for sudden laughter. A uniform tenor of friendship encompasses highest and lowest. Rare the house that does not scorn a needy friend; rare the house that does not trample contemptuously on a humble dependant. Though his mind be clean and his life unimpeachable, still his probity will rank as low as his poverty; and no patron seeks to have at his side a retainer got by pure affection but one whom cursed gain has brought him: no one confers largess on a true friend in order to guide him on an equal footing and in turn be guided by him, but one hires [a] the wretched man for a trumpery wage to have the power of practising shameful witticisms at the festal board.[b] Far has such a disgrace, far has a plight of this sort fled, worshipful Piso, from your house. In your gentleness and freedom from sharp asperity, laying aside pride everywhere, you are reckoned as but one among your friendly peers: you teach obedience, as you court love by loving. The whole house rings with the varied accomplishments of its frequenters: zeal is the motive force everywhere; for you find no satisfaction in a clumsy uneducated band of clients, whose forte lies in trivial services and whose one ability is to walk before a patron when the common herd are cleared away. No, it is a wide

[b] Juvenal, writing at the beginning of the second century A.D., draws parallel pictures of the relations between patron and client: *e.g.* with 115–116 and 118–119 *cf.* Juv. III. 152–153, *nil habet infelix paupertas durius in se quam quod ridiculos homines facit,* and with 122–124 *cf.* X. 46 *defossa in loculos quos sportula fecit amicos.*

sed virtus numerosa iuvat. tu pronus in omne
pectora ducis opus, seu te graviora vocarunt
seu leviora iuvant. nec enim facundia semper
adducta cum fronte placet: nec semper in armis
bellica turba manet, nec tota classicus horror
nocte dieque gemit, nec semper Gnosius arcum
destinat, exempto sed laxat cornua nervo,
et galea miles caput et latus ense resolvit.
ipsa vices natura subit variataque cursus
ordinat, inversis et frondibus explicat annum.
non semper fluidis adopertus nubibus aether
aurea terrificis obcaecat sidera nimbis:
cessat hiemps, madidos et siccat vere capillos;
ver fugit aestates; aestatum terga lacessit
pomifer autumnus, nivibus cessurus et undis.
ignea quin etiam superum pater arma recondit
et Ganymedeae repetens convivia mensae
pocula sumit ea, qua gessit fulmina, dextra.
temporibus servire decet: qui tempora certis
ponderibus pensavit, eum si bella vocabunt,
miles erit; si pax, positis toga vestiet armis.
hunc fora pacatum, bellantem castra decebunt.
felix illa dies totumque canenda per aevum,
quae tibi, vitales cum primum traderet auras,
contulit innumeras intra tua pectora dotes.
mira subest gravitas inter fora, mirus omissa
paulisper gravitate lepos. si carmina forte

146 frondibus S : frontibus *Beck, Baehrens*.
151 nubibus S : nimbis P : nebulis *Wernsdorf* : nivibus *Barth.*
157 vestiet p n^2 : gestiet S n^1 (*secundum Ullmanum* vestiet n, *non ex* gestiet *corr., ut Baehrens dicit*).

range [a] of good qualities that pleases you. Your own keenness leads the mind to every sort of work, whether the call has come from graver pursuits, or lighter pursuits are to your fancy; for the eloquence of the serious brow does not charm at every season: not for ever does the warlike band remain under arms: nor does the trumpet's alarum blare all night and day: not for ever does the Cretan aim his bow, but, freeing its string, he relaxes its horns: and the soldier unbinds helmet from head and sword from flank. Nature herself undergoes alternations, in varied form ordering her courses, unfolding the year with the change of the leaf. Not for ever does ether, shrouded in streaming clouds, darken the golden stars with dreadful rains. Winter flags and in the springtime dries his dripping locks. Spring flees before the summer-heats: on summer's heels presses fruit-bearing autumn, destined to yield to snow and flood. Yea, the Sire of the Gods stores away his fiery weapons, and, seeking again the banquet at the table served by Ganymede, he grasps the goblet in the right hand wherewith he wielded the thunderbolt. 'Tis meet to obey the seasons: whoso has weighed the seasons [b] with sure weights, he, if war calls him, will be a soldier; if peace, he will lay down his arms and his dress will be the gown. Him the law-court in peace, the camp in war will befit. Happy that day, for all time worthy of song, which, so soon as it gave you the breath of life, conferred on you countless gifts within your breast. A wondrous dignity upholds you in court; a wondrous wit, when for the moment dignity is dropped. If

[a] *Cf.* 66 *numerosa laude.*
[b] Here *tempora* is used in the sense of "the fit times."

nectere ludenti iuvit fluitantia versu,
Aonium facilis deducit pagina carmen;
sive chelyn digitis et eburno verbere pulsas,
dulcis Apollinea sequitur testudine cantus,
et te credibile est Phoebo didicisse magistro.
ne pudeat pepulisse lyram, cum pace serena
publica securis exultent otia terris,
ne pudeat: Phoebea chelys sic creditur illis
pulsari manibus, quibus et contenditur arcus;
sic movisse fides saevus narratur Achilles,
quamvis mille rates Priameius ureret heros
et gravis obstreperet modulatis bucina nervis:
illo dulce melos Nereius extudit heros
pollice, terribilis quo Pelias ibat in hostem.

arma tuis etiam si forte rotare lacertis
inque gradum clausis libuit consistere membris
et vitare simul, simul et captare petentem,
mobilitate pedum celeres super orbibus orbes
plectis et obliquis fugientem cursibus urges:
et nunc vivaci scrutaris pectora dextra,
nunc latus adversum necopino percutis ictu.
nec tibi mobilitas minor est, si forte volantem
aut geminare pilam iuvat aut revocare cadentem
et non sperato fugientem reddere gestu.
haeret in haec populus spectacula, totaque ludos

[171] nec S: ne *Baehrens*. si S: sic *Baehrens*.
[177] ibat in hostem PS: iverat hasta *Schrader*, *Baehrens*.

mayhap it is your pleasure to twine in sportive verse the unpremeditated lay, then an easy page draws out the Aonian song; or, if you smite the lyre with finger and ivory quill, sweet comes the strain on a harp worthy of Apollo: well may we believe you learned under Phoebus' tuition. Blush not to strike the lyre: mid peace serene let national tranquillity rejoice in a care-free world: blush not: so, 'tis believed, Apollo's strings are played by the hands which also stretch the bow. Even so fierce Achilles is related to have touched the lyre, albeit the hero son of Priam (Hector) burned a thousand ships, and the war-trumpet clashed harshly with the well-tuned strings. The hero sprung from Nereus [a] beat out sweet melody with the thumb 'neath which the menacing spear from Pelion [b] sped against the foe.

If moreover you have chosen mayhap to whirl weapons from the shoulder and take your stand, limbs taut in fixed position, and at the same moment both avoid and hit your adversary, then with nimbleness of foot you swiftly interlace circle upon circle; with slantwise rush you press on your retreating opponent; now your vigorous right hand lunges at his breast, now your unexpected thrust strikes his exposed flank. No less is your nimbleness, if mayhap it is your pleasure to return the flying ball [c] or recover it when falling to the ground, and by a surprising movement get it within bounds again in its flight. To watch such play the populace remains stockstill, and the

[a] Achilles, son of Thetis, and grandson of Nereus.

[b] *Pelias*, sc. *hasta*: the spear of Achilles was so called because its shaft came from Pelion. The phrase *Pelias hasta* occurs in Ovid, *Her.* iii. 126, and in Pentadius, *De Fortuna*, 29–30.

[c] Excursus X in Wernsdorf's *Poet. Lat. Min.*, iv. pp. 398–404, deals with *lusus pilae* at Rome.

turba repente suos iam sudabunda relinquit.
te si forte iuvat studiorum pondere fessum
non languere tamen lususque movere per artem,
callidiore modo tabula variatur aperta
calculus et vitreo peraguntur milite bella,
ut niveus nigros, nunc et niger alliget albos.
sed tibi quis non terga dedit? quis te duce cessit
calculus? aut quis non periturus perdidit hostem?
mille modis acies tua dimicat: ille petentem,
dum fugit, ipse rapit; longo venit ille recessu,
qui stetit in speculis; hic se committere rixae
audet et in praedam venientem decipit hostem;
ancipites subit ille moras similisque ligato
obligat ipse duos; hic ad maiora movetur,
ut citus ecfracta prorumpat in agmina mandra
clausaque deiecto populetur moenia vallo.
interea sectis quamvis acerrima surgant
proelia militibus, plena tamen ipse phalange
aut etiam pauco spoliata milite vincis,
et tibi captiva resonat manus utraque turba.
  sed prius emenso Titan versetur Olympo,
quam mea tot laudes decurrere carmina possint.
felix et longa iuvenis dignissime vita

[203] et fracta S: effracta *doctus quidam*: ecfracta *Baehrens*.
[204] *fortasse* quassaque *Maehly*.
[207] etiam S: tantum *Baehrens*.
[209] versetur PS: mersetur *Wernsdorf*: vergetur *Baehrens*.

---

[a] Excursus XI, *ibid.*, pp. 404–419, deals with the *ludus latrunculorum*, a game with a resemblance to chess or draughts.

[b] *i.e.* instead of advancing, this "soldier" lets himself be stopped and then, when he looks penned in, suddenly breaks out. Another explanation is that one counter "undergoes a double attack" (*mora* technically meaning "check"), *i.e.* is in danger from two opposing pieces, but by a further move endangers two enemies.

whole crowd, sweating with exertion, suddenly abandons its own games. If mayhap you please, when weary with the weight of studies, to be nevertheless not inactive but to play games of skill, then on the open board [a] in more cunning fashion a piece is moved into different positions and the contest is waged to a finish with glass soldiers, so that white checks the black pieces, and black checks white. But what player has not retreated before you? What piece is lost when you are its player? Or what piece before capture has not reduced the enemy? In a thousand ways your army fights: one piece, as it retreats, itself captures its pursuer: a reserve piece, standing on the alert, comes from its distant retreat—this one dares to join the fray and cheats the enemy coming for his spoil. Another piece submits to risky delays [b] and, seemingly checked, itself checks two more: this one moves towards higher results, so that, quickly played and breaking the opponent's defensive line,[c] it may burst out on his forces and, when the rampart is down, devastate the enclosed city.[d] Meanwhile, however fierce rises the conflict among the men in their divided ranks, still you win with your phalanx intact or deprived of only a few men, and both your hands rattle with the crowd of pieces you have taken.

But the Sun-God would complete his circuit after measuring the heavens, ere my lays could traverse so many merits. Fortunate youth, most worthy of

[c] *Mandra*, a herd of cattle, was taken by Scaliger for the *equites* of the *ludus latrunculorum*. Some suggest that, as a piece, the *latro* had higher value than pieces in the *mandra*. In the sense of "enclosure," *mandra* might mean the line of less valuable pieces (like "pawns"). R. G. Austin, "Roman Board Games," *Greece and Rome*, Oct. 1934, takes *mandra* as "any solid phalanx barring the enemy's advance."

[d] The πόλις of a similar Greek game.

eximiumque tuae gentis decus, accipe nostri
certus et hoc veri complectere pignus amoris.
quod si digna tua minus est mea pagina laude,
at voluisse sat est: animum, non carmina, iacto.
tu modo laetus ades: forsan meliora canemus
et vires dabit ipse favor, dabit ipsa feracem
spes animum: dignare tuos aperire Penates,
hoc solum petimus. nec enim me divitis auri
imperiosa fames et habendi saeva libido
impulerunt, sed laudis amor. iuvat, optime, tecum
degere cumque tuis virtutibus omne per aevum
carminibus certare meis: sublimior ibo,
si famae mihi pandis iter, si detrahis umbram.
abdita quid prodest generosi vena metalli,
si cultore caret? quid inerti condita portu,
si ductoris eget, ratis efficit, omnia quamvis
armamenta gerat teretique fluentia malo
possit ab excusso dimittere vela rudenti?

ipse per Ausonias Aeneia carmina gentes
qui sonat, ingenti qui nomine pulsat Olympum
Maeoniumque senem Romano provocat ore,
forsitan illius nemoris latuisset in umbra
quod canit, et sterili tantum cantasset avena
ignotus populis, si Maecenate careret.
qui tamen haut uni patefecit limina vati
nec sua Vergilio permisit numina soli:
Maecenas tragico quatientem pulpita gestu

237 numina S: nomina P: carmina *Lachmann*: somnia *Baehrens*.

[a] *Cf.* Ennius' *Musae quae pedibus magnum pulsatis Olympum*: or the idea may be that Virgil's fame rises and "strikes" the heavens.

[b] L. Varius Rufus, who with Plotius Tucca edited the *Aeneid*, was an epic and elegiac as well as a tragic author:

long life, distinguished ornament of your clan, assured of my loyalty, accept and welcome this pledge of true affection. Yet, if my page falls short of your renown, the intent is enough. I vaunt my aspiration, not my poetry. Do you but lend your joyful presence: perchance I shall sing better lays and your very favour will give strength, the very hope will give a fertile spirit: deign to throw open your home: this is my sole request. For it is no imperious hunger for rich gold, no savage lust of possession that has prompted me, but love of praise. I fain, noble sir, would dwell with you, and through all my life hold rivalry in my songs with your excellences: more lofty will be my way, if you are now opening for me the path of fame, if you are removing the shadow (of obscurity). What profits the hidden vein of precious metal, if it lack the miner? What can a vessel do, buried in some sluggish haven, if it lack captain, though it carry all its tackle, and could loosen its flapping sails on the shapen mast from the slackened rope?

The very bard who through Italian peoples makes his poem on Aeneas resound, the bard who in his mighty renown treads [a] Olympus and in Roman accents challenges the old man Maeonian, perchance his poem might have lurked obscure in the shadow of the grove, and he might have but sung on a fruitless reed unknown to the nations, if he had lacked a Maecenas. Yet it was not to one bard only that he opened his doors, nor did he entrust his (imperial) divinities to Virgil alone: Maecenas raised to fame Varius,[b] who shook the stage with tragic mien;

Hor. *Od.* I. vi. 1 and Porphyrion *ad loc.*; *Sat.* I. x. 44; *A.P.* 55; Quintilian X. i. 98; Mart. VIII. xviii. 7; Tac. *Dial.* xii. 6.

erexit Varium, Maecenas alta tonantis
eruit et populis ostendit nomina Graiis. 240
carmina Romanis etiam resonantia chordis,
Ausoniamque chelyn gracilis patefecit Horati.
o decus, in totum merito venerabilis aevum,
Pierii tutela chori, quo praeside tuti
non umquam vates inopi timuere senectae. 245
quod si quis nostris precibus locus, et mea vota
si mentem subiere tuam, memorabilis olim
tu mihi Maecenas tereti cantabere versu.
possumus aeternae nomen committere famae,
si tamen hoc ulli de se promittere fas est 250
et deus ultor abest; superest animosa voluntas
ipsaque nescio quid mens excellentius audet.
tu nanti protende manum: tu, Piso, latentem
exsere. nos humilis domus, at sincera, parentum
et tenuis fortuna sua caligine celat. 255
possumus impositis caput exonerare tenebris
et lucem spectare novam, si quid modo laetus
adnuis et nostris subscribis, candide, votis.
est mihi, crede, meis animus constantior annis,
quamvis nunc iuvenile decus mihi pingere malas 260
coeperit et nondum vicesima venerit aestas.

240 nomina Graiis S: Troica Macri *Baehrens.*

[a] A divine power hostile to pride is suggested, but not named; *cf.* Sen. *H.F.* 385, *sequitur superbos ultor a tergo deus*; Ovid, *Met.* XIV. 750, *quam iam deus ultor agebat.* The idea resembles that of Nemesis, and it is noteworthy that Ovid, *Met.* XIV. 693–694 mentions the *dei ultores* and, independently, the "mindful wrath" of Nemesis.

Maecenas drew out the grand style of the thundering poet and revealed famous names to the peoples of Greece. Likewise he made known to fame songs resonant on Roman strings and the Italian lyre of graceful Horace. Hail! ornament of the age, worshipful deservedly for all time, protection of the Pierian choir, beneath whose guardianship never did poet fear for an old age of beggary.

But if there is any room for entreaties of mine, if my prayers have reached your heart, then you, Piso, shall one day be chanted in polished verse, to be enshrined in memory as my Maecenas. I can consign a name to everlasting renown, if after all 'tis right for any man to promise this of himself, and if the avenging god is absent:[a] there is abundance of spirited will, and the mind itself ventures on something of surpassing quality. Do you stretch out your hand to a swimmer:[b] do you, Piso, bring to the light one who is obscure. The home of my sires, humble but true, along with its slender fortune hides me in its own darkness. I can clear my head of its enshrouding burden, I can behold fresh light, if you, my fair-souled friend, do but cheerfully approve and support my aspirations. I have, trust me, a spirit firmer than my years, though youth's comeliness has just begun to shade my cheeks and my twentieth summer is not yet at hand.

[b] The appeal of this young poet contrasts with Johnson's famous sarcasm: "Is not a patron, my lord, one who looks with unconcern on a man struggling for life in the water, and, when he has reached ground, encumbers him with help?"

EINSIEDELN ECLOGUES

INTRODUCTION

TO EINSIEDELN ECLOGUES

THE Einsiedeln pastorals, so called after the tenth-century manuscript at Einsiedeln from which H. Hagen first published them in 1869, have already been touched upon in connexion with Calpurnius Siculus. These two incomplete poems date almost certainly from the early years of Nero's reign (A.D. 54–68). In the first, the emperor is an Apollo and a Jupiter and the inspired author of a poem on the taking of Troy. In the second, one of the shepherds is convinced that with the emperor's accession the Golden Age has returned. This poem, the earlier and the more artistic of the two, in its opening "*quid tacitus, Mystes?*" either echoes or is echoed by the opening of Calpurnius Siculus' fourth eclogue, "*quid tacitus, Corydon?*" On the ground of the *laudata chelys* of i. 17, it has been argued that the author's muse was already popular at court and that it might have been worth while for Calpurnius Siculus, a humbler person and a junior poet, to pay him the compliment of imitation.[a] The argument proceeds to identify the author of the Einsiedeln poems with the eminent Calpurnius Piso on the ground that, if Calpurnius Siculus' patron "Meliboeus"

[a] This is Groag's theory, P. W. *Realencycl.* III. 1379: it is contradicted by Skutsch, P. W. *Realencycl.* V. 2115.

was really Piso,[a] then it is appropriate that he, as the speaker at *Eclogue* iv. 1, should appear to quote "*quid tacitus?*" from himself. Besides, in spite of Piso's later complicity in the conspiracy against Nero, he had been at one time on intimate terms with the emperor,[b] and might well have indulged in pastoral panegyrics upon him. This implies that the Einsiedeln poems preceded the Calpurnian eclogues. But if the *gaudete ruinae* and *laudate rogos* of Einsied. i. 40–41 could be taken to indicate composition after the fire of Rome in A.D. 64, then it is hard to picture Piso so praising Nero on the verge of his plot against him. However this may be, the eulogies upon Nero are in the manner of court literature during the opening years of his reign, as is evident from the tone of Seneca's praises in his *Apocolocyntosis* and *De Clementia.* Much learned speculation has been spent on the pieces. It has generally been felt needless to assert (as Hagen, Buecheler and Birt have done) two separate authors for them; and, while Lucan, as well as Piso, has been put forward as the writer, the balance of opinion tends to agree that there is not enough evidence on which to dogmatise. Ferrara[c] thinks it possible that the two pieces are by Calpurnius Siculus. There are, it is true, resemblances between the Einsiedeln pair and his eclogues; but the very fact that the adulation of Nero in the first piece and the restoration of the

[a] It must be remembered that a case can be made out for regarding "Meliboeus" as Seneca. Some, on the other hand, consider all such identifications to be futile (see introd. to Calpurnius Siculus).

[b] Tacitus, *Ann.* XV. 52.

[c] In *Calpurnio Siculo e il panegirico a Calpurnio,* Pavia, 1905.

Golden Age in the second are themes in common with the fourth and first Calpurnian eclogues militates rather against than for identity of authorship. At least, it is arguable that a writer with aspirations after originality would not go on harping on the same string. In one way, indeed, there is a departure from pastoral usage, which normally confines speakers to complete hexameters: the second poem has this amount of individuality in structure, that the interlocutors sometimes start speaking in the middle of a line (ii. 1; 4; 5 and 6).

EDITIONS

H. Hagen, in *Philol.* 28 (1869), pp. 338 *sqq.* (the first publication of the text).
A. Riese, in *Anthol. Latina*, Nos. 725 and 726.
E. Baehrens, in *P.L.M.* III, 60–64.
C. Giarratano, with *Bucolica* of Calpurnius and Nemesianus (Paravia ed.). Turin, 1924.

RELEVANT WORKS

R. Peiper. *Praefationis in Senecae tragoedias supplem.* Breslau, 1870. (First established the Neronian date.)
F. Buecheler. *Rh. Mus.* 26 (1871), 235.
O. Ribbeck. *Rh. Mus.* 26 (1871), 406, 491.
Th. Birt. *Ad historiam hexametri latini symbola*, p. 64. [Argues, like Hagen and Buecheler, that the two poems are by different authors.] Bonn, 1876.
E. Groag, in P. W. *Realencycl.* III. (1899) col. 1379. [Considers Calpurnius Piso the author.]

F. Skutsch, in P. W. *Realencycl.* V. (1905) col. 2115. [Considers Groag's conjecture unfounded.]
A. Maciejczyk. *De carminum Einsidlensium tempore et auctore.* Diss. Greifswald, 1907.
S. Loesch. *Die Einsiedler Gedichte: eine litterarhistorische Untersuchung* (w. text and a facsimile). Diss. Tübingen, 1909. [These last two writers argue for Lucan's authorship.]
J. Hubaux. *Les thèmes bucoliques dans la poésie latine,* Bruxelles, 1930, pp. 228 *sqq.*

For a fuller list see Schanz, *Gesch. d. röm. Lit.*

SIGLUM

E = Codex Einsiedlensis 266: saec. x.

Baehrens' transpositions of lines are not followed, nor all of his emendations.

INCERTI CARMINA BUCOLICA

I

THAMYRAS LADAS MIDAS

Th. Te, formose Mida, iam dudum nostra requirunt
iurgia: da vacuam pueris certantibus aurem.
Mi. haud moror: et casti nemoris secreta voluptas
invitat calamos: imponite lusibus arcem.
Th. praemia si cessant, artis fiducia muta est.
La. sed nostram durare fidem duo pignora cogunt:
vel caper ille, nota frontem qui pingitur alba,
vel liber hic et mobilibus circumdata bullis
fistula, silvicolae munus memorabile Fauni.
Th. sive caper placeat seu Fauni ponere munus,
elige utrum perdas: sed erit, puto, certius omen
fistula damnato iam nunc pro pignore dempta.

THAMYRAS LADAS MIDAS *Hagen*: [illegible]
³ et casti *Baehrens* (cf. *Ilias Lat.* 40) [illegible]
E: et [illegible] *Peiper*: [illegible]
⁴ [illegible] *Hagen*, *Riese*.
⁷ nota . . . alba *Hagen*: notam . . . albam E.
⁸ bullis E, *corr. Hagen*.
⁹ [illegible] : munus et memorabile E.
¹¹ [illegible] E.
¹³ [illegible] *Baehrens*: templa est E.

INCERTI CARMINA BUCOLICA

I

THAMYRA : LADAS : MIDA

Th. Te, formose Mida, iam dudum nostra requirunt
iurgia: da vacuam pueris certantibus aurem.
Mi. haud moror; et casti nemoris secreta voluptas
invitat calamos: imponite lusibus artem.
Th. praemia si cessant, artis fiducia muta est.
La. sed nostram durare fidem duo pignora cogent:
vel caper ille, nota frontem qui pingitur alba,
vel levis haec et mobilibus circumdata bullis
fistula, silvicolae munus memorabile Fauni.
Th. sive caprum mavis vel Fauni ponere munus, 1
elige utrum perdas; sed erit, puto, certius omen
fistula damnato iam nunc pro pignore dempta.

THAMIRA E: THAMYRA *Hagen*: *cf.* Thamyras, 21.
[3] et casti *Baehrens* (*cf.* Tac. *Germ.* 40 *castum nemus*) : et cusu E: et lusu *Hagen*: excusum *Gundermann*.
[5] nulla *Hagen, Ribbeck*.
[7] nota . . . alba *Hagen*: notam . . . albam E.
[8] nobilibus E, *corr. Hagen*.
[9] munus venerabile *Baehrens*: munus et memorabile E.
[11] set *Baehrens*: et E.
[12] dempta *Baehrens*: empta est E.

EINSIEDELN ECLOGUES

I

[The personages are Thamyras and Ladas as contending shepherds, and Midas as umpire.]

Th. Long have our contests called for you, my handsome Midas; lend a leisured ear to competing swains.

Mi. I am ready: the sequestered charm of the holy wood is an invitation to pipings: lay skill upon your minstrelsy.

Th. If prizes are lacking, the confidence of skill is dumb.

La. Nay, two stakes will make our confidence endure: either yonder he-goat, whose forehead is decked with the white mark, or this light pipe set round with moveable knobs,[a] the memorable gift of Faunus, denizen of the woods.

Th. Whether you prefer to stake the he-goat or Faunus' gift, choose which of the two you are to lose; but the surer omen, I fancy, will be the pipe which, instead of being a stake, is as good as taken away from the rejected competitor.

[a] The *bullae* might control the musical notes by closing or opening the perforations; but they might merely be decorative. Hubaux (*Les thèmes bucoliques*, p. 230) thinks of " une flûte ornée de verroteries."

La. quid iuvat insanis lucem consumere verbis?
iudicis e gremio victoris gloria surgat.
Th. praeda mea est, quia Caesareas me dicere laudes 15
mens iubet: huic semper debetur palma labori.
La. et mi sidereo cor movit Cynthius ore
laudatamque chelyn iussit variare canendo.
Mi. pergite, io pueri, promissum reddere carmen;
sic vos cantantes deus adiuvet! incipe, Lada, 20
tu prior; alternus Thamyras imponet honorem.
La. maxime divorum caelique aeterna potestas,
seu tibi, Phoebe, placet temptare loquentia fila
et citharae modulis primordia iungere mundi
carmine uti virgo furit et canit ore coacto, 25
fas mihi sit vidisse deos, fas prodere mundum:
seu caeli mens illa fuit seu solis imago,
dignus utroque ⟨deo⟩ stetit ostro clarus et auro

17 mi s. cor movit (commovit *olim*) *Baehrens*: me s. corrumpit E, *Giarratano*.
20 cantantes E: certantes *Baehrens*.
21 imponit E: imponet *Baehrens*: imponat *Hagen*.
22 caelique *Hagen*: ceterique E.
23 temptare *Peiper*: emitare E.
24 *versum qui est* 24 *in* E *post* 31 *traiecit Baehrens*.
25 carmine uti *Baehrens*: carminibus E.
26 mundo *Hagen, Baehrens*: mundum E.
28 utraque *Peiper*. *post* stetit, dux *addidit Baehrens*: deus *Peiper*: *ante* stetit, deo *addidit Krickenberg*: Nero *Buecheler*.

[a] *i.e.* to Nero's merits.

La. What avails it to waste the daylight in wild words? Let the winner's fame rise from the umpire's bosom.

Th. The spoil is mine, because my mind prompts me to recount a Caesar's praises: to such a task the prize is ever due.

La. My heart too hath Apollo stirred with celestial lips and bade me sing changing strains to my lyre which has already won praise.

Mi. Proceed, my lads, to render the promised song: so may God aid you as ye sing! Ladas, begin—you first: Thamyras in turn will bring his tribute.[a]

La. Greatest of gods, eternal ruler of the sky,[b] whether, Phoebus, it is thy pleasure to make trial of the eloquent strings and set to melodies on the lyre the first principles of the world, even as in song the maiden-priestess raves and chants with lips o'er-mastered, so may I be allowed to have looked on gods, allowed to reveal the story of the universe:[c] whether that mind was the mind of the sky or likeness of the sun,[d] worthy of both divine principles Apollo took his place, brilliant in purple and gold, and

[b] Some have taken this as addressed to Jupiter; but Ladas is concerned with Phoebus alone (17–18), while Thamyras is concerned with the emperor (15–16). This seems to preclude the idea supported by some scholars that the emperor (instead of Apollo) is the subject of *stetit* in 28.

[c] Ladas prays for inspiration like that of the Pythian prophetess: *cf.* Lucan, V. 88–99, on Apollo as guardian of eternal fate at Delphi, a passage containing noticeable parallelisms of expression to the verses here given to Ladas.

[d] The reference is to Apollo as the omniscient god of divination (Lucan V. 88 *caeli . . . deus omnia cursus aeterni secreta tenens*) and as the Sun-God.

intonuitque manu. talis divina potestas
quae genuit mundum septemque intexuit oris 3
artificis zonas et totas miscet amore.
talis Phoebus erat, cum laetus caede draconis
docta repercusso generavit carmina plectro:
caelestes ulli si sunt, hac voce loquuntur!
venerat ad modulos doctarum turba sororum. . . . 3
Th. huc huc, Pierides, volucri concedite saltu:
hic Heliconis opes florent, hic vester Apollo est!
tu quoque Troia sacros cineres ad sidera tolle
atque Agamemnoniis opus hoc ostende Mycenis!
iam tanti cecidisse fuit! gaudete, ruinae, 4
et laudate rogos: vester vos tollit alumnus!
. . . .
⟨*venerat en et Maeonides, cui*⟩ plurima barba

[30] orbis *Hagen*: oris E.
[31] totas *Baehrens*: toto E: totum *Riese*.
[35] *versum qui est* 35 *in* E *post* 41 *traiecit Baehrens.* sororum *Hagen*: sonarum E.
[42] *hic versus totus et* 43 *ex maiore parte desunt in* E.
[43] *explevit Baehrens ut supra.*

[a] Apollo's power, from a Stoic stand-point, was *totius pars magna Iovis* (Lucan, V. 95). The *artifex*, or contriver of the *mundus*, is the δημιουργός of Platonic philosophy. According to Plutarch, Thales and Pythagoras divided the heavens into five zones, Pythagoras dividing the earth into five corresponding zones (*De Placitis Philosophorum*, 2, 12 and 3, 14). The Stoic Poseidonius gave Parmenides as originator of the division into five zones (Strabo, *Geog.* II. ii. 2). Poseidonius himself recognized seven zones (Strabo, II. ii. 3 [C. 95]), and his influence acts directly or indirectly on this passage.

sped thunder with his hand. Such was the divine power which has begotten the world and has inwoven with the seven borders the artificer's zones [a] and blends them all with love.[b] Such was Phoebus, when, rejoicing in the slaughter of the dragon,[c] he produced learned minstrelsy to the beat of the plectrum: if there are any dwellers in heaven, they speak with voice like this. The band of the learned sisterhood had come to the sounds of the music. . . .

Th. Hither, hither, ye Pierian Muses, approach in the fleet dance! Here flourishes the wealth of Helicon; here is your own Apollo! You too, O Troy, raise your hallowed ashes to the stars,[d] and display this work to Agamemnon's Mycenae! Now has it proved of such value to have fallen! Rejoice, ye ruins; praise your funeral pyres: 'tis your nurseling that raises you again! . . . ⟨Lo! Homer too had come,

[b] The principle of attraction in the universe descended from the *Theogony* of Pherecydes to Stoic philosophy. This physical φιλία of the Greeks is echoed in Lucan, IV. 189–191, *nunc ades aeterno complectens omnia nexu, o rerum mixtique salus, Concordia, mundi, et sacer orbis amor*. The difficulties of the passage 22 *sqq*. are discussed by Loesch, *Die Einsiedler Gedichte* (1909), pp. 34–42.

[c] *i.e.* the serpent Python sent to torment Latona, *cf.* Lucan, V. 80.

[d] The reference might be, some have argued, to Nero's poem on Troy, from which according to common gossip he recited the episode of the fall of the city (Ἅλωσις Ἰλίου) on the occasion of the great fire at Rome, A.D. 64: Tac. *Ann*. xv. 39; Suet. *Ner*. 38; Dio, lxii. 18. But it would not be a tactful allusion, and there are difficulties in placing the poem so late.

albaque caesaries pleno radiabat honore.
ergo ut divinis implevit vocibus aures, 45
candida flaventi discinxit tempora vitta
Caesareumque caput merito velavit amictu.
haud procul Iliaco quondam non segnior ore
stabat et ipsa suas delebat Mantua cartas.

* * *

II

Glyceranus : Mystes

Gl. Quid tacitus, Mystes? *My.* curae mea gaudia turbant:
cura dapes sequitur, magis inter pocula surgit,
et gravis anxietas laetis incumbere gaudet.
Gl. non satis accipio. *My.* nec me iuvat omnia fari.
Gl. forsitan imposuit pecori lupus? *My.* haud timet hostes 5
turba canum vigilans. *Gl.* vigiles quoque somnus adumbrat.
My. altius est, Glycerane, aliquid, non quod patet: erras.
Gl. atquin turbari sine ventis non solet aequor.
My. quod minime reris, satias mea gaudia vexat.

[45] implentur . . . aurae *Baehrens*: implevit aures E.
[46] discinxit *Hagen*: distinxit E.
[47] velavit *Peiper*: celabit E.
II. [7] non quod patet *Baehrens*: non non pat̄ E.

whose⟩ full beard and white hair shone in undimmed honour. So when he filled the poet's ears with accents divine, he undid the golden circlet from his fair brow and veiled the emperor's head with its deserved attire. Hard by stood Mantua,[a] erstwhile as forceful as the lips which sang of Ilion; but now with her own hands she began to tear her writings to shreds.

[The poem is incomplete. Probably Thamyras' verses are unfinished and certainly the judgement of Midas is lacking.]

II

A Dialogue between Glyceranus and Mystes.

Gl. Why silent, Mystes? *My.* Worries disturb my joys: worry pursues my meals: it rises even more amid my cups: a load of anxiety enjoys burdening my happy hours.

Gl. I don't quite take you. *My.* Well, I don't like to tell the whole.

Gl. Mayhap a wolf has tricked your cattle? *My.* My watchful band of dogs fears not enemies. *Gl.* Sleep can o'ershadow even the watchful.

My. 'Tis something deeper, Glyceranus—no open trouble: you are wrong.

Gl. Yet the sea is not usually disturbed without winds.

My. You may not think it, but 'tis satiety that plagues my joys.

[a] Virgil's birthplace, now eclipsed by Nero's ministrelsy! This gross sycophancy contrasts with the reverential homage shown towards Virgil both in Calp. Sic. iv. 62–63 and in *Laus Pisonis* 230 *sqq.* It suggests different authorship.

Gl. deliciae somnusque solent adamare querellas. 10
My. ergo si causas curarum scire laboras—
Gl. quae spargit ramos, tremula nos vestiet umbra
ulmus, et en tenero corpus summittere prato
herba iubet: tu dic, quae sit tibi causa tacendi.
My. cernis ut attrito diffusus cespite pagus 15
annua vota ferat sollennesque incohet aras?
spirant templa mero, resonant cava tympana palmis,
Maenalides teneras ducunt per sacra choreas,
tibia laeta canit, pendet sacer hircus ab ulmo
et iam nudatis cervicibus exuit exta. 20
ergo num dubio pugnant discrimine nati
et negat huic aevo stolidum pecus aurea regna?
Saturni rediere dies Astraeaque virgo
tutaque in antiquos redierunt saecula mores.
condit secura totas spe messor aristas, 25
languescit senio Bacchus, pecus errat in herba,
nec gladio metimus nec clausis oppida muris
bella tacenda parant; nullo iam noxia partu
femina quaecumque est hostem parit. arva iuventus

[15] cespite pagus *Baehrens*: cortice fagus E.
[16] inchoet *Baehrens*: imbuet E: imbuat *Hagen*: induat *Peiper*.
[21] nunc *Baehrens*: num E.
[24] tutaque *Baehrens*: totaque E.

---

[a] Maenalus in Arcadia was especially associated with Pan.
[b] *i.e.* the present generation has no handicap in the struggle of life: there is no conflict between man and nature, because the Golden Age has returned.
[c] The very cattle must own that the blessings of the Golden Age belong to the present era.

Gl. Pleasure and drowsihead are commonly in love with complaints.

My. Well then, if you are intent on knowing the reasons for my pangs——

Gl. There is an elm-tree with outspread branches which will cover us with its quivering shade, and, look! the green-sward bids us lie down on the soft meadow: *you* must tell what is your reason for silence.

My. Do you see how the villagers, outspread o'er the well-worn turf, offer their yearly vows and begin the regular altar-worship? Temples reek of wine; the hollow drums resound to the hands; the Maenalids [a] lead the youthful ring-dances amid the holy rites; joyful sounds the pipe; from the elm hangs the he-goat doomed to sacrifice, and with neck already stripped lays his vitals bare. Surely then the offspring of to-day fight with no doubtful hazard? [b] Surely the blockish herd denies not to these times the realms of gold? [c] The days of Saturn have returned with Justice the Maid: [d] the age has returned in safety to the olden ways. With hope unruffled does the harvester garner all his corn-ears; the Wine-god betrays the languor of old age; the herd wanders on the lea; we reap with no sword, nor do towns in fast-closed walls prepare unutterable war: there is not any woman who, dangerous in her motherhood, gives birth to an enemy.[e] Unarmed

[d] Line 23 imitates Virg. *Ecl.* iv. 6, *iam redit et Virgo, redeunt Saturnia regna.*

[e] No foeman can be born, as war is at an end.

nuda fodit tardoque puer domifactus aratro
miratur patriis pendentem sedibus ensem.
est procul a nobis infelix gloria Sullae
trinaque tempestas, moriens cum Roma supre-
mas
desperavit ⟨opes⟩ et Martia vendidit arma.
nunc tellus inculta novos parit ubere fetus,
nunc ratibus tutis fera non irascitur unda;
mordent frena tigres, subeunt iuga saeva leones:
casta fave Lucina: tuus iam regnat Apollo!

[32] est *Baehrens*: sed E.
[34] opes *add. Peiper*: *om.* E.
[37] sueta *Baehrens*: sęva E.

our youth can dig the fields, and the boy, trained to the slow-moving plough, marvels at the sword hanging in the abode of his fathers. Far from us is the luckless [a] glory of Sulla and the threefold crisis [b] when dying Rome despaired of her final resources and sold her martial arms. Now doth earth untilled yield fresh produce from the rich soil, now are the wild waves no longer angry with the unmenaced ship: tigers gnaw their curbs, lions endure the cruel yoke: be gracious, chaste Lucina: thine own Apollo now is King.[c]

[The poem thus relates the shepherd's *gaudia* but not the *curae* of verse 1.]

[a] Sulla was traditionally regarded as *felix*.

[b] The allusion seems to be to (1) the first capture of Rome by a Roman army when Sulla took the city in 88 B.C.; (2) Marius' reign of terror in 87 when slaves from the *ergastula* were armed (*Martia vendidit arma*), and (3) the occupation of Rome by Sulla in 82.

[c] This last line is taken from Virgil, *Ecl.* iv. 10. Lucina, goddess of childbirth, is here not Juno, but Diana, who as the Moon-goddess is sister to the Sun-god Apollo. He is the deity of the tenth Sibylline era which Virgil in *Ecl.* iv. identifies with the Golden Age.

PRECATIO TERRAE
AND
PRECATIO OMNIUM HERBARUM

INTRODUCTION

TO PRECATIO TERRAE AND PRECATIO OMNIUM HERBARUM

Both these prayers afford interesting glimpses into features of ancient religion much older than the poems themselves. It is characteristic of the worship of the Earth-Goddess that they should exhibit a recognition of her as the source of life and energy and nourishment, an anticipation of a final refuge in her at death,[a] and a confidence in her power to give help and healing. The divinity of the Earth-Mother was believed to be communicated to the dead, who were by inhumation absorbed into her. The words of the first *Precatio* find a full parallel in the epitaph—

> mortua heic ego sum et sum cinis, is cinis terrast :
> sein est terra dea, ego sum dea, mortua non sum.[b]

The return of the body to Mother Earth was a natural notion for a primitive agricultural folk, since much of the religious ritual of such peoples must be connected with the land. Earth had to be propitiated that she might grant increase to crops and cattle;

[a] With ll. 12–14 of the first *Precatio*, *cf. mater genuit materque recepit* in Buecheler, *Carmina lat. epigraphica*, No. 809 : *cf.* also the traditional sepulchral inscription *sit tibi terra levis*, and the spirit of the prayer to Tellus which ends the first elegy on Maecenas (141 *sqq.*, p. 134 *supra*).

[b] Buecheler, *op. cit.*, No. 1532 : *cf.* 974.

and at funerals the pig was sacrificed to the Corn-Goddess to secure her favour in receiving the dead. It is, then, intelligible that the Di Manes and Tellus Mater should sometimes be coupled; *e.g.* Decius in his *devotio* (Livy VIII. ix. 8) named them together. So Romans came to look on the tomb as an eternal home [a] where the spirit of the dead should abide, still a member of the old clan, still in some kind of communion with the living through the offering of sacrifice and food.

An excellent plastic illustration of the *Precatio Terrae* may be found in the allegorical relief of Tellus Mater, from the walls of the Ara Pacis Augustae decreed by the Senate to the emperor Augustus in 13 B.C. It is symbolic of peace and plenty, and characteristically representative of the fusion of Eastern with Western elements in Graeco-Roman art. Baehrens, indeed, would ascribe both the *Precationes* to the same period as the Ara Pacis (*Miscell. Crit.*, Groningen, 1878, pp. 107-113). Under the name of Antonius Musa we have a treatise "de herba betonica" in a Leyden MS. (Leidensis), a Breslau MS. (Vratislaviensis), and two Florentine MSS. (Laurentiani). These four also contain the two *Precationes* in senarii. The *Precatio Omnium Herbarum* is in one MS. (Laur. 11th cent.) ascribed to Musa: on this ground Baehrens concludes that both poems are by him. If this were convincing, it would settle their date as Augustan; but the argument is weak, and there are features in the poems suggestive of a later period. *Maiestas tua*, for instance, in lines 25 and 32 of the

[a] Buecheler, *op. cit.*, No. 59 *suae gnatae, sibeique, uxori hanc constituit domum aeternam ubei omnes pariter aevom degerent*: *cf.* 1488.

first piece, has a post-Augustan ring; and it is noteworthy that the word *maiestas* comes three times in the *Precatio Omnium Herbarum.*

SIGLA

(following Baehrens, *P.L.M.* I. pp. 137–138)

A = codex Leidensis (M.L.V.Q. 9), saec. VI.
B = codex Vratislaviensis (cod. bibl. univers. III. F. 19), saec. XI.
C = codex Laurentianus (plut. lxxiii. 41), saec. XI ineunte.
D = codex Laurentianus (plut. lxxiii. 16), saec. XIII.

PRECATIO TERRAE

Dea sancta Tellus, rerum naturae parens,
quae cuncta generas et regeneras indidem,
quod sola praestas gentibus vitalia,
caeli ac maris diva arbitra rerumque omnium,
per quam silet natura et somnos concipit, 5
itemque lucem reparas et noctem fugas:
tu Ditis umbras tegis et immensum chaos
ventosque et imbres tempestatesque attines
et, cum libet, dimittis et misces freta
fugasque soles et procellas concitas, 10
itemque, cum vis, hilarem promittis diem.
tu alimenta vitae tribuis perpetua fide,
et, cum recesserit anima, in tete refugimus:
ita, quicquid tribuis, in te cuncta recidunt.
merito vocaris Magna tu Mater deum, 15
pietate quia vicisti divom numina;
tuque illa vera es gentium et divom parens,
sine qua nil maturatur nec nasci potest:
tu es Magna tuque divom regina es, dea.
te, diva, adoro tuumque ego numen invoco, 20
facilisque praestes hoc mihi quod te rogo;
referamque grates, diva, tibi merita fide.
exaudi ⟨me⟩, quaeso, et fave coeptis meis;

[2] sidus *codd.*: indidem *Baehrens*: in dies *Buecheler*.
[3] tutela *codd.*: vitalia *Baehrens*.
[10] solem *codd.*: soles *Baehrens*.
[17] ver et BC: vere A: vero D: vera es *Baehrens*.

A LITANY TO EARTH

Goddess revered, O Earth, of all nature Mother, engendering all things and re-engendering them from the same womb, because thou only dost supply each species with living force, thou divine controller of sky and sea and of all things, through thee is nature hushed and lays hold on sleep, and thou likewise renewest the day and dost banish night. Thou coverest Pluto's shades and chaos immeasurable: winds, rains and tempests thou dost detain, and, at thy will, let loose, and so convulse the sea, banishing sunshine, stirring gales to fury, and likewise, when thou wilt, thou speedest forth the joyous day. Thou dost bestow life's nourishment with never-failing faithfulness, and, when our breath has gone, in thee we find our refuge: so, whatsoe'er thou bestowest, all falls back to thee. Deservedly art thou called Mighty Mother of Gods, since in duteous service thou hast surpassed the divinities of heaven, and thou art that true parent of living species and of gods, without which nothing is ripened or can be born. Thou art the Mighty Being and thou art queen of divinities, O Goddess. Thee, divine one, I adore and thy godhead I invoke: graciously vouchsafe me this which I ask of thee: and with due fealty, Goddess, I will repay thee thanks. Give ear to me, I pray, and favour my undertakings: this which I seek of

hoc quod peto a te, diva, mihi praesta volens.
herbas, quascumque generat maiestas tua, 25
salutis causa tribuis cunctis gentibus:
hanc ⟨nunc⟩ mihi permittas medicinam tuam.
veniat medicina cum tuis virtutibus:
quidque ex his fecero, habeat eventum bonum,
cuique easdem dedero quique easdem a me accepe-
rint, 30
sanos eos praestes. denique nunc, diva, hoc mihi
maiestas praestet ⟨tua⟩, quod te supplex rogo.

PRECATIO OMNIUM HERBARUM

Nunc vos potentes omnes herbas deprecor.
exoro maiestatem vestram, quas parens
tellus generavit et cunctis dono dedit:
medicinam sanitatis in vos contulit
maiestatemque, ut omni generi ⟨identidem⟩ 5
humano sitis auxilium utilissimum.
hoc supplex exposco ⟨et⟩ precor: ve⟨locius⟩
⟨huc⟩ huc adeste cum vestris virtutibus,
quia, quae creavit, ipsa permisit mihi,
ut colligam vos; favit hic etiam, cui 10
medicina tradita est. quantumque vestra ⟨nunc⟩
virtus potest, praestate medicinam bonam
causa salutis. gratiam, precor, mihi
praestetis per virtutem vestram, ut omnibus
in rebus, quicquid ex vobis ⟨ego⟩ fecero, 15

[28] veni ad me cum A: veniat me cum BCD: veniat medicina cum *Baehrens*: veni veni ad me *Buecheler*.
[10] favente (-tem A) hoc *codd.*: favit hic *Baehrens*.
[15] viribus ACD: virtutibus B: in rebus *Baehrens*.

thee, Goddess, vouchsafe to me willingly. All herbs soever which thy majesty [a] engendereth, for health's sake thou bestowest upon every race: entrust to me now this healing virtue of thine: let healing come with thy powers: whate'er I do in consonance therewith, let it have favourable issue: to whomso I give those same powers or whoso shall receive the same from me, all such do thou make whole. Finally now, O Goddess, let thy majesty vouchsafe to me what I ask of thee in prayer.

A PRAYER TO ALL HERBS

With all you potent herbs do I now intercede; and to your majesty make my appeal: ye were engendered by Mother Earth, and given for a gift to all. On you she has conferred the healing which makes whole, on you high excellence, so that to all mankind you may be time and again an aid most serviceable. This in suppliant wise I implore and entreat: hither, hither swiftly come with all your potency, forasmuch as the very one who gave you birth has granted me leave to gather you: he also to whom the healing art is entrusted has shown his favour.[b] As far as your potency now extends, vouchsafe sound healing for health's sake. Bestow on me, I pray, favour by your potency, that in all things, whatsoever I do according to your will, or for what-

[a] *maiestas tua* (in lines 25 and 32) sounds post-Augustan: *maiestas* had already become a title of respect for an emperor in Phaedrus II. 5. 23. *Cf.* in the following poem, *maiestatem vestram* addressed to the *herbae* in line 2: *cf.* lines 5 and 18 and Juvenal's *templorum quoque maiestas praesentior*, XI. 111, for a "mystic presence" in temples.

[b] *i.e.* Paean, Apollo as deity of healing.

cuive homini dedero, habeatis eventus bonos
et effectum celerrimum. ut semper mihi
liceat favente maiestate vestra vos
colligere, ...
ponamque vobis fruges et grates agam 2
per nomen Matris, quae vos iussit nascier.

[21] maiestatis *codd.* : Matris *Baehrens.* nasci *codd.* : nascier *Riese.*

soever man I prescribe, ye may have favourable issues and most speedy result. That I may ever be allowed, with the favour of your majesty, to gather you . . . and I shall set forth the produce of the fields for you and return thanks through the name of the Mother who ordained your birth.

AETNA

INTRODUCTION

TO AETNA

THE poem on Aetna has many claims on the attention of readers. It was placed among the minor works of Virgil by manuscript tradition, though this assignation, which came to be disputed by the time of Donatus, finds few scholars to support it now. But whatever its authorship and its date,[a] *Aetna* was written by an author who must win respect by reason of his earnest enthusiasm for the study of nature. He is in quest of a *vera causa* to explain volcanic action, and in his concentration of purpose, coupled with his disdain for mythology, there rings, notwithstanding his errors, a note half-suggestive of scientific modernity. If he despises mythology as no true explanation (though, like Lucretius, accepting it as an ornament), the author also despises sightseers who gad about the world to the neglect of the wonders of nature near their homes. His is a call to observe: " study the colossal work of nature the artist " (*artificis naturae ingens opus adspice*, 601). Basing his observations and theories upon Aetna specially—because Vesuvius was mistakenly considered extinct (431–432)—he argues that the controlling motive force behind eruptions is air operating in the *vacua* with which the earth is honeycombed,

[a] See J. Wight Duff, *A Literary History of Rome in the Silver Age*, 1927, pp. 338–339.

and that the volcanic fire gets a nutritive material in the lava-stone (*lapis molaris*).

There are digressions from which the poem gains in attractiveness. One passage (224–273) utters a stirring proclamation of the majesty of physical research in contrast with mankind's ignoble cares. Again, towards the conclusion, the poet turns from theorising about physical phenomena to an episode (604–646) which centres in the human quality of heroic devotion shown by two brothers who rescue their parents from a sea of fire during an appalling eruption.

The difficulty of the poem itself is partly textual, partly stylistic—the former becomes evident in the *apparatus criticus*; the latter, in great measure, arises from a striving after brevity, a tendency to overload words and phrases, a fondness for metaphor and for personification, and perhaps an occasional adoption of expressions from the *sermo plebeius* of Rome.[a] These points resemble characteristics of the "Silver" Latinity of the early empire. The terseness, too, in mythological references, where details are taken for granted as well known, suggests some degree of lateness in period,[b] and is consistent with Buecheler's verdict that the poem must be later than Ovid and Manilius and with Munro's testimony regarding its versification. But it must have been composed before A.D. 63, as the terrible earthquake which devastated the towns close to Vesuvius in that year could not have been overlooked by a didactic poet who had the volcanic zone of Campania under

[a] See J. M. Stowasser, *Zur Latinität des Aetna* in *Zeitschrift für d. oesterr. Gymn.*, 51 (1900), p. 385.

[b] E. Bickel, *Rhein. Mus.* lxxix. 3 (1930).

consideration and dismissed it as inactive (431–432). Similarities to expressions in Seneca's *Naturales Quaestiones* of A.D. 65 do not prove the contention that *Aetna* came after that work; for both authors may well have used a common source. A summer visit to the volcano may have turned the poet to study Posidonian theories[a]: congruity of subject must have directed him to read Lucretius and Manilius, while in the use of the hexameter he had before him as models both Virgil and Ovid.

There is no clear way of deciding the authorship. Seneca's letter to his friend Lucilius Junior (*Epist.* lxxix. 4–7), once widely accepted as proof that Lucilius composed the work, implies nothing beyond a prediction that Lucilius was to insert a passage about Aetna in a projected poem on Sicily.

EDITIONS

J. B. Ascensius. *Virgilii Opera.* Paris, 1507.
Jos. Scaliger. In *Virgilii Appendix.* Leyden, 1573.
J. Le Clerc (Gorallus). *Aetna* c. notis et interpret. Amsterdam, 1703, 1715.
J. C. Wernsdorf. *Lucilii Junioris Aetna* in *Poetae Latini Minores.* Altenburg, 1780–1799.
F. Jacob. *Lucilii Junioris Aetna* (Latin notes; translation in German hexameters). Leipzig, 1826.

[a] *e.g.* on πνεῦμα (= *spiritus*) as a volcanic agent: cf. *Aetna*, 213, 344. Poseidonius (*c.* 130–50 B.C.), born at Apamea in Syria, was a traveller of encyclopaedic knowledge, whose works are now lost. Apart from eminent services to eclectic Stoicism, he devoted much attention to physical science. A great authority on earthquakes and volcanoes, he is constantly quoted by Strabo (*c.* B.C. 63–25 A.D.) in his *Geography* (see index to Loeb ed., vol. viii). Seneca in the *Nat. Quaest.* often cites him and his pupil Asclepiodotus. For a full account of his influence on *Aetna* see Sudhaus' ed. pp. 59–81.

H. A. J. Munro. *Aetna* revised emended and explained. Cambridge, 1867.

E. Baehrens. In *Poetae Latini Minores*, Vol. II. Leipzig, 1880.

S. Sudhaus. *Aetna* erklärt (German prose trans.). Leipzig, 1898.

Robinson Ellis. *Aetna* with textual and exegetical commentary (English prose translation). Oxford, 1901.

—— *Aetna* ("incerti auctoris carmen"): in Postgate's *Corpus Poetarum Latinorum*, Vol. II. London, 1905.

J. Vessereau. *Aetna* avec traduction et commentaire. Paris, 1905.

M. L. De Gubernatis. *Aetna carmen Vergilio adscriptum* (recens. et interpret.). Turin, 1911: also an edition in Paravia series.

F. Vollmer. In *Poetae Latini Minores*, Vol. I, ed. 2. Leipzig, 1927.

E. Schwartz. Berlin, 1933. (With a limited apparatus, which claims for the editor some emendations made earlier by others: *e.g.* Ellis' *varie*, 184; Baehrens' *moles, frustra*, 489; Vessereau's *iunctas*, 509.)

RELEVANT WORKS

A. De Rooy. *Coniecturae in Martialis libr. xiv. et Severi Aetnam.* Utrecht, 1764.

F. C. Matthiae. In *Neue Bibliothek der schönen Wissenschaften*, 59 (collation of Gyraldinian variants). 1797.

M. Haupt. In *Opuscula.* Leipzig, 1875–76. (His text of *Aetna* at end of his edition of Virgil.)

J. Maehly. *Beiträge zur Kritik des Lehrgedichts Aetna.* Basel, 1862.

B. Kruczkiewicz. *Poema de Aetna Vergilio esse tribuendum.* Cracow, 1883.

P. R. Wagler. *De Aetna poemate quaestiones criticae.* Berlin, 1884. (With index verborum.)

R. Unger. *Aetna* (suggested readings). *Journal of Philology*, xvii. 34, pp. 152–154. Cambridge, 1888.

L. Alzinger. *Studia in Aetnam collata.* Leipzig, 1896.

J. Franke. *Res metrica Aetnae carminis.* Diss. Marburg, 1898.

R. Hildebrandt. *Beiträge zur Erklärung des Gedichtes Aetna.* Leipzig, 1900.

S. Sudhaus. *Zur Ueberlieferung des Gedichtes Aetna* in *Rh. Mus.* lx. pp. 574–583. Frankfurt-a-M. 1905.

E. Herr. *De Aetnae carminis sermone et de tempore quo scriptum sit.* Marburg, 1911.

E. Bickel. *Apollon und Dodona* (ein Beitrag zur Datierung, etc.) in *Rheinisches Museum*, lxxix. 3. Frankfurt-a-M. 1930.

SIGLA

C = Cantabrigiensis: in Cambridge University Library, Kk. v. 34, 10th century (considered by Ellis the best codex). See note at end of this introduction.

S = fragmentum Stabulense, now in Paris, 17177, 10th or 11th century. (Besides about 260 fairly complete lines, it has about 86 more in a truncated form.)

Z = a lost archetype whose text is represented (see Vollmer's *stemma codicum*) by three related MSS. of the 15th century: viz.

H = Helmstadiensis 332,
A = Arundelianus 133, in British Museum,
R = Rehdigeranus, 125 in the city Library, Breslau.

V = Vaticanus 3272 (lines 1–434 *fecundius aethna*). 15th century.

Exc. = florilegia of excerpts, 11th to 13th cent.

(Two are in Paris, 7647 and 17903, and one in the Escorial, Q. 1. 14.)

G = readings of a lost codex used by Lilius Gyraldus (Giglio Giraldi) in the 16th century and represented by N. Heinsius' collation for lines 138–287, and by a copy of lines 272–287 surviving in codex Laurentianus 33. 9. [The value of the recorded Gyraldinian readings for those 150 lines has been estimated differently by critics. Some are attractive, but it is difficult to see how others, though plausible on the surface, could ever have been corrupted into what C gives. Schwartz [a] has recently suggested that alterations and errors in G may be due not to a late humanist, but to a Carolingian " corrector."]

codd. = general consensus of MSS.

A text of *Aetna*, in view of the unsatisfactory evidence of the manuscripts, must be eclectic. Some passages are frankly matter for despair, and are incurable by the licence of emendation, or rather rewriting, in which Baehrens allowed himself to indulge. But there are other passages where

[a] ed. 1933, p. 8.

Robinson Ellis' scholarship, ingenuity, and palaeographical knowledge enabled him to make conjectures of a high degree of probability. Many of these are here adopted.

The corrupt state of the tradition has necessitated what may appear to be a considerable apparatus criticus, but it does not profess to be exhaustive.

Note on C

The text in C is neatly, though often inaccurately, written on vellum as part of a miscellaneous volume which begins with a patristic comment on the story of the prodigal son and contains extracts from Ausonius among others, with the *Culex* immediately preceding the "*Aethna*" at the end. These poems are both ascribed to Virgil in the manuscript. Besides the handwriting, several points suggest its insular or Saxon origin. It has many corruptions, such as unintelligent division of words (*e.g.* 66, *infert edivis*; 114 *inclusis olidum*), dittographies (*e.g.* 240 *cura aestatae perit, cura aestas*), haplographies (*e.g.* 599 *etiam illa manus* for *et iam mille manus*), and other blunders like 107 *crebrer*; 472 *repit* for *recipit*; 566 *ignobilis* for *sic nobilis*; 595 *camilli* for *capilli*. But in spite of defects, its date and its preservation of many sound readings constitute it a most valuable contribution to the text. All the readings reported as from C in the apparatus criticus have been specially verified for the purpose of this edition.

AETNA

AETNA mihi ruptique cavis fornacibus ignes
et quae tam fortes volvant incendia causae,
quid fremat imperium, quid raucos torqueat aestus,
carmen erit. dexter venias mihi carminis auctor
seu te Cynthos habet seu Delo est gratior Hyla
seu tibi Dodone potior, tecumque faventes
in nova Pierio properent a fonte sorores
vota: per insolitum Phoebo duce tutius itur.

aurea securi quis nescit saecula regis?
cum domitis nemo cererem iactaret in arvis
venturisque malas prohiberet fructibus herbas,
annua sed saturae complerent horrea messes,
ipse suo flueret Bacchus pede mellaque lentis
penderent foliis et pinguis Pallas olivae
secretos amnes ageret: tum gratia ruris:
non cessit cuiquam melius sua tempora nosse.

[5] illa SAR *om.* H: ila C: Hyla *Munro.*
[6] dodona CSH^2A: do bona H^1: do dodona R: Dodone *Ald.* 1517, *Vollmer*: Ladonis *Munro, Ellis.*
[10] lactaret CS.
[14] pingui *codd.*: pinguis H^2.
[15] cum V: tum *ceteri codd.*: securos omnis aleret cum gratia ruris *Baehrens*: secretos amnis ageret cum gratia ruris *Vollmer.*

AETNA

Aetna shall be my poetic theme and the fires that break from her hollow furnaces. My poem shall tell what those mighty causes are which roll conflagrations on their way, what it is that chafes at governance, or whirls the clamorous heat-currents. Come with favour to be my inspirer in song, whether Cynthos [a] be thy dwelling-place, or Hyla [b] please thee more than Delos, or Dodona [c] be thy favourite: and with thee let the sister-Muses hasten from the Pierian spring to forward my new emprise. On an unwonted track 'tis safer going if Apollo guide.

Who knows not of the Golden Age of the care-free King [d]? when no man subdued fields to his will or sowed grain in them or fended harmful weeds from the crops which were to come; when plenteous harvests filled the barns to last the year; when, with no tread but his own, Bacchus ran into wine; when honies dripped from clinging leaves, and Pallas made flow her own especial streams of rich olive-oil: then had the country graciousness. To none was it e'er vouchsafed to know more joyously his own times.

[a] *Cynthos*, the rocky hill-shrine of Apollo on Delos.

[b] *Hyla* or *Hyle*, forest-land in Cyprus, is rightly inferred from Lycophron's epithet for Apollo—Ὑλάτης.

[c] E. Bickel, *Rhein. Mus.* lxxix. 3 (1930), defends Apollo's association with Dodona, traditionally the oracle of Zeus.

[d] Saturn.

ultima quis tacuit iuvenum certamina, Colchos?
quis non Argolico deflevit Pergamon igni
impositam et tristi natorum funere matrem
aversumve diem sparsumve in semine dentem?
quis non periurae doluit mendacia puppis,
desertam vacuo Minoida litore questus?
quicquid in antiquum iactata est fabula carmen.

fortius ignotas molimur pectore curas,
qui tanto motus operi, vis quanta perennis
explicet in denso flammas et trudat ab imo
ingenti sonitu moles et proxima quaeque
ignibus irriguis urat—mens carminis haec est.

principio ne quem capiat fallacia vatum,
sedes esse dei tumidisque e faucibus ignem
Vulcani ruere et clausis resonare cavernis
festinantis opus. non est tam sordida divis
cura, neque extremas ius est demittere in artes
sidera: subducto regnant sublimia caelo
illa, neque artificum curant tractare laborem.

19 matrem H²AR: mentem CSH¹: mensam *Schwartz*.
20 semine *codd.*: semina *Scaliger*.
25 qui tanto CSH¹: quis tantos H²AR. operi CS: operit H: reperit AR. vis quanta *Ellis*. qu(a)e CSH: quis A: quamvis R. tanta *codd.*: causa *Ald.* 1517.

Who has not told[a] of the Colchians—mellay of warriors on farthest soil? Who but has uttered a dirge for Pergamos set on her blazing Argive pyre and the mother mourning the poignant slaying of her sons, or the day that turned its course in horror, or the dragon's tooth sown mid the sprinkling of seed? Who has not lamented the lying signal of the ship that kept not troth, or chanted the plaint of Minos' daughter forlorn on a deserted shore?—yes, every form in which legend has been thrown into ancient song.

More gallantly I set my spirit toiling on a task untried; what are the forces for this mighty working, how great the energy which releases in dense array the eternal flames, thrusts masses of rock from the lowest depth with gigantic noise and burns everything near in rills of fire—this is the burden of my lay.

First, let none be deceived by the fictions poets tell—that Aetna is the home of a god, that the fire gushing from her swollen jaws is Vulcan's fire, and that the echo in that cavernous prison comes from his restless work. No task so paltry have the gods. To meanest crafts one may not rightly lower the stars; their sway is royal, aloft in a remote heaven; they reck not to handle the toil of artisans.

[a] The mythological topics here briefly dismissed as hackneyed subjects of poetry are, in the order of mention, Jason's Argonautic expedition to Colchis; the burning of Troy by the Greeks; Hecuba's loss of her sons; the retreat of the Sun-God from the "banquet of Thyestes" on human flesh; the crop of warriors which sprang from the dragon's teeth sown by Cadmus; the fatal failure of Theseus to keep his compact with his father to hoist sails of good omen in the event of a successful return to Athens; and Theseus' desertion in Naxos of King Minos' daughter, Ariadne, who had enabled him to thread the labyrinth in Crete.

discrepat a prima facies haec altera vatum:
illis Cyclopas memorant fornacibus usos,
cum super incudem numerosa in verbera fortes
horrendum magno quaterent sub pondere fulmen
armarentque Iovem: turpe est sine pignore carmen.
  proxima vivaces Aetnaei verticis ignes
impia sollicitat Phlegraeis fabula castris.
temptavere (nefas) olim detrudere mundo
sidera captivique Iovis transferre gigantes
imperium et victo leges imponere caelo.
his natura sua est alvo tenus, ima per orbes
squameus intortos sinuat vestigia serpens.
construitur magnis ad proelia montibus agger:
Pelion Ossa gravat, summus premit Ossan Olympus:
iam coacervatas nituntur scandere moles,
impius et miles metuentia comminus astra
provocat, infestus cunctos ad proelia divos
provocat, admotis per inertia sidera signis.
Iuppiter e caelo metuit dextramque coruscam
armatus flamma removet caligine mundum.
incursant vasto primum clamore Gigantes,
his magno tonat ore Pater, geminantque faventes
undique discordi sonitum simul agmine venti.

[39] flumen CSH[1]: fulmen H[2]AR.
[49] creat *codd.*: ciet *De Gubernatis* (*Paravia ed.*): gravat *Jacob*: onerat *Baehrens*: terit *Ald.* 1517.
[52] infestus CS: infensus AR: inde Iris . . . convocat *Baehrens* (an illustration of his arbitrary changes).
[53] admotisque tertia C: admotis ad territa sidera signis *Haupt*: admotisque terit iam sidera signis *Sudhaus*: admotis per inertia *Ellis*.
[54] e caelo *codd.*: et caelo *Bormans, Sudhaus, Vollmer*.
[58] discordes comitum *codd.*: discordi sonitum *Jacob, Ellis*.

There is this second form of poetic error, different from the first. Aetna's furnaces, it is declared, are those the Cyclopes used, when, employing their strength in rhythmic strokes upon the anvil, they forged the dread thunderbolt beneath their heavy hammers and so gave Jupiter his panoply—a graceless tale with ne'er a pledge of truth.

Next, there is a sacrilegious legend which molests with Phlegra's [a] warfare the ever-living fires of Aetna's summit. In olden time the giants essayed impiously to thrust down the stars from the firmament, then capturing Jove to place his sovereignty elsewhere and impose their laws on vanquished heaven. These monsters have man's nature down to the belly; below 'tis a scaly serpent that forms the tortuous windings of their steps. Great mountains are built into a pile for waging the battle. Ossa weighs down Pelion; Olympus, topmost of the three, lies heavy on Ossa. Now they strive to climb the mountain-masses heaped in one; the sacrilegious host challenges to close fight the alarmed stars—challenges in hostile array all the gods to battle: the standards advance through constellations paralysed. From heaven Jupiter shrinks in alarm; weaponing his glittering right hand with flame, he withdraws the firmament in gloom. With mighty outcry the Giants begin their onset; hereat thunders the deep voice of the Sire, and therewithal from every quarter the supporting winds with their discordant host redouble the noise. Thick burst the

[a] It was fabled that the Earth-born brood of the Giants, in their rebellion against the gods, sought to scale heaven by piling Mount Ossa on Pelion and then Olympus on Ossa. They were discomfited by Jupiter's lightnings on the Phlegraean plain in Macedonia.

densa per attonitas rumpuntur flumina nubes,
atque in bellandum quae cuique potentia divum
in commune venit: iam patri dextera Pallas
et Mars laevus erat: iam cetera turba deorum
stant utrimque decus. validos tum Iuppiter ignes
increpat et iacto proturbat fulmine montes.
illinc devictae verterunt terga ruinae
infestae divis acies, atque impius hostis
praeceps cum castris agitur Materque iacentis
impellens victos. tum pax est reddita mundo,
tum Liber cessata venit per sidera: caelum
defensique decus mundi nunc redditur astris.
gurgite Trinacrio morientem Iuppiter Aetna
obruit Enceladon, vasto qui pondere montis
aestuat et petulans exspirat faucibus ignem.

haec est mendosae vulgata licentia famae.
vatibus ingenium est: hinc audit nobile carmen.
plurima pars scaenae rerum est fallacia: vates
sub terris nigros viderunt carmine manes
atque inter cineres Ditis pallentia regna:
mentiti vates Stygias undasque canesque.
hi Tityon poena stravere in iugera foedum;
sollicitant illi te circum, Tantale, cena
sollicitantque siti; Minos, tuaque, Aeace, in umbris

[59] flumina CS : fulmina Z, *Munro, Ellis.*

[62] s(a)evus CSHA : scaevus R : laevus *Bormans.*

[63] stant CSH^1A : stat H^2R. utrimque CS : utrumque Z. deus CZ : de . . S : tuens *Baehrens, Vessereau* : verens *Ellis* : stant ut cuique decus *Unger.*

[64] victo CSH^1 : vinctos H^2 : victor AR : iacto *ed. Ascens.* 1507.

[66] infert(a)e S : infest(a)e Z : infert edivis (*sic*) C.

[69] tum liber *codd.* : tunc imber *Vollmer.* cessat CS : c(a)essa H^1A : cressa H^2 : celsa R : tum nimbo cessante nitet *Baehrens* : Liber cessata *Ellis, Vessereau* : cessat : lenit per sidera caelum *De Gubernatis* (*Paravia ed.*).

torrents through the astonied clouds: all the warlike prowess of one and every god joins the common cause. Already was Pallas at her father's right and Mars at his left: already the rest of the gods take their stand, a glory on either flank. Then Jupiter discharges the din of his puissant fires: he hurls his bolt and lays the mountains low. From that scene the falling throng fled vanquished, the armies embattled against heaven: headlong the godless foe is driven, his camp with him, and Mother Earth urging her prostrate sons back to the fight they have lost. Then peace is restored to the firmament: then mid stars at rest comes Bacchus: the sky and the honour of a world preserved are now restored to the stars. As in the Sicilian sea Enceladus lies dying, Jupiter whelms him under Aetna. Beneath the mountain's mighty weight he tosses feverishly, and rebellious breathes fire from his throat.

Such is the widespread licence of faulty rumour. Bards have genius: so their lay wins high renown. 'Tis well-nigh all delusion that the stage gives us. Bards have beheld in poetry dark ghosts in the underworld and the pale realm of Dis amid the ashes of the dead. Bards have sung false lays of Stygian wave and Stygian hound. Some have stretched over many an acre Tityus ugly in his punishment: others torment you, Tantalus, with a banquet spread around—torment you too with thirst. They sing of your judgements, Minos, and yours,

---

[73] petulans Z: petula in se CS: patulis *edd. ant., Baehrens.*
[79] canentes *codd.*: canesque *Scaliger.*
[81] p(o)ena CSAR: cena *Baehrens; Ellis.*

iura canunt, idemque rotant Ixionis orbem—
quicquid et interius; falsi sibi conscia terra est.
nec tu, terra, satis: speculantur numina divom
nec metuunt oculos alieno admittere caelo.
norunt bella deum, norunt abscondita nobis
coniugia et falsa quotiens sub imagine peccet
taurus in Europen, in Ledam candidus ales
Iuppiter, ut Danaae pretiosus fluxerit imber:
debita carminibus libertas ista; sed omnis
in vero mihi cura: canam quo fervida motu
aestuet Aetna novosque rapax sibi congerat ignes.
  quacumque immensus se terrae porrigit orbis
extremique maris curvis incingitur undis,
non totum ex solido est: ducit namque omnis
    hiatum,
secta est omnis humus, penitusque cavata latebris
exiles suspensa vias agit; utque animanti
per tota errantes percurrunt corpora venae
ad vitam sanguis omnis qua commeat eidem,
terra voraginibus conceptas digerit auras.
scilicet aut olim diviso corpore mundi
in maria ac terras et sidera, sors data caelo
prima, secuta maris, deseditque infima tellus
sed tortis rimosa cavis; et qualis acervus
exsilit imparibus iactis ex tempore saxis,

[84] quicquid interius *codd.*: in terris *Baehrens.* sibi conscia CS: consortia Z. terrent *codd.*: texent *De Gubernatis* (*Paravia ed.*): terra est *Ald.* 1517: quidquid et infernist, falsi consortia adhaerent *Ellis.*

[88] peccent *codd.*: peccet *Schrader.*

[96] non totum et solido desunt namque omnis hiatu CS: solidum . . . hiatus R: non totum ex solido est, ducit namque omnis hiatum *Ellis*: non totum et solido densum est *Vollmer*: solidum et densum *Gercke.*

[100] idem *codd.*: eidem *Ellis.*

Aeacus, in the world of shades: they also set Ixion's wheel revolving—and whatsoe'er is deeper hid; earth is conscious of the falsehood. Nor yet do you, O earth, suffice them: they spy on the divine powers: they are not afraid to let their eyes peer into a heaven where they have no portion. They know the wars of gods, their unions hidden from us, all the sins of Jove in deceitful guise, as a bull to trick Europa, a white swan for Leda, a streaming shower of precious ore for Danaë. Such freedom must be accorded to poetry; but with truth alone is my concern. I will sing the movement that makes fervent Aetna boil and greedily gather its own stores of fire renewed.

Wherever the earth's vast sphere extends, girt with the curving waves of farthest ocean, it is not solid all in all. Everywhere the ground has its long line of fissure, everywhere is cleft and, hollowed deeply with secret holes, hangs above narrow passages which it makes.[a] As in a living creature veins run through the whole body with wandering course, along which passes every drop of blood to feed life for the selfsame organism, so the earth by its chasms draws in and distributes currents of air. Either, I mean, when of old the body of the universe was divided into sea, earth and stars, the first portion was given to the sky, then followed that of the sea, and earth sank down lowest of the three, albeit fissured by winding hollows; and, even as a heap springs out of stones of uneven shape

[a] *suspensa*: *cf. pendeat in sese*, 108.

ut crebro introrsus spatio vacuata † charybdis
pendeat in sese, simili quoque terra figura
in tenuis laxata vias, non omnis in artum
nec stipata coit: sive illi causa vetusta est,
nec nata est facies, sed liber spiritus intrat
et fugiens molitur iter, seu lympha perenni
edit humum limo furtimque obstantia mollit;
aut etiam inclusi solidum vicere vapores,
atque igni quaesita via est; sive omnia certis
pugnavere locis; non est hic causa dolendi
dum stet opus causae. quis enim non credit inanes
esse sinus penitus, tantos emergere fontes
cum videt ac totiens imo se mergere hiatu?
non ille ex tenui quocumque agat: apta necesse est
confluvia errantes arcessant undique venas
et trahat ex pleno quod fortem contrahat amnem.
flumina quin etiam latis currentia rivis
occasus habuere suos: aut illa vorago

107 vacat acta CS: vacuata *Ald.* 1517: vacefacta *Buecheler* (cf. Lucret. vi. 1005, multusque văcēfit). charibdis C: carinis *corr. in* charims S: carambos V.

108 simili *codd.*: similis *Ellis.* futur(a)e *codd.*: futura est *Vollmer*: figura *Ald.* 1517: figurae *Ellis.*

112 nympha CS: lympha Z. perenni *codd.*: perennis *Ellis.*

114 videre *codd.*: exedere *Ald.* 1517: vicere *Sevin*: rupere *Jacob*: fudere *Munro*: solvere *Birt.*

116 dolendi *codd.*: docendi *Ald.* 1517: docenda *Clericus*: docendi, dum stet opus, causas *Munro.*

117 credit CS: credat *Ald.* 1517. (In 118–122 textual difficulties have possibly been increased by the loss of a line after 119: Munro and Ellis mark a lacuna.)

119 torrens Z: torres (n superscribed) C: totiens *Haupt.* uno CSZ: imo V, *Haupt.*

120 non Z: nam CS. vocemque *codd.*: vacuoque *Scaliger*: quocumque *Sudhaus*: nam mille ex tenui vocuoque (*sic*) agitata *Munro*: non ille ex tenui violens veget; arta *Ellis.*

thrown at random, so as to form a charybdis [a] hollowed with frequent interstices within and hanging upon itself, even so in like configuration the earth, too, loosened into tiny channels, does not all unite compactly or into narrow compass. Or maybe the cause of it is indeed ancient, though the formation is not coeval with its origin, but some air enters unchecked and works a road as it escapes: or water has eaten away the ground with the mud it perpetually makes and stealthily softens what blocks its course. Or again hot vapours cribbed and confined have overcome solidity and fire has sought a path for itself: or all these forces may have striven in their assigned places. No cause is here for mourning our ignorance, so long as the working of the true cause stands assured. Who does not believe that there are gulfs of emptiness in earth's recesses, when he sees springs so mighty emerge and so often plunge again in the depth of a chasm? That chasm could not speed it from any slender source: fit confluents must needs summon from everywhere their wandering ducts and the chasm draw from a full source the making of a mighty river. Moreover, rivers running with broad currents have found their own places of sinking. Either an abyss has snatched them headlong down

[a] No editor has found a satisfactory reading here. What is wanted is a feminine noun agreeing with *vacuata* and meaning a loosely compacted heap with hollows in it: *charybdis*, "a whirlpool," does not express this. Clericus invented *corymbis* (fem.) for this passage from *κόρυμβος*, "a peak" or "cluster," and Gronov suggested *corymbas* (*κορυμβάς*, "a string running round a net").

121 cum fluvio C: cum fluvia S: confluit AR: confluvia H¹, *and modern editors*.
122 et trahat CSH: extrahat AR: ut trahat *Munro*.

derepta in praeceps fatali condidit ore,
aut occulta fluunt, tectis adoperta cavernis,
atque inopinatos referunt procul edita cursus.
quod ni diversos emittat terra canales,
hospitium fluvio det semita, nulla profecto
fontibus et rivis constet via, pigraque tellus
conferta in solidum segni sub pondere cesset.
quod si praecipiti conduntur flumina terra,
condita si redeunt, si quaedam incondita surgunt,
haud mirum clausis etiam si libera ventis
spiramenta latent. certis tibi pignora rebus
atque oculis haesura tuis dabit ordine tellus.
immensos plerumque sinus et iugera pessum
intercepta licet densaeque abscondita nocti
prospectare: procul chaos ac sine fine ruinae.
cernis et in silvis spatiosa cubilia retro
antraque demersas penitus fodisse latebras?
incomperta via est operum; tantum effluit intra . . .
argumenta dabunt ignoti vera profundi,
tu modo subtiles animo duce percipe curas
occultique fidem manifestis abstrahe rebus.
nam quo liberior quoque est animosior ignis

128 si *codd.*: ni *Jacob*: nisi *Vollmer*.

129 fluvium CS: fluminum Z: fluviorum *Ald.* 1517: fluviis *Birt*: fluvio *Baehrens*. aut CSHA: haud *Clericus*: et det *Baehrens*: det *Ellis*.

131 conserta *codd.*: conferta *Ald.* 1517.

133 si qua etiam CSR: si quae etiam V: et iam *Scaliger*: si quaedam *Munro*.

138 densaque . . . nocte G.

139 Vollmer punctuates after *procul*.

140 spatioque *codd.*: spatiosa *Ald.* 1517.

141 demissa pedibus CZ: dimiss apedibus (*sic*) S: demersas penitus G.

142 Munro and Ellis mark a lacuna after this line. operum CSZ: aer *Jacob*. effluit intra CSZ: effugit ultra G.

and buried them in its fateful jaws, or they flow unseen, o'er-arched by closed caverns, then, coming to light far away, renew their unexpected course. If earth did not let out channels in different places, if some path did not give welcome to a river, truly no road would be assured for springs and streams, and sluggish earth, packed in a dense mass, would be rendered idle by its unmoving weight. But if rivers are buried in a sheer abyss of earth, if some which are buried come back to light and others without such burial rise from earth, no wonder is it that confined winds have liberating vents which are concealed. Proofs of this through facts indisputable, proofs which hold the eye, the earth will give you in due order. Oftentimes you may look out on vast cavities and tracts of land cut off ruinously and plunged into thick darkness; 'tis far-flung chaos and unending debris. Moreover, do you see how in forests there are lairs and caves of widely receding space which have dug far down their deep-sunk coverts? Undiscovered is the route of such working: only within there is an outflow. . . .[a] These (caves) will furnish true proofs of a depth unknown to us. Let but your mind guide you to a grasp of cunning research: from things manifest gather faith in the unseen. For as fire is always more unfettered and

[a] Some part of the argument about the hidden forces of air is lost. The reasoning seems to be that, though the process of working is unascertained, yet anyone entering such caverns will be conscious of the efflux of air.

145 occultamque *codd.* : occultique *Baehrens.*

semper in inclusis nec ventis segnior ira est,
sub terra penitusque novent hoc plura necesse est,
vincla magis solvant, magis hoc obstantia pellant.
nec tamen in rigidos exit contenta canales
vis animae flammaeve: ruit qua proxima cedunt
obliquumque secat qua visa tenerrima caula est.
hinc terrae tremor, hinc motus, ubi densus hiantes
spiritus exagitat venas cessantiaque urget.
quod si spissa foret, solido si staret in omni,
nulla daret miranda sui spectacula tellus,
pigraque et in pondus conferta immobilis esset.
sed summis si forte putas concrescere causis
tantum opus et summis alimentum viribus, ora
qua patula in promptu cernis vastosque recessus,
falleris et nondum tibi lumine certa liquet res.
namque illuc quodcumque vacans hiat impetus omnis:
at sese introitu solvunt adituque patenti
conversae languent vires animosque remittunt.

148 movent CSH : movet AR : novent *Ellis.*

151 verrit CS : ruit G.

152 causa est CSH[1] : causa (*om.* est) AR : massa est *Munro* : caula est *Clericus* : crusta est *Haupt* : secant quae causa tenerrima caussa est G (faulty enough to justify Ellis' remark "the fondest admirer of Gyr. will not claim much for it here.")

158 subitis G : summis CSZ. concrescere G : concredere CS : concedere *Ellis.*

159 et subitis G : et summis CSZ : adsumptis *Ellis* : ex subitis alimenti incursibus *Unger*. oris CSZ : ora ? G, *Munro.*

160 qu(a)e CSZ : qua *Ellis.* patula G : valida CSZ. vastosque G : validosque CSAR : validosaque H.

161 falleris et G : fallere sed CSZ. certo tibi lumine res est G : tibi lumine certaque retro CSZ : tibi lumine certa liquet res *Ellis.*

162 illis G : illic H[2] : illuc CSH[1] : illud AR. quaecumque G : quodcunque CSARH[2] : quocumque H[1]. vacant hiatibus G : vacat hiat impetus CS : vagantur hiatibus *Baehrens* : vacans hiat, impetus *Ellis.*

more furious in confined spaces, and as the rage of the winds is no less vehement there, so to this extent, underground and in earth's depths, must fire and wind cause greater changes, all the more loose their bonds, all the more drive off what blocks their course. Yet 'tis not into unyielding channels that the pent-up force of air or flame escapes. It hurtles on only where the nearest barriers give way, and cuts its course sideways just where the enclosure seems most frail. Hence comes the trembling, the quaking of earth, when compressed air stirs the pores till they gape and drives sluggish matter before it. But if earth had no openings, if its frame were entirely solid, it would give the eye no marvellous visions of its inner self; inert and packed into a weighty mass, it would remain immovable. But if perhaps you think that this mighty action is a growth from causes at the surface and its nourishment a growth from surface strength[a] at the point where you perceive before you outstretched clefts and vast chasms—if so, you are wrong: the case is not yet clear to you, established in its true light. For all the onslaught of the winds makes for any open vacuum, but at their entry their forces slacken; altered by the spacious access to the chasm, they turn feeble and relax their spirit. For when the

[a] Ellis' reading *concedere* means "is a yielding to forces at the surface." Conjecturing *adsumptis* in the next line, he takes *alimentum* as gen. plur.; the meaning then would be: "when a powerful addition of materials feeding the flame has been received." In either case, provided *summis* of 158 is right, the author is opposing the theory that eruptions can be caused by agencies near the surface.

---

163 et CSZ : set *Ellis* : at *Vessereau*.
164 conceptae G : conversae CSZ : conruptae *Baehrens*.

quippe ubi quod teneat ventos acuatque morantes 165
in vacuo desit cessant, tantumque profundi
explicat errantes et in ipso limine tardant.
angustis opus est turbare in faucibus illos.
fervet opus densaque premit premiturque ruina
nunc Euri Boreaeque Notus, nunc huius uterque. 170
hinc venti rabies, hinc saevo quassat hiatu
fundamenta soli: trepidant urbesque caducae
inde, neque est aliud, si fas est credere, mundo
venturam antiqui faciem veracius omen.

haec primo cum sit species naturaque terrae, 175
introrsus cessante solo trahit undique venas
Aetna: sui manifesta fides et proxima vero est.
non illic duce me occultas scrutabere causas,
occurrent oculis ipsae cogentque fateri.
plurima namque patent illi miracula monti. 180
hinc vasti terrent aditus merguntque profundo,
corrigit hinc artus penitus quos exigit ultra.
hinc spissae rupes obstant discordiaque ingens.
inter opus nectunt varie mediumque coercent
pars igni domitae, pars ignes ferre coactae, 185

165 qui teneat G: contineat CZ: quod teneat *Haupt*. ventosa qua quaeque CS: ventos aquasque (? qua quasque) G: ventos acuatque *Munro*.

166 defit G: desint CSHA: desinit R: desit *Ellis*.

168 turbanti G: turbant in CSH: turbare R, *Ellis*. illos CSZ: illo G.

171 quassa meatu *Wernsdorf, Maehly*: quassa boatu *Unger*.

175 immo G: primo CZ: imo *Matthiae*.

176–177 Punctuation varies according as stop is placed after *venas, Aetna* or *sui*.

178 caulas *Baehrens*. 180 spiracula *Baehrens*.

182 porrigit G: corrigit CZ. artus GCZ: artos *Maehly*. exaestuat G: quos exigit CS.

183 spissae CZ: scissae G.

184 aliae G: varies CH[1]: varios H[2]AR: varie *Ellis*.

vacuum contains nothing to stop the winds or spur them in their delay, they flag; all the great abyss deploys them drifting to and fro, and on the very threshold they lose their speed. It must needs be in narrow gullies that the winds work their havoc. Hot glows the work:[a] now the South Wind presses or is pressed on by the thick swoop of the East Wind and the North: now, again, both these winds by a current from the South. Hence the wind's fury: hence it can shatter the foundations of the ground with cruel cleavage. For that reason do cities totter in panic, and, if such belief be not impious, there is no truer presage that the universe will return to its primeval appearance.[b]

As this from the beginning has been the character and nature of the earth, everywhere Aetna runs channels into its interior, while the surface-soil remains inert: Aetna is the plain and truest proof of its own nature. There, with my guidance, you will not have to search for hidden causes: they will of themselves leap into your vision and force acknowledgement; for that mountain has countless marvels apparent to every eye. On this side are vast openings which terrify and plunge in an abyss, on another side the mountain rearranges its limbs projected too far. Elsewhere thick crags bar the path, and enormous is the confusion. They make a chequered weaving of their work and hem it round—some rocks quite subdued by fire, others compelled to

[a] The phrase *fervet opus* occurs twice in Virgil: *Georg.* IV. 169; *Aen.* I. 436. *Cf.* other Virgilian echoes such as *manifesta fides*, 177, *Aen.* II. 309; III. 375; *volvuntur ab imo*, 200 and *volvuntur in imo, Aen.* VI. 581.

[b] *i.e.* chaos: *antiqui sc. mundi.*

[ut maior species et ne succurrat inanis].
haec illi sedes tantarumque area rerum est,
[haec operis visenda sacri faciesque domusque].
  nunc opus artificem incendi causamque reposcit—
non illam parvi aut tenuis discriminis; ignes
mille sub exiguo ponent tibi tempore veram.
res oculique docent; res ipsae credere cogunt.
quin etiam tactu moneant, contingere tuto
si liceat; prohibent flammae, custodiaque ignis
illi operum est arcens aditus, divinaque rerum
cura sine arbitrio, eadem procul omnia cernes.
nec tamen est dubium penitus quid torqueat
    Aetnam,
aut quis mirandus tantae faber imperet arti.
pellitur exustae glomeranter nimbus harenae,
flagrantes properant moles, volvuntur ab imo
fundamenta, fragor tota nunc rumpitur Aetna,
nunc fusca pallent incendia mixta ruina.
ipse procul magnos miratur Iuppiter ignes,
neve sepulta novi surgant in bella Gigantes,
neu Ditem regni pudeat neu Tartara caelo
vertat, in occulto tacitus tremit; omniaque extra
congeries operit saxorum et putris harenae.

[186] aetne C: aethne S: ethnae R. The line is repeated after 195 in CSZ.

[187–188] This is the order in G: CSZ omit 188.

[190] parvi aut tenuis discriminis ignes CSZ (ingens *Ellis*): parvo aut tenui discrimine signis G (signes *Heinsius*).

[191] ponent tibi Z: ibi S: ponentibus C. vera CSZ: veram *Munro*. exiguum venient tibi pignora tempus G.

[192] oculique docent CZ: oculos ducent G. cogunt CSAR: cogent GH[1].

[193] moneant AV: moneat CS: moneam G (?), *Munro, Ellis*.

[195] operum C: operi G.

[197] torqueat CSZ: torreat G.

endure fires yet [to make its look more imposing and its mental picture no unreal one]. Such is Aetna's seat, the field of phenomena so mighty: [such the enticing form and home of its hallowed activity].

Now my task demands who is the maker and what the cause of the conflagration—no cause that of slight or trivial import. A thousand fires in a moment of time will set before you the true cause. Facts and your eyes instruct you: facts unaided compel belief. Nay, they would instruct you by touch, were it safe to touch. But flames forbid it; Aetna's activity has the protection of fire which prevents approach, and the divine control over all is without witness; all such things you will descry from a distance. But there is no doubt what racks Aetna within or who is the marvellous artificer that directs handiwork so great. A cloud of burnt sand is driven in a whirl; swiftly rush the flaming masses; from the depth foundations are upheaved. Now bursts a crash from Aetna everywhere: now the flames show ghastly pale as they mingle with the dark downpour. Afar off even Jupiter marvels at the mighty fires and trembles speechless in his secret haunt, lest a fresh brood of Giants be rising to renew long-buried war or lest Pluto be growing ashamed of his kingdom and be changing hell for heaven; while outside all is covered with heap on heap of rock and crumbling

---

[199] exutae CZ: exhaustae G: exustae *ed. Ascens.* 1507. glomeratur CHAV: glomerantur SR: glomeratim G: glomeranter *Ellis.*

[206] tantum premit CSZ: tremit G: tacitus tremit *Baehrens, Ellis.*

quae nec sponte sua veniunt nec corporis ullis
sustentata cadunt robusti viribus: omnes
exagitant venti turbas et vortice saevo
in densum collecta rotant volvuntque profundo.
hac causa exspectata ruunt incendia montis.
spiritus inflatis nomen, languentibus aer.
nam prope nequicquam per se est violentia: semper
ingenium velox igni motusque perennis,
verum opus auxilium est ut pellat corpora: nullus
impetus est ipsi; qua spiritus imperat, audit;
hic princeps magnoque sub hoc duce militat ignis.
nunc, quoniam in promptu est operis natura solique,
unde ipsi venti? quae res incendia pascit?
cum subito cohibentur, inest quae causa silenti?
subsequar. immensus labor est, sed fertilis idem.
digna laborantis respondent praemia curis.
non oculis solum pecudum miranda tueri
more, nec effusos in humum grave pascere corpus,
nosse fidem rerum dubiasque exquirere causas,
ingenium sacrare caputque attollere caelo,
scire quot et quae sint magno natalia mundo
principia (occasus metuunt an saecula pergunt

208 veniunt G: faciunt CSZ.
211 collecta G: coniecta CSZ.
212 expectata CSZ: expectanda G. ruunt CZ: terunt G. montis Z: mortis C (*Ellis cites* montis *in error, Proleg.* lxxviii).
213 inflat iis *Maehly*. momen *Scaliger*.
214 par est CZ: pars est G: per se est *Wagler*.
217 audit CSHR²: audis AR¹: audet G.
221 cum CSZ: cur G. cohibetur inest CSZ: cohibent iners G: cohibent vires *Heinsius*. silenti CSZ: silendi G.
223 laborantis *Exc.*, CSZ: laboratis G.
227 *sic* G: sacra per ingentem capitique attollere caelum CSZ.

sand. They come not so of their own accord: unsupported by the strength of any powerful body they fall. It is the winds which arouse all these forces of havoc: the rocks which they have massed thickly together they whirl in eddying storm and roll from the abyss. For this reason the rush of fire from the mountain is no surprise. Winds when swollen are called "spirit," but "air" when sunk to rest.[a] The violence of flame unaided is almost ineffectual; true, fire has always a natural velocity and perpetual motion, but some ally is needed for the propulsion of bodies. In itself it has no motive energy: where spirit is commander, it obeys. Spirit is emperor: fire serves in the army of this great captain.[b]

Now, since the character of Aetna's activity and of the soil is manifest, whence come the winds themselves? What feeds the conflagration? When they are suddenly arrested, what is the inherent cause of the hush? I shall follow up the inquiry. Infinite is the toil, yet fruitful too. Just rewards match the worker's task. Not cattle-like to gaze on the world's marvels merely with the eye, not to lie outstretched upon the ground feeding a weight of flesh, but to grasp the proof of things and search into doubtful causes, to hallow genius, to raise the head to the sky, to know the number and character of natal elements in the mighty universe (do they dread extinction or

[a] Ellis justifiably defended this line against attack, *Jrnl. Philol.* xvi. 301, citing the parallel doctrine of Seneca, *Nat. Quaest.* II. i. 3 (*cum motus terrae fiat spiritu, spiritus autem sit aer agitatus* . . .): VI. xxi. and xxii.

[b] The imperial note in the Latin of 217–218 is unmistakable.

---

[228] natalia *Exc.*, CS: fatalia G.

et firma aeterno religata est machina vinclo?) 230
solis scire modum et quanto minor orbita lunae est
(haec brevior cursu ut bis senos pervolet orbes,
annuus ille meet): quae certo sidera currant
ordine quaeve suo derrent incondita gyro:
scire vices etiam signorum et tradita iura 235
[sex cum nocte rapi, totidem cum luce referri],
nubila cur Phatne caelo denuntiet imbres,
quo rubeat Phoebe, quo frater palleat igni,
tempora cur varient anni (ver, prima iuventa,
cur aestate perit? cur aestas ipsa senescit 240
autumnoque obrepit hiemps et in orbe recurrit?);
axem scire Helices et tristem nosse cometen,
Lucifer unde micet quave Hesperus, unde Bootes,
Saturni quae stella tenax, quae Martia pugnax,
quo rapiant nautae, quo sidere lintea tendant; 245
scire vias maris et caeli praediscere cursus;
quo volet Orion, quo Sirius incubet index,
et quaecumque iacent tanto miracula mundo
non disiecta pati, nec acervo condita rerum,
sed manifesta notis certa disponere sede 250
singula, divina est animi ac iucunda voluptas.

232 pervolet *Exc.*, CSZ: pervolat G. Ellis inserts *ut*.
233 movet GHR: monet CSA: meet *Exc.*
234 suos servent G: suo errant CSZ: suo derrent *Ellis*. motus G: cura CSAR: gyris *Haupt*: gyro *Schrader*: guro (? circo) *Ellis*.
236 omitted in all MSS. except G.
237 caelo terris *Exc.*, CSZ: Panope caelo G: Phatne caelo *Matthiae*.
245 tendant *Exc.*, CSAR: pandant G.
247 volet *Exc.*, CSZ: vocet G. setius CS: secius H: serus AR: Sirius *Ald.* 1517. incubet *Exc.*, CSAR: excubet G.
249 digesta *Exc.*, CSZ: disiecta *Ellis*: congesta G.

[a] *i.e.* six zodiacal signs rise by day, six by night.

go on through the ages, and is the fabric fixed secure with everlasting chain?), to know the limit of the sun's track and the measure by which the moon's orbit falls short thereof (so that in her shorter course she flies through twelve rounds while he has a yearly path), to know what stars run in constant order and which stray irregularly from their true orbit, to know likewise the changes of the zodiac-signs and their immemorial laws [that six be sped during the night and as many return with the dawn],[a] to know why lowering Phatne[b] gives celestial warning of rain, what is the nature of the Moon-Goddess' red and her brother's pallid fire, why the year's seasons vary (why does spring, its youthful prime, die with the advent of summer? why does summer itself turn old, why does winter creep upon autumn and return in the season's cycle?), to know the axle of Helice,[c] to discern the ill-omened comet, to see on what side gleams the Morning-Star, where the Evening-Star, and whence the Bear-Keeper, and which is Saturn's steadfast star and which the warlike star of Mars, under what constellation the sailor must furl or spread his sails, to know the paths of the sea and learn betimes the courses of the heavens, whither Orion is hastening, over what land broods Sirius with warning sign; in fine, to refuse to let all the outspread marvels of this mighty universe remain unordered or buried in a mass of things, but to arrange them each clearly marked in the appointed place—all this is the mind's divine and grateful pleasure.

[b] The Manger-constellation (Φάτνη) which Aratus associates with storm. Panope, the reading in G, being a fine-weather divinity, is unsuitable here.

[c] The Great Bear.

sed prior haec hominis cura est cognoscere terram
et quae tot miranda tulit natura notare.
haec nobis magis affinis caelestibus astris.
nam quae mortali spes quaeve amentia maior 255
in Iovis errantem regno perquirere velle,
tantum opus ante pedes transire et perdere segnem.
torquemur miseri in parvis premimurque labore:
scrutamur rimas et vertimus omne profundum.
quaeritur argenti semen, nunc aurea vena. 260
torquentur flamma terrae ferroque domantur,
dum sese pretio redimant; verumque professae
tum demum vilesque tacent inopesque relictae.
noctes atque dies festinant arva coloni;
callent rure manus, glebarum expendimus usum. 265
fertilis haec segetique feracior, altera viti.
haec platanis humus, haec herbis dignissima tellus,
haec dura et melior pecori silvisque fidelis.
aridiora tenent oleae, sucosior ulmis
grata: leves cruciant animos et corpora causae 270
horrea uti saturent, tumeant et dolia musto,

[252] hominis Z (? S): dominis C: omni G.
[253] et qu(a)e nunc CSH: et quae tot *Pithou*: quaeque in ea G.
[254] magna CSZ: magis G.
[255] mortalis spes est quaeve CSH: mortali cuiquam est G.
[256] velle CSZ: divos G.
[258] premimurque *Exc.*, CSZ: terimurque G.
[263] viles taceant CSZ: tum demum humilesque iacent (*unmetrical*) G: vilesque iacent *Maehly*: vilesque tacent *Wight Duff*.
[265] expendimus usum G: expellimur usu *Exc.*, CSZ: expendimur usu *Schwartz*.
[267] platanis *Exc.*, CSZ: plantis G.

Yet this is man's more primary task—to know the earth and mark all the many wonders nature has yielded there. This is for us a task more akin than the stars of heaven. For what kind of hope is it for mortal man, what madness could be greater—that he should wish to wander and explore in Jove's domain and yet pass by the mighty fabric before his feet and lose it in his negligence? We torture ourselves wretchedly over little things: we let toil weigh us down: we peer into crannies and upturn every depth. The quest is now for a germ of silver, now for a vein of gold. Parts of the earth are tortured with flame and tamed with iron till they ransom themselves at a price[a]; and, when they have owned their secret, they are silenced[b] and abandoned to contempt and beggary. Day and night farmers hasten on the cultivation of their fields; hands grow hard with rural toil; we ponder the use of different soils. One is fertile and is more fruitful for corn, another for the vine; this is the soil for plane-trees, this the worthiest of grass crops; this other is hard and better for grazing and trusty to a tree-plantation. The drier parts are held by the olive; elms like a soil more moist. Trivial motives torture men's minds and bodies—to have their barns overflowing, their wine-casks swelling with must, and their haylofts rising

[a] In man's quest for gold and silver, regions of earth are "put to the torture" by the processes of mining and smelting until they buy themselves off by the ore they have yielded (*sese pretio redimant*).

[b] *i.e.* the rest is silence after the truth (*i.e.* where their hidden treasures lie) has been extorted from them: *tacent* gives a better contrast than *iacent*.

---

268 dura et *Exc.*: duro G: diviti CSZ.

plenaque desecto surgant faenilia campo:
sic avidi semper, qua visum est carius, itis.
  implendus sibi quisque bonis est artibus: illae
sunt animi fruges, haec rerum maxima merces: 27
scire quid occulto terrae natura coercet,
nullum fallere opus, non mutum cernere sacros
Aetnaei montis fremitus animosque furentes,
non subito pallere sono, non credere subter
caelestes migrasse minas aut Tartara rumpi, 28
nosse quid impediat ventos, quid nutriat illos,
unde repente quies et muto foedere pax sit;
cur crescant animi, penitus seu forte cavernae
introitusque ipsi servent, seu terra minutis
rara foraminibus tenues in se abstrahat auras 28
(plenius hoc etiam rigido quia vertice surgens
illinc infestis atque hinc obnoxia ventis,
undique diversas admittere cogitur auras,
et coniuratis addit concordia vires);
sive introrsus agunt nubes et nubilus Auster, 29
seu fortes flexere caput tergoque feruntur,
praecipiti deiecta sono premit unda fugatque
torpentes auras pulsataque corpora denset.

[273] avidi GCS: avidis *Matthiae*. qua visum est CSZ: quovis est G. ipsis G: istis CSZ: itis *Ellis*: sic avidi semper quaestus: est carius istis *Unger*.

[277] multos CS: multo Z: mutos *Scaliger*: multum G: mutum *Haupt*: motum *Postgate*.

[281] impediat CSZ: intendat G. illos C: ignes GH²: ignis AR.

[282] multo *codd.*: muto *Oudin* (who also suggested *inulto*): iuncto *Mencken, Vollmer*: nullo *Unger*.

[283] concrescant GCSZ: cur crescant *Scaliger, Pithou*. forte CSZ: porta G.

[284] servent GCZ: fervent S: sorbent *Sudhaus*.

[285] tenues G: neve CSZ: nivis in sese *Ellis*.

[286] surgens G: surgit CSZ.

higher, charged with the full reapings of the field. So do ye tread the path of greed where sight reveals aught more precious.

Everyone should imbue himself with noble accomplishments. They are the mind's harvest, the greatest guerdon in the world—to know what nature encloses in earth's hidden depth, to give no false report of her work, not to gaze speechless on the mystic growls and frenzied rages of the Aetnaean mount, not to blench at the sudden din, not to believe that the wrath of the gods has passed underground to a new home, or that hell is breaking its bounds; to learn what hinders winds, what nurtures them, whence their sudden calm and the silent covenant of their truce, why their furies increase, whether it chance that caverns deep down or the very inlets conserve them or that the earth, porous by reason of its minute openings, draws off into itself thin draughts of air (and this in fuller measure because Aetna, rising with its stiff peak, is exposed on this side and on that to hostile winds and of necessity admits gales all round from different quarters and their concert brings more strength to their league), or whether they are driven inwards by clouds and the cloud-laden South Wind, or whether they have gallantly encircled the summit and sweep on behind; then the water from the clouds, streaming down with headlong noise, presses on the sluggish air-currents, drives them before it, and with its buffeting condenses

---

[291] forte *codd.*: fortes *Ellis.*
[292] una CSZ: ima *Birt*: unda *Scaliger, Pithou.*
[293] torrentes *codd.*: torpentes *De Rooy, Munro, Ellis.*

nam veluti sonat ora diu Tritone canoro—
pellit opus collectus aquae victusque moveri
spiritus et longas emugit bucina voces;
carmineque irriguo magnis cortina theatris
imparibus numerosa modis canit arte regentis,
quae tenuem impellens animam subremigat unda:
haud aliter summota furens torrentibus aura
pugnat in angusto et magnum commurmurat Aetna.
credendum est etiam ventorum exsistere causas
sub terra similis harum quas cernimus extra;
ut, cum densa premant inter se corpora, turbam
elisa in vacuum fugiant et proxima secum
momine torta trahant tutaque in sede resistant.
quod si forte mihi quaedam discordia tecum est,

294 ora diu H: ore diu AR: ora duc C: hora duci *Munro*: hora deo *Maehly*: hora deis *Alzinger*: hora die *Haupt*: sonituro horam *Schwartz*: urna ciens Tritona canorum *Ellis*. tritone CH: tritona AR. canoro Z: cancro C.
304 cremant CSZ: premunt *Gronov*: premant *Baehrens*.
306 nomina CSZ: momine *Gronov*: agmina *Sudhaus*. tota CSZ: torta *Jacob*.

[a] The two similes illustrate from mechanical examples the theory of the action of water and air in Aetna. In the first example, the readings suggested give a choice among a variety of contrivances. If *ora* is read, the Siren-like horn might be on the sea-shore, or on the Tiber-bank during one of Julius Caesar's *naumachiae*, or at Lake Fucinus when the emperor Claudius exhibited a naval spectacle in A.D. 53 (Suet. *Claud.* xxi). If *duci* were a certain correction and if it were then clear that only Claudius was meant, the passage would assist (as some have tried to make it assist) in dating the poem. The reading *hora* implies a hydraulic time-machine for announcing the hour to gods or men (*deo?, deis?, duci?*). Ellis' *urna* is meant to denote a hydraulic vessel fitted to work the "Triton." The second comparison is concerned with a

their elements. For just as the shore echoes for long the tuneful Triton-horn—the machinery [a] is set in motion by a volume of water and the air which is perforce moved thereby, and then the trumpet bellows forth its prolonged blare; just as in some vast theatre a water-organ, whose musical modes harmonise through their unequal pipes, sounds its water-worked music thanks to the organist's skill, which starts a small draught of air while causing a rowing movement in the water below [b]—even so the wind, dislodged by the rushing streams, raves and struggles in its narrow space and Aetna murmurs loudly with the blast.

Besides, we must believe that beneath the earth there arise causes of winds like those we see above ground; so that, whenever closely massed particles press against each other, they are forced out into a free space and escape the crush, and by their motive energy whirl and drag what is nearest along in their course, halting only when a safe position is reached.

But perhaps you may be at variance with me in

hydraulic organ of a sort known in Rome from Cicero's time (*Tusc. Disp.* III. 18 (43), *hydrauli hortabere ut audiat voces potius quam Platonis?* *i.e.* "will you advise him to listen to the notes of a water-organ rather than to the words of Plato?"). The invention is ascribed to Ctesibius, a barber of Alexandria, *circ.* 200 B.C. Nero was almost madly interested in water-organs (Suet. *Nero* xli and liv).

[b] *i.e.* probably with a pedal. A mosaic found near Trier last century gives a representation of a water-organ (Wilmowsky, *Röm. Villa zu Nennig*, Bonn, 1864–65). There the position of the organ-player is consistent with his using his hands to play and his feet on a pedal to set the water in motion. In May 1931, a handsome hydraulic organ dating from A.D. 288 was discovered at Aquincum on the Danube, the capital of Lower Pannonia (now Alt-Ofen, part of Buda Pest).

principiis aliis credas consurgere ventos:
non dubium rupes aliquas penitusque cavernas
proruere ingenti sonitu, casuque propinquas 310
diffugere impellique animas: hinc crescere ventos:
aut umore etiam nebulas effundere largo,
ut campis agrisque solent quos alluit amnis.
vallibus exoriens caligat nubilus aer:
flumina parva ferunt auras, vis proxima vento est: 315
eminus adspirat fortes et verberat umor.
atque haec in vacuo si tanta potentia rorum est,
hoc plura efficiant infra clusique necesse est.
his agitur causis extra penitusque: coactu
exagitant ventos: pugnant in faucibus: arte 320
pugnantis suffocat iter. velut unda profundo
terque quaterque exhausta graves ubi perbibit Euros,
ingeminant fluctus et primos ultimus urget:
haud secus, adstrictus certamine, tangitur ictu
spiritus involvensque suo sibi pondere vires 325
densa per ardentes exercet corpora venas,
et, quacumque iter est, properat transitque morantem,
donec confluvio veluti siponibus actus
exsilit atque furens tota vomit igneus Aetna.

310 provehere CSH: proruere *Ald.* 1517.
312 effundere CSZ: se effundere *Baehrens.*
316 fortis CSZ: fontis V. 317 rerum CZ: rorum *Jacob.*
319 coactus C: coactu *Ellis.*
326 ardentes CSZ: artantes *Jacob.* vires CZ: venas *Ald.* 1517: fauces *Sudhaus*: gyros *Ellis.*

---

[a] 307–329. The reasoning takes the form of an answer to a possible objector who suggests that there may be causes for winds in Aetna other than those already set forth (283–306). The argument is that you must allow that rock-falls underground generate air-currents; and, just as river vapours in valleys emit air (more perceptibly in hot climates, Munro says here; *cf.* also Lucret. VI. 476 *sqq.*), so the effect of moisture (*cf.*

your belief that winds rise from other causes.[a] It is undoubted (I claim) that there are rocks and caverns far below which fall forward with enormous crash, and that their fall disperses and sets in motion air-currents hard by: hence the gathering of winds. Again, fogs with their ample vapour pour out air, as they commonly do in plains and fields watered by a river. Rising from valleys the air makes a sombre cloud: rivulets bring gusts whose force is like the force of winds. Moisture from a distance breathes on the air-currents and whips them into strength. And, if a free space lets moisture have such power, its effects must be greater in proportion when within confined limits underground. These are the causes above and below ground which are at work. By compression they rouse the winds; they strive in narrow gorges; in that close strife their channel strangles them. As when a wave, drawn up again and again from the deep, has drunk full of the East Wind's violence, the billows redouble their number and the first are pushed on by the last, in that same way the (volcanic) wind feels the impact of the struggle which compresses it, wraps its own strength within its heavy mass and impels its close-packed particles through fiery passages. Wherever a path is found, it speeds on, ignoring any wind that would stay its course, until, driven by the confluent air-stream, as by so many forcing-pumps,[b] it leaps forth and all over Aetna discharges itself in blasts of angry fire.

the clouds of 290–293) within confined caverns underground must be far more potent. Two analogies are cited—waves under strong gales and the *siphon* forcing water on burning houses.

[b] *Sipo* (*sipho*, *sifo* = σίφων) was the tube of a fire-engine used to pump up water.

quod si forte putas isdem decurrere ventos
faucibus atque isdem pulsos remeare, notandas
res oculis locus ipse dabit cogetque negare.
quamvis caeruleo siccus Iove fulgeat aether,
purpureoque rubens surgat iubar aureus ostro,
illinc obscura semper caligine nubes
pigraque defuso circum stupet umida vultu,
prospectans sublimis opus vastosque receptus.
non illam videt Aetna nec ullo intercipit aestu;
obsequitur quacumque iubet levis aura, reditque.
placantes etiam caelestia numina ture
summo cerne iugo, vel qua liberrimus Aetnae
introspectus hiat, tantarum semina rerum,
si nihil irritet flammas stupeatque profundum.
huicne igitur credis torrens ut spiritus ille
qui rupes terramque rotat, qui fulminat ignes,
cum rexit vires et praeceps flexit habenas,
praesertim ipsa suo declinia pondere, numquam

[341] (a)ethnae AR : aethna C : etna H (? ablative).
[342] inprospectus CSZ : introspectus *Schrader*.
[344] huịṇc C : huicne *Ellis* : hinc *Scaliger, Baehrens*.
[345] notat CSZ : rotat *Jacob*.
[347] declivia CZ : declinia *Ellis*. All lines after 346 are missing in S.

[a] 330–358. This passage aims at disproving the idea that the wind which in an eruption issues from the crater has been constantly entering the mountain by the same avenue. Two arguments refute the notion: (1) the cloud which hangs invariably over the summit would be displaced by any wind

But if haply you imagine that the winds run down the same passage as that by which they are expelled and return, Aetna's own region will give your eyes facts for their notice and so compel denial.[a] However brilliant the atmosphere, however rainless under the blue sky, though the dawn rise with golden beams and blush with crimson tint, yet in that quarter there is always a cloud of impenetrable gloom and of slow movement that hangs lumpishly around, moist in its showery countenance, looking forth from its height on the mountain's state[b] and its vast recesses. Aetna ignores it and never dislodges it with any discharge of heat; wherever the bidding of a light breeze sends it, the cloud obeys, but then comes back. Further, look for yourself at worshippers who on the highest spur, just where there gapes open the freest view of the mountain's interior—source of such mighty upheavals—propitiate with incense the deities of heaven, provided nothing arouses the flames and the abyss remains in stupor. Do you then accept this as proving how that rushing volcanic "spirit," the whirler of crags and soil, the darter of fires, is, when once it has controlled its powers and put a sudden check on the reins, never known to pluck asunder bodies of matter or dislodge them from their strong arch, even though by their

passing down the crater; (2) the custom of worshippers to assemble at the crater and there offer incense would be impossible, if there were powerful winds blowing into the mountain. This, then, is ocular evidence of calm against any theory that winds from without cause volcanic explosions.

[b] *opus* here is not much more than "condition." It implies the activity, actual or latent, of the mountain, its "working": *cf.* 142, 188, 219, 277, 566. An alternative sense would be "fabric," "formation" as in 257.

corpora diripiat, validoque absolverit arcu?
quod si fallor, adest species: tantusque ruinis
impetus attentos oculorum transfugit ictus, 3
nec levis adstantes igitur ferit aura movetque
sparsa liquore manus sacros ubi ventilat ignes;
verberat ora tamen pulsataque corpora nostris
incursant: adeo in tenui vim causa repellit.
non cinerem stipulamve levem, non arida sorbet 35
gramina, non tenues placidissimus excit apludas:
surgit odoratis sublimis fumus ab aris:
tanta quies illi est et pax innoxia rapti.
  sive peregrinis igitur propriisve potentes
coniurant animae causis, ille impetus ignes 36
et montis partes atra subvectat harena,
vastaque concursu trepidantia saxa fragores
ardentesque simul flammas ac fulmina rumpunt.

348 diripiant CHA: diripiat R: deripiat *Clericus.* absolveret CZ: absolverit *Scaliger.* arcu CZ: aestu *vel* actu *Wernsdorf.*
351 nec levitas tantos CZ: nec levis astantes *Ellis* (*in note*).
354 *Ellis marks a lacuna after this line.*
356 humus excita praedas C: exit humus apredas H: exit humor † ap̄ndas AR: placidissimus excit apludas *Ellis.*
357 adoratis CAR: odoratus H: odoratis *Scaliger.*

---

[a] The passage is difficult. Taking *ut* with Birt and Sudhaus as "how," we may paraphrase it: "noting the calm on Aetna's summit, you can understand how the *spiritus,* so powerful when roused, fails to displace any part of the crater (*arcu*) when quiescent." [Sudhaus renders "von dem Felsrande des Kraters," but *arcu,* if the right reading, may mean an arched cavern and not the crater-curve.] Ellis propounds a different view, suggesting that *huicne credis ut numquam diripiat* may mean "Can you believe, on the showing of this, the impossibility of the *spiritus,* when in a milder form, tearing down masses of rock?"

[b] *Cf. ventilat ignem,* Juv. III. 253: *ventilet aurum* I. 28.

[c] *Cf.* Virg. *G.* IV. 6, *in tenui labor.* The connexion of

weight they have a natural tendency to fall?[a] Still, if I am wrong, appearance supports me: and such a great downward coursing rush eludes the eager glance of the eye. And so neither are they who stand near the crater struck and moved by the light wind, when the purified hand of the priest brandishes the sacred torches;[b] yet it strikes their faces, and bodies set in motion invade our bodies: in so slight an instance there is a cause which repels force.[c] The air in its complete calm[d] draws up no cinder or light stubble, stirs no parched grass or thin bits of chaff. Straight on high rises the smoke from the incense-perfumed[e] altars: so profound is that sleep of the air, a peace guiltless of ravin.

Whether then it is through extraneous or internal causes that the winds make their puissant alliance, that volcanic rush carries up amid black sand streams of fire and pieces of the mountain: huge rocks shiver as they clash and burst into explosions together with blazing flames and lightning flashes; as when forests

thought is not easy to follow. It has just been claimed that even powerful volcanic agencies may elude notice (349–350); and the parallel is cited of the air-current made by the priest in his lustration striking the worshippers' faces without their being aware of the impact. *Corpora* = "atoms": *nostris* = "our human bodies," which suffer the impact of atoms of air unconsciously. The extremely condensed *adeo in tenui vim causa repellit* is literally "in so slight an instance a cause repels force," *i.e.* keeps it from being felt. The "slight instance" is the priestly sprinkling of water and his waving the lustral fire: "force" may be said to be "repelled," if it is not allowed free play, and the worshippers are apparently unconscious of its operation. The proper explanation of *causa* is obscure, and Ellis may be right in suspecting a lacuna after *repellit.*

[d] *i.e.* on Aetna's summit between eruptions.

[e] *adoratis,* "venerated," the reading of C, makes quite good sense.

haud aliter quam cum prono iacuere sub Austro
aut Aquilone fremunt silvae, dant bracchia nodo 365
implicitae ac serpunt iunctis incendia ramis.
nec te decipiant stolidi mendacia vulgi,
exhaustos cessare sinus, dare tempora rursus
ut rapiant vires repetantque in proelia victi.
pelle nefas animi mendacemque exue famam: 370
non est divinis tam sordida rebus egestas
nec parvas mendicat opes nec corrogat auras.
praesto sunt operae, ventorum examina, semper:
causa latet quae rumpat iter cogatque morari.
saepe premit fauces magnis exstructa ruinis 375
congeries clauditque vias luctamine ab imo,
et spisso veluti tecto sub pondere praestat
haud similes, teneros cursu, cum frigida monti
desidia est tutoque licet discedere, ventos.
post, ubi conticuere, mora velocius urgent: 380
pellunt oppositi moles ac vincula rumpunt.
quicquid in obliquum est, frangunt iter: acrior ictu
impetus exoritur; magnis operata rapinis
flamma micat, latosque ruens exundat in agros:
sic cessata diu referunt spectacula venti. 385
nunc superant quaecumque regant incendia silvae,
quae flammas alimenta vocent, quid nutriat Aetnam.
incendi poterunt illis vernacula causis
materia appositumque igni genus utile terrae.

370 animi CZ: animo *Ald.* 1517.
377 et scisso C: et spisso *Jacob.* pr(a)estat CZ: pressat *Baehrens.*
378 haud similis teneros cursu CV: haud simili strepere hos cursu *Munro*: aut simili tenet occursu *Ellis.*
380 conticuere CAR: convaluere mora, velocius *Morel.*
385 si CZ: sic *Maehly.*

[a] *Silvae*, "materials" = Greek ὕλη in the sense of "mass," "stuff." The plural here is noticeable.

have fallen beneath the swoop of the South wind or when they moan under a Northern gale, they intertwine their arms in a knot and with the union of the branches the fire creeps on. Do not let yourself be deceived by the blockish rabble's falsehood that the activity of the mountain recesses flags through loss of power, that mere time lets them capture their forces again and after subjection fetch them back into battle. Banish the disgraceful thought and spurn lying rumour. Such squalid poverty fits not things divine nor begs for mean supplies nor solicits doles of air. Ever at hand are workers, the swarming band of the winds: there is an unseen cause enough to interrupt the free passage and compel a stoppage. Often a pile heaped up with huge fallen boulders chokes the gullies: it bars the ways against the struggle below, and beneath its weight, under a massive roof as it were, shows the winds unlike their former selves, gentle in their current, while the mountain is in cold inaction and the onlooker may still depart in safety. Later, after their silent spell, they press on the swifter for the delay: they dislodge the masses of rock which they face: they burst their bonds. Whatever slants across their path, they break a way through: their fury rises fiercer for each impact. Flame glitters with widespread havoc for its work, and in its rush wells far across the country-side: so after long quiescence the winds renew their brave displays.

Now there remain to be discussed all the materials [a] which govern the conflagration, what fuels summon the flames, what is Aetna's food. There is native material capable of being kindled by these causes; also a serviceable sort of earth which fire finds

uritur adsidue calidus nunc sulphuris umor, 390
nunc spissus crebro praebetur alumine sucus.
pingue bitumen adest et quicquid comminus acris
irritat flammas: illius corporis Aetna est.
atque hanc materiam penitus discurrere, fontes
infectae crispantur aquae radice sub ipsa. 395
pars oculis manifesta iacet, quae robore dura est
ac lapis: in pingui fervent incendia suco.
quin etiam varie quaedam sine nomine saxa
toto monte liquent: illis custodia flammae
vera tenaxque data est. sed maxima causa molaris 400
illius incendi lapis est: is vindicat Aetnam.
quem si forte manu teneas ac robore cernas,
nec fervere putes, ignem nec spargere posse.
sed, simul ac ferro quaeras, respondet et ictu
scintillat dolor. hunc multis circum inice flammis 405
et patere extorquere animos atque exue robur.
fundetur ferro citius; nam mobilis illi
et metuens natura mali est, ubi cogitur igni.
sed simul atque hausit flammas, non tutior hausti
ulla domus, servans aciem duransque tenaci 410
saepta fide: tanta est illi patientia victo;

[395] eripiantur CH: eripiant AR: excipiantur *Vollmer*: crispantur *Ellis*: testantur *Maehly*: evincant tibi *Morel in supplem. novae editionis*.
[401] est si C: est sic R: est; is *Munro*.
[408] coritur C: cogitur V, *Munro*.
[411] tutum CZ: tanta *Scaliger*: bruta *Ellis*.

---

[a] The accus. and infin. construction *materiam discurrere* depends on a verb implied in *crispantur*.
[b] Springs of water at the foot of Aetna with a sulphurous or bituminous taste testify to the presence of inflammable substances in the mountain. The author proceeds (398–425) to argue that stones which liquefy, especially the lava-stone (*lapis molaris*) point to the same conclusion. Though a chief

proper to its use. At one time the hot liquid of sulphur burns continuously; at another a fluid presents itself thickened with copious alum; oily bitumen is at hand and everything that by close encounter provokes flames to violence. Of such substance is Aetna composed. And to show [a] that this fuel is scattered deep within the mountain, we find springs of tainted water rippling at its very base.[b] Some of this fuel lies obvious to the sight; in its solid part it is hard—a stone; but it contains an oily juice in which burns fire. Moreover, in divers places all over the mountain there are rocks of no specific name which liquefy. To them has been given a true and steadfast guardianship of flame. But the paramount source of that volcanic fire is the lava-stone. It above all claims Aetna for its own. If perchance you held it in your hand and tested it by its firmness, you would not think it could burn or discharge fire, but no sooner do you question it with iron than it replies, and sparks attest its pain beneath the blow. Throw it into the midst of a strong fire, and let it wrest away its proud temper: so strip it of its strength. It will fuse quicker than iron, for its nature is subject to change and afraid of hurt under pressure from fire. But once it has absorbed the flames, there is no safer home for what is absorbed; preserving its edge, it hardens with steadfast fidelity what it confines. Such is its endurance after being

cause of volcanic conflagration, the lava-stone externally does not look inflammable; if struck, however, with an iron bar, it gives off sparks, and in a powerful furnace is more quickly fusible than iron. Its great characteristic is its stubborn retention of fire: this marks it off from other substances which, once burnt out, cannot be rekindled.

vix umquam redit in vires atque evomit ignem.
totus enim denso stipatus robore carbo
per tenues admissa vias incendia nutrit
cunctanterque eadem et pigre concepta remittit. 415
nec tamen hoc uno quod montis plurima pars est,
vincit et incendi causam tenet ille: profecto
miranda est lapidis vivax animosaque virtus.
cetera materies quaecumque est fertilis igni,
ut semel accensa est, moritur nec restat in illa 420
quod repetas: tantum cinis et sine semine terra est.
hic semel atque iterum patiens ac mille perhaustis
ignibus instaurat vires, nec desinit ante
quam levis excocto defecit robore pumex
in cinerem putresque iacet dilapsus harenas. 425
cerne locis etiam: similes adsiste cavernas.
illic materiae nascentis copia maior.
sed genus hoc lapidis (certissima signa coloris)
quod nullas adiunxit opes, elanguit ignis.
dicitur insidiis flagrasse Aenaria quondam 430
nunc exstincta super, testisque Neapolin inter
et Cumas locus ex multis iam frigidus annis,
quamvis aeternum pingui scatet ubere sulphur.

413 cardo C: tardans AR: tarde H: carbo *Ellis*.
418 lapidum CZ: lapidis *De Rooy*.
425 iacet Z: iacit C. delapsus CZ: dilapsus *Scaliger*.
429 et languit CH: elanguit *Jacob*.
433 pinguescat et CH: pingui scatet *Ellis*.

---

[a] There is an apparent inconsistency between l. 412 and the statements of 418 and 422 *sqq*. The partial burning of successive eruptions (422–423) is to be contrasted with a complete burning out of the lava-stone (411–412 and 424–425); or

overpowered. Rarely does it ever go back to its old strength and belch out fire.[a] Throughout it is a carbonised block packed with a density of strength; narrow are the channels through which it receives and feeds its fires; slowly and unwillingly it releases them when collected. Yet not for this sole reason that lava forms the greatest part of the mountain does it remain triumphant and control the cause of volcanic fire. In truth the thing to marvel at is the vitality and pluck of the stone. Every other substance productive of fire dies after it has been lighted: nothing remains therein to be recovered—merely ashes and earth with not a seed of flame. But this lava-stone, submissive time and again, after absorbing a thousand fires, renews its strength and fails not till its heart is burnt out, and, now a light pumice-stone, has collapsed into cinders scattering a crumbling sand in its fall.

Judge likewise by special places; take your stand by similar volcanic hollows. These have a larger store of natural fuel. But because this species of stone—colour attests this most surely—has nowhere contributed its resources, the fire has died away. Aenaria,[b] we are told, once blazed out in sudden treachery, though to-day its summit is quenched. Another witness is the region [c] between Neapolis and Cumae, now cooled for many a year, though sulphur wells forth unceasingly in rich abundance.

it may be that 412 implies only an *immediate* return to former strength.

[b] Monte Epomeo (Latin *Epopeus*), the chief mountain of Ischia (Latin *Aenaria*) has been noted for sudden outbreaks.

[c] *locus* = Solfatara. Its character in antiquity is described by Lucretius (vi. 747–8), Strabo 246 (= V. 4. 6. *ad fin.*) and Petronius, *Satyr.* 120, line 67 *sqq.*

in mercem legitur, tanto est fecundius Aetna.
insula, cui nomen facies dedit ipsa rotunda, 43
sulphure non solum nec obesa bitumine terra est:
et lapis adiutat generandis ignibus aptus,
sed raro fumat qui vix si accenditur ardet,
in breve mortales flammas quod copia nutrit.
insula durat et a Vulcani nomine sacra, 44
pars tamen incendi maior refrixit et alto
iactatas recipit classes portuque tuetur.
quae restat minor et dives satis ubere terra est,
sed non Aetnaeo vires quae conferat illi.
atque haec ipsa tamen iam quondam exstincta fuisset,
ni furtim aggereret Siculi vicinia montis 44
materiam silvamque suam, pressove canali
huc illuc ageret ventos et pasceret ignes.
  sed melius res ipsa notis spectataque veris
occurrit signis nec temptat fallere testem. 4
nam circa latera atque imis radicibus Aetnae
candentes efflant lapides disiectaque saxa
intereunt venis, manifesto ut credere possis
pabula et ardendi causam lapidem esse molarem,
cuius defectus ieiunos colligit ignes. 45
ille ubi collegit flammas iacit et simul ictu

440 durata CZ: durat adhuc *Scaliger*: durat et a *Vollmer*.
444 Aetnaei *codd.*: Aetnaeo *Ellis*. illi CZ: igni *Haupt*.

---

[a] *Rotunda* is a translation of στρογγύλη, the Greek name represented by the modern Stromboli.
[b] Trachytic lava, not the *lapis molaris* of Aetna.
[c] In the Lipari islands Vulcano (Ἱερὰ Ἡφαίστου) is the southernmost, as Stromboli is the northernmost.
[d] or "to act the counterfeit witness."

It is gathered for merchandise, so much more plentiful is it here than on Aetna. The isle whose name comes from its own round shape [a] is land that waxes fat not merely in sulphur and bitumen; a stone [b] is found besides, fitted to beget fire, which aids eruption. But it rarely gives out smoke; if kindled, it burns with difficulty; for the supply feeds but for a little the short-lived flames. There survives too the island sanctified by Vulcan's name.[c] Most of its fire, however, has grown cold, and now the isle welcomes sea-tossed fleets and shelters them in its haven. What remains is the smaller portion—soil fairly rich in the abundance of its fuel, but not such as could match its power with that of Aetna's great supply. And yet this very island would long ago have been extinct had not its neighbour, the Sicilian mountain, always been secretly providing it with its own fuel and material, or through some sunken channel been driving the winds this way and that to feed the flames.

But better than any signs and tested by real proofs, true fact encounters us: it seeks not to deceive the watcher.[d] Round the sides and at the lowest base of Aetna rocks fume with white heat and scattered boulders cool down in their pores, enabling you to believe the evidence that the lava-stone is food and cause of the burning:[e] its failure gathers only starveling fires. When it has gathered flames, it discharges them and in the moment of

[e] *Cf.* Plin. *N.H.* xxxvi. 137, *molarem quidam pyriten vocant*: Grattius, *Cyn.* 404, *vivum lapidem.* The *lapis molaris* is appropriately called *pyrites*, "firestone" (πυρίτης) or *vivus lapis*, "the live stone," in virtue of its characteristic conservation of fire: *cf.* note on 395.

materiam accendit cogitque liquescere secum.
haud equidem mirum ⟨in⟩ facie quam cernimus extra;
si lenitur opus, res stat: magis uritur illic
sollicitatque magis vicina incendia saxum 460
certaque venturae praemittit pignora flammae.
nam simul atque movet vires turbamque minatur,
diffugit extemploque solum trahit: † ictaque ramis †. . . .
et grave sub terra murmur demonstrat et ignes.
tum pavidum fugere et sacris concedere rebus 465
par rere: e tuto speculaberis omnia collis.
nam subito effervent onerosa incendia raptis,
accensae subeunt moles truncaeque ruinae
provolvunt atque atra rotant examina harenae.
illinc incertae facies hominumque figurae: 470
pars lapidum domita, stanti pars robora pugnae
nec recipit flammas; hinc indefessus anhelat
atque aperit se hostis, decrescit spiritus illinc—
haud aliter quam cum laeto devicta tropaeo
prona iacet campis acies et castra sub ipsa. 475
tum si quis lapidum summo pertabuit igni,
asperior sopito et quaedam sordida faex est,
qualem purgato cernes desidere ferro:
verum ubi paulatim exsiluit sublata caducis

458 in *Vollmer*: *om.* CZ. facie que (*sic*) C: scate quod AR: scaterest *Ellis*.
459 restat *codd.*: res stat *Wight Duff*.
462 minatus C: minatur *Ulitius*.
463 exemploque C: extemploque Z. ictaque ramis CZ: actaque rima *Clericus*: undique rimans *Vessereau*.
466 parere CHR: par rere A. e *Scaliger*: et CZ. collis CZ: colli *ed. Ascens.* 1507.
469 atque atra *codd.*: adque astra *Ellis*. sonant *codd.*: rotant *Wight Duff*: volant *De Rooy*.
471 stanti C: stantis *Munro*.

impact kindles other fuel, forcing it to melt in a common blaze. No marvel is there in the appearance presented outside; if the action is abating, the upheaval is at a standstill. The more potent fire is in the crater: there the lava tempts more winningly all inflammable bodies within reach and sends sure forewarnings of the conflagration to come. For as soon as it stirs its forces, and threatens havoc, it flies in different directions, dragging at once the soil with it: smitten in its branches . . .[a] while the eruption is announced by a deep rumbling underground accompanied with fire. Then shall you think fit to flee in panic and yield place to the divine event. From the safety of a hill you will be able to observe all. For on a sudden the conflagration blazes out, loaded with its spoils; masses of burning matter advance; mutilated lumps of falling rock roll forth and whirl dark shoals of sand. They present vague shapes in human likeness—some of the stones suggest the defeated warrior, some a gallant host armed for a standing fight, unassailed by the flames; on one side pants the enemy unwearied and deploys his forces, on another the breath of fury wanes, even as when an army, vanquished in the victor's joyous triumph, lies prostrate on the field right to the gates of the camp. Then any stone that a surface fire has liquefied becomes, when the fire is quenched, more rugged—a sort of dirty slag like what you will see drop from iron when smelted. But when a heap has

[a] There may be a lacuna after *minatur* (462) as Munro thought, and there must be a lacuna after *ictaque ramis* (463), if that is the right reading.

---

472 hinc defensus C : hinc indefessus *Ellis*.
477 sopita es CH¹ : s. est H²AR : sopito *Maehly*.

congeries saxis, angusto vertice surgunt; 48
sic veluti in fornace lapis torretur et omnis
exustus penitus venis subit altius umor:
amissis opibus levis et sine pondere pumex
excutitur: liquor ille magis fervere magisque
fluminis in speciem mitis procedere tandem 48
incipit et pronis demittit collibus undas.
illae paulatim bis sena in milia pergunt.
quippe nihil revocat, certis nihil ignibus obstat,
nulla tenet (frustra) moles, simul omnia pugnant.
nunc silvae rupesque natant, hic terra solumque, 49
ipse adiutat opes facilesque sibi induit amnis.
quod si forte cavis cunctatus vallibus haesit,
utpote inaequales volvens perpascitur agros;
ingeminat fluctus et stantibus increpat undis,
sicut cum rapidum curvo mare † cernulat aestu, 49
ac primum tenues † undas agit, ulteriores . . .
progrediens late diffunditur et † succernens . . .
flumina consistunt ripis ac frigore durant,
paulatimque ignes coeunt ac flammea messis
exuitur facies. tum prima ut quaeque rigescit 50
effumat moles atque ipso pondere tracta
volvitur ingenti strepitu; praecepsque sonanti
cum solido inflixa est, pulsatos dissipat ignes,

486 primis Z: prunis C: pronis *Munro*.
488 curtis CH: certis *Wernsdorf*.
489 frustra moles CHA: moles, frustra s. obvia p. *Baehrens*.
490 notant CAR: natant *Baehrens*. haec tela *codd.*: nunc terra *Haupt*: hic terra *Ellis*: *perhaps* hinc . . . hinc.
491 ipsa *codd.*: ipse *Scaliger, Ellis*.
494 ingeminant CZ: ingeminat *ed. Ven.* 1475.
495 curvo CA: turbo *Vollmer*. cernulus *codd.*: cernimus *Munro*: cernulat *Jacob, Ellis*.
496 imas C: simas H: undas *Baehrens*: simans *Ellis*: rimas *Morel*: tenuis sinuans agit unda priores *Jacob*.

gradually sprung up raised from fallen rocks, they mount in a narrow-pointed pyramid. Just as a stone is calcined in a furnace and its moisture all burnt out inside and through the pores it steams on high, so the lava-stone loses its substance and is turned out a light pumice of inconsiderable weight: the lava-liquid begins to boil hotter and at last to advance more in the fashion of a gentle stream, as it lets its waves course down the slopes of the hills. By stages the waves advance some twice six miles. Nay, nothing can recall them: nothing checks these determined fires: no mass can hold them—'tis vain: all is war together. Now woodland and crag, here again earth and soil are in the flood. The lava-river itself aids their supplies and adjusts the compliant material to its own course. But if perhaps in some deep valley it lags and stops, its rolling volume browses leisurely over the fields uneven as they are. Then it redoubles its billows and chides the laggard waves; as when a violent sea plunges headforemost with curving swell; and first it urges on its feeble waves, others beyond . . . advancing, it spreads far and wide, and choosing (what to envelop). . . . The lava-streams come to a standstill inside their margins and harden as they cool; slowly the fires shrink and the appearance of a waving harvest of flame is lost. Each mass in turn, as it stiffens, emits fumes, and, dragged by its very weight, rolls on with enormous din; whenever it has crashed pell-mell into some solid substance which resounds with the impact, it spreads abroad the fires of the concussion and shines with

---

497 succernens CZ: succrescunt *Jacob*: sua certis *Schwartz*.
503 inflexa CZ: inflixa *Scaliger*.

et qua disclusa est candenti robore fulget.
emicat examen plagis, ardentia saxa 505
(scintillas procul ecce vides, procul ecce ruentes)
incolumi fervore cadunt: verum impetus ignes
Simaethi quondam ut ripas traiecerit amnis,
vix iunctas quisquam fixo dimoverit illas.
vicenos persaepe dies iacet obruta moles. 510
sed frustra certis disponere singula causis
temptamus, si firma manet tibi fabula mendax,
materiam ut credas aliam fluere igne, favillae
flumina proprietate simul concrescere, sive
commixtum lento flagrare bitumine sulphur. 515
nam posse exusto cretam quoque robore fundi
et figulos huic esse fidem, dein frigoris usu
duritiem revocare suam et constringere venas.
sed signum commune leve est atque irrita causa
quae trepidat: certo verum tibi pignore constat. 520
nam velut arguti natura est aeris, et igni
cum domitum est constans eademque et robore salvo,
utraque ut possis aeris cognoscere partem;
haud aliter lapis ille tenet seu forte madentes
effluit in flammas sive est securus ab illis 525

506 esse . . . esse CZ: ecce . . . ecce *Scaliger*. fides C: fide Z: vides *Haupt*: este pedes *Ellis*.
507 verum CZ: fert *Baehrens*. ignes *codd.*: ingens *Baehrens*, *Ellis*: igni est *Vessereau*.
509 iunctis *codd.*: uncis *Ellis*: iunctas *Vessereau*.
516 post . . . fundit CZ: posse . . . fundi *Wernsdorf*. exustam CHA: exusto *Sudhaus*.
521 ignis CZ: igni *Scaliger*.
522 constat CZ: constans *Haupt*.
523 ultraque CH: utramque AR: utraque *Munro*. portam CZ: partem *Clericus*.

white-glowing core wherever it has been opened out. A host of sparks flash forth at every blow: the glowing rocks (look, you see the flashes in the distance—look, raining down in the distance!) fall with undiminished heat. Yet, though the rush has been known to throw its fires across the banks of the river Simaethus,[a] hardly will anyone part those banks when once united by the hard-set lava. Very often for twenty days on end a mass of rock lies buried. But in vain I try to marshal each effect with its determined cause, if a lying fable remains unshaken in your mind, leading you to believe that it is a different substance which liquefies in fire, that the lava-streams harden in virtue of their cindery property, or that what burns is a mixture of sulphur and glutinous bitumen. For clay also, they assert, can fuse when its inner material is burnt out, and potters are a testimony to this: then by the process of cooling it recovers its hardness and tightens its pores. But this analogous indication is unimportant—an ineffectual reason given on hasty grounds. An unfailing token makes the truth evident to you. For as the essence of gleaming copper, both when fused with fire and when its solidity is unimpaired, remains constant and ever the same, so that in either state you may distinguish the copper portion, in no other way the lava-stone, whether dissolved into liquid flames or kept safe from them, retains and preserves

[a] The Simaethus or Symaethus in Eastern Sicily drains a considerable part of the island. The impetuosity of the lava-flood, carrying it over the bed of the river, is contrasted with the rigid immobility which marks it when solidified (507–510). The hard masses are described as lying immovable for twenty days together, blocking the river. D'Orville preferred to read *pedes* "buried twenty feet in the ground."

conservatque notas nec vultum perdidit ignis.
quin etiam externa † immotus color ipse refellit,
non odor aut levitas: putris magis ille magisque,
una operis facies eadem perque omnia terra est.
nec tamen infitior lapides ardescere certos, 530
interius furere accensos: haec propria virtus.
quin ipsis quaedam Siculi cognomina saxis
imposuere † rhytas et iam ipso nomine signant
fusilis esse notae: numquam tamen illa liquescunt,
quamvis materies foveat sucosior intus, 535
ni penitus venae fuerint commissa molari.
quod si quis lapidis miratur fusile robur,
cogitet obscuri verissima dicta libelli,
Heraclite, tui: nihil insuperabile ab igni,
omnia quo rerum natura semina iacta. 540
sed nimium hoc mirum? densissima corpora saepe
et solido vicina tamen compescimus igni.
non animos aeris flammis succumbere cernis?
lentitiem plumbi non exuit? ipsaque ferri
materies praedura tamen subvertitur igni. 545
spissaque suspensis fornacibus aurea saxa
exsudant pretium: et quaedam fortasse profundo

[527] quin etiam *codd.*: quin speciem *Ellis.* externam multis *codd.*: externa immotus *A. M. Duff.*
[531] propala CZ: propria *ed. Ven.* 1475.
[533] fridicas C: frichas AR: chytas *or* rhytas *Scaliger*: Ϝρύδας (= frydas) *Ellis* (*in notes*).
[539] gigni CZ: ab igni *Scaliger.*
[540] quae *codd.*: cui *Jacob*: quo *Scaliger.*
[544] lenitiem C: lentitiem A: lenticiem HR.

[a] The editorial *externa immotus* meets the difficulty of finding a noun to agree with *externam* (either substituted in the text for *etiam*, or understood like *materiam* or *naturam*). *Externa refellit* = "refutes the idea of alien substances," though the object of *refellere* is usually a person or such a word as *verbum*

its characteristics, and fire has not ruined its look. Moreover, the very constancy of its colour, not its smell or lightness, disproves any foreign elements.[a] The stone crumbles more and more, but its mode of working has the same look and the earth therein is unchanged throughout. I do not, however, deny that specific stones take fire and when kindled burn fiercely within. It is a quality proper to them. The Sicilians have given those very stones a name, *rhytae*, and by the title itself record that they are of a fusible character.[b] Yet although these stones have a somewhat juicy substance to preserve heat within, they never liquefy unless they have been brought deeply into touch with the pores of the lava-stone. But if anyone wonders that the core of stone can be fused, let him ponder those truest of sayings in thy mysterious book, O Heraclitus,[c] "naught is unconquerable by fire, in which all the seeds of the universe are sown." But is this too great a marvel? Bodies of thickest grain and well-nigh solid we nevertheless often subdue by fire. Do you not see how copper's sturdy spirit yields to flame? Does not fire strip away the toughness of lead? Even iron's substance, hard though it be, is yet undone by fire. Massive nuggets of gold sweat out their rich ore in vaulted furnaces; and mayhap there lie in the depths of earth undis-

or *mendacium*. *Immotus color* leads up to *una operis facies eadem* in 529; and the awkward *multis* disappears. For metrical parallel see 479.

[b] Scaliger based his suggestion of *rhytas* on ῥυτός (ῥεῖν) "flowing," "fluid," hence applicable to fusible substances.

[c] Heraclitus of Ephesus, one of the early Ionian philosophers, held that heat is the inherent principle of existence and that everything is in a perpetual flux. By the obscurity of his writings on physics he earned the name of "the dark" (σκοτεινός).

incomperta iacent similique obnoxia sorti.
nec locus ingenio est: oculi te iudice vincent.
nam lapis ille riget, praeclususque ignibus obstat, 550
si parvis torrere velis caeloque patenti.
candenti pressoque agedum fornace coerce;
nec sufferre potest nec saevum durat in hostem.
vincitur et solvit vires captusque liquescit.
quae maiora putas artem tormenta movere 555
posse manu? quae tanta putas incendia nostris
sustentare opibus quantis fornacibus Aetna
uritur, arcano numquam non fertilis igni?
sed non qui nostro fervet moderatior usu
sed caelo propior, vel quali Iuppiter ipse 560
armatus flamma est. his viribus additur ingens
spiritus, adstrictis elisus faucibus: ut cum
fabriles operae rudibus contendere massis
festinant, ignes quatiunt follesque trementes
exanimant, pressoque instigant agmine ventum. 565
haec operis forma est, sic nobilis uritur Aetna:
terra foraminibus vires trahit, urget in artum
spiritus, incendi via fit per maxima saxa.

magnificas laudes operosaque visere templa
divitiis hominum aut arces memorare vetustas 570
traducti maria et taetris per proxima fatis
currimus, atque avidi veteris mendacia famae

549 ingenium CZ: ingenio *ed. Ven.* 1475.
555 autem C: aurem AR: artem *Ellis.*
558 ac sacro C: a sacro AR: arcano *Ellis.*
565 examinant CH^{1}AR: exanimant H^2.
566 fama *codd.*: forma *Wolf.*
568 vivit *codd.*: via fit *Baehrens.*
570 sacras C: arcas *Ellis*: artes *vel* arces *Vessereau.*

covered minerals subject to similar ordinance. No place this for ingenuity: be you the judge and your eyes will triumph. The lava-stone is rigid; its surface barrier resists all fire, if you seek to burn it with small fires and in the open air. Well then, confine it in a narrow white-hot furnace—it cannot endure or stand firm against that fierce foe. It is vanquished: it relaxes its strength; in its captor's grip it melts. Now, what greater engines, think you, can skill apply with the hand, or what fires can it support with our human resources to compare with the mighty furnaces with which Aetna burns, ever the mother of secret fire? Yet her fire is not of the limited heat within our own experience, but more akin to that of heaven or the kind of flame with which Jupiter himself is armed. With these mighty forces is allied the gigantic volcanic spirit forced out of straitened jaws, as when mechanics hasten to pit their strength against masses of natural iron, they stir the fires and, expelling the wind from panting bellows, rouse the current in close array. Such is the manner of its working: so goes far-famed Aetna's burning. The earth draws in forces through her perforations; volcanic spirit compresses these into narrow space, and the path of conflagration lies through the mightiest rocks.

Over the paths of the sea, through all that borders on ghastly ways of death, we hasten to visit the stately glories of man's achievement and temples elaborate with human wealth or to rehearse the story of antique citadels. Keenly we unearth the false-

---

571 traducti CHA: tracti R. maria *De Rooy*: materia CZ. terris CZ: terras *De Rooy*: taetris *Scaliger*.

eruimus cunctasque libet percurrere gentes.
nunc iuvat Ogygiis circumdata moenia Thebis
cernere: quae fratres, ille impiger, ille canorus. . . .
condere, felicesque alieno intersumus aevo. 576
invitata piis nunc carmine saxa lyraque,
nunc gemina ex uno fumantia sacra vapore
miramur septemque duces raptumque profundo.
detinet Eurotas illic et Sparta Lycurgi 580
et sacer in bellum numerus, sua turba, trecenti.
nunc hic Cecropiae variis spectantur Athenae
carminibus gaudentque soli victrice Minerva.
excidit hic reduci quondam tibi, perfide Theseu,
candida sollicito praemittere vela parenti; 585
tu quoque Athenarum carmen, iam nobile sidus,
Erigone; sedes vestra est: Philomela canoris
evocat in silvis et tu, soror, hospita tectis

586 tam CZ: iam *Ald.* 1534.
587–8 Erigone edens questus P. canoras en volat in silvas *Maass*: Erigonae es, dequesta senem: P. canoris plorat Ityn silvis *Ellis*. evocat CZ: eiulat *Jacob*; en vocat *Munro*.

---

[a] The mythological allusions in lines 574–579 are to the miraculous building of Thebes when the stones obeyed the call of the "pious" brethren Amphion and Zethus; the never-ending hatred of Eteocles and Polynices, the sons of Oedipus, shown in the separation of even the flames on their altar; the seven champions who marched from Argos upon Thebes; the gulf in the earth which swallowed Amphiaraus.

[b] *piis*: Amphion and Zethus are called *pii*, not because they fortified Thebes, but because they avenged on Dirce her maltreatment of their mother Antiope. To furnish Thebes with walls and towers Zethus brought up the stones with his strong arms, and Amphion fitted them together by the music of his lyre.

[c] Eurotas was the river of Sparta and Lycurgus her legendary lawgiver.

hoods told by ancient legend[a] and we like to speed our course through every nation. Now 'tis our joy to see the walls which gird Ogygian Thebes, the walls reared by the brothers, the active one (Zethus) and the tuneful one (Amphion) . . . and so for a happy hour we live in a bygone age. We marvel now at the stones charmed into place by duteous sons,[b] with song and lyre, now at the sacrificial reek sundered as it rose from a single altar-steam, now at the seven chiefs and him whom the chasm snatched away. There the Eurotas and the Sparta of Lycurgus[c] arrest us and the troop consecrated to war, the Three Hundred, the band true to themselves.[d] Here again in manifold poetry is Cecropian Athens shown to us and her joy that Minerva won her soil.[e] Here once upon a day, faithless Theseus, your promise escaped your mind, to hoist, as you were nearing home, the white sail for an advance signal to your anxious father.[f] You too, Erigone, were an Athenian lay, henceforth a star of renown; Athens is the home of you and yours.[g] Philomela's call fills the groves with song and you, her sister (Procne), find a guest's

[d] The three hundred Spartans who laid down their lives fighting against the Persians in the pass at Thermopylae, 480 B.C.

[e] Athens is called "Cecropian" after her legendary king Cecrops. Athene (identified with Minerva) by her gift of the olive won the land belonging to Athens and so ousted Poseidon. The marble sculptures in the western pediment of the Parthenon recorded this rivalry.

[f] *Cf.* 21–22 *supra* for another reference to Theseus' return from Crete.

[g] *Vestra* ("of you and yours") alludes to her father Icar(i)us and the faithful hound which became Sirius. Erigone hanged herself for grief at her father's death. The theme was treated in a once celebrated poem by Eratosthenes.

acciperis, solis Tereus ferus exsulat agris.
miramur Troiae cineres et flebile victis 59
Pergamon exstinctosque suo Phrygas Hectore: parvum
conspicimus magni tumulum ducis: hic et Achilles
impiger et victus magni iacet Hectoris ultor.
quin etiam Graiae fixos tenuere tabellae
signave; nunc Paphiae rorantes arte capilli, 59
sub truce nunc parvi ludentes Colchide nati,
nunc tristes circa subiectae altaria cervae
velatusque pater, nunc gloria viva Myronis
et iam mille manus operum turbaeque morantur.

haec visenda putas terrae dubiusque marisque: 60
artificis naturae ingens opus aspice: nulla
tu tanta humanae plebis spectacula cernes,
praecipueque vigil fervens ubi Sirius ardet.
insequitur miranda tamen sua fabula montem

[595] paflae CZ: Paphiae *Ald.* 1517. parte CZ: arte *Scaliger*: patre *Haupt*: matre *Baehrens, Ellis.*
[599] turb(a)eque CHA: tabulaeque *Ellis.*
[602] cum CZ: tu *Clericus.* humanis *codd.*: humanae *Ellis.* Ph(o)ebus CZ: rebus *Ald.* 1534: plebis *Ellis* ("*ex* plebeis *quod est in Rehd.* 60").

---

[a] Procne, wife of the Thracian King Tereus, avenged his violation of her sister Philomela by slaying their son Itys or Itylus and serving his flesh to Tereus as food. Legend changed Philomela into a nightingale, Procne into a swallow.

[b] *suo Hectore sc. exstincto.* Either (1) instrumental ablat., "through their Hector," he being by his death the cause of their destruction or (2) ablat. absolute, "their Hector having been destroyed": see Munro's note (which cites Cic. *Pro Mil.* 47, *iacent suis testibus*, "they are prostrated by the evidence of their own witnesses,") and Th. Maguire's discussion, *Journal of Philology*, III. (1871), pp. 232 *sqq.*

[c] The picture meant is the Venus Anadyomene by Apelles.

welcome in the home, while cruel Tereus lives an exile in the deserted fields.[a] We wonder at Troy in ashes and her citadel bewept by the vanquished, the Phrygians' doom owing to the fall of Hector.[b] We behold the humble burial-mound of a mighty leader: and here lie vanquished alike untiring Achilles and (Paris) the avenger of heroic Hector. Moreover, Greek paintings or sculptures have held us entranced. Now the Paphian's tresses dripping (so art shows them),[c] now the little boys playing at the feet of the pitiless Colchian,[d] a sad group with a father veiled around the altar of the substituted hind,[e] now the life-like glory of Myron's art,[f] yea a thousand examples of handiwork and crowds of masterpieces make us pause.

These attractions you think you must visit—wavering between land and sea. But look upon the colossal work of the artist nature. You will behold no sights so great belonging to the human rabble—(this you will find) especially if you keep watch when the Dogstar is blazing in his heat. Yet there is a wonderful story of its own which attends the mountain: it is

The traditional treatment of the tresses survives to some extent in Botticelli's "Nascita di Venere."

[d] The Medea of Timomachus (3rd cent. B.C.), a celebrated picture in which the painter represented the mother deliberating whether she should kill her children to revenge herself on Jason.

[e] The masterpiece of Timanthes (about 400 B.C.) in which he painted the sacrifice of Iphigenia, expressing woe on the faces of the bystanders, but veiling the face of the grief-stricken father, Agamemnon. The *cerva*, according to one form of the legend, was at the last moment miraculously substituted for the victim.

[f] The bronze cow by Myron, a greatly admired work (Cic. *Verr*. IV. lx. 135).

nec minus ille pio quam sonti est nobilis igni. 605
nam quondam ruptis excanduit Aetna cavernis,
et velut eversis penitus fornacibus ingens
evecta in longum lapidis fervoribus unda,
haud aliter quam cum saevo Iove fulgurat aether
et nitidum obscura caelum caligine torquet. 610
ardebant agris segetes et mollia cultu
iugera cum dominis; silvae collesque rubebant.
vixdum castra putant hostem movisse, tremebant
et iam finitimae portas evaserat urbis.
tum vero, ut cuique est animus viresque rapinae, 615
tutari conantur opes: gemit ille sub auro,
colligit ille arma et stulta cervice reponit,
defectum raptis illum sua carmina tardant,
hic velox minimo properat sub pondere pauper,
et quod cuique fuit cari fugit ipse sub illo. 620
sed non incolumis dominum sua praeda secuta est:
cunctantes vorat ignis et undique torret avaros,
consequitur fugisse ratos et praemia captis
concremat: ac nullis parsura incendia pascunt
vel solis parsura piis. namque optima proles 625

605 quamquam sors nobilis ignis CZ: quam quo sons, n. ignist *Baehrens*: quam sonti n. ignist *Maehly*.
607 ignes CZ: ingens *Scaliger*.
608 lapidis CH: rapidis AR.
610 c(a)elum CZ: telum *Postgate*.
611 mil(l)ia CZ: mollia *Scaliger*: mitia *Heinsius*.
612 urebant C: virebant Z: ruebant *Wagler*: rubebant *Munro, Ellis*.
619 nimio CZ: minimo *Auratus, Pithou*.
623 ratis CZ: ratos *Ald*. 1517.
624 concrepat CZ: concremat *Auratus, Pithou*.
625 dees CH: piis *Ald*. 1517.

[a] The eruption was historic. Aelian, quoted in Stobaeus' *Florilegium*, 79, 38, p. 456 (Gaisford), places it in Olympiad

no less famous for a fire of goodness than for one of guilt. Once Aetna burst open its caverns and glowed white-hot[a]: as though its deep-pent furnaces were shattered, a vast wave of fire gushed forth afar upborne by the heat of the lava-stone, just as when the ether lightens under the fury of Jupiter and plagues the bright sky with murky gloom. Corn-crops in the fields and acres soft-waving under cultivation were ablaze with their lords. Forests and hills gleamed red. Scarce yet can they believe the foe has struck camp; yet they were quaking and he had already passed the gates of the neighbouring city. Then every man strives to save his goods with such courage and strength as avails him to snatch at them. One groans beneath a burden of gold; another collects his arms and piles them again about his foolish neck; another, faint under what he has seized, has his flight hindered by his poems![b] Here the poverty-stricken man hastens nimbly beneath the lightest of loads: everyone makes for safety with what he held dear upon his shoulders. But his spoil did not follow each owner safe to the end: fire devours them as they linger: it envelops the greedy ones in flame. They think they have escaped, but the fire catches them: it consumes its prisoners' booty: and the conflagration feeds itself, set on sparing none or only the dutiful. Two noble sons,

81 (= 456–453 B.C.). He gives the names of the Catanaean youths who saved their parents from the flames as Philonomos and Kallias: *cf. n.* on 629 *infra*.

[b] 616–618. The satire at the expense of those who try to save their goods at the risk of life culminates in the glance at a poet struggling under a load of his own works. There is also a satiric undertone in the picture of tourists (569–600), who are curious sightseers rather than students of nature.

Amphinomus fraterque pari sub munere fortes
cum iam vicinis streperent incendia tectis,
adspiciunt pigrumque patrem matremque senecta
eheu! defessos posuisse in limine membra.
parcite, avara manus, dulces attollere praedas: 63
illis divitiae solae materque paterque:
hanc rapient praedam. mediumque exire per ignem
ipso dante fidem properant. o maxima rerum
et merito pietas homini tutissima virtus!
erubuere pios iuvenes attingere flammae 63
et quacumque ferunt illi vestigia cedunt.
felix illa dies, illa est innoxia terra.
dextra saeva tenent laevaque incendia: fertur
ille per obliquos ignes fraterque triumphans,
tutus uterque pio sub pondere sufficit: illa 64
et circa geminos avidus sibi temperat ignis.
incolumes abeunt tandem et sua numina secum
salva ferunt. illos mirantur carmina vatum,
illos seposuit claro sub nomine Ditis,
nec sanctos iuvenes attingunt sordida fata: 64
securae cessere domus et iura piorum.

626 Amphion CH: Amphinomus AR. fontis CH: fortis (*nom. plur.*) A.
628 senemque CZ: senecta *Scaliger*: sedentem *Barth*: senentem *Baehrens*: sequentem *Ellis*.
630 manduces *corr. in* manducens C: manus dites *Ald.* 1517: manus dulces *Ellis*.
632 rapies C: raperest *Munro*: rapient *Ellis*.
638 dextera CZ. tenet CH: tenent AR. fervent HR: ferunt *corr. in* fervent C: fertur *Buecheler*.
639 fratremque CZ: fraterque *ed. Ascens.* 1507.
640 sufficit *codd.*: substitit *Baehrens*.
646 sed curae C: securae *Munro, Ellis, Vessereau*.

Amphinomus and his brother, gallantly facing an equal task, when fire now roared in homes hard by, saw how their lame father and their mother had sunk down (alas!) in the weariness of age upon the threshold.[a] Forbear, ye avaricious throng, to lift the spoils ye love! For *them* a mother and a father are the only wealth: this is the spoil they will snatch from the burning. They hasten to escape through the heart of the fire, which grants safe-conduct unasked. O sense of loving duty, greatest of all goods, justly deemed the surest salvation for man among the virtues! The flames held it shame to touch those duteous youths and retired wherever they turned their steps. Blessed is that day: guiltless is that land. Cruel burnings reign to right and left. Flames slant aside as Amphinomus rushes among them and with him his brother in triumph: both hold out safely under the burden which affection laid on them. There—round the couple—the greedy fire restrains itself. Unhurt they go free at last, taking with them their gods in safety. To them the lays of bards do homage: to them under an illustrious name has Ditis[b] allotted a place apart. No mean destiny touches the sacred youths: their lot is a dwelling free from care, and the rightful rewards of the faithful.

[a] Claudian, *Carmina Minora*, XVII (L), has an elegiac poem on the statues of the two brothers, Amphinomus and Anapius at Catina now Catania. For allusions to their *pietas cf.* Strabo, vi. 2. 3 (C. 269), who calls the second brother Anapias; Sen. *Benef.* III. 37. 2; Martial, VII. 24. 5; Sil. Ital. XIV. 197. Hyginus, *Fab.* 254, gives them different names. Their heads appear on both Sicilian and Roman coins, *e.g.* Head, *Hist. Num.* 117; *Brit. Mus. Cat.*

[b] Ditis (more commonly Dis in the nominative) is Pluto, god of the under-world.

FLORUS

INTRODUCTION

TO FLORUS

There is considerable plausibility in the arguments which have been advanced in favour of regarding three apparently different Flori, namely the historian, the rhetor and the poet as one and the same person. The acceptance of these arguments commits us to taking the correct name to have been P. Annius Florus, as the rhetor was called, and to explaining as confusions the "Julius Florus" or "Annaeus Florus" found in the MSS. of the historian.[a] We no longer possess the rhetor's dialogue discussing the problem whether Virgil was more an orator than a poet (*Vergilius orator an poeta*), but from a Brussels manuscript containing an introduction to the lost theme important facts about the author's life are recoverable.[b] He was born in Africa about 74 A.D. While at Rome in his younger days under Domitian he entered for the Capitoline competition in poetry, but owing to jealousy was denied the wreath of victory. This injustice so rankled in his heart that he left Rome for distant wanderings which ended with his settlement at Tarraco in Spain. One day in Trajan's

[a] One MS. has "L. Annei Flori."

[b] F. Ritschl, *Rhein. Mus.* I. 302; O. Jahn, *Flori epitome*, Leipzig, 1852, p. xli; edn. by K. Halm, Leipzig, 1854, p. 106; edn. by O. Rossbach, Leipzig, 1896, p. 183. See J. Wight Duff, *A Lit. Hist. of Rome in Silver Age*, p. 644.

reign a friend twitted him with his long absence from the capital, telling him that his poems had won appreciation there. By Hadrian's time he was once more in Rome, enjoying the Emperor's regard in virtue of his literary abilities and possibly because of some common links with Spain also. The intimacy was so close that it emboldened Florus to address Hadrian in a few extant trochaic lines of persiflage upon his craze for travel—*Ego nolo Caesar esse*—to which we have the imperial repartee *Ego nolo Florus esse.*[a] Happily there is more poetry in his hexameters upon spring-roses and in some at least of his trochaic tetrameters. This is the quality which has lent support to the conjecture hazarded by certain scholars, that Florus was the author of one of the most romantic poems in Latin, the *Pervigilium Veneris*. Certainly that poem would have been signally appropriate during the principate of Hadrian, who resuscitated the cult of Venus on a scale of great magnificence.[b] We cannot, however, be sure that the *Pervigilium Veneris* belongs to the second century: and a rival hypothesis claims it for the fourth century, laying stress upon its resemblance to the manner of Tiberianus.[c]

In the codex Salmasianus of the Latin *Anthologia* (Parisinus, 10318) twenty-six trochaic tetrameters appear under the superscription *Flori de qualitate vitae*. The codex Thuaneus (Parisinus 8071) has, instead of *Flori*, *Floridi*, a corruption due to a mistake in the succeeding word. Five hexameters in the codex Salmasianus also bear the heading *Flori*.

[a] Spartianus, *Hadrian*, xvi.

[b] See Introduction, p. 344, to Loeb edition of Catullus, Tibullus and *Pervigilium Veneris*.

[c] See Introduction to Tiberianus, *infra*, p. 555.

TEXTS OF FLORUS' VERSE

P. Burman. *Anthol. Lat.* Lib. II. No. 97; III. Nos. 288–291. Amsterdam, 1759.

[Burman ascribes 97, *Ego nolo* . . ., to "Julius Florus"; 288, *O quales* . . ., 289, *Aut hoc risit* . . ., and 290, *Hortus erat* . . ., to an unknown author; and 291, *Venerunt aliquando rosae* . . ., to "Florus." Baehrens and Buecheler follow these ascriptions.]

J. C. Wernsdorf. *Poetae Latini Minores*, III. pp. 483–488. Altenburg, 1782.

L. Mueller. *Rutilius Namatianus*, etc., p. 26 *sqq.* Leipzig, 1870.

E. Baehrens. *Poet. Lat. Min.*, IV. pp. 279, 346 *sqq.* Leipzig, 1882.

F. Buecheler and A. Riese. *Anthologia Latina*, I. i. pp. 119–121, and pp. 200–202. Leipzig, 1894.

RELEVANT WORKS

O. Mueller. *De P. Annio Poeta et de Pervig. Ven.* diss. Berlin, 1855.

F. Eyssenhardt. *Hadrian und Florus.* Berlin, 1882.

G. Costa. *Floro e Adriano, Bollettino di filol.* 13 (1907), p. 252.

FLORUS

I

Ego nolo Caesar esse,
ambulare per Britannos
. . . .
Scythicas pati pruinas.

II–IX. De Qualitate Vitae

II

Bacche, vitium repertor, plenus adsis vitibus,
effluas dulcem liquorem, comparandum nectari,
conditumque fac vetustum, ne malignis venulis
asperum ducat saporem, versus usum in alterum.

III

Mulier intra pectus omnis celat virus pestilens;
dulce de labris loquuntur, corde vivunt noxio.

II. De Qualitate Vitae *codd.*: Vitium *L. Mueller.*
II. 1 vitium *codd.*: vini tu *L. Mueller.*

---

[a] The numbering I–XIII follows L. Mueller's edition: No. XIV is taken from Baehrens.

[b] The Latin is given by Spartianus, *Hadrian* xvi: also Hadrian's retort (see p. 444). As the latter is in four lines, it may be assumed that Florus' third line is lost.

FLORUS

I[a]

I'VE no mind to be a Caesar,
Strolling round among the Britons,
. . . .
Victim of the Scythian hoar-frosts.[b]

II–IX. THE QUALITY OF LIFE[c]

II

Bacchus, of the vine revealer, let thy fullness aid the vine:
Send the dulcet juice aflowing which no nectar can outshine.
Grant it ever-mellowing storage lest in veins inimical
It produce a smack of roughness turned to vinegar withal.

III

Every woman in her bosom hides a poisonous pestilence:
Though the lips speak ne'er so sweetly, yet the heart contrives offence.

[c] The MS. heading for the 26 verses in II–IX is so inappropriate that Lucian Mueller by emending *vitae* into *vitium* suggested that it meant "On the Nature of Vines" and was applicable only to poem II.

IV

Sic Apollo, deinde Liber sic videtur ignifer:
ambo sunt flammis creati prosatique ex ignibus;
ambo de donis calorem, vite et radio, conferunt;
noctis hic rumpit tenebras, hic tenebras pectoris.

V

Quando ponebam novellas arbores mali et piri,
cortici summae notavi nomen ardoris mei.
nulla fit exinde finis vel quies cupidinis:
crescit arbor, gliscit ardor: animus implet litteras.

VI

Qui mali sunt non fuere matris ex alvo mali,
sed malos faciunt malorum falsa contubernia.

VII

Sperne mores transmarinos, mille habent offucia.
cive Romano per orbem nemo vivit rectius:
quippe malim unum Catonem quam trecentos
    Socratas.

V. [3] fit *codd.*: fit iam *L. Mueller*: facta *Baehrens.*

---

[a] *Cf.* Juvenal II. 83, *nemo repente fuit turpissimus*, " no one became an absolute villain in a moment," and St. Paul's quotation from Menander, I. *Cor.* xv. 33 *φθείρουσιν ἤθη χρήσθ' ὁμιλίαι κακαί*, " evil communications corrupt good manners."

IV

So Apollo and then Bacchus are fire-bringers, I opine:
Both the gods are flame-created; in their birth the fires take part.
Both confer their heat for guerdon, by the sunbeam or the vine;
One dispels the long night's darkness, one the darkness of the heart.

V

When my young pear-trees I planted, when I planted apple-trees,
On the bark the name I gravéd of the sweetheart who is mine.
Never henceforth will my passion find an end or find its ease.
As the tree grows, so my zeal glows: love-dreams through each letter shine.

VI

Rascals have not been so always—rascals from their mother's womb;
But false comradeship with rascals brings one to a rascal's doom.[a]

VII

Shun the morals brought across seas; they've a thousand trickeries.
None in all the world lives straighter than a citizen of Rome.
Why, I prize one Cato more than fifteen score like Socrates.

VIII

Tam malum est habere nummos, non habere quam
malum est;
tam malum est audere semper quam malum est
semper pudor;
tam malum est tacere multum quam malum est
multum loqui;
tam malum est foris amica quam malum est uxor
domi;
nemo non haec vera dicit, nemo non contra facit.

IX

Consules fiunt quotannis et novi proconsules;
solus aut rex aut poeta non quotannis nascitur.

X

De Rosis

Venerunt aliquando rosae. per veris amoeni
ingenium una dies ostendit spicula florum,
altera pyramidas nodo maiore tumentes,
tertia iam calathos, totum lux quarta peregit
floris opus. pereunt hodie nisi mane leguntur.

XI

De Rosis

A, quales ego mane rosas procedere vidi!
nascebantur adhuc neque erat par omnibus aetas.
prima papillatos ducebat tecta corymbos,
altera puniceos apices umbone levabat,
tertia iam totum calathi patefecerat orbem,

VIII

'Tis as bad possessing money as to live in penury;
Just as bad perpetual daring as perpetual modesty;
Just as bad is too much silence as too much loquacity;
Just as bad the girl you visit as the wife at home can be.
None can say that this is falsehood: none but does the contrary.

IX

Every year we get fresh consuls, every year proconsuls too:
Only patrons, only poets, are not born each year anew.

X

Roses in Springtime

Roses are here at last: thanks to the mood
Of lovely Spring, one day shows barbs of bloom;
A second, pyramids more largely swoln;
A third reveals the cup: four days fulfil
Their task of flowering. This day seals their doom
Unless the morning brings a gatherer.

XI

Roses

What roses have I seen come with the morn!
Scarce born they were, yet not alike in age:
One showed the breast-like buds that hid the flower,
One shot its purple crest from swelling heart,
A third had opened full its rounded cup,

quarta simul nituit nudati germine floris.
dum levat una caput dumque explicat altera nodum,
sic, dum virgineus pudor exsinuatur amictu,
ne pereant lege mane rosas: cito virgo senescit.

XII

De Rosa

Aut hoc risit Amor aut hoc de pectine traxit
purpureis Aurora comis aut sentibus haesit
Cypris et hic spinis insedit sanguis acutis.

XIII

De Rosis

Hortus erat Veneris, roseis circumdatus herbis,
gratus ager dominae, quem qui vidisset amaret.
dum puer hic passim properat decerpere flores
et velare comas, spina libavit acuta
marmoreos digitos: mox ut dolor attigit artus
sanguineamque manum, tinxit sua lumina gutta.
pervenit ad matrem frendens defertque querellas:
" unde rosae, mater, coeperunt esse nocentes?
unde tui flores pugnare latentibus armis?
bella gerunt mecum. floris color et cruor unum
est!"

A fourth was bright with well-grown naked bloom,
One rears its head, while one untwines its coil:
So, while their maiden virtue's chastely garbed,
At dawn pull roses fresh: maids soon grow old.

XII

The Rose

The rose was Cupid's smile, or from her comb
Dawn drew it forth—Dawn of the lustrous hair,
Or haply Venus was by briars caught
And on the sharp thorns this her blood remained.

XIII

Venus' Rose-Garden

Venus a garden had, rose-bushes round—
Its lady's darling plot; once seen, beloved.
Her boy, in random haste to cull the blooms
And crown his tresses, pricked with pointed thorn
His marble fingers. Soon, as pain stabbed limbs
And blood-stained hand, the tear-drop bathed his eye.
In rage he seeks his mother with his plaints:
" Whence comes it, mother, that the roses hurt?
Whence fight thy flowers with hidden arms? They war
On me: the flower's hue is the same as blood!"

XIV

De Musis

Clio saecla retro memorat sermone soluto.
Euterpae geminis loquitur cava tibia ventis.
voce Thalia cluens soccis dea comica gaudet.
Melpomene reboans tragicis fervescit iambis.
aurea Terpsichorae totam lyra personat aethram.
fila premens digitis Erato modulamina fingit.
flectitur in faciles variosque Polymnia motus.
Uranie numeris scrutatur sidera mundi.
Calliope doctis dat laurea serta poetis.

---

[a] Ascribed to Florus, Baehrens, *P.L.M.* IV. p. 279. *Cf.* the verses which have come down under the name of Cato, *P.L.M.* III. p. 243: see *infra*, p. 634.

The Muses in Hesiod (*Theog.* 36–103, 915–918) are the nine daughters of Zeus and Mnemosyne, born in Pieria. Sometimes represented as linked together in a dance, they formed an allegory of the connexion among the liberal arts. For

XIV

The Nine Muses [a]

Clio records past ages in her prose.
Euterpe's hollow reed makes double sound.
Voice-famed Thalia revelling loves the sock.
Melpomene's notes in tragic iambs seethe.
Terpsichore's golden lyre thrills all the sky.
Strings touched by Erato sweet love-songs make.
Polymnia's odes suit swift and varying moods.[b]
Urania scans the stars of heaven in verse.
Calliope crowns epic bards with bays.

their functions and varying symbols in literature and art see "Musen" in Roscher's *Ausführliches Lexikon der gr. und röm. Mythologie* and "Musai" in P. W. Realencyclopädie.

[b] *Motus* is here taken of the mind. But it is possible to take it of bodily movement ("P. sways her body in easy and in varied movements"); for a province assigned at a late period to Polymnia was that of pantomime: see p. 635, note *b*.

HADRIAN

INTRODUCTION

TO HADRIAN

P. Aelius Hadrianus, who was born in A.D. 76, reigned as Trajan's successor from 117 till his death in A.D. 138. His contradictory traits of character, summarised by Spartianus [a] in his *Vita*, indicated a restlessness of temperament which was reflected in the physical restlessness of the perpetually travelling Emperor. He took genuine interest in army organisation, in agricultural prospects, in building schemes, and (as shown during his visit to Britain, where *Pons Aelii* [b] commemorated his name) in the establishment of frontier-lines. Prose and verse attracted his dilettante tastes: in Latin he felt a preference for archaic writers—for Ennius rather than Virgil, for Cato rather than Cicero, and for Coelius Antipater rather than Sallust: towards Hellenic thought and literature he was so much drawn that his courtiers secretly nicknamed him "Graeculus." Inscriptions have preserved fragments of his military addresses, and at one time collections of his speeches were in existence. His autobiographic books, which whether from modesty or another motive he caused to be published under the names of his literary freedmen, became the direct or indirect [c] source of much in

[a] *Hadr*. xiv. [b] at Newcastle-upon-Tyne.

[c] J. Dürr, *Die Reisen d. Kaisers Hadrian*, 1881; and J. Plew, *Quellenuntersuchungen zur Gesch. d. Kaisers H.*, 890.

the life by Spartianus. A lost miscellany of his appeared under the forbidding title of *Catachannae*,[a] and he dabbled in both Greek and Latin poetry: most things by starts and nothing long, he was an epitome of contemporary culture. Possessed of an excellent memory, readiness in speech, and considerable humour, he loved to engage in discussions with the professors of the day. Sometimes he deferred to them, sometimes browbeat them; yet though he was a tormenting catechiser, he conferred generous benefactions upon teachers. Moreover, he established a library at his spacious villa whose ruins still impress the tourist under the slopes of Tivoli: he had another library at Antium, and a third at his famous academy in Rome, the Athenaeum.

The mediocrity of most of the surviving verse ascribed to him reconciles us to the rejection of the uncertain pieces. When the poet Florus took the risk of chaffing his imperial majesty on his mania for travelling (*ego nolo Caesar esse*),[b] he incurred nothing worse than the retort in the quatrain beginning *Ego nolo Florus esse*. Spartianus[c] is our authority for the simple lines of death-bed farewell

[a] Spartianus, *Hadrian* xvi, mentions this lost work as being in the manner of Antimachus, *Catac(h)annas* (in different MSS. *catacannos, catacrianos, catacaymos*), *libros obscurissimos Antimachum imitando scripsit*: perhaps Hadrian aped the learning of the Greek epic poet until he became obscure. *Catachanna*, in Fronto (ed. Naber, p. 35 and p. 155) was applied to a fruit-tree inoculated with alien buds (resembling the extraordinarily engrafted tree of Pliny *N.H.* XVII. 120) and to a style blended of elements from Cato and Seneca. Unger, *Jahrb. Phil.* 119 (1879), p. 493, connected it with καταχήνη, "derision", and it is therefore defined in *Thesaurus Ling. Lat.* III col. 586, as "res risu digna."

[b] Spartianus, *Hadr.* xvi.

[c] *Ibid.* xxv.

to his soul, where genuine feeling, echoed in tender diminutives, has bequeathed an immortal challenge to translators in many languages.[a] The lines purporting to have been inscribed on the grave of the Emperor's favourite hunting-steed Borysthenes have been suspected. That an inscription was written is clear from Dio Cassius.[b] It is true that he does not say whether it was in Latin or Greek; but, on the whole, it seems fair to accept the testimony of Pithoeus that he found the Latin lines in an ancient manuscript.

EDITIONS

P. Burman. *Anthologia Veterum Lat. Epigram. et Poem.* Vol. I. Lib. II, Nos. 96, 98; Vol. II. Lib. IV, No. 399. Amsterdam, 1759–73.

L. Mueller. In a section *De Poetis Saeculi Urbis Conditae X* which is appended to his edition of Namatianus. Leipzig, 1870. [L. Mueller accepts as genuine only "ego nolo Florus esse . . .," "animula vagula . . ." and the verse "lascivus versu, mente pudicus eras," ten lines in all.]

E. Baehrens. *P.L.M.* Vol. IV. pp. 111 *sqq.* Leipzig, 1882. [Baehrens prints five poems ascribed to Hadrian, of which only that on Borysthenes has been included in the present edition.]

F. Buecheler and A. Riese. *Anthologia Latina*, I. i. pp. 306–7, Leipzig, 1894. I. ii. p. 132, Leipzig, 1906. [The "Hadrianic" poems in the above

[a] *Translations . . . of Dying Hadrian's Address to his Soul*, collected by D. Johnston, Bath, 1876.
[b] lxix. 10.

collection are identical with three in Baehrens: as their authenticity is questionable, they are not included in the present edition.]

RELEVANT WORKS

F. Gregorovius. *Der Kaiser Hadrian*, ed. 2. Stuttgart, 1884 (Eng. tr., London, 1898).

J. Dürr. *Die Reisen des Kaisers Hadrian.* Vienna, 1881.

S. Dehner. *Hadriani Reliquiae*, particula I. Diss. Bonn, 1883. (For *adlocutiones* to the army.)

J. Plew. *Quellenuntersuchungen zur Geschichte des Kaisers Hadrian* (pp. 11–53 on the *Vita* by Spartianus). Strassburg, 1890.

W. Weber. *Untersuchungen zur Gesch. d. K. Hadrian.* Leipzig, 1907.

B. Henderson. *Life and Principate of Hadrian.* London, 1923 ("Literary Activities," pp. 240 *sqq.*).

J. Wight Duff. *A Literary Hist. of Rome in the Silver Age.* London, 1927. (Sketch of Literature in the reign of Hadrian, pp. 628–649.)

HADRIAN

I

Ego nolo Florus esse,
ambulare per tabernas,
latitare per popinas,
culices pati rotundos.

II

Lascivus versu, mente pudicus eras.

III

Animula vagula blandula,
hospes comesque corporis,
quae nunc abibis in loca,
pallidula, rigida, nudula,
nec ut soles dabis iocos?

---

[a] Spartianus, *Hadr.* xvi : see Florus' lines, p. 426.

HADRIAN

I

Retort to Florus [a]

I've no mind to be a Florus
Strolling round among the drink-shops,
Skulking round among the cook-shops,
Victim of fat-gorged mosquitoes.

II

On a Poet-friend

Your lines were wanton but your heart was clean.[b]

III

Hadrian's Dying Farewell to his Soul

Dear fleeting sweeting, little soul,
My body's comrade and its guest,
What region now must be thy goal,
Poor little wan, numb, naked soul,
Unable, as of old, to jest?

[b] Apuleius, *Apolog.* xi, cites the Latin as from Hadrian's own pen to honour the tomb of his friend Voconius.

IV

Borysthenes Alanus,
Caesareus veredus,
per aequor et paludes
et tumulos Etruscos
volare qui solebat,
Pannonicos nec ullus
apros eum insequentem
dente aper albicanti
ausus fuit nocere:
sparsit ab ore caudam
vel extimam saliva,
ut solet evenire.
sed integer iuventa
inviolatus artus
die sua peremptus
hic situs est in agro.

IV. [4] et ruscos *Masdeus*: et ocres *Baehrens*.
[6–11] Pannonicos in apros (nec ullus insequentem dente aper albicanti ausus fuit notare) sparsit ab ore caldam vel extimam salivam *Baehrens*: Pannonicos nec ullus † apros insequentem *cod.*: apros eum insequentem *Scriverius*.
[10–11] caudam *cod.*: caldam *Casaubon*. extimam salivam *cod.*: extima saliva *Scriverius*. *Hos versus transposuit Riese*.

IV

On his Favourite Hunting-horse

Borysthenes the Alan [a]
Was mighty Caesar's steed:
O'er marshland and o'er level,
O'er Tuscan hills, with speed
He used to fly, and never
Could any rushing boar
Amid Pannonian boar-hunt
Make bold his flank to gore [b]
With sharp tusk whitely gleaming:
The foam from off his lips,
As oft may chance, would sprinkle
His tail e'en to the tips.
But he in youthful vigour,
His limbs unsapped by toil,
On his own day extinguished,
Here lies beneath the soil.

[a] Alanus, belonging to the Ἀλανοί, warlike Scythians on the Tanais and Palus Maeotis.

[b] *nocere* governing the accusative is one of the suspicious points in these lines. Baehrens emends to *notare*.

IV

[illegible]

Borysthenes the Alan

O'er Tuscan hills, [illegible]

Make bold his [illegible][b]

His tail e'en to the tip.

His limbs unstripp'd by toil,

NEMESIANUS

INTRODUCTION

TO NEMESIANUS

Towards the end of the third century A.D., M. Aurelius Olympius Nemesianus wrote bucolic and didactic poetry. He has already been mentioned in the introductions to Calpurnius Siculus and Grattius. His four eclogues for long passed under Calpurnius' name, and of his hexameter poem on the chase 325 verses have survived. He belonged to Carthage, as his designation *Carthaginiensis* in MSS. implies; and, when he says of the Spanish people *gens ampla iacet trans ardua Calpes culmina* (*Cyn.* 251–252), his attitude is that of an African author. It is recorded [a] that he won fame in poetic contests and in several kinds of literature. A love for the open air fitted him to attempt pastoral poetry, and it is in keeping with this that at the outset of his didactic poem he should echo the almost conventional renunciation of mythology to be found in Virgil, Martial and Juvenal, and should disdain it as something hackneyed, preferring to "roam the glades, the green tracts and open plains." [b] But he contemplates a more epic task when, in addressing Numerianus and Carinus, the brother emperors who were the sons of Carus, he announces his intention [c] to compose a narrative of their triumphant exploits. Of the two, Numerianus

[a] Vopiscus, *Carus, Numerianus et Carinus*, xi.
[b] *Cyn.* 48–49. [c] *Cyn.* 63–78.

was at least a good speaker and had himself entered the field of poetry. The *Cynegetica* may be assigned to the period which elapsed between the death of Carus in 283 A.D. and that of Numerianus in 284; and, if we decide that in *Cynegetica* 58–62 Nemesianus is referring to his eclogues as lighter performances than his ambitious literary voyage into didactic poetry, then we may date his pastorals as earlier.

The four pastoral poems, traditionally coupled with the seven by Calpurnius, are now by general consent separated from them. In the first, Tityrus declines on the ground of age Timetas' invitation to show his poetic skill, but instead prevails on him to repeat a song inscribed by Timetas on the bark of a tree. This takes the form of a eulogy on the dead Meliboeus, who is introduced as a sort of analogue to the Meliboeus honoured by Calpurnius as his patron. But the real cue is taken from the praises of Daphnis in Virgil's fifth eclogue. Nemesianus' second eclogue, in which two shepherd lads complain that their sweetheart Donace is shut up at home by her parents, has drawn elements from Calpurnius' second and third poems. Nemesianus' third eclogue introduces Pan surprised by three rustics, who, after trying his pipe in vain, are entertained by Pan's own minstrelsy in praise of Bacchus. This eclogue is modelled on Virgil's sixth, where Silenus, caught asleep, had to pay the forfeit of a song. In the last eclogue, attractive for its glimpses of country scenes, Lycidas and Mopsus deplore the pains of unreturned affection. This is the one pastoral in which Nemesianus employs the prettily recurrent burden or refrain of the Theocritean tradition which Virgil followed in his *Pharmaceutria* or eighth eclogue. Here, then, the Virgilian influence acts directly on him; for the refrain is not one of Calpurnius' devices.

In the incomplete *Cynegetica* of 325 hexameters the first 102 lines are introductory: the remainder handles needful preliminaries to the chase rather than the chase itself—first hunting-dogs, their rearing, feeding, training, diseases and breeds; then horses, their qualities, breeds and maintenance; finally implements such as nets and snares. It will be noted that the order here is not the same as in Grattius.[a] Though Grattius was more expert in hunting than the Carthaginian poet was, it may be felt to be an advantage for Nemesianus that he enters less into details, and, if not so concentrated on imparting instruction as Grattius was, for this very reason has more chance of giving pleasure to a reader.

The diction and the metre of Nemesianus benefit undoubtedly in standard from the conscious imitation of Virgil as a model. Among the more noticeable metrical points, some of them due to his late period, are the shortened *-o* in *devotiŏ* (*Cyn.* 83) and *exercetŏ* (*Cyn.* 187),[b] the single occurrence of hiatus *catuli huc* (*Cyn.* 143) and the close of a hexameter in *fervida zonae* (*Cyn.* 147). Elision is not overdone: some 52 elisions (very many of them in *-que* or *atque*) occur in the 325 lines of the *Cynegetica.*[c]

[a] It has been pointed out in the Introduction to Grattius that according to some he did, according to others he did not, influence Nemesianus.

[b] *Cf.* such shortenings in Nemesianus' eclogues as *exspectŏ* (ii. 26), *coniungŏ* (iii. 14), *mulcendŏ* (i. 53), *laudandŏ* (ii. 80).

[c] Keene counts 39 elisions in the four eclogues, *i.e.* in 319 lines. Elision is much less frequent in Calpurnius.

There are in it a few rare words such as *inocciduus* (105) and *cibatus* (160); but in the main the diction is classical. And, in respect of both language and metre, broadly similar features characterise the pastoral and the didactic poetry of Nemesianus.

EDITIONS

Eclogues

For the chief editions and relative literature see the works given under Calpurnius Siculus, pp. 214–215.

E. Baehrens' text: *P.L.M.* III. pp. 176–190.
H. Schenkl's text is given in Postgate's *Corp. Poet. Lat.*, 1905, II. pp. 565–568.

Cynegetica

For editions, which usually combine Nemesianus with Grattius, see the list given under Grattius, pp. 146–147.

E. Baehrens' text: *P.L.M.* III. pp. 190–202.
J. P. Postgate's text is given in *Corp. Poet. Lat.*, II. 1905, pp. 569–571.
D. Martin. *Cynegetica of Nemesianus* (with comment.). Cornell Univ., U.S.A., 1917.

RELEVANT WORKS

M. Fiegl. *Des Grattius Faliskus Cynegetica: seine Vorgänger u. seine Nachfolger.* [Holds that Nemesianus borrowed from Grattius: P. J. Enk in his ed. of Grattius and in *Mnemos.* 45 (1917) supports this: so does F. Muller in *Mnemos.* 46 (1918). G. Curcio in his ed. of Grattius opposes the view.]

P. Monceaux. *Les Africains : Étude sur la littérature latine d'Afrique.* Paris, 1894.

SIGLA

For the *Eclogues* see the Sigla for Calpurnius Siculus, pp. 216–217.

For the *Cynegetica* :

A = Parisinus 7561, saec. x.

[B = Parisinus 4839, saec. x.]

This codex, disfigured by many worthless readings, was collated by Baehrens out of respect for its age: it is ignored by Postgate in *C.P.L.* and its readings are not recorded in this edition.

C (Baehrens) = σ (Postgate) Vindobonensis 3261, saec. xvi.

This codex contains Nemesianus after Ovid's *Halieutica* and before Grattius' *Cynegetica.* σ denotes that it was written by Sannazarius, as shown by H. Schenkl, *Supplementband der Jahrbücher für klass. Philol.* xxiv, 1898, pp. 387–480.

NEMESIANI CARMINA

ECLOGAE I

TIMETAS : TITYRUS

Tim. Dum fiscella tibi fluviali, Tityre, iunco
texitur et raucis immunia rura cicadis,
incipe, si quod habes gracili sub harundine carmen
compositum. nam te calamos inflare labello
Pan docuit versuque bonus tibi favit Apollo.
incipe, dum salices haedi, dum gramina vaccae
detondent, viridique greges permittere campo
dum ros et primi suadet clementia solis.

Tit. hos annos canamque comam, vicine Timeta,
tu iuvenis carusque deis in carmina cogis? 1
diximus et calamis versus cantavimus olim,
dum secura hilares aetas ludebat amores.
nunc album caput et veneres tepuere sub annis,
iam mea ruricolae dependet fistula Fauno.
te nunc rura sonant; nuper nam carmine victor 1
risisti calamos et dissona flamina Mopsi

11 et calamis versus V *nonnulli* : et calamis et versu NGA : et calamis et versum aptavimus *Baehrens.*

---

[a] The hybrid alternative title "Epiphunus" (ἐπὶ and *funus*) refers to the obituary lament on Meliboeus.

NEMESIANUS

ECLOGUE I

TIMETAS : TITYRUS [a]

Tim. While, Tityrus, you are weaving a basket with river rushes, and while the country-side is free from the harsh-toned grasshoppers,[b] strike up, if you've got any song set to the slender reed-pipe. Pan has taught your lips to blow the reeds and a kind Apollo has given you the grace of verse. Strike up, while the kids crop the willows and the cows the grass, while the dew and the mildness of the morning sun urge you to let your flocks into the green meadow-land.

Tit. Neighbour Timetas, do you constrain these years of mine and hoary hair to sing, you a young man beloved of the gods? Time was when I found words; time was when I sang verses to the reeds, so long as my care-free youth uttered the merry lays of love. Now my head is white and passion has cooled beneath the years. Already hangs my pipe devoted to the country-haunting Faunus. With your fame the country now resounds. Victor in song of late, when I was judge, you mocked the pipes of Mopsus

[b] It is morning and the cicalas are not yet noisy.

iudice me. mecum senior Meliboeus utrumque
audierat laudesque tuas sublime ferebat;
quem nunc emeritae permensum tempora vitae
secreti pars orbis habet mundusque piorum. 20
quare age, si qua tibi Meliboei gratia vivit,
dicat honoratos praedulcis tibia manes.

Tim. et parere decet iussis et grata iubentur.
namque fuit dignus senior, quem carmine Phoebus, 24
Pan calamis, fidibus Linus aut Oeagrius Orpheus
concinerent totque acta viri laudesque sonarent.
sed quia tu nostrae laudem deposcis avenae,
accipe quae super haec cerasus, quam cernis ad amnem,
continet, inciso servans mea carmina libro.

Tit. dic age; sed nobis ne vento garrula pinus 30
obstrepat, has ulmos potius fagosque petamus.

Tim. hic cantare libet; virides nam subicit herbas
mollis ager lateque tacet nemus omne: quieti
adspice ut ecce procul decerpant gramina tauri.

omniparens aether et rerum causa, liquores, 35
corporis et genetrix tellus, vitalis et aer,
accipite hos cantus atque haec nostro Meliboeo
mittite, si sentire datur post fata quietis.
nam si sublimes animae caelestia templa
sidereasque colunt sedes mundoque fruuntur, 40
tu nostros adverte modos, quos ipse benigno

[37] hos cantus N: hos calamos V, *Baehrens.*

and his discordant blasts. With me the aged Meliboeus had heard you both, and he extolled your merits on high. He has fulfilled the span of life's campaign, and dwells now in a part of that secluded sphere, the heaven of the blest. Wherefore, come, if you have a living gratitude to Meliboeus, let the dulcet strains of your flute tell of his glorified spirit.

Tim. 'Tis right to obey your commands, and your commands are pleasing. The old man deserved that the poetry of Phoebus, the reeds of Pan, and the lyre of Linus or of Orpheus, son of Oeagrus, should join in his praises and should extol all the glorious deeds of the hero. But since you ask but the praise my pipe can give, hear now what the cherry-tree you see beside the river keeps upon this theme; it preserves my lay in the carving on its bark.

Tit. Come, speak: but lest the pine, made garrulous by the wind, trouble us with its noise, let us seek rather these elms and beeches.

Tim. Here 'tis my pleasure to sing: for underneath us the soft fields spread their carpeting of green sward, and far and wide all the grove is still. Look! see in the distance how the bulls are quietly browsing in the grass.

Ether, parent of all; water, primal cause of things; and earth, mother of body; and life-giving air! accept ye these strains; waft these words to our loved Meliboeus, if those at rest are permitted to have feeling after death. For if souls sublime dwell in the celestial precincts and the starry abodes, if the heavens are their lot, do thou, Meliboeus, give ear to

pectore fovisti, quos tu, Meliboee, probasti.
longa tibi cunctisque diu spectata senectus
felicesque anni nostrique novissimus aevi
circulus innocuae clauserunt tempora vitae. 45
nec minus hinc nobis gemitus lacrimaeque fuere
quam si florentes mors invida carperet annos;
nec tenuit tales communis causa querellas.
"heu, Meliboee, iaces mortali frigore segnis
lege hominum, caelo dignus canente senecta 50
concilioque deum. plenum tibi ponderis aequi
pectus erat. tu ruricolum discernere lites
adsueras, varias patiens mulcendo querellas.
sub te iuris amor, sub te reverentia iusti
floruit, ambiguos signavit terminus agros. 55
blanda tibi vultu gravitas et mite serena
fronte supercilium, sed pectus mitius ore.
tu calamos aptare labris et iungere cera
hortatus duras docuisti fallere curas;
nec segnem passus nobis marcere iuventam 60
saepe dabas meritae non vilia praemia Musae.

[47] pelleret V: carperet NGA: velleret *Glaeser*: tolleret *Heinsius*: perderet *Burman*.
[49] mortali NG: letali V, *Baehrens*.
[50] canente *codd.*: callente *Baehrens*.
[53] patiens *codd.*: pacans *Maehly*, *Baehrens*, *H. Schenkl*, *Giarratano*: sapiens *Burman*.
[54] ruris N²GV: iuris N¹, *Martellius*. iusti V, N (*in margine*): iuris G (*corr. ex* ruris), N (*corr. ex* viris).

my lays, which your own kind heart cherished and your judgement approved. An advanced old age, long esteemed by all, and happy years and the final cycle in our human span closed the period of your life which injured none. Neither did this make our tears and lamentations less sore than if churlish death had plucked the years of your prime: nor did the common cause[a] check dirges such as these: "Ah, Meliboeus, in that chill which awaits all men you lie strengthless, obeying the law of all flesh, worthy though you are of heaven in your hoary age and worthy of the council of the gods. Your heart was full of firmness fairly balanced. With patient ear and soothing word for diverse plaints, you were wont to judge the disputes of the peasants. Under your guidance flourished a love of law and a respect for justice; disputed land was marked with a boundary line. You had a courteous dignity in your countenance and kindly brow with an unruffled forehead; but still kindlier than your face was your heart. You urged me to adapt the reed-pipe to my lips and to fashion it with wax, and so taught me to beguile oppressive cares. You would not suffer my youth to languish in idleness; guerdons of no mean price you often gave to my Muse if she quitted herself well. Often

[a] *i.e.* that all men are mortal: *cf. Hamlet* I. ii:
"Thou know'st 'tis common; all that lives must die,
Passing through nature to eternity";
Tennyson, *In Memoriam*, vi:
"Loss is common to the race—
And common is the commonplace."

saepe etiam senior, ne nos cantare pigeret,
laetus Phoebea dixisti carmen avena.
felix o Meliboee, vale! tibi frondis odorae
munera dat lauros carpens ruralis Apollo;
dant Fauni, quod quisque valet, de vite racemos,
de messi culmos omnique ex arbore fruges;
dat grandaeva Pales spumantia cymbia lacte,
mella ferunt Nymphae, pictas dat Flora coronas:
manibus hic supremus honos. dant carmina Musae,
carmina dant Musae, nos et modulamur avena:
silvestris te nunc platanus, Meliboee, susurrat,
te pinus; reboat te quicquid carminis Echo
respondet silvae; te nostra armenta loquuntur.
namque prius siccis phocae pascentur in arvis
hirsutusque freto vivet leo, dulcia mella
sudabunt taxi, confusis legibus anni
messem tristis hiemps, aestas tractabit olivam,
ante dabit flores autumnus, ver dabit uvas,
quam taceat, Meliboee, tuas mea fistula laudes."

Tit. perge, puer, coeptumque tibi ne desere carmen.
nam sic dulce sonas, ut te placatus Apollo
provehat et felix dominam perducat in urbem.
iamque hic in silvis praesens tibi fama benignum
stravit iter, rumpens livoris nubila pennis.

[67] messi *Maehly*: messe NGA: campo V: messo *Burman.*
[73–74] reboant . . . silvae (*nom. plur.*) *Baehrens.*
[74] armenta *codd.*: arbusta *Haupt, Baehrens.*
[76] hirsutusque V *nonnulli*: vestitusque NG V *plerique*: insuetusque *Heinsius*: villosusque *C. Schenkl.*
[78] tractabit GV: tractavit N: iactabit *Burman*: praestabit *Haupt, Baehrens.*

too, lest singing might irk us, you sang joyfully despite your years to a flute inspired by Phoebus. Farewell, blessed Meliboeus; Apollo of the country-side plucks the laurel and offers you gifts of fragrant foliage. The Fauns offer, each according to his power, grape-clusters from the vine, harvest-stalks from the field, and fruits from every tree. Time-honoured Pales offers bowls foaming with milk; the Nymphs bring honey; Flora offers chaplets of varied hue. Such is the last tribute to the departed. Songs the Muses offer: the Muses offer song: and we play your praises on the flute. Your name, Meliboeus, is in the whisper of the forest plane-tree and the pine: every tuneful answer that echo makes to the woodland resounds your name. 'Tis you our herds have upon their lips. For first will seals browse in the dry meadow, the shaggy lion live in the sea, and yew-trees drip sweet honey; first will the year confound its laws and winter's gloom control the harvest and summer the olive-crop; autumn will yield blossoms, spring will yield grapes, ere your praises, Meliboeus, are hushed upon my flute."

Tit. Forward, my boy, leave not off the music you have begun. Your melody is so sweet that a favourable Apollo bears you onward and is your auspicious guide into the queen of cities.[a] For propitious fame has here in the woods made smooth a kindly path for you, her pinions piercing the clouds of malice.

[a] *i.e.* the imperial capital, Rome: *cf.* II. 84.

sed iam sol demittit equos de culmine mundi,
flumineos suadens gregibus praebere liquores.

II

Idas : Alcon

Formosam Donacen puer Idas et puer Alcon
ardebant rudibusque annis incensus uterque
in Donaces venerem furiosa mente ruebant.
hanc, cum vicini flores in vallibus horti
carperet et molli gremium compleret acantho,
invasere simul venerisque imbutus uterque
tum primum dulci carpebant gaudia furto.
hinc amor et pueris iam non puerilia vota:
quis anni ter quinque† hiemes et cura iuventae.
sed postquam Donacen duri clausere parentes, 10
quod non tam tenui filo de voce sonaret
sollicitumque foret pinguis sonus, improba cervix
suffususque rubor crebro venaeque tumentes,
tum vero ardentes flammati pectoris aestus
carminibus dulcique parant relevare querella; 15
ambo aevo cantuque pares nec dispare forma,
ambo genas leves, intonsi crinibus ambo.
atque haec sub platano maesti solatia casus
alternant, Idas calamis et versibus Alcon.

[4] callibus *G. Hermann.*

[6] venerisque H V *nonnulli*: venerique V *nonnulli*: veneris NG. imbutus *codd.*: immitis *ed. Ald.* 1534.

[9] anni *codd.*: actae *Heinsius*: aevi *Hartel.* hiemes et cura iuventae *codd. plerique*: hiemes et cruda iuventa *Haupt*: et mens et cura iuventae *Summers*: increscit cura iuvencae *Baehrens*: *alii alia.*

[18] haec sub *Glaeser*: hic sub NG: hi sub AH, *Baehrens*: sub hac V: hinc sub *H. Schenkl.*

But now the sun is driving his steeds down from the arch of heaven and prompting us to give our flocks the river waters.

ECLOGUE II

IDAS : ALCON

Young Idas and young Alcon had a burning passion for the fair Donace; both, ablaze in their inexperienced years, rushed with frenzied spirit into their love for Donace. Her they assailed together, when she was gathering flowers in the neighbouring garden vales and filling her lap with soft acanthus. Then first initiated, they both snatched the joys of Venus by a sweet robbery. Hence came love,[a] and the boys felt longings beyond their boyish age. Their years were only fifteen winters, yet they had the pangs of early manhood. But after her stern parents had imprisoned Donace, because her voice had lost its fine music, and its thickened sound caused anxious thought, because her neck grew coarse, and spreading blushes came and went and her veins showed larger,[b] then truly the youths made ready to relieve the burning heat of a love-enflamed heart with the sweet plaint of their minstrelsy—both of them equal in age and song, of well-matched comeliness, both smooth in cheek, both of unshorn locks. And beneath a plane-tree—Idas on the flute followed by Alcon in his verse—they poured out this solace for their sad plight.

[a] *Cf.* Grattius, *Cyneget.* 283–284.
[b] The reasons given are traditional signs of lost maidenhood.

I. "quae colitis silvas, Dryades, quaeque antra, Napaeae, 2
et quae marmoreo pede, Naiades, uda secatis
litora purpureosque alitis per gramina flores:
dicite, quo Donacen prato, qua forte sub umbra
inveniam, roseis stringentem lilia palmis?
nam mihi iam trini perierunt ordine soles, 2
ex quo consueto Donacen exspecto sub antro.
interea, tamquam nostri solamen amoris
hoc foret aut nostros posset medicare furores,
nulla meae trinis tetigerunt gramina vaccae
luciferis, nullo libarunt amne liquores; 3
siccaque fetarum lambentes ubera matrum
stant vituli et teneris mugitibus aera complent.
ipse ego nec iunco molli nec vimine lento
perfeci calathos cogendi lactis in usus. 3
quid tibi, quae nosti, referam? scis mille iuvencas
esse mihi, nosti numquam mea mulctra vacare.
ille ego sum, Donace, cui dulcia saepe dedisti
oscula nec medios dubitasti rumpere cantus
atque inter calamos errantia labra petisti.
heu, heu! nulla meae tangit te cura salutis? 4
pallidior buxo violaeque simillimus erro.
omnes ecce cibos et nostri pocula Bacchi
horreo nec placido memini concedere somno.
te sine, vae misero, mihi lilia fusca videntur

[32] aera NH V *plerique*: ethera G: aethera *Ulitius, Baehrens.*
[44] fusca NGA: nigra V, *Baehrens.*

---

[a] Line 35 closely follows Calpurnius, *Ecl.* III. 65.
[b] Lines 37–39 are copied from Calpurnius, *Ecl.* III. 55 *sqq.*

Idas. "Ye Dryads who haunt the woodland, Napaean nymphs who haunt the caves, and Naiads whose marble-white feet cleave the watery strands, who nourish the gleaming flowers athwart the sward, say, in what meadow or haply 'neath what shade shall I find Donace pulling lilies with her rosy hands? Three succeeding days are now lost to me, while I have been awaiting Donace in the grotto that was our tryst. Meanwhile, as if this were consolation for my love or could heal my passion, my cows for three morns have touched no grass, nor sipped the waters from any stream. Calves stand licking the dry udders of their new-delivered mothers and fill the air with their tender lowing. And for myself, neither of soft sedge nor of pliant osier have I made baskets for the purposes of curdling milk. Why should I relate to you what you know? [a] You are aware I have a thousand heifers; you know my milk-pails are never empty. I am he to whom, Donace, you gave many a tender kiss, whose strains half-sung you did not hesitate to interrupt by seeking my lips, as they strayed o'er the reed-pipe. [b] Alack, alack, are you touched by no thought for my health? Paler than the box-tree and most like unto the (white) violet I stray. See, I shrink from all food and from the goblets of our loved Bacchus, nor do I mind me to yield myself to gentle sleep. Ah, without you, [c] to my unhappy sight lilies are grey and roses pale

[c] *Cf.* 44–48 with the passage which it imitates, Calp. *Ecl.* III. 51–54.

pallentesque rosae nec dulce rubens hyacinthus, 4
nullos nec myrtus nec laurus spirat odores.
at si tu venias, et candida lilia fient
purpureaeque rosae, et dulce rubens hyacinthus;
tunc mihi cum myrto laurus spirabit odores.
nam dum Pallas amat turgentes unguine bacas, 5
dum Bacchus vites, Deo sata, poma Priapus,
pascua laeta Pales, Idas te diligit unam."

haec Idas calamis. tu, quae responderit Alcon
versu, Phoebe, refer: sunt curae carmina Phoebo.

A. "o montana Pales, o pastoralis Apollo, 5
et nemorum Silvane potens, et nostra Dione,
quae iuga celsa tenes Erycis, cui cura iugales
concubitus hominum totis conectere saeclis:
quid merui? cur me Donace formosa reliquit?
munera namque dedi, noster quae non dedit Idas,
vocalem longos quae ducit aedona cantus; 6
quae licet interdum, contexto vimine clausae
cum parvae patuere fores, ceu libera ferri
norit et agrestes inter volitare volucres,
scit rursus remeare domum tectumque subire, 6
viminis et caveam totis praeponere silvis.
praeterea tenerum leporem geminasque palumbes
nuper, quae potui, silvarum praemia misi.

[48] et dulce rubens V *nonnulli*: *sed sine hiatu* tunc dulce rubens *V alii*: dulce atque rubens *Baehrens*.

[50] unguine N^1GA: sanguine N^2V.

[51] vites V: uvas NG. Deo *Glaeser*: deus *codd.*

[54] curae *Haupt*: aurea *codd.*

[62] clausae *Haupt*: clausa *codd.*: caveae *Maehly*.

[64] norit *Wernsdorf*: novit *codd.*

and the hyacinth has no sweet blush, nor do myrtle or laurel breathe any fragrance; but if you come, lilies will grow white once more, the roses be red, and the hyacinth regain its sweet blush; then for me will laurel with myrtle breathe fragrance forth. For while Pallas loves the olive-berries that swell with fatness, while Bacchus loves the vines, Deo [a] her crops, Priapus his fruits and Pales the joyous pastures, Idas loves you alone."

So Idas on the pipes. O Phoebus, recount what Alcon answered in verse. Over poetry Phoebus presides.

A. " O Pales, lady of the hills, Apollo of the pasture-land, Silvanus, lord of the groves, and my Dione [b] whose citadel is the lofty ridge of Eryx, whose province it is throughout the aeons to rivet the love-unions of mankind; what fate have I merited? Why has fair Donace deserted me? I gave her gifts, such as our friend Idas never gave—a tuneful nightingale that trills its songs hour after hour: and, although sometimes, when the little cage-doors—barred with woven osier—are opened, it can fly forth as if free and wing its way among the birds of the field, yet it knows how to return home again and enter its abode and prefer the cage of osier to all the woods that are. Besides, of late I sent her what spoils of the forest I could, a young hare and a

[a] Deo is Δηώ, Demeter, the corn-goddess.

[b] Dione, strictly mother of Venus, is here identified with Venus, whose temple on Mount Eryx in N.W. Sicily gave her the epithet of " Erycina."

et post haec, Donace, nostros contemnis amores?
forsitan indignum ducis, quod rusticus Alcon 70
te peream, qui mane boves in pascua duco.
di pecorum pavere greges, formosus Apollo,
Pan doctus, Fauni vates et pulcher Adonis.
quin etiam fontis speculo me mane notavi,
nondum purpureos Phoebus cum tolleret ortus 75
nec tremulum liquidis lumen splenderet in undis:
quod vidi, nulla tegimur lanugine malas;
pascimus et crinem; nostro formosior Ida
dicor, et hoc ipsum mihi tu iurare solebas,
purpureas laudando genas et lactea colla 80
atque hilares oculos et formam puberis aevi.
nec sumus indocti calamis: cantamus avena,
qua divi cecinere prius, qua dulce locutus
Tityrus e silvis dominam pervenit in urbem.
nos quoque te propter, Donace, cantabimur urbi, 85
si modo coniferas inter viburna cupressos
atque inter pinus corylum frondescere fas est."

sic pueri Donacen toto sub sole canebant,
frigidus e silvis donec descendere suasit
Hesperus et stabulis pastos inducere tauros. 90

89 descendere N: discedere G: descendere *vel* discedere V: decedere *Baehrens*.

pair of wood-pigeons. And after this, Donace, do you despise my passion? Perhaps you think it shame that the clownish Alcon should pine with love for you, I who lead oxen to their morning pasturage. Gods have fed herds of cattle, beauteous Apollo, skilled Pan, prophetic Fauns, and fair Adonis. Nay, I have remarked myself in a fountain's mirror of a morning, before Phoebus raised aloft the splendour of his uprising, and when no quivering light shone in the clear waters. As far as I saw, no down covers my cheeks; I let my hair grow; men call me more handsome than our Idas, and this indeed you were wont to say to me on oath,[a] while praising [b] the radiance of my cheeks, the milky whiteness of my neck, the laughter in my eyes and the comeliness of my manhood. Nor am I without skill on the reed-pipe. I sing on a flute whereon gods have sung ere now, whereon Tityrus made sweet music and so advanced from the woodland to the imperial city.[c] Me too on your account, Donace, the city will celebrate, if only the cypress with its cones be allowed to burst into leaf among the osiers or the hazel among the pines."

So the boys sang of Donace throughout the day until chilly evening bade them come down from the woods and lead the full-fed bulls to their stalls.

[a] Line 79 is repeated from Calp. III. 62.
[b] With *laudandŏ* (80) *cf.* Nemes. *Ecl.* I. 53, *mulcendŏ*.
[c] "Tityrus" means Virgil. Among frequent reminiscences of the *Eclogues* one is appropriately near; line 86 is based on *inter viburna cupressi* of Virg. *Ecl.* I. 25.

III

Bacchus[a]

Nyctilus atque Micon nec non et pulcher Amyntas
torrentem patula vitabant ilice solem,
cum Pan venatu fessus recubare sub ulmo
coeperat et somno laxatus sumere vires;
quem super ex tereti pendebat fistula ramo. 5
hanc pueri, tamquam praedem pro carmine possent
sumere fasque esset calamos tractare deorum,
invadunt furto; sed nec resonare canorem
fistula quem suerat nec vult contexere carmen,
sed pro carminibus male dissona sibila reddit, 10
cum Pan excussus sonitu stridentis avenae
iamque videns " pueri, si carmina poscitis " inquit,
" ipse canam: nulli fas est inflare cicutas,
quas ego Maenaliis cera coniungo sub antris.
iamque ortus, Lenaee, tuos et semina vitis 15
ordine detexam: debemus carmina Baccho."
haec fatus coepit calamis sic montivagus Pan:
" te cano, qui gravidis hederata fronte corymbis
vitea serta plicas quique udo palmite tigres
ducis odoratis perfusus colla capillis, 20
vera Iovis proles; nam cum post sidera caeli
sola Iovem Semele vidit Iovis ora professum,
hunc pater omnipotens, venturi providus aevi,

[4] laxatas G: lassatas N V *plerique*: lassatus V *nonnulli*: laxatus *Hoeufft*.
[6] praedem *Titius*: praedam *codd.*
[11] cum NG: tum V.
[21] iam tunc *codd.*: nam tunc *Burman*: nam cum *Baehrens*.

---

[a] Bacchus is the subject of Pan's song: some editors prefer " Pan " as the title.

ECLOGUE III

Bacchus [a]

Nyctilus and Mycon and likewise fair Amyntas were shunning the scorching heat of the sun beneath a spreading ilex, when Pan, fatigued in the chase, set himself to recline under an elm and gain strength by sleep's recreation. From a rounded bough above him hung his pipe. This the boys seized by stealth, as though they could take it to be a surety for a song, as though 'twere right to handle the reed-pipes of gods. But neither would the pipe sound its wonted music, nor would it weave its song, but instead of songs it rendered vilely discordant screeches, till Pan was awakened by the din of the strident pipe, and, now seeing them, said, "Boys, if songs ye call for, I myself will sing. No man may blow upon the hemlock stalks which I fashion with wax within Maenalian caves.[b] And now, O God of the winepress, I will unfold in order due the story of thy birth and the seeds of the vine. Song is our debt to Bacchus."

With these words, Pan the mountain-ranger began thus upon the reeds: "Thee I sing, who plaitest vine-wreaths with berried clusters hanging heavy on thine ivy-circled brow, who leadest tigers with juice-soaked vine-branch, thy perfumed hair flowing o'er thy neck, true offspring of Jove. For when Semele alone, save the stars of heaven, saw Jove wearing Jove's own countenance, this child did the Almighty Father, careful for future ages, carry till

[b] The Arcadian mountain-range of Maenalus was sacred to Pan.

pertulit et iusto produxit tempore partus.
hunc Nymphae Faunique senes Satyrique procaces, 25
nosque etiam Nysae viridi nutrimus in antro.
quin et Silenus parvum veteranus alumnum
aut gremio fovet aut resupinis sustinet ulnis,
evocat aut risum digito motuve quietem
allicit aut tremulis quassat crepitacula palmis. 30
cui deus arridens horrentes pectore setas
vellicat aut digitis aures adstringit acutas
applauditve manu mutilum caput aut breve mentum
et simas tenero collidit pollice nares.
interea pueri florescit pube iuventus 35
flavaque maturo tumuerunt tempora cornu.
tum primum laetas extendit pampinus uvas:
mirantur Satyri frondes et poma Lyaei.
tum deus 'o Satyri, maturos carpite fetus'
dixit 'et ignotos primi calcate racemos.' 40
vix haec ediderat, decerpunt vitibus uvas
et portant calathis celerique elidere planta
concava saxa super properant: vindemia fervet
collibus in summis, crebro pede rumpitur uva
nudaque purpureo sparguntur pectora musto. 45
tum Satyri, lasciva cohors, sibi pocula quisque
obvia corripiunt: quae fors dedit, arripit usus.
cantharon hic retinet, cornu bibit alter adunco,

[27] veteranus *O. Schubert*: veneratus *codd.*
[37] extendit G: ostendit NVH.
[40] primi NG: pueri V: proni *Baehrens.*
[45] rubraque NG: udaque V *nonnulli*: nudaque V *reliqui.*
[47] arripit NG: hoc capit V: occupat *Ulitius, Baehrens.*

[a] The story of Semele's perishing amid the lightnings of Jupiter's tremendous epiphany and of the preservation of her child, Bacchus, in Jupiter's thigh till he reached the due hour of birth is alluded to in Nemes. *Cyneg.* 16 *sqq.*

its full time and bring forth at the due hour of birth.[a] This child the Nymphs, the aged Fauns and wanton Satyrs, and I as well, did nurture in the green cave of Nysa.[b] Nay, the veteran Silenus, too, fondles his little nursling in his bosom, or holds him in his cradling arms, or wakes a smile with his finger, or woos repose by rocking him, or shakes rattles in tremulous hands. Smiling on him, the god plucks out the hairs which bristle on his breast, or with the fingers pulls his peaked ears, or pats with the hand his crop-horned[c] head or his short chin, and with tender thumb pinches his snub nose. Meanwhile the boy's youth blooms with the coming of manhood, and his yellow temples have swollen with full-grown horns. Then first the tendril outspreads the gladsome grapes. Satyrs are amazed at the leaves and fruitage of Lyaeus. Then said the god, 'Pluck the ripe produce, ye Satyrs, be first to tread the bunches whose full power ye know not.'

Scarce had he uttered these words, when they snatched the grapes from the vines, carried them in baskets and hastened to crush them on hollowed stones with nimble foot. On the hill-tops the vintage goes on apace, grapes are burst by frequent tread, and naked breasts are besprinkled with purple must. Then the wanton troop of Satyrs snatched the goblets, each that which comes his way. What chance offers, their need seizes. One keeps hold of a tankard; another drinks from a curved horn; one

[b] Nysa, the fabled birthplace of Bacchus, was by some accounts placed in Arabia Felix, by others in India.

[c] "crop-horned" (*cf.* "crop-eared") is meant to suggest the stumpy or cropped horns with which Silenus was represented. Wernsdorf, following Heinsius, took *mutilum* as "bald": *cf. turpe pecus mutilum,* Ovid, *A.A.* III. 249.

concavat ille manus palmasque in pocula vertit,
pronus at ille lacu bibit et crepitantibus haurit 50
musta labris; alius vocalia cymbala mergit
atque alius latices pressis resupinus ab uvis
excipit; at potus (saliens liquor ore resultat)
evomit, inque umeros et pectora defluit umor.
omnia ludus habet cantusque chorique licentes; 55
et venerem iam vina movent: raptantur amantes
concubitu Satyri fugientes iungere Nymphas
iamiamque elapsas hic crine, hic veste retentat.
tum primum roseo Silenus cymbia musto
plena senex avide non aequis viribus hausit. 60
ex illo venas inflatus nectare dulci
hesternoque gravis semper ridetur Iaccho.
quin etiam deus ille, deus Iove prosatus ipso,
et plantis uvas premit et de vitibus hastas
integit et lynci praebet cratera bibenti." 65

haec Pan Maenalia pueros in valle docebat,
sparsas donec oves campo conducere in unum
nox iubet, uberibus suadens siccare fluorem
lactis et in niveas adstrictum cogere glebas.

52 *hunc versum post* 53 *collocant codices plerique.*

53 at potus *codd. plerique*: aes potum *Baehrens*: at potis *ed. Ald.* 1534. saliensque liquore G, *Baehrens*: rediens liquor ore *Maehly.*

54 evomit NGH: spumeus V: ebibit *Baehrens, qui hunc versum cum* 52 *coniungit.*

63 prosatus ipso V *multi*: natus ab ipso V *pauci*, *Baehrens.*

65 integit NG: ingerit V.

hollows his hands and makes a cup of his palms; another, stooping forward, drinks of the wine-vat and with smacking lips drains the new wine; another dips therein his sonorous cymbals, and yet another, lying on his back, catches the juice from the squeezed grapes, but when drunk (as the welling liquid leaps back from his mouth) he vomits it out, and the liquor flows over shoulders and breasts. Everywhere sport reigns, and song and wanton dances. And now love is stirred by the wine; amorous satyrs are seized with desire to unite in intercourse with the fleeing nymphs, whom, all but escaped, one captor holds back by the hair, another by the dress. Then first did old Silenus greedily quaff bowls full of rosy must, his strength not equal to the carousal. And ever since that time he rouses mirth, his veins swollen with the sweet nectar and himself heavy with yesterday's Iacchus.[a] And indeed that god renowned, the god sprung from very Jove, presses the grape-clusters with his feet, enwreaths the spear-like thyrsi from the vine-wands, and proffers a mixing bowl to a lynx that drinks thereof."

So Pan taught the boys in the Maenalian vale, until night bade them drive together the sheep scattered o'er the plain, urging them to drain the udders of their milk-flow and curdle and thicken it into snow-white clots of cheese.

[a] *i.e.* his debauch on the gifts of the Wine-god.

IV

Lycidas : Mopsus

Populea Lycidas nec non et Mopsus in umbra,
pastores, calamis ac versu doctus uterque
nec triviale sonans, proprios cantabat amores.
nam Mopso Meroe, Lycidae crinitus Iollas
ignis erat; parilisque furor de dispare sexu
cogebat trepidos totis discurrere silvis.
hos puer ac Meroe multum lusere furentes,
dum modo condictas vitant in vallibus ulmos,
nunc fagos placitas fugiunt promissaque fallunt
antra nec est animus solitos alludere fontes. 10
cum tandem fessi, quos dirus adederat ignis,
sic sua desertis nudarunt vulnera silvis
inque vicem dulces cantu luxère querellas.

M. immitis Meroe rapidisque fugacior Euris,
cur nostros calamos, cur pastoralia vitas 15
carmina? quemve fugis? quae me tibi gloria victo?
quid vultu mentem premis ac spem fronte serenas?
tandem, dura, nega: possum non velle negantem.
cantet, amat quod quisque: levant et carmina curas.

[10] ad ludere *Maehly, Baehrens.*
[11] durus NGA: lusus *vel* luxus V: dirus *H. Schenkl*: torridus *Baehrens.* ederat NG V *plerique, Baehrens*: adederat V *nonnulli.*
[13] dixere *vulgo*: duxere V *plerique*: luxere *Glaeser*: mulsere *Maehly.*
[18] non *codd.*: iam *Baehrens*: nam *C. Schenkl.*

---

[a] An alternative title is "Eros."
[b] From Virg. *Aen.* IV. 477, *spem fronte serenat.*

ECLOGUE IV

Lycidas: Mopsus [a]

The shepherds, Lycidas and Mopsus too, both of them skilled on the reed-pipes and in verse, were singing each of his own love in the poplar shade, uttering no common strain. For Mopsus the flame was Meroe, for Lycidas 'twas Iollas of the flowing locks; and a like frenzy for a darling of different sex drove them wandering restlessly through all the groves. The youth and Meroe sorely mocked these shepherds in their desperate passion; now they would shun the valley-elms which had been made a trysting-place; anon they would avoid the beeches where they fixed to meet, fail to be at the promised cave, or have no mind to sport by the wonted springs; until at length in weariness, consumed by the dread fire of love, Mopsus and Lycidas thus laid bare their wounds to the solitary groves, and by turns wailed forth in song their sweet complaints.

M. Pitiless Meroe, more elusive than the rushing East wind, why do you avoid my pipes, why my shepherd songs? Or whom do you shun? What glory does my conquest bring to you? Why conceal your mind under your looks, why show fair hope on your brow? [b] At last, O heartless maid, refuse me; I may cease to want her who refuses me.

Let each sing of what he loves: song too relieves love's pangs.[c]

[c] The device of a refrain follows the examples in Theocritus, *Idyll.* I. and II. and Virgil, *Eclog.* VIII. It is effectively used in the trochaics of the *Pervigilium Veneris*: '*cras amet qui numquam amavit quique amavit cras amet.*'

L. respice me tandem, puer o crudelis Iolla. 20
non hoc semper eris: perdunt et gramina flores,
perdit spina rosas nec semper lilia candent
nec longum tenet uva comas nec populus umbras:
donum forma breve est nec se quod commodet annis.
cantet, amat quod quisque: levant et carmina curas. 25
M. cerva marem sequitur, taurum formosa iuvenca,
et Venerem sensere lupae, sensere leaenae
et genus aerium volucres et squamea turba
et montes silvaeque, suos habet arbor amores:
tu tamen una fugis, miserum tu prodis amantem.
cantet, amat quod quisque: levant et carmina curas. 31
L. omnia tempus alit, tempus rapit: usus in arto est.
ver erat, et vitulos vidi sub matribus istos,
qui nunc pro nivea coiere in cornua vacca.
et tibi iam tumidae nares et fortia colla, 35
iam tibi bis denis numerantur messibus anni.
cantet, amat quod quisque: levant et carmina curas.
M. huc, Meroe formosa, veni: vocat aestus in umbram.
iam pecudes subiere nemus, iam nulla canoro
gutture cantat avis, torto non squamea tractu 40
signat humum serpens: solus cano. me sonat omnis
silva, nec aestivis cantu concedo cicadis.

[30] prodis NG: perdis V.

L. Turn your gaze on me at last, Iollas, cruel boy. You will not be ever thus. Herbs lose their bloom, thorns lose their roses, nor are lilies always white; the vine keeps not its leaf for long nor the poplar its shady foliage. Beauty is a short-lived gift nor one that lends itself to age.

Let each sing of what he loves: song too relieves love's pangs.

M. The doe follows the buck, the comely heifer the bull, wolves have felt the stirring of love, lionesses have felt it, and the tribes of the air, the birds, and the throng of scaled creatures, and mountains and woods—and trees have their own loves. You alone flee from love; you betray your hapless lover.

Let each sing of what he loves: song too relieves love's pangs.

L. Time nurtures all things, time snatches them away; enjoyment lies within narrow bounds. 'Twas spring, and I saw beneath their mothers yonder calves, which now have met in horned battle for the snow-white cow. For you, already your nostrils swell, already your neck grows strong, already you count your years by twenty harvests.

Let each sing of what he loves: song too relieves love's pangs.

M. Come hither, fair Meroe; the heat calls us to the shade. Now the herds have found cover in the wood; now there is no bird that sings from tuneful throat; the scaly serpent marks not the ground with its sinuous trail. Alone I sing, all the wood resounds with my strain, nor do I yield in song to the summer cicalas.

cantet, amat quod quisque: levant et carmina curas.

L. tu quoque, saeve puer, niveum ne perde colorem
sole sub hoc: solet hic lucentes urere malas. 4
hic age pampinea mecum requiesce sub umbra;
hic tibi lene fluens fons murmurat, hic et ab ulmis
purpureae fetis dependent vitibus uvae.
cantet, amat quod quisque: levant et carmina curas.

M. qui tulerit Meroes fastidia lenta superbae, 5
Sithonias feret ille nives Libyaeque calorem,
Nerinas potabit aquas taxique nocentis
non metuet sucos, Sardorum gramina vincet
et iuga Marmaricos coget sua ferre leones.
cantet, amat quod quisque: levant et carmina curas. 5

L. quisquis amat pueros, ferro praecordia duret,
nil properet discatque diu patienter amare
prudentesque animos teneris non spernat in annis,
perferat et fastus. sic olim gaudia sumet,
si modo sollicitos aliquis deus audit amantes. 6
cantet, amat quod quisque: levant et carmina curas.

M. quid prodest, quod me pagani mater Amyntae

[46] hic V *plerique, Leo, Giarratano*: hac G, *Baehrens.*
[47] virens NG, *H. Schenkl*: fluens V *plerique.*

---

[a] *Sithonias* means "Thracian"; *Sardoa gramina,* bitter herbs from Sardinia; *Marmaricos,* belonging to the north of Africa between Egypt and the Syrtes.

Let each sing of what he loves: song too relieves love's pangs.

L. You too, cruel youth, destroy not your snow-white colour under this sun; it is wont to scorch fair cheeks. Come, rest here with me beneath the shadow of the vine. Here you have the murmur of a gently running spring, here too on the supporting elms hang purple clusters from the fruitful vines.

Let each sing of what he loves: song too relieves love's pangs.

M. The man who can endure proud Meroe's unresponsive disdain will endure Sithonian snows and Libyan heat, will drink sea-water, and be unafraid of the hurtful yew-tree's sap; he will defy Sardinian herbs and will constrain Marmaric lions to bear his yoke.[a]

Let each sing of what he loves: song too relieves love's pangs.

L. Whoe'er loves boys, let him harden his heart with steel. Let him be in no haste, but learn for long to love with patience. Let him not scorn prudence in tender years. Let him even endure disdain. So one day he will find joy, if so be that some god hearkens to troubled lovers.

Let each sing of what he loves: song too relieves love's pangs.

M. What boots it[b] that the mother of Amyntas

[b] Lines 62–72 draw upon the magical ideas in the *Pharmaceutriae* of Theocritus, *Idyll.* II, and its adaptation by Virgil, *Ecl.* VIII. 64–109. From Virgil come the odd numbers, fillets of wool, frankincense, burning of laurel, ashes thrown in a stream, the many-coloured threads, herbs of virtue, and charms to affect the moon or a snake or corn-crops.

ter vittis, ter fronde sacra, ter ture vaporo,
incendens vivo crepitantes sulphure lauros, 6
lustravit cineresque aversa effudit in amnem, 6
cum sic in Meroen totis miser ignibus urar?
cantet, amat quod quisque: levant et carmina curas.

L. haec eadem nobis quoque versicoloria fila
et mille ignotas Mycale circumtulit herbas;
cantavit, quo luna tumet, quo rumpitur anguis, 7
quo currunt scopuli, migrant sata, vellitur arbos.
plus tamen ecce meus, plus est formosus Iollas.
cantet, amat quod quisque: levant et carmina curas.

CYNEGETICA

Venandi cano mille vias; hilaresque labores
discursusque citos, securi proelia ruris,
pandimus. Aonio iam nunc mihi pectus ab oestro
aestuat: ingentes Helicon iubet ire per agros,
Castaliusque mihi nova pocula fontis alumno
ingerit et late campos metatus apertos
imponitque iugum vati retinetque corymbis
implicitum ducitque per avia, qua sola numquam

[64] *versus qui sunt in codicibus* 64 *et* 65 *transposuit Hauptius.*
[68] quoque NGA: quae V.
Cyn. [5] alumnus *Ulitius, Baehrens.*

[a] The notion, imitating Virgil, *Ecl.* VIII. 82 (*fragiles incende bitumine lauros*), is that the laurels are kindled with divine fire, bitumen being reckoned a product of lightning.

from our village purified me thrice with chaplets, thrice with sacred leaves, thrice with reeking incense, while she burnt crackling laurel[a] with live sulphur, and, turning her face away, cast the ashes into the river? what boots it when my unhappy heart burns thus for Meroe in all the fires of love?

Let each sing of what he loves: song too relieves love's pangs.

L. Round me also this self-same dame, Mycale, carried threads of varied colour and a thousand strange herbs. She uttered the spell which makes the moon grow large, the snake to burst, rocks to run, crops to change their field, and trees to be uprooted: yet more, lo! still more beautiful is my Iollas.[b]

Let each sing of what he loves: song too relieves love's pangs.

THE CHASE

The thousand phases of the chase I sing; its merry tasks do we reveal, its quick dashes to and fro—the battles of the quiet country-side. Already my heart is tide-swept by the frenzy the Muses[c] send: Helicon bids me fare through widespread lands, and the God of Castaly presses on me, his foster-child, fresh draughts from the fount of inspiration: and, after far roaming in the open plains, sets his yoke upon the bard, holding him entangled with ivy-cluster, and guides him o'er wilds remote, where never

[b] *i.e.* despite all incantations, Iollas retains a beauty which exerts an irresistible power over Lycidas.

[c] Aonia = Boeotia, associated with the Muses through Mount Helicon.

trita rotis. iuvat aurato procedere curru
et parere deo: virides en ire per herbas
imperat: intacto premimus vestigia musco;
et, quamvis cursus ostendat tramite noto
obvia Calliope faciles, insistere prato
complacitum, rudibus qua luceat orbita sulcis.
  nam quis non Nioben numeroso funere maestam
iam cecinit? quis non Semelen ignemque iugalem
letalemque simul novit de paelicis astu?
quis magno recreata tacet cunabula Baccho,
ut pater omnipotens maternos reddere menses
dignatus iusti complerit tempora partus?
sunt qui sacrilego rorantes sanguine thyrsos
(nota nimis) dixisse velint, qui vincula Dirces
Pisaei⟨que⟩ tori legem Danaique cruentum
imperium sponsasque truces sub foedere primo
dulcia funereis mutantes gaudia taedis.
Biblidos indictum nulli scelus; impia Myrrhae

[13] facilest *Pithoeus, Baehrens.*
[14] non placito *Baehrens*: complacito AC: complacitum *H. Schenkl.*
[20] complerit *vulgo*: compellere AC.
[21] sacrilegos orantes A: sacrilego rorantes C.

---

[a] Lines 8–14: for this almost conventional claim to be original, *cf.* Lucret. I. 926, *avia Pieridum peragro loca nullius ante trita solo*; Virg. *G.* III. 291–293; Hor. *Od.* III. i. 2–4; Milton, *P.L.* I. 16.

[b] Juno (here strikingly called *paelex,* "concubine") tempted Semele into the fatal request that Jupiter should appear to her in all his glory.

[c] After Semele perished amidst the flames of her lover Jupiter's visitation, the god kept her unborn child, Bacchus, in his thigh until his birth was due: *cf.* Nem. *Ecl.* III. 21–24.

wheel marked ground.[a] 'Tis joy to advance in gilded car and obey the God: lo, 'tis his behest to fare across the green sward: we print our steps on virgin moss; and, though Calliope meet us pointing to easy runs along some well-known path, it is our dear resolve to set foot upon a mead where the track lies clear mid furrows hitherto untried.

For ere now who has not sung of Niobe saddened by death upon death of her children? Who does not know of Semele and of the fire that was at once bridal and doom for her—as the outcome of her rival's [b] craft? Who fails to record the cradling renewed for mighty Bacchus—how the Almighty Sire deigned to restore his mother's months and fulfilled the time of regular pregnancy.[c] Poets there are whose taste is to tell the hackneyed tales of Bacchic wands dripping with unholy blood,[d] or Dirce's bonds,[e] and the terms imposed for the wooing at Pisa,[f] and Danaus' bloody behest, and the merciless brides who, fresh from plighted troth, changed sweet joys to funeral torches.[g] No poet fails to tell of Biblis' criminal passion;[h] we know of Myrrha's

[d] *i.e.* of Pentheus, King of Thebes, torn to pieces by his mother and other Bacchanalian devotees.

[e] Dirce was tied to a savage bull by Amphion and Zethus out of revenge for her part in the maltreatment of their mother, Antiope: *cf. Aetna*, 577.

[f] To escape prophesied death at the hands of a son-in-law, Oenomaus, King of Elis and Pisa, proclaimed that he would give his daughter, Hippodamia, in marriage only to the suitor who should win a chariot-race against his supernatural steeds.

[g] The fifty Danaides, with the exception of Hypermestra, carried out the command of their father, Danaus, to kill their bridegrooms on their marriage-night.

[h] *i.e.* for her brother Caunus.

conubia et saevo violatum crimine patrem
novimus, utque Arabum fugiens cum carperet arva
ivit in arboreas frondes animamque virentem.
sunt qui squamosi referant fera sibila Cadmi 30
stellatumque oculis custodem virginis Ius
Herculeosque velint semper numerare labores
miratumque rudes se tollere Terea pinnas
post epulas, Philomela, tuas; sunt ardua mundi
qui male temptantem curru Phaethonta loquantur 35
exstinctasque canant emisso fulmine flammas
fumantemque Padum, Cycnum plumamque senilem
et flentes semper germani funere silvas.
Tantalidum casus et sparsas sanguine mensas
condentemque caput visis Titana Mycenis 40
horrendasque vices generis dixere priores.
Colchidos iratae sacris imbuta venenis
munera non canimus pulchraeque incendia Glauces,
non crinem Nisi, non saevae pocula Circes,

[27] foedo *vel* scaevo *Ulitius.*
[30] quis quã osi A.
[32] *fort.* memorare *Postgate.*
[33] se tollere ad aera (*sive* aethera) *Baehrens* : s&oller&acerea A : sustollere *Burman* : rudi s. t. T. pinna *Heinsius.*
[43] incendia *Pithoeus* : ingentia AC.

---

[a] Myrrha (or Zmyrna), daughter of King Cinyras, was metamorphosed into a fragrant tree.

[b] Juno, jealous of Jupiter's love for Io, consigned her to the guardianship of Argus of the hundred eyes, afterwards transformed into a peacock.

[c] Procne and Philomela punished Tereus for his unfaithfulness by serving to him as food Itys, his son by Procne. When Procne was changed into a swallow and Philomela into a nightingale, Tereus became a hoopoe to pursue them: *cf. Aetna*, 589.

[d] The fiery ruin which overtook Phaëthon in the Sun-God's chariot was lamented by Cycnus, who was changed into a

impious amour, of her father defiled with cruel crime, and how, traversing in her flight the fields of Araby, she passed into the greenwood life of the leafy trees.[a] There are some who relate the fierce hissing of Cadmus turned to a scaly serpent, and Maiden Io's gaoler starred with eyes,[b] or who are fain for ever to recount the labours of Hercules, or Tereus' wonderment that after your banquet, Philomela,[c] he could raise wings as yet untried; there are others whose theme is Phaethon's ill-starred attempt upon the heights of the universe in the Sun's chariot, and whose song is of flames quenched in the thunderbolt launched forth, and of the river Padus reeking, of Cycnus and the plumage of his old age, of the (poplar-)trees for ever weeping by reason of a brother's death.[d] Bards ere now have told of the misfortunes of the Tantalids, the blood-besprinkled tables, the Titan Sun hiding his face at the sight of Mycenae and the dread vicissitudes of a race.[e] We do not sing of gifts imbued with the accursed poison of the angry Colchian dame[f] and of the burning of fair Glauce; not of Nisus' lock;[g] not of cruel Circe's

swan, and by his sisters, the Heliades, who were changed into poplars.

[e] Blood-guilt was transmitted through Pelops, son of Tantalus, and through his sons Atreus and Thyestes to Agamemnon and his son Orestes. Atreus, King of Mycenae, avenged himself for the seduction of his wife on his brother by slaying his two sons and setting their flesh before their father. From this "banquet of Thyestes" the Sun hid his face in horror: *cf. Aetna*, 20.

[f] The sorceress Medea from Colchis, infuriated by Jason's desertion of her for Glauce, sent to her bridal gifts which consumed her with fire.

[g] On the purple lock of Nisus, King of Megara, the safety of his kingdom depended. His betrayal by his daughter is told in *Ciris* (*Appendix Vergiliana*).

nec nocturna pie curantem busta sororem:
haec iam magnorum praecepit copia vatum,
omnis et antiqui vulgata est fabula saecli.
nos saltus viridesque plagas camposque patentes
scrutamur totisque citi discurrimus arvis
et varias cupimus facili cane sumere praedas;
nos timidos lepores, imbelles figere dammas
audacesque lupos, vulpem captare dolosam
gaudemus; nos flumineas errare per umbras
malumus et placidis ichneumona quaerere ripis
inter harundineas segetes faelemque minacem
arboris in trunco longis praefigere telis
implicitumque sinu spinosi corporis erem
ferre domum; talique placet dare lintea curae,
dum non magna ratis, vicinis sueta moveri
litoribus tutosque sinus percurrere remis,
nunc primum dat vela notis portusque fideles
linquit et Adriacas audet temptare procellas.
mox vestros meliore lyra memorare triumphos
accingar, divi fortissima pignora Cari,
atque canam nostrum geminis sub finibus orbis
litus et edomitas fraterno numine gentes,
quae Rhenum Tigrimque bibunt Ararisque remotum

[58] cursu (= *cursui*) *Baehrens*: curae AC: cymbae *Heinsius*.
[65] gemini *Heinsius*.

---

[a] Circe's potions and spells transformed men into beasts.
[b] Antigone buried her brother Polynices in defiance of the edict of Creon.
[c] *eres* (= *ericius*, *ericinus* or *erinaceus*) corresponds to the Greek *ἐχῖνος*.
[d] This passage dates the *Cynegetica*. For the Emperor Carus and his sons, Carinus and Numerianus, see Gibbon,

cups;[a] nor yet of the sister[b] whose conscience contrived a (brother's) burial by night: in all this ere now a band of mighty bards has forestalled us, and all the fabling of an ancient age is commonplace.

We search the glades, the green tracts, the open plains, swiftly coursing here and there o'er all the fields, eager to catch varied quarries with docile hound. We enjoy transfixing the nervous hare, the unresisting doe, the daring wolf or capturing the crafty fox; our heart's desire is to rove along the river-side shades, hunting the ichneumon on the quiet banks among the crops of bulrushes, with the long weapon to pierce in front the threatening polecat on a tree-trunk and bring home the hedgehog[c] entwined in the convolution of its prickly body: for such a task it is our resolve to set sail, while our little barque, wont to coast by the neighbouring shore and run across safe bays with the oar, now first spreads its canvas to southern winds, and, leaving the trusty havens, dares to try the Adriatic storms.

Hereafter I will gird myself with fitter lyre to record your triumphs, you gallant sons of deified Carus,[d] and will sing of our sea-board beneath the twin boundaries of our world,[e] and of the subjugation, by the brothers' divine power, of nations that drink from Rhine or Tigris or from the distant source of the Arar or look upon the wells of

Decline and Fall, ch. xii. They succeeded their father on his death in A.D. 283. In 284 Carinus celebrated elaborate games at Rome in the name of himself and Numerian; but the brothers never saw each other after their father died. Numerian's death in 284 during his return journey with his army from Persia prevented him from enjoying the triumph decreed to the young emperors at Rome.

[e] *Fines* are the limits set by Ocean on East and West.

principium Nilique vident in origine fontem;
nec taceam, primum quae nuper bella sub Arcto
felici, Carine, manu confeceris, ipso
paene prior genitore deo, utque intima frater
Persidos et veteres Babylonos ceperit arces,
ultus Romulei violata cacumina regni;
imbellemque fugam referam clausasque pharetras
Parthorum laxosque arcus et spicula nulla.

haec vobis nostrae libabunt carmina Musae,
cum primum vultus sacros, bona numina terrae,
contigerit vidisse mihi: iam gaudia vota
temporis impatiens sensus spretorque morarum
praesumit videorque mihi iam cernere fratrum
augustos habitus, Romam clarumque senatum
et fidos ad bella duces et milite multo
agmina, quis fortes animat devotio mentes:
aurea purpureo longe radiantia velo
signa micant sinuatque truces levis aura dracones.

tu modo, quae saltus placidos silvasque pererras,
Latonae, Phoebe, magnum decus, heia age suetos
sume habitus arcumque manu pictamque pharetram
suspende ex umeris; sint aurea tela, sagittae;
candida puniceis aptentur crura cothurnis;

68 vident *Johnson*: bibunt AC.
69 primum AC: prima *Baehrens*.

---

[a] The war maintained against the Sarmatians by Carus after Probus' death was left to Carinus to finish, when Carus had to face the Persian menace in the East. In his Gallic campaign also, Carinus showed some degree of soldierly ability.

[b] Numerian is here flatteringly associated with the exploits of Carus, who after subduing Mesopotamia carried his vic-

the Nile at their birth; nor let me fail to tell what campaigns you first ended, Carinus, beneath the Northern Bear [a] with victorious hand, well-nigh outstripping even your divine father, and how your brother [b] seized on Persia's very heart and the time-honoured citadels of Babylon, in vengeance for outrages done to the high dignity of the realms of Romulus' race.[c] I shall record also the Parthians' feeble flight, their unopened quivers, unbent bows and unavailing arrows.

Such strains shall my Muses consecrate to you both, as soon as it is my fortune to see your blest faces, kindly divinities of this earth. Already my feelings, intolerant of slow time and disdainful of delay, anticipate the joys of my aspiration, and I fancy I already discern the majestic mien of the brothers, and therewith Rome, the illustrious senate, the generals trusted for warfare, and the marching lines of many soldiers, their brave souls stirred with devotion. The golden standards gleam radiant afar with their purple drapery, and a light breeze waves the folds of the ferocious dragons.[d]

Only do thou, Diana, Latona's great glory, who dost roam the peaceful glade and woodland, come quickly, assume thy wonted guise, bow in hand, and hang the coloured quiver from thy shoulder; golden be the weapons, thine arrows; and let thy gleaming feet be fitted with purple buskins; let thy cloak

torious arms to Ctesiphon. Numerian's subsequent retreat surprised the Persians.

[c] The reference is to violations of the Eastern frontiers of the Empire. *Cacumina regni* is taken, with Wernsdorf, to mean *fastigium et maiestatem imperii Romani*.

[d] They were military emblems from Trajan's time.

sit chlamys aurato multum subtegmine lusa
corrugesque sinus gemmatis balteus artet
nexibus; implicitos cohibe diademate crines.
tecum Naiades faciles viridique iuventa
pubentes Dryades Nymphaeque, unde amnibus umor,
adsint, et docilis decantet Oreadas Echo.
duc age, diva, tuum frondosa per avia vatem:
te sequimur, tu pande domos et lustra ferarum.
huc igitur mecum, quisquis percussus amore
venandi damnas lites pavidosque tumultus
civilesque fugis strepitus bellique fragores
nec praedas avido sectaris gurgite ponti.

principio tibi cura canum non segnis ab anno
incipiat primo, cum Ianus, temporis auctor,
pandit inocciduum bis senis mensibus aevum.
elige tunc cursu facilem facilemque recursu,
seu Lacedaemonio natam seu rure Molosso,
non humili de gente canem. sit cruribus altis,
sit rigidis, multamque trahat sub pectore lato
costarum sub fine decenter prona carinam,
quae sensim rursus sicca se colligat alvo,
renibus ampla satis validis diductaque coxas,
cuique nimis molles fluitent in cursibus aures.
huic parilem submitte marem, sic omnia magnum,
dum superant vires, dum laeto flore iuventas

[96] decantet Oreadas *vulgo*: dicant oreades A: decantet oreades C.
[98] domos C: dolos A.
[99] huc *Ulitius*: hinc AC.
[100] avidos AC: pavidos *vel* rabidos *Ulitius*: rabidos *Baehrens*: rapidos *Postgate*.

---

[a] Lines 91–93 are discussed in a special excursus by Wernsdorf. With *lusa cf.* Virg. *G.* II. 464, *illusasque auro vestes*, "garments fancifully embroidered with gold."

be richly tricked with golden thread,[a] and a belt with jewelled fastenings tighten the wrinkled tunic-folds: restrain thine entwined tresses with a band. In thy train let genial Naiads come and Dryads ripening in fresh youth and Nymphs who give the streams their water, and let the apt pupil Echo repeat the accents of thine Oreads.[b] Goddess, arise, lead thy poet through the untrodden boscage: thee we follow; do thou disclose the wild beasts' homes and lairs. Come hither then with me, whosoever, smitten with the love of the chase, dost condemn lawsuits and panic-stricken turmoil, or dost shun the din in cities and the clash of war, or pursuest no spoils on the greedy surge of the deep.

At the outset your diligent care of your dogs[c] must start from the beginning of the year, when Janus, author of the march of time, opens for each twelve months the never-ceasing round. At that season you must choose a bitch obedient to speed forward, obedient to come to heel, native to either the Spartan or the Molossian[d] country-side, and of good pedigree.[e] She must stand high on straight legs; with a comely slope let her carry, under a broad breast, where the ribs end, a width of keel that gradually again contracts in a lean belly: she must be big enough with strong loins, spread at the hips, and with the silkiest of ears floating in air as she runs. Give her a male to match, everywhere similarly well-sized, while strength holds sway, while

[b] *i.e.* the surroundings should reverberate to the voices of the attendant mountain-nymphs.

[c] On dogs generally see note on Grattius, *Cyneg.* 151.

[d] *Cf.* Grattius, *Cyneg.* 181, 197, 211–212.

[e] On the mating of dogs *cf.* Grattius, *Cyneg.*, esp. 263–284.

corporis et venis primaevis sanguis abundat.
namque graves morbi subeunt segnisque senectus,
invalidamque dabunt non firmo robore prolem.
sed diversa magis feturae convenit aetas:
tu bis vicenis plenum iam mensibus acrem
in venerem permitte marem; sit femina, binos
quae tulerit soles. haec optima cura iugandis.
mox cum se bina formarit lampade Phoebe
ex quo passa marem genitalia viscera turgent,
fecundos aperit partus matura gravedo,
continuo largaque vides strepere omnia prole.
sed, quamvis avidus, primos contemnere partus
malueris; mox non omnes nutrire minores.
nam tibi si placitum populosos pascere fetus,
iam macie tenues sucique videbis inanes
pugnantesque diu, quisnam prior ubera lambat,
distrahere invalidam lassato viscere matrem.
sin vero haec cura est, melior ne forte necetur
abdaturve domo, catulosque probare voluntas,
quis nondum gressus stabiles neque lumina passa
luciferum videre iubar, quae prodidit usus
percipe et intrepidus spectatis annue dictis.
pondere nam catuli poteris perpendere vires
corporibus⟨que⟩ leves gravibus praenoscere cursu.
quin et flammato ducatur linea longe

122 *hic in codicibus sequuntur* 224–230, *quos traiecit Hauptius, Schradero viam praemonstrante.*

---

[a] *Soles* stands here for *annos*, *i.e.* annual revolutions of the sun according to the ancient cosmology.

[b] Wernsdorf, following Barth, explains *passa* as meaning *aperta* (from *pandere*, not from *pati*).

bodily youth is in its joyous flower and blood abounds in the veins of early life. For burdensome diseases creep on and sluggish age, and they will produce unhealthy offspring without steadfast strength. But for breeding a difference of age in the parents is more suitable: you should release the male, keen for mating, when he has already completed forty months: and let the female be two full years old.[a] Such is the best arrangement in their coupling. Presently when Phoebe has completed the round of two full moons since the birth-giving womb fertilised by the male began to swell, the pregnancy in its due time reveals the fruitful offspring, and straightway you see all round an abundant noisy litter. Yet, however desirous of dogs, you must make up your mind to put no value on the first set born; and of the next set you must not rear all the young ones. For if you decide to feed a crowd of whelps, you will find them thin with leanness and beggared of strength, and, by their long tussle to be first to suck, harassing a mother weakened with teat outworn. But if this is your anxiety, to keep the better sort from being killed or thrown out of the house, if it is your intention to test the puppies before even their steps are steady or their eyes have felt[b] and seen the light-bearing sunbeam, then grasp what experience has handed on, and assent fearlessly to well-tried words. You will be able to examine the strength of a puppy by its weight and by the heaviness of each body know in advance which will be light in running.[c] Furthermore, you should get a series of flames made in a

[c] 138–139: the parallel in Grattius, *Cyn.* 298–299, is one of the points suggesting that Nemesianus had read Grattius.

circuitu signet⟨que⟩ habilem vapor igneus orbem,
impune ut medio possis consistere circo:
huc omnes catuli, huc indiscreta feratur
turba: dabit mater partus examen, honestos
iudicio natos servans trepidoque periclo.
nam postquam conclusa videt sua germina flammis,
continuo saltu transcendens fervida zonae
vincla, rapit rictu primum portatque cubili,
mox alium, mox deinde alium. sic conscia mater
segregat egregiam subolem virtutis amore.
hos igitur genetrice simul iam vere sereno
molli pasce sero (passim nam lactis abundans
tempus adest, albent plenis et ovilia mulctris),
interdumque cibo cererem cum lacte ministra,
fortibus ut sucis teneras complere medullas
possint et validas iam tunc promittere vires.
sed postquam Phoebus candentem fervidus axem
contigerit tardasque vias Cancrique morantis
sidus init, tunc consuetam minuisse saginam
profuerit tenuesque magis retinere cibatus,
ne gravis articulos depravet pondere moles.
nam tum membrorum nexus nodosque relaxant
infirmosque pedes et crura natantia ponunt,
tunc etiam niveis armantur dentibus ora.

[142] ut *Johnson*: in AC.
[144] examen AC: examine *vulgo.*
[145] exitio *Scaliger.* trepidosque *Baehrens*: *fort.* trepidansque *Postgate.*

---

[a] *Cf.* Grattius, *Cyn.* 307, *lacte novam pubem facilique tuebere maza.* For the use of the goddess' name by metonymy for bread *cf.* Gratt. *Cyn.* 398: also *Aetna*, 10.

[b] In the long days of midsummer the sun might be fancied to cross the sky more slowly. *Morantis* refers to the almost

wide circuit with the smoke of the fire to mark a convenient round space, so that you may stand unharmed in the middle of the circle: to this all the puppies, to this the whole crowd as yet unseparated must be brought: the mother will provide the test of her progeny, saving the valuable young ones by her selection and from their alarming peril. For when she sees her offspring shut in by flames, at once with a leap she clears the blazing boundaries of the fire-zone, snatches the first in her jaws and carries it to the kennel; next another, next another in turn: so does the intelligent mother distinguish her nobler progeny by her love of merit. These then along with their mother, now that it is clear spring, you are to feed on soft whey (for everywhere the season that abounds in milk has come, and sheepfolds are white with brimming milk-pails): at times, too, add to their food bread with milk,[a] so that they may be able to fill their young marrows with powerful juices and even at that time give promise of vigorous strength.

But after the burning Sun-God has reached the glowing height of heaven, entering on his slow paths and on the sign of the lingering Crab,[b] then it will be useful to lessen their regular fattening food and retain the more delicate nourishment,[c] so that the weight of heavy bulk may not overstrain their limbs; for that is when they have the connecting joints of the body slack, and plant on the ground unstable feet and swimming legs: then too their mouths are furnished with snowy teeth. But you should not

imperceptible lengthening and shortening of the days before and after the solstice.

[c] *i.e.* the *molle serum* of l. 152.

sed neque conclusos teneas neque vincula collo 165
impatiens circumdederis noceasque futuris
cursibus imprudens. catulis nam saepe remotis
aut vexare trabes, laceras aut mandere valvas
mens erit, et teneros torquent conatibus artus
obtunduntve novos arroso robore dentes 170
aut teneros duris impingunt postibus ungues;
mox cum iam validis insistere cruribus aetas
passa, quater binos volvens ab origine menses,
illaesis catulos spectaverit undique membris,
tunc rursus miscere sero Cerealia dona 175
conveniet fortemque dari de frugibus escam.
libera tunc primum consuescant colla ligari
concordes et ferre gradus clausique teneri.
iam cum bis denos Phoebe reparaverit ortus,
incipe non longo catulos producere cursu, 180
sed parvae vallis spatio septove novali.
his leporem praemitte manu, non viribus aequis
nec cursus virtute parem, sed tarda trahentem
membra, queant iam nunc faciles ut sumere praedas.
nec semel indulge catulis moderamina cursus, 185
sed donec validos etiam praevertere suescant
exerceto diu venandi munere, cogens
discere et emeritae laudem virtutis amare.
nec non consuetae norint hortamina vocis,
seu cursus revocent, iubeant seu tendere cursus. 190
quin etiam docti victam contingere praedam
exanimare velint tantum, non carpere sumptam.
sic tibi veloces catulos reparare memento

[168] mandere *Heinsius*: pandere AC.
[187] munera *Ulitius*: munere AC. *sic interpunxit Postgate.*

keep them shut up, nor impatiently put chains on their neck, and from want of foresight hurt their future running powers. For often young dogs, when kept separate, will take to worrying the timber-fittings, or to gnawing the doors till they are torn, and in the attempt they twist their tender limbs or blunt their young teeth by chewing at the wood or drive their tender nails into the tough door-posts. Later, when time, revolving eight months from their birth, now lets them stand on steady legs and sees the whelps everywhere with limbs unharmed, then it will be suitable again to mix the gifts of Ceres with their whey and have them given strengthening food from the produce of the fields. Only then must they be trained to have their free necks in leash, to run in harmony or be kept on chain. When Phoebe has now renewed twenty monthly risings, start to bring out the young dogs on a course not over-long but within the space of a small valley or enclosed fallow. Out of your hand let slip for them a hare, not of equal strength nor their match in speed of running, but slow in moving its limbs, so that they may at once capture an easy prey. Not once only must you grant the whelps these limited runs, but until they are trained to outstrip strong hares, exercise them long in the task of the chase, forcing them to learn and love the praise due to deserving merit. Likewise they must recognise the urgent words of a well-known voice, whether calling them in or telling them to run full-speed. Besides, when they have been taught to seize the vanquished prey, they must be content to kill, not mangle, what they have caught. By such methods see that you recruit your swift dogs every season,

semper et in parvos iterum protendere curas.
nam tristes morbi, scabies et sordida venis 19
saepe venit multamque canes discrimine nullo
dant stragem: tu sollicitos impende labores
et sortire gregem suffecta prole quotannis.
quin acidos Bacchi latices Tritonide oliva
admiscere decet catulosque canesque maritas 20
unguere profuerit tepidoque ostendere soli,
auribus et tineas candenti pellere cultro.
  est etiam canibus rabies, letale periclum.
quod seu caelesti corrupto sidere manat,
cum segnes radios tristi iaculatur ab aethra 20
Phoebus et attonito pallens caput exserit orbe;
seu magis, ignicomi candentia terga Leonis
cum quatit, hoc canibus blandis inviscerat aestus,
exhalat seu terra sinu, seu noxius aer
causa mali, seu cum gelidus non sufficit umor 21
torrida per venas concrescunt semina flammae:
quicquid id est, imas agitat sub corde medullas
inque feros rictus nigro spumante veneno
prosilit, insanos cogens infigere morsus.
disce igitur potus medicos curamque salubrem. 21
tunc virosa tibi sumes multumque domabis
castorea, attritu silicis lentescere cogens;
ex ebore huc trito pulvis sectove feratur,
admiscensque diu facies concrescere utrumque:
mox lactis liquidos sensim superadde fluores, 22

[199] olivo AC: oliva *vulgo.* Tritonide . . . *Postgate qui cum Housmano* olivo *ut interpretamentum eiecit.*
[207] sed *Baehrens*: seu AC.

---

[a] The reference is to the heat of the sun on entering the sign of Leo.

and again direct your anxious thoughts towards the young ones. For they have melancholy ailments, and the filthy mange often comes on their veins, and the dogs cause widespread mortality without distinction: you must yourself expend anxious efforts on them and every year fill up your pack by supplying progeny. Besides, the right thing is to blend tart draughts of wine with Minerva's olive-fruit, and it will do good to anoint the whelps and the mother dogs, expose them to the warm sun, and expel worms from their ears with the glittering knife.

Dogs also get rabies, a deadly peril. Whether it emanates from taint in a heavenly body when the Sun-God shoots but languid rays from a saddened sky, raising a pallid face in a world dismayed; or whether, rather, in striking the glowing back of the fire-tressed Lion,[a] he drives deep into our friendly dogs his feverish heats, whether earth breathes forth contagion from its bosom, or harmful air is the cause of the evil, or whether, when cool water runs short, the torrid germs of fire grow strong throughout the veins—whatever it is, it stirs the inmost marrow beneath the heart, and with black venomous foam darts forth into ferocious snarls, compelling the dog to imprint its bites in madness. Learn, therefore, the curative potions and the treatment that brings health. In such cases you will take the fetid drug got from the beaver and work it well, forcing it to grow viscous with the friction of a flint: to this should be added powder from pounded or chopped ivory, and by a long process of blending you will get both to harden together: next put in gradually the liquid flow of milk besides, to enable you to pour

ut non cunctantes haustus infundere cornu
inserto possis Furiasque repellere tristes
atque iterum blandas canibus componere mentes.
sed non Spartanos tantum tantumve Molossos
pascendum catulos: divisa Britannia mittit 2[a]
veloces nostrique orbis venatibus aptos.
nec tibi Pannonicae stirpis temnatur origo,
nec quorum proles de sanguine manat Hibero.
quin etiam siccae Libyes in finibus acres
gignuntur catuli, quorum non spreveris usum. 23
quin et Tuscorum non est externa voluptas
saepe canum. sit forma illis licet obsita villo
dissimilesque habeant catulis velocibus artus,
haud tamen iniucunda dabunt tibi munera praedae,
namque et odorato noscunt vestigia prato 23
atque etiam leporum secreta cubilia monstrant.
horum animos moresque simul naresque sagaces
mox referam; nunc omnis adhuc narranda supellex
venandi cultusque mihi dicendus equorum.
cornipedes igitur lectos det Graecia nobis 24
Cappadocumque notas referat generosa propago
† armata et palmas superet grex omnis avorum.

224–230 *post* 122 *in codicibus.*
231 extrema AC: externa *Wight Duff.*
242 armata et palmas nuper grex AC: *fortasse* superet *Postgate*: "*locus vexatissimus totius poematii*" *Wernsdorf, qui proponit* harmataque (= ἅρματα) et palmas numeret: armenti et palmas numeret *Gronov*: Martius et palmas superans *Burman.*

---

[a] For British dogs see Grattius, 174 *sqq.* and note there: *divisa Britannia* is an allusion to Virg. *Ecl.* I. 66, *penitus toto divisos orbe Britannos.*

in through an inserted horn doses which do not stick in the throat, and so banish the melancholy Furies, and settle the dogs' minds once more to friendliness.

But it is not only Spartan whelps or only Molossian which you must rear: sundered Britain sends us a swift sort, adapted to hunting-tasks in our world.[a] You should not disdain the pedigree of the Pannonian breed, nor those whose progeny springs from Spanish blood. Moreover, keen whelps are produced within the confines of dry Libya, and their service you must not despise. Besides, Tuscan dogs often give a satisfaction not foreign to us.[b] Even allowing that their shape is covered with shaggy hair and that they have limbs unlike quick-footed whelps, still they will give you an agreeable return in game; for they recognise the tracks on the meadow, though full of scents, and actually point to where a hare lies hid. Their mettle and their habits as well, and their discerning sense of smell I shall record presently;[c] for the moment the whole equipment of the chase[d] has to be explained, and I must deal with the attention due to horses.

So then let Greece send us choice horny-hoofed coursers, and let a high-mettled breed recall the traits of the Cappadocians, and let the whole stud be soundly equipped and surpass the victorious racing-palms of their ancestors. Theirs is surface

[b] Burman gives the choice between *summa* and *minima* as equivalents to *extrema*. *Non . . . externa* seems to fit better the only Italian dogs in the passage.

[c] This shows the incomplete state in which Nemesianus has been transmitted; for these subjects are not treated in his extant work.

[d] The *supellex venandi* corresponds to Grattius' *arma*, *i.e.* nets, traps, hunting-spears, caps and so forth.

illis ampla satis levi sunt aequora dorso
immodicumque latus parvaeque ingentibus alvi,
ardua frons auresque agiles capitisque decori 24
altus honos oculique vago splendore micantes ;
plurima se validos cervix resupinat in armos ;
fumant umentes calida de nare vapores,
nec pes officium standi tenet, ungula terram
crebra ferit virtusque artus animosa fatigat. 25
quin etiam gens ampla iacet trans ardua Calpes
culmina, cornipedum late fecunda proborum.
namque valent longos pratis intendere cursus,
nec minor est illis Graio quam in corpore forma ;
nec non terribiles spirabile flumen anheli 25
provolvunt flatus et lumina vivida torquent
hinnitusque cient tremuli frenisque repugnant,
nec segnes mulcent aures, nec crure quiescunt.
sit tibi praeterea sonipes, Maurusia tellus
quem mittit (modo sit gentili sanguine firmus) 26
quemque coloratus Mazax deserta per arva
pavit et adsiduos docuit tolerare labores.
nec pigeat, quod turpe caput, deformis et alvus
est ollis quodque infrenes, quod liber uterque,
quodque iubis pronos cervix deverberet armos. 26
nam flecti facilis lascivaque colla secutus
paret in obsequium lentae moderamine virgae :
verbera sunt praecepta fugae, sunt verbera freni.

[245] decori *Baehrens* : decoris A : capitique decoro C.

---

[a] One of the fabled Pillars of Hercules, in Hispania Baetica, now the Rock of Gibraltar. Nemesianus, writing from the standpoint of an African, thinks of all Spain (*gens ampla*) as beyond Calpe.

wide enough on their smooth back, an enormous extent of side, and neat belly for their huge size, a forehead uplifted, quick ears, high pride of comely head, and eyes sparkling with restless gleam; an ample neck falls back on powerful shoulders; moist breath steams from hot nostrils, and, while the foot does not maintain its duty to stand still, the hoof repeatedly strikes the earth and the horse's spirited mettle tires its limbs. Moreover, beyond the soaring peaks of Calpe [a] lies a vast country, productive far and wide of fine coursers. For they have the strength to make long runs across the prairies,[b] and their beauty is no less than that in a Grecian body; panting they roll forth terrifying snorts, a flood of breath; they shoot out spirited glances; all a-quiver they raise whinnyings and fight against the bridle, never giving their ears smooth rest nor their legs repose. Besides, you may select the courser sent by Mauretania (if he be a stout descendant of good stock), or the horse which the dusky Mazax tribesman [c] has reared in desert fields and taught to undergo ceaseless toil. No need to repine at their ugly head and ill-shapen belly, or at their lack of bridles, or because both breeds have the temper of freedom, or because the neck lashes the sloping shoulders with its mane. For he is an easy horse to guide, and, following the turn of an unconfined neck, complies obediently under the control of a limber switch: its strokes are the orders for speed, its strokes are

[b] The commendation of Spanish horses is supported by Martial I. xlix. 21–25: *cf.* XIV. cxcix. But, according to Oppian, *Cyneg.* I. 284–286, the Iberian horses, although fleet (*θοοί*), were found wanting in staying power (*δρόμον ἐν παύροισιν ἐλεγχόμενοι σταδίοισιν*).

[c] Belonging to the Numidian tribe of Mazaces in Africa.

quin et promissi spatiosa per aequora campi
cursibus acquirunt commoto sanguine vires 27
paulatimque avidos comites post terga relinquunt.
haud secus, effusis Nerei per caerula ventis,
cum se Threicius Boreas superextulit antro
stridentique sono vastas exterruit undas,
omnia turbato cesserunt flamina ponto: 27
ipse super fluctus spumanti murmure fervens
conspicuum pelago caput eminet: omnis euntem
Nereidum mirata suo stupet aequore turba.
horum tarda venit longi fiducia cursus,
his etiam emerito vigor est iuvenalis in aevo. 28
nam quaecumque suis virtus bene floruit annis,
non prius est animo quam corpore passa ruinam.
pasce igitur sub vere novo farragine molli
cornipedes venamque feri veteresque labores
effluere adspecta nigri cum labe cruoris. 28
mox laetae redeunt in pectora fortia vires
et nitidos artus distento robore formant;
mox sanguis venis melior calet, ire viarum
longa volunt latumque fuga consumere campum.
inde ubi pubentes calamos duraverit aestas 29
lactentesque urens herbas siccaverit omnem
messibus umorem culmisque aptarit aristas,
hordea tum paleasque leves praebere memento:
pulvere quin etiam puras secernere fruges

269 permissi *Heinsius*.
276 pater fluctus (*id est Neptunus*) *Baehrens*: super fluctus AC. marmore *Heinsius*.
282 passa *vulgo*: posse AC.
292 culmisque armarit *Burman*: culmusque *Baehrens, Postgate*: aptarit *Wight Duff*.

as bridles too. Nay, once launched across the spacious levels of the plain, with blood stirred, the steeds win fresh strength in the race, leaving by degrees their eager comrades behind. Even so, on the outburst of the winds across the blue waters of Nereus, when Thracian Boreas has uprisen o'er his cavern and with shrill howling dismayed the dreary waves, all the blasts on the troubled deep give way to him: himself[a] aglow mid foaming din, above the billows he o'ertops them in mastery manifest upon the sea: the whole band of the Nereids is mazed in wonderment as he passes over their watery domain.

These horses are slow to attain confidence in prolonged running; also, theirs is youthful vigour even in age that has served its time. For no quality which has bloomed full at its due period suffers collapse in spirit ere physical powers fail. In the fresh spring-time, then, feed the coursers on soft mash, and, lancing a vein, watch old-standing ailments flow out with the ooze of the tainted blood. Soon strength returns joyously to their gallant hearts, moulding the sleek limbs with strength diffused: soon a better blood runs warm in their veins, and they wish for long stretches of road, and to make the broad plain vanish in their career. Next, when summer has hardened the ripening stalks and, scorching the juicy blades, has dried all the moisture for harvest and joined corn-ears to stems, then be sure to furnish barley and light chaff: moreover, there must be care to winnow the produce free from dust, and to run the hands

[a] Boreas.

cura sit atque toros manibus percurrere equorum, 295
gaudeat ut plausu sonipes laetumque relaxet
corpus et altores rapiat per viscera sucos.
id curent famuli comitumque animosa iuventus.
  nec non et casses idem venatibus aptos
atque plagas longoque meantia retia tractu 300
addiscant raris semper contexere nodis
et servare modum maculis linoque tenaci.
linea quin etiam, magnos circumdare saltus
quae possit volucresque metu concludere praedas,
digerat innexas non una ex alite pinnas. 305
namque ursos magnosque sues cervosque fugaces
et vulpes acresque lupos ceu fulgura caeli
terrificant linique vetant transcendere septum.
has igitur vario semper fucare veneno
curabis niveisque alios miscere colores 310
alternosque metus subtegmine tendere longo.
dat tibi pinnarum terrentia milia vultur,
dat Libye, magnarum avium fecunda creatrix,
dantque grues cycnique senes et candidus anser,
dant quae fluminibus crassisque paludibus errant 315
pellitosque pedes stagnanti gurgite tingunt.
hinc mage puniceas nativo munere sumes:
namque illic sine fine greges florentibus alis
invenies avium suavique rubescere luto
et sparsos passim tergo vernare colores. 320
his ita dispositis hiemis sub tempus aquosae
incipe veloces catulos immittere pratis,
incipe cornipedes latos agitare per agros.

---

[a] *Cf.* Grattius, *Cynegeticon*, 75–88 (the "formido").
[b] *e.g.* the ostrich.
[c] *i.e.* aquatic fowl.

over the horses' muscles, so that the courser may enjoy being patted and relax his body in pleasure and quickly pass the nourishing juices throughout his frame. This must be the task of the servants and brave young attendants.

Besides they too must learn always to weave with knots far enough apart the hollow nets fit for the chase, and the toils set on tracks, and the nets which run in a long stretch; they must learn to preserve the right size for the openings between the knots and for the binding cord. Moreover, the line which can enclose great glades and by reason of terror shut in winged game as prey must carry here and there, entwined on it, feathers of different birds.[a] For the colours, like lightning-flashes, frighten bears, big boars, timid stags, foxes and fierce wolves, and bar them from surmounting the boundary of the cord. These then you will always be careful to diversify with various hues, mixing other colours with the whites, and thus stretching all along the line one terror after another. In feathers you draw a thousand means of fright from the vulture, from Africa, fertile mother of great-sized birds,[b] from cranes and aged swans and the white goose, from fowl that haunt rivers and thick marshes and dip webbed feet in standing pools. Of these[c] you will rather take birds with red plumage by nature's gift; for among the former you will find endless flocks of birds with bright-hued wings, their colours reddening with pleasant orange tint and gleaming everywhere in flecks upon the back. With such arrangements made towards the season of rainy winter, begin to send your swift dogs across the meadows; begin to urge your horses over the broad

venemur dum mane novum, dum mollia prata
nocturnis calcata feris vestigia servant. 325

TWO FRAGMENTS ON BIRD-CATCHING ASCRIBED TO NEMESIANUS

Introduction

Gybertus Longolius (de Longueil, 1507–1543), in a *Dialogus de avibus* printed at Cologne in 1544, is the authority for ascribing the two following fragments to Nemesianus. He records that they were surreptitiously copied by a young friend of his, Hieronymus Boragineus of Lübeck, from a poem *De Aucupio* by Nemesianus "in bibliotheca porcorum (*sic*) Salvatoris Bononiensis." This account is not

---

VERSUS DE AUCUPIO

I

. . . et tetracem, Romae quem nunc vocitare taracem
coeperunt. avium est multo stultissima ; namque
cum pedicas necti sibi contemplaverit adstans,
immemor ipse sui tamen in dispendia currit.
tu vero adductos laquei cum senseris orbes 5
appropera et praedam pennis crepitantibus aufer.
nam celer oppressi fallacia vincula colli
excutit et rauca subsannat voce magistri

---

[a] a black grouse. The bird is identified with the *urogallus* by Longolius. Pliny's form is *tetras*.

fields. Let us go hunting while the morning is young, while the soft meads retain the tracks imprinted by the wild beasts of the night.

---

free from suspicion, any more than certain points in the Latinity and prosody of the lines. *Contemplaverit* in l. 3 may be an archaistic return to the active form of the verb as used in early Latin; but the metrical quantity of *notae* which Longolius read in l. 13 and of *gulae* in the last line of all is unclassical, and the frequent elision of a long vowel (ll. 5, 6, 14 and 27) is noticeable. Teuffel considers the lines a late production, though they are usually printed along with the *Cynegetica*.

E. Baehrens' text, *P.L.M.* III. pp. 203–204.
J. P. Postgate's text, *C.P.L.* II. p. 572.

FRAGMENTS ON BIRD-CATCHING

I

. . . and the *tetrax*,[a] which they have now begun to call *tarax* at Rome. It is far the silliest of birds; for although it has perched and has watched the snare laid for it, yet reckless of self it darts upon its own hurt. You, however, on finding the circles of the noose drawn tight, must hasten up and carry off your prey with its whirring wings. For it is quick to shake off the treacherous bonds of the neck when caught, deriding [b] with hoarse cry the hunter's

[b] *Subsannare*, a late Latin verb, used by Tertullian, and in the Vulgate.

consilium et laeta fruitur iam pace solutus.
hic prope † Peltinum ⟨ad⟩ radices Apennini
nidificat, patulis qua se sol obicit agris,
persimilis cineri collum, maculosaque terga
inficiunt pullae cacabantis imagine guttae.
Tarpeiae est custos arcis non corpore maior
nec qui te volucres docuit, Palamede, figuras.
saepe ego nutantem sub iniquo pondere vidi
mazonomi puerum, portat cum prandia, circo
quae consul praetorve novus construxit ovanti.

II

cum nemus omne suo viridi spoliatur honore,
fultus equi niveis silvas pete protinus altas
exuviis: praeda est facilis et amoena scolopax.
corpore non Paphiis avibus maiore videbis.
illa sub aggeribus primis, qua proluit umor,
pascitur, exiguos sectans obsonia vermes.
at non illa oculis, quibus est obtusior, etsi
sint nimium grandes, sed acutis naribus instat:
impresso in terram rostri mucrone sequaces
vermiculos trahit et vili dat praemia gulae.

[10] Pelt(u)inum *Buecheler*: Pentinum *Longolius*: Pontinum *Ulitius*. in radicibus *Burman*: et radices *Haupt*: ad radices *Baehrens*.
[12] dorsum *Longolius* : collum *Gesner*.
[13] notae *Longolius* : guttae *Ulitius*.
[17] mazonomi *Gesner* : mazonoim *Longolius*. circo *Burman*: cirro *Longolius*.
[21] facilis praeda est et amoena *Riese*.
[28] atque gulae d. pr. vili *Wernsdorf*.

[a] The geese of the Capitol saved it from surprise by the Gauls, in 390 B.C., Livy, V. xlvii.

design and now in freedom delighting in the joy of peace. Near Peltinum by the foot of the Apennine range it builds its nest where the sun presents himself to the outspread lands: at the neck it is very like ashes in colour, and its spotted back is marked with dark flecks in the fashion of a partridge. The guardian of the Tarpeian citadel[a] is no larger in size, nor the bird that taught you, Palamedes, winglike letters.[b] Often have I seen a slave swaying beneath the unfair weight of a huge dish of such dainties,[c] as he carries the collation which a consul or a new praetor has furnished for the circus at a fête.

II

When the woodland everywhere is despoiled of its green honours, make straight for the deep forest, mounted on the snow-white housing of your steed. The snipe is an easy and an agreeable prey. You will find it no larger in body than Venus' doves. It feeds close to the edge of embankments, by the wash of the water, hunting tiny worms, its favourite fare. But its pursuit thereof is rather with keen-scented nose than with the eyes, in which its sense is rather dull, too big for the body though they be. With the point of the beak driven into the ground it drags out the little worms which needs must follow, therewith rewarding an appetite cheap to satisfy.[d]

[b] Palamedes was said to have invented some of the Greek letters (Υ, Θ, Ξ, Φ, Χ) by observing the flight of cranes: *cf.* Martial, IX. xiii. 7, XIII. lxxv.; Ausonius, *Idyll.* xii. (*Technopaegnion de literis monosyllabis*) 25; Pliny *N.H.* VII. 192.

[c] For the *mazonomus* (μαζονόμος) see Hor. *Sat.* II. viii. 86.

[d] For the unclassical lengthening of *gŭla,* Wernsdorf cites as a parallel from Nemesianus' fellow-African Luxorius, *quid festinus abis gula impellente, sacerdos?*

[2] i.e. the goose [illegible]: cf. Hor. Sat. II. viii. 88.

[3] For the [illegible] of [illegible] "Moorland" [illegible].

REPOSIANUS

AND SOME CONTEMPORARIES

INTRODUCTION

TO REPOSIANUS, MODESTINUS, "CUPIDO AMANS" AND PENTADIUS

The codex Salmasianus [a]—a title which records the previous ownership of Claude de Saumaise—is the chief authority for the surviving poems by three authors of the third century here selected from it —Reposianus, Modestinus and Pentadius, with the additional piece *Cupido Amans* by an unknown hand. The codex represents, though imperfectly, the extensive and varied *Anthologia Latina* compiled from poets of different periods, originally in twenty-four books, at Carthage in the time of the Vandal kings about A.D. 532. Owing to the disappearance of the first eleven quaternions, half-a-dozen books at the beginning are lost except in so far as the missing contents are represented by codex Leid. Voss. Q. 86 [" V "], by codex Paris. 8071 (or Thuaneus, " T "), both of the ninth century, and by other MSS.[b] The 182 hexameters by Reposianus on the *liaison* between Mars and Venus depend solely on the codex Salmasianus; for Modestinus we have the additional authority of T; and for Pentadius we have V as well as S and T.

Reposianus' theme is the discovery of the intrigue

[a] It is also the manuscript for Florus' poems, see p. 424.

[b] See Baehrens' prolegomena *P.L.M.* IV. pp. 3–54; Buecheler and Riese, *Anth. Lat.* I. i. praefatio, pp. xii. *sqq.*

between the Goddess of Love and the God of War by the injured husband, as first related in European literature by Homer, *Odyssey* VIII. 266–366. The Roman poet exhibits a turn for description, especially in depicting the flowery grove where the lovers meet; but there is in him a certain poverty of style—a certain want of variety in language, in thought and in structure. Manifestly he overdoes the use of *forte* (*e.g.* 68, 83, 87, 95, 114, 121, 126, 156, 166). The archaism *mage* of line 9 is an artificiality which he shares with Nemesianus (*Cyneg.* 317), with Sulpicius Lupercus Servasius and other late poets. The most noticeable metrical points are his use of *tuo* (93) as a monosyllable and *gratiosa* (126) as a trisyllable. A few turns of phrase suggest the Lucretian picture of Mars in Venus' lap (Lucret. I. 31–40); but Reposianus shows signs of independence in treating his sensuous theme. Thus, he alters the scene of the amour from the traditional house of the Fire-God, Vulcan, to a forest, which gives the cue for his introduction of some beauties in external nature (33–50). Further, the chains fastened upon the offending lovers are not, according to earlier forms of the fable, prepared as a trap in anticipation of their continued guilt, but fashioned at Vulcan's forge after Phoebus has informed him of Venus' infidelity.

The three longer pieces by Pentadius, *On Fortune*, *On the Coming of Spring* and *On Narcissus*, have "echoic" lines: the rest are short epigrams. Among these the quatrain *On Woman's Love*, beginning *Crede ratem ventis*, may be a tetrastichon combining a pair of independent elegiac distichs. It has been ascribed to a variety of authors besides Pentadius—to Marcus Cicero, to his brother, to Petronius, to Ausonius, and to Porphyrius, the panegyrist of Constantine. The epigram has been claimed for Quintus Cicero [a] as a vigorous expression of a thought which might have been in his mind after his divorce (*Ad Att.* XIV. 13. 3). But it cannot be argued that either the situation or the reflection was by any means peculiar to him.

EDITIONS

Reposianus : P. Burman. *Anthol. Lat.* Lib. I. No. 72. Amsterdam, 1759.
J. C. Wernsdorf. *Poet. Lat. Min.* IV. pp. 319 *sqq.* Altenburg, 1785.
E. Baehrens. *Poet. Lat. Min.* IV. pp. 348 *sqq.* Leipzig, 1882.
F. Buecheler and A. Riese. *Anth. Lat.* I. i. No. 253. Leipzig, 1894.

Modestinus : P. Burman. *Anthol. Lat.* Lib. I. No. 31.
E. Baehrens. *Poet. Lat. Min.* IV. p. 360.
F. Buecheler and A. Riese. *Anth. Lat.* I. i. No. 273, p. 217.

Pentadius : P. Burman. *Anthol. Lat.* Lib. I. Nos. 139, 141, 165; III. No. 105; V. No. 69.
J. C. Wernsdorf. *Poet. Lat. Min.* III. pp. 262–80, pp. 405–407.
E. Baehrens. *Poet. Lat. Min.* IV. pp. 343–5, 358–9.
F. Buecheler and A. Riese. *Anth. Lat.* I. i. Nos. 234–5, 265–8.

[a] Jas. Stinchcomb, "The Literary Interests of a Roman Magnate," *Class. Weekly*, Oct. 3, 1932.

INTRODUCTION TO REPOSIANUS

SIGLA

S = codex Salmasianus sive Parisinus 10318: saec. vii.

T = codex Thuaneus sive Parisinus 8071: saec. ix. exeunte.

V = codex Vossianus L.Q. 86: medio saec. ix.

REPOSIANUS

De Concubitu Martis et Veneris

Discite securos non umquam credere amores.
ipsa Venus, cui flamma potens, cui militat ardor,
quae tuto posset custode Cupidine amare,
quae docet et fraudes et amorum furta tuetur,
nec sibi securas valuit praebere latebras. 5
improbe dure puer, crudelis crimine matris,
pompam ducis, Amor, nullo satiate triumpho!
quid conversa Iovis laetaris fulmina semper?
ut mage flammantes possis laudare sagittas,
iunge, puer, teretes Veneris Martisque catenas: 10
gestet amans Mavors titulos et vincula portet
captivus, quem bella timent! utque ipse veharis,
iam roseis fera colla iugis submittit amator:
post vulnus, post bella potens Gradivus anhelat
in castris modo tiro tuis, semperque timendus 15
te timet et sequitur qua ducunt vincla marita.
ite, precor, Musae: dum Mars, dum blanda Cythere
imis ducta trahunt suspiria crebra medullis

[a] *conversa*, either thrown back by the power of love or exchanged for the disguises which Jove used in his amours.

[b] *mage*, an artificial archaism, as in Sulpicius Lupercus Servasius, II. (*De Cupiditate*) 16, and in the *Dicta Catonis*, *Praef*. II. 2, *Distich*. II. 6; IV. 42.

[c] An ancient form of *Mars*: his surname *Gradivus* (14) marks him as god of the march (*gradus*).

[d] *Cythere* (*cf*. 172), a late Latin collateral form of *Cytherea* (153), refers to the birth of Venus from the sea at the island

REPOSIANUS

The Intrigue of Mars with Venus

Learn ye the creed that amours are never free from care. Venus herself of the potent flame, Venus of the blazing campaign, who might indulge love with Cupid as her safe warden, instructress in deceits, protectress of the stealth of love, did not avail to furnish herself with a secure lurking-place. Harsh tyrant Boy, cruel in a mother's fault, O Love, you lead your victorious procession, never sated with any triumph! Why do you always rejoice that Jove's thunderbolts have been reversed? [a] That you may the better [b] praise your flaming arrows, draw tight, Boy, the well-woven chains of Venus and of Mars: let Mavors [c] in love wear the label of a slave, let him whom wars do dread be a prisoner bearing bonds! To let you ride triumphant, the lover yields his savage neck to a rosy yoke. After wounds dealt and battles fought, pcwerful Gradivus pants as a new-enlisted recruit in your camp; he that should ever be feared fears you, following where wedlock's bonds do lead. Pray, come, ye Muses: while Mars, while alluring Cythere [d] draw fast-following sighs from the depth

of Cythera. *Cypris* (35, 79, 141, 146) recalls her cult in Cyprus, and *Paphie*, Reposianus' favourite epithet for Venus (23, 50, 61, 64, 80, 105, 109, 136, 139, 178), alludes to her temple at Paphos in Cyprus. Reposianus shares the epithets *Cythere*, *Cypris* and *Paphie* with Ausonius (4th cent. A.D.), though *Paphie* is used by Martial.

dumque intermixti captatur spiritus oris,
carmine doctiloquo Vulcani vincla parate, 20
quae Martem nectant Veneris nec bracchia laedant
inter delicias roseo prope livida serto.
namque ferunt Paphien, Vulcani et Martis amorem,
inter adulterium nec iusti iura mariti
indice sub Phoebo captam gessisse catenas. 25
illa manu duros nexus tulit, illa mariti
ferrea vincla sui. quae vis fuit ista doloris?
an fortem faciebat amor? quid, saeve, laboras?
cur nodos Veneri Cyclopia flamma paravit?
de roseis conecte manus, Vulcane, catenis! 30
nec tu deinde liges, sed blandus vincla Cupido,
ne palmas duro nodus cum vulnere laedat.
lucus erat Marti gratus, post vulnera Adonis
pictus amore deae; si Phoebi lumina desint,
tutus adulterio, dignus quem Cypris amaret, 35
quem Byblos coleret, dignus quem Gratia servet.

22 divitias S: delicias *Burman*. prope S: modo *Baehrens*.
26 manus S: manu *Schrader*: Venus *Baehrens*.
32 comodus S: nodus cum *Baehrens, alii alia*.
34 pictus S: dictus *vel* lectus *vel* dignus *Wernsdorf*: huius *Baehrens*: laetus *Riese* (*in not*.).

---

[a] *i.e.* arms so delicate that rose-leaves might almost make them black and blue.

[b] Addressed to Vulcan as the injured husband of Venus.

[c] *i.e.* to fashion iron chains.

[d] After the death of her beloved Adonis from a wound inflicted by a boar in the forest, Venus might be imagined to dislike all woods. The passage implies that she made an exception in the case of the grove where she met her lover Mars, and so it is "decorated," "lit up" by the beautiful presence of the enamoured goddess. *pictus* may be right, though *amore* is less directly instrumental than the concrete ablatives in Lucr. V. 1395–1396, *anni tempora pingebant viridantes floribus herbas*; Sen. *Med.* 310, *stellisque quibus pingitur*

of their being, and while they woo the breath of intermingled kisses, do ye with dulcet strain make ready Vulcan's bonds to twine round Mars and yet do no hurt to Venus' arms that mid their dalliance are half-discoloured with the pressure of even a garland of roses.[a]

The tale is told that the Paphian goddess, darling of Vulcan and of Mars, amid her adulterous intercourse and rights usurped by one not her lawful husband, was 'neath the revealing Sun-god caught, and wore the chains. She bore on her hand the cruel coils, she bore the iron bonds of her own husband. What was that violence in your resentment?[b] Did love make strength?[c] Why toil, O ruthless one? Why did the flame of the Giants' forge prepare entanglements for Venus? Rather, Vulcan, make the linking for the hands from chains of roses! And then *you* must not tie the bonds, but coaxing Cupid must, lest the knotting hurt the palms and inflict harsh pain.

There was a grove dear to Mars, adorned[d] by the goddess' love after Adonis' death-wound; if only sunlight were lacking, safe for unlawful passion, meet for the Cyprian's affection, meet for worship from Byblos,[e] meet for the regard of one of the Graces.[f]

aether; Pentadius, *De Adventu Veris*, line 11, *floribus innumeris pingit sola flatus Eoi*: *cf.* Lucr. II. 374–5, *concharum genus . . . videmus pingere telluris gremium.* The metaphorical use seems a not unnatural extension from the idea of *pingunt* in 38, or in *sic mea flaventem pingunt vineta Garumnam* (of vineyards throwing their green reflection on the yellow Garonne), Auson. *Mosella* 160, or in *quis te naturae pinxit color? ib.* 110.

[e] This Phoenician coast-town was the chief seat of the worship of Adonis: *cf.* 66 and *Bybliades*, 90.

[f] *Cf.* line 51. The singular is used in Ovid. *Met.* VI. 429.

vilia non illo surgebant gramina luco:
pingunt purpureos candentia lilia flores;
ornat terra nemus: nunc lotos mitis inumbrat,
nunc laurus, nunc myrtus. habent sua munera rami; 40
namque hic per frondes redolentia mala relucent.
hic rosa cum violis, hic omnis gratia odorum,
hic inter violas coma mollis laeta hyacinthi:
dignus amore locus, cui tot sint munera rerum.
non tamen in lucis aurum, non purpura fulget: 45
flos lectus, flos vincla tori, substramina flores;
deliciis Veneris dives Natura laborat.
texerat hic liquidos fontes non vilis harundo,
sed qua saeva puer componat tela Cupido.
hunc solum Paphie puto lucum fecit amori: 50
hic Martem exspectare solet. quid Gratia cessat,
quid Charites? cur, saeve puer, non lilia nectis?
tu lectum consterne rosis, tu serta parato
et roseis crinem nodis subnecte decenter.
haec modo purpureum decerpens pollice florem, 55
cum delibato suspiria ducat odore.
ast tibi blanda manus ⟨flores⟩ sub pectore condat!
tunc ne purpurei laedat te spina roseti,
destrictis teneras foliis constringe papillas!
sic decet in Veneris luco gaudere puellas: 60
ut tamen illaesos Paphiae servetis amores,

39 locos vitis S: lotos mitis *Burman.*
40 rami *Baehrens, Riese*: lauri *vulgo.*
41 lilia pendent S: mala relucent *Baehrens.*
52 licia *vulgo.*
56 diligatum . . . odorem S: delibat eum . . . odorem *Baehrens*: delibato . . . odore *Klappius.*

---

[a] There are no purple coverlets.

No common herbage grew within that grove: white lilies set off its bright-hued flowers. The earth gives adornment to the woodland: now the mild lotus casts its shade, now the laurel, now the myrtle. The boughs have their own gifts; for here mid leafage fragrant apples shine out. Here the rose is neighbour to violets, here is every charm of scent, here among the violets are the joyous bells of the delicate hyacinth. Meet for love is a place which hath such wealth of boons. Still, gold there is none in all the grove, no gleam of purple [a]: flowers are the bed, flowers the frame of the couch, flowers the support beneath. Rich Nature toils for Venus' luxury. Here had no common reeds shaded the crystal wells, but such as those whence young Cupid fashions his cruel weapons. I trow our Lady of Paphos made this grove for naught but love. Here 'tis her way to wait for Mars. Why be the Graces slow to come—the sisterhood of the Charites? [b] Why, cruel Boy, do you not twine lilies? Nay, *you* must strew the couch with roses, *you* must make garlands ready and with rosy knots bind up Venus' hair in seemly wise.[c] Even as her finger culls the bright-hued bloom, let her draw long sighs as she drinks in its fragrance. But for thyself let a caressing hand store the flowers beneath thy bosom! Then, lest a thorn of the bright-hued rose-bush hurt thee, strip off the leaves ere thou bind together the tender buds! [d] Even thus 'tis seemly that maids rejoice within the grove of Venus: yet that ye may preserve amours uninjured for the Paphian,

[b] The Greek Χάριτες corresponded to the Latin *Gratiae*.
[c] Wernsdorf thinks *tu* is addressed to one of the Graces.
[d] For *papillae* as rosebuds *cf. Pervig. Ven.* 14 and 21.

vincula sic mixtis caute constringite ramis,
ne diffusa ferat per frondes lumina Titan.
his igitur lucis Paphie, dum proelia Mavors
horrida, dum populos diro terrore fatigat, 65
ludebat teneris Bybli permixta puellis.
nunc varios cantu divom referebat amores
inque modum vocis nunc motus forte decentes
corpore laeta dabat, nunc miscens † denique plantas,
nunc alterna movens suspenso pollice crura, 70
molliter inflexo subnitens poplite sidit.
saepe comam pulchro collectam flore ligabat
ornans ambrosios divino pectine crines.

dum ludos sic blanda Venus, dum gaudia miscet 74
et dum flet, quod sera venit sibi grata voluptas, 76
et dum suspenso solatia quaerit amori: 75
ecce furens post bella deus, post proelia victor 77
victus amore venit. cur gestas ferrea tela?
ne metuat Cypris, comptum decet ire rosetis.
a, quotiens Paphie vultum mentita furentis 80
lumine converso serum incusavit amantem!
verbera saepe dolens minitata est dulcia serto
aut, ut forte magis succenso Marte placeret,
amovit teneris suspendens oscula labris
nec totum effundens medio blanditur amore. 85

decidit aut posita est devictis lancea palmis
et, dum forte cadit, myrto retinente pependit.
ensem tolle, puer, galeam tu, Gratia, solve; 88

82 mentita S: minitata *Higtius*.
84 atmovet S: admovit *vulgo*: amovit *Wakkerus*.

---

[a] An imitation of Virg. *Georg.* IV. 347.

carefully knit together bonds of branches intertwined to keep the Sun-god from shedding a flood of light through the foliage. In these woodlands, then, the Paphian used to sport amid a bevy of tender damsels from Byblos, while Mavors plied savage warfare, while he wearied the nations with dread alarm. Now she would rehearse in song the chequered amours of the gods [a] and to the vocal measure now joyously, as it befell, made seemly movements with her body; now in turn plying intricate steps, now on light fantastic toe moving alternate feet, she sinks down resting upon gracefully bended haunch. Oft she would bind her hair close-drawn with pretty blooms, ordering ambrosial tresses with comb divine.

While thus sweet Venus engages in various sports and joys, and turns to tears for that her darling pleasure cometh late, and seeks some solace for her love deferred, behold in frenzy after warfare comes the god, after his battles the vanquisher vanquished by love. Why dost thou wear weapons of steel? Lest Cypris feel alarm, 'tis seemly to come with roses garlanded. Ah, how often did the Paphian's look feign anger as her averted eye reproached her lover's tardiness! Oft, piqued, did she threaten sweet lashes from festoons of flowers, or, mayhap the more to please when Mars was afire with passion, withheld those kisses which she poised on tender lips, alluring in the midst of love by checking love's full flood.

Down fell his lance or with love-vanquished hands was laid aside, and, as it happened to fall, hung on a myrtle-bough which caught it. Take, Boy, his sword: let one of the Graces unlace his helmet: ye

solvite, Bybliades, praeduri pectora Martis:
haec laxet nodos, haec ferrea vincula temptet
loricaeque moras, vos scuta et tela tenete.
nunc violas tractare decet. laetare, Cupido,
terribilem divum tuo solo numine victum:
pro telis flores, pro scuto myrtea serta,
et rosa forte loco est gladii, quem iure tremescunt!
iverat ad lectum Mavors et pondere duro
floribus incumbens totum turbarat honorem.
ibat pulchra Venus vix presso pollice cauta,
florea ne teneras violarent spicula plantas,
et nunc innectens, ne rumpant oscula, crinem,
nunc vestes fluitare sinens, vix lassa retentat,
cum nec tota latet nec totum nudat amorem.
ille inter flores furtivo lumine tectus
spectat hians Venerem totoque ardore tremescit.
incubuit lectis Paphie. proh sancte Cupido,
quam blandas voces, quae tunc ibi murmura fundunt!
oscula permixtis quae tunc fixere labellis!
quam bene consertis haeserunt artubus artus!
stringebat Paphiae Mavors tunc pectore dextram
et collo innexam ne laedant pondera laevam,
lilia cum roseis supponit candida sertis.
saepe levi cruris tactu commovit amantem
in flammas, quas diva fovet. iam languida fessos
forte quies Martis tandem compresserat artus;
non tamen omnis amor, non omnis pectore cessit
flamma dei: trahit in medio suspiria somno

[95] iura S: iure *Riese*: bella *Baehrens*.
[101] sinũ S: sinens *Oudendorp*. laxa S: lassa *Baehrens*.
[103] tectus S: tectam *Baehrens*.
[104] motoque *Baehrens*.

---

[a] *Cf.* Lucret. I. 36, of Mars in Venus' lap, *pascit amore avidos inhians in te, dea, visus*.

damsels of Byblos, unlace the breast of stalwart Mars—let one slacken the knots, one try the iron bands which guard his breastplate, you others keep the shield and weapons. 'Tis the fitting moment to handle violets. Rejoice, O Cupid, that the awe-inspiring god is conquered by your divinity alone: instead of weapons there be flowers, instead of shield the myrtle wreaths; the rose, it so befalls, takes the place of the sword at which men have cause to tremble!

Mavors had come to the couch and resting his hard weight upon the flowers disordered all their gracefulness. Fair Venus came scarce leaving footprint in her caution lest the prickly flowers should mar her tender feet, and, now entwining her tresses lest kisses might ruffle them, now letting her robes flow loose, can scarce confine them in her languor: she is not wholly hid nor wholly bares her charms. He in his covering of flowers with stealthy eye gazes agape at Venus, quivering in the full flame of passion.[a] The Paphian goddess sank upon the couch. Ah! Cupid the august, how coaxing the words, what the murmurs they then did utter there! What kisses did they then imprint upon commingled lips! How well did limb clasp limb in close embrace! Then Mavors drew his right hand from the Paphian's breast and lest his weight should hurt the left arm twined around her neck, sets white lilies and rose-wreaths underneath. Oft the leg's light touch stirred the lover into flames by the goddess fanned. At last, it befell, the languor of repose had mastered the weary limbs of Mars; yet did not all love's rapture, yet did not all the flame, quit the god's breast: amidst his slumber he heaves sighs and from the

et venerem totis pulmonibus ardor anhelat.
ipsa Venus tunc tunc calidis succensa venenis
uritur ardescens, nec somnia parta quieta.
o species quam blanda! o quam bene presserat artus 12
nudos forte sopor! niveis suffulta lacertis
colla nitent: pectus gemino quasi sidere fulget.
non omnis resupina iacet, sed corpore flexo
molliter et laterum qua se confinia iungunt.
Martem respiciens deponit lumina somno, 12
sed gratiosa, decens. pro lucis forte Cupido
Martis tela gerit; quae postquam singula ⟨lustrat⟩,
loricam clipeum gladium galeaeque minacis
cristas, flore ligat; tunc hastae pondera temptat
miraturque suis tantum licuisse sagittis. 13
iam medium Phoebus radiis possederat orbem,
iam tumidis calidus spatiis libraverat horas:
flammantes retinebat equos. proh conscia facti
invida lux! Veneris qui nunc produntur amores
lumine, Phoebe, tuo! stant capti iudice tanto 13
Mars Amor et Paphie, ramisque inserta tremescunt
lumina, nec crimen possunt te teste negare.
viderat effusis Gradivum Phoebus habenis
in gremio Paphiae spirantem incendia amoris.
o rerum male tuta fides! o gaudia et ipsis 14
vix secura deis! quis non, cum Cypris amaret,

120 *sic Baehrens*: o quam blanda quies S, *Riese.*
122 turget S: fulget *Baehrens.*
124 quo . . . iungant *Baehrens.*
127 regens S: gerit *Riese.* tela; rigens *Baehrens.* lustrat *Burman, Baehrens*; *om.* S: vidit *vulgo*: sumpsit *Riese.*
132 *sic Burman*: iam mediis *Maehly*: dimidiis *Riese.* calidum spatium . . . horis *Baehrens, Riese.*
136 ramis cum *Baehrens.*

---

[a] The manuscript reading *quam blanda quies* seems an over-bold contradiction of the preceding line.

depths of his lungs hot passion still pants love. Venus herself then, even then, enkindled with glowing poison, is afire and burns: she wins no restful dreams. How winning the sight![a] How fit the slumber that has o'ercome the naked limbs! A fair neck rests on snowy arms: the breast seems lit up by a pair of stars. Not wholly on her back is she reclined, but with a gentle bend of the body where side meets side. Looking at Mars, she drops her eyes in sleep, charming as ever, comely.[b] In front of the grove meanwhile Cupid is handling Mars' weapons: and after scanning them one by one, breastplate, shield, sword, plumes of the threatening helmet, he binds them each with flowers; then tests the spear's weight, marvelling that his own arrows have been allowed such power.

Already had Phoebus taken possession of the mid-world with his rays, already in the heat of his proud course had he balanced the hours of day and was restraining his flaming steeds. Ah! envious day-light privy to the deed! What love-intrigues of Venus are now betrayed, O Phoebus, by thy sun-shine! With a judge so mighty there stand as prisoners Mars and Love and Paphos' queen; shed through the branches, sunbeams quiver; they cannot disown their guilt confronted by thy testimony. From his chariot in full career Phoebus had espied Gradivus breathing love's fires in the Paphian goddess' lap. O ill-placed confidence! O joys even for the very gods scarce free from care! Who but would hope, when Cypris was in love, that loving

[b] Baehrens marks a lacuna here because of the abrupt transition.

praeside sub tanto tutum speraret amare?
criminis exemplum si iam de numine habemus,
quid speret mortalis amor? quae vota ferenda?
quod numen poscat, quo sit securus, adulter? 145
Cypris amat, nec tuta tamen! compressit habenas
Phoebus et ad lucos tantummodo lumina vertit
et sic pauca refert: "nunc spargis tela, Cupido;
nunc nunc, diva Venus, nati devicta sagittis
das mihi solamen; sub te securus amavi: 150
fabula, non crimen, nostri dicentur amores."
haec ait et dictis Vulcanum instigat amaris:
"dic ubi sit Cytherea decens, secure marite!
te exspectat lacrimans, tibi castum servat amorem?
vel si forte tuae Veneris fera crimina nescis, 155
quaere simul Martem, cui tu modo tela parasti."
dixit et infuso radiabat lumine lucum
inque fidem sceleris totos demiserat ignes.
haeserat Ignipotens stupefactus crimine tanto.
iam quasi torpescens (vix sufficit ira dolori) 160
ore fremit maestoque modo gemit ultima pulsans
ilia et indignans suspiria pressa fatigat.
antra furens Aetnaea petit. vix iusserat, omnes
incubuere manus, multum dolor addidit arti.
quam cito cuncta gerunt ars numen flamma maritus 165
ira dolor! nam vix causam tunc forte iubendo

142 amorem *vulgo*.
148 sparge tela S: spargis *Riese*: sparge o *Baehrens*.
150 da S: das *Oudendorp*. securus S: si lusus *Baehrens*.

[a] Apollo mischievously argues that Venus' example has shown him that conscience need not trouble a lover: so his own amours will be handed down as entertaining stories, not moral offences.

should be safe 'neath overseer so mighty? If now we take our pattern of wrongdoing from deity, what may a mortal's love expect? What prayers must be offered? What deity should a paramour entreat for an easy mind? Cypris is in love, yet not in safety. Phoebus held tight his reins and towards the grove turned but his eyes, uttering these brief words: "Now dost thou shower thy darts, O Cupid; now, now, divine Venus, quite vanquished by thy son's arrows, thou givest me solace; 'neath thy power I have learned to love care-free. My amours will be recounted for a fable, not a crime." [a]

So speaking he stirs up Vulcan with bitter words: "Say, heedless husband, where is the comely Lady of Cythera! Does she await thee in tears, preserving her chaste love for thee? Or, if mayhap thou knowest not the wild offences of thy Venus, search at the same time for Mars, whom of late thou didst provide with weapons." As he spoke, he lit up the grove with a flood of light, sending straightway his full fires down in proof of guilt. The Lord of Fire was at a loss, stunned by so great a crime: now half-benumbed (anger scarce meets his pain) he growls aloud, and groaning in melancholy wise convulses his sides to their very depth and wrathfully heaves sigh on sigh unceasing.[b] In his frenzy he makes for the cavern-forge of Aetna. Scarce were his orders given, when all hands fell to work—much did resentment add to skill. How quickly is all accomplished by skill, deity, flame, husband, anger, pain! Scarce in the moment of his ordering had he explained the

[b] *Cf.* phrases like Virg. *Aen.* IX. 415, *longis singultibus ilia pulsat*; VIII. 94, *noctemque diemque fatigant*; Sil. Ital. XII. 496, *curasque ita corde fatigat.*

dixerat, et vindex coniunx iam vincla ferebat.
pervenit ad lucos, non ipsi visus Amori,
non Chariti: totas arti mandaverat iras.
vincula tunc manibus suspenso molliter ictu 17(
illigat et teneris conectit bracchia palmis.
excutitur somno Mavors et pulchra Cythere.
posset Gradivus validos disrumpere nexus,
sed retinebat amor, Veneris ne bracchia laedat.
tunc tu sub galea, tunc inter tela latebas, 17
saeve Cupido, timens. stat Mavors lumine torvo
atque indignatur, quod sit deprensus adulter.
at Paphie conversa dolet non crimina facti;
sed quae sit vindicta sibi tum singula volvens
cogitat et poenam sentit, si Phoebus amaret. 18(
iamque dolos properans decorabat cornua tauri,
Passiphaae crimen mixtique cupidinis iram.

MODESTINUS

Forte iacebat Amor victus puer alite somno
myrti inter frutices pallentis roris in herba.

176 stans S: stat *Burman*: flat *Baehrens*.
180 sancit *Baehrens*. 181 reparans *Baehrens*.
182 Passifę S.

[a] *i.e.* for the full satisfaction of his anger he depended on the skill at the forge with which the avenging chains were made.

[b] Reposianus departs from the traditional story according to which the lovers were entrapped in a snare previously contrived by the Fire-god: see *Odyss.* viii. 276 *sqq.*; Ovid. *Met.* IV. 176 *sqq.*; *Ars. Am.* II. 577 *sqq.*; Statius, *Silv.* I. ii. 59–60. He also substitutes a grove for the Fire-god's house as the scene of the amour.

reason before the avenging husband was already bringing the chains. He reaches the grove, unseen by Love himself, unseen by any Grace: to his art he had entrusted all his rage.[a] Then with light soft touch he bound the chains upon the sleepers' hands, linking their arms with gentle movement.[b] Mars shakes himself free of sleep: so too the fair Cytherean. Gradivus well might burst asunder the strong bonds, but love restrained him lest he hurt Venus' arms. Then did *you* lurk hidden 'neath Mars' helmet, then did you lurk among his weapons, cruel Cupid, in cowardice. Mavors stands sullen of look, chafing because he is an adulterer caught. But the Paphian feels no grief that her guilty deed has turned awry: instead, she thinks of what revenge is hers, revolving point by point, and feels it were fit penalty if Phoebus fell in love: and now, hastening forward her guile, she set to ornament the horns of the bull which would mean Pasiphaë's guilt and the wrath involved in blended lust.[c]

MODESTINUS

Cupid Asleep

Young Love lay once with wingéd sleep o'ercome
Mid myrtle shrubs where pale dew soaked the grass.

[c] The fable ran that Venus took revenge on Phoebus through his offspring. Pasiphaë, daughter of the Sun-god, and wife of Minos, king of Crete, was the victim of Venus, who caused her to become enamoured of the bull: *cf.* Virg. *Aen.* VI. 25, *Pasiphaē mixtumque genus prolesque biformis* (in reference to the Minotaur).

Here, as occasionally elsewhere, *cupido* (= "desire") is masculine: there is no need to personify it as "Cupid," nor to adopt the suggestion in Burman of *mixtaeque libidinis.*

hunc procul emissae tenebrosa Ditis ab aula
circueunt animae, saeva face quas cruciarat.
"ecce meus venator!" ait "hunc" Phaedra "ligemus!" 5
crudelis "crinem" clamabat Scylla "metamus!"
Colchis et orba Procne "numerosa caede necemus!"
Didon et Canace "saevo gladio perimamus!"
Myrrha "meis ramis," Euhadneque "igne crememus!"
"hunc" Arethusa inquit Byblisque "in fonte necemus!" 10
ast Amor evigilans dixit "mea pinna, volemus."

AUCTOR INCERTUS

Cupido Amans

Quis me fervor agit? nova sunt suspiria menti.
anne aliquis deus est nostro vehementior arcu?
quem mihi germanum fato fraudante creavit
diva parens? satis an mea spicula fusa per orbem
vexavere polum laesusque in tempore mundus 5
invenit poenam? sed si mea vulnera novi,

Cupido Amans: [3] fato S: furto *Wakkerus*: partu *Baehrens*.

---

[a] The ten victims of unhappy love are represented as making allusions to their own misfortunes. Thus Phaedra seems to see a second Hippolytus, eager for the chase; Scylla remembers the lock she treacherously clipped from her father's head; Dido and Canace recall their death by a sword; Myrrha her transformation into a tree; Euhadne or Evadne her suicide on a blazing pyre; Byblis and Arethusa their metamorphosis into a fountain.

ANONYMOUS

Round him came ghosts, from Pluto's gloomy hall
Set free, ghosts whom his cruel brand had scorched.[a]
" Look! 'tis my hunter! " Phaedra said: " bring
 bonds! "
But ruthless Scylla cried " Let's shear his hair! "
The Colchian dame [b] and Procne sore-bereaved
Said " We must make him die full many a death! "
Dido and Canace urged death by steel:
" Nay, by my branches! " Myrrha claimed. " Let's
 burn
Him in the fire! " Euhadne thought his due.
Byblis and Arethusa wished him drowned.
But Love awoke and said " My wings, let's fly! "

ANONYMOUS

Cupid in Love [c]

What is the glow of passion that impels me? Sighs be new for me to think of. Can it be that some god has mightier force than Cupid's bow? To whom by some trick of fate has my goddess mother given birth to be a brother for me? Have my darts, shot through the globe, harassed the heavens enough, and an injured world at the fit moment discovered a penalty? Nay, if I know wounds of my

[b] Medea.

[c] This poem by an unknown author was first printed by Burman, *Anth. Lat.* I. Lib. I. No. 30 immediately before Modestinus' poem (. . . " ex Divionensi codice primi producimus et Salmasianis schedis "). It is here included as a companion picture to " Cupid Asleep." See Buecheler–Riese, *Anth. Lat.* I. i. No. 240, p. 197; Baehrens, *P.L.M.* IV. pp. 345–346.

hic meus est ignis: meus est, qui parcere nescit.
in furias ignesque trahor! licet orbe superno,
Iuppiter, et salsis undis, Neptune, tegaris,
abdita poenarum te cingant Tartara, Pluton, 10
impositum rumpemus onus! volitabo per axem
mundigerum caelique plagas pontique procellas
umbriferumque Chaos; pateant adamantina regna,
torva venenatis cedat Bellona flagellis!
poenam mundus amet: stupeat vis maior! anhelat 15
in se saevus Amor fraudemque in vulnere quaerit!

PENTADIUS

I

De Fortuna

Res eadem adsidue momento volvitur uno
  atque redit dispar res eadem adsidue.
vindice facta manu Progne pia dicta sorori,
  impia sed nato vindice facta manu.
carmine visa suo Colchis fuit ulta maritum, 5
  sed scelerata fuit carmine visa suo.
coniugis Eurydice precibus remeabat ad auras,
  rursus abit vitio coniugis Eurydice.

[9] ex altis S: et salsis *Wakkerus*: exultes *Riese*.
[10] poenarum *vulgo*: terrarum *Maehly*: Taenarium *Baehrens*. te cingant *Oudendorp*: est ingum (*sic*) S.
[15] vix S: vis *schedae*: mox *Baehrens*: stupeat, vincatur, anhelet *Riese*.
[16] vulnera *Baehrens*.
Pentadius: [3, 4] functa *L. Mueller, Baehrens*: facta *codd.*
[5, 6] visa *codd.*: fisa *Baehrens*: nisa *Riese*.

dealing, this is my own fire—that fire of mine which knows not how to spare. Into a frenzy of fires am I dragged! Although thou, O Jupiter, be concealed in the sphere above, and thou, O Neptune, in the salt-sea waves, although the hidden Hell of punishment encircle thee, Pluto, we will burst the burden laid on us! I will fly across the axis that supports the world, through the tracts of the sky and the tempests of ocean, and through shadowy Chaos: let adamantine realms ope wide, let the War-Goddess, sullen mid her envenomed whips, retreat! Let the world love its punishment! Let mightier force stand mazed!—So pants fell Cupid inly and, though himself wounded,[a] aims at guile.

PENTADIUS

I

On Changing Fortune

The same thing constantly rolls on with uniform movement, and unlike its old self returns the same thing constantly. By her avenging hand,[b] legend says, Progne proved loyal to her sister but proved disloyal to her son by her avenging hand. Through her incantation the Colchian (Medea) was seen to have revenged herself on her husband, but she was seen to be guilt-stained through her incantation. Her consort's entreaties all but won Eurydice's return to upper air: again is Eurydice lost through the fault

[a] Cupid forgets his own wound in his desire to do mischief.

[b] Progne or Procne: *cf.* Nemes. *Cyneg.* 33. She avenged on her husband King Tereus his outrage on her sister Philomela by slaying Itys her own son by Tereus: *cf.* Nem. *Cyn.* 33–34.

sanguine poma rubent Thisbae nece tincta repente:
  candida quae fuerant, sanguine poma rubent. 10
Daedalus arte sua fugit Minoia regna,
  amisit natum Daedalus arte sua.
munere Palladio laeti qua nocte fuere,
  hac periere Phryges munere Palladio.
nate quod alter ades caelo, sunt gaudia Ledae; 15
  sed maeret mater, nate quod alter abes.
hostia et ipse fuit diri Busiridis hospes
  Busirisque aris hostia et ipse fuit.
Theseus Hippolyto vitam per vota rogavit,
  optavit mortem Theseus Hippolyto. 20
stipite fatifero iuste quae fratribus usa est,
  mater saeva fuit stipite fatifero.
sola relicta toris flevisti in litore, Cnosis;
  laetaris caelo sola relicta toris.
aurea lana fuit, Phrixum quae per mare vexit; 25
  Helle qua lapsa est, aurea lana fuit.

[9] tristi nece *codd.*: Thysbaeo tincta *Heinsius*: Thisbae nece *L. Mueller*.

[17, 18] saepe *codd.*: et ipse *Heinsius*: sacra *Baehrens*.

[23] litore *codd.*: in litore *vulgo*: litora (*coniungendum cum* sola) *Baehrens*.

---

[a] Heinsius saw that the reference was to the trysting-place of Pyramus and Thisbe, and altered the *tristi* of the manuscripts. L. Mueller's *Thisbae* saves *nece*.

[b] Castor and Pollux, Leda's twins, were granted an alternate immortality; when changed into the constellation Gemini, one had to be above the horizon, the other below. This is the one instance among these Latin "echoic" verses in which the opening of a couplet is not exactly repeated at the close. Here there is the slight change of *ades* to *abes*.

[c] The Egyptian king who sacrificed strangers was in turn immolated by Hercules.

of her consort. Red with blood is the fruit suddenly stained by Thisbe's death:[a] the fruit which once was white is red with blood. By his skill (in flying) Daedalus escaped from the realms of Crete: his son (Icarus) was lost to Daedalus by his skill. Minerva's gift ruined the Trojans on that same night in which they were gladdened by Minerva's gift (of the wooden horse). O son, because thou, the one twin, art present in the sky, Leda feels joy; but her maternal heart is sore, O son, because thou, the other twin, art not present.[b] A victim of dread Busiris[c] was the stranger his very self, and Busiris at the altar his very self was a victim. For Hippolytus Theseus sought long life in his prayers; yet Theseus' (final) prayer was death for Hippolytus.[d] A fatal brand Althaea used justly for avenging her brothers, and a cruel mother she proved herself with that same fatal brand.[e] Left alone on thy couch, O Cretan lady, thou didst weep upon the strand; thou now rejoicest in the sky because thou wast left alone on thy couch.[f] The Golden Fleece it was which bore Phrixus o'er the sea: that from which (his sister) Helle fell was the Golden Fleece.[g] The Tantalid

[d] *i.e.* after the false charge brought against Hippolytus by Phaedra.

[e] Althaea avenged her brothers, whom her son Meleager had slain, by burning the brand on which his life depended (*impietate pia est*, Ovid, *Met.* VIII. 477): *cf.* Rutilius, II. 53.

[f] Ariadne, deserted by Theseus, was consoled by Bacchus and eventually made a constellation.

[g] Phrixus, in danger of death by sacrifice through the malignity of his stepmother Ino, escaped overseas with his sister Helle on the ram of the Golden Fleece provided by Zeus. Helle was drowned by falling from the ram into the strait which was called the Hellespont after her; but her brother reached Colchis in safety.

Tantalis est numero natorum facta superba,
natorum afflicta † Tantalis est numero.
Pelias hasta fuit, vulnus grave quae dedit hosti;
hoc quae sanavit, Pelias hasta fuit. 30
per mare iacta ratis pleno subit ostia velo,
in portu mersa est per mare iacta ratis.
lux cito summa datur natusque exstinguitur infans
atque animae eximiae lux cito summa datur.
sunt mala laetitiae diversa lege creata, 35
iuncta autem adsidue sunt mala laetitiae.

II

De Adventu Veris

Sentio, fugit hiemps; Zephyrisque animantibus orbem
iam tepet Eurus aquis: sentio, fugit hiemps.
parturit omnis ager, persentit terra calores,
germinibusque novis parturit omnis ager.
laeta virecta tument, folio sese induit arbor: 5
vallibus apricis laeta virecta tument.
iam Philomela gemit modulis, Ityn impia mater
oblatum mensis iam Philomela gemit.
monte tumultus aquae properat per levia saxa,
et late resonat monte tumultus aquae. 10
floribus innumeris pingit sola flatus Eoi,

27–28 afflicta *codd.* (*contra metrum*): *fortasse* infelix *Wight Duff. Metri causa coniecit Oudendorp* T. e numero . . . afflicta est T. e numero.

32 versa *codd.*: mersa *Heinsius.*

34 prima *codd.* (*corruptum*): primae *Oudendorp*: pretium *Heinsius*: *fortasse* eximiae *A. M. Duff.*

35 e lege creandi *Baehrens.*

36 autem *Riese*: etiam *Baehrens.*

(Niobe) grew proud over the number of her children: in the number of her children grief crushed the Tantalid. Achilles' spear[a] it was which dealt the enemy a heavy blow: what also cured the wound was Achilles' spear. The sea-tost barque enters the river-mouth under full sail; but in harbour sinks the sea-tost barque. Soon is the final day assigned and the new-born child cut off: likewise to illustrious life soon is the final day assigned. Evils and joy are made on a different pattern: yet are they constantly linked—evils and joy.

II

On the Arrival of Spring

Winter, I feel, has fled; and while Zephyrs quicken the world, Eurus is already genial on the waters: winter, I feel, has fled. Every field is in travail: earth feels thrills of warmth throughout: with the new buds every field is in travail. Green copses swell joyously: the tree robes herself with leaves: in sunlit dales green copses swell joyously. Now doth Philomel lament in tuneful notes; now, for that Itys was served at the board,[b] doth the impious mother Philomel lament. From the hill the tumultuous stream speeds among the smooth-worn stones: far and wide resounds from the hill the tumultuous stream. With flowers beyond all count the breath of the Orient wind decks the ground; and vales like

[a] See note on *Laus Pisonis*, 177.
[b] *i.e.* as food to Tereus. Philomela here takes the place of Procne: *cf. De Fortuna*, 3–4.

Tempeaque exhalant floribus innumeris.
per cava saxa sonat pecudum mugitibus Echo,
voxque repulsa iugis per cava saxa sonat.
vitea musta tument vicinas iuncta per ulmos ;
fronde maritata vitea musta tument.
nota tigilla linit iam garrula luce chelidon ;
dum recolit nidos, nota tigilla linit.
sub platano viridi iucundat somnus in umbra,
sertaque texuntur sub platano viridi.
tunc quoque dulce mori, tunc fila recurrite fusis :
inter et amplexus tunc quoque dulce mori.

III

NARCISSUS

Cui pater amnis erat, fontes puer ille colebat,
laudabatque undas, cui pater amnis erat.
se puer ipse videt, patrem dum quaerit in amne,
perspicuoque lacu se puer ipse videt.
quod Dryas igne calet, puer hunc irridet amorem ;
nec putat esse decus, quod Dryas igne calet.
stat stupet haeret amat rogat innuit adspicit ardet
blanditur queritur stat stupet haeret amat.
quodque amat, ipse facit vultu prece lumine fletu ;
oscula dat fonti, quodque amat ipse facit.

[14] visque T : usque V : bisque S : voxque *corr. Salmasius, Baehrens.*
[19] iucunda *codd.* : iucundat *Meyer.*

[a] *musta,* usually of new wine, here by metonymy means the clusters containing the promise of wine.
[b] *i.e.* in the spring season restore the by-gone days of youth.
[c] The River-god Cephisus was the father of Narcissus, who fell in love with his own reflection in water. The story is beautifully told by Ovid, *Met.* III. 346–510.

Tempe are fragrant with flowers beyond all count. Mid hollow rocks resounds Echo to the lowing herd; the note reverberated by the heights mid hollow rocks resounds. Wine-filled clusters [a] swell, linked among their neighbour elms: mid married leafage wine-filled clusters swell. The familiar roof-timber already at daybreak is being smeared with mud by the twittering swallow; as she repairs her nest, she smears the familiar roof-timber. Under the green plane-tree sleep takes pleasure in the shade: and garlands are a-twining under the green plane-tree. Then too 'twere sweet to die: then run, ye threads of destiny, back on the spindles: [b] amid embraces then too 'twere sweet to die.

III

Narcissus

The youth who had a river for sire [c] was ever fond of fountains: the waters won praise from him who had a river for sire. The youth beholds himself as he seeks his sire in the river; in the translucent pool the youth beholds himself. When a Dryad is fired with passion, the youth flouts such love: he deems it ne'er an honour that a Dryad is fired with passion. He stands astonished; halts and falls in love, questions, nods, gazes all aflame; now coaxing, now reproaching, he stands astonished; halts and falls in love. And what he loves, himself he makes [d] in look, entreaty, eye and tears; prints kisses on the fountain, and what he loves, himself he makes.

[d] *i.e.* he makes his own reflection, with which he is in love.

IV

Narcissus

Hic est ille, suis nimium qui credidit undis,
  Narcissus vero dignus amore puer.
cernis ab irriguo repetentem gramine ripas,
  ut per quas periit cernere possit aquas.

V

Chrysocome

Chrysocome gladium fugiens stringente marito
  texit adulterium iudice casta reo.

VI

De Femina

Crede ratem ventis, animum ne crede puellis;
  namque est feminea tutior unda fide.
femina nulla bona est, vel, si bona contigit una,
  nescio quo fato est res mala facta bona.

IV. [1] undis *codd.*: umbris *Baehrens.*
[4] crescere *codd.*: cernere *Baehrens* (*in not.*).

---

[a] The *Anthologia Latina* contains also two elegiac couplets on Narcissus (Baehrens, *P.L.M.* IV. p. 305 and p. 340); but their authorship is uncertain. The *Tumulus Hectoris* given to Pentadius in Cabaret-Dupaty's *Poetae Minores* is by Baehrens assigned to Pompilianus (*P.L.M.* IV. p. 149), while the *Tumulus Acidis* is of uncertain authorship (*P.L.M.* V. p. 404).

IV

Narcissus [a]

This is he who trusted overmuch in the pools which were his kin—the youth Narcissus, worthy of no counterfeit love. You behold him making again from the moist meadow for the river-banks in hope of beholding the waters which wrought his doom.[b]

V

Goldilocks

Chrysocome escaping from the sword as her husband drew it (to punish her) veiled her adultery by being found innocent when the culprit acted as judge.[c]

VI

On Woman's Love [d]

Trust to the winds thy barque, but to a girl
Never thy heart's affections; for the swirl
Of ocean wave is less to be eschewed
Than woman's faith. No woman can be good,
Or if a good one comes, then freakish fate
Good out of ill has managed to create.

[b] *crescere* would imply his perennial growth as a flower after metamorphosis.

[c] Convinced of her infidelity, her husband had been within an ace of killing her; but in court the judge pronounced her not guilty—he had been her partner in the offence!

[d] Variously ascribed to the Ciceros, to Ausonius and other poets besides Pentadius. See Introduction.

IV

Narcissus

This is he who trusted overmuch in the pool, which were his [illegible] worthy of no [illegible] love. [illegible] behold him [illegible] again from [illegible] river-banks [illegible] hope of beholding the [illegible] which wrought his doom.[1]

V

Chrysocome

Chrysocome, [illegible] as her husband drew it (in [illegible]) [illegible] by being found innocent [illegible] judge.[2]

VI

On Woman's Love[3]

Trust to the [illegible] to a girl
Nor [illegible] thy heart [illegible] for the [illegible]
Of [illegible] less [illegible]
Than woman's [illegible] No [illegible] be good,
Or if [illegible] good [illegible] fate,
[illegible] has managed to create.

[1] [illegible] would imply [illegible]
[2] Convinced of her [illegible] her husband had been within an ace of killing [illegible] not guilty—he had [illegible] in the crime.
[3] Variously ascribed to [illegible] and other poets besides Pentadius. See Introduction.

TIBERIANUS

INTRODUCTION

TO TIBERIANUS

From Jerome's Chronicle (ad ann. 2352) we learn that Tiberianus, "vir disertus," was a governor in Gaul as "praefectus praetorio" in A.D. 335. Possibly he is the same as the Tiberianus whom we find holding official positions in Africa and Spain slightly earlier in the fourth century. His poetry is represented by a few surviving poems and quotations. The feeling for the beauty of nature pervading the twenty trochaic tetrameters[a] in his *Amnis ibat* gives some countenance to Baehrens' suggestion that he composed the metrically similar *Pervigilium Veneris*;[b] and the almost entire avoidance of quadrisyllabic endings in that poem bears, it has been argued, a resemblance to the manner of Tiberianus.[c] His authorship of the twenty-eight hexameters on the pernicious influence of gold is attested by Servius' citation of its third line on *Aeneid* VI. 136. The twelve hendecasyllabics

[a] Tiberianus apparently uses greater metrical licence than is found in the *Pervigilium Veneris*. He allows an anapaest in the fifth foot, if either Baehrens' *violarum sub spiritu* or Garrod's *violarum suspiritu* is accepted in line 7, and a spondee in the fifth foot, if the MS. readings are correct in lines 6 and 14.

[b] See Introduction to Florus for the contention that the *Pervigilium* is much earlier: *cf.* also Introduction to the poem in Loeb ed. of Catullus, Tibullus and *Pervig. Ven.*

[c] See Appendix to J. A. Fort's ed. of *Pervig. Ven.*, Oxford, 1922.

on a bird may be somewhat less confidently ascribed to him. Based on different manuscript authority is the poem purporting to be translated from Greek into Latin " a quodam Tiberiano," and in its invocation of the Supreme Being blending Orphic, Pythagorean and Platonic elements. There are, besides, a few fragments referred explicitly to Tiberianus by Servius and Fulgentius.[a]

EDITIONS

M. Haupt. *Ovidii Halieutica*, etc. Leipzig, 1838. [Haupt first printed poem No. iv " Omnipotens . . ."][b]

E. Baehrens. *Unedirte lateinische Gedichte*, p. 27 *sqq.* Leipzig, 1877.

—— *Poet. Lat. Minores*, III. pp. 263–269. Leipzig, 1881.

F. Buecheler and A. Riese. *Anthologia Latina*, I. ii. Nos. 490, 719*b*, 809–810.

The text here given is in the main that of Baehrens, with the chief departures indicated.

SIGLUM for Poems I–III.

H = codex Harleianus 3685 : saec. xv. (Containing also various medieval verses.)

[a] These scraps are given by Baehrens, *P.L.M.* III. 269, and are included in this edition.

[b] See also L. Quicherat, *Biblioth. de l'école des chartes*, IV. p. 267 *sq.*

TIBERIANUS

SIGLA for Poem IV.

R = Reginensis 215: saec. ix. (Collated by Baehrens.)
P = Parisinus 2772: saec. x–xi. (Collated by Quicherat and by Riese.)
S = Parisinus 17160: saec. xii. (Collated by Baehrens.)
V = Vindobonensis 143: saec. xiii. (Used by Haupt.)

TIBERIANUS

I

Amnis ibat inter arva valle fusus frigida,
luce ridens calculorum, flore pictus herbido.
caerulas superne laurus et virecta myrtea
leniter motabat aura blandiente sibilo.
subter autem molle gramen flore adulto creverat:
et croco solum rubebat et lucebat liliis,
et nemus fragrabat omne violarum ⟨sub⟩ spiritu.
inter ista dona veris gemmeasque gratias
omnium regina odorum vel colorum Lucifer
auriflora praeminebat, flamma Diones, rosa.
roscidum nemus rigebat inter uda gramina:
fonte crebro murmurabant hinc et inde rivuli,
antra muscus et virentes intus ⟨hederae⟩ vinxerant,
qua fluenta labibunda guttis ibant lucidis.

[6] tum croco *Baehrens* : et croco H.
[7] violarum spiritu H (*contra metrum*) : sub *addidit Baehrens* : spiritu violarii *Fort.*
[10] *sic Garrod* (*Oxford Book of Latin Verse*) : auro flore praeminebat forma dionis H : aureo flore eminebat cura Cypridis *Baehrens.*
[13] hederae *addidit Mackail* : myrtus *Baehrens* : *om.* H.
[14] qua *Ziehen* : quae H, *Baehrens, qui hunc versum ante* 13 *transposuit.* guttis ibant lucidis H : gurgite i. lucido *Fort.*

TIBERIANUS

I

THROUGH the fields there went a river; down the airy glen it wound,
Smiling mid its radiant pebbles, decked with flowery plants around.
Dark-hued laurels waved above it close by myrtle greeneries,
Gently swaying to the whispers and caresses of the breeze.
Underneath grew velvet greensward with a wealth of bloom for dower,
And the ground, agleam with lilies, coloured 'neath the saffron-flower,
While the grove was full of fragrance and of breath from violets.
Mid such guerdons of the spring-time, mid its jewelled coronets,
Shone the queen of all the perfumes, Star that loveliest colours shows,
Golden flame of fair Dione, passing every flower—the rose.
Dewsprent trees rose firmly upright with the lush grass at their feet:
Here, as yonder, streamlets murmured tumbling from each well-spring fleet.
Grottoes had an inner binding made of moss and ivy green,
Where soft-flowing runlets glided with their drops of crystal sheen.

has per umbras omnis ales plus canora quam putes
cantibus vernis strepebat et susurris dulcibus;
hic loquentis murmur amnis concinebat frondibus,
quis melos vocalis aurae musa Zephyri moverat.
sic euntem per virecta pulchra odora et musica
ales amnis aura lucus flos et umbra iuverat.

II

Aurum, quod nigri manes, quod turbida versant
flumina, quod duris extorsit poena metallis!
aurum, quo pretio reserantur limina Ditis,
quo Stygii regina poli Proserpina gaudet!
aurum, quod penetrat thalamos rumpitque pudorem,
qua ductus saepe illecebra micat impius ensis!
in gremium Danaes non auro fluxit adulter
mentitus pretio faciem fulvoque veneno?
non Polydorum hospes saevo necat incitus auro?
altrix infelix, sub quo custode pericli
commendas natum? cui regia pignora credis?
fit tutor pueri, fit custos sanguinis aurum!
immitis nidos coluber custodiet ante
et catulos fetae poterunt servare leaenae.
sic etiam ut Troiam popularet Dorica pubes,
aurum causa fuit . . . .
. . . . pretium dignissima merces:
infami probro palmam convendit adulter.

[a] Jupiter: *cf.* Sulpicius Lupercus Servasius, II. 7–8 (*De Cupiditate*).

[b] Polydorus, son of Priam, was murdered by Polymnestor, King of Thrace, for the gold which Priam had sent with Polydorus: *cf.* Virgil, *Aeneid* III. 41–57, esp. *auri sacra fames.*

[c] Paris gave his judgement in favour of Venus for the promise of Helen's love, and his award of the golden apple to her thus led to the Trojan war.

Through those shades each bird, more tuneful than belief could entertain,
Warbled loud her chant of spring-tide, warbled low her sweet refrain.
Here the prattling river's murmur to the leaves made harmony,
As the Zephyr's airy music stirred them into melody.
To a wanderer through the coppice, fair and filled with song and scent,
Bird and river, breeze and woodland, flower and shade brought ravishment.

II

O Gold, whirled onward by dark hell and muddy rivers, wrested by the convict from cruel mines: gold, the bribe unbarring Pluto's doors, and the delight of Proserpine, queen of the Stygian world! gold which invades the marriage-bower and shatters chastity, and at whose enticement the unholy sword often flashes from scabbard drawn! Was it not in golden stream that to Danaë's lap there came the adulterer [a] who masked his appearance in his bribe of yellow poison? Was not barbarous gold the motive when Polydorus [b] was slain by his host? Unhappy nurse, under what guardian against danger dost thou entrust a son? To whom dost thou commit children of royal line? Gold becomes protector of the boy, gold the guardian of the blood! Sooner will ruthless serpent guard nestlings, and lionesses be ready to save the whelps of a newly delivered dam. So too for Troy's destruction by the young manhood of Greece the reason lay in gold . . . a bribe the worthiest recompense. At the price of infamous scandal the paramour sold his award.[c]

denique cernamus, quos aurum servit in usus.
auro emitur facinus, pudor almus venditur auro,
tum patria atque parens, leges pietasque fidesque:
omne nefas auro tegitur, fas proditur auro.
porro hoc Pactolus, porro fluat et niger Hermus?
aurum, res gladii, furor amens, ardor avarus,
te celent semper vada turbida, te luta nigra,
te tellus mersum premat infera, te sibi nasci
Tartareus cupiat Phlegethon Stygiaeque paludes!
inter liventes pereat tibi fulvor harenas,
nec post ad superos redeat faex aurea puros!

III

Ales, dum madida gravata nube
udos tardius explicat volatus,
decepta in medio repente nisu
capta est pondere depremente plumae:
cassato solito vigore pennae,
quae vitam dederant, dedere letum;
sic, quis ardua nunc tenebat alis,
isdem protinus incidit ruinae.
quid sublimia circuisse prodest?
qui celsi steterant, iacent sub imis!
exemplum capiant, nimis petendo
qui ventis tumidi volant secundis.

III. [1] madida g. pennis H: madidis g. p. *Garrod*: madida g. nube *Baehrens*.
[7] ac *Baehrens*.
[9] sublima circuisse H: sublima requisiisse *Baehrens*.
[10] sub ictu *Baehrens*.
[12] vanis t. tonant H: ventis t. volant *Rohde*.

Let us then see for what uses gold doth serve. It is the buying-price of crime, it is the sale-price of kind modesty, of fatherland and parent, of laws and piety and faith: all guilt is hidden by gold, by gold all righteousness betrayed. With it must Pactolus still flow on, and likewise the dark Hermus-stream?[a] O gold, thou murderous thing, thou frenzied madness and passionate greed, let muddy shallows and a stream's dark silt conceal thee evermore; let earth below whelm and bury thee, let Tartarean Phlegethon and the Stygian pools covet thy birth for themselves! Perish thy yellow gleam among the sombre sands! Never hereafter let the golden dregs return to clean-handed men of the world above!

III

A bird with drenching rain o'erweighted,
Hindered by wet, her flight abated,
And sudden, mid her efforts foiled,
Was caught as 'neath her load she toiled.
When her old strength of wing grew nought,
What once brought life now ruin brought:
So pinions used for soaring high
Straight dashed her on the ground to die.
What boots it round the heavens to fly?
Who stood exalted, lowest lie!
Learn this, who aim beyond the scale
And haughtily ride the favouring gale.

[a] The golden sands of the Lydian river Hermus and its tributary, the Pactolus, were renowned in antiquity.

IV

Omnipotens, annosa poli quem suspicit aetas,
quem sub millenis semper virtutibus unum
nec numero quisquam poterit pensare nec aevo,
nunc esto affatus, si quo te nomine dignum est,
quo sacer ignoto gaudes, quom maxima tellus 5
intremit et sistunt rapidos vaga sidera cursus.
tu solus, tu multus item, tu primus et idem
postremus mediusque simul mundique superstes.
nam sine fine tui labentia tempora finis.
altus ab aeterno spectas fera turbine certo 10
rerum fata rapi vitasque involvier aevo
atque iterum reduces supera in convexa referri,
scilicet ut mundo redeat quod partubus haustus
perdiderit refluumque iterum per tempora fiat.
tu (siquidem fas est in temet tendere sensum 15
et speciem temptare sacram, qua sidera cingis
immensus longamque simul complecteris aethram)
fulmineis forsan rapida sub imagine membris
flammifluum quoddam iubar es, quo cuncta coruscans
ipse vides nostrumque premis solemque diemque. 20
tu genus omne deum, tu rerum causa vigorque,
tu natura omnis, deus innumerabilis unus,
tu sexu plenus toto, tibi nascitur olim

[8] mundique superstes RS: mundoque superstans *Baehrens.*

[10] altus et *Baehrens.* spectans *codd.*, *Baehrens*: spectas *Riese.*

[13] austrum R: abstrum P: abstui S: astra V: haustum *Quicherat*: haustus *Baehrens.*

[18] fulgentis . . . Phoebi *Baehrens.*

[19] choruscas S: coruscant R: coruscas P, *Baehrens*: coruscans *Riese.*

[20] ipse vides *codd.*: ipseque das *Baehrens.*

IV

Almighty Being, to whom heaven's age, ancient of years, showeth reverence, whom for ever One amid a thousand attributes, no man shall e'er have power to appraise in number or in time, now be thou addressed if under any name it is fitting to address thee; yet even in name unknown thou hast thy hallowed joy, when mightiest earth shuddereth and wandering constellations stay their rapid courses. Thou art alone, yet in thyself many, thou art first and likewise last, and midway in time withal, outliving the world. For without end for thyself, thou bringest the gliding seasons to an end. On high from everlasting thou beholdest the cruel destinies of the world awhirl in their predestined cycle, living souls in the coils of time, and again on their return restored to the vault above,[a] doubtless so that there may come back to the world what it has lost, exhausted by births, and that this may again flow through the seasons of time. Thou (if indeed it is allowed towards thee to direct the senses and essay to grasp the hallowed beauty wherewith in thine immeasurable power thou dost invest the stars and dost embrace withal the far-stretched upper air) in some quick guise mayhap with lightning limbs art like a flame-flowing radiance wherewith thou dost cause to flash all the world beneath thine own eyes and speedest onward the sunlight of our day. Thou art the whole kindred of the gods, thou art the cause and energy of things, thou art all nature, one god beyond reckoning, thou art full of the whole of sex, for thee cometh to birth upon a day here a god, here

[a] *Cf.* Virg. *Aen.* VI. 241, *supera ad convexa ferebat.*

hic deus hic mundus, domus haec hominumque deumque,
lucens, augusto stellatus flore iuventae. 25
quem (precor, adspires), qua sit ratione creatus,
quo genitus factusve modo, da nosse volenti;
da, Pater, augustas ut possim noscere causas,
mundanas olim moles quo foedere rerum
sustuleris animamque levi quo maximus olim 30
texueris numero, quo congrege dissimilique,
quidque id sit vegetum, quod per cita corpora vivit.

FRAGMENTA

1. *Servius ad Verg. Aen. VI.* 532:

Tiberianus etiam inducit epistolam vento allatam ab antipodibus, quae habet: "superi inferis salutem."

2. Fulgentius, *Mythologiarum I.* 26:

. . . unde Tiberianus: "Pegasus hinniens transvolat aethram."

3. Fulgentius, *Mythologiarum III.* 7:

nam et Tiberianus in Prometheo ait, deos singula sua homini tribuisse.

4. Fulgentius, *Vergiliana Continentia*, p. 154:

. . . memores Platonis sententiae, cuius hereditatem Diogenes Cynicus invadens nihil ibi plus aurea lingua invenit, ut Tiberianus in libro de Socrate memorat.

24 hic deus hic mundus *codd.*: hic cunctus m. *Baehrens.* domus hic *codd.*: d. haec *Riese*: d. una *Baehrens.*

a world—this home of men and gods—lucent, starred with the majestic bloom of youth. Touching this world (vouchsafe thy favour, I pray), grant to a willing mind the knowledge of the principles on which it was created, the manner of its origin and making. Grant, O Sire, that I may have power to learn causes majestic, by what alliance of things [a] thou didst of old upraise the world's masses of matter, and of what light texture, intimate yet dissimilar, thou didst of old in thy might weave the soul, and what that vigorous element is which in quick-moving bodies constitutes life.

Fragments

1. Tiberianus also introduces a letter brought by the wind from the antipodes, with the words "Those above greet those beneath."

2. Hence Tiberianus says: "Pegasus neighing flies across the upper air."

3. For Tiberianus too says in the Prometheus that the gods have assigned to a man his individual traits.

4. (We used "golden" of brilliant eloquence), recalling the utterance of Plato on whose inheritance Diogenes the Cynic encroached and found there nothing more than a golden tongue, as Tiberianus records in his book on Socrates.

[a] Or "law of nature."

5. Fulgentius, *Expositio sermonum antiquorum*, p. 183:

sudum dicitur serenum. Tiberianus: "Aureos subducit ignes sudus ora Lucifer."

[6. *Servius ad Verg. Aen. VIII.* 96:

ostendit adeo perspicuam fuisse naturam fluminis ut in eo apparerent imagines nemorum, quas Troianae naves secabant. Tiberianus:

"natura sic est fluminis,
ut obvias imagines
receptet in lucem suam."]

6 [3] Tiberianus *Baehrens*: Terentianus *vulgo*.

5. The word *sudum* means serene: *e.g.* Tiberianus: "Lucifer, serene to look on, draws away his golden fires."

[6. He shows that so transparent was the nature of the river that in it appeared clear reflections of the woods across which the Trojan vessels cut their way, as Tiberianus says:

> "Such is the nature of the stream
> That images which meet it seem
> Clear-mirrored in its own bright gleam."] [a]

[a] The ascription of this to Tiberianus depends on Baehrens' suggestion that Terentianus in Servius' text is a blunder for Tiberianus.

SULPICIUS LUPERCUS SERVASIUS JUNIOR

INTRODUCTION

TO SERVASIUS

The codex Leidensis Vossianus of Ausonius contains two poems ascribed to Sulpicius Lupercus Serbastus Junior. Schryver (Scriverius) altered "Serbastus" to "Sebastus," which Baehrens retains; Wernsdorf printed "Servastus," and Riese proposed "Servasius." From this schoolman author, whose very name is imperfectly known, there are thus preserved three Sapphic stanzas on the transitoriness of everything in nature and a longer elegiac complaint on the ruinous result which the prevalence of money-getting produces upon rhetorical studies. The archaisms *mage* and *fundier* (II. 16 and 18), artificially introduced into these laboured verses of the fourth century, contribute to the effect of unreality.

EDITIONS

P. Burman. *Anthol. Lat.* Lib. III. No. 97 (*De Vetustate*). Amsterdam, 1759.

J. C. Wernsdorf. *Poet. Lat. Min.* III. p. 235 and p. 408. Altenburg, 1782.

E. Baehrens. *Poet. Lat. Min.* IV. Nos. 118–119 (pp. 107–109). Leipzig, 1882.

F. Buecheler and A. Riese. *Anthol. Latina* I. ii. Nos. 648–649. Leipzig, 1906.

(The main departures from Baehrens' text are indicated.)

INTRODUCTION TO SERVASIUS

SIGLUM

E (Baehrens' siglum) = codex nobilissimus Ausonii, Leidensis Vossianus 111: saec. viii–ix.

(In West-Gothic writing it contains, after its text of Ausonius, other poems including the two ascribed to Sulpicius Lupercus " Serbastus.")

SULPICIUS LUPERCUS SERVASIUS JUNIOR

I

De Vetustate

Omne quod Natura parens creavit,
quamlibet firmum videas, labascit:
tempore ac longo fragile et caducum
 solvitur usu.

amnis insueta solet ire valle, 5
mutat et rectos via certa cursus,
rupta cum cedit male pertinaci
 ripa fluento.

decidens scabrum cavat unda tofum,
ferreus vomis tenuatur agris, 10
splendet attrito digitos honorans
 anulus auro.

II

De Cupiditate

Heu misera in nimios hominum petulantia census!
 caecus inutilium quo ruit ardor opum,
auri dira fames et non expleta libido
 ferali pretio vendat ut omne nefas!

SULPICIUS LUPERCUS SERVASIUS JUNIOR

I

The Work of Time

All that Nature ever bore,
Firm to look at, time makes hoar,
Frail and fleeting more and more,
  Its strength in service losing.

Streams fresh valley-routes pursue,
Ancient courses change to new,
When their banks are broken through
  By floods' persistent oozing.

Cascades make rough tufa yield;
Ploughs wear thinner in the field;
Rings that jewelled fingers wield
  Show gold rubbed bright by using.

II

Greed

Alas for the wretched craving after excessive incomes! What is the end on which the blind passion for useless wealth rushes, so that the cursed hunger for gold and greed unsatisfied may barter any enormity for a recompense fraught with destruction?

sic latebras Eriphyla viri patefecit, ubi aurum 5
accepit, turpis materiam sceleris;
sic quondam Acrisiae in gremium per claustra puellae
corruptore auro fluxit adulterium.
o quam mendose votum insaturabile habendi
imbuit infami pectora nostra malo! 10
quamlibet immenso dives vigil incubet auro,
aestuat augendae dira cupido rei.
heu mala paupertas numquam locupletis avari!
dum struere immodice quod tenet optat, eget.
quis metus hic legum quaeve est reverentia veri, 15
crescenti nummo si mage cura subest?
cognatorum animas promptum est patrumque cruorem
fundier: affectus vincit avara fames.
divitis est, semper fragiles male quaerere gazas:
nulla huic in lucro cura pudoris erit. 20
istud templorum damno excidioque requirit;
hoc caelo iubeas ut petat: inde petet.

mirum ni pulchras artes Romana iuventus
discat et egregio sudet in eloquio,
ut post iurisonae famosa stipendia linguae 25
barbaricae ingeniis anteferantur opes.
at qui sunt, quos propter honestum rumpere foedus
audeat illicite pallida avaritia?

[16] crescenti nummo *vulgo*: crescentis nummi *Baehrens.*
[17] fratrumque *cod., Baehrens*: patrumque *vulgo.*
[21] exitioque *vulgo.*
[25] iurgisonae clamosa impendia *Heinsius.*
[27] atqui *vulgo.*

---

[a] Amphiaraus, for whom it meant death to take part in the Theban War, was betrayed by his wife for a golden necklace: *cf.* Hor. *Od.* III. xvi. 11–13: Statius, *Theb.* IV. 187–213.

Thus it was that Eriphyla betrayed her husband's [a] hiding-place when she received the gold that was the cause of her foul crime: thus it was that long ago through prison-bars there rained in corrupting gold an adulterous stream on the lap of Acrisius' daughter.[b] How culpably the unquenchable longing for possession stains our hearts with scandalous wickedness! However boundless the gold o'er which Dives broods wakefully, within there seethes the accursed lust for adding to his wealth. Alas for the baleful poverty of the miser who is never rich! His desire for a limitless heap of what he holds makes him a beggar. What fear is here of laws, what respect for what is fair, if 'neath his growing bullion-heap there lurk still more the pains of greed? Taking the lives of kinsmen, shedding a father's blood comes readily to his mind: miserly hunger masters feeling. An evil quest after frail treasures is ever the rich man's way: in the matter of gain he will have no qualms of shame. Such gain it is he pursues, though it mean loss or destruction to temples:[c] bid him seek this in heaven and from heaven he will fetch it.[d]

It is not unlikely that the young men of Rome learn fine accomplishments and sweat at distinguished rhetoric only in order that, after the glorious campaigns [e] of an eloquent lawyer's tongue, they may prize barbaric wealth above talent. Yet who are those (glib pleaders) thanks to whom pale avarice ventures on the forbidden crime of breaking an

[b] Danaë: cf. Hor. *Od.* III. xvi. 1–8; and Tiberianus' poem on gold, II. 7–8.

[c] *i.e.* he sacrilegiously robs or fires them.

[d] An echo of Juvenal III. 78, *in caelum iusseris, ibit.*

[e] Heinsius' emendation (meaning literally "the bawling outlay of a loud litigious tongue") gets rid of ă before *stipendia.*

Romani sermonis egent, ridendaque verba
  frangit ad horrificos turbida lingua sonos. 30
sed tamen ex cultu appetitur spes grata nepotum?
  saltem istud nostri forsan honoris habent?
ambusti torris species, exesaque saeclo
  amblant ut priscis corpora de tumulis!
perplexi crines, frons improba, tempora pressa, 35
  exstantes malae deficiente gena,
simataeque iacent pando sinuamine nares,
  territat os nudum caesaque labra tument.
defossum in ventrem propulso pondere tergum
  frangitur et vacuo crure tument genua. 40
decolor in malis species, hoc turpius illud,
  quod cutis obscure pallet in invidiam.

29 egens *vulgo*.
31 ultu *cod.*: vultu *Scaliger*: cultu *Oudendorp*.
34 amblant ut *Baehrens*: abtantur *cod.*: abduntur *vulgo*: aptantur *Vinetus*.
38 caesaque *cod.*: scissaque *vel* fissaque *Heinsius*: crassaque *Wernsdorf*.
41 discolor *cod.*: *corr. Heinsius*. in manibus *cod.*: in malis *Baehrens*.

honourable compact? They are beggared of Latin style, and their confused jargon minces ridiculous words to an accompaniment of shocking sounds. Yet does their dress prompt the younger generation to indulge pleasing hopes (of legacies)? [a] Have they mayhap such a share at least of our Roman dignity? No, theirs is the appearance of a burnt-out firebrand: they walk like skeletons gnawed by time from ancient graves! Their hair is tangled, forehead impudent, temples thin, jaws protruding while their cheeks are sunken, and their flattened nostrils rest on a tip-tilted curve: the toothless mouth is a terror and the chapped lips are swollen. Forced down by the impetus of weight, back sinks to belly; and the knees swell on a shrunken leg. Sallow is the look of their jaws, and it is an uglier feature that the skin wears a mysterious pallor suggestive of envy.

[a] *i.e.* Can it be said for the misers that they dress well and in accordance with their wealth?

DICTA CATONIS

INTRODUCTION

TO DICTA CATONIS

In the educational training of the Middle Ages, when Donatus supplied the rudiments, an early and safe reading-book was the compendium of practical ethics which passed under the name of "Cato." Here was a work with much of the unimpeachable but hackneyed morality of the copy-book headline, and a useful repertory of material for adorning the letters of a young student desirous of creating a good impression when he wrote home. It is significant that Chaucer accounts for the foolish marriage of the carpenter in the *Miller's Tale* by remarking that "he knew not Catoun, for his wit was rude." This *vade mecum* of proverbial wisdom has, however, bequeathed an extraordinary number of enigmas: its title and the meaning of the title, the date of different *strata* in our collections, the proportion borne by what we now possess to the larger *corpus* of *Dicta Catonis* once in existence, the relation of the single lines to the couplets, the disentanglement of pagan elements from Christian additions or alterations, and the textual criticism of what has been handed down to us, all constitute problems of considerable difficulty.

Inscriptional evidence proves that about the end of the second century A.D. some of the proverbs were well enough known to be quoted.[a] It is likely that an unknown author gave to his collection of wise saws the title of *Cato*, as an echo of the moral instruction addressed generations earlier by Cato the Censor to his son. The name "Dionysius," sometimes added, rests upon a doubtful testimony by Scaliger to the effect that it existed in a manuscript belonging to Bosius. If "Dionysius" has to be considered at all, it may be explained, on Haupt's theory,[b] as due to a contamination of Cato's name with that of Dionysius, whose *Periegesis*, translated by Priscian, might have immediately preceded Cato in Bosius' manuscript.

By the fourth century we have evidence that the *Disticha* enjoyed an extensive vogue, and the Irish monk Columbanus at the turn of the sixth century had access to a large body of moral verses whence to draw part of the collection of separate hexameters to which he added many lines from Christian sources. But wide use did not guarantee the preservation of the text. Some *disticha* became less popular for school-work than others; extracts, excisions and transpositions were made; and couplets were, by intention or chance, reduced to single lines (*monosticha*) amidst the confusion into which the collection had fallen by the eighth century. It is, then, not an unreasonable supposition that a re-editing of the Catonian *corpus* took place in the Carolingian era; and it is possible that the brief verses prefixed to Books II, III and IV of the *Disticha* date from that period. Our present collection opens with a

[a] *Distich.* II. 3 is used in *C.I.L.* VI. 11252.

[b] M. Haupt, *Opusc.* I. 376. *Cf.* Boas, *Phil. Woch.* 1930, 649 *sqq.*

prose preface ostensibly directing its precepts to a son (*fili karissime*) in what we might call a Cato-like manner, and between this preface and the *Disticha* are 57 brief prose *sententiae*, some only two words long. About these opinion is sharply divided. It has been, on the one hand, argued that some of them may be the oldest part of the sayings, that some may even go back to Cato the Censor himself, and that some at least were expanded later into *disticha*; on the other hand, it has been argued that these *breves sententiae* may have constituted a summary introduction based, as excerpts, upon a once much fuller collection of verse sayings.[a]

Despite the excisions and alterations to which Christian re-editing subjected the inferior ethics of the original collection, there have survived evident traces not merely of antiquity (*e.g.* in the prose sentences *foro par(c)e* or *ad praetorium stato*), but of pagan principles in the religious thought or the practical advice. Thus, in the *Disticha* the polytheistic *an di sint* of II. 2 must be the original text, and is combined with monotheism (*mitte arcana dei*) in one manuscript only: II. 12, on divination, and IV. 38, on sacrifice, may be called pre-Christian, while IV. 14, on cleansing by a victim's blood, may possibly be directed against the doctrine of the atonement. Occasionally the ring is that of worldly cunning, I. 26, or selfishness in I. 11 and in the second line of III. 12. A wife's tears, III. 20, or her complaints about her husband's favourite slave, I. 8, must not, readers are enjoined, be too

[a] Skutsch, in *P.W. Realencycl.* V., on "Dicta Catonis," maintains the priority of the prose sentences in opposition to Bischoff.

much regarded. But, taken all in all, it is a sound if homely morality that is preached—respect for the lessons of books and of life, diligence in work, loyalty to friends, avoidance of quarrels, bravery in misfortune, temperance in prosperity, and—as Stoicism had taught—consideration for slaves.

In the maxims can be discerned the human experience of many generations, some of it going back to Greek originals and some of it touched with a literary reminiscence of Horace or Ovid. On the whole, the language is simple and clear, as befits proverbial wisdom, so that an archaism like *mage* (*Praef.* II. 2; *Distich.* II. 6; IV. 42) or a compound like *officiperdi* (IV. 42) stands out as something unusual. The closing distich emphasises the brevity aimed at in the couplets. Yet the very condensation led to a monotony of clause-structure and of expression; and this monotony is not redeemed by any great metrical variety in the hexameters. The prevailing merit, however, remains of a neat intelligibility which suited both teacher and taught; and this ensured for the collection its long career as an educational manual. " Catho " was one of the books printed during the early years of Caxton's work at Westminster. The distichs were paraphrased by Caxton's contemporary, Benedict Burgh, who expanded each couplet into the Chaucerian seven-lined stanza or rhyme-royal. Both text and paraphrase are extant in many fifteenth-century MSS., *e.g.* the Harleian 4733, and the volume, handsomely illustrated with coloured miniatures, which is now Peniarth MS. 481 in the National Library of Wales, Aberystwyth. The educational vogue of these *disticha moralia* is exemplified by their use during the eighteenth century in Scotland as an adjunct to Ruddiman's *Rudiments of the Latin Tongue*: they were, for example, included among the *Prima Morum et Pietatis Praecepta*, printed as a schoolbook at Edinburgh in 1784.

EDITIONS

D. Erasmus. *Disticha moralia titulo Catonis . . . mimi Publiani . . . cum scholiis Erasmi.* (?) London, 1514.

M. Corderius. *Catonis Disticha Lat. et Gall. interpret.* Oliva, 1561.

P. Pithou. *Catonis Disticha.* Paris, 1577.

M. Corderius. *Disticha moralia nomine Catonis inscripta c. Gall. interpretatione . . . et Graeca Planudae interpretatione.* Paris, 1585.

Jos. Scaliger. *P. Syri sentent. et Dion. Catonis disticha graece redd.* Leyden, 1598.

P. Scriverius. *Dionysii Catonis Disticha.* Amsterdam, 1635 and 1636.

M. Z. Boxhorn. *Catonis Disticha.* Amsterdam, 1646.

O. Arntzen. Utrecht 1735; Amst. 1754 (with the dissertations of Boxhorn, Cannegieter, and Withof).

F. Hauthal. Berlin, 1869.

E. Baehrens. *Poet. Lat. Min.* III. pp. 205–246. Leipzig, 1881.

G. Némethy. Ed. 2. Budapest, 1895.

RELEVANT WORKS

F. Zarncke. *Der Deutsche Cato.* Leipzig, 1852.

H. J. Mueller. *Symbolae ad emendandos scriptores Latinos. II. Quaestiones Catonianae.* Berlin, 1876.

J. Nehabs. *Der altenglische Cato.* Berlin, 1879.
M. O. Goldberg. *Die Catonischen Distichen während des Mittelalters in englischen und französischen Literatur.* Leipzig, 1883.
E. Bischoff. *Proleg. zu Dionysius Cato.* Diss. Erlangen, 1890.
F. Skutsch. *Pauly-Wissowa, Realencycl.* V. (1905) *s.v.* "Dicta Catonis."
E. Stechert. *De Catonis quae dicuntur distichis.* Greifswald, 1912.
M. Boas. *Der Codex Bosii der Dicta Catonis* in *Rhein. Mus.* 67 (1912), pp. 67–93.

For a list of translations into other languages see M. Schanz, *Gesch. der röm. Lit.*, ed. 3, 1922, pp. 38–39: to which may be added *The Distichs of Cato* translated into couplets, with introductory sketch by Wayland J. Chase, Madison, U.S.A., 1922.

SIGLA FOR DISTICHA

(As in Baehrens, *P.L.M.* III. 206–211.)

A = codex biblioth. capit. Veronensis 163: saec. ix. (Imperfect and in confused order, though preserving many good readings.[a])
B = codex Matritensis 14, 22: saec. ix. (Contains *disticha* up to I. 27, 1.)
C = codex Turicensis 78: saec. ix.
D = codex scholae medicinalis Montepessulanae 306: saec. ix.

[a] On this, the oldest codex, see K. Schenkl, *Zeitschr. für österr. Gymn.* 24 (1873), p. 485; C. Cipolla, *Riv. di filol.* 8 (1880).

E = codex Vossianus L.Q. 86: saec. ix.[a]
F = codex Ambrosianus C 74: saec. x. [The last four are from a common original, CD and EF showing close agreement.]
ς = codices inferiores, including Reginenses and Parisini.

[The codex Matritensis is regarded by M. Boas, along with Paris. 8093 saec. ix and Vaticanus Reg. 2078 saec. x, as representing a Spanish-Gallic tradition of the vulgate collection, in contrast to a "Neben-vulgata" and "Vor-vulgata" represented by Paris. 9347, Monacensis 19413 saec. xi, Vaticanus Barber. 8, 41 saec. xiii–xiv. See references at close of the Sigla given for the *Monosticha*.]

The main departures from Baehrens' text are indicated in the apparatus criticus.

[a] See H. J. Mueller, *op. cit.*, pp. 17 *sqq.*

CATO

I. COLLECTIO DISTICHORUM VULGARIS

Prologus

Cum animadverterem quam plurimos graviter in via morum errare, succurrendum opinioni eorum et consulendum famae existimavi, maxime ut gloriose viverent et honorem contingerent. nunc te, fili karissime, docebo quo pacto morem animi tui componas. igitur praecepta mea ita legito, ut intellegas. legere enim et non intellegere neglegere est.

Deo supplica.
Parentes ama.
Cognatos cole.
Datum serva.
Foro parce. 5
Cum bonis ambula.
Antequam voceris, ne accesseris.
Mundus esto.
Saluta libenter.
Maiori concede. 10

Incp̄ dicta marci catonis ad filium suum A : Marci Catonis ad filium salutem *litt. mai. rubr.* B : Incipiunt libri Catonis philosophi *litt. mai.* D : *tit. om.* C : *totum prologum om.* EF.

Prologus : [2] graviter in via morum BC ς *omnes* : gravitate murum A.

Sententiolae : [5] parce A : pare B ς *nonnulli* : para CD ς *nonnulli*.

CATO

I. THE COMMON COLLECTION OF DISTICHS

Prologue

As I noticed the very great number of those who go seriously astray in the path of conduct, I decided that I should come to the aid of their belief and take thought for their reputation, so that they might live with the utmost glory and attain honour. Now I will teach you, dearest son, how to fashion a system for your mind. Therefore, so read my precepts as to understand; for to read and not to understand is to give them the go-by.[a]

Pray to God.
Love your parents.
Respect your kindred.
Guard what is given you.
Avoid the market-place.[b]
Walk in good company.
Don't approach, until you're invited.
Be tidy.
Salute willingly.
Yield to your senior.

[a] On the manuscript authority for the order of these *sententiolae* see Baehrens, *P.L.M.* III. pp. 206 and 214–215.

[b] This seems to anticipate Bacon's warning against *idola fori*, misconceptions due to the careless notions of the crowd.

Magistratum metue.
Verecundiam serva.
Rem tuam custodi.
Diligentiam adhibe.
Familiam cura. 15
Mutuum da.
Cui des videto.
Convivare raro.
Quod satis est dormi.
Coniugem ama. 20
Iusiurandum serva.
Vino tempera.
Pugna pro patria.
Nihil temere credideris.
Meretricem fuge. 25
Libros lege.
Quae legeris memento.
Liberos erudi.
Blandus esto.
Irascere ob rem ⟨gravem⟩. 30
Neminem riseris.
In iudicio adesto.
Ad praetorium stato.
Consultus esto.
Virtute utere. 35
Trocho lude.
Aleam fuge.
Litteras disce.

22 te tempera ς *pauci.*

Honour a magistrate.
Preserve your modesty.
Guard your own property.
Practise diligence.
Take trouble for your household.
Be willing to lend.
Consider to whom you should give.
Let your banquets be few.
Sleep as much as suffices.
Love your wife.
Keep an oath.
Be moderate with wine.
Fight for your country.
Believe nothing rashly.
Shun a harlot.
Read books.
Remember what you read.
Instruct your children.
Be kind.
Be angry for a serious cause.
Mock no one.
Support a friend in the law-court.
Maintain your standing at the praetor's residence.[a]
Be conversant with the law.
Practise virtue.
Play with the hoop.
Eschew dice.
Study literature.

[a] The *praetorium* may be the official residence of a provincial governor, or the headquarters in a camp, or sometimes a great private mansion (*e.g.*, Juvenal I. 75). The advice here apparently is "keep in with the powers that be" or "keep in with your patron." Erasmus took *praetorium* of a law-court, explaining "multa enim discuntur in agendis causis."

Bono benefacito.
Tute consule.
Maledicus ne esto.
Existimationem retine.
Aequum iudica.
Nihil mentire.
Iracundiam rege.
Parentem patientia vince.
Minorem ne contempseris.
Nihil arbitrio virium feceris.
Patere legem quam ipse tuleris.
Benefici accepti esto memor.
Pauca in convivio loquere.
Miserum noli irridere.
Minime iudica.
Alienum noli concupiscere.
Illud aggredere quod iustum est.
Libenter amorem ferto.
Liberalibus stude.

CATONIS DISTICHA

LIBER I

1. Si deus est animus, nobis ut carmina dicunt,
hic tibi praecipue sit pura mente colendus.
2. Plus vigila semper neu somno deditus esto;
nam diuturna quies vitiis alimenta ministrat.
3. Virtutem primam esse puto, compescere linguam:
proximus ille deo est qui scit ratione tacere.
4. Sperne repugnando tibi tu contrarius esse:
conveniet nulli qui secum dissidet ipse.

[40] tute *corruptum videtur*: *fortasse* tuta consule *A. M. Duff.*
[2, 1] neu A: nec BCDEF: ne ς.

Do good to a good man.
Give safe advice.
Do not be abusive.
Hold fast to your reputation.
Judge fairly.
Tell no lie.
Control your anger.
Overcome your parent with patience.
Do not despise a younger man.
Do nothing with the caprice of might.
Accept the law which you yourself made.
Bear in mind a benefit received.
Say little at a banquet.
Do not deride the wretched.
Judge not at all.
Do not covet what is another's.
Undertake what is fair.
Show affection gladly.
Put zeal into noble pursuits.

THE DISTICHS OF CATO

BOOK I

1. If God be spirit, as bards represent,
   He must be worshipped with a clean intent.
2. Watch always more: sleep must not thee entice:
   Prolonged inaction serves up food for vice.
3. To rule the tongue I reckon virtue's height:
   He's nearest God who can be dumb aright.
4. Avoid the clash of inconsistency:
   Who fights with self, with no one will agree.

5. Si vitam inspicias hominum, si denique mores,
cum culpant alios: nemo sine crimine vivit.
6. Quae nocitura tenes, quamvis sint cara, relinque:
utilitas opibus praeponi tempore debet.
7. Clemens et constans, ut res expostulat, esto:
temporibus mores sapiens sine crimine mutat.
8. Nil temere uxori de servis crede querenti:
semper enim mulier quem coniunx diligit odit.
9. Cum moneas aliquem nec se velit ille moneri,
si tibi sit carus, noli desistere coeptis.
10. Contra verbosos noli contendere verbis:
sermo datur cunctis, animi sapientia paucis.
11. Dilige sic alios, ut sis tibi carus amicus;
sic bonus esto bonis, ne te mala damna sequantur.
12. Rumores fuge neu studeas novus auctor haberi;
nam nulli tacuisse nocet, nocet esse locutum.
13. Spem tibi polliciti certam promittere noli:
rara fides ideo est, quia multi multa loquuntur.
14. Cum te aliquis laudat, iudex tuus esse memento;
plus aliis de te quam tu tibi credere noli.
15. Officium alterius multis narrare memento;
at quaecumque aliis benefeceris ipse, sileto.
16. Multorum cum facta senex et dicta reprendis,
fac tibi succurrant iuvenis quae feceris ipse.
17. Ne cures, si quis tacito sermone loquatur:
conscius ipse sibi de se putat omnia dici.
18. Cum fueris felix, quae sunt adversa caveto:
non eodem cursu respondent ultima primis.

12, 1 neu studeas *Baehrens*: ne studeas A: ne (nec D) incipias *ceteri omnes*.

13, 1 polliciti A: promissi BCDE: promissam F (*et sic* CE *m.* 2 *corr.*).

5. Test but the life and ways of them who blame
Their fellows; all, you'll find, have faults the same.
6. Gear that may harm forgo, however dear:
Wealth yields to usefulness in time of fear.
7. Be mild or firm as circumstances claim:
A sage may change his outlook free from blame.
8. A wife's complaints about the slaves mistrust:
Her husband's favourite wakens her disgust.
9. In warning one who fain would not attend,
Drop not the endeavour, should he be your friend.
10. To fight the wordy you must words eschew:
Speech is bestowed on all, sound sense on few.
11. Love other men; yet be your own true friend:
Do good to good men so no loss attend.
12. Shun tattling, and the newest thing to say
Seek not: closed lips hurt no one—speaking may.
13. Think not hopes built on promises are sure:
Much said by many seldom proves secure.
14. When someone praises you, be judge alone:
Trust not men's judgement of you, but your own.
15. Let others' kindness frankly be revealed;
Your own good turns to others keep concealed.
16. When you, grown old, blame what folk do or say,
Think what you did in your own youthful day.
17. Reck not of what the whispering lip lets fall:
Self-conscious men think they're the talk of all.
18. In happy hours beware the hapless lot:
What the start promises, the end is not.

19. Cum dubia et fragilis nobis sit vita tributa,
 in morte alterius spem tu tibi ponere noli.
20. Exiguum munus cum dat tibi pauper amicus,
 accipito laetus, plene et laudare memento.
21. Infantem nudum cum te natura crearit,
 paupertatis onus patienter ferre memento.
22. Ne timeas illam quae vitae est ultima finis:
 qui mortem metuit, quod vivit, perdit id ipsum.
23. Si tibi pro meritis nemo succurrit amicus,
 incusare deos noli, sed te ipse coerce.
24. Ne tibi quid desit, quod quaesisti, utere parce;
 utque, quod est, serves, semper tibi desse putato.
25. Quod dare non possis, verbis promittere noli,
 ne sis ventosus, dum vir bonus esse videris.
26. Qui simulat verbis nec corde est fidus amicus,
 tu quoque fac simules: sic ars deluditur arte.
27. Noli homines blando nimium sermone probare:
 fistula dulce canit, volucrem dum decipit auceps.
28. Cum tibi sint nati nec opes, tunc artibus illos
 instrue, quo possint inopem defendere vitam.
29. Quod vile est, carum, quod carum, vile putato:
 sic tu nec cupidus nec avarus nosceris ulli.
30. Quae culpare soles ea tu ne feceris ipse:
 turpe est doctori, cum culpa redarguat ipsum.
31. Quod iustum est petito vel quod videatur honestum;
 nam stultum petere est quod possit iure negari.
32. Ignotum tibi tu noli praeponere notis:
 cognita iudicio constant, incognita casu.

24, 1 quod quaesisti *Baehrens*: quod quaeris A.
25, 1 verbis promittere noli *Baehrens*: nec bis (*ex* vis *corr. m.* 2) promittere noli A: noli promittere verbis *Columb.*
30, 2 redarguat *Baehrens*: arguat A: redarguit *ceteri codd.*

19. Our life is but a frail uncertain breath:
    Rest not thy hopes, then, on another's death.
20. When your poor friend gives of his poverty,
    Accept well pleased and thank him handsomely.
21. A naked babe since nature fashioned thee,
    With patience bear the load of poverty.
22. Fear not lest life's concluding lap be nigh:
    He makes his life no life who dreads to die.
23. If no friend helps you as your deeds demand,
    Tax not the gods but hold yourself in hand.
24. Save up your gains lest you go short some day:
    To keep possessions, fancy they're away.
25. Utter no promise that you can't redeem,
    Lest you inconstant prove, while kind you seem.
26. The glib dissembler, faithless friend at heart,
    See that you copy: so art baffles art.
27. Approve not men who wheedling nothings say:
    Fowlers pipe sweetly to delude their prey.
28. Since sons you have—not wealth—such training give
    Their minds that they, though poor, unharmed may live.
29. Hold dear the cheap, and cheaply hold the dear:
    So none can say you hunt or hoard your gear.
30. Do not yourself what you are wont to blame:
    When sin convicts the preacher's self, 'tis shame.
31. Ask what is right or fair to human eye:
    Fools ask what others rightly may deny.
32. Do not the unknown o'er the known advance:
    Known things on judgement hang, unknown on chance.

32, 1 notis noli praeponere amicis *Baehrens.*

33. Cum dubia in certis versetur vita periclis,
pro lucro tibi pone diem quicumque sequetur.
34. Vincere cum possis, interdum cede sodali,
obsequio quoniam dulces retinentur amici.
35. Ne dubita, cum magna petes, impendere parva:
his etenim pressos contingit gloria raro.
36. Litem inferre cave, cum quo tibi gratia iuncta est:
ira odium generat, concordia nutrit amorem.
37. Servorum culpa cum te dolor urguet in iram,
ipse tibi moderare, tuis ut parcere possis.
38. Quem superare potes interdum vince ferendo;
maxima enim est hominum semper patientia virtus.
39. Conserva potius, quae sunt iam parta, labore:
cum labor in damno est, crescit mortalis egestas.
40. Dapsilis interdum notis et largus amicis
cum fueris, dando semper tibi proximus esto.

LIBER II

Telluris si forte velis cognoscere cultus,
Vergilium legito; quodsi mage nosse laboras
herbarum vires, Macer haec tibi carmina dicit;

35, 2 pressos contingit gloria raro *Baehrens*: rebus coniungit gratia caros *codd. omnes, sine sensu.*

40, 1 largus *edd. vett.*: carus *codd.* 2 cum ς *nonnulli*: dum CDEF ς *nonnulli.* dando *Par.* 2772 *m.* 1, *Regin.* 2078 *in ras.*: felix *codd. ceteri, quod ortum videtur ex* I. 18, 1.

33. Since our frail life through dangers sure must run,
 Count every day that comes as something won.
34. Yield to your mate some points you well might score:
 Compliance keeps your friends attached the more.
35. In mighty aims small cost you must not spare;
 For those whom trifles cramp high fame is rare.
36. Beware of strife with one close linked to thee:
 Anger breeds hate, love feeds on harmony.
37. If, stung by slaves' misdeeds, you've angry grown,
 Control yourself and so hurt not your own.
38. Sometimes put up with him you might beat down;
 Of human virtues patience is the crown.
39. What you have won conserve at cost of pains:
 Want must increase, when labour brings no gains.
40. Though sometimes on your friends you lavish gear,
 In giving always to yourself keep near.[a]

BOOK II

If perchance you fain would acquaint yourself with farming, read Virgil; but if your struggle rather is to know the virtue of herbs, this is the poetry that Macer[b] offers you; if you long to know

[a] The self-regarding morality of this distich advises the generous man never to depart too far from his own interest.

[b] The didactic poet Aemilius Macer of Verona (d. 16 B.C.) wrote a work *De Herbis* (Ovid, *Trist.* IV. x. 43–44).

si Romana cupis et Punica noscere bella,
Lucanum quaeres, qui Martis proelia dixit; 5
si quid amare libet vel discere amare legendo,
Nasonem petito; sin autem cura tibi haec est,
ut sapiens vivas, audi quae discere possis,
per quae semotum vitiis deducitur aevum:
ergo ades et quae sit sapientia disce legendo. 10

1. Si potes, ignotis etiam prodesse memento:
utilius regno est meritis acquirere amicos.
2. An di sint caelumque regant, ne quaere doceri:
cum sis mortalis, quae sunt mortalia cura.
3. Linque metum leti; nam stultum est tempore in omni,
dum mortem metuas, amittere gaudia vitae.
4. Iratus de re incerta contendere noli:
impedit ira animum, ne possis cernere verum.
5. Fac sumptum propere, cum res desiderat ipsa;
dandum etenim est aliquid, dum tempus postulat aut res.
6. Quod nimium est fugito, parvo gaudere memento:
tuta mage est puppis modico quae flumine fertur.
7. Quod pudeat, socios prudens celare memento,
ne plures culpent id quod tibi displicet uni.

[4] romam velis et p. cognuscere (*sic*) A: civica *pro* punica *Scriverius.*

[2, 1] *codd. omnes habent:* mitte arc(h)ana dei caelumque inquirere quid sit, *nisi quod* C *unus ante versum* 2 *inserit:* an dii sint caelum qui (i *ex corr.*) regant nequere (*sic*) doceri; *haec altera versus forma genuina iudicanda est, cum prior illa colorem christianum prae se ferat.*

of Roman and Punic[a] warfare, you will seek Lucan, who has recounted the combats of Mars; if your fancy is to have a love-affair or by reading learn how to love, make for Ovid. But if your serious aim is a life of wisdom, hear what you may learn of things that ensure a course of life divorced from vice. Come then and, as you read, learn what wisdom is.

1. To help even strangers, if you can, take pains:
   A crown counts less than friends whom kindness gains.
2. Ask not if Gods exist or are Heaven's kings:
   As thou art mortal, think of mortal things.
3. Cease fearing death: 'tis folly day by day,
   For fear of death, to cast life's joys away.
4. Temper in fighting rival claims eschew:
   Temper bars minds from seeing what is true.
5. Make haste to spend when so the case desires;
   For something must be given, as need requires.
6. Pleased with small store, take care to avoid the extreme:
   Safer the craft that sails a moderate stream.
7. What makes you blush 'fore friends decline to own,
   Lest many blame what you dislike alone.[b]

[a] If *Punica* be the right reading, did an erroneous superscription on a manuscript of Lucan mislead the author of these lines? (*Cf.* H. Blass, *Rhein. Mus.* xxxi. p. 134.) Or has a verse referring to a poet other than Lucan, *e.g.* Silius Italicus, dropped out of the text? Lucan's *Pharsalia* narrated the civil war between Caesar and Pompey; Silius' *Punica* the struggle of Rome against Hannibal.

[b] One of the many prudential maxims: to confess openly a secret fault may invite ill-natured comment about what is really your own concern.

8. Nolo putes pravos homines peccata lucrari:
temporibus peccata latent, et tempore parent.
9. Corporis exigui vires contemnere noli:
consilio pollet cui vim natura negavit.
10. Cui scieris non esse parem, pro tempore cede.
victorem a victo superari saepe videmus.
11. Adversum notum noli contendere verbis:
lis verbis minimis interdum maxima crescit.
12. Quid deus intendat, noli perquirere sorte:
quid statuat de te, sine te deliberat ille.
13. Invidiam nimio cultu vitare memento:
quae si non laedit, tamen hanc sufferre molestum est.
14. Esto animo forti, cum sis damnatus inique:
nemo diu gaudet qui iudice vincit iniquo.
15. Litis praeteritae noli maledicta referre:
post inimicitias iram meminisse malorum est.
16. Nec te collaudes nec te culpaveris ipse;
hoc faciunt stulti, quos gloria vexat inanis.
17. Utere quaesitis modice: cum sumptus abundat,
labitur exiguo quod partum est tempore longo.
18. Insipiens esto, cum tempus postulat aut res:
stultitiam simulare loco, prudentia summa est.
19. Luxuriam fugito, simul et vitare memento
crimen avaritiae; nam sunt contraria famae.
20. Nolito quaedam referenti credere saepe:
exigua est tribuenda fides, qui multa loquuntur.

8, 2 tempore si *Baehrens* : temporibus *codd. omnes.*
14, 1 ferto *Baehrens* : esto *codd.*
18, 1 ipsum A, *Baehrens* : aut res *ceteri codd.* 2 ioco *Baehrens* : loco *codd.* cum tempore laus est A : prudentia summa est *ceteri codd.*

8. Think not that wicked men find wrongdoing gain:
At times the wrong lies hid—in time 'tis plain.
9. Strength housed in little frame do not disdain:
In counsel men of slight physique may reign.
10. When you're outmatched, to meet the case, retreat:[a]
Oft-times the vanquished will the victor beat.
11. In wordy war do not engage thy friend;
For trivial words in mighty strife may end.
12. What God intendeth seek not to divine:
His plans for thee require no aid of thine.
13. Proud pomp will rouse men's jealousy, be sure:
Though it mayn't hurt, it's irksome to endure.
14. When judged unfairly, your own courage trust:
None long has joy who wins through judge unjust.
15. The quarrel past, its bitter words ignore:
'Tis ill to think of wrath, when strife is o'er.
16. Praise not yourself, nor to yourself take blame:
Fools do so, plagued by love of empty fame.[b]
17. Make temperate use of gains: when all is cost,
What took long time to get is quickly lost.
18. Play the fool's part, if time or need advise:
To act the fool at times is truly wise.
19. Flee luxury, avoiding all the same
The charge of avarice: both blot a name.
20. Trust not those who for ever news relate:
Slight faith is due to tongues that glibly prate.

[a] *Cf.* the French *reculer pour mieux sauter*.

[b] The second line refers more obviously to the first part of the preceding line, but insincere self-depreciation may be the form of vanity known as "fishing for compliments."

21. Quae potus peccas ignoscere tu tibi noli;
nam crimen vini nullum est, sed culpa bibentis.
22. Consilium arcanum tacito committe sodali,
corporis auxilium medico committe fideli.
23. Successu indignos noli tu ferre moleste:
indulget Fortuna malis, ut vincere possit.
24. Prospice qui veniant casus hos esse ferendos:
nam levius laedit, quicquid praevidimus ante.
25. Rebus in adversis animum submittere noli:
spem retine; spes una hominem nec morte relinquit.
26. Rem tibi quam nosces aptam dimittere noli:
fronte capillata, post est Occasio calva.
27. Quod sequitur specta quodque imminet ante videto:
illum imitare deum, partem qui spectat utramque.
28. Fortius ut valeas, interdum parcior esto:
pauca voluptati debentur, plura saluti.
29. Iudicium populi numquam contempseris unus:
ne nulli placeas, dum vis contemnere multos.
30. Sit tibi praecipue, quod primum est, cura salutis;
tempora nec culpes, cum sis tibi causa doloris.
31. Somnia ne cures; nam mens humana quod optat,
dum vigilans sperat, per somnum cernit id ipsum.

[23, 1] successus nolito indigni (*vel* indignos) ferre *Baehrens*. [2] vincere A: laedere *ceteri codd.*

[26, 1] noris *Baehrens*: noscis CDEF ς *plerique*: nosces ς *pauci*: scieris A.

[30, 2] sit *codd.*: sis ς *pauci*.

[31, 2] vigilat *codd. omnes*: vigilans *edd. vet.* verum *Baehrens*: sperat *codd. omnes*.

21. Your faults in drink should not your pardon win:
The wine is guiltless: 'tis the drinker's sin.
22. Trust secret plans to friend who guards his speech,
And bodily treatment to a faithful leech.
23. Chafe not against men's undeserved success:
To bring it low Luck smiles on wickedness.
24. Ills, as they come, prepare to undergo:
What we've foreseen deals us a lighter blow.
25. Let not your courage droop in darkest hours:
Hope on; for hope alone at death is ours.[a]
26. Do not let slip the thing that suits your mind:
Chance wears a forelock, but is bald behind.[b]
27. Observe the past and what impends foresee,
Like Janus, facing both ways equally.
28. For growth in strength, at times eat food in measure;
You owe more to your health than to your pleasure.
29. Ne'er stand alone to flout the general view:
If you flout many, none may care for you.
30. Your health, the chief thing, guard with might and main:
Don't blame the season for your self-caused pain.
31. Reck not of dreams; in things which men pursue,
Sleep sees the hopes of waking hours come true.

[a] This is probably an instance where Christian thought has coloured the *Disticha*: "hope alone does not desert man—not even in death."

[b] The Latin is quoted by Wm. Herman in letter to Cornelius Gerard, A.D. 1494: *cf.* P. S. Allen, *Erasmi Epistolae* (1906), no. 36.

LIBER III

Hoc quicumque volet carmen cognoscere lector,
cum praecepta ferat quae sunt gratissima vitae,
commoda multa feret; sin autem spreverit illud,
non me scriptorem, sed se fastidiet ipse.

1. Instrue praeceptis animum, ne discere cessa;
nam sine doctrina vita est quasi mortis imago.
2. Cum recte vivas, ne cures verba malorum:
arbitrii non est nostri quid quisque loquatur.
3. Productus testis, salvo tamen ante pudore,
quantumcumque potes, celato crimen amici.
4. Sermones blandos blaesosque cavere memento:
simplicitas veri forma est, laus ficta loquentis.
5. Segnitiem fugito, quae vitae ignavia fertur;
nam cum animus languet, consumit inertia corpus.
6. Interpone tuis interdum gaudia curis,
ut possis animo quemvis sufferre laborem.
7. Alterius dictum aut factum ne carpseris umquam,
exemplo simili ne te derideat alter.
8. Quod tibi sors dederit tabulis suprema notato,
augendo serva, ne sis quem fama loquatur.
9. Cum tibi divitiae superant in fine senectae,
munificus facito vivas, non parcus, amicis.
10. Utile consilium dominus ne despice servi:
si prodest, sensum nullius tempseris umquam.
11. Rebus et in censu si non est quod fuit ante,
fac vivas contentus eo quod tempora praebent.

III *prologum ita habet* A: *ceteri codices interponunt distichon primum inter versum* 2 *et versum* 3 *prologi*.

4, 2 forma *Barth*: fama *codd. omnes*: norma *Scriverius*. laus f. loquentis A: fraus f. loquendi CDEF ς.

BOOK III

Any reader who decides to study this poem will reap many advantages, as it offers maxims most acceptable for life; but if he spurn it, he will show disdain not for me, its author, but for himself.

1. Fail not to learn: equip your mind with rules;
   Count as but death the life that never schools.
2. Mind not ill tongues, if you live straight of soul:
   A neighbour's words are not in our control.
3. If called to witness, hide as best you can
   A friend's misdeeds, but be an honest man.
4. Beware of softly whispered flatteries:
   Frankness is mark of truth, flattery of lies.
5. Shun slackness, which means idling all your days:
   With lazy minds sloth on the body preys.
6. Sandwich occasional joys amidst your care
   That you with spirit any task may bear.
7. Another's word or act ne'er criticise,
   Lest others mock at you in selfsame wise.
8. A heritage bequeathed to you by will
   Keep and increase: so save your good name still.
9. If you've abundant wealth, as old age ends,
   Be generous, not close-fisted, with your friends.
10. Sound counsel from your slave do not despise:
    Spurn no man's view at all, if it is wise.
11. If goods and income are not what they were,
    Live satisfied with what the times confer.

8, 2 auge servando *vel* augendo cura ne segnem *Withof*.

12. Uxorem fuge ne ducas sub nomine dotis,
nec retinere velis, si coeperit esse molesta.
13. Multorum disce exemplo, quae facta sequaris,
quae fugias: vita est nobis aliena magistra.
14. Quod potes id temptato, operis ne pondere pressus
succumbat labor et frustra temptata relinquas.
15. Quod factum scis non recte, nolito silere,
ne videare malos imitari velle tacendo.
16. Iudicis auxilium sub iniqua lite rogato:
ipsae etiam leges cupiunt ut iure regantur.
17. Quod merito pateris patienter ferre memento,
cumque reus tibi sis, ipsum te iudice damna.
18. Multa legas facito, perlectis neglege multa;
nam miranda canunt, sed non credenda poetae.
19. Inter convivas fac sis sermone modestus,
ne dicare loquax, cum vis urbanus haberi.
20. Coniugis iratae noli tu verba timere;
nam lacrimis struit insidias, cum femina plorat.
21. Utere quaesitis, sed ne videaris abuti:
qui sua consumunt, cum dest, aliena sequuntur.
22. Fac tibi proponas mortem non esse timendam:
quae bona si non est, finis tamen illa malorum est.
23. Uxoris linguam, si frugi est, ferre memento;
namque malum est non velle pati nec posse tacere.
24. Aequa diligito caros pietate parentes,
nec matrem offendas, dum vis bonus esse parenti.

14, 2 inceptata *Baehrens*: temptata *s nonnulli*.
15, 2 velle inritare *Baehrens*.
16, 2 rogentur (*i.e.* adeantur) *Baehrens*: regantur E *m.*1.
18, 1 facito tum lectis *Baehrens*: factorum lectis CD.
23, 2 tacere *codd.*: carere *Withof*.

12. Do not for dowry's sake espouse a wife,
Nor wish to keep her, if she causes strife.
13. From men's behaviour learn what to pursue
Or shun. The life of others gives the cue.
14. Try what you can, lest by hard task foredone
You fail and drop what you've in vain begun.
15. Do not conceal ill deeds within your ken,
Lest silence look like aping wicked men.
16. If sued unfairly, ask the judge for aid:
The very laws would fain be justly swayed.
17. What you deserve to bear, with patience bear:
And, when you're judge of self, you must not spare.
18. Read much, but, having read, with much dispense;
Bards' themes are wonders, but revolt the sense.
19. Upon your talk, at dinners, set a bit,
Lest you're dubbed "rattle," when you'd fain be "wit."
20. Fear not the words your angry wife may say:
A weeping woman plots but to waylay.
21. Use your estate, yet shun extravagance:
Want follows waste and begs for maintenance.
22. Be this thy motto—"I do not dread death":
Death, if no boon, our troubles finisheth.
23. A thrifty wife may talk and talk: endure:
Lost patience and loud brawling are no cure.
24. Love both your parents, one as much as other:
To please your father never wound your mother.

LIBER IV

Semotam a curis si vis producere vitam
nec vitiis haerere animi, quae moribus obsunt,
haec praecepta tibi saepe esse legenda memento:
invenies, quo te possis mutare, magistrum.

1. Despice divitias, si vis animo esse beatus;
quas qui suspiciunt, mendicant semper avari.
2. Commoda Naturae nullo tibi tempore derunt,
si contentus eo fueris quod postulat usus.
3. Cum sis incautus nec rem ratione gubernes,
noli Fortunam, quae non est, dicere caecam.
4. Dilige † te ornari, sed parce dilige formam,
quam nemo sanctus nec honestus captat habere.
5. Cum fueris locuples, corpus curare memento:
aeger dives habet nummos, se non habet ipsum.
6. Verbera cum tuleris discens aliquando magistri,
fer patris imperium, cum verbis exit in iram.
7. Res age quae prosunt; rursus vitare memento,
in quis error inest nec spes est certa laboris.
8. Quod donare potes gratis concede roganti;
nam recte fecisse bonis in parte lucrorum est.
9. Quod tibi suspectum est confestim discute quid sit;
namque solent, primo quae sunt neglecta, nocere.
10. Cum te detineat veneris damnosa libido,
indulgere gulae noli, quae ventris amica est.

4, 1 olens nardum *Baehrens*: denarium *codd.*: te ornari *Cannegieter*. defuge odorem *Baehrens*: dilige formam *codd.* 2 quem *codd.* (*quod non congruit cum* formam): quam *vulgo*. habere *codd.*: ab aere *Scaliger*.

BOOK IV

If you would lead a long life divorced from anxieties, and not cling to faults in the mind which harm character, then remember that you must often read these rules. You will find a teacher through whom you will be able to transform yourself.

1. Scorn wealth, if you would have a mind care-freed:
   Its votaries are but beggars in their greed.
2. Ne'er will you lack supplies from Nature's hands,
   If you're content with that which need demands.
3. Reckless, haphazard steersman of your lot,
   Do not call Fortune blind: blind she is not.
4. Love neatness: showiness love not amain,
   Which good and honest folk seek not to gain.
5. Yourself, when you grow rich, treat well; for pelf
   The invalid owns, but does not own himself.
6. At school you sometimes bear the teacher's cane:
   So 'gainst a father's angry words don't strain.[a]
7. Do what is helpful; but from things recoil
   Where hazard leaves dim hope to honest toil.
8. Give gratis what you can upon request:
   Befriending friends may be as gain assessed.
9. Test quickly what it is that you suspect:
   Men end by suffering from what they neglect.
10. When on some ruinous amour forced to spend,
    Indulge not gluttony, the belly's friend.[b]

[a] *verbera* and *verbis* make an excellent contrast in the Latin.

[b] *i.e.* love in itself is ruinous enough; but expensive feasts given in honour of a sweetheart may prove ruinous to health and purse.

11. Cum tibi praeponas animalia bruta timore,
unum hominem scito tibi praecipue esse timendum.
12. Cum tibi praevalidae fuerint in corpore vires,
fac sapias: sic tu poteris vir fortis haberi.
13. Auxilium a notis petito, si forte labores;
nec quisquam melior medicus quam fidus amicus.
14. Cum sis ipse nocens, moritur cur victima pro te?
stultitia est morte alterius sperare salutem.
15. Cum tibi vel socium vel fidum quaeris amicum,
non tibi fortuna est hominis sed vita petenda.
16. Utere quaesitis opibus, fuge nomen avari:
quid tibi divitiae, si semper pauper abundes?
17. Si famam servare cupis, dum vivis, honestam,
fac fugias animo quae sunt mala gaudia vitae.
18. Cum sapias animo, noli ridere senectam;
nam quoicumque seni puerilis sensus inhaeret.
19. Disce aliquid; nam cum subito Fortuna recessit,
ars remanet vitamque hominis non deserit umquam.
20. Prospicito tecum tacitus quid quisque loquatur:
sermo hominum mores et celat et indicat idem.
21. Exerce studio quamvis perceperis artem:
ut cura ingenium, sic et manus adiuvat usum.
22. Multum venturi ne cures tempora fati:
non metuit mortem qui scit contemnere vitam.
23. Disce sed a doctis, indoctos ipse doceto:
propaganda etenim est rerum doctrina bonarum.

11, 1 bruta *Arntzen*: cuncta *codd.* timore D: timere *ceteri codd.*

16, 2 divitias DF, *Baehrens*: divitiae C.

18, 2 cuicumque seni *edd. vet.*: quocumque sene *codd.*: quicumque senet *Scaliger*. pueri bis *Withof*. inhaeret *Baehrens*: in illo est *codd.*

11. When fear of brute beasts harasses your mind,
Know what you most should dread is human kind.
12. If you have bodily strength in high degree,
Add wisdom: so win fame for bravery.
13. In straits ask those you know their aid to lend;
No doctor can surpass a trusty friend.
14. Why dies a victim for you in your sin?
Grace through another's blood fools hope to win.
15. Seeking a mate or friend who will be true,
A man's life, not his fortune, you must view.
16. Employ your gains: earn not a niggard's name:
What boots your wealth, if you're in want the same?
17. If throughout life you'd keep an honoured name,
Shun in your thought the joys which end in shame.
18. Don't mock old age, though you've a gifted brain:
Old age must ever show a childish vein.
19. Learn something; for when Luck is sudden gone,
Art stays nor ever leaves man's life alone.
20. Look quietly out on what the city says:
Men's talk at once reveals and hides their ways.
21. Practise with zeal an art once learned: as pains
Help talent, so the hand, used deftly, trains.
22. For fated hours to come show small concern:
He fears not death who knows how life to spurn.
23. Learn from the learnéd, but the unlettered teach:
Far should the spread of wholesome knowledge reach.

24. Hoc bibe quo possis si tu vis vivere sanus:[1]
morbi causa mali minima est quaecumque voluptas.[2]
25. Laudaris quodcumque palam, quodcumque probaris,
hoc vide ne rursus levitatis crimine damnes.
26. Tranquillis rebus semper diversa timeto,
rursus in adversis melius sperare memento.
27. Discere ne cessa: cura sapientia crescit,
rara datur longo prudentia temporis usu.
28. Parce laudato; nam quem tu saepe probaris,
una dies, qualis fuerit, ostendit, amicus.
29. Non pudeat, quae nescieris, te velle doceri:
scire aliquid laus est, culpa est nil discere velle.
30. Cum venere et baccho lis est et iuncta voluptas:
quod lautum est animo complectere, sed fuge lites.
31. Demissos animo et tacitos vitare memento:
quod flumen placidum est, forsan latet altius unda.
32. Dum fortuna tibi est rerum discrimine prava,[1]
alterius specta cui sit discrimine peior.
33. Quod potes id tempta; nam litus carpere remis
utilius multo est quam velum tendere in altum.
34. Contra hominem iustum prave contendere noli;
semper enim deus iniustas ulciscitur iras.
35. Ereptis opibus noli maerere dolendo,
sed gaude potius, tibi si contingat habere.
36. Est iactura gravis quaesitum amittere damno;
sed tibi cum valeat corpus, superesse putato.

[24, 1] hoc adhibe vitae quo possis v. s. *Baehrens*. [2] mali est nimia est *Baehrens*.

[32, 1] tibist rerum *Baehrens*: rerum tibi sit A: tua rerum tibi *ceteri codd.* discrimine prava *Baehrens*: discrimine peior A: displicet ipsi *ceteri codd.*

24. If you'd live healthy, drink in temperate measure:
Oft ill diseases spring from trivial pleasure.
25. What you've approved and lauded openly,
Shun the reproach of damning flightily.
26. When all is calm, dread ever fortune's change:
Then, in bad times, your hope towards good must range.
27. Fail not to learn; for wisdom grows by pains:
Mere long-drawn waiting rarely prudence gains.
28. Praise sparingly; for him you oft commend—
One day reveals how far he has been friend.
29. Blush not to wish, where ignorant, to be taught:
Knowledge wins praise: drones wish to study naught.
30. With love and wine are strife and pleasure knit:
Take to your heart the joy: the strife omit.
31. Gloomy and silent men take care to shun;
Still waters haply all too deep may run.
32. When fortune at a crisis serves thee ill,
Look at that other who is served worse still.
33. Try only what you can: 'tis wiser far
To row inshore than sail beyond the bar.
34. Strive not unfairly 'gainst an upright man:
On wrath unjustified God sets a ban.
35. When robbed of wealth, in anguish sorrow not:
Rather rejoice in what falls to thy lot.
36. To part with what toil won the loss is sore:
Yet think, if health be thine, thou hast full store.

33, 2 utilius multo est A: tutius est multo ς.
36, 1 quaesitum a. damno A: quae sunt a. dam(p)nis *celeri codd.*

37. Tempora longa tibi noli promittere vitae:
quocumque incedis, sequitur Mors corporis umbra.
38. Ture deum placa, vitulum sine crescat aratro:
ne credas gaudere deum, cum caede litatur.
39. Cede locum laesus Fortunae, cede potenti:
laedere qui ⟨potuit⟩ poterit prodesse aliquando.
40. Cum quid peccaris, castiga te ipse subinde:
vulnera dum sanas, dolor est medicina doloris.
41. Damnaris numquam post longum tempus amicum:
mutavit mores, sed pignora prima memento.
42. Gratior officiis, quo sis mage carior, esto,
ne nomen subeas quod dicunt officiperdi.
43. Suspectus cave sis, ne sis miser omnibus horis;
nam timidis et suspectis aptissima mors est.
44. Cum servos fueris proprios mercatus in usus
et famulos dicas, homines tamen esse memento.
45. Quam primum rapienda tibi est occasio prona,
ne rursus quaeras iam quae neglexeris ante.
46. Morte repentina noli gaudere malorum:
felices obeunt quorum sine crimine vita est.
47. Cum coniunx tibi sit, ne res et fama laboret,
vitandum ducas inimicum nomen amici.
48. Cum tibi contigerit studio cognoscere multa,
fac discas multa a vita te scire doceri.
49. Miraris versus nudis me scribere verbis?
hoc brevitas fecit, sensu uno iungere binos.

45, 1 prona *Baehrens*: prima *codd.* 2 iam quae *Baehrens*: quae iam *codd.*

48, 2 multa a vita *Baehrens*: multa vita *codd.* te scire *Baehrens*: nescire *codd.* doceri EF: docere C.

49, 2 sensu uno iungere *Baehrens*: sensu (-sum *m.* 2 *corr.*) coniungere A: sensus coniungere *ceteri codd.*

37. Thyself to promise years of life forbear;
    Death, like thy shadow, dogs thee everywhere.
38. Spare calves to plough: heaven's grace with incense gain:
    Think not God loves the blood of victims slain.
39. When stricken, yield to Fortune, yield to power:
    Who once could hurt may help in happier hour.
40. For faults committed, oft yourself arraign:
    In treating wounds, the cure for pain is pain.
41. Never condemn your friend of many a year:
    If changed his ways, think how he once was dear.
42. Show gratitude to bind affection's tie:
    Lest "ingrate" be the name you justify.
43. Earn not suspicion lest you live in grief:
    Suspected cravens find in death relief.
44. When you've bought slaves to serve your own sweet will,
    Though servants called, they're men, remember, still.
45. The lucky chance you must secure with speed,
    Lest you go seeking what you failed to heed.
46. Joy not when knaves come by a sudden end:
    Their death is blest whose life you can commend.
47. Having a wife, wouldst save thy gear and fame?
    Beware the friend who is but friend in name.
48. Great knowledge you have gained from books, you own:
    Yet note that life has lessons to be known.
49. You wonder that I write in these bare lines?
    Terseness the couplet in one thought combines.[a]

[a] An apology for the unadorned language of the distichs: the aim at brevity has prevented expansion, the object being to clinch one general thought in a couplet (or, if *sensus coniungere binos* be read, "to combine two allied thoughts").

II. CODICUM TURICENSIS ET VERONENSIS APPENDIX

1. LAETANDUM est vita, nullius morte dolendum;
cur etenim doleas a quo dolor ipse recessit.
2. Quod scieris opus esse tibi, dimittere noli;
oblatum auxilium stultum est dimittere cuiquam.
3. Perde semel, socium ingratum quom noveris esse;
saepe dato, quom te scieris bene ponere dona.
4. Dissimula laesus, si non datur ultio praesens:
qui celare potest odium pote laedere quem vult.
5. Qui prodesse potest non est fugiendus amicus,
si laesit verbo: bonitas sine crimine nil est.
6. Contra hominem astutum noli versutus haberi:
non captare malos stultum est, sed velle cluere.
7. Dat legem Natura tibi, non accipit ipsa.
8. Quod tacitum esse velis verbosis dicere noli.
9. Fortunae donis parvum tribuisse memento:
non opibus bona fama datur, sed moribus ipsis.

5, 2 nihil est A: *an* nulla est? *Baehrens in not.*
6, 2 velle cluere *Baehrens*: velle nocere A *sine sensu.*

SIGLA FOR MONOSTICHA

(As used by Baehrens in constituting his text.)

[For the contribution of single lines from each manuscript, see *P.L.M.* III. pp. 212–213.]

A = Vaticano-Palatinus 239: saec. x.
B = Vaticano-Reginensis 711: saec. xi.
C = Vaticano-Reginensis 300: saec. xi.

II. APPENDIX OF ADDITIONAL LINES FROM ZÜRICH AND VERONA MSS. (= C and A)

1. Find joy in life; grieve for the death of none.
   Why grieve for him from whom all grief has gone?
2. Never let slip the thing you know you need:
   They're fools who fail the proffered aid to heed.
3. Your friend, ungrateful proved, dismiss with haste:
   Give often, when you know your gifts well placed.
4. Conceal your wrong, if vengeance must be slow:
   Who hides his hate can injure any foe.
5. Your useful friend, though by his words annoyed,
   Drop not; there is no goodness unalloyed.
6. To outwit craft, court not for guile a name:
   Trap rogues you may, but not therefrom seek fame.
7. On you falls Nature's law, not on herself.
8. Don't tell a chatterbox what you'd keep quiet.
9. As slight in worth the gifts of Fortune view:
   To character, not wealth, renown is due.

D = Parisinus 8069: saec. xi.
E = Voravensis 111: saec. xii.
F = Marbodi codex S. Gatian. Turonensis 164.

[For the Cambridge MS. in Gonville and Caius College, saec. ix, see H. Schenkl, *Wien. Sitzungsber.* 143 (1901). For further views on the MSS. see M. Boas, *Mnemos.* 43 (1915), 44 (1916); *Philol.* 74 N.F. 28 (1917); *Rhein. Mus.* 72 (1917).]

III. COLLECTIO MONOSTICHORUM

Utilibus monitis prudens accommodet aurem.
Non laeta extollant animum, non tristia frangant.
Dispar vivendi ratio est, mors omnibus una.
Grande aliquid caveas timido committere cordi.
Numquam sanantur deformis vulnera famae.
Naufragium rerum est mulier male fida marito.
Tu si animo regeris, rex es; si corpore, servus.
Proximus esto bonis, si non potes optimus esse.
Nullus tam parcus, quin prodigus ex alieno.
Audit quod non vult, qui pergit dicere quod vult.
Non placet ille mihi, quisquis placuit sibi multum.
Nulli servitium si defers, liber haberis.
Vel bona contemni docet usus vel mala ferri.
Ex igne ut fumus, sic fama ex crimine surgit.
Paulisper laxatus amor decedere coepit.
Splendor opum sordes vitae non abluit umquam.
Improbus officium scit poscere, reddere nescit.
Irridens miserum dubium sciat omne futurum.
Mortis imago iuvat somnus, mors ipsa timetur.
Quanto maior eris, tanto moderatior esto.
Alta cadunt odiis, parva extolluntur amore.
Criminis indultu secura audacia crescit.
Quemlibet ignavum facit indignatio fortem.
Divitiae trepidant, paupertas libera res est.
Haut homo culpandus, quando est in crimine casus.
Fac quod te par sit, non alter quod mereatur.
Dissimilis cunctis vox vultus vita voluntas.
Ipsum se cruciat, te vindicat invidus in se.
Semper pauperies quaestum praedivitis auget.
Magno perficitur discrimine res memoranda.
Terra omnis patria est, qua nascimur et tumulamur.

---

[a] *i.e.* the very fact of envying a man is in itself (*in se*) a testimony to his merit.

CATO

III. COLLECTION OF SINGLE LINES

Let prudence to sound warnings lend an ear.
Gladness must not transport, nor sorrow break.
Life's way will vary: death is one for all.
Trust not a faint heart with some high emprise.
The wounds of base repute are never cured. 5
The wife who tricks her husband wrecks the home.
King art thou, ruled by mind; by body, slave.
If short of best, then emulate the good.
No thrift but will be free with others' gear.
Say all you like; you'll hear what you mislike. 10
Who much hath pleased himself doth not please me.
To none subservient, you are reckoned free.
Life's rule is—spurn your goods and face your ills.
As fire gives smoke, a charge gives rise to talk.
Love gradually relaxed begins to go. 15
Wealth's glitter never washed a foul life clean.
Rascals can ask a service, but not give.
Mockers at woe should know the future's hid.
Death's copy, sleep, delights: death's self affrights.
The greater you are, be all the more restrained. 20
Hate ruins high things, love exalts the small.
Give rein to guilt, and daring grows secure.
Wrath forces any coward to be brave.
Where wealth brings panic, poverty is free.
Man's not to blame when fortune is arraigned. 25
Act as befits you, not as men deserve.
In voice, look, life and will all are unlike.
Self-racking Envy clears you in herself.[a]
The rich man's gain aye grows by poverty.
Great crises foster deeds enshrined in thought. 30
All the Earth's our home; there we are born and buried.

Aspera perpessu fiunt iucunda relatu.
Acrius appetimus nova quam iam parta tenemus.
Labitur ex animo benefactum, iniuria durat.
Tolle mali testes: levius mala nostra feremus. 35
Saepe labor siccat lacrimas et gaudia fundit.
Tristibus afficiar gravius, si laeta recorder.
Quid cautus caveas aliena exempla docebunt.
Condit fercla fames, plenis insuavia cuncta.
Doctrina est fructus dulcis radicis amarae. 40
Cum accusas alium, propriam prius inspice vitam.
Qui vinci sese patitur pro tempore, vincit.
Dum speras, servis, cum sint data praemia sensis.
Nemo ita despectus, quin possit laedere laesus.
Ille nocet gravius quem non contemnere possis. 45
Quod metuis cumulas, si velas crimine crimen.
Consilii regimen virtuti corporis adde.
Cum vitia alterius satis acri lumine cernas
nec tua prospicias, fis verso crimine caecus.
Suffragium laudis quod fert malus, hoc bonus odit. 50
Si piget admissi, committere parce pigenda.
Quod nocet interdum, si prodest, ferre memento:
dulcis enim labor est, cum fructu ferre laborem.
[Laetandum est vita, nullius morte dolendum:
cur etenim doleas, a quo dolor ipse recessit?] 55
Spes facit illecebras visuque libido movetur.
Non facit ipse aeger quod sanus suaserit aegro.
Ipsos absentes inimicos laedere noli.
Ulcus proserpit quod stulta silentia celant.

43 *solus habet* A. cum data sint A. sensis *Baehrens*: saevis A: servis *Mai*.

---

[a] *Cf.* Tennyson's "For a sorrow's crown of sorrow is remembering happier things" and Dante's "nessun maggior dolore che ricordarsi del tempo felice nella miseria."

[b] *i.e.* you are a slave if you cherish extravagant hopes, because your thoughts have no freedom from the imaginary

[T]hings hard to bear grow pleasant to relate.
[K]eener our zest for the new than our grasp on the old.
[A] good turn slips the mind, a wrong endures.
[N]o witness near—we'll easier bear our ills. 35
[W]ork often dries the tear and spreads delight.
[M]emory of joys will aggravate my woes.[a]
[C]aution and care you'll learn from others' case.
[H]unger is sauce: no dishes please the gorged.
[L]earning is pleasant fruit from bitter root. 40
[E]re you accuse, your own life first inspect.
[W]ho at fit moment yields is conqueror.
[Y]our hopes enslave you; for your thoughts are bribed.[b]
[N]one so despised as cannot hurt when hurt.[c]
[T]he man you could not slight can harm you more.[d] 45
[C]loak crime with crime and you increase your fear.
[T]o bodily courage add the sway of thought.
[W]hen with sharp eye another's faults you mind,
[N]ot seeing yours, you're blamed in turn as blind.
[P]raise voted to the bad disgusts the good. 50
[I]f irked by what you've done, don't do what irks.
[H]arm sometimes must be borne, if found to suit;
[F]or sweet the toil of bearing toil with fruit.
[Find joy in life; grieve for the death of none.
[W]hy grieve for him from whom all grief has gone?][e] 55
[H]ope makes allurements: lust is stirred by sight.
[W]hat you prescribe when well, you drop when sick.
[D]on't hurt e'en enemies behind their backs.
[S]ores spread in stealth by foolish silence hid.

[a]dvantages you are counting on and allotting to yourself [a]s if already won.

[c] *i.e.* the veriest craven will retaliate: "even a worm will [t]urn."

[d] The thought is not very deep: the man with no chinks [i]n his armour is one to be reckoned with.

[e] In D: also in Appendix from Zürich and Verona MSS. *[s]upra.*

Nemo reum faciet qui vult dici sibi verum. 6
Vincere velle tuos satis est victoria turpis.
Nonnumquam vultu tegitur mens taetra sereno.
Quisque miser casu alterius solatia sumit.
Vera libens dicas, quamquam sint aspera dictu.
Vir constans quicquid coepit complere laborat. 6
Iniustus, qui sola putat proba quae facit ipse.
Omne manu factum consumit longa vetustas.
Haut multum tempus mentis simulata manebunt.
Quicquid inoptatum cadit, hoc homo corrigat arte.
Durum etiam facilem facit adsuetudo laborem. 7
Robur confirmat labor, at longa otia solvunt.
Ut niteat virtus, absit rubigo quietis.
Sat dulcis labor est, cum fructu ferre laborem.
Magni magna parant, modici breviora laborant.
Ne crede amissum, quicquid reparare licebit. 7
Non pecces tunc cum peccare impune licebit.
Tristis adest messis, si cessat laeta voluptas.
Absentum causas contra maledicta tuere.

68 haut multum E : haud ullum CF. mentis E : vanitas CF : bonitas *Riese* : gravitas *vel* virtus *Buecheler*.

IV. LINES FROM COLUMBANUS

Which may be regarded as Catonian

Under the name of the Irish monk Columbanus (A.D. 543–615) there has come down a *carmen monostichon* in 207 verses constituting a set of rules for life (*praecepta vivendi*). While many are of Christian origin, Baehrens selects about a quarter of these as being Catonian in source; and Manitius thinks considerably more might be claimed under this head.[a] Baehrens bases his text on Canisius in

None him arraigns who wants truth said to him. 60
'Tis a poor win to seek to beat your own.
Calm looks do sometimes cloak a loathsome mind.
Another's woe consoles all wretched folk.
Speak the truth freely, though the truth be hard.
The steadfast strive to end a task begun. 65
Unfair the man who approves his own acts only.
Long lapse of time consumes all handiwork.
The mind's pretences will not long endure.
Let man by skill make good unwelcome chance.
Hard work grows easy to the practised hand. 70
Long leisure saps the strength which work upbuilds.
That worth may shine, let rest be free from rust.
Sweet task it is to face a task and win.[a]
The great aim high ; plain folk ply humbler tasks.
Whate'er may be recovered think not lost. 75
Sin not in the hour when you may safely sin.
Sad reaping comes, if joyful pleasure wanes.
Champion the absent 'gainst backbiting tongues.

[a] *Cf.* line 53 *supra.*

---

his *Thesaurus* (Amsterdam, 1725),[b] who used a *codex Frisingensis*. It gives the ascription to Columbanus —*incipit libellus cuiusdam sapientis et ut fertur beati Columbani*. In the word *sapientis* may be detected an echo of "Cato the Philosopher."[c] Other manuscripts are the *codices Sangallenses*, *Lugdunensis* 190, and *Parisinus* 8092.

[a] *Gesch. der latein. Lit. des Mittelalters*, I. (1911), pp. 181 *sqq.*: *cf.* E. Dümmler, *Poet. lat. aevi Karolini*, I. 275–281.

[b] First ed. Ingolstad, 1601.

[c] The Disticha are entitled in the Parisinus 2659, saec. ix. *liber (quartus) Catonis philosophi*. The Montepessulanus has *libri Catonis philosophi*.

IV. EX COLUMBANO QUAE VIDENTUR CATONIS ESSE

Corporis exsuperat vires prudentia mentis.
Ne tua paeniteat caveas victoria temet.
Vir bonus esse nequit nisi qui siet omnibus aequus.
Non tu quaeso iocis laedas nec carmine quemquam.
Sit servus mentis venter, sit serva libido.
Eripe, si valeas, non suggere tela furenti.
Saepe nocet puero miratio blanda magistri.
Cum sapiente loquens perpaucis utere verbis.
Egregios faciet mentis constantia mores.
Felix, qui causam loquitur prudentis in aurem.
Tantum verba valent, quantum mens sentiat illa.
Non erit antiquo novus anteferendus amicus.
Moribus egregiis facias tibi nomen honestum.
Cui prodest socius qui non prodesse probatur?
Res se vera quidem semper declarat honeste.
Actibus aut verbis noli tu adsuescere pravis.
Praemeditata animo levius sufferre valebis.
Quae subito adveniunt multo graviora videntur.
Felix, alterius cui sunt documenta flagella.
Praemia non capiet, ingrato qui bona praestat.
Omnis paulatim leto nos applicat hora.
Ante diem mortis nullus laudabilis exstat.
Doctor erit magnus, factis qui quod docet implet.
Quod tibi vis fieri, hoc alii praestare memento.
Quod tibi non optes, alii ne feceris ulli.
Corripe prudentem: reddetur gratia verbis.
Plus tua quam alterius damnabis crimina iudex.

---

[a] *Cf.* Publilius Syrus, line 2.

IV. LINES FROM COLUMBANUS

Presumably of Catonian origin

Foresight of mind surpasses bodily strength.
Take care your victory bring you no regrets.
He can't be good who is not fair to all.
Wound no one, pray, with either jest or verse.
Let appetite and lust be slaves of mind. 5
Seize, if you can, a madman's arms : lend none.
A teacher's flattering wonder harms a boy.
Talking with sages, use but scanty words.
Firmness of mind will make fine character.
Blest he who states his case to wisdom's ear. 10
As the heart feels, so much the worth of words.
New friends must not be set before the old.
By noble traits make yours an honoured name.
Who gains by friend who stands no test of use?
Truth ever honourably declares herself. 15
Do not grow used to evil acts or words.
You'll bear more lightly what the mind fore-knew.
Far heavier seem the strokes which sudden fall.
Blest he who from another's scourging learns.
Goods given to ingrates will bring no reward. 20
Each hour slow moving steers us nearer death.
Praiseworthy none stands out till day of death.
Great teacher he who as he teaches acts.
As you'd be treated, see you treat another.[a]
What you'd not like yourself, don't do to any. 25
Reprove the wise: your words will bring you thanks.
Thy faults, when judge, condemn more than another's.

Sis bonus idque bonis, laesus nec laede nocentem.
Vir prudens animo est melior quam fortis in armis.
Divitias animo iniustas attendere noli. 30
Semper avarus amat mendacia furta rapinas.
Invidiae maculat famam mala pestis honestam.
Nil sine consilio facias: sic facta probantur.
Instanter facias, sors quae tibi tradat agenda.
Improperes numquam, dederis munuscula si qua. 35
Omnia pertractet primum mens verba loquelae.
Sic novus atque novum vinum veterascat amicus.
Alma dies noctem sequitur somnosque labores.
Tempora dum variant, animus sit semper honestus.
Corripe peccantem, noli at dimittere, amicum. 40
Observat sapiens sibi tempus in ore loquendi;
insipiens loquitur spretum sine tempore verbum.
Iam magnum reddis modico tu munus amico,
si ipsum ut amicus amas: amor est pretiosior auro.
Dives erit semper, dure qui operatur in agro. 45
Otia qui sequitur, veniet huic semper egestas.
Omnibus est opibus melior vir mente fidelis.
Qui bona sectatur prima bene surgit in hora.
Multorum profert sapientis lingua salutem.
Hostili in bello dominatur dextera fortis. 50
Lingua ligata tibi multos acquirit amicos.
Diligit hic natum, virga qui corripit illum.

41 forte *Baehrens*: in ore *cod. Fris.*
50 hostili *Baehrens*: hostibus *cod. Fris.*
51 ligata tibi *Baehrens*: placata sibi *cod. Fris.*

Treat well the good: though harmed, harm not the bad.
Men sage in mind excel the brave in arms.
To unfair money-getting give no heed. 30
Greed ever loves lies, theft and robbery.
Fair fame is soiled by envy's cursed plague.
Do naught uncounselled: so are deeds approved.
What chance hands you to do, do earnestly.
Never upbraid for any gifts you give. 35
Thought, words and language first must handle all.[a]
Let time mature new friends just like new wine
Kind day comes after night, toil after sleep.
Times change: let honour always rule the mind.
Reprove, but don't let go, your erring friend. 40
Wise men respect the hour for utterance;
Fools out of season utter worthless trash.
To a humble friend you give a handsome gift
In friendly love: love counts for more than gold.
Rich he'll be ever who toils hard afield. 45
The quest of ease will in its trail bring want.
The man of trusty mind excels all wealth.
Who aims at gear is smart to rise at dawn.
The sage's tongue reveals the health of many.[b]
In fighting foes, the strong right hand is lord. 50
A tongue fast bound procures you many a friend.[c]
He loves his son who chides him with the rod.[d]

[a] *i.e.* reflection and discussion should precede action.
[b] *i.e.* gives advice which, if acted on, will secure the general welfare.
[c] *i.e.* silence may be golden in avoiding offence to others.
[d] This may be influenced by the Scriptures: *e.g. Prov.* xiii. 24 "He that spareth his rod hateth his son; but he that loveth him chasteneth him betimes."

LINES ON THE MUSES

The lines on the Muses were well known in the Middle Ages, and, according to Baehrens, may well be the work of the composer of the *Disticha*. They are found in the following, among other, MSS. :—

A = Turicensis 78 : saec. ix.
B = Caroliruhensis 36 f. : saec. ix–x.

CATONIS DE MUSIS VERSUS

Clio gesta canens transactis tempora reddit.
dulciloquis calamos Euterpe flatibus urguet.
comica lascivo gaudet sermone Thalia.
Melpomene tragico proclamat maesta boatu.
Terpsichore affectus citharis movet impetrat auget.
plectra gerens Erato saltat pede carmine vultu.
signat cuncta manu loquiturque Polymnia gestu.
Urania ⟨arce⟩ poli motus scrutatur et astra.
carmina Calliope libris heroica mandat.
mentis Apollineae vis has movet undique Musas,
in medioque sedens complectitur omnia Phoebus.

[3] comicolas civo A : lascivio E.
[5] impetrat *Baehrens* : imperat *codd. omnes.*
[7–9] *ita ponunt* DE : 8, 9, 7 *collocant* ABC *et ceteri omnes.*
[8] Urania arce poli *Baehrens* : Urania poli *codd. omnes* (poliq. B) : Uranie caeli *vulgo.*
[11] medioque sedens *Baehrens* : medio residens *codd. omnes* (*aut* 10 *aut* 11 *spurium putat Riese*).

---

[a] *Cf.* p. 434, *supra*, lines *De Musis* ascribed to Florus. The ascription of the above verses to "Cato" is doubtful. Burman, *Anthol. Lat.*, *Lib. I.* No. 74, gives the heading "Musarum

CATO

C = Vossianus L.Q. 33: saec. x.
D = Cantabrigiensis, Collegii S. Trinit. O. 4. 11: saec. x–xi.
E = Parisinus 7930: saec. xi.

The title in A is simply *Nomina Musarum* ; but two MSS. ascribe the lines to Cato, viz. B *Versus Catonis de musis vel nominibus philorum* (*sic*) and C *Incipiunt versus Catonis philosophi de novem musis.*

LINES ON THE MUSES[a]

To recreate the past is Clio's theme:
Euterpe plies the pipes with tuneful breath
Thalia's joy is playful comedy:
Melpomene utters woe with tragic cry:
Terpsichore's lute moves, wins and swells the heart:
Lyric the song, dance, smile of Erato:
Polymnia's hand marks all—she speaks in act:[b]
Urania scans the sky and moving stars:
Calliope records heroic lays.
Apollo's varied thought each Muse inspires:[c]
So Phoebus, mid them throned, combines their charms.

Inventa" and cites the parallel lines from the *Anthologia Graeca.*

[b] Polymnia or Polyhymnia was traditionally the Muse of sacred song, but varied provinces were at different periods assigned to her—rhetoric and even agriculture and geometry. A wall-painting from Herculaneum associated her with μύθους (*fabulas*). It was a late development to assign *pantomimus* to her patronage, and the line refers to the expression of everything by gesture.

[c] Apollo, as their patron, was known as *Musagetes.*

EPITAPH ON VITALIS THE MIME-ACTOR

This poem is subjoined to the *Disticha Catonis* in the following manuscripts:

A = Turicensis 78: saec. ix.
B = Reginensis 2078: saec. ix–x.
C = Parisinus 2772: saec. x–xi.
D = Reginensis 1414: saec. xi.
E = Parisinus 8319: saec. xi.

A gives no title: D gives *Epitaphium Vitalis Mimi Filii Catonis*, which Baehrens accepts: BC give

---

EPITAPHIUM VITALIS MIMI [FILII CATONIS]

Quid tibi, Mors, faciam, quae nulli parcere nosti?
  nescis laetitiam, nescĭs amare iocos.
his ego praevalui toto notissimus orbi,
  hinc mihi larga domus, hinc mihi census erat.
gaudebam semper. quid enim, si gaudia desint, 5
  hic vagus ac fallax utile mundus habet?
me viso rabidi subito cecidere furores;
  ridebat summus me veniente dolor.
non licuit quemquam curis mordacibus uri
  nec rerum incerta mobilitate trahi. 10
vincebat cunctos praesentia nostra timores
  et mecum felix quaelibet hora fuit.
motibus ac dictis, tragica quoque veste placebam
  exhilarans variis tristia corda modis.
fingebam vultus, habitus ac verba loquentum, 15
  ut plures uno crederĕs ore loqui.

[2] amara *coni. Burman.*
[9] curis mordacibus uri *Baehrens*: mordacibus urere curis *codd.* (ordac. B. curris B, C *m.* 1).

Epitafium filii Cat(h)onis; and E *Epitaphiũ Vitalis mimi.* Burman, *Anth. Lat.*, *Lib.* IV. No. 20, and Meyer, *Anth. vet. Lat.*, 1173, have the poem under the heading *Vitalis mimi.* Its late period is shown in the shortening of the final syllable in *nescis* l. 2 and *crederes* l. 16. The German monk Ermenrich of the ninth century, writing to Grimald, cites *nescis* as a trochee "in epitaphio Catonis Censorini dicentis" (where *dicentis*, it may be guessed, is an attempt to include the lines as among *Dicta Catonis*).

EPITAPH ON VITALIS THE MIME-ACTOR

How shall I treat thee, Death, who sparest none?
Thou knowst not mirth, knowst not the love of fun:
Yet all the world in these my merit knew—
Hence came my mansion, hence my revenue.
I always wore a smile: if smiles be lost,
What boots a world in wayward trickery tossed?
At sight of me wild frenzy met relief:
My entrance changed to laughter poignant grief.
None felt the canker of anxiety
Nor worried mid this world's uncertainty.
O'er every fear my presence won success:
An hour with me was ever happiness.
In tragic rôle my word and act could please,
Cheering in myriad ways hearts ill at ease:
Through change in look, mien, voice I so could run
That many seemed to use the lips of one.

---

[13] veste *Buecheler*: verba *codd.*: voce *Pithoeus.*
[15] angebam CD. loquentũ E *corr.*: loquentur *codd.*
[16] crederis *codd.*, *nisi quod in* A e *supra* i *m.* 1 *est positum.*

ipse etiam, quem nostra oculis geminabat imago,
  horruit in vultus se magis isse meos.
o quotiens imitata meos per femina gestus
  vidit et erubuit totaque muta fuit! 20
ergo quot in nostro vivebant corpore formae,
  tot mecum raptas abstulit atra dies.
quo vos iam tristi turbatus deprecor ore,
  qui titulum legitis cum pietate meum:
"o quam laetus eras, Vitalis" dicite maesti, 25
  "sint tibi di tali, sint tibi fata modo!"

19 meos per femina *Baehrens*: meo ≣ se ≣ femine A: meos es semina BCD: meo se femina E. gestus *Baehrens*: gestu *codd.*

20 muta *Baehrens*: mata CD: mota E: nata B: compta A *interpolate.*

21 vivebant *Goetz*: videbantur *codd.* (videantur E): ridebant *Hauthal.*

The man whose double on the stage I seemed
Shrank, as my looks his very own he deemed.
How oft a woman whom my gestures played
Saw herself, blushed, and held her peace dismayed!
So parts which I made live by mimicry
Dark death hath hurried to the grave with me.[a]
To you who with compassion read this stone
I utter my request in saddened tone:
Say sadly: " Glad, Vitalis, did you live:
Such gladness may the Gods and fates thee give! "

[a] *abstulit atra dies* (22) is from Virg. *Aen.* VI. 429.

---

22 raptas *Pithoeus*: raptor *codd.* (rapitor E).
24 titulum *Burman, Schrader*: tumulum *codd.*
26 di tali *Baehrens*: vitalis *codd., nisi quod* vitalis *m.* 1 *in* dii tales *corr.* A. fata *Heinsius*: laeta *codd. e glossa.*

The man whose double on the stage I seemed
Drunk as my looks his very own he deemed.
How oft a woman whom my gestures moved
Saw herself, blushed and held her grace disproved!
So parts which I made live by mimicry
Dark death hath buried to the grave with me.[a]
To you who with compassion read this stone,
I after my request with saddened tone
Say sadly, "O [illegible] did you live?"
Such gladness may the Gods and Fates thee give!

[a] abstulit atra dies (?) [illegible], from Virg. Aen. VI. 429.

[illegible]

[illegible]

[illegible]

PHOENIX

INTRODUCTION

TO PHOENIX

It is not surprising that poets and historians, Latin as well as Greek, should have felt the magnetism of legends concerning the phoenix, a strange Eastern bird of brilliantly varied plumage, reappearing in loneliness at long cyclic intervals after an aromatic and musical death, which was at once a mysterious loss and a mysterious renewal of life. Even in its pagan forms—for it varied considerably in detail—the story had undeniable attraction.[a] The earliest reference traceable is one in Hesiod[b] to the bird's longevity. Herodotus' contact with Egypt impelled him to mention the story of its re-emergence at Heliopolis every 500 years—a cyclic period doubled and even further increased by other

[a] See W. H. Roscher *Ausführliches Lexicon der griech. u. röm. Mythologie*, 1902–1909, III. 2. col. 3450–3472 for an account of the Phoenix (Φοῖνιξ) in literature and in both pagan and Christian art, *e.g.* on coins as a symbol of eternity and rejuvenation. Here it must suffice to select some representative references: Herod. II. 73; Ovid *Am.* II. vi. 54, *Met.* XV. 392–407; Stat. *Silv.* II. iv. 36; Sen. *Epist.* xlii. 1; Pliny, *N.H.* X. 3–5; Tac. *Ann.* VI. 28; Aur. Vict. *De Caesaribus* 4; Claudian, *De Cons. Stil.* II. 414–420, *Carm. min.* xxvii (xliv).

[b] Fragm. 163 (222), 3–4, ed. Goettling, 1878 = Loeb ed. of Hesiod, etc., p. 74. αὐτὰρ ὁ φοῖνιξ ἐννέα μὲν κόρακας (sc. γηράσκεται), "the phoenix lives nine times longer than the raven." The idea is echoed in the "reparabilis ales" of Ausonius, Bk. VII. *Eclog.* v. 5–6 (Loeb ed.).

authorities. Ovid fitted the description of the nest into the last book of his *Metamorphoses*; and at a subsequent date Statius conceived the fancy of a still happier phoenix untouched by the lethargy of age. The rarity of the fabulous bird struck Seneca as a good analogy to the infrequent occurrence of a perfect Stoic sage. Pliny in his *Natural History* touches with considerable minuteness upon the bird's nest of spices, its habits, and the growth of its offspring; while the news that it had been seen in Egypt in the year A.D. 34 draws from Tacitus an account of its periodic death and the transport of the father's body by the new phoenix to the altar of the Sun. Towards the end of the classical period we note the continued attraction of the theme for Claudian, not only in an elaborate simile of half a dozen lines in his *De Consulatu Stilichonis*, but also in the 110 hexameters which he almost certainly modelled upon our extant elegiac *Phoenix*. This is most commonly ascribed to Lactantius, the pupil of Arnobius in oratory, who was professor of rhetoric at Nicomedia early in the fourth century and who later in the West became the instructor of Prince Crispus by the invitation of Constantine. As his conversion from paganism did not divorce him from ancient culture, Lactantius attained distinction among early Christian authors for the beauty and eloquence of his Latin style.

But no more surprising than the semi-romantic pagan appeal of the phoenix fable is the fact that Christian writers should have found an added symbolic fascination in such features as its Oriental paradise and its resurrection to life through death. *Prima facie*, then, there seems little to startle one in the ascription to Lactantius; but, in fact, the authorship of the *Phoenix* has long been under discussion. It is easy to discover in the poem both pagan and Christian constituents. Baehrens indeed argues that the pagan element is enough to invalidate the traditional ascription (supported by certain MSS.[a] of the poem) to so unquestionably Christian an author. To meet this objection Brandt has argued that the *Phoenix* was composed by Lactantius before his conversion; and Pichon, who minimises the Christian colour, is so sure that the pagan touches would have been unacceptable to a Christian, that he holds the only possible alternatives to be the composition of the poem either by Lactantius at a pre-Christian stage or by a different author who was pagan. Yet such "contamination" of conflicting strains does not seem to be an insuperable barrier to the prevailing belief: indeed it is rather to be expected in the age and circumstances of Lactantius. Baehrens, who, like Ribbeck, rejects the Lactantian authorship, is not convinced by Dechent's study of similarities in phraseology between our poem and the unquestioned works of Lactantius. As regards the testimony by Gregory of Tours[b] in the sixth century to a poem on the phoenix which he summarises and ascribes to Lactantius, Baehrens eventually concluded[c] that Gregory

[a] See the Sigla.

[b] *De cursu stellarum* 12, p. 861. Our poem is quoted eight times under the name of Lactantius in a short anonymous treatise *de dubiis nominibus* (between Isidore of Seville and the ninth century); and it is significant that Alcuin cites Lactantius as a Christian poet in his list of books in the library at York (F. Dümmler, *Poet. lat. aev. Carol.* I. p. 204).

[c] *P.L.M.* III. pp. 250–252.

had not before him the same poem as we have, but a lost one by Lactantius. On Jerome's authority we know that Lactantius wrote a ὁδοιπορικόν from Africa to Nicomedia, presumably when he went on Diocletian's invitation to teach rhetoric in that city; and it is Baehrens' suggestion that into this narrative of his own journey eastwards he might have appropriately worked an account of the fabled Oriental bird, using our extant poem (according to Baehrens, by a pagan) but adding Christian colour. The hypothesis next assumes that after the supposed disappearance of Lactantius' poem monkish copyists made an incorrect ascription of the surviving poem to the "Christian Cicero," being misled by the outward resemblances in it to Christian ideas and by the knowledge that a *Phoenix* had actually been composed by Lactantius. It will be noted that the monks, if this guess be true, did not find the paganism of the poem so much of a stumbling-block as Baehrens and Pichon have done. But the majority of critics, including Ebert, Manitius, Riese, Birt and Dechent, have been satisfied with a less elaborate theory and have accepted our poem as Lactantius' authentic work.

For English readers the *Phoenix* possesses special historical and literary interest as the basis of an early Anglo-Saxon *Phoenix* in alliterative accentual verse. Its author, whether the Northumbrian Cynewulf or not—for here too there is a dispute—undoubtedly modelled the earlier portion of his poem upon the extant Latin poem. Here again, as in the original, we meet the earthly paradise, partly a plain, partly "a fair forest where fruits fall not" (*wuduholt wynlic, waestmas ne dreosað*).

Here too, familiar as in the ancient source, are the bird's unrivalled notes of song, its flight to the Syrian palm-tree in the fullness of a thousand years, the building of its nest, its own admirable beauty, its strange death and birth to fresh life. But the adaptation is free. The English borrower omits as he wishes. Phaethon and Deucalion vanish. Phoebus' car becomes "God's candle." Even the texture of the Anglo-Saxon proem on the far Eastern land where the marvellous bird dwells is interwoven with Biblical thought. Such expansion is still more noticeable in the later part, where a transition is made from the mystery of the phoenix's sex and birth to analogies with the life of the elect; and, when the ways of the phoenix are treated as symbolic of the Christian life, the English poem departs entirely from the Latin original.

EDITIONS

Apart from editions of Lactantius (*e.g. ed. princeps*, Rome, 1468; M. Thomasius, Antwerp, 1570; Gallaeus, Leyden, 1660):

Gryphiander. Jena, 1618.
Burman. In his *Claudian.* Amsterdam, 1760.
Wernsdorf. In *P.L.M.* III. Altenburg, 1782.
A. Martini. Lüneburg, 1825.
H. Leyser. Quedlinburg, 1839.
A. Riese. In *Anthol. Lat.* 1863; ed. 2. Leipzig, 1906.
L. Jeep. In his *Claudian*, vol. ii. Leipzig, 1879.
E. Baehrens. In *P.L.M.* III. Leipzig, 1881.

INTRODUCTION TO

RELEVANT WORKS

A. Ebert. In *Allgemeine Geschichte der Lit. des Mittelalters im Abendlande.* Leipzig, 1874, ed. 2, 1889.

G. Goetz. In *Acta Societ. philol. Lips.* V. p. 319 *sqq.*

H. Klapp. In *Progr. gymn. Wandsbeckiani.* 1875.

A. Riese. *Ueber den Phoenix des Lactantius, Rh. Mus.* xxxi. 1876.

H. Dechent. *Ueber die Echtheit des Phoenix von Lactantius, Rh. Mus.* xxxv. 1880, pp. 39–55.

M. Manitius. In *Geschichte der christl.-latein. Poesie.* Stuttgart, 1891.

O. Ribbeck. In *Geschichte der röm. Dichtung,* III. p. 364. Stuttgart, 1892.

S. Brandt. *Zum Phoenix des Lactantius, Rh. Mus.* xlvii. 1892.

A. Knappitsch. *De Lactantii Ave Phoenice.* Graz, 1896.

R. Pichon. *Lactance : Étude sur le mouvement philosophique et religieux sous le règne de Constantin.* Paris, 1901.

C. Pascal. *Sul carme de ave Phoenice.* Naples, 1904.

———. *I carmi De Phoenice* in *Letteratura latina medievale*: Nuovi Saggi. Catania, 1909.

C. Landi. *De Ave Phoenice : il carme e il suo autore* in *Atti e memorie di Padova,* 31, 1914–1915.

SIGLA

(As in Baehrens' *P.L.M.* III. pp. 247–249.)

A = Parisinus 13048: saec. viii, scriptura langobardica exaratus inter Venantii Fortunati poemata, fol. 47a–48b versus 1–110, sine titulo exhibens.

PHOENIX

B = codex bibliothecae capitularis Veronensis 163: saec. ix, continens Claudianum maxime cuius post "Phoenicem" legitur nostrum carmen, fol. 14ª–19ᵇ, cum hac inscriptione *item Lacta(n)tii de eadem ave.*

C = Vossianus L.Q. 33: saec. x: fol. 73ª–75ᵇ, *versus Lactantii de ave Phoenice* habet.

O = consensus codicum melioris notae vel communis archetypus.

CODICES INTERPOLATI

D = codex Cantabrigiensis [Bibl. Univers. Gg. 5.35]: saec. xi, qui inter multa poemata christiana fol. 168ª–170ᵇ, habet "Phoenicem" praemisso titulo: *Incipit libellus de fenice, paradisi ut fertur habitatrice. Quidam ferunt Lactantium hunc scripsisse libellum.*

E = Bodleianus F. 2. 14: saec. xii, fol. 126ᵇ–128ᵇ, sine inscriptione libellum continens.

ς = pauca quae correctiora leguntur in codicibus saeculo xiv maximeque xv scriptis.

[For the large number of late and inferior manuscripts see A. Martini's edition, 1825.]

DE AVE PHOENICE

Est locus in primo felix oriente remotus,
qua patet aeterni maxima porta poli,
nec tamen aestivos hiemisve propinquus ad ortus,
sed qua Sol verno fundit ab axe diem.
illic planities tractus diffundit apertos, 5
nec tumulus crescit nec cava vallis hiat,
sed nostros montes, quorum iuga celsa putantur,
per bis sex ulnas imminet ille locus.
hic Solis nemus est et consitus arbore multa
lucus perpetuae frondis honore virens. 10
cum Phaethonteis flagrasset ab ignibus axis,
ille locus flammis inviolatus erat;
et cum diluvium mersisset fluctibus orbem
Deucalioneas exsuperavit aquas.
non huc exsangues Morbi, non aegra Senectus 15
nec Mors crudelis nec Metus asper adest
nec Scelus infandum nec opum vesana Cupido
aut Ira aut ardens caedis amore Furor;
Luctus acerbus abest et Egestas obsita pannis
et Curae insomnes et violenta Fames. 20
non ibi tempestas nec vis furit horrida venti
nec gelido terram rore pruina tegit;

16 adest AB : adit CDE.

18 aut metus O (*cf. v.* 16) : aut Mars *edd. vet.* : Venus *Oudendorp* : Pavor *Goetz* : Letum *Riese* : huc meat *Birt* : aut Ira *Baehrens.*

PHOENIX

There is a far-off land, blest amid the first streaks of dawn, where standeth open the mightiest portal of the everlasting sky, yet not beside the risings of the summer or the winter Sun, but where he sheds daylight from the heavens in spring. There a plain spreads out its open levels; no knoll swells there, no hollow valley gapes, yet that region o'ertops by twice six ells our mountains whose ridges are reckoned high. Here is the grove of the Sun, a woodland planted with many a tree and green with the honours of eternal foliage. When the sky went ablaze from the fires of Phaethon's car, that region was inviolate from the flames;[a] it rose above the waters on which Deucalion sailed, when the flood had whelmed the world in its waves.[b] Hither no bloodless Diseases come, no sickly Eld, nor cruel Death nor desperate Fear nor nameless Crime nor maddened Lust for wealth or Wrath or Frenzy afire with the love of murder; bitter Grief is absent and Beggary beset with rags and sleepless Cares and violent Hunger.[c] No tempest raveth there nor savage force of wind: nor does the hoar-frost shroud the ground in chilly

[a] For Phaethon's disastrous driving of the car of his father Apollo see Ovid, *Met.* II. 1–332.

[b] Deucalion's ark saved him and Pyrrha during the primeval deluge.

[c] The personifications are largely based on Virg. *Aen.* VI. 274 *sqq.*

nulla super campos tendit sua vellera nubes
nec cadit ex alto turbidus umor aquae.
sed fons in medio, quem vivum nomine dicunt, 25
perspicuus, lenis, dulcibus uber aquis;
qui semel erumpens per singula tempora mensum
duodeciens undis irrigat omne nemus.
hic genus arboreum procero stipite surgens
non lapsura solo mitia poma gerit. 30
hoc nemus, hos lucos avis incolit unica Phoenix,
unica, si vivit morte refecta sua.
paret et obsequitur Phoebo memoranda satelles:
hoc Natura parens munus habere dedit.
lutea cum primum surgens Aurora rubescit, 35
cum primum rosea sidera luce fugat,
ter quater illa pias immergit corpus in undas,
ter quater e vivo gurgite libat aquam.
tollitur ac summo considit in arboris altae
vertice, quae totum despicit una nemus, 40
et conversa novos Phoebi nascentis ad ortus
exspectat radios et iubar exoriens.
atque ubi Sol pepulit fulgentis limina portae
et primi emicuit luminis aura levis,
incipit illa sacri modulamina fundere cantus 45
et mira lucem voce ciere novam,
quam nec aedoniae voces nec tibia possit
musica Cirrheis adsimulare modis;

[25] sed O: est *Baehrens.*
[32] sed O: si (= siquidem) *Baehrens.*
[33] memoranda O: veneranda *Baehrens.*
[47] voces O: fauces *Baehrens.*

damp. Above the plains no cloud stretches its fleece, nor falleth from on high the stormy moisture of rain. But there is a well in the midst, the well of life they call it, crystal-clear, gently-flowing, rich in its sweet waters: bursting forth once for each several month in its season, it drenches all the grove twelve times with its flood. Here is a kind of tree that rising with stately stem bears mellow fruits which will not fall to the ground.

In this grove, in these woods, dwells the peerless bird,[a] the Phoenix, peerless, since she lives renewed by her own death. An acolyte worthy of record,[b] she yields obedience and homage to Phoebus: such the duty that parent Nature assigned to her for observance. Soon as saffron Aurora reddens at her rising, soon as she routs the stars with rosy light, thrice and again that bird plunges her body into the kindly waves, thrice and again sips water from the living flood. Soaring she settles on the topmost height of a lofty tree which alone commands the whole of the grove, and, turning towards the fresh rising of Phoebus at his birth, awaits the emergence of his radiant beam. And when the Sun has struck the threshold of the gleaming portal and the light shaft of his first radiance has flashed out, she begins to pour forth notes of hallowed minstrelsy and to summon the new day in a marvellous key which neither tune of nightingale nor musical pipe could rival in

[a] "alone of its kind," "unparalleled": *cf.* Ovid *Am.* II. vi. 54, *et vivax phoenix, unica semper avis.*

[b] In most accounts the phoenix appears as a male bird (*pater*, etc.). Contrast, however, Ovid's *unica avis* (*l.c.*) with Claudian's *Titanius ales* (*Carm. Min.* xxvii.7) and his *idem* (masc.) in *De Cons. Stil.* II. 415. Aurelius Victor, *De Caesaribus* 4, has *quam volucrem* in reference to the phoenix.

sed neque olor moriens imitari posse putetur
nec Cylleneae fila canora lyrae.[b] 50

postquam Phoebus equos in aperta effudit Olympi
atque orbem totum protulit usque means,
illa ter alarum repetito verbere plaudit
igniferumque caput ter venerata silet.
atque eadem celeres etiam discriminat horas 55
innarrabilibus nocte dieque sonis,
antistes luci nemorumque verenda sacerdos
et sola arcanis conscia, Phoebe, tuis.
quae postquam vitae iam mille peregerit annos
ac sibi reddiderint tempora longa gravem, 60
ut reparet lapsum spatiis vergentibus aevum,
adsuetum nemoris dulce cubile fugit;
cumque renascendi studio loca sancta reliquit,
tunc petit hunc orbem, Mors ubi regna tenet.
derigit in Syriam celeres longaeva volatus, 65
Phoenicen nomen cui dedit ipsa vetus,
securosque petit deserta per avia lucos,
hic ubi per saltus silva remota latet.
tum legit aerio sublimem vertice palmam,
quae Graium Phoenix ex ave nomen habet, 70
in quam nulla nocens animans prorepere possit,
lubricus aut serpens aut avis ulla rapax.

49 sed O : et *Baehrens*.
60 ac si A : ac se BCDE : et sic *Barth* : ac sibi *Hoeufft*.
65 dirigit O : derigit *Baehrens*.
66 vetus DE : vaetus A : vetustas BC : Venus *Heinsius*.
68 sic ubi post DE : hic ubi per *edd. vet.*
70 Graium A : gratum *ceteri*.
71 prorepere A : proripere B : prorumpere *ceteri*.

---

[a] From Cirrha near Parnassus.
[b] An allusion to Mercury's early association with Mount Cyllene in Arcadia.

Cirrhean [a] modes; nay, let not the dying swan be thought capable of imitating it, nor yet the tuneful strings of Cyllenean [b] lyre.

After Phoebus has given his steeds the rein into the open heavens and in ever onward course brought forth his full round orb,[c] then that bird with thrice repeated beat of the wing yields her applause, and after three obeisances to the fire-bearing prince holds her peace. She it is also who marks off the swift hours by day and night in sounds which may not be described, priestess of the grove and awe-inspiring ministrant of the woods, the only confidant of thy mysteries, Phoebus. When she has already fulfilled a thousand years of life [d] and long lapse of time has made it burdensome to her, she flees from her sweet and wonted nest in the grove, so that in the closing span she may restore her bygone existence, and when in passion for re-birth she has left her sacred haunts, then she seeks this world where Death holds sovereignty. Despite her length of years she directs her swift flight into Syria, to which she herself of old gave the name of "Phoenice," and seeks through desert wilds the care-free groves, here where the sequestered woodland lurks among the glades. Then she chooses a palm-tree towering with airy crest which bears its Greek name "Phoenix" from the bird: against it no hurtful living creature could steal forth, or slippery serpent, or any bird of

[c] Possibly "revealed the whole wide world" (*cf.* Virg. *Aen.* IV. 118).

[d] Tac. *Ann.* VI. 28 gives 500 years as the usually accepted length of the Phoenix-cycle, but he mentions also 1461 years (*i.e.* the "magnus annus" $= 365\frac{1}{4} \times 4$). Martial V. vii. 2 gives *decem saecula*, and Pliny 1000 years, a round figure adopted by Claudian and Ausonius.

tum ventos claudit pendentibus Aeolus antris,
  ne violent flabris aera purpureum,
neu concreta Noto nubes per inania caeli
  submoveat radios solis et obsit avi.
construit inde sibi seu nidum sive sepulcrum:
  nam perit ut vivat, se tamen ipsa creat.
colligit huic sucos et odores divite silva,
  quos legit Assyrius, quos opulentus Arabs,
quos aut Pygmeae gentes aut India carpit
  aut molli generat terra Sabaea sinu.
cinnamon hic auramque procul spirantis amomi
  congerit et mixto balsama cum folio.
non casiae mitis nec olentis vimen acanthi
  nec turis lacrimae guttaque pinguis abest.
his addit teneras nardi pubentis aristas
  et sociat murrae vim, Panachaea, tuae.
protinus instructo corpus mutabile nido
  vitalique toro membra vieta locat.
ore dehinc sucos membris circumque supraque
  inicit exsequiis immoritura suis.
tunc inter varios animam commendat odores,
  depositi tanti nec timet illa fidem.

79 hinc O: huc *Riese*: huic *Baehrens*.
88 panacea ς *Wernsdorf*.
90 quieta CDE: quiete AB: vieta *Heinsius*.

---

[a] *Cf.* Claudian, *Carm. Min.* xxvii. 44, *bustumque sibi partumque futurum.*

[b] The Pygmies were considered legendary dwarfs of Egypt or Ethiopia: the allusions are to both African and Asiatic spices.

[c] *terra Sabaea* = Arabia Felix, whose chief town Saba was famed for its myrrh and frankincense.

[d] *Cf.* Ovid, *Met.* XV. 398, *nardi lenis aristas.*

prey. Then Aeolus imprisons the winds in over-arching grottoes, lest their blasts harass the bright-gleaming air, or the cloud-wrack from the South banish the sunrays throughout the empty tracts of heaven and do harm to the bird. Thereafter she builds herself a cradle or sepulchre [a]—which you will—for she dies to live and yet begets herself. She gathers for it from the rich forest juicy scented herbs such as the Assyrian gathers or the wealthy Arabian, such as either the Pygmaean races or India [b] culls or the Sabaean [c] land produces in its soft bosom. Here she heaps together cinnamon and effluence of the aromatic shrub that sends its breath afar and balsam with its blended leaf. Nor is there lacking a slip of mild casia or fragrant acanthus or the rich dropping tears of frankincense. Thereto she adds the tender ears [d] of downy spikenard, joining as its ally the potency of thy myrrh, Panachaea.[e] Forthwith in the nest she has furnished she sets her body that awaits its change—withered limbs on a life-giving couch: thereafter with her beak she casts the scents on her limbs, around them and above, being appointed to die in her own funeral.[f] Then she commends her soul [g] amid the varied fragrances without a fear for the trustworthiness of

[e] The usual form is *Panchaïa*, a fabled island east of Arabia, famous for precious stones and myrrh. *Cf.* Virg. *Georg.* II. 139: Plin. *N.H.* X. 4.

[f] This paradoxical idea is introduced by the preceding lines which picture the bird as laying out her own body, and, by throwing perfumes on herself, performing a ritual usually assigned to mourners: *immoritura* is echoed in 95, *corpus genitali morte peremptum.*

[g] One of the Christian notes in the poem: *cf.* 64, *hunc orbem mors ubi regna tenet.* With 94 *cf.* 2 Timothy I. 12.

interea corpus genitali morte peremptum 95
aestuat et flammam parturit ipse calor,
aetherioque procul de lumine concipit ignem:
flagrat et ambustum solvitur in cineres.
quos velut in massam cineres umore coactos
conflat; et effectum seminis instar habet. 100
hinc animal primum sine membris fertur oriri,
sed fertur vermi lacteus esse color:
creverit immensum subito cum tempore certo
seque ovi teretis colligit in speciem,
inde reformatur quali fuit ante figura 105
et Phoenix ruptis pullulat exuviis:
ac velut agrestes, cum filo ad saxa tenentur,
mutari tineae papilione solent.
non illi cibus est nostro consuetus in orbe
nec cuiquam implumem pascere cura subest; 110
ambrosios libat caelesti nectare rores,
stellifero tenues qui cecidere polo.
hos legit, his alitur mediis in odoribus ales,
donec maturam proferat effigiem.
ast ubi primaeva coepit florere iuventa, 115
evolat ad patrias iam reditura domus.
ante tamen, proprio quicquid de corpore restat,
ossaque vel cineres exuviasque suas,

99 in more ABC: in morte D, *Wernsdorf*: in monte E: umore *Ritschl, Baehrens*: *alii alia.*

103 it tener in densum duratus *Baehrens*: *alii alia.*

107–108 *post* 102 *ponit Baehrens.*

108 pinnae AB: pennae *ceteri*: tineae *Didacus Couarruvias episcopus Segobiensis, teste Thomasio*: *cf. Ovid, Met.* XV. 372–4.

109 concessus O: consuetus *Baehrens.*

110 *in verbis* cura subest *desinit codex* A.

a deposit so great. Meanwhile her body, by birth-giving death destroyed, is aglow, the very heat producing flame and catching fire from the ethereal light afar: it blazes and when burned dissolves into ashes. These ashes she welds together, as if they were concentrated by moisture in a mass, possessing in the result what takes the place of seed.[a] Therefrom, 'tis said, rises a living creature first of all without limbs, but this worm is said to have a milky colour: when suddenly at the appointed hour it has grown enormously, gathering into what looks like a rounded egg, from it she is remoulded in such shape as she had before, bursting her shell and springing to life a Phoenix: 'tis even so that larvae in the country fastened by their threads[b] to stones are wont to change into a butterfly. Hers is no food familiar in this world of ours: 'tis no one's charge to feed the bird as yet unfledged: she sips ambrosial dews of heavenly nectar fallen in a fine shower from the star-bearing sky. Such is her culling, such her sustenance, encompassed by fragrant spices until she bring her appearance to maturity. But when she begins to bloom in the spring-time of her youth, she flits forth already bent on a return to her ancestral abodes. Yet ere she goes, she takes all that remains of what was her own body—bones or ashes and the shell that was hers—and stores it

[a] The simile from metallurgy seems violent as applied to a substance endowed with the seeds of life. With *umore coactos* *cf.* Virg. *G.* IV. 172–173 *stridentia tingunt aera lacu,* of dipping metal in the blacksmith's watertank.

[b] The passage, like Ovid, *Met.* XV. 372–4, has silkworms in view. Thomasius thought *saxa* should be *taxa,* presumably in the sense of yew branches, an invention of which Wernsdorf does not approve.

unguine balsameo murraque et ture soluto
  condit et in formam conglobat ore pio. 120
quam pedibus gestans contendit Solis ad urbem
  inque ara residens ponit in aede sacra.
mirandam sese praestat praebetque videnti:
  tantus avi decor est, tantus abundat honor.
principio color est qualis sub sidere caeli 125
  mitia quem corio punica grana tegunt;
qualis inest foliis, quae fert agreste papaver,
  cum pandit vestes Flora rubente polo.
hoc umeri pectusque decens velamine fulget,
  hoc caput, hoc cervix summaque terga nitent; 130
caudaque porrigitur fulvo distincta metallo,
  in cuius maculis purpura mixta rubet;
alarum pennas lux pingit discolor, Iris
  pingere ceu nubes desuper acta solet;
albicat insignis mixto viridante smaragdo 135
  et puro cornu gemmea cuspis hiat;

[121] ortus O (*e versu* 41): urbem *ed. Gryphiandri* 1618.
[123] vehentes B: vehentis E: videnti *vulgo*: verendam *Baehrens*.
[124] ubi B: ibi CDE: avi *Heinsius*.
[125–6] principio O: puniceus *Heinsius*: purpureus *Burman*: praecipuus *Baehrens*: qualis sub sidere caeli O: qualis sub cortice laevi *Heinsius*. qu(a)e croceo BE: qui croceo CD: quem croceum *Heinsius*: quae corio *Goetz*. legunt O: tegunt *Heinsius*: quali sunt, sidere Cancri mitia quae corio, Punica, grana tegunt *Baehrens*.
[128] flore O: Flora *vulgo*. caelo BC: polo B *m*. 2: flore rubente novo *Baehrens*.
[131] fulvo BC: flavo DE. distenta BC: distincta DE: *cf. vers*. 141.

in balsam oil, myrrh, and frankincense set free,[a] rounding it into ball-shape with loving beak. Bearing this in her talons she speeds to the City of the Sun,[b] and perching on the altar sets it in the hallowed temple. Marvellous is her appearance and the show she makes to the onlooker: such comeliness has the bird, so ample a glory. To begin with, her colour is like the colour which beneath the sunshine of the sky ripe pomegranates cover under their rind[c]; like the colour in the petals of the wild poppy when Flora displays her garb at the blush of dawn. In such a dress gleam her shoulders and comely breast: even so glitter head and neck and surface of the back, while the tail spreads out variegated with a metallic yellow, amid whose spots reddens a purple blend. The wing-feathers are picked out by a contrasted sheen, as 'tis the heaven-sent rainbow's way to illuminate the clouds. The beak is of a fine white with a dash of emerald green, glittering jewel-like in its clear horn as it opens. You would take

[a] *i.e.* dissolved from the form of roundish tears of gum resin.

[b] The usual form of the legend, as in Ovid, Mela and Tacitus, gives Heliopolis as the destination, *i.e.* a westward instead of the eastward flight suggested by *solis ad ortus* of the MSS. Pliny, *N.H.* X. 4, has *in Solis urbem.*

[c] The text of 125–126 is difficult. Wernsdorf reads *principio color est, qualis sub cortice laevi* (= *levi*), *mitia quem croceum punica grana legunt.* Baehrens' text is given in the apparatus criticus. The editors do not consider either reading satisfactory. For *qualis* followed by the relative *cf.* Liv. VIII. 39, *acies qualis quae esse instructissima potest*: Calp. Sic. iv. 160, *talis erit qualis qui* . . .

---

133 harum inter pennas insigneque desuper iris DE: clarum *Wernsdorf*: alarum *Ritschl.* lux pingit discolor, Iris *Baehrens.*

134 aura O: alta ς: acta *Heinsius, Baehrens.*

ingentes oculos credas geminos hyacinthos,
quorum de medio lucida flamma micat;
aptata est toto capiti radiata corona
Phoebei referens verticis alta decus; 140
crura tegunt squamae fulvo distincta metallo,
ast ungues roseo tingit honore color.
effigies inter pavonis mixta figuram
cernitur et pictam Phasidis inter avem.
magnitiem terris Arabum quae gignitur ales 145
vix aequare potest, seu fera seu sit avis.
non tamen est tarda, ut volucres quae corpore magno
incessus pigros per grave pondus habent,
sed levis ac velox, regali plena decore:
talis in adspectu se tenet usque hominum. 150
huc venit Aegyptus tanti ad miracula visus
et raram volucrem turba salutat ovans.
protinus exsculpunt sacrato in marmore formam
et titulo signant remque diemque novo.
contrahit in coetum sese genus omne volantum, 155
nec praedae memor est ulla nec ulla metus.
alituum stipata choro volat illa per altum
turbaque prosequitur munere laeta pio.
sed postquam puri pervenit ad aetheris auras,
mox redit; illa suis conditur inde locis. 160
a fortunatae sortis finisque volucrem,
cui de se nasci praestitit ipse deus!

139 aequataq; O: aptatur *Oudendorp*: aptata est *Ritschl*: arquata est *Baehrens.* noto BD: notho C: nota E: toto *Wernsdorf*: croceo *Klapp*: summo *vel* nitido *Ritschl*: rutilo *Baehrens.*

161 ad B: at C: a *Is. Vossius*: sat *Baehrens.* filisque volucrum BC: fatique volucrem *edd. vet.*: finisque volucrem *Is. Vossius.*

for twin sapphires those great eyes from between which shoots a bright flame. All over the head is fitted a crown of rays, in lofty likeness to the glory of the Sun-god's head. Scales cover the legs, which are variegated with a metallic yellow, but the tint which colours the claws is a wonderful rose. To the eye it has a blended semblance between the peacock's appearance and the rich-hued bird from Phasis.[a] Its size[b] the winged thing that springs from the Arabs' lands is scarce able to match, whether wild animal it be or bird.[c] Yet 'tis not slow like large-sized birds which are of sluggish movement by reason of their heavy weight, but 'tis light and swift, filled with a royal grace: such is its bearing ever to the eyes of men. Egypt draws nigh to greet the marvel of so great a sight and the crowd joyfully hails the peerless bird. Straightway they grave its form on hallowed marble and with a fresh title mark both the event and the day.[d] Every breed of fowl unites in the assemblage: no bird has thoughts of prey nor yet of fear. Attended by a chorus of winged creatures, she flits through the high air, and the band escorts her, gladdened by their pious task. But when the company has reached the breezes of ether unalloyed, it presently returns: she then ensconces herself in her true haunts. Ah, bird of happy lot and happy end to whom God's own will has granted birth from herself! Female or

[a] The pheasant.

[b] *magnitiem* is unparalleled.

[c] *ales* is a reference to the ostrich or *strouthiocamelos*, which was so called from its camel-like neck, and which might be considered either land animal or bird.

[d] *i.e.* in their joy over the periodic return of the Phoenix.

femina vel mas haec, seu neutrum, seu sit utrumque,
felix quae veneris foedera nulla colit:
mors illi venus est, sola est in morte voluptas: 165
ut possit nasci, appetit ante mori.
ipsa sibi proles, suus est pater et suus heres,
nutrix ipsa sui, semper alumna sibi—
ipsa quidem, sed non eadem quia et ipsa nec ipsa est,
aeternam vitam mortis adepta bono. 170

163 *sic Heinsius et Wernsdorf*: *discrepant codices*: femina seu mas est seu neutrum: belua felix *Baehrens.*
164 colit O: coit *Baehrens.*
169 *sic* ς *et Wernsdorf*: *omiserunt* et CD: non ⟨eadem est⟩ eademque nec ipsa est *Baehrens.*

male she is, which you will—whether neither or both, a happy bird, she regards not any unions of love: to her, death is love; and her sole pleasure lies in death: to win her birth, it is her appetite first to die. Herself she is her own offspring, her own sire and her own heir, herself her own nurse, her own nurseling evermore—herself indeed, yet not the same; because she is both herself and not herself, gaining eternal life by the boon of death.

AVIANUS

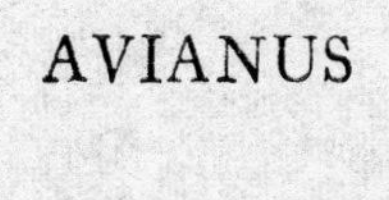

INTRODUCTION

TO THE FABLES OF AVIANUS

In most of the extant MSS. the name of the author of these forty-two fables is given (in the genitive) *Aviani*. Two of our principal MSS. (A and *Rawl.*), however, have *Avieni*. If one may judge from inscriptions, Avianius was a commoner name than Avianus. Between Avienus and Avienius there is not enough material on which to form a judgement. Since, however, there is no trace of the ending *-ii* in any of our MSS., we may venture to limit ourselves to the question of Avianus as against Avienus.

The suggestion has been made that the writer of the fables was identical with Rufius Festus Avienus, author of works entitled *Aratea* and *Descriptio Orbis Terrae*. Chronology agrees, it is true; but there are two grave objections: the fables and the *Aratea* are poles asunder in style; and the author of the *Aratea* is designated in full in the MSS. *Rufi Festi Avieni*, while the prevailing description of the fabulist is simply *Aviani*. A more possible suggestion is that our fabulist was the Avienus who took part in the symposium described in the *Saturnalia* which was written early in the fifth century by Macrobius Theodosius. The theory appears more likely, if we agree that *ad Theodosium* in the title of the dedicatory letter means Macrobius Theodosius[a] and neither of the emperors named Theodosius, although two MSS. (*Rawl.* and *Reg.*) have *imperatorem* in apposition to *Theodosium.* Other arguments are given by Ellis (*Proleg.* p. xiv) in favour of this particular Avienus; but nothing in the way of proof is forthcoming, and the prevalence of "Avi*a*ni" in the MSS. militates against it. It seems, then, best to conclude that the fables are the work of an unknown Avianus, who wrote about A.D. 400 in the lifetime of Macrobius and dedicated his work to him.

Cannegieter and Lachmann, denying that the Theodosius of the preface was either of the emperors or Macrobius, argued that Avianus lived in the middle of the second century A.D. Cannegieter based his theory partly on the fact that the preface omits Julius Titianus (a fabulist of about A.D. 200 mentioned by Ausonius) from the list of Avianus' predecessors. Therefore, he held, Avianus must have preceded Titianus. This argument from silence is demolished by Wernsdorf's reply that Avianus' list of fabulists does not profess to be exhaustive. But Cannegieter (like Lachmann in the following century) argued from Avianus' style also. The first impression is that of general metrical correctness marred by some glaring licences and of a Latinity, partly Augustan, partly Silver, combined with a number of violent departures from classical usage. Therefore, according to Cannegieter and Lachmann, the original

[a] This hypothesis, originally propounded by Pithou, *Poemat. Vet.* p. 474, has been accepted by many scholars, including Voss, *De Histor. Latinis* ii. 9; Wernsdorf, *P.L.M.* V. 669; L. Müller, *De Phaedri et Av. Libellis*, 32; Baehrens, *P.L.M.* V. 31; Unrein, *De Aviani Aetate*, 60.

Avianus lived in the second century and wrote in classical Latin and in correct metre, while schoolmasters, rhetoricians, interpolators and copyists are responsible for the depravations.

Since Lachmann's day, however, the date of Babrius[a] the fabulist, whom Avianus mentions and upon whom (as we shall see) he models a great part of his work, has been established by Otto Crusius.[b] Babrius, we now know, wrote under Severus Alexander (222–235 A.D.); and so Avianus must belong to a subsequent age. Moreover, arguments from style really support the view that Avianus flourished about 400 A.D. Many couplets, it may be conceded, particularly in the "promythia" and "epimythia," employed to introduce or conclude some fables, as we now have them, are quite late additions; others can be plausibly emended into classical Latin. Still, there remain some violations of prosody,[c] both defying emendation and occurring in couplets which cannot be dismissed as interpolations without destroying the sense of the fable; while much of the late Latin (see Ellis, *Proleg.* xxx *sqq.*) is embedded in the core of a fable, and must therefore come from the original Avianus. These violations of prosody and this late Latin prevent us from putting the period of Avianus earlier than the later part of the fourth century.

[a] Valerius Babrius composed two books of fables in Greek scazons. The dedication of one of his books is to the son of Severus Alexander. We have in all 137 fables along with fragments. There is in the Bodleian a Greek prose paraphrase of many of his fables, including some no longer extant in Babrius: see W. G. Rutherford, *Babrius*, London 1883.

[b] *De Babrii Aetate*, *Leipz. Stud.* II. 238.

[c] *Cf.* remarks on metre later in Introduction.

Avianus in his preface or dedicatory letter makes no claim to be original. He claims that he has put into elegiac verse 42 fables from the Aesopic collection—a collection from which Socrates and Horace[a] had drawn to illustrate moral maxims and which Phaedrus[b] and Babrius had abridged in their Latin and Greek iambics respectively. It is strange that Avianus should mention Phaedrus and Babrius together in such a way as to suggest he was no more indebted to one than to the other. The truth is that he owes practically nothing to Phaedrus and nearly everything to Babrius. Avianus 2, 5, 9, 34, 37 are respectively more or less similar in subject-matter to Phaedrus II. vi, I. xi, V. ii, IV. xxiv, III. vii. In fable 37 Avianus is as near to Phaedrus as he is to Babrius and (though a lion has taken the place of a wolf) Phaedrian influence may be admitted; the other four Avianus could have composed without reading Phaedrus. Fables 2, 9, 34 are much closer to Babrius than to Phaedrus, and 5, which is not in our Babrius, is closer to the Aesopic prose version. As for single lines, apart from Av. xi. 10 and xxxi. 12 (which perhaps are echoes of Phaedrus I. v. 1 and IV. vi. 13) there is scarcely a trace of indebtedness to the first-century fabulist. The case is very different in regard to Babrius.[c] With a few exceptions the 42 fables can be traced to a Babrian source—either to the scazons of Babrius or to the Greek prose

[a] *Cf.* notes on the dedicatory letter.

[b] Phaedrus, of Thracian origin, composed his five books in Latin iambic senarii. His first two books were written under Tiberius (14–37 A.D.); see J. Wight Duff, *Lit. Hist. of Rome in Silver Age*, pp. 133–154.

[c] The Greek text of the extant Babrian versions is given in Ellis' commentary.

paraphrase now in the Bodleian. Probably, if our Babrius were complete, we should be able to account for all Avianus' *fabulae.* In most cases Avianus' version is longer than that of Babrius. Avianus expands his Babrian material, sometimes to make an alteration in the story (*e.g.* 32, 35, 36), but more often to elaborate the descriptive element with poetical diction which contains frequent echoes of Virgil or Ovid. Thus a strained, even grotesque, artificiality displaces the simple directness of Babrius. For a forcible instance, one may examine fable 7, which is based on Babrius 104. Here Avianus takes four lines (3–6) to paraphrase λάθρη κύων ἔδακνε, virtually repeats in lines 9 and 10 the preceding couplet, and introduces the Virgilian *crepitantia aera*, perhaps as a tardy recognition of χαλκεύσας in Babrius' opening line. Then the couplet 15–16

> " Infelix, quae tanta rapit dementia sensum,
> munera pro meritis si cupis ista dari ? "

represents ὦ τάλαν, τί σεμνύνῃ; and combines a mock-heroic imitation of Virgil with a colloquial post-classical use of *si cupis* for " if you want to make out that . . ." Other expansions, largely descriptive, are observable in most fables where the Babrian original has survived (*e.g.* in 14, 18, 34). To such expansions throughout the fables a very noticeable contribution is made by Avianus' habit of drawing poetical phrases freely from Virgil and, to a less extent, from Ovid. They may be pleasantly picturesque reminiscences like *glaucas salices* (xxvi. 6) and *querulo ruperat arva sono* of the grasshopper (xxxiv. 12);[a] or they may lend a quaint epic turn to the story

[a] *Cf.* Virg. *Georg.* IV. 182; III. 328.

as in *pependit onus* (ix. 8), *rumpere vocem* (xiv. 11, xxv. 13), *surgentes demoror austros* (xvi. 15), *generis fiducia vestri* (xxiv. 11);[a] or they may be still more positively mock-heroic as in *circumstetit horror* of the ass in the lion's skin (v. 9) and *lacrimis obortis* of a weeping fish (xx. 5).[b]

Mingled with this poetical language of a pre-Avianian age we have frequent instances of a degenerate Latin. These have been collected and tabulated by Ellis (*Proleg.* xxxvi *sqq.*). The use of *nimius* for *magnus*, of *tanti* for *tot*, and of *datur* for *dicitur*, are among the most noticeable as far as single words are concerned. Indirect statement is sometimes introduced by *quod* or expressed by the subjunctive without a conjunction. *Que* and *atque* according to the manuscripts (though emendation is generally possible) may be used illogically to connect participles with finite verbs; and the gerundive once or twice does the work of a future participle passive.

To the prosody of Avianus a reference has already been made. In general, he gives us correct Ovidian elegiacs. Occasionally, according to the traditional text, at the end of the first half of a pentameter, hiatus is admitted or a short syllable takes the place of a long one (Ellis xxiv–xxv). In most of these cases the text can be easily emended and Avianus himself absolved from a metrical fault. Some other violations of classical prosody (*velĭs* iii. 6; *nŏlam* vii. 8; *dispăr* xi. 5; *herĕs* xxxv. 14) cannot be explained away; they come from Avianus' own hand and attest

[a] *Cf.* Ovid, *Her.* ix. 98, *Rem. Am.* 18, *Fasti* II. 760; Virg. *Aen.* II. 129, etc.; III. 481; I. 132.
[b] *Cf.* Virg. *Aen.* II. 559; XI. 41.

the decline of metrical strictness at the end of the fourth century.

There is no trace of Christian influence in the Fables. Pagan gods and sacrifices are introduced after a pre-Christian fashion in 4, 8, 14, 22, 23, 32, 36 and 42.

The popularity of Avianus in the schools of the Middle Ages is attested by accretions, paraphrases, scholia and quotations. As rhetorical exercises, promythia or epimythia were composed at the beginning or end of many fables to point the moral. A few of these came to be included in the text. Some epimythia (those contained in the earliest MSS.), it is likely, come from Avianus himself; but the four promythia (to fables 5, 7, 8, 34) are probably the work of a rhetorician, although, being contained in the tenth century MSS., they are of an early date. A number of undoubtedly spurious epimythia (found only in later MSS.) are omitted in most editions. Froehner prints them separately in his edition of 1862. Paraphrases were often made of Avianus. One collection entitled *Apologi Aviani*[a] is attached to two of the later Paris MSS. Here the paraphrast usually turns the first half or more of each fable into prose and ends by copying the last few lines of Avianus' own version, so that occasionally his work is useful for determining the text. Alexander Neckam (1157–1217) composed verse paraphrases, perhaps of the whole of Avianus, entitling his work *Novus Avianus*. His versions of the first six fables are contained in a St. Germain MS. of the thirteenth century.[b] Scholia of varying

[a] Published by Froehner in his ed. of Avianus 1862.

[b] Published by Edelestand du Meril (*Poésies Inédites*, 260–267) and afterwards by Froehner, *op. cit.*

extent and value are included in nearly all MSS. of Avianus, indicating the assiduity with which he was studied. He is extensively quoted or alluded to by medieval grammarians and anthologists,[a] and the fables were to be found in many libraries of the Middle Ages.[b]

EDITIONS

H. Cannegieter. Amsterdam, 1731.
J. A. Nodell. Amsterdam, 1787.
K. Lachmann. Berlin, 1845.
W. Froehner. Leipzig, 1862.
E. Baehrens. In *Poetae Latini Minores*, Vol. V. Leipzig, 1883.
R. Ellis. Oxford, 1887.
L. Hervieux. In *Fabulistes latins*. iii. Paris, 1894.

RELEVANT WORKS

T. Wopkens. *Observationes Criticae.* Amsterdam, 1736, VII. ii, pp. 197–253.
J. H. Withof. *Encaenia Critica.* 1741.
J. C. Wernsdorf. In *P. L. M.*, V. 2, pp. 663 *sqq*.
K. Lachmann. *De aetate Fl. Aviani.* Berlin, 1845 = *Kl. Schriften*, II. 51.
E. Baehrens, *Miscell. Critica.* Groningen, 1878.
K. Schenkl. *Ztschr. f. österr. Gymn.* xvi. 397.
O. Unrein. *De Aviani aetate.* Jena, 1885.
Draheim. *De Aviani elegis*, *J. f. Philologie*, cxliii. 509.
J. E. B. Mayor. *Class. Rev.* I. (1887), 188 *sqq*.

[a] Manitius, *Gesch. der lat. Lit. des Mittelalters*, Index, *s.v.* Avianus; *Philologus* LI (1892), 533 *sqq*.
[b] G. Becker, *Catalogi Bibliothecarum Antiqui*, 306.

F. Heidenhain. *Zu den Apologi Aviani. Progr.* Strassburg, 1894.
Jenkinson. *Fables of Avianus, The Academy*, XLV. (1894), 129.
O. Crusius. *De Babrii Aetate, Leipz. Stud.*, II. 238.
—— *Avian und die sogenannten Apologi Aviani, Philologus* LIV. (1895), 474–488.
—— s.v. *Avianus* in Pauly-Wissowa, *Realencyclop.*

SIGLA

(following Ellis in the main)

A = Paris. 8093: saec. ix.
P = Paris. 13206: saec. ix.
C = Paris. 5570: saec. ix (Froehner), x (Ellis), xi (Baehr.).
O = Oxon. Auct. F. 2. 14: saec. xi.
Rawl. = Oxon. B. N. Rawl. 111: saec. xi–xii.
X = Oxon. Auct. F. 5. 6: *circ.* 1300.
G = Cantab. Trinity, Gale 0. 3. 5: saec. xii.
Pet[1]. = Cantab. Peterhouse, 4 (fabulis i–xxii dereptis): saec. xiii–xiv.
Pet[2]. = Cantab. Peterhouse, 25 (continens Avianum et Maximianum): saec. xiii–xiv.
B = Londin. Brit. Mus. Harl. 4967: saec. xiii.
b = Londin. Brit. Mus. 21, 213 (saepe interpolatus): saec. xiii.
b[2] = Londin. Brit. Mus. A. xxxi (xvii–xxi omissis): *circ.* 1300.
b[3] = Londin. Brit. Mus. 10090 (interpolatus).
T = Trevirensis. 1464 (continens Avianum et Prudentium): saec. x.
V = Lugdun. Batav. Vossianus L.Q. 86: saec. ix.

W = Lugdun. Batav. Vossianus L.O. 15: saec. xi.
Ashb. [= B in Baehrens' ed.] = Ashburnhamensis (Libri 1813): saec. xi–xii.
Reg. = Reginensis. 1424: saec. xi.
L = Laurentianus, lxviii 24: saec. xi.
S = Fragmentum Sangallense. 1396: saec. xi.
K = Fragmentum Karoliruhense (ab Froehnero adhibitum): saec. ix.
Cab. = readings reported by Cabeljau from a " codex vetustissimus " and reprinted by Cannegieter in D'Orville's *Miscellanea Nova*, 1734.
Paraphr. = readings of the paraphrast, author of the *apologi Aviani.*

Of the MSS. Baehrens collated the Leyden manuscripts V and W, the Trèves one, T, the Florence one, L, and the Ashburnhamensis (his B). G was collated for Baehrens by H. A. J. Munro. Baehrens cites the readings of the Paris MSS. P, A, C and of the Carlsruhe fragment, K, from Froehner's edition. Ellis based his text largely on a personal examination of the three Paris codices, those at Oxford, and those in the British Museum, besides T and S. The most important MSS. are C, Rawl., G, B (in Ellis' sigla, *i.e.* Harl. 4967), T and V.

FABULAE AVIANI

EPISTULA EIUSDEM AD THEODOSIUM

Dubitanti mihi, Theodosi optime, quoinam litterarum titulo nostri nominis memoriam mandaremus, fabularum textus occurrit, quod in his urbane concepta falsitas deceat et non incumbat necessitas veritatis. nam quis tecum de oratione, quis de poemate loqueretur, cum in utroque litterarum genere et Atticos Graeca eruditione superes et Latinitate Romanos? huius ergo materiae ducem nobis Aesopum noveris, qui responso Delphici Apollinis monitus ridicula orsus est, ut legenda firmaret. verum has pro exemplo fabulas et Socrates divinis operibus indidit et poemati suo Flaccus aptavit, quod in se sub iocorum communium specie vitae argumenta contineant.

Titulus: Incipiunt fabulae Aviani poetae: epistola eiusdem ad Theodosium C: ad imperatorem Theodosium *Reg.*: ad Teodosium imperatorem *Rawl.*

[4] falsitas *codd.*: salșitas *Baehrens.* veritatis *codd.*: severitatis *Lachmann.*

[10] legenda *codd.*: sequenda *Lachmann.*

---

[a] *i.e.* probably Macrobius Theodosius, author of the *Saturnalia*: see Introduction. The tone of the dedication suits a literary addressee.

[b] The historical "Aisopos" was a slave in Samos, 6th cent. B.C., who used beast-stories to convey moral lessons. Later generations freely ascribed to him a mass of fables, and the supposed Aesopic fables were collected about 300 B.C. by

THE FABLES OF AVIANUS

DEDICATORY LETTER TO THEODOSIUS [a]

I WAS in doubt, most excellent Theodosius, to what class of literature I should entrust the memory of my name, when the narration of fables occurred to my mind; because in these, fiction, if gracefully conceived, is not out of place, and one is not oppressed by the necessity of adhering to the truth. Who could speak in your company on oratory or on poetry? In both these divisions of literature you outstrip the Athenians in Greek learning as well as the Romans in mastery of Latin. My pioneer in this subject, you must know, is Aesop,[b] who on the advice of the Delphic Apollo started droll stories in order to establish moral maxims. Such fables by way of example have been introduced by Socrates [c] into his inspired works and fitted by Horace [d] into his poetry, because under the guise of jests of general application they contain illustrations

Demetrius of Phaleron. The authority for Avianus' statement that Aesop was advised by the Delphic oracle is unknown.

[c] The reference is to Plato's dialogues (*Socraticis sermonibus*, Hor. *Od.* III. xxi. 9–10) which represent much of Socrates' teaching. In Plato's *Phaedo*, 60–61, Socrates says a dream led him to turn Aesopic fables into verse. Avianus here refers to apologues in fable style: *e.g.* of Grasshoppers, *Phaedr.* 259; of Plenty and Poverty, *Symp.* 203; of Prometheus and Epimetheus, *Protag.* 320–321.

[d] *e.g.* the Town Mouse and the Country Mouse in *Sat.* II. vi.

quas Graecis iambis Babrius repetens in duo volumina coartavit. Phaedrus etiam partem aliquam quinque in libellos resolvit. de his ego ad quadraginta et duas in unum redactas fabulas dedi, quas rudi Latinitate compositas elegis sum explicare conatus. habes ergo opus, quo animum oblectes, ingenium exerceas, sollicitudinem leves totumque vivendi ordinem cautus agnoscas. loqui vero arbores, feras cum hominibus gemere, verbis certare volucres, animalia ridere fecimus, ut pro singulorum necessitatibus vel ab ipsis ⟨in⟩animis sententia proferatur. ⟨vale.⟩

I

De Nutrice et Infante

Rustica deflentem parvum iuraverat olim,
ni taceat, rabido quod foret esca lupo.
credulus hanc vocem lupus audiit et manet ipsas
pervigil ante fores, irrita vota gerens.
nam lassata puer nimiae dat membra quieti;
spem quoque raptoris sustulit inde fami.

[16] ergo *plerique*: ego OP.
I. [1] iuvaverat *Pet.*[2]: iuraverat *cett. codd.*: iurgaverat *Froehner secutus Cabellavium.*
[6] *sic Wopkens*: fami (*ex* -mes *corr.*) T: famis PVm^1W: fames Vm^2 *cum cett.*

---

[a] See Introduction and note.
[b] *Ibid.*
[c] *Cf.* Phaedrus, I. *prol.* 6–7 *quod arbores loquantur non tantum ferae, fictis iocari nos meminerit fabulis,* and Babrius,

of life. They were taken up by Babrius[a] in Greek choliambics and abridged into two volumes. A considerable portion also was expanded by Phaedrus[b] to a length of five books. I have compressed forty-two of these into one book for publication—writing in unembellished Latin and attempting to set them forth in elegiacs. You have, therefore, a work to delight the mind, to exercise the brain, to relieve anxiety—one that will give you a wary knowledge of the whole course of life. I have made trees talk,[c] beasts growl in conversation with men, birds engage in wordy disputes, and animals laugh, so that to meet the needs of each individual a maxim may be proffered even by inanimate things. Farewell.

I

The Nurse and her Child

Once upon a time when her little boy was crying, a peasant-woman had sworn that if he were not quiet he would be given as a tit-bit[d] for a ravenous wolf. A credulous wolf overheard these words and waited on guard close in front of the cottage doors, cherishing hopes in vain. For the child let a deep sleep come over his weary limbs, and besides deprived the hungry robber thereby of his expectation. The wolf

praef. 9 ἐλάλει δὲ πέτρη καὶ τὰ φύλλα τῆς πεύκης. In Avianus, pine and bramble argue xix, and a reed speaks xvi. His other remarks in this sentence are illustrated by the following: tigress challenges hunter xvii; lion and hunter dispute xxiv; crane and peacock quarrel xv; fox laughs vi; ant laughs xxxiv; and among "inanimate things" a jar speaks xi; a statue xxiii and a trumpet xxxix.

[d] *quod foret esca* replaces the classical accus. and infin. *Cf.* xxv. 16.

hunc ubi silvarum repetentem lustra suarum
ieiunum coniunx sensit adesse lupa,
" cur " inquit " nullam referens de more rapinam
languida consumptis sic trahis ora genis ? " 10
" ne mireris " ait " deceptum fraude maligna
vix miserum vacua delituisse fuga:
nam quae praeda, rogas, quae spes contingere posset,
iurgia nutricis cum mihi verba darent ? "[a]

haec sibi dicta putet seque hac sciat arte notari, 15
femineam quisquis credidit esse fidem.

II

De Testudine et Aquila

Pennatis avibus quondam testudo locuta est,
si quis eam volucrum constituisset humi,
protinus e Rubris conchas proferret harenis,
quis pretium nitido cortice baca daret:
indignum, sibimet tardo quod sedula gressu 5
nil ageret toto proficeretque die.
ast ubi promissis aquilam fallacibus implet,
experta est similem perfida lingua fidem;
et male mercatis dum quaerit sidera pennis,
occidit infelix alitis ungue fero. 10

II. [2] volucrem PA*m*[2]: volucrum A*m*[1] *cum ceteris codd.*
[6] perficeretque ACOTW *Ash.*: proficeretque *Pet.*[2] G *Rawl.* B b b[2] *Cab.*
[10] occidit *plerique codd.*: excidit *Baehrens.*

[a] *verba darent* in the classical sense of tricking. Contrast ix. 20; xxiv. 10; xxxvii. 2; xxxviii. 6, where the sense is simply that of speaking.

repaired to the lair in his native woods, and his mate, seeing him arrive famished, said, "Why don't you bring back the usual prey? Why are your cheeks wasted and your jaws so drawn and emaciated?" "A mean trick took me in," he said; "so don't be surprised that I have been hard put to it to skulk pitifully away—with no spoil. What kill, do you ask, could come my way? what prospect could there be, when a scolding nurse befooled me?"[a]

Let anyone who believes in a woman's sincerity reflect that to him these words are spoken and that it is he whom this lesson censures.

II

The Tortoise and the Eagle

Once a tortoise said to the feathered birds that if one of the swift fliers could carry her away and set her safe on the ground[b] she would at once from the sands of the Erythraean Sea produce shells[c] on which their bright-crusted pearl conferred a value. She felt it an outrage that, despite her diligence, her slow pace prevented her doing anything or making any progress the whole day. She loaded an eagle with false promises, but her untruthful tongue found a broken troth to match her own. While soaring aloft on the wings whose aid she had bought so ill, the wretched tortoise met her death by the bird's

[b] Line 2 presents difficulties. It has *eam* for *se*; *quis* implying the rare masc. gender for *volucrum*; and *constituisset* involving a latent idea. The alternative *volucrem* means that the tortoise asked to be made a bird: this is accepted by Baehrens, who reads *ibi* for *humi*.

[c] Late Latin for *se prolaturam esse conchas*.

tum quoque sublimis, cum iam moreretur, in auras
  ingemuit votis haec licuisse suis;
nam dedit exosae post haec documenta quieti
  non sine supremo magna labore peti.

sic quicumque nova sublatus laude tumescit, 15
  dat merito poenas, dum meliora cupit.

III

De Cancro et Matre Eius

Curva retro cedens dum fert vestigia cancer,
  hispida saxosis terga relisit aquis.
hunc genetrix facili cupiens procedere gressu
  talibus alloquiis emonuisse datur:
"ne tibi transverso placeant haec devia, nate, 5
  rursus in obliquos neu velis ire pedes,
sed nisu contenta ferens vestigia recto
  innocuos proso tramite siste gradus."
cui natus "faciam, si me praecesseris" inquit,
  "rectaque monstrantem certior ipse sequar. 10
nam stultum nimis est, cum tu pravissima temptes,
  alterius censor si vitiosa notes."

[12] licuisse *plerique codd.*: libuisse *Cannegieter*.
III. [3] procedere CT: praecedere *plerique codd.*
[4] praemonuisse *codd.*: emonuisse *Ellis*.
[12] ut *codd.*: si *Ellis* (*servans metrum*).

cruel talons. Then it was that, raised on high,[a] in the hour of death, she filled the breezes with her moaning plaint that such had been the answer to her prayers. For she gave surly sloth a warning for the future that great achievement is only reached by the utmost toil.

So anyone elated and puffed up with new-found glory pays a just penalty in hankering after what is too high for him.

III

The Crab and its Mother

While a crab was walking backwards and tracing its crooked way, it banged its scaly back in the rocky pools. Its mother, eager to go forward with step unhindered, is said to have delivered a warning to it in such words as these: "Don't go zigzag and choose these crooked ways, my child, and don't seek to move backwards and slantwise on your feet. Step out vigorously with straightforward effort and plant your footsteps safely in the onward path." "I will do so," the young crab replied, "if you go ahead of me; and, if you show me the correct road, I will follow the more surely. For it is exceedingly foolish of you, when you are attempting the most crooked of courses yourself, to set up as censor and criticise the faults of another."

[a] *sublimis* is emphatic: *cf.* the application in 15–16. *sublimes,* the variant in several MSS., goes with *auras,* "breezes of heaven."

IV

De Vento et Sole

Immitis Boreas placidusque ad sidera Phoebus
  iurgia cum magno conseruere Iove,
quis prior inceptum peragat: mediumque per aequor
  carpebat solitum forte viator iter.
convenit hanc potius liti praefigere causam, 5
  pallia nudato decutienda viro.
protinus impulsus ventis circum tonat aether
  et gelidus nimias depluit imber aquas:
ille magis lateri duplicem circumdat amictum,
  turbida submotos quod trahit aura sinus. 10
sed tenues radios paulatim increscere Phoebus
  iusserat, ut nimio surgeret igne iubar,
donec lassa volens requiescere membra viator
  deposita fessus veste sederet humi.
tunc victor docuit praesentia numina Titan, 15
  nullum praemissis vincere posse minis.

V

De Asino Pelle Leonis Induto

[Metiri se quemque decet propriisque iuvari
  laudibus, alterius nec bona ferre sibi,
ne detracta gravem faciant miracula risum,
  coeperit in solitis cum remanere malis.]

IV. [1] sidera *codd.*: cetera *Lachmann*: ludicra *Baehrens.*
[3] aequor *Cm*[1]: orbem *cett. codd.*
V. [4] solitis *Pet.*[2] b: solis *plerique codd.*

IV

The Wind and the Sun

Savage Boreas and gentle Phoebus joined strife in the presence of the stars with great Jupiter, to decide which should first achieve his task; and over the midst of the plain it happened a traveller was plying his wonted way. They agree to preface their dispute with this case for trial—to get the man stripped by tearing off his cloak.[a] Straightway with the onset of the wind the sky thunders around, and the chill rain-storm pours down torrents of water. The traveller folds his cloak double and draws it round his sides all the more, because the tempestuous blast pushes the folds aside and tugs at them. But Phoebus had bidden his penetrating rays grow stronger little by little, so that his splendour might emerge in excessive heat,—until the traveller, anxious to rest his weary limbs, threw down his cloak and sat on the ground exhausted. Then in his triumph the Titan taught the assembled gods[b] that no one can win victory by an advance guard of threats.

V

The Donkey in the Lion's Skin

[Everyone should take his true measure and be content with his own merits, and not claim for himself his neighbour's goods, lest the stripping of the finery lead to painful ridicule as soon as he is left in possession of his usual defects.]

[a] *nudato* is proleptic. [b] *i.e.* the stars and Jupiter.

Exuvias asinus Gaetuli forte leonis
  repperit et spoliis induit ora novis.
aptavitque suis incongrua tegmina membris
  et miserum tanto pressit honore caput.
ast ubi terribilis mimo circumstetit horror
  pigraque praesumptus venit in ossa vigor,
mitibus ille feris communia pabula calcans
  turbabat pavidas per sua rura boves.
rusticus hunc magna postquam deprendit ab aure,
  correptum vinclis verberibusque domat;
et simul abstracto denudans corpora tergo
  increpat his miserum vocibus ille pecus:
"forsitan ignotos imitato murmure fallas;
  at mihi, qui quondam, semper asellus eris."

VI

De Rana et Vulpe

Edita gurgitibus limoque immersa profundo
  et luteis tantum semper amica vadis,
ad superos colles herbosaque prata recurrens
  mulcebat miseras turgida rana feras,
callida quod posset gravibus succurrere morbis
  et vitam ingenio continuare suo;
nec se Paeonio iactat cessisse magistro,
  quamvis perpetuos curet in orbe deos.

[5] getuli *plerique codd.*: defuncti PV.
[9] mimo *Cannegieter*: animo *plerique codd.*: animū *Ashb.*
VI. [1] limoque W *Nevelet*: olimque *cett. codd.*
[7] P(a)eonio *plerique codd.*: Paeoni *Lachmann.*

It happened that a donkey discovered a Gaetulian lion's skin and clothed his face with the new-found spoil. To his own limbs he fitted the ill-assorted covering and burdened his wretched head with trappings so majestic. But when the grim appearance, awe-inspiring in its mimicry,[a] enveloped him, and the courage he had assumed in advance entered his sluggish bones, then, trampling the pasture which he shared with the tame animals, he drove the scared cattle in confusion over their fields. The farmer, after catching him by his long ear, hustled him off and subdued him by tying him up and thrashing him; and as he stripped the stolen skin off his body he scolded the poor beast with these words: "Perhaps your mimic roar may cheat strangers. To me you will always be a donkey as before."

VI

The Frog and the Fox

Sprung from pools, immersed in depths of mud, the constant friend of naught but miry shallows, a distended frog, revisiting the hills above and the grassy meadows, sought to comfort the afflicted beasts with the assurance that her leech-craft could relieve their sore diseases and her genius could prolong their lives. Her boast was that she had never been surpassed by the Paeonian master,[b] though he attended the ever-

[a] *mimo* goes with *terribilis* as an ablative. The reading *animū* tempts one to suggest *mimum*: "when the awful appearance enveloped this farcical actor" (*i.e.* the ass). For the diction *cf.* Virg. *Aen.* II. 559, *me . . . circumstetit horror.*

[b] Paeon was the Master Healer: *cf.* Rut. Namat. I. 75 *Paeoniam artem.*

tunc vulpes pecudum ridens astuta quietem,
verborum vacuam prodidit esse fidem: 10
"haec dabit aegrotis" inquit "medicamina membris,
pallida caeruleus cui notat ora color?"

VII

De Cane qui noluit Latrare

[Haud facile est pravis innatum mentibus ut se
verberibus dignas suppliciove putent.]

Forte canis quondam nullis latratibus horrens
nec patulis primum rictibus ora trahens,
mollia sed pavidae submittens verbera caudae, 5
concitus audaci vulnera dente dabat.
hunc dominus, ne quem probitas simulata lateret,
iusserat in rabido gutture ferre nolam.
faucibus innexis crepitantia subligat aera,
quae facili motu signa cavenda darent. 10
haec tamen ille sibi credebat praemia ferri,
et similem turbam despiciebat ovans.
tunc insultantem senior de plebe superbum
aggreditur tali singula voce monens:
"infelix, quae tanta rapit dementia sensum, 15
munera pro meritis si cupis ista dari?

[10] vacuam *codd.*: vanam *Cannegieter.*

VII. [2] muneribus *codd.*: verberibus *Withof*: vulneribus *Froehner in not.*

[8] nolam *plerique codd.*: molam Vm^1W: notam *Cab.*

[14] singula voce *codd.*: monens *plerique codd.*: sibila voce movens *Lachmann*: voce severa monens *Baehrens*: cingula voce moves? *Ellis.*

lasting gods in turn. Then a cunning vixen, laughing at the acquiescence of the cattle, disclosed the futility of giving credence to words: "Is physic," she asked, "going to be prescribed for diseased limbs by this frog, whose pale face is sicklied o'er with a livid hue?"

VII

The Dog that would not Bark

[Not readily is it the nature of evil dispositions to believe themselves deserving of stripes and punishment.]

It happened once there was a dog with no gruff bark, that did not open its mouth in a wide gape as a first sign of mischief, but put its soft-wagging tail in fear beneath it, and then would fly into a fury and snap recklessly with its teeth. To prevent anyone being taken unawares by its pretended good character, its master had made it wear a bell [a] round its savage throat. He fastened its neck and tied the tinkling brass underneath to give signals of warning by its ready motion. The dog, however, believed this was worn by it as a reward, and triumphantly began to look down on the crowd of dogs like itself. Then an older dog of humble rank accosted the swaggerer in its exaltation, giving each word of advice [b] after the following strain: "Wretch, what is this monstrous madness that steals away your senses, if indeed you will have it that those rewards are given you for your

[a] *nolam* elsewhere has a long *o*.
[b] Ellis' reading is attractive, "tali cingula voce moves?" "what, so loud in shaking your collar?"

non hoc virtutis decus ostentatur in aere,
nequitiae testem sed geris inde sonum."

VIII

De Camelo et Iove

[Contentum propriis sapientem vivere rebus
nec cupere alterius fabula nostra monet,
indignata cito ne stet Fortuna recursu
atque eadem minuat quae dedit ante rota.]

Corporis immensi fertur pecus isse per auras 5
et magnum precibus sollicitasse Iovem:
turpe nimis cunctis irridendumque videri,
insignes geminis cornibus ire boves,
et solum nulla munitum parte camelum
obiectum cunctis expositumque feris. 10
Iuppiter irridens postquam sperata negavit,
insuper et magnae sustulit auris onus.
"vive minor merito, cui sors non sufficit" inquit,
"et tua perpetuum, livide, damna geme."

IX

De Duobus Sociis et Ursa

Montibus ignotis curvisque in vallibus artum
cum socio quidam suscipiebat iter,

VIII. [3] det . . . recursum *Baehrens* (*ex* recursū *in* W).
[5] auras *plerique codd.*: aras b: arva *Pet.*[2]: Afros *Withof.*

deserts? This is not an ornament of merit displayed in a brass setting: no, by wearing it you carry a sound as witness of your bad character."

VIII

Jupiter and the Camel

[Our fable counsels a man if he be wise to live contented with his own property and not to covet what belongs to another, lest Fortune be angry and run quickly back to a standstill, and the same wheel that once bestowed favours end in lessening them.]

The story goes that an animal of vast bulk went through the air and besought high Jove with entreaties, saying that everyone thought it a monstrous scandal and theme for ridicule that oxen should strut about in the glory of a pair of horns, while the camel alone should be undefended in every quarter, at the mercy of all the animal world and open to their attacks. Jupiter, mocking the camel, after refusing the expected boon, went further and relieved it of the weight of its large ears, saying, "Live beneath your deserts, as you are not satisfied with your lot; bewail your loss for ever, you jealous creature."

IX

The two Companions and the Bear

A man was once journeying along a narrow road with a companion among unknown hills and in

11 adridens *vel* arridens *plerique codd.*: irridens B *Rawl. Pet.*[2]: at ridens *Cannegieter*.

securus, cum quodque malum Fortuna tulisset,
 robore collato posset uterque pati.
dumque per inceptum vario sermone feruntur,
 in mediam praeceps convenit ursa viam.
horum alter facili comprendens robora cursu
 in viridi trepidum fronde pependit onus;
ille trahens nullo iacuit vestigia gressu,
 exanimem fingens, sponte relisus humi.
continuo praedam cupiens fera saeva cucurrit
 et miserum curvis unguibus ante levat;
verum ubi concreto riguerunt membra timore
 (nam solitus mentis liquerat ossa calor),
tunc olidum credens, quamvis ieiuna, cadaver
 deserit et lustris conditur ursa suis.
sed cum securi paulatim in verba redissent,
 liberior iusto, qui fuit ante fugax:
"dic, sodes, quidnam trepido tibi rettulit ursa?
 nam secreta diu multaque verba dedit."
"magna quidem monuit, tamen haec quoque maxima iussit,
 quae misero semper sunt facienda mihi:
'ne facile alterius repetas consortia,' dixit,
 'rursus ab insana ne capiare fera.'"

X

De Calvo Equite

Calvus eques capiti solitus religasse capillos
 atque alias nudo vertice ferre comas,

IX. [3] quodcumque *plerique codd.* : cum quodque *Baehrens.* [5] inceptum *plerique codd.* : incertum T : inseptum *Ellis.* [6] convenit *codd.* : en venit *Canneg.* : convolat *Baehrens.*
X. [1] religasse PVW *Ashb. Rawl.* : religare *plerique codd.*

winding valleys. He felt safe because, whatever adversity Fortune might bring, both would be able to unite their strength and face it. While with varied conversation they were pursuing the journey they had started, a she-bear came headlong to meet them in the middle of the way. One of the travellers with an easy run grasped an oak branch and suspended his panic-stricken weight among the green foliage. The other, without advancing his course a single step, feigned death, and lay down, throwing himself intentionally on the ground. At once, eager for the spoil, the savage beast ran up and, to start with, lifted the poor man in her crooked claws. But when icy fear stiffened his limbs (for the usual vital warmth had left his bones), then the bear, thinking him a rank corpse, abandoned him in spite of her hunger and vanished into her own haunts. But after they recovered their nerve and gradually resumed their talk, the man who before had run away grew now over-merry and said, "Tell me, please, what was it the bear told you when you were trembling there? She spoke much with you in a long private talk." "Yes, she gave me important advice, but laid also this command especially on me, and I, poor wretch, must always carry it out. 'Be chary of returning to partnership with another,' she said, 'lest a rabid beast get hold of you a second time.'"

X

The Bald Horseman

A bald horseman, accustomed to fasten hair to his head and wear strange locks on his bare crown,

ad Campum nitidis venit conspectus in armis
  et facilem frenis flectere coepit equum.
huius ab adverso Boreae spiramina praeflant 5
  ridiculum populo conspiciente caput;
nam mox deiecto nituit frons nuda galero,
  discolor apposita quae fuit ante coma.
ille sagax, tantis quod risus milibus esset,
  distulit admota calliditate iocum, 10
"quid mirum" referens "positos fugisse capillos,
  quem prius aequaevae deseruere comae?"

XI

De Duabus Ollis

Eripiens geminas ripis cedentibus ollas
  insanis pariter flumen agebat aquis.
sed diversa duas ars et natura creavit:
  aere prior fusa est, altera ficta luto.
dispar erat fragili et solidae concordia motus, 5
  incertumque vagus amnis habebat iter.
ne tamen allisam confringeret, aerea testa
  iurabat solidam longius ire viam.

[5] praeflant *Ellis*: perfl ≡ ant *Ashb.*: praestant *cett. codd.*
[8] apposita *codd.*: ab posita *Baehrens.*
XI. [4] facta CX b² *Pet.*² *Reg.*: ficta *plerique codd.*
[6] vagans B, *Ellis*: vagus *cett. codd.*
[7] elisam *codd.*: allisam *Barth, Baehrens*: illisam *Schenkl.*
[8] solitam *codd.*: solidam *Ellis*: sociam *Nevelet.* longius *codd.*: comminus *Canneg.*: urgebat coctam, comminus *Baehrens.*

came to the Campus[a] conspicuous in shining armour and began manœuvring his nimble horse with the bridle. The blasts of the North wind driving against him blew upon the front of his head and made it a figure of fun in the sight of the people. For soon his wig flew off and his uncovered forehead shone brightly, which just before had another hue while the false hair was fixed on. As the horseman saw that he was the laughing-stock of so many thousands, he shrewdly brought cunning to his aid and turned away the jest from himself. "Why be surprised," he remarked, "that my assumed locks have gone, when my natural hair deserted me first?"

XI

The two Jars

Two jars were once swept away by a river owing to a collapse of its banks and were being carried down together in the wild current. Different craftsmanship and material had created the two; the first was of fused bronze, the other of moulded clay. The brittle and the solid jar kept up an uneven harmony of progress,[b] while the meandering river took its wayward course. The bronze jar, however, swore to pursue its metallic route at a distance from the other lest it should strike against it and smash it to pieces. The

[a] *i.e.* the *Campus Martius*, the ancient open exercise-ground of Rome: *cf.* Hor. *Sat.* I. vi. 126 *fugio Campum lusumque trigonem.*

[b] *dispăr*: *cf.* xxiii. 8, and *impăr*, xviii. 10. The oxymoron *dispar concordia* means that in general the pots kept together, but irregularly so. Each in turn might drop behind and afterwards catch up.

illa timens ne quid levibus graviora nocerent,
et quia nulla brevi est cum meliore fides, 10
"quamvis securam verbis me feceris" inquit,
"non timor ex animo decutiendus erit;
nam me sive tibi seu te mihi conferat unda,
semper ero ambobus subdita sola malis."

XII

De Rustico et Thesauro

Rusticus impresso molitus vomere terram
thesaurum sulcis prosiluisse videt.
mox indigna animo properante reliquit aratra,
gramina compellens ad meliora boves.
continuo supplex Telluri construit aras, 5
quae sibi depositas sponte dedisset opes.
hunc Fortuna novis gaudentem provida rebus
admonet, indignam se quoque ture dolens:
"nunc inventa meis non prodis munera templis
atque alios mavis participare deos; 10
sed cum surrepto fueris tristissimus auro,
me primam lacrimis sollicitabis inops."

XIII

De Hirco et Tauro

Immensum taurus fugeret cum forte leonem
tutaque desertis quaereret antra viis,

[14] subruta sola modis *Lachmann.*
XII. [4] semina *plerique codd.*: gramina *Canneg.*: *fortasse* vimina *vel* stramina *Ellis.*

clay jar, through fear that it might be an instance of the light damaged by the heavy, and because weakness has no confidence in dealings with the stronger, said, "Though you relieve me of anxiety as far as your promises go, still I cannot shake my mind clear of fear. For whether the water brings me up against you or you against me, I shall always be the sole victim of either disaster."

XII

The Peasant and the Treasure

On breaking up the earth by the impact of his plough a peasant noticed a treasure-hoard leap into view from the furrows. Presently with quickened heart he abandoned the plough, now disesteemed, and drove his oxen to better pastures. At once with vows he raised altars in honour of Earth, since she unasked had given him the wealth entrusted to her. As he rejoiced in his new estate, Fortune with an eye to the future gave him a warning; for she was piqued that he did not think her also deserving of incense. "For the moment you neglect to hand over your treasure-trove to any temple of mine, and prefer to share it with other gods; but when the gold is stolen and you are in the depths of grief, I shall be the first whom you will tearfully entreat in your beggary."

XIII

The Goat and the Bull

It happened once that a bull was running away from a mighty lion, seeking by lonely paths for some

speluncam reperit, quam tunc hirsutus habebat
  Cinyphii ductor qui gregis esse solet.
ast ubi submissa meditantem irrumpere fronte
  obvius obliquo terruit ore caper,
tristis abit longaque fugax de valle locutus
  (nam timor expulsum iurgia ferre vetat):
"non te demissis saetosum, putide, barbis,
  illum, qui super est consequiturque, tremo;
nam si discedat, nosces, stultissime, quantum
  discrepet a tauri viribus hircus olens."

XIV

De Simia

Iuppiter in toto quondam quaesiverat orbe,
  munera natorum quis meliora daret.
certatim ad regem currit genus omne ferarum,
  permixtumque homini cogitur ire pecus;
sed nec squamigeri desunt ad iurgia pisces
  vel quicquid volucrum purior aura vehit.
inter quos trepidae ducebant pignora matres,
  iudicio tanti discutienda dei.
tunc brevis informem traheret cum simia natum,
  ipsum etiam in risum compulit ire Iovem.

XIII. [3] repetit C *Rawl. m*[1].
[5] post *plerique codd.*: ast BX *Pet.*[2] b[2].
[7] longaque *plerique codd.*: longeque *Canneg.*: longumque *Ellis.* valle (vale P) *codd.*: calle *Lachmann.*
XIV. [4] homini *codd.*: cicur *Baehrens.*
[7] inter quos *codd.*: in tergo *Baehrens.*

safe cavern, when he discovered a cave which was then occupied by a shaggy goat accustomed to lead the Cinyphian herd.[a] Thereupon, when the goat met him and with sidelong look frightened him out of his intention to lower his head and burst in, he went off mournfully and in his flight sent a reply from the far reaches of the valley (fear forbade him to quarrel over his rebuff). "It's not you I tremble at, you stinking creature, with your bristly hair and trailing beard; it's that lion—which is still to come and which follows in my track. If he abandons the chase, you'll learn, you arrant fool, the difference between a bull in his strength and a smelly goat."

XIV

The Monkey

Jupiter had once inquired through the whole world which animal it was that could present the gift of the finest offspring. In eager rivalry there hastened to the king every sort of creature of the wild, and every beast that has dealings with man was constrained to come. Nor did the scale-covered fish fail to contest their claim, or any bird borne on the clearer air. Among this gathering nervous mothers led up their progeny to be inspected at the judgement-seat of the powerful god. Just then, as a dwarfish monkey pulled forward her ugly offspring, she forced even Jove himself to laugh. But for all her

[a] The epithet refers to the long-haired goats bred in the Mauritanian territory washed by the Cinyps.

hanc tamen ante alios rupit turpissima vocem,
dum generis crimen sic abolere cupit:
" Iuppiter hoc norit, maneat victoria si quem;
iudicio superest omnibus iste meo."

XV

De Grue et Pavone

Threiciam volucrem fertur Iunonius ales
communi sociam conteruisse cibo—
namque inter varias fuerat discordia formas,
magnaque de facili iurgia lite trahunt—
quod sibi multimodo fulgerent membra decore, 5
caeruleam facerent livida terga gruem;
et simul erectae circumdans tegmina caudae
sparserat arcatum sursus in astra iubar.
illa licet nullo pennarum certet honore,
his tamen insultans vocibus usa datur: 10
" quamvis innumerus plumas variaverit ordo,
mersus humi semper florida terga geris:
ast ego deformi sublimis in aera penna
proxima sideribus numinibusque feror."

[11] haec BX *Rawl.* : hec *Ashb.* : hanc *cett. codd.*

XV. [2] contenuisse P : continuisse *vel* continuasse *cett. codd.* : conripuisse *Froehner* : commonuisse *vel* detinuisse *vel* conteruisse *Ellis.*

[7] agmina *Ellis.*

[8] arcanum *codd.* : arcatum *Barth.* rursus *codd.* : sursus *Lachmann.*

ugliness the monkey flung out these words before others could speak, anxious by so doing to remove the reproach upon her race: "Let Jupiter determine whether victory is in store for anyone; to *my* mind the little monkey before you beats the lot."

XV

The Crane and the Peacock

The story goes that Juno's bird disparaged the Thracian fowl,[a] when she shared their joint feeding-ground. For a quarrel had arisen involving their different kinds of beauty and they were protracting a long argument on a case easy to settle. The peacock contended that the parts of his body gleamed in manifold loveliness, but that a dingy back gave the crane a dun colour, and at the word he arrayed about him the canopy of his uplifted tail and shot an arc of light upwards to the sky. The crane, though unable to rival the other in any glory of plumage, is nevertheless said to have used these words in mockery: "Countless may be the array of colours variegating your plumage, yet you, the wearer of that gaudy tail, are for ever kept close to earth. But I soar aloft into the air on my wing for all its ugliness, and am wafted nigh to the stars and heavenly powers."

[a] *i.e.* the crane: *cf.* Ovid, *A. A.* iii. 182, *Threiciamve gruem*; Virg. *Aen.* X. 265, *Strymoniae grues.*

XVI

De Quercu et Harundine

Montibus e summis radicitus eruta quercus
    decidit insani turbine victa Noti,
quam tumidis subter decurrens alveus undis
    suscipit et fluvio praecipitante rapit.
verum ubi diversis impellitur ardua ripis, 5
    in fragiles calamos grande residit onus.
tunc sic exiguo conectens caespite ramos
    miratur liquidis quod stet harundo vadis:
se quoque tam vasto necdum consistere trunco,
    ast illam tenui cortice ferre minas. 10
stridula mox blando respondens canna susurro
    seque magis tutam debilitate docet.
" tu rabidos " inquit " ventos saevasque procellas
    despicis et totis viribus acta ruis.
ast ego surgentes paulatim demoror Austros 15
    et quamvis levibus provida cedo Notis;
in tua praeruptus se effundit robora nimbus,
    motibus aura meis ludificata perit."

haec nos dicta monent magnis obsistere frustra,
    paulatimque truces exsuperare minas. 20

XVI. [9] necdum *plerique codd.*: rectum C *Reg.*: rectam *Ellis.* consistere *plerique codd.*: non sistere *Ellis.*
[17] offendit *codd. praeter* X: se effundit *Lachmann.*
[19] frusta b: lustra B: rebus b[3]: frustra *cett. codd.*: fluxa *Ellis.*

XVI

The Oak and the Reed

An oak was torn up by its roots, a victim of the mad South Wind's whirling force, and fell down from the mountain heights. A river-channel, flowing below in high spate, took it and bore it off in the headlong current. But after the tall trunk had been thrust from bank to bank, its mighty bulk came to rest among slender reeds. Then it marvelled that a reed, fastening its stalks in but a tiny tuft, should stand firm in the flowing water; it marvelled that, for all its massive trunk, even it could not yet[a] stand unmoved, while the reed with its slender rind endured the menaces of nature.[b] Presently the creaking reed, answering with meek whisper, declared that its weakness increased its safety. "You," it said, "scorn the ravening winds and cruel tempests, and fall beneath the onset of their full strength. I keep in dalliance the gradually rising Auster and, with an eye to the future, let myself be swayed by Notus, however light his breath. Against your strength the rain-storm hurls itself sheer; but, baffled by my motion, the breeze sinks into nothing."

This teaches us that it is in vain we resist the mighty and that it is by slow degrees that we surmount the fury of their menaces.

[a] *necdum.* The years in which the *truncus* had grown *tam vastus* had not yet made it strong enough to resist the storm. *Cf.* J. E. B. Mayor, *C. R.* I. (1887) p. 191.

[b] *miratur* (8) is first followed by *quod stet* to express indirect statement, then by two accus. and infin. clauses (9–10).

XVII

De Venatore et Tigride

Venator iaculis haud irrita vulnera torquens
turbabat trepidas per sua lustra feras.
tum pavidis audax cupiens succurrere tigris
verbere commoto iussit adesse minax.
ille tamen solito contorquens tela lacerto 5
"nunc tibi, qualis eam, nuntius iste refert."
et simul emissum transegit vulnere ferrum,
praestrinxitque citos hasta cruenta pedes.
molliter at fixum traheret cum saucia telum,
a trepida fertur vulpe retenta diu, 10
nempe quis ille foret, qui talia vulnera ferret,
aut ubinam iaculum delituisset agens.
illa gemens fractoque loqui vix murmure coepit
(nam solitas voces ira dolorque rapit):
"nulla quidem medio convenit in aggere forma 15
quaeque oculis olim sit repetenda meis,
sed cruor et validis in nos directa lacertis
ostendunt aliquem tela fuisse virum."

XVIII

De Quattuor Iuvencis et Leone

Quattuor immensis quondam per prata iuvencis
fertur amicitiae tanta fuisse fides,

XVII. [2] pavidas BGOX *Rawl. Ashb. Pet.*[2]: rapidas L: rabidas *cett. codd.*: trepidas *Lachmann.*

[4] commoto O: commotas *plerique codd.* minas *codd.*: minax *Froehner.*

[6] eram *plerique codd.*: eam T*m*[2], *Froehner.*

[11] dum quis *plerique codd.*: quis deus *Baehrens*: nempe quis *Ellis.*

XVII

The Hunter and the Tigress

A huntsman who dealt effective wounds with the javelins he discharged used to drive the wild animals in terrified confusion through their coverts. Then a bold tigress, eager to succour the panic-stricken beasts, lashing with her tail in threatening wise, bade him come up against her. But he hurled as usual his missile from his shoulder, saying, "That is the messenger which in this hour tells you my prowess as I go my way"; and at that moment the weapon which he discharged pierced and wounded her, and the blood-stained shaft grazed her swift feet. When the wounded tigress was gently drawing forth the tight-fixed weapon, she is said to have been kept in converse a long time by a fox asking in dismay, who was the man that could deal such wounds or where had he hid himself to shoot his javelin. The tigress with moans and broken growls found speech with difficulty; for rage and pain robbed her of her usual utterance; "No shape that my sight could afterwards recall confronted me in the middle of the road,[a] but the blood and the weapon aimed at me by a powerful arm show that it was some man of might."

XVIII

The Four Oxen and the Lion

Once among four huge oxen in the meadows there existed, as the story goes, so trusty a bond of affection,

[a] Servius on Virg. *Aen.* V. 273, *viae deprensus in aggere*, explains *agger est media viae eminentia coaggeratis lapidibus strata*: *cf.* Rut. Namat. I. 39 *Aurelius agger* = *Via Aurelia.*

ut simul emissos nullus divelleret error,
  rursus et e pastu turba rediret amans.
hos quoque collatis inter se cornibus ingens 5
  dicitur in silvis pertimuisse leo,
dum metus oblatam prohibet temptare rapinam
  et coniuratos horret adire boves;
et quamvis audax factisque immanior esset,
  tantorum solus viribus impar erat. 10
protinus aggreditur pravis insistere verbis,
  collisum cupiens dissociare pecus.
sic postquam dictis animos disiunxit acerbis,
  invasit miserum diripuitque gregem.
tunc quidam ex illis "vitam servare quietam 15
  qui cupit, e nostra discere morte potest;
neve cito admotas verbis fallacibus aures
  impleat aut veterem deserat ante fidem."

XIX

De Abiete ac Dumis

Horrentes dumos abies pulcherrima risit,
  cum facerent formae iurgia magna suae,
indignum referens cum istis certamen haberi,
  quos meritis nullus consociaret honor:
"nam mihi deductum surgens in nubila corpus 5
  verticis erectas tollit in astra comas,
puppibus et patulis media cum sede locamur,
  in me suspensos explicat aura sinus;
at tibi deformem quod dant spineta figuram,
  despectum cuncti praeteriere viri." 10

XVIII. [4] ovans WBX b *Pet.*[2]: amans *cett. codd.*
[9] sed *codd.*: et *vulgo.*
[14] invasit BX *Pet.*[2]: invadit *cett. codd.*
XIX. [3] cunctis *codd.*: cum istis *Baehrens*: dumis *Ellis.*
[4] quos GTOX *Reg. Rawl.*: quod *cett. codd.*

that on being sent from their stalls together no straying would sunder them, and then again the group would return from pasture still friends. Now, before these oxen, with their horns united in line, a mighty lion in the forest is said to have quailed, so long as fear forbade him to make trial of the quarry facing him, and he shrank from approaching the allied cattle; and, though courageous and more savage in his deeds, he was no match by himself for the strength of such powerful beasts. Thereupon he began to urge evil counsels, anxious to divide the herd by making them quarrel. So after he had sown disunion with embittering words, he rushed upon the poor herd and tore them limb from limb. Then one of them said, "Anyone who wants to preserve an untroubled life may learn from our death. Let him not be in a hurry to suffer a ready ear to be filled with guile, or to desert over soon an ancient loyalty."

XIX

The Pine and the Bramble Bush

A very lovely pine made mockery of a prickly bramble bush in a serious dispute touching their claims to beauty. The pine said it was unfair it should have to contend with such as no title brought by merit into its own class. "For my tapering trunk rises towards the clouds, and rears starward the lofty foliage of my tree-top; and when I am placed on the ship's open deck in the centre, the sails unfurled by the wind hang upon me. But you—everyone passes you by with scorn, because your growth of thorns gives you an ugly appearance." The bramble

ille refert: "nunc laeta quidem bona sola fateris
  et nostris frueris imperiosa malis;
sed cum pulchra minax succidet membra securis,
  quam velles spinas tunc habuisse meas!"

XX

De Piscatore et Pisce

Piscator solitus praedam suspendere saeta
  exigui piscis vile trahebat onus.
sed postquam superas captum perduxit ad auras
  atque avido fixum vulnus ab ore tulit,
"parce, precor" supplex lacrimis ita dixit obortis; 5
  "nam quanta ex nostro corpore dona feres?
nunc me saxosis genetrix fecunda sub antris
  fudit et in propriis ludere iussit aquis.
tolle minas, tenerumque tuis sine crescere mensis:
  haec tibi me rursum litoris ora dabit: 10
protinus immensi depastus caerula ponti
  pinguior ad calamum sponte recurro tuum."
ille nefas captum referens absolvere piscem,
  difficiles queritur casibus esse vices:
"nam miserum est" inquit "praesentem amittere
    praedam, 15
  stultius et rursum vota futura sequi."

XX. [6] damna *codd.*: dona *Lachmann.*
[14] casibus *codd.*: cassibus *Froehner, Baehrens, Ellis.*

rejoins: "True, now you rejoice and all you profess is fair, and in your domineering way you take pleasure in my defects. But in that day when the threatening axe shall hew your fine limbs, how you would then wish that you had possessed my thorns!"

XX

The Angler and the Fish

A fisherman who used to catch his prey hanging on a horsehair line was drawing in a tiny fish of trumpery weight. But after he had brought his catch up into the air and the fish had been pierced with a wound [a] through its hungry mouth, in entreaty amid starting tears it said, "Have mercy, I pray you; for how much gain will you derive from my flesh? Just now has a fertile mother spawned me 'neath the rocky caves, and bidden me disport myself in our own waters. Banish your fell designs; I am young; let me grow up for your table. This bank of the shore will give me to you again. In a little time, when I have fed on the blue waters of the boundless deep, I shall willingly return the fatter to your rod." The fisherman, declaring it a crime to let go a fish once caught, complained that hazards are beset with turns incalculable: "It is a pity," he said, "to lose the spoil in hand, and a worse folly to start afresh in pursuit of future hopes."

[a] *vulnus ferre* here means to endure a wound: contrast XVII. 11, where it means to deal a wound.

XXI

De Alite et Messione

Parvula progeniem terrae mandaverat ales,
qua stabat viridi caespite flava seges.
rusticus hanc fragili cupiens decerpere culmo
vicinam supplex forte petebat opem.
sed vox implumes turbavit credita nidos, 5
suasit et e laribus continuare fugam.
cautior hos remeans prohibet discedere mater:
"nam quid ab externis proficietur?" ait.
ille iterum caris operam mandavit amicis;
at genetrix rursum tutior inde manet. 10
sed postquam curvas dominum comprendere falces,
frugibus et veram sensit adesse manum,
"nunc" ait, "o miseri, dilecta relinquite rura,
cum spem de propriis viribus ille petit."

XXII

De Cupido et Invido

Iuppiter ambiguas hominum praediscere mentes
ad terras Phoebum misit ab arce poli.
tunc duo diversis poscebant numina votis;
namque alter cupidus, invidus alter erat.

XXI. [5] credula *plerique codd.*: sedula b: credita *Withof*: acredula (*in casu vocativo*) *Ellis*.
[6] suaserat e X: suaserat et *cett. codd.*: suasit et e *Ellis*.
XXII. [4] invidus *codd.* (*contra metrum*): lividus *Withof*.

---

[a] Babrius makes the bird a lark. Gellius, *N. A.* ii. 29, who paraphrases the fable from Ennius' trochaic septenarii,

XXI

The Bird and the Reaping of the Corn

A tiny little bird [a] had entrusted her young to the ground where with its root-stem green stood the yellow corn-crop. It so happened that a farmer wanting to cut the corn from its fragile stalk begged and prayed for a neighbour's help. Now these words, which the unfledged nestlings believed, struck panic into them and counselled instant flight from their home. Their mother was more wary; on her return she told them not to go away, saying, "What good will come from outsiders?" The farmer once more entrusted the task to his dear friends; but the mother again stayed where she was, all the safer for that reason. But when she perceived that the owner was gripping the curved sickle and that his true hand was near the crops, she said, "Now, my poor dears, abandon the fields you love so well, now that he seeks the fulfilment of his hopes from his own powers."

XXII

The Greedy Man and the Jealous Man

Jupiter sent Phoebus to the earth from the citadel of the sky to discover in advance the doubtful hearts of mankind. Just then two men were beseeching the gods to satisfy different desires, for one had a covetous and the other a jealous nature. The Sun-

describes it as *cassita,* "helmeted" or "crested." Ellis' *acredula* strictly means a nightingale. While the Ennian moral is explicitly "Do not expect friends to do what you can do yourself," it is noticeable that Avianus gives no epimythion.

his sese medium Titan scrutatus utrumque 5
obtulit et precibus cum peteretur, ait:
"praestant di facilis; quae namque rogaverit unus,
protinus haec alter congeminata feret."
sed cui longa iecur nequeat satiare cupido,
distulit admotas in nova damna preces, 10
spem sibi confidens alieno crescere voto
seque ratus solum munera ferre duo.
ille ubi captantem socium sua praemia vidit,
supplicium proprii corporis optat ovans;
nam petit exstinctus sic lumine degeret uno, 15
alter ut hoc duplicans vivat utroque carens.
tum sortem sapiens humanam risit Apollo,
invidiaeque malum rettulit ipse Iovi,
quae, dum proventis aliorum gaudet iniquis,
laetior infelix et sua damna cupit. 20

XXIII

De Venditore et Baccho

Venditor insignem referens de marmore Bacchum
expositum pretio fecerat esse deum.
nobilis hunc quidam funesta in sede sepulcri
mercari cupiens compositurus erat;

[6] confiteretur X: ut peteretur *cett.*: cum peteretur *Ellis*: Iuppiter aecus *Lachmann*.

[7] praestabit C *Reg.*: praestandi *cett. codd.*: praestandist *Baehrens*: praestant di *Ellis*. facilis *codd.* nam quae speraverit VW: nam quaeque rogaverit *plerique codd.*: quae namque rogaverit *Ellis*.

[15] ut *plerique codd.*: sic *Ellis*.

---

[a] Ellis' conjecture and interpretation have been followed, though *facilis* is a rare form for the nom. plur. (See Neue, *Formenlehre d. lat. Sprache*, II. 1875, pp. 34 *sqq.*)

God, scrutinising both, presented himself as a mediator between them, and when entreated with prayers said, "The gods being kind grant fulfilment;[a] for what one of you asks, that shall the other forthwith receive, doubled." But the one, whose far-reaching desires could not satisfy his heart, put off addressing his prayer—with a surprising loss as the sequel.[b] He was sure the desires of the other would increase his own prospects, calculating that in his single person he was thus winning two boons. The other, when he saw his companion grasping at his own prizes, gleefully prayed for a punishment to be inflicted on his own body. For he asked that he might lose one eye for the rest of his life in order that the other, doubling this misfortune, might live deprived of both. Then Apollo, learning the truth, smiled at human lot, and with his own lips reported to Jupiter the curse of jealousy, which, as it rejoices in other people's untoward fortunes, is unlucky enough the more gladly to desire its own harm also.

XXIII

The Salesman and his Statue of Bacchus[c]

A trading craftsman who had fashioned a fine Bacchus in marble had put up the god for sale. A nobleman who wanted to buy it intended to place it in the funereal resting-place containing his tomb.

[b] *i.e.* the loss of both his eyes, described later.

[c] The fable is so full of difficulties that Ellis questions its authenticity. The use of the participles in lines 1 and 4 marks the deterioration of syntax; *expositum fecerat esse* cannot be called good Latin; and the obscurity of lines 7–9 led Baehrens to rewrite them with more than usual infelicity.

alter adoratis ut ferret numina templis,
redderet et sacro debita vota loco.
" nunc " ait " ambiguum facies de mercibus omen,
cum spes in pretium munera dispar agit,
et me defunctis seu malis tradere divis,
sive decus busti seu velis esse deum ; 10
subdita namque tibi est magni reverentia sacri
atque eadem retines funera nostra manu."

convenit hoc illis, quibus est permissa potestas,
an prodesse magis seu nocuisse velint.

XXIV

De Venatore et Leone

Certamen longa protractum lite gerebant
venator quondam nobilis atque leo.
hi cum perpetuum cuperent in iurgia finem,
edita continuo forte sepulcra vident.
illic docta manus flectentem colla leonem 5
fecerat in gremio procubuisse viri.
" scilicet affirmas pictura teste superbum
te fieri ? exstinctam nam docet esse feram."
ille graves oculos ad inania signa retorquens
infremit et rabido pectore verba dedit : 10

XXIII. 9 et me licet addere vivis *Baehrens*.
11 fati *plerique codd.* : facti AGO *m. pr.* b *Pet.*[2] : sati P : sacri *Ellis* : fani *Baehrens*.
14 prodesse X : praestare *plerique codd.*
XXIV. 4 contigue *Baehrens* (*in not.*) : continuo *codd.* fronte *Ellis* : forte *codd.*
7 affirmans *plerique codd.* : affirmas *Ellis.*
8 se *codd.* : te *Ellis.*

Another wished to present[a] the god in the temple where he worshipped and in the hallowed precincts to fulfil a vow that was owing. "Now," said the statue, "you will make a puzzling forecast about your wares, when two far different prospects set a price upon your work,[b] and you will be in doubt whether you prefer to consign me to the dead or to the gods, whether you wish me to adorn a tomb or to be a deity. To your arbitrament is submitted the reverence of a great religious act; in your hand also you hold my death-warrant."[c]

This is applicable to those who have it in their power to do a good or a bad turn according as they wish.[d]

XXIV

The Hunter and the Lion

A huntsman of renown and a lion were once engaged in a contest protracted by long dispute. As they desired to put an end once for all to their quarrel, they saw on the instant, it so happened, a lofty tombstone. Thereon a cunning hand had represented a lion bowing its neck in submission and prostrate in a man's embrace. "Can you really assert that the evidence of that work of art makes you proud? Why, it shows the death of the beast." The lion, turning downcast eyes to the unreal figures, growled and in fierceness of heart broke into speech:

[a] *ut ferret* depends on *mercari cupiit* supplied from *mercari cupiens.*

[b] *munera* seems more suitably translated as "result of your employment" than as "gift."

[c] *i.e.* to make of me a sepulchral ornament.

[d] *i.e.* the salesman had the option of benefiting or injuring the statue.

"irrita te generis subiit fiducia vestri,
  artificis testem si cupis esse manum.
quod si nostra novum caperet sollertia sensum,
  sculperet ut docili pollice saxa leo,
tunc hominem adspiceres oppressum murmure
    magno, 15
  conderet ut rabidis ultima fata genis."

XXV

De Puero et Fure

Flens puer extremam putei consedit ad undam,
  vana supervacuis rictibus ora trahens.
callidus hunc lacrimis postquam fur vidit obortis,
  quaenam tristitiae sit modo causa rogat.
ille sibi abrupti fingens discrimina funis 5
  hac auri queritur desiluisse cadum.
nec mora, sollicitam traxit manus improba vestem:
  exutus putei protinus ima petit.
parvulus exiguo circumdans pallia collo
  sentibus immersus delituisse datur. 10
sed post fallaci suscepta pericula voto
  tristis ut amissa veste resedit humi,
dicitur his sollers vocem rupisse querellis
  et gemitu summos sollicitasse deos:
"perdita, quisquis erit, post haec bene pallia credat, 15
  qui putat in liquidis quod latet urna vadis."

15 expressum marmore *Lachmann.*
XXV. 6 atque *plerique codd.*: ac C *Reg.*: hac *Froehner.*
16 natat *vel* natet *codd.*: latet *Wight Duff.*

---

[a] *latet* implies that the thief ought not to have been fool enough to be cheated by the boy's story about letting a golden pitcher drop into the well: he had not paused (*nec mora,* 7)

"Vain is the confidence in your human birth that has entered into you, if you desire to have for a witness an artist's hand. If *our* ingenuity admitted of an extra sense, allowing a lion to engrave stones with skilful touch, then you would behold how the man, overwhelmed by a loud roar, closed his final destiny in ravening jaws."

XXV

The Boy and the Thief

A boy sat down in tears at the edge of the water of a well, deceitfully opening wide his mouth in groundless blubbering. A smart thief, on seeing him with tears starting from his eyes, asked what was the cause of his distress now. The boy pretended his rope had parted in two; thereby, he sobbed, his golden pitcher had fallen down the well. At once the rascal's hand dragged off his hampering garment, and, when stripped, he made straight for the bottom of the well. The youngster, so the story has it, put the cloak round his own little neck, plunged into the brambles and was lost to sight. But when, after encountering danger on a deceptive hope, he had seated himself again on the ground, miserable over the loss of his cloak, the shrewd knave (so the story goes) gave utterance to these laments and made moaning supplication to the high gods: "Henceforth let anyone, whoever he be, who thinks a jar lies hid in clear water,[a] reckon that he has richly deserved to lose his cloak."

to see if the gold was visible in the water. *Natet* or *natat* implies that anyone who expected a jar to be floating at the bottom of a well would be served right by losing his cloak.

XXVI

De Capella et Leone

Viderat excelsa pascentem rupe capellam,
  comminus esuriens cum leo ferret iter,
et prior " heus " inquit " praeruptis ardua saxis
  linque nec hirsutis pascua quaere iugis;
sed cytisi croceum per prata virentia florem 5
  et glaucas salices et thyma grata pete."
illa gemens " desiste, precor, fallaciter " inquit
" securam placidis instimulare dolis.
vera licet moneas, maiora pericula tollas,
  tu tamen his dictis non facis esse fidem: 10
nam quamvis rectis constet sententia verbis,
  suspectam hanc rabidus consiliator habet."

XXVII

De Cornice et Urna

Ingentem sitiens cornix adspexerat urnam,
  quae minimam fundo continuisset aquam.
hanc enisa diu planis effundere campis,
  scilicet ut nimiam pelleret inde sitim,
postquam nulla viam virtus dedit, admovet omnes 5
  indignata nova calliditate dolos;
nam brevis immersis accrescens sponte lapillis
  potandi facilem praebuit unda viam.

XXVI. [8] instimulare b [2] *et paraphr.*: insimulare *plerique codd.*: insinuare *Cab.*
[12] rabidus *Ashb.*: gravidus *cett. codd.*: pravus *Baehrens.* habes b[3], *Lachmann, Ellis*: habet *cett. codd.*

XXVI

The Lion and the Goat

A hungry lion while passing near by had spied a she-goat grazing on a rocky height. He opened conversation with "Ho, there! leave these steeps with their precipitous crags and don't look for pasture on prickly ridges. No, you should go through the green meadows in quest of the yellow lucerne-flower and pale green willow and sweet thyme." "Please stop," said the goat with a groan, "your lying attempts to rouse me from my security with your gentle wiles. Though your advice has truth in it, though you suppress the greater dangers, yet you do not make me trust what you say. For however correct your words be and however sound their meaning, yet a famished counsellor has his meaning under suspicion."

XXVII

The Crow and the Jar

A thirsty crow had spied a huge jar containing a very little water at the bottom. Long did the crow strive to spill this water on the level plain, to banish, of course, thereby her excessive thirst; but, when no valiant effort could provide a way, she lost her temper and with fresh cunning applied all her crafty devices. She threw pebbles in, and the low level of water rose naturally and so supplied an easy way of drinking.

viribus haec docuit quam sit prudentia maior,
qua coeptum cornix explicuisset opus. 10

XXVIII

De Rustico et Iuvenco

Vincla recusanti dedignantique iuvenco
aspera mordaci subdere colla iugo
rusticus obliqua succidens cornua falce
credidit insanum defremuisse pecus,
cautus et immenso cervicem innectit aratro 5
(namque erat hic cornu promptior atque pede),
scilicet ut longus prohiberet verbera temo
neve ictus faciles ungula saeva daret.
sed postquam irato detractans vincula collo
immeritam vacua calce fatigat humum, 10
continuo eversam pedibus dispergit harenam,
quam † in domini Boreas ora sequentis agat.
tunc hic informi squalentes pulvere crines
discutiens imo pectore victus ait:
"nimirum exemplum naturae derat iniquae, 15
qua fieri posset quis ratione nocens."

XXVII. [10] volucris *plerique codd.*: cornix *Ellis* (*servans metrum*).

XXVIII. [9] bos quom *Baehrens*: postquam *codd.*

[10] vacuo (*masc.*) *nonnulli codd., Ellis.*

[12] quam ferus in domini ora *plerique codd.*: q. in d. aura ferens ora *Lachmann*: q. feriens Boreas ora *Withof*: q. in d. Boreas ora *Baehrens in not.* agat ACPT b: agit *cett. codd.*

[13] sic *codd.*: hic *Lachmann.*

[16] cum *codd.*: quis *Baehrens.*

This fable has proved the superiority of foresight over stout efforts, as by it the crow accomplished the task she had undertaken.

XXVIII

THE FARMER AND HIS OX

There once was an ox that chafed at ropes and shirked submitting its rebellious neck to the grip of the yoke. The farmer cut its horns with a knife used slantwise and thought the frenzied animal had abated its rage. Carefully he fastened its neck to the weighty plough (for it was over-ready with horn and hoof), doubtless so that the long pole might obstruct any butting and that its cruel hoof might find it difficult to kick. But when the animal, its neck angrily struggling against the straps, worried the inoffensive earth with impotent hoof, its feet at once churned up the sand broadcast for the North wind to blow into its master's face as he followed. Then the farmer, while he shook his locks begrimed with unsightly dust, said, in deep discomfiture of heart, "Truly, I needed an instance of a vicious temper to show how anyone could contrive to do mischief." [a]

[a] This new instance proved how a low nature, in spite of all precautions, could work harm.

XXIX

De Viatore et Satyro

Horrida congestis cum staret bruma pruinis
 cunctaque durato stringeret arva gelu,
haesit in adversa nimborum mole viator;
 perdita nam prohibet semita ferre gradum.
hunc nemorum custos fertur miseratus in antro 5
 exceptum Satyrus continuisse suo.
quem simul adspiciens ruris miratur alumnus
 vimque homini tantam protinus esse pavet;
nam gelidos artus vitae ut revocaret in usum,
 afflatas calido solverat ore manus. 10
sed cum depulso coepisset frigore laetus
 hospitis eximia sedulitate frui,
namque illi agrestem cupiens ostendere vitam
 silvarum referens optima quaeque dabat,
obtulit et calido plenum cratera Lyaeo, 15
 laxet ut infusus frigida membra tepor.
ille ubi ferventem labris contingere testam
 horruit, algenti rursus ab ore reflat.
obstipuit duplici monstro perterritus hospes
 et pulsum silvis longius ire iubet: 20
" nolo " ait " ut nostris umquam successerit antris,
 tam diversa duo qui simul ora ferat."

XXIX. [8] protinus *codd.*: pectoris *Lachmann*: providus *Froehner.*
[10] foverat *Lachmann*: solverat *plerique codd.*
[11] sed cum *codd.*: donec *Baehrens.*
[18] sufflat *vel* suflat *codd.*: reflat *Schenkl.*

XXIX

The Traveller and the Satyr

When mid-winter stood bristling with thick frost and bound every field in hardened ice, a traveller came to a halt in a heavy barrier of mist; for the losing of his path prevented his advance. They say one of the guardians of the woodland, a Satyr, felt pity and gave him welcome and shelter in his cave. This nurseling of the country [a] looked upon him wondering the while, and straightway was afeared to see a mortal possess power so great. For, to bring back his chilled limbs to the tasks of life, the traveller had blown into his hands and thawed them with his warm breath. But it was different when he had banished the cold and had delightedly begun to enjoy his host's generous attentions; since, anxious to show him how they lived in the country, the Satyr kept bringing out and serving all the best that the woodland yielded; he set before him also a bowl full of warm wine so that its pervasive heat might loosen the chilliness of his limbs. The traveller, fearing to touch the glowing cup with his lips, blew this time with a cooling breath. His host was alarmed and astounded at the double miracle, and driving him from the woods bade him begone still further off. "I desire no one," he said, "ever to approach my cave who owns at the same moment two such different sorts of mouth."

[a] The Satyr is called *ruris alumnus* as one of the ape-like and goat-footed demigods of the forest: *cf.* Ovid *Met.* I. 192–3 *sunt mihi semidei, sunt rustica numina Nymphae, Faunique Satyrique et monticolae Silvani*; ib. VI. 392-3 *ruricolae, silvarum numina, Fauni et Satyri fratres.*

XXX

De Sue et Illius Domino

Vastantem segetes et pinguia culta ruentem
liquerat abscisa rusticus aure suem,
ut memor accepti referens monumenta doloris
ulterius teneris parceret ille satis.
rursus in exsculpti deprensus crimine campi 5
perdidit indultae perfidus auris onus.
nec mora, praedictae segeti caput intulit horrens;
poena sed insignem congeminata facit.
tunc domini captum mensis dedit ille superbis,
in varias epulas plurima frusta secans. 10
sed cum consumpti dominus cor quaereret apri,
impatiens fertur quod rapuisse cocus,
rusticus hoc iustam verbo compescuit iram,
affirmans stultum non habuisse suem—
nam cur membrorum demens in damna redisset, 15
atque uno totiens posset ab hoste capi?

haec illos descripta monent, qui saepius ausi
numquam peccatis abstinuere manus.

XXX. [5] exculpti G: excepti *cett. codd.*: excerpti *Guiet.*
[7] praedictae *plerique codd.*: praedator *Lachmann*: praevetitae *Baehrens.*
[8] quod O *Rawl., Pet.*[2]: sed *cett. codd.* indignum *codd.*: indictum *Cab.*: insignem *Lachmann.*

XXX

The Pig and its Owner

A pig was ruining a farmer's corn and trampling his fertile fields; so he cut its ear off and let it go, hoping that, carrying home a reminder of the pain suffered, it would remember in future and keep off the tender crops. It was caught again in the crime of grubbing up the soil, and for its thieving lost the ear it had—the one previously spared. Immediately afterwards it thrust its mutilated [a] head into the aforementioned corn; but the twice-repeated punishment made it a marked trespasser.[b] This time the farmer, having captured it, gave it for its owner's sumptuous banquet, cutting a great number of slices for the various dishes. But when they had been eating the boar and the owner asked for its heart, which the ravenous cook is said to have purloined, then the farmer soothed his reasonable anger with these words, remarking that the pig was stupid and never had a heart [c]—for why had it been mad enough to return just to lose parts of its body? why let itself be caught so many times by the same enemy?

This sketch is a warning to those who have ventured too often and never kept their hands off iniquity.

[a] *Horrens* is glossed in the Trèves MS. as *truncatum*.

[b] If *indignum* of the MSS. is kept, the sense is that the two previous punishments made this new trespass by the pig an outrage. Nothing, therefore, but death could meet the case.

[c] The *cor* was considered the seat of understanding.

XXXI

De Mure et Bove

Ingentem fertur mus quondam parvus oberrans
ausus ab exiguo laedere dente bovem.
verum ubi mordaci confecit vulnera rostro,
tutus in anfractus conditur inde suos.
ille licet vasta torvum cervice minetur, 5
non tamen iratus quem petat esse videt.
tunc indignantem mus hoc sermone fatigans
distulit hostiles calliditate minas:
"non quia magna tibi tribuerunt membra parentes,
viribus effectum constituere tuis. 10
disce tamen brevibus quae sit fiducia rostris,
ut faciat quicquid parvula turba cupit."

XXXII

De Aratore et Bobus

Haerentem luteo sub gúrgite rusticus axem
liquerat et nexos ad iuga tarda boves,
frustra depositis confidens numina votis
ferre suis rebus, cum resideret, opem.
cui rector summis Tirynthius infit ab astris 5
(nam vocat hunc supplex in sua vota deum):

XXXI. [7] iusto *codd.*: mus hoc *Withof*: lusor *Ellis*. [11] monstris *plerique codd.*: membris B: rostris *Froehner*. [12] ut W *Reg.*, *Pet.*[1]: et *plerique codd.* faciat *plerique codd.*: facias *Pet.*[1], B *m. sec.*, *paraphr.*

XXXII. [3] depositis *plerique codd.*: dispositis PX *Rawl.* b[2].

[a] For *ab cf.* Ovid. *Met.* viii. 513, *invitis correptus ab ignibus arsit.*

XXXI

The Mouse and the Ox

They tell how once upon a time a little mouse on its wanderings ventured with [a] its tiny teeth to attack a mighty ox. When its nibbling mouth finished biting, it thereupon hid safely in its winding hole. Though the ox made sullen threats with his huge neck, yet for all his anger he could not see that there lived an enemy for him to attack. Then the mouse dispersed [b] the foe's threats with its cleverness, bantering the enraged ox with these words: "Because your parents transmitted strong limbs to you, it does not follow that they added efficiency to your strength. Learn, however, the self-reliance that our tiny mouths possess, and learn how our pigmy band does whatever it wants."

XXXII

The Ploughman and his Oxen [c]

A peasant had left his cart sticking in a muddy pool and his oxen fastened to a yoke that would not move. He trusted in vain that thanks to the vows he lodged the gods would assist his fortunes though he sat idle himself. From the starry heights he was addressed by the Lord of Tiryns [d] (for he was one of the gods whom his entreaties invoked to further his prayers).

[b] *Cf.* x. 10.
[c] This represents *De aratore et bobus, Rawl.* Other titles are *De rustico et axe,* O, and *De pigro Tyrint(h)ium frustra orante,* C.
[d] Hercules.

"perge laborantes stimulis agitare iuvencos,
  et manibus pigras disce iuvare rotas.
tunc quoque congressum maioraque viribus ausum
  fas superos animis conciliare tuis. 10
disce tamen pigris non flecti numina votis
  praesentesque adhibe, cum facis ipse, deos."

XXXIII

De Ansere Ova Aurea Pariente

Anser erat cuidam pretioso germine feta,
  ovaque quae nidis aurea saepe daret.
fixerat hanc volucri legem Natura superbae,
  ne liceat pariter munera ferre duo.
sed dominus, cupidum sperans vanescere votum, 5
  non tulit exosas in sua lucra moras,
grande ratus pretium volucris de morte referre,
  quae tam continuo munere dives erat.
postquam nuda minax egit per viscera ferrum
  et vacuam solitis fetibus esse videt, 10
ingemuit tantae deceptus crimine fraudis;
  nam poenam meritis rettulit inde suis.

sic qui cuncta deos uno male tempore poscunt,
  iustius his etiam vota diurna negant.

[10] animis *codd.*: athlis *Baehrens*.
XXXIII. [5] cupidus . . . augescere *Wopkens*.

"Go on and drive your bullocks with the goad through their difficulties, and learn to aid with your hands the sluggish wheels. After you have come to grips and used your strength for greater efforts, then it is allowable also to win the gods over to your wishes. Learn, however, that the deities are not swayed by indolent vows: bring the gods to your help by acting yourself."

XXXIII

The Goose that laid the Golden Eggs

A man owned a goose teeming with precious offspring, one that often laid golden eggs in its nest. Nature had ordained this rule for the noble bird, that it should not lay more than one egg at the same time. But the owner, anticipating the disappearance of his greedy expectations,[a] could not brook delays, hateful when his profits were considered;[b] he thought to win a handsome prize by killing the bird, rich as it was in such unfailing bounty. When he plunged his dread knife into its open[c] breast, and found the bird empty of the usual eggs, he groaned aloud, tricked by the iniquity of so gross a fraud; for thereupon he ascribed the punishment to his own deserts.

So to those wicked enough to ask the gods for everything at once, they refuse the more justly even the prayers of a single day.

[a] The golden harvest, he feared, was too good to last.

[b] He wished more than one golden egg at a time.

[c] *nuda* = *nudata.* Ellis explains as "stript of feathers" to make the opening with more dexterity.

XXXIV

De Formica et Cicada

[Quisquis torpentem passus transisse iuventam
nec timuit vitae providus ante mala,
confectus senio, postquam gravis adfuit aetas,
heu frustra alterius saepe rogabit opem.]

Solibus ereptos hiemi formica labores 5
distulit et brevibus condidit ante cavis.
verum ubi candentes suscepit terra pruinas
arvaque sub rigido delituere gelu,
pigra nimis tantos non aequans corpore nimbos
in laribus propriis umida grana legit. 10
discolor hanc precibus supplex alimenta rogabat,
quae quondam querulo ruperat arva sono:
se quoque, maturas cum tunderet area messes,
cantibus aestivos explicuisse dies.
parvula tunc ridens sic est affata cicadam 15
(nam vitam pariter continuare solent):
"mi quoniam summo substantia parta labore est,
frigoribus mediis otia longa traho;
at tibi saltandi nunc ultima tempora restant,
cantibus est quoniam vita peracta prior." 20

XXXIV. [9] pigranimis KTV : pigra nimis *plerique codd.* tanto (= *tam parvo*) T *Rawl.*, *Pet.*[2] : tantos GC*m*[2].
[11] decolor A*m*[1]KPT : discolor A*m*[2] *Ashb.*

XXXIV

The Ant and the Grasshopper

[The man that has allowed his youth to go by in idleness and has not taken anxious precautions against the ills of life—that man, foredone with years, will in the presence of burdensome old age often ask in vain, alas, for a neighbour's help.]

An ant reserved for the winter the fruits of toil snatched during sunny hours and stored them betimes in her tiny hole. But when earth assumed its white robe of hoar frost and fields lay hid beneath unyielding ice, then, quite idle and unfit bodily to face the rain-storms, she picked out the moistened grain in her own abode. A grasshopper in her varied hues, who before had cleft the fields with plaintive note, amid prayers and supplications begged the ant for food. For her part, she said, when the threshing-floor was bruising the ripened harvest, she had worked out the summer days in song. Then with a laugh the tiny ant thus addressed the grasshopper (for their wont is to prolong their life equally)[a]: " Since *my* subsistence has been secured by dint of hardest toil, I draw out long days of ease in the midst of the frost. But *you* now have your last days left for dancing, since your past life was spent in song."[b]

[a] *i.e.* continue their life from year to year, as neither dies in the winter.

[b] The ant's ironic gibe is that, as the grasshopper has been an inveterate singer, she can conclude her days in dancing with her song as an accompaniment.

XXXV

De Simiae Gemellis

Fama est quod geminum profundens simia partum
  dividat in varias pignora nata vices;
namque unum caro genetrix educit amore,
  alteriusque odiis exsaturata tumet.
coeperit ut fetam gravior terrere tumultus, 5
  dissimili natos condicione rapit:
dilectum manibus vel pectore gestat amico,
  contemptum dorso suscipiente levat.
sed cum lassatis nequeat consistere plantis,
  oppositum fugiens sponte remittit onus. 10
alter at hirsuto circumdans bracchia collo
  haeret et invita cum genetrice fugit.
mox quoque dilecti succedit in oscula fratris,
  servatus vetulis unicus heres avis.

sic multos neglecta iuvant, atque ordine verso 15
  spes humiles rursus in meliora refert.

XXXVI

De Vitulo et Bove

Pulcher et intacta vitulus cervice resultans
  scindentem adsidue viderat arva bovem.
" non pudet heus " inquit " longaevo vincula collo
  ferre nec haec positis otia nosse iugis?
cum mihi subiectas pateat discursus in herbas 5
  et nemorum liceat rursus opaca sequi."

XXXV. [11] ad P : et *Pet.*[1] : ab *cett. codd.* : at *vulgo*.
[16] *fortasse* rursus spes humiles *Ellis*.
XXXVI. [4] haec positis *Ellis* : expositis *codd.*

XXXV

The Monkey's Twins

The story goes that a monkey gave birth to twin offspring and assigned her children each to a different destiny. One the mother reared in fond affection, and she rankled with superabundant hatred for the other. When a perilous attack began to alarm the mother she hurried her young apes off, meting out unequal treatment. The favourite she carried in her paws or her tender bosom; the despised one she lifted up and carried on her back. But when she could not stand upright on her wearied feet, in mid-flight she gladly let go the one that burdened her in front. But the other, throwing his arms round his mother's hairy neck, clung to her and shared her escape against her will. Besides, he soon succeeded to the caresses his favoured brother had enjoyed, and survived to be sole heir to his ancient lineage.

Thus do many come to like what once they slighted; and hope, changing the order of things, carries the lowly back into happier fortune.

XXXVI

The Calf and the Ox

A fine calf, skipping to and fro and never yoked as yet, had seen an ox busily ploughing the fields. "You there," he said, "are you not ashamed to have your aged neck fastened, unable to throw off the yoke and know the leisure that is mine? For I am free to range at will over the low-lying pasture, and then again I can make for the shade of the

at senior, nullam verbis compulsus in iram,
  vertebat solitam vomere fessus humum,
donec deposito per prata liceret aratro
  molliter herboso procubuisse toro. 10
mox vitulum sacris innexum respicit aris
  admotum cultro comminus ire popae.
" hanc tibi " testis ait " dedit indulgentia mortem,
  expertem nostri quae facit esse iugi.
proderit ergo graves quamvis perferre labores, 15
  otia quam tenerum mox peritura pati."

est hominum sors ista, magis felicibus ut mors
  sit cita, cum miseris vita diurna negat.

XXXVII

De Cane et Leone

Pinguior exhausto canis occurrisse leoni
  fertur et insertis verba dedisse iocis.
" nonne vides duplici tendantur ut ilia tergo
  luxurietque toris nobile pectus ? " ait.
" proximus humanis ducor post otia mensis, 5
  communem capiens largius ore cibum."

[11] sertis *Cannegieter.*
[13] testis CK *Reg.* : tristis *cett. codd.*
[18] miseris B *m. pr.*: miseros *cett. codd.* negat B b^2 *m. sec.*: regat *cett. codd.* : necat *Ellis.*

---

[a] The epimythion 17–18 is perhaps spurious, as it partly contradicts lines 15–16, which may be taken to point the moral and which advocate endurance.
[b] *verba dare* has not necessarily in late Latin the classical sense of gulling : *cf.* ix. 20, xxxviii. 6 : contrast i. 14.

grove." But the old ox, not at all angered by the words, went on wearily turning the soil as usual with the share, till he was allowed to drop the plough and to lie at his ease on a grassy bed in the meadows. Soon afterwards he saw the calf brought by a leading-string to the sacrificial altar and coming close to the knife of the priest's attendant. As he witnessed this he said, "Such is the death given you by the forbearance that leaves you free from my yoke. So then it will be better to endure toil however burdensome than to experience when young an ease that is soon to be lost."

This is the lot of mortals; death comes swift to the happier ones, while the daily life of the unfortunate refuses them death.[a]

XXXVII

The Dog and the Lion

A well-fed dog is said to have met an exhausted lion and to have addressed[b] him with taunts in his words: "Don't you see," he said, "how my flanks dilate under my back's double ridge[c] and my fine breast has handsome muscles? When resting-time has come, I am brought close up to the tables where men eat, my mouth getting in ample measure the fare my master shares with me." "But what is that

[c] Heinsius explained *duplici tergo* as *lato tergo*, like Virgil's *duplex agitur per lumbos spina*, *G.* III. 87 (of a horse), where Servius interprets "aut revera duplex aut lata." The depression along the back of a horse in good condition gives the appearance of a double spine. Ellis suggests that *tergo* is used of the ridge or projecting surface of the skin covering the dog's flanks, which is called "double" from inequalities produced by outstanding muscle or fat.

"sed quod crassa malum circumdat guttura ferrum?"
"ne custodita fas sit abire domo.
at tu magna diu moribundus lustra pererras,
donec se silvis obvia praeda ferat. 10
perge igitur nostris tua subdere colla catenis,
dum liceat faciles promeruisse dapes."
protinus ille gravem gemuit collectus in iram
atque ferox animi nobile murmur agit.
"vade" ait "et meritis nodum cervicibus infer, 15
compensentque tuam vincula dura famem;
at mea cum vacuis libertas redditur antris,
quamvis ieiunus quae libet arva peto.
has illis epulas potius laudare memento,
qui libertatem postposuere gulae." 20

XXXVIII

De Pisce et Phycide

Dulcibus e stagnis fluvio torrente coactus
aequoreas praeceps piscis obibat aquas.
illic squamigerum despectans improbus agmen
eximium sese nobilitate refert.
non tulit expulsum patrio sub gurgite phycis 5
verbaque cum salibus asperiora dedit:
"vana laboratis aufer mendacia dictis,
quaeque refutari te quoque teste queant.

XXXVII. 7–8 *hos versus post* 10 *collocavit Cannegieter, post* 12 *Schenkl et Baehrens, post* 14 *Barth.*
7 quo *Cannegieter*: quod *codd.*
13 gemitu *codd.*: gemuit *Baehrens.*
16 compescant BX *Pet.*1 *Pet.*2
XXXVIII. 5 phycis *Cannegieter*: phoecis CK: phocas GLOT *Rawl. Pet.*2

villainous bit of iron round your brawny throat?" "That's to prevent my leaving the house I have been guarding. But you for a long time wander through the wilds dying of hunger, until your victim meets you in the jungle. Proceed, therefore, to bow your neck to the chains I wear, till you can earn an easy-won feast." At once the lion with a growl worked himself into a violent rage and in haughty spirit uttered a lordly roar. "Begone," he said, "set bonds on your neck as it deserves, and may the galling chains take the place of hunger in your case; but when I am restored still free to my solitary den, famished though I be, I make for any field I please. Mind you commend such junketing more especially to those who have sacrificed independence for gluttony."

XXXVIII

The Fish and the Lamprey

Driven by the rush of a river out of its fresh pools, a fish darted headlong to the waters of the sea. There it arrogantly looked down on the ranks of scaly fish and averred that its high birth gave it distinction. A lamprey in its ancestral depths could not endure the *émigré*, and spoke [a] to it sharply in satiric vein. "Away with empty falsehoods from your affected language! away with what can be disproved even on your own evidence! For I will

[a] *Cf.* note on *verba dedisse*, xxxvii. 2.

---

[6] salibus *codd. fere omnes contra metrum*: sociis G: salsis *Lachmann*: ? sannis *Ellis*: probris asperiora *vel* salibus liberiora *Withof*.

nam quis eat potior populo spectante probabo,
  si pariter captos umida lina trahant. 10
tunc me nobilior magno mercabitur emptor,
  te simul aere brevi debile vulgus emet."

XXXIX

De Milite Arma Cremante

Voverat attritus quondam per proelia miles
  omnia suppositis ignibus arma dare,
vel quae victori moriens sibi turba dedisset
  vel quicquid profugo posset ab hoste capi.
interea votis fors adfuit, et memor arma 5
  coeperat accenso singula ferre rogo.
tunc lituus rauco deflectens murmure culpam
  immeritum flammis se docet isse pyrae.
" nulla tuos " inquit " petierunt tela lacertos,
  viribus affirmes quae tamen acta meis ; 10
sed tantum ventis et cantibus arma coegi,
  hoc quoque submisso (testor et astra) sono."
ille resultantem flammis crepitantibus addens
  " nunc te maior " ait " poena dolorque rapit ;

[9] erit *codd.* : eat *Baehrens.*
XXXIX. [8] esse prius *codd.* : piis *Canneg.* : cibum *Withof* : in flammis se d. esse pyrae *Froehner* : isse pyrae *Ellis.*
[13] resultantem *codd.* : reluctantem *ed. vetus.*
[14] dolorque *plerique codd.* : colorque B : calorque *Ellis.*

prove to you who passes for better in the eyes of the people, should a dripping net catch and land us both at the same time. In that case a purchaser of high rank will pay a lot for me, while the feeble rabble will give but a brass farthing for you."

XXXIX

The Soldier who Burned the Weapons

Once upon a time a soldier worn out in the wars had vowed to light a fire and devote to it all his arms, both those yielded to him in his hour of victory by numbers of dying combatants and aught that could be taken from the foe in flight. Time passed and chance favoured his hopes; so, mindful of his vow, he kindled a pyre and began bringing his weapons to it one by one. At that moment a trumpet with a harsh blare, deprecating all guilt, declared that it went innocent to the flaming pyre. "Never," it said, "were your brawny arms struck by missiles which you could, by way of plea, assert were hurled by strength of mine. No, I only mustered the weapons of war with wind and note, and that only (the stars be my witness) in a sound subdued." The soldier added the trumpet to the crackling flames and made it bounce, saying, "Now a severer punishment[a] and pain hurries

[a] "A severer punishment" (Ellis says "an extra severity of punishment") befalls the trumpet; for, whereas the weapons only suffer the burning, it suffers first the violence of being thrown against the weapons and is then destroyed by fire. This supports *resultantem* rather than *reluctantem*, which otherwise is a good suggestion.

nam licet ipse nihil possis temptare nec ausis, 15
saevior hoc, alios quod facis esse malos."

XL

De Pardo et Vulpe

Distinctus maculis et pulchro pectore pardus
inter consimiles ibat in ora feras;
sed quia nulla graves variarent terga leones,
protinus his miserum credidit esse genus.
cetera sordenti damnans animalia vultu 5
solus in exemplum nobilitatis erat.
hunc arguta novo gaudentem vulpis amictu
corripit et vanas approbat esse notas:
"vade" ait "et pictae nimium confide iuventae,
dum mihi consilium pulchrius esse queat, 10
miremurque magis quos munera mentis adornant,
quam qui corporeis enituere bonis."

XLI

De Imbre et Testa

Impulsus ventis et pressa nube coactus
ruperat hibernis se gravis imber aquis;
cumque per effusas stagnaret turbine terras,
expositum campis fictile pressit opus:
mobile namque lutum tepidus prius instruit aer, 5
discat ut admoto rectius igne coqui.

XL. [2] inira CK : in ira A *m. pr.* : mira P : inire GLT *Rawl.*, *Reg.* : in arva A *m. sec.* V *m. sec.* BX *Petrenses* : in ora *Ellis* : abnuit ire *Lachmann*.

you off. For, though you cannot yourself attack at all or venture on anything, you are a more cruel foe in that you make others dangerous."

XL

The Leopard and the Fox

A fine-breasted leopard in his dappled glory went to parade himself among the beasts which were his compeers. But because the surly lions had no varied hues upon their back, he straightway formed the belief that theirs was a sorry tribe. Condemning all the other animals as mean-looking, he took himself for the one pattern of noble breed. As he was rejoicing in the garb of youth, a wily vixen chid him and showed the uselessness of his markings. "Go," said she, "keep your excessive confidence in your gorgeous youthfulness, so long as I can surpass you in fine counsel, and so long as we can admire those adorned by gifts of intellect more than those who shine in bodily charms."

XLI

The Shower and the Jar

Impelled by the winds, a heavy rain-storm had gathered with the pressure of cloud upon cloud and burst in wintry torrents. And as its whirling deluge made a lake over the widespread lands, it struck some potter's work set outside in the fields; for warm air shapes the plastic clay beforehand, to train it for being baked more perfectly when fire is applied.

tunc nimbus fragilis perquirit nomina testae.
immemor illa sui "Amphora dicor" ait;
"nunc me docta manus rapiente volumina gyro
molliter obliquum iussit habere latus." 10
"hactenus hac" inquit "liceat constare figura:
nam te subiectam diluet imber aquis."
et simul accepto violentius amne fatiscens
pronior in tenues victa cucurrit aquas.
infelix, quae magna sibi cognomina sumens 15
ausa pharetratis nubibus ista loqui!

haec poterunt miseros posthac exempla monere,
subdita nobilibus ne sua fata gemant.

XLII

De Lupo et Haedo

Forte lupum melior cursu deluserat haedus,
proxima vicinis dum petit arva casis;
inde fugam recto tendens in moenia cursu
inter lanigeros adstitit ille greges.
impiger hunc raptor mediamque secutus in urbem 5
temptat compositis sollicitare dolis:
"nonne vides" inquit, "cunctis ut victima templis
immitem regemens morte cruentet humum?
quod nisi securo valeas te reddere campo,
ei mihi, vittata tu quoque fronte cades." 10

XLI. [9] nunc *codd.*: nam *edd.*
[16] pharetratis *codd.*: foret tantis *Cab.*, *Baehrens*: foret atris *Wopkens*: *fortasse* erat iratis *Ellis.*
[18] ne B: ut *cett. codd.*

---

[a] *i.e.* conceitedly elated by its beauty as described in 9–10, it forgets what a frail thing it is.

Then the rain-cloud asked the name of the brittle jar, which, forgetting itself,[a] said, "My name is Amphora. As you see me now, a craftsman's hand, by means of the wheel's swift revolutions, has ordained the gentle slope of my side." "Till now, but no more," said the other, "think yourself permitted to bear this shape, for rain is about to whelm you in its waters and wash you away." And thereupon, taking in the wild rush of the flood, and cracking open, the jar yielded and dashed headlong into the flowing waters. Ill-fated one, to take a proud name to itself and venture to speak thus to clouds which have their quivers in readiness!

This example will serve in future to warn the wretched not to lament their destiny when it is under the control of the great.

XLII

The Wolf and the Kid

It happened that a kid, while making for the fields which lay nearest to some neighbouring huts, had baffled a wolf by faster running. Then, directing his flight straight for the city walls, he came to a halt among flocks of wool-clad sheep. The beast of prey was unwearied and, pursuing the kid into the heart of the town, tried to lure him with studied wiles. "Do you not see," he said, "how in all the temples a victim amid repeated groans stains the pitiless ground with its life-blood?[b] But if you are not able to return to the safety of the meadow, ah me, you too will die with the sacrificial fillet round your brow."

[b] The fable, Ellis points out, belongs to a time when sacrifices in heathen temples might still take place: *cf.* the pagan atmosphere of XXIII and XXXVI (see also Introd.).

ille refert: "modo quam metuis, precor, exue curam
  et tecum viles, improbe, tolle minas;
nam sat erit sacrum divis fudisse cruorem
  quam rabido fauces exsaturare lupo."

sic quotiens duplici subeuntur tristia casu, 15
  expedit insignem promeruisse necem.

XLII. [13] sat erit *plerique codd.*: satius *Withof.*

The kid replied, " Just drop, I pray you, the anxiety which is your dread, and take yourself off and your trumpery threats too, you rogue. I shall be content to pour out my blood in a sacrifice to the gods rather than gorge the throat of a ravenous wolf."

So every time we face disaster of twofold hazard, it is the noble death which it is expedient to achieve.

RUTILIUS NAMATIANUS

INTRODUCTION

TO RUTILIUS NAMATIANUS

The last of the classical Latin poets, Claudius Rutilius Namatianus, or (as is quite possibly the correct order for his name) Rutilius Claudius Namatianus, belonged to a Gallo-Roman family[a] and was born late in the fourth century, most likely at Toulouse. His father, almost certainly the Lachanius of his poem, and more or less plausibly identified with different official Claudii of the period, passed through a distinguished public career and had been honoured with a statue at Pisa, a visit to which is described with filial pride.[b] Rutilius held high appointments under the emperor Honorius, who reigned A.D. 395–423. We must, however, beware of being misled by distinctions spuriously thrust upon him in the title of the Bologna edition; he was not a *vir consularis*, though he was a *vir clarissimus*; he had been neither a *tribunus militum* nor a *praefectus praetorii*, but he had attained to the influential positions of *magister officiorum*[c] and *praefectus urbis*.[d] It can be shown that he held the former office in A.D. 412 and that he immediately

[a] I. 20. [b] I. 575–596. [c] I. 563.
[d] I. 157–160 and 427.

preceded his friend Albinus [a] as prefect of the city for part of the year A.D. 414.

Educated on the lines of the ancient learning, Rutilius, as his poem indicates, was a man of literary knowledge and taste, an adherent of paganism, and influenced by Stoic philosophy. The times in which he lived had brought devastation again and again into Italy at the hands of northern barbarians. In A.D. 410, six years before he undertook the journey back to his native Gaul which makes the subject of his poem *De Reditu Suo*,[b] Rome had witnessed in a three days' sack the culmination of the third siege of the city by Alaric, King of the Visigoths.

That same year men had seen the burial of the Gothic chief under the diverted waters of the Busento; and in 412 Ataulf, the successor of Alaric, had withdrawn his Goths from Italy into Gaul, whence he had been forced across the Pyrenees into Spain to meet his death by assassination in 415. Soon afterwards, under their King Walia, the Visigoths concluded peace with Rome; but years of merciless ravage had left in Italy and Gaul scenes of depressing desolation which are reflected in our author's realistic allusions.[c] The misery of it all touched him closely as he was planning his route in 416 from the one devastated country to the other, and so he decided to coast northwards from the mouth of the Tiber rather than face the dangerous roads and broken bridges of Italy. The motive for his journey has been questioned: it is at least more likely that he

[a] I. 466–474.

[b] A slightly more satisfactory title than the alternative *Itinerarium*.

[c] I. 21, 39–42.

may have wished to inspect some property of his own in Gaul than that his paganism had somehow lost him favour in Rome.[a]

It was autumn when he started from the city, and in the extant portion of the poem we can read an entertaining elegiac journal for two months from September 22nd to November 21st, A.D. 416,[b] when his second book breaks off at the 68th line after the arrival at Luna. This was something more elaborate as a travel-poem than Horace's journey to Brundusium or Ovid's sketch of his voyage in the *Tristia* or Statius' send-off to his patron bound for Egypt.[c] We may guess that the composition of the poem followed not long after the time of the journey; but our knowledge of the author and of his fortunes stops short with the interruption of his work. Only half-a-dozen lines before the end, as we now have it, the author had contemplated the continuance of his narrative. Is the conclusion lost or was it never written?

A brief summary will enable us to follow him on his voyage so far as his poetic record runs. A long exordium (1–164) is largely a rhetorical eulogy on

[a] H. Schenkl, *Rh. Mus.* 66 (1911), pp. 393 *sqq.*, argues that Rutilius' attacks on Christian monks do not prove his pagan creed, and it is true that some Christians have censured monasticism severely. But this is not the whole case. Rutilius' tone elsewhere seems inconsistent with Christian belief. Labriolle quite reasonably distinguishes it from that of a professing Christian like Ausonius, *Rev. des études latines*, 6 (1928), pp. 30 *sqq.*

[b] Carcopino, *Rev. des études lat.*, 6, 180 *sqq.*, 1928, argues for 16th Oct. 417 as the date of the departure from Rome. Both Helm and Préchac agree in their editions.

[c] Hor. *Sat.* I. v (partly suggested by Lucilius' *Iter Siculum*); Ovid, *Trist.* I. x; Stat. *Silv.* III. ii.

the majestic greatness of Rome and her gift of unifying nations. After the start from the city (165) Rutilius was weather-bound for fifteen days at Ostia in the harbour of Claudius and Trajan. When his sailors had once found a fair wind, the coasting and mainly daylight voyage began, and, as related in Book I, lasted six days (or, according to Vessereau, seven). The first day (217–276) brings them to Centumcellae, where they spend the night. On the second day (277–312) they sail at dawn, pass off the mouth of the Munio and the pinewoods of Graviscae, sighting Cosa before putting into Portus Herculis at nightfall. On the third day (313–348), sailing still earlier, before sunrise, they coast along Monte Argentario, pass the island of Igilium (recently a refuge for fugitives from the Goths), touch, without staying, at the Umbro mouth, and are forced, when overtaken by night, to bivouac ashore. The fourth day (349–428) finds them compelled to take to oars in the morning: and after sighting Ilva (Elba), whose mines suggest to the poet the praises of iron, they land in a state of fatigue before midday at Faleria, where they chance upon an Osiris fête in progress. Their most unpleasant experiences with an extortionate landlord, a Jew, lead to an outburst against Judaism. Subsequent rowing brings them to Populonia, where they are rejoiced to get news from Rome. With the fifth day (429–510) we have the distant view of Corsica chronicled, and when Capraria rises in sight, the opportunity is seized for an onslaught on the monasticism of its inhabitants. The travellers later reach Volaterrana Vada. A visit is paid to the villa of a good friend, Albinus, and the processes of the neighbouring salt-pans are described. The welcome meeting with Victorinus, a friend from Toulouse, compensates for the delay caused by a gale. During the early part of the sixth day [a] (511–540) they find themselves off the dangerous rocks of Gorgon island, the home of a hermit whom Rutilius regards as one of a group of misguided fanatics, more bewitched, he thinks, than the victims of Circe's enchantments. They next arrive at the villa Triturrita, built on an artificial causeway near a harbour protected by a curious barrier of seaweed. Here, in spite of the inducement to proceed with the voyage in fair weather, an interruption is made, as Rutilius cannot resist the temptation to visit his friend Protadius in the neighbouring town: so Protadius' merits, Pisa itself and the statue erected there to his own father are in turn touched upon. This voluntary delay (541–614) is followed by a compulsory one (615–644); for on coming back to Triturrita, the travellers being storm-stayed have to occupy their time in a boar-hunt: and for the moment horn and song appear to be echoed in one of Rutilius' couplets.[b] A long stay is made in this district, Book I ending in a description of violent and continued storm.

Book II in its 68 lines narrates only the voyage from Portus Pisanus to Luna, but it also contains a description of Italy, a furious invective against the dead general Stilicho, and an account of the marble quarries in the Luna district.

[a] Vessereau makes this the seventh day, as he estimates that the distance from Populonia to Vada and the visit to Albinus would need more than a single day. The sixth day may therefore have been spent at the villa; but the poem does not clearly indicate this.

[b] 629–630.

His poem, in some ways the better for those digressions which make it more than a journal of travel, exhibits Rutilius as a man with an eye for the scenery of the Italian coast, interested in the affairs of the places touched at during his voyage northwards, and stirred by warm affection for friends [a] no less than by frankly expressed dislike for Jews, Christian monks and Stilicho. It is pleasant to note his joy at meeting friends and his regret at parting: it is an equally human trait that he is a good hater. His tender Stoic melancholy, coloured rather than seared by the memory of Rome's recent capture by the Goths, does not prevent him from cherishing an optimistic confidence in her recovery, even as in long-past history she had recovered after the Allia and Cannae. And so in his encomium upon the imperial city, sincere enough in feeling and yet in phrasing more rhetorical than poetic, Rutilius has uttered the swan-song of Rome.

Nor is it a song unworthy of the classical tradition. His Latin has a prevailing lucidity which befits his theme; and, despite the influence of Virgil and Ovid, his work, thanks to concentration upon his own experiences, which are narrated in a vivid and realistic style, bears a definitely individual mark. But it is rare for this individual note of his to show itself in mere linguistic usage such as *decessis* (if that be the true reading at I. 313) or the archaistic *propudiosa* (I. 388). As to metre, it is true that *amphitheatrum* is not a Virgilian ending for a hexameter, nor *sollicitudinibus* an Ovidian ending for a pentameter.[b] It is true also that Rutilius is too free

[a] See notes on the translation.

[b] There are some sixteen exceptions in Rutilius to the dissyllabic close of a pentameter.

in his employment of spondees. There is, further, little *enjambement* between hexameter and pentameter, so that his lines tend to be monotonously self-contained.[a] Yet, on the whole his versification must be called graceful,[b] and at times his elegiac couplets gain greatly in strength by a kind of Propertian force which Rutilius succeeds in conferring upon the pentameter.

EDITIONS

J. B. Pius. Editio princeps. Bologna, 1520.

Onuphrius Panvinius. In his *Reipublicae Romanae Commentarii*. Venice, 1558.

J. Castalio. Rome, 1582.

C. Barth. Frankfort, 1623.

Th. J. Almeloveen (c. not. variorum). Amsterdam, 1687.

P. Burman. *P. L. M.* II. pp. 1–184. Leyden, 1731.

C. T. Damm. Brandenburg, 1760.

J. C. Wernsdorf. *P. L. M.* V. i. pp. 1–202. Altenburg, 1788.

A. W. Zumpt. Berlin, 1840.

L. Mueller. Leipzig, 1870.

Itasius Lemniacus (A. v. Reumont). Berlin, 1872.

E. Baehrens. *P. L. M.* V. pp. 3–30. Leipzig, 1883.

[a] Usually hexameter and pentameter constitute a unity, as in I. 65–66, or the second line takes up and completes the first, as in I. 91–92, 331–332. Only occasionally does a sentence run into more than one distich, as in I. 403–408, 519–522.

[b] The elisions are 61 in 712 lines. There are no elisions of a long vowel before a short, nor of a monosyllable, nor at the caesura, nor in the second half of a pentameter.

J. Vessereau (text, French prose transln. and essays). Paris, 1904.
C. H. Keene (Eng. verse transln. by G. F. Savage-Armstrong). London, 1907.
G. Heidrich (introd. and crit. appar.). Vienna, 1911.
V. Ussani. Florence, 1921.
R. Helm. Heidelberg, 1933.
J. Vessereau and F. Préchac (texte établi et traduit). Paris, 1933.

RELEVANT WORKS

E. Gibbon. *Decline and Fall of the Roman Empire* (esp. chaps. xxviii–xxxi for historical background).
T. Hodgkin. *Italy and her Invaders*, Vol. I. Oxford, 1880–1899.
Fr. Mueller. *De Rutilio Namatiano stoico*, progr. Soltquellae (= Saltwedel), 1882.
H. Schiller. *Geschichte der röm. Kaizerzeit*, II. Gotha, 1887.
P. Monceaux. *Les Africains : étude sur la littér. latine d'Afrique.* Paris, 1894.
C. Hosius. *Die Textgeschichte des Rutilius*, *Rh. Mus.* 51 (1896), pp. 197–210.
P. Rasi. *In Cl. Rut. Namatiani libros adnotationes metricae.* Turin, 1897.
S. Dill. *Roman Society in the last Century of the Wn. Empire.* London, 1905.
R. Pichon. *Les derniers écrivains profanes* (ch. v, " un grand fonctionnaire gallo-romain : le poète Rut. Nam."). Paris, 1906.
H. Schenkl. *Ein spätrömischer Dichter u. sein Glaubensbekenntnis*, *Rh. Mus.* 66 (1911), pp. 393–416.

P. de Labriolle. *Rut. Nam. et les moines* in *Rev. des études latines*, VI. pp. 30–41. Paris, 1928.
J. Carcopino. *À propos du poème de Rut. Nam.* in *Rev. des études latines*, VI. pp. 180–200. Paris, 1928.
M. L. W. Laistner. *Thought and Letters in Wn. Europe*, A.D. 500–900 (opening chapter on "Empire and its Invaders"). London, 1931.
E. S. Duckett. *Latin Writers of the Fifth Century.* New York, 1931.

SIGLA

V = Codex Vindobonensis 277 (olim 387), qui, post membranas vetustas Ovidii Halieutica et Grattii Cynegetica continentes, foliis 84^{a}–93^{b} saeculi xvi nostrum carmen habet.
[·*f*· = the symbol accompanying some of the marginal corrections in the Vienna MS.: it has been variously interpreted as *fortasse* (L. Mueller, Baehrens), *fiat* (Hosius), or *fuit* (Purser).]
B = editio princeps, Bononiae anno 1520 emissa.
R = Codex Romanus: saec. xvi, Romae anno 1891 repertus.

On these three sources of the text, two MSS. and the editio princeps, a few notes are desirable. Baehrens in his edition of 1883 based his text upon the Vienna manuscript (now denoted by V, the collation of which by Huemer was called c by Baehrens) and upon Mau's collation of the editio princeps published by Battista Pio at Bologna in 1520 (here denoted by B but in Baehrens by b). Since Baehrens' time a second manuscript, denoted by R, has become available: it was discovered in the library of the Duke of Sermoneta at Rome in 1891. V and R, both written in the sixteenth century, are indirectly and independently derived from an archetype found at Bobbio in 1494 or 1493. This archetype may be conjectured to have been written in Lombardic characters in the eighth or ninth century; but it has been lost since its removal from Bobbio in 1706. In 1495 Inghiramius, surnamed Phaedrus of Volaterra, afterwards librarian at the Vatican, made a copy of it at Bobbio and took it to Rome before 1506. About that time the poet Sannazaro had brought with him from France to Italy the newly-discovered *Halieutica* of Ovid and *Cynegetica* of Grattius and of Nemesianus; and in his enthusiasm for new works he either acquired or transcribed Phaedrus' copy of the manuscript. According to Baehrens and to Vessereau, V is Sannazaro's copy, though, according to Hosius, the descent of V is traceable back through Sannazaro and then through Phaedrus to the codex Bobiensis. The Vienna MS. is on paper, of the sixteenth century, bound up at the end of a volume immediately after Ovid's *Halieutica*, also on paper and preceded by seven older manuscripts on vellum of smaller dimensions than the paper MSS. Among these vellum MSS. certain lines of Eucheria and another copy of the *Halieutica*, with Sidonius Apollinaris and Grattius, have been identified with the actual poems which Sannazaro brought from France.

The editio princeps published by Battista Pio at Bologna in 1520 has a value for determining the text, as it represents Phaedrus' copy according to Hosius, and thus offers a testimony earlier than Sannazaro's copy and its derivative V.

R is dated by Vessereau a quarter of a century after V, *i.e.* in 1530, as he holds V to be Sannazaro's copy. Hosius, who collated R in *Rh. Mus.* (1896), vol. li, inferred that it was written within 30 or 40 years of the discovery of Rutilius' poem in 1493.[a] The corruptions shared by V and R prove their common descent, but R cannot have come from Phaedrus' copy (represented in the editio princeps B), because R sometimes preserves the true reading in contrast with V and B. On the other hand, a consensus of V and R virtually establishes a reading in the lost codex Bobiensis of the eighth century.

[a] The comparative value of V and R is hard to estimate. Keene points out that while R has the advantage in I. 178 *tenet*, 211 *curae*, 235 *largo*, 265 *lymphas*, 461 *algam*, 552 *utramque*, V has the superiority in I. 22 *miseranda*, 232 *Inui*, 317 *ternis*, 573 *Elide*, II. 62 *propositum*. R certainly has serious disfigurements due to one or other of its three hands. Recently L. Bartoli (*Athenaeum* ix. 3, 1931), writing on the two codices, has awarded the palm to the Vienna manuscript.

RUTILIUS NAMATIANUS

DE REDITU SUO

LIBER PRIMUS

VELOCEM potius reditum mirabere, lector,
  tam cito Romuleis posse carere bonis.
quid longum toto Romam venerantibus aevo?
  nil umquam longum est quod sine fine placet.
o quantum et quotiens possum numerare beatos 5
  nasci felici qui meruere solo!
qui Romanorum procerum generosa propago
  ingenitum cumulant urbis honore decus!
semina virtutum demissa et tradita caelo
  non potuere aliis dignius esse locis. 10
felices etiam qui proxima munera primis
  sortiti Latias obtinuere domos!
religiosa patet peregrinae Curia laudi,
  nec putat externos quos decet esse suos;
ordinis imperio collegarumque fruuntur 15
  et partem Genii quem venerantur habent:

[5] quater *Heinsius, Mueller, Baehrens.*

---

[a] *Potius* supports the view that the opening of the poem is lost.

[b] The poet is to praise Rome at length (3–164). He claims that nothing can be tedious in the eulogy of a city which every age has held in honour—the *urbs aeterna* calls for eternal veneration.

RUTILIUS NAMATIANUS

A VOYAGE HOME TO GAUL

BOOK I

Rather [a] will you marvel, reader, that my quick return journey (to Gaul) can so soon renounce the blessings of the city of Romulus. What is too long for men who spend all time in venerating Rome? [b] Nothing is ever too long that never fails to please. How greatly and how often can I count those blest who have deserved birth in that happy soil! Those highborn scions of Roman nobility crown their honourable birth with the lustre of the Capital! On no other land could the seeds of virtues have been more worthily let fall by heaven's assignment. Happy they too who, winning meeds next to the first, have enjoyed Latin homes! [c] The Senate-house, though fenced with awe, yet stands open to foreign merit, nor deems those strangers who are fittingly its own. They share the power of their colleagues in the senatorial order, and possess part of the sacred Genius [d] which they revere, even

[c] *i.e.* though not born in Rome, like those in 5–6.

[d] The *Genius* is the indwelling spirit of the Roman People, shared by such provincials as were admitted into the senate. Their union is compared with the heavenly council under the presidency of the supreme god (Jupiter is not named).

quale per aetherios mundani verticis axes
concilium summi credimus esse dei.

at mea dilectis fortuna revellitur oris,
indigenamque suum Gallica rura vocant. 20
illa quidem longis nimium deformia bellis,
sed quam grata minus, tam miseranda magis.
securos levius crimen contemnere cives:
privatam repetunt publica damna fidem.
praesentes lacrimas tectis debemus avitis: 25
prodest admonitus saepe dolore labor.
nec fas ulterius longas nescire ruinas
quas mora suspensae multiplicavit opis:
iam tempus laceris post saeva incendia fundis
vel pastorales aedificare casas. 30
ipsi quin etiam fontes si mittere vocem
ipsaque si possent arbuta nostra loqui,
cessantem iustis poterant urgere querelis
et desideriis addere vela meis.
iam iam laxatis carae complexibus urbis 35
vincimur et serum vix toleramus iter.

electum pelagus, quoniam terrena viarum
plana madent fluviis, cautibus alta rigent.
postquam Tuscus ager postquamque Aurelius agger,
perpessus Geticas ense vel igne manus, 40
non silvas domibus, non flumina ponte coercet,
incerto satius credere vela mari.

[17] aetherias . . . arces *Baehrens.*
[22] veneranda R: miseranda VB.
[34] verba *vir doctus apud Wernsdorf*: *accepit Baehrens.*
[37] vetabant *Baehrens.*

as from ethereal pole to pole of the celestial vault we believe there abideth the council of the Deity Supreme.

But 'tis my fortune that is plucked back from the well-loved land; the fields of Gaul summon home their native.[a] Disfigured they are by wars immeasurably long, yet the less their charm, the more they earn pity. 'Tis a lighter crime to neglect our countrymen when at their ease: our common losses call for each man's loyalty. Our presence and our tears are what we owe to the ancestral home: service which grief has prompted ofttimes helps. 'Tis sin further to overlook the tedious tale of disasters which the delay of halting aid has multiplied: now is the time after cruel fires on ravaged farms to rebuild, if it be but shepherds' huts. Nay, if only the very springs could utter words, if only our very trees[b] could speak, they well might spur my laggard pace with just complaints and give sails to my yearning wishes. Now that the dear city slackens her embrace, my homeland wins, and I can scarce feel patient with a journey deferred so late.

I have chosen the sea, since roads by land, if on the level, are flooded by rivers; if on higher ground, are beset with rocks. Since Tuscany and since the Aurelian highway,[c] after suffering the outrages of Goths with fire or sword, can no longer control forest with homestead or river with bridge, it is better to entrust my sails to the wayward sea.

[a] Rutilius feels the call of his ravaged estates in Gaul: see Introduction.

[b] *arbuta* is not used here in the restricted sense of *arbutus*.

[c] The Via Aurelia was the road by the coast of Etruria to the Italian Riviera. *Cf.* sense of *agger* in *medio in aggere*, Avianus, xvii. 15.

crebra relinquendis infigimus oscula portis:
  inviti superant limina sacra pedes.
oramus veniam lacrimis et laude litamus, 45
  in quantum fletus currere verba sinit:

"exaudi, regina tui pulcherrima mundi,
  inter sidereos Roma recepta polos,
exaudi, genetrix hominum genetrixque deorum,
  non procul a caelo per tua templa sumus: 50
te canimus semperque, sinent dum fata, canemus:
  sospes nemo potest immemor esse tui.
obruerint citius scelerata oblivia solem,
  quam tuus ex nostro corde recedat honos.
nam solis radiis aequalia munera tendis, 55
  qua circumfusus fluctuat Oceanus.
volvitur ipse tibi, qui continet omnia, Phoebus
  eque tuis ortos in tua condit equos.
te non flammigeris Libye tardavit harenis,
  non armata suo reppulit Ursa gelu: 60
quantum vitalis natura tetendit in axes,
  tantum virtuti pervia terra tuae.
fecisti patriam diversis gentibus unam:
  profuit iniustis te dominante capi.
dumque offers victis proprii consortia iuris, 65
  urbem fecisti quod prius orbis erat.

"auctores generis Venerem Martemque fatemur,
  Aeneadum matrem Romulidumque patrem:

52 sospes VRB: hospes *Cuperus, Baehrens.*
58 ortus VB: ortas R: ortos *Castalio.*
64 iniustis VB: inustis R: invitis *Juretus, Damm, Mueller, Baehrens*: invictis *Castalio*: infestis *Schrader.*

[a] Baehrens' alteration to *nutrix* is purely arbitrary, even in the light of *altricem* in 146.

Repeated kisses I imprint on the gates I have to leave: unwillingly my feet cross the honoured threshold. In tears I beseech pardon (for my departure) and offer a sacrifice of praise, so far as weeping allows the words to run:

"Listen, O fairest queen of thy world, Rome, welcomed amid the starry skies, listen, thou mother [a] of men and mother of gods, thanks to thy temples we are not far from heaven: thee do we chant, and shall, while destiny allows, for ever chant. None can be safe if forgetful of thee. Sooner shall guilty oblivion whelm the sun than the honour due to thee quit my heart: for thy benefits extend as far as the sun's rays, where the circling Ocean-flood bounds the world. For thee the very Sun-God who holdeth all together [b] doth revolve: his steeds that rise in thy domains he puts in thy domains to rest. Thee Africa hath not stayed with scorching sands, nor hath the Bear, armed with its native cold, repulsed thee. As far as living nature hath stretched towards the poles, so far hath earth opened a path for thy valour. For nations far apart thou hast made a single fatherland; under thy dominion captivity hath meant profit even for those who knew not justice: [c] and by offering to the vanquished a share in thine own justice, thou hast made a city of what was erstwhile a world.

"As authors of our race we acknowledge Venus and Mars—mother of the sons of Aeneas, father of

[b] *Cf. Einsied. Ecl.* I. 29–31 and note *b*, p. 329 *supra*.
[c] *iniustis* has its point in relation to *iuris*, l. 65.

mitigat armatas victrix clementia vires,
convenit in mores nomen utrumque tuos: 70
hinc tibi certandi bona parcendique voluptas:
quos timuit superat, quos superavit amat.
inventrix oleae colitur vinique repertor
et qui primus humo pressit aratra puer;
aras Paeoniam meruit medicina per artem, 75
factus et Alcides nobilitate deus:
tu quoque, legiferis mundum complexa triumphis,
foedere communi vivere cuncta facis.
te, dea, te celebrat Romanus ubique recessus
pacificoque gerit libera colla iugo. 80
omnia perpetuo quae servant sidera motu,
nullum viderunt pulchrius imperium.
quid simile Assyriis conectere contigit armis?
Medi finitimos condomuere suos;
magni Parthorum reges Macetumque tyranni 85
mutua per varias iura dedere vices.
nec tibi nascenti plures animaeque manusque,
sed plus consilii iudiciique fuit.
iustis bellorum causis nec pace superba
nobilis ad summas gloria venit opes. 90
quod regnas minus est quam quod regnare mereris:
excedis factis grandia fata tuis.

[70] numen *Barth, Baehrens.*
[76] fretus VRB (*in marg.* factus · f · V): factus *multi editores*: cretus *Canneg.*: fertur *Baehrens*: fretus it *Barth.*
[81] perpetuos . . . motus VRB: *corr. Baehrens.*
[84] condomuere *Mueller*: cum domuere VRB.

---

[a] *i.e.* of the two divinities Venus and Mars.
[b] The three alluded to are Athene (Minerva), Bacchus, and Triptolemus.

the scions of Romulus: clemency in victory tempers armed strength: both names [a] befit thy character: hence thy noble pleasure in war and in mercy: it vanquishes the dreaded foe and cherishes the vanquished. The goddess who found the olive-tree is worshipped, the deity too who discovered wine, and the youth who first drove the ploughshare in the soil; [b] the healing art through the skill of the god Paeon [c] won altars: Hercules by his renown was made divine: thou, too, who hast embraced the world in triumphs fraught with law, dost make all things live under a common covenant. Thee, O goddess, thee every nook of the Roman dominion celebrates, beneath a peaceful yoke holding necks unenslaved. The stars, which watch all things in their unceasing motion, never looked on a fairer empire. What like unto thy power did it fall to Assyrian arms to link in one? The Persians only subdued neighbours of their own. The mighty Parthian kings and Macedonian monarchs [d] imposed laws on each other through varying changes. It was not that at thy birth thou hadst more souls and hands: but more prudence and more judgement were thine. By wars for justifiable cause and by peace imposed without arrogance thy renowned glory reached highest wealth. That thou reignest is less than that thou deservest to reign: thy deeds surpass thine exalted destiny. To review thy high

[c] *Paeŏniam:* the Greek adjective is παιώνιος. Rutilius is not, however, unclassical here; for Ingram (*Hermathena* ix. 407) illustrates the use of *Paeonius* in Virgil, Ovid, and other poets: *cf.* Avianus vi. 7, *Paeonio magistro.*

[d] The Seleucid kings of Syria, who succeeded to part of the empire won by Alexander of Macedon, and whose wars with Parthia brought sometimes victory, sometimes defeat.

percensere labor densis decora alta tropaeis
  ut si quis stellas pernumerare velit;
confunduntque vagos delubra micantia visus: 95
  ipsos crediderim sic habitare deos.
quid loquar aerio pendentes fornice rivos,
  qua vix imbriferas tolleret Iris aquas?
hos potius dicas crevisse in sidera montes;
  tale giganteum Graecia laudet opus. 100
intercepta tuis conduntur flumina muris;
  consumunt totos celsa lavacra lacus.
nec minus et propriis celebrantur roscida venis
  totaque nativo moenia fonte sonant.
frigidus aestivas hinc temperat halitus auras, 105
  innocuamque levat purior unda sitim.
nempe tibi subitus calidarum gurges aquarum
  rupit Tarpeias hoste premente vias.
si foret aeternus, casum fortasse putarem:
  auxilio fluxit, qui rediturus erat. 110
quid loquar inclusas inter laquearia silvas,
  vernula qua vario carmine ludit avis?
vere tuo numquam mulceri desinit annus;
  deliciasque tuas victa tuetur hiemps.

[96] credideris hic *Burman.* [109] externus R.
[111] inter VRB : subter *Baehrens.*
[112] quae VR: qua *Castalio.* ludat VRB: ludit *Panv.*: laudat *Baehrens.*

---

[a] The aqueducts of Rome, massive enough to be called "Cyclopean" (*giganteum opus*, 100), like the masonry at Tiryns or of the Lion Gateway at Mycenae. In the time of Frontinus, who was *curator aquarum* A.D. 97–106, there were nine aqueducts; later, this number was increased.

[b] The hyperbole means that hardly any rainbow in the sky could reach the same height as the span of the arches of the aqueducts. Burman suggested that *quo* might be clearer than *qua*.

honours amid crowded trophies were a task like endeavouring to reckon up the stars. The glittering temples dazzle the wandering eyes: I could well believe such are the dwelling-places of the very gods. What shall I say of streams suspended on airy arches,[a] where scarce the Rainbow-Goddess could raise her showery waters?[b] You might rather call them mountains grown up to the sky: such a structure Greece would praise, as giant-wrought. Rivers[c] diverted are lost sight of within thy walls: the lofty baths consume whole lakes.[d] No less are thy dewy meads filled also with their own rivulets, and all thy walls are a-babble with springs from the soil. Hence a breath of coolness tempers the summer air, and the crystal well relieves a harmless thirst. Nay, once a sudden torrent of waters seething hot broke forth, when thine enemy[e] trod the roads by the Capitol: had it lasted for ever, mayhap I had deemed this mere chance; but it was to save thee that it flowed; for it came only to vanish. Why speak of woods enclosed amid thy panelled palaces,[f] where native birds sport with varied song? In the spring that is thine never does the year fail in its mildness: baffled winter respects thy charms.

[c] *e.g.* water from the Anio supplied the aqueducts called *Anio Vetus* and *Anio Novus*.

[d] *celsa* refers to the imposing loftiness of the public baths; *lacus* to such lakes as Alsietinus, Sabatinus (Lago di Bracciano) and Sublacensis (near Subiaco), from which water was brought into Rome by aqueducts and stored in large cisterns.

[e] Legend had it that when Titus Tatius and his Sabines reached the gate of Janus under the Capitol, the god sent out boiling water from the earth and discomfited the enemy.

[f] The reference is to gardens enclosed within colonnades which had panelled ceilings.

"erige crinales lauros seniumque sacrati 115
  verticis in virides, Roma, refinge comas.
aurea turrigero radient diademata cono,
  perpetuosque ignes aureus umbo vomat!
abscondat tristem deleta iniuria casum:
  contemptus solidet vulnera clausa dolor. 120
adversis sollenne tuis sperare secunda:
  exemplo caeli ditia damna subis.
astrorum flammae renovant occasibus ortus;
  lunam finiri cernis, ut incipiat.
victoris Brenni non distulit Allia poenam; 125
  Samnis servitio foedera saeva luit;
post multas Pyrrhum clades superata fugasti;
  flevit successus Hannibal ipse suos:
quae mergi nequeunt nisu maiore resurgunt
  exsiliuntque imis altius acta vadis; 130
utque novas vires fax inclinata resumit,
  clarior ex humili sorte superna petis.
porrige victuras Romana in saecula leges,
  solaque fatales non vereare colos,
quamvis sedecies denis et mille peractis 135
  annus praeterea iam tibi nonus eat.
quae restant nullis obnoxia tempora metis,
  dum stabunt terrae, dum polus astra feret!
illud te reparat quod cetera regna resolvit:
  ordo renascendi est crescere posse malis. 140

116 recinge VRB, *Vessereau*: refinge *Heinsius et fere omnes*.
137 maestis *Baehrens*.

[a] *Cf.* Lucan I. 185–190, where Roma, wearing a mural crown, appears to Caesar at the Rubicon, *turrigero canos effundens vertice crines*.

[b] Four examples of recovery are cited: (1) the defeat of Rome at the Allia in 390 B.C. was soon avenged by the death of Brennus, the Gallic leader; (2) the subjection of the Samnites compensated for the severe terms imposed by them

"Raise, O Rome, the triumphal laurels which wreathe thy locks, and refashion the hoary eld of thy hallowed head to tresses fresh and fair. Golden let the diadem flash on thy tower-crowned helmet[a]; let the golden buckler belch forth perpetual fires! Let forgetfulness of thy wrongs bury the sadness of misfortune; let pain disregarded close and heal thy wounds. Amidst failure it is thy way to hope for prosperity: after the pattern of the heavens losses undergone enrich thee. For flaming stars set only to renew their rising; thou seest the moon wane to wax afresh. The Allia did not hinder Brennus' penalty; the Samnite paid for a cruel treaty by slavery; after many disasters, though defeated, thou didst put Pyrrhus to flight; Hannibal himself was the mourner of his own successes.[b] Things which cannot be sunk rise again with greater energy, sped higher in their rebound from lowest depths; and, as the torch held downward regains fresh strength, so from lowly fortune thou dost soar more radiant aloft. Spread forth the laws that are to last throughout the ages of Rome: alone thou needst not dread the distaffs of the Fates, though with a thousand years and sixteen decades o'erpast, thou hast besides a ninth year in its course.[c] The span which doth remain is subject to no bounds, so long as earth shall stand firm and heaven uphold the stars! That same thing builds thee up which wrecks all other realms: the law of thy new birth is the power to thrive upon thine ills.

on the Romans at the Caudine Forks, 321 B.C.; (3) King Pyrrhus' successes in his invasion changed to disaster at Beneventum, 275 B.C.; (4) Hannibal's victories in the Second Punic War ended in defeat.

[c] The year 1169 of Rome gives the date A.D. 416.

"ergo age, sacrilegae tandem cadat hostia gentis:
  submittant trepidi perfida colla Getae.
ditia pacatae dent vectigalia terrae:
  impleat augustos barbara praeda sinus.
aeternum tibi Rhenus aret, tibi Nilus inundet, 145
  altricemque suam fertilis orbis alat.
quin et fecundas tibi conferat Africa messes,
  sole suo dives, sed magis imbre tuo.
interea et Latiis consurgant horrea sulcis,
  pinguiaque Hesperio nectare prela fluant. 150
ipse triumphali redimitus harundine Thybris
  Romuleis famulas usibus aptet aquas;
atque opulenta tibi placidis commercia ripis
  devehat hinc ruris, subvehat inde maris.

"pande, precor, gemino placatum Castore pontum; 155
  temperet aequoream dux Cytherea viam,
si non displicui, regerem cum iura Quirini,
  si colui sanctos consuluique patres;
nam quod nulla meum strinxerunt crimina ferrum,
  non sit praefecti gloria, sed populi. 160
sive datur patriis vitam componere terris,
  sive oculis umquam restituere meis,
fortunatus agam votoque beatior omni,
  semper digneris si meminisse mei."

---

[a] For the ancient idea that the north wind brought to Africa rain-clouds gathered in Italy *cf.* Stat. *Theb.* VIII. 411; Lucan, III. 68–70; IX. 420–423.

[b] The prayer is that traffic and trade may revive, now that Alaric has withdrawn.

[c] The name of either of the twin Dioscuri may do duty for the other: *cf.* Hor. *Od.* III. xxix. 64, *geminusque Pollux*; in Catull. iv. 27 both are invoked, but only one named, *gemelle*

"Come, then, let an impious race fall in sacrifice at last: let the Goths in panic abase their forsworn necks. Let lands reduced to peace pay rich tribute and barbarian booty fill thy majestic lap. Evermore let the Rhineland plough for thee, for thee the Nile o'erflow; and let a teeming world give nurture to its nurse. Yea, let Africa proffer to thee her fertile harvests, rich in her own sun, but richer for thy showers.[a] Meanwhile may granaries too arise to house the furrow-crops of Latium, and with the nectar of the West may sleek wine-presses flow. Let Tiber's self, garlanded with triumphal reed, apply his waters to serve the needs of Romulus' race, and 'twixt his peaceful banks bear for thee down-stream the wealthy cargoes of the fields and up-stream those of the sea.[b]

"Outstretch, I pray, the level main lulled to rest 'neath Castor and his twin brother; [c] be our Lady of Cythera the guide to smooth my watery path, if I found favour when I administered Quirinus' laws,[d] if to the venerable senators I showed respect and from them asked advice; for that ne'er a crime unsheathed my magisterial sword must be the people's, not the prefect's, boast.[e] Whether 'tis granted to lay my life to rest in ancestral soil or whether thou shalt one day be restored to my eyes, blest shall my life be, lucky beyond all aspiration, if thou deign always to remember me."

Castor et gemelle Castoris. There was a temple of Castor and Pollux at Ostia, and one of Venus on the island at the Tiber-mouth; hence the allusion to *Cytherea.*

[d] Rutilius had been *praefectus urbis* in A.D. 414; *cf.* I. 423–428; 467–468.

[e] The absence of capital punishment during Rutilius' prefecture was a credit to the Roman people.

his dictis iter arripimus : comitantur amici : 165
dicere non possunt lumina sicca " vale."
iamque aliis Romam redeuntibus haeret eunti
Rufius, Albini gloria viva patris;
qui Volusi antiquo derivat stemmate nomen
et reges Rutulos teste Marone refert. 170
huius facundae commissa palatia linguae:
primaevus meruit principis ore loqui.
rexerat ante puer populos pro consule Poenos;
aequalis Tyriis terror amorque fuit.
sedula promisit summos instantia fasces: 175
si fas est meritis fidere, consul erit.
invitum tristis tandem remeare coegi:
corpore divisos mens tamen una tenet.

tum demum ad naves gradior, qua fronte bicorni
dividuus Tiberis dexteriora secat. 180
laevus inaccessis fluvius vitatur harenis;
hospitis Aeneae gloria sola manet.

166 non possum sicca dicere luce vale *nonnulli editores.*
175 imitantia V : imitatio RB (*sic etiam in marg.* V, *sed expunctum*) : instantia *Mueller.*
178 ter et (*in marg.* tenet · f ·) V : tenet R.
180 secat V : petit R.

---

[a] Ceionius Rufius Volusianus belonged to an official family of ancient pedigree. He had been proconsul of Africa with his headquarters at Carthage (I. 173), and as a youthful imperial quaestor had performed the duty of reading before the senate communications from the Emperor (I. 171). Rutilius expresses his delight over the news of his friend's appointment to the city prefecture (I. 415–428).

[b] Rufius Albinus, prefect of the city in A.D. 390, should be distinguished from the Albinus of I. 466.

With these words we take the road: our friends attend. Eyes cannot tearless say "good-bye." And now while others wend their way back to Rome, Rufius,[a] the living glory of his father Albinus,[b] clings close to me on my way. He draws his name from the ancient pedigree of Volusus, citing Rutilian princes on the witness of Virgil.[c] To his power of eloquence was entrusted the imperial palace: in youth he was the fitting spokesman of the emperor. Still earlier, a mere stripling, he had governed as pro-consul the Carthaginian peoples and among the Tyrian folk inspired dread and love alike. His zealous energy gave promise of highest office: if it is permitted to trust desert, a consul he will be. In the end I sadly forced him to go back reluctant: yet, though in body severed, one mind keeps us linked.

Then at length I proceed to the ships,[d] where with twy-horned brow the branching Tiber cleaves his way to the right.[e] The channel on the left is avoided for its unapproachable sands: its one remaining boast is to have welcomed Aeneas.[f] And now the

[c] The family claimed descent from the Volusus addressed by Turnus, prince of the Rutuli, in *Aeneid* XI. 463.

[d] There were several boats (*cymbae* I. 219) used by Rutilius' company on their coasting voyage northwards: *cf.* I. 559, *puppibus ergo meis.*

[e] About eighteen miles from Rome and some miles from the sea the Tiber branches so as to form the Isola Sacra (*cf. Aeneid* VIII. 727, *Rhenusque bicornis,* referring to the two mouths of the Rhine: the "horn" idea is associated with the bull-like force of rivers in flood). At the mouth of the left branch was Ostia, the ancient port of Rome, which in time became blocked up with silt and sand. On the right branch harbour-works were undertaken by the Emperor Claudius and improved by Trajan.

[f] For Aeneas' landing see *Aeneid* VII. 29 *sqq.*

et iam nocturnis spatium laxaverat horis
  Phoebus Chelarum pallidiore polo.
cunctamur temptare salum portuque sedemus, 185
  nec piget oppositis otia ferre moris,
occidua infido dum saevit gurgite Plias
  dumque procellosi temporis ira calet.
respectare iuvat vicinam saepius urbem
  et montes visu deficiente sequi, 190
quaque duces oculi grata regione fruuntur,
  dum se, quod cupiunt, cernere posse putant.
nec locus ille mihi cognoscitur indice fumo,
  qui dominas arces et caput orbis habet
(quamquam signa levis fumi commendat Homerus, 195
  dilecto quotiens surgit in astra solo);
sed caeli plaga candidior tractusque serenus
  signat septenis culmina clara iugis.
illic perpetui soles atque ipse videtur
  quem sibi Roma facit purior esse dies. 200
saepius attonitae resonant Circensibus aures;
  nuntiat accensus plena theatra favor:
pulsato notae redduntur ab aethere voces,
  vel quia perveniunt vel quia fingit amor.

[188] cadit VRB: calet *Mueller*: cadet *Ussani*.
[191] feruntur *Baehrens*.

---

[a] The Scorpion is next to Libra among the signs of the Zodiac: the sun enters Libra at the autumnal Equinox. Poets use either *Chelae* (claws) or *Libra* (balance) in reference to this season.

sun in the paler sky of the Scorpion's Claws had lengthened the space of the night-watches.[a] We hesitate to make trial of the sea; we tarry in the haven, unreluctant to endure idleness amid the delays which bar our voyage, so long as the setting Pleiad storms upon the treacherous main, and the anger of the squally season is hot.[b] It is a joy to look back many a time at the city still near, and with scarce availing sight to trace its hills, and look where the guiding eyes[c] feast on that dear scene, fancying they can see what they desire to see. Nor is yonder place, which holds the imperial citadels and the world's capital, recognised by me in virtue of the smoke which marks it out (and yet 'tis the signs of light smoke which Homer[d] praises whensoever it rises starward from a well-loved land); nay rather a fairer tract of sky and a serene expanse marks the clear summits of the Seven Hills. There 'tis lasting sunshine: the very daylight which Rome makes for herself seems purer than all else. Time and again our spell-bound ears ring with the noise of the Circus games;[e] a blaze of cheers proclaims the crowded theatre: familiar shouts are sent back by the echoing air, whether it is that they really reach us or that affection fancies so.

[b] If *cadit*, 188, is kept in the sense of "subsides," it involves taking *dum* as "while" in 187 and as "until" in 188 (unless *cadit* can here mean "descends" or "swoops" upon the sea). *Calet* is accepted from L. Mueller.

[c] *Cf. oculique duces rem credere cogunt, Aetna* 189. He can just make out the hills of Rome, and part of the city he can see in imagination only, his eyes directing him to where it should be.

[d] *Cf. Odyss.* I. 57–59; X. 29–30.

[e] The *Ludi Romani* began in Rutilius' time on Sept. 21 and so fit into the autumnal setting of his voyage.

explorata fides pelagi ter quinque diebus, 205
  dum melior lunae se daret aura novae.
tum discessurus studiis urbique remitto
  Palladium, generis spemque decusque mei.
facundus iuvenis Gallorum nuper ab arvis
  missus Romani discere iura Fori. 210
ille meae secum dulcissima vincula curae,
  filius affectu, stirpe propinquus, habet:
cuius Aremoricas pater Exuperantius oras
  nunc postliminium pacis amare docet;
leges restituit libertatemque reducit 215
  et servos famulis non sinit esse suis.

solvimus Aurorae dubio, quo tempore primum
  agnosci patitur redditus arva color.
progredimur parvis per litora proxima cymbis,
  quorum perfugio crebra pateret humus. 220
aestivos penetrent oneraria carbasa fluctus:
  tutior autumnus mobilitate fugae.
Alsia praelegitur tellus, Pyrgique recedunt—
  nunc villae grandes, oppida parva prius.
iam Caeretanos demonstrat navita fines: 225
  aevo deposuit nomen Agylla vetus.
stringimus ⟨hinc effractum⟩ et fluctu et tempore Castrum:
  index semiruti porta vetusta loci.

[205] explorata VRB: expectata *Schrader.*
[206] fideret VRB: se daret *Heinsius*: *alii alia* (*e.g.* sideret, funderet).
[211] cunę V: curę R.
[227] *lacunam alii aliter suppleverunt*: hinc exesum *Barth*: hinc effractum *Keene in not.*: expugnatum *Baehrens.*

---

[a] Palladius, the last of Rutilius' circle to take leave of him before his voyage, was a young relative of his who had come

Thrice five days we watched the trust to be placed in the sea, until a new moon's more favourable breeze should present itself. Then on the eve of going I send back to his studies and the city Palladius, the hope and honour of my race.[a] That eloquent youth had been sent of late from the lands of the Gauls to learn the laws of the Roman courts. My son in affection and kinsman by blood, he holds the fondest ties of my regard. Even now his father Exuperantius trains the Armoric sea-board to love the recovery of peace; he re-establishes the laws, brings freedom back and suffers not the inhabitants to be their servants' slaves.[b]

In the half-dawn we weigh anchor, at the hour of day when colour is first restored and lets the fields grow visible. In little boats we make way along the nearest shores, so that a beach might always lie open as refuge for them. Let cargo-ships 'neath canvas plough through the summer waves: safer is autumn if we have quickness to escape. The Alsian land is skirted, and Pyrgi fades into the distance[c]—to-day large country-houses, in earlier days small towns. Now the sailor points out the bounds of Caere: the ancient Agylla has lost its name through time.[d] Next we coast by Castrum, shattered both by wave and time: an age-worn gateway marks the half-ruined place. O'er it

from Gaul to study law in Rome. His father, Exuperantius, had restored order to the Armorican regions in Gaul, which had followed the example of revolt from the empire set by Britain in A.D. 407.

[b] The reference is most probably to a servile insurrection which Exuperantius checked.

[c] Alsium, now Palo, was an ancient Etrurian town. Pyrgi, now Santa Severa, was a seaport for Caere.

[d] Caere, now Cervetri, had Agylla as its Greek name.

praesidet, exigui formatus imagine saxi,
  qui pastorali cornua fronte gerit: 230
multa licet priscum nomen deleverit aetas,
  hoc Inui castrum fama fuisse putat,
seu Pan Tyrrhenis mutavit Maenala silvis
  sive sinus patrios incola Faunus init;
dum renovat largo mortalia semina fetu, 235
  fingitur in venerem pronior esse deus.

ad Centumcellas forti defleximus Austro:
  tranquilla puppes in statione sedent.
molibus aequoreum concluditur amphitheatrum,
  angustosque aditus insula facta tegit; 240
attollit geminas turres bifidoque meatu
  faucibus artatis pandit utrumque latus.
nec posuisse satis laxo navalia portu;
  ne vaga vel tutas ventilet aura rates,
interior medias sinus invitatus in aedes 245
  instabilem fixis aera nescit aquis;
qualis in Euboicis captiva natatibus unda
  sustinet alterno bracchia lenta sinu.

nosse iuvat tauri dictas de nomine thermas;
  nec mora difficilis milibus ire tribus. 250

[229–230] *distichon post* 232 *posuit Damm.*
[232] Inui VB : Iani R.
[235] dumve novat *Baehrens.* longo V : largo RB. semina VRB : saecula *Mueller.*
[250] difficilis VRB : distantis (*sc.* thermas) *Baehrens.*

---

[a] Rutilius confuses Castrum Novum in Etruria with Castrum Inui in Latium: *cf. Aen.* VI. 775. *Init* in 234 is an attempt to explain the name Inuus, here identified with the Greek Pan or the Latin Faunus.

[b] For *dum* causal, assigning a reason, *cf.* Plaut. *Trin.* 1149–50 *dum vereor sermonem interrumpere, solus sto*; and Cic. *Ad Att.*

stands guard, fashioned as a little statue in stone, the figure of one with horns upon his shepherd's brow: although long years have blotted out the earliest name, legend considers this was once "Castrum Inui,"[a] whether it be that Pan exchanged Maenalus for Tuscan woods or that Faunus comes in to haunt his native dells: since[b] he reneweth the offspring of mankind with plenteous births, the god is represented over-prone to venery.

To Centumcellae[c] we changed our tack before a strong South wind: our ships find mooring in the calm roadstead. An amphitheatre of water is there enclosed by piers, and an artificial island shelters the narrow entrances; it rears twin towers and extends in both directions so as to leave a double approach with narrow channels. Nor was it enough to construct docks of wide harbourage; to keep the vagrant breeze from rocking the craft even when safe in port, an inner basin has been coaxed into the very midst of the buildings, and so, with its surface at rest, it knows naught of the wayward wind, like the water imprisoned in Cumae's baths[d] which buoys up the unhurried arms plied by the swimmer in alternate sweep.

We pay a pleasant visit to the hot springs named after a bull:[e] the distance of three miles seems no

I. xvi. 2 *qui* (*sc. Hortensius*) *dum veritus est . . . non vidit illud. . . .* Rutilius I. 443 may also be a parallel.

[c] Now Civita Vecchia. The port was constructed under Trajan: see the description in Plin. *Ep.* VI. xxxi. 15–17.

[d] Cumae, on the bay of Naples, was partly settled by Euboeans: *cf.* Virg. *Aen.* VI. 2: *Euboicis Cumarum allabitur oris.*

[e] Aquae or Thermae Taurianae, three miles N. of Civita Vecchia.

non illic gustu latices vitiantur amaro
  lymphave fumifico sulphure tincta calet:
purus odor mollisque sapor dubitare lavantem
  cogit qua melius parte petantur aquae.
credere si dignum famae, flagrantia taurus 255
  investigato fonte lavacra dedit,
ut solet excussis pugnam praeludere glaebis,
  stipite cum rigido cornua prona terit:
sive deus, faciem mentitus et ora iuvenci,
  noluit ardentis dona latere soli; 260
qualis Agenorei rapturus gaudia furti
  per freta virgineum sollicitavit onus.
ardua non solos deceant miracula Graios!
  auctorem pecudem fons Heliconis habet:
elicitas simili credamus origine lymphas, 265
  Musarum ⟨ut⟩ latices ungula fodit equi.
haec quoque Pieriis spiracula comparat antris
  carmine Messallae nobilitatus ager;
intrantemque capit discedentemque moratur
  postibus affixum dulce poema sacris. 270
hic est qui primo seriem de consule ducit,
  usque ad Publicolas si redeamus avos;

253 labantem VB, *corr. Simler*: molisque . . . labentem R.
261 tecti *Baehrens*.
263 solos . . . Graios V: solum . . . Graiis R.
265 en medicas *Baehrens*. nymphas V *et pler. edd. vett.*: lymphas *corr. Castalio et sic legitur in* R.
266 ut *addidit Damm*.

---

[a] *i.e.* whether for drinking or bathing.

[b] The bull that unearthed the hot wells may have been a disguised god, just as, according to the myth, the bull that carried off to Crete Europa, the daughter of the Phoenician king Agenor, was really Jupiter.

[c] The fountain Hippocrene on Mount Helicon in Boeotia,

troublesome delay. There the wells are not spoiled by a brackish flavour, nor is the water coloured and hot with fuming sulphur: the pure smell and delicate taste make the bather hesitate for what purpose the waters should better be used.[a] If the legend deserves credit, it was a bull that first revealed these hot baths by tracking out the source, when, tossing aloft the sods, as is a bull's way to prelude a fight, he grazed his downbent horns upon a hard tree-stump: or else a god, counterfeiting an ox-like shape and visage, would not permit the gift of the warm soil to lurk unseen; like the god who, bent on snatching stolen joys from his theft of Agenor's daughter, bore across the seas the terror-stricken maid.[b] Not Greeks alone must have the glory of marvels which o'ertop belief! The fount of Helicon has for its begetter an animal:[c] let us believe that through like origin these waters were drawn forth, as the steed's hoof dug out the Muses' well. The land also, blazoned in Messalla's poetry,[d] has these outlets to vie with the Pierian grots: and his sweet lines, affixed to the hallowed portals, capture the eye of him who enters, and makes him linger as he leaves. This is the man who traces his descent from the first consul, if we go back as far as his ancestors the Publicolae: he too with his nod as

sacred to the Muses, was fabled to have been produced by a stroke of the hoof of the winged horse Pegasus.

[d] Valerius Messalla, praetorian prefect in A.D. 396, is often mentioned in the Code of Theodosius. He claimed descent from Valerius Publicola, who became colleague to Junius Brutus on the retirement of Tarquinius Collatinus; so that "primo de consule," 271, is not literally accurate. Symmachus (VII. 81–92) addresses letters to him, and Sidonius Apollinaris admired his intellectual qualities (*Carm.* 9, 302).

hic et praefecti nutu praetoria rexit.
  sed menti et linguae gloria maior inest.
hic docuit qualem poscat facundia sedem: 275
  ut bonus esse velit, quisque disertus erit.

roscida puniceo fulsere crepuscula caelo:
  pandimus obliquo lintea flexa sinu.
paulisper litus fugimus Munione vadosum:
  suspecto trepidant ostia parva salo. 280
inde Graviscarum fastigia rara videmus,
  quas premit aestivae saepe paludis odor;
sed nemorosa viret densis vicinia lucis,
  pineaque extremis fluctuat umbra fretis.
cernimus antiquas nullo custode ruinas 285
  et desolatae moenia foeda Cosae.
ridiculam cladis pudet inter seria causam
  promere, sed risum dissimulare piget.
dicuntur cives quondam migrare coacti
  muribus infestos deseruisse Lares! 290
credere maluerim Pygmaeae damna cohortis
  et coniuratos in sua bella grues.
haud procul hinc petitur signatus ab Hercule portus:
  vergentem sequitur mollior aura diem.

[277] fulsere VB: luxere R.

---

[a] Quintilian repeatedly insists on character as indispensable in an orator: I. *proem.* 9–10 (*qui esse nisi vir bonus non potest*); II. ii. (the whole section); II. xv. 1; XII. i. 1 (*is qui a M. Catone finitur, vir bonus dicendi peritus*): *cf.* Cic. *de Orat.* II. 85.

prefect held praetorian control. Yet greater glory dwells in his mind and tongue. He has shown what kind of dwelling-place eloquence demands: each man's power in oratory will depend on his desire to be good.[a]

The half-light of dewy morn gleamed from a purple sky; we spread our sails bent in curves slantwise; and for a time give a wide berth to the shore which the Munio[b] blocks with shoals: the narrow river-mouth heaves restlessly with treacherous surf. Thereafter we sight the scattered housetops of Graviscae,[c] plagued often with a marshy smell in summer-time; and yet the wooded neighbourhood is green with close-grown groves, and pine-tree shadows wave o'er the margin of the sea. Then we descry, all unguarded now, desolate Cosa's ancient ruins and unsightly walls.[d] 'Tis with a qualm that I adduce mid serious things the comic reason for its downfall; but I am loath to suppress a laugh. The story runs that once upon a time the townsfolk were forced to migrate and left their homes behind because rats infested them! I'd sooner believe in losses suffered by the Pygmies' infantry[e] and in cranes leagued solemnly to fight their wars. Not far from here we make the port which the name of Hercules distinguishes: a softer breeze follows

[b] Now the Mignone.

[c] Graviscae, the port of Tarquinii, being in the Maremma, had unhealthy air. Like its pine-groves, this small place has disappeared.

[d] Cosa is now Ansedonia: its harbour was the Portus Herculis, now Porto Ercole.

[e] The first mention of Milton's "small infantry warred on by cranes" is in Homer, *Iliad* III. 3–6.

inter castrorum vestigia sermo retexit 295
Sardoam Lepido praecipitante fugam;
litore namque Cosae cognatos depulit hostes
virtutem Catuli Roma secuta ducis.
ille tamen Lepidus peior civilibus armis
qui gessit sociis impia bella tribus, 300
qui libertatem Mutinensi Marte receptam
obruit auxiliis urbe pavente novis.
insidias paci moliri tertius ausus
tristibus excepit congrua fata reis.
quartus, Caesareo dum vult irrepere regno, 305
incesti poenam solvit adulterii.
nunc quoque—sed melius de nostris fama queretur:
iudex posteritas semina dira notet.
nominibus certos credam decurrere mores?
moribus an potius nomina certa dari? 310
quicquid id est, mirus Latiis annalibus ordo,
quod Lepidum totiens reccidit ense malum.

necdum discussis pelago permittimur umbris:
natus vicino vertice ventus adest.

302 pavente V: gemente R: favente B.
313 decessis VRB: discussis *Almeloveen*: detersis *Heinsius*. permittitur VRB: permittimur *Castalio*.

---

[a] Four Lepidi are here alluded to: (1) M. Aemilius Lepidus, declared a public enemy by the Senate in 77 B.C., was after his defeat at the Mulvian Bridge pursued by Catulus into Etruria. He eventually fled from Portus Herculis to Sardinia. (2) His son, M. Aemilius Lepidus, who had long wavered

declining day. Amid the traces of his camp our conversation weaves again the tale of Lepidus in headlong flight to Sardinia;[a] for 'twas from Cosa's shore that Rome, following the lead of valiant Catulus, drove off the foes of her own blood. Yet was that Lepidus more a villain, who mid civil strife, in a confederacy of three, waged impious warfare; whose reinforcements—to the city's dread—crushed the freedom recovered in battle at Mutina. A third of the name ventured to contrive a plot against the peace and met a fate that fits luckless defendants. A fourth, aiming at a stealthy inroad on imperial power, paid the penalty of foul adultery. To-day also—but of the Lepidi of our day fame will draw up a better indictment: let posterity be the judge to brand the ill-omened stock. Am I to believe that definite characters descend from names or rather that definite names are given to characters? However that be, it is a strange routine in the chronicles of Latium that misfortune has so often recurred through the sword of the Lepidi.[b]

The shades of night as yet are undispelled when we entrust ourselves to the sea. Born of the neighbouring hill-crest, a breeze befriends us. Mount

between Mark Antony and the Senate, joined forces with Antony after the battle of Mutina in 44 B.C. The allusion in l. 300 is to his membership of the triumvirate with Antony and Octavian. (3) The triumvir's son plotted in 30 B.C. to murder Octavian, but was arrested and sent to Octavian, then in the East, where he was put to death. (4) M. Aemilius Lepidus was the second husband of Drusilla, Caligula's sister. He conspired against his imperial brother-in-law, and had illicit relations with Agrippina and Livilla, two other sisters of the emperor. He was executed in A.D. 39.

[b] *Lepidum*: genit. plur. rather than adjectivally with *malum*.

tenditur in medias mons Argentarius undas 315
ancipitique iugo caerula curva premit;
transversos colles bis ternis milibus artat;
circuitu ponti ter duodena patet:
qualis per geminos fluctus Ephyreius Isthmos
Ionias bimari litore findit aquas. 320
vix circumvehimur sparsae dispendia rupis,
nec sinuosa gravi cura labore caret:
mutantur totiens vario spiramina flexu:
quae modo profuerant vela repente nocent.
eminus Igilii silvosa cacumina miror, 325
quam fraudare nefas laudis honore suae.
haec proprios nuper tutata est insula saltus,
sive loci ingenio seu domini genio,
gurgite cum modico victricibus obstitit armis
tamquam longinquo dissociata mari: 330
haec multos lacera suscepit ab urbe fugatos,
hic fessis posito certa timore salus.
plurima terreno populaverat aequora bello
contra naturam classe timendus eques:

317 ternis VB: denis R.
322 cura VRB: terra *Almeloveen, Baehrens.*

---

[a] Monte Argentario, a rugged peninsular promontory over 20 miles in circuit, has two peaks (*ancipiti iugo*)—the southern one above Porto Ercole, and the northern one above Porto S. Stefano.

[b] The promontory of Monte Argentario is likened to the isthmus of Corinth (= *Ephyre,* frequently in the poets from Homer onwards). In strict accuracy, the Ionian sea lies on one side only of the isthmus, the Aegean being on the other side.

[c] Igilium, now Giglio, was, as an island, reasonably safe from invasion by the Goths (l. 329), whether in A.D. 408

Argentarius juts out amidst the waves and with two-fold ridge[a] confines the blue waters of its bays, shortening the road across the hills to twice three miles, while its extent round by sea is three times twelve, even as the Corinthian isthmus betwixt twin floods cleaves the Ionian deep with shores which two seas wash.[b] We just succeed in doubling that long round of scattered crags, nor are the helmsman's anxious détours without heavy toil—so often puffs of wind change with each varying tack: the sails which helped a moment since are suddenly a drag. Far off I marvel at Igilium's [c] forest heights: 'twere sinful to cheat the island [d] of the homage which its fame deserves. Of late this isle defended its own glades, whether by natural position or by the emperor's supernatural powers,[e] when, though severed only by a moderate channel, it bade defiance to triumphant arms as if isolated by the far-dividing sea. It welcomed many refugees from mangled Rome: here might the weary drop their fear and find sure safety. A cavalry, which against nature's law spelt terror on shipboard, had harried many a sea with warfare suited to the land.[f] It is a miracle

when Alaric advanced to his first siege of Rome or in the following years. It offered refuge to fugitives from Rome when the city was sacked by Alaric in A.D. 410 (see l. 331).

[d] *quam*: *sc. insulam*, though its name Igilium is neuter.

[e] The alternatives (emphasized by a play on words) are that the island may have been protected either by the *ingenium* (= *natura*) *loci* or by the indwelling *Genius* of Honorius, which is viewed as a presiding *Fortuna* guarding the island against attack.

[f] The Gothic cavalry was reinforced by that of the Huns under Alaric's brother-in-law Ataulf. They sailed from island to island on marauding expeditions.

unum mira fides vario discrimine portum 335
tam prope Romanis, tam procul esse Getis.
tangimus Umbronem; non est ignobile flumen,
quod tuto trepidas excipit ore rates:
tam facilis pronis semper patet alveus undis,
in pontum quotiens saeva procella ruit. 340
hic ego tranquillae volui succedere ripae;
sed nautas avidos longius ire sequor.
sic festinantem ventusque diesque reliquit:
nec proferre pedem nec revocare licet.
litorea noctis requiem metamur harena: 345
dat vespertinos myrtea silva focos:
parvula subiectis facimus tentoria remis:
transversus subito culmine contus erat.

lux aderat: tonsis progressi stare videmur,
sed cursum prorae terra relicta probat. 350
occurrit Chalybum memorabilis Ilva metallis,
qua nihil uberius Norica glaeba tulit;
non Biturix largo potior strictura camino,
nec quae Sardonico caespite massa fluit.
plus confert populis ferri fecunda creatrix 355
quam Tartessiaci glarea fulva Tagi.

339 pronis *om.* R.
343 festinantem VRB: festinantes *Schrader, Baehrens.*
352 qua nihil . . . gleba V: qua mihi . . . terra R.

[a] *i.e.* at the time of the sack of Rome and of the Gothic sea-raids.
[b] *metari* is the regular verb for laying out a camp.
[c] Lit. "mines of the Chalybes." The Χάλυβες of Pontus were renowned for their working of steel (χάλυψ).
[d] Noricum, between the Danube and the Alps, corresponded to a great part of Styria and Carinthia and included the district round Salzburg. Its steel was famed: *cf.* Hor. *Od.* I. xvi. 9–10, *Noricus ensis.*

to believe that a single haven at crises different[a] should be so near the Romans, and for the Goths so far. We touch at Umbro's mouth: no inconsiderable stream, it welcomes panic-stricken barques at a safe entrance: such easy approach does the river-bed with its descending current ever offer, as often as a cruel tempest bursts upon the deep. Here I was minded to land upon the peaceful shore; but, as the mariners were greedy for further progress, I e'en follow: so, speeding on, I find that with day-light the breeze has failed: neither forward nor backward can we make way. So on the sand of the beach we mark out[b] our resting-place for the night: a myrtle wood provides our evening fires. We raise our little tents with oars as props: a pole set cross-wise helped to form a hastily fashioned roof.

Day came: though pushing on with oars, we seem to be at a standstill, and yet the receding land proves the movement of the bow. Across our course lies Elba, famous for its iron mines:[c] than it Norican[d] soil has produced no richer yield; nor is the wrought metal of the Bituriges preferable, though smelted in great furnaces;[e] nor the molten mass which pours from the Sardinian ore.[f] More good is done to the world by teeming earth which gives birth to iron than by the golden gravel washed down by the Tagus in the distant West;[g] for deadly gold is the

[e] The Bituriges of Gallia Aquitanica have left their name in Bourges. *Strictura*, wrought metal, implied smelting which could be carried out where firewood was abundant. Ore from Ilva (the modern Elba), which was short of fuel, had to be taken to furnaces on the mainland.

[f] *caespes*, lit. the clod or lump containing ore: *cf. glaeba*, 352.

[g] From Tartessus in Spain *Tartessiacus* gets its meaning of "Western."

materies vitiis aurum letale parandis:
  auri caecus amor ducit in omne nefas:
aurea legitimas expugnant munera taedas,
  virgineosque sinus aureus imber emit: 360
auro victa fides munitas decipit urbes:
  auri flagitiis ambitus ipse furit.
at contra ferro squalentia rura coluntur;
  ferro vivendi prima reperta via est:
saecula semideum, ferrati nescia Martis, 365
  ferro crudeles sustinuere feras:
humanis manibus non sufficit usus inermis,
  si non sint aliae ferrea tela manus.
his mecum pigri solabar taedia venti,
  dum resonat variis vile celeuma modis. 370

lassatum cohibet vicina Faleria cursum,
  quamquam vix medium Phoebus haberet iter.
et tum forte hilares per compita rustica pagi
  mulcebant sacris pectora fessa iocis:
illo quippe die tandem revocatus Osiris 375
  excitat in fruges germina laeta novas.
egressi villam petimus lucoque vagamur:
  stagna placent septo deliciosa vado.

357 fatale *Burman*: ferale *Baehrens*.
371 laxatum *Castalio*: lassantem *Baehrens*.
373 fagi VRB: pagi *Castalio*.
377 lucoque vagamur V: lŭtoque vagamus (*contra metrum*) R: petimusque luthoque vagamur B: ludoque vacamus *Wernsdorf*.

[a] The allusion in l. 360 is to the myth of Danaë and in l. 361 to the bribery employed by Philip of Macedon to capture cities. *Cf.* the attack on gold by Tiberianus, pp. 560–563 *supra*.

substance that makes vice: blind lust of gold leads into every crime: golden gifts carry by storm the troth of wedded brides: a golden shower can buy the maid's embraces:[a] loyalty sapped by gold betrays the well-walled town: by scandalous misuse of gold ambition itself pursues its wild career. But not so iron: it is with iron that neglected fields are tilled; by iron was the first way of living found. Races of demigods, who knew not iron-harnessed Mars, by iron faced the charge of savage beasts. For human hands their unarmed use is not enough, if iron weapons lent not other hands. Such thoughts of mine beguiled the weariness of a laggard wind, and all the time in varied notes the boatswain's trumpery refrain rang out.

The neighbouring Faleria[b] checks our weary course, though Phoebus scarce had reached his mid career. That day it happened merry village-bands along the country cross-roads soothed their jaded hearts with festal observances; it was in truth the day when, after long time restored, Osiris wakes the happy seeds to yield fresh produce.[c] Landing, we seek lodging,[d] and stroll within a wood; we like the ponds which charm with their shallow enclosed

[b] It is now Falese, or Porto di Faliesi.

[c] The worship of Osiris, introduced from Egypt in republican times, passed through vicissitudes of favour and disfavour, but spread widely through the Roman Empire. A vegetation-deity and patron of agriculture, Osiris was also a suffering hero and became god of the dead. The priests of his sister-wife Isis mourned his death or joyfully celebrated his periodic resuscitation. Here he gives a fertilizing stimulus to autumnal sowings.

[d] *Villam* here seems to mean an "inn": *cf. villicus* or *vilicus* as "innkeeper," I. 623.

ludere lascivos intra vivaria pisces
  gurgitis inclusi laxior unda sinit. 380
sed male pensavit requiem stationis amoenae
  hospite conductor durior Antiphate!
namque loci querulus curam Iudaeus agebat,
  humanis animal dissociale cibis:
vexatos frutices, pulsatas imputat algas, 385
  damnaque libatae grandia clamat aquae.
reddimus obscaenae convicia debita genti
  quae genitale caput propudiosa metit:
radix stultitiae, cui frigida sabbata cordi,
  sed cor frigidius religione sua. 390
septima quaeque dies turpi damnata veterno,
  tamquam lassati mollis imago dei.
cetera mendacis deliramenta catastae
  nec puerum in somnis credere posse reor.
atque utinam numquam Iudaea subacta fuisset 395
  Pompeii bellis imperiisque Titi!
latius excisae pestis contagia serpunt,
  victoresque suos natio victa premit.

adversus surgit Boreas; sed nos quoque remis
  surgere certamus, dum tegit astra dies. 400
proxima securum reserat Populonia litus,
  qua naturalem ducit in arva sinum.

379 inter VRB: intra *Schrader*.
382 dirior *Drakenborch*: crudior *Mueller*.
394 pueros omnes VB: puer õnes R: pueros parvos *vel* teneros *coniec. Baehrens*: pueros et anus *Keene in not.*: puerum in somnis *A. M. Duff*.
395 Iudea capta R.
396 imperioque B, *Baehrens*.

[a] The savage king of the Laestrygones devoured one of Ulysses' men and sank all his ships except that on which Ulysses sailed (*Odyss.* X. 114–132).

basin. The spacious waters of the imprisoned flood permit the playful fish to sport inside these preserves. But we were made to pay dear for the repose of this delightful halting-place by a lessee who was harsher than Antiphates as host! [a] For a crabbed Jew was in charge of the spot—a creature that quarrels with sound human food.[b] He charges in our bill for damaging his bushes and hitting the seaweed, and bawls about his enormous loss in water we had sipped. We pay the abuse due to the filthy race that infamously practises circumcision: a root of silliness they are: chill Sabbaths are after their own heart, yet their heart is chillier than their creed. Each seventh day is condemned to ignoble sloth, as 'twere an effeminate picture of a god fatigued.[c] The other wild ravings from their lying bazaar methinks not even a child in his sleep could believe. And would that Judaea had never been subdued by Pompey's wars and Titus' military power.[d] The infection of this plague, though excised, still creeps abroad the more: and 'tis their own conquerors that a conquered race keeps down.[e]

Against us rises a North wind; but we too strive with oars to rise, while daylight shrouds the stars. Close at hand Populonia opens up her safe coast, where she draws her natural bay well inland. No

[b] The taboo of the pig as unclean was unintelligible to Romans, whose cuisine included fifty different ways of serving swine's flesh.

[c] The reference is to the teaching of the Hebrew scriptures: *e.g. Genesis* ii. 2–3; *Exodus* xx. 9–11, xxxiv. 21.

[d] The Maccabean monarchy fell after Pompey's three months' siege of Jerusalem, 63 B.C. Titus captured Jerusalem in A.D. 70.

[e] *Cf.* Hor. *Epist.* II. i. 156, *Graecia capta ferum victorem cepit.*

non illic positas extollit in aethera moles
  lumine nocturno conspicienda Pharos;
sed speculam validae rupis sortita vetustas, 405
  qua fluctus domitos arduus urget apex,
castellum geminos hominum fundavit in usus,
  praesidium terris indiciumque fretis.
agnosci nequeunt aevi monumenta prioris:
  grandia consumpsit moenia tempus edax. 410
sola manent interceptis vestigia muris:
  ruderibus latis tecta sepulta iacent.
non indignemur mortalia corpora solvi:
  cernimus exemplis oppida posse mori.

laetior hic nostras crebrescit fama per aures: 415
  consilium Romam paene redire fuit.
hic praefecturam sacrae cognoscimus urbis
  delatam meritis, dulcis amice, tuis.
optarem verum complecti carmine nomen,
  sed quosdam refugit regula dura pedes. 420
cognomen versu † ⟨veniet⟩, carissime Rufi:
  illo te dudum pagina nostra canit.
festa dies pridemque meos dignata Penates
  poste coronato vota secunda colat:

421 cogn. versu veneris VB: cognomen venens (*om.* versu *contra metrum*) R: Veneri (*vocativus*) *Pith.*, *Burman*: cognomen serva, Veneri *Barth*, *Schrader*: c. versus servet *Damm*: c. versu dederis *Mueller*: c. versu capitur *Baehrens*: c. versu veniet *Vessereau*: c. v. veneror *Helm*: c. v. vehĕris *Préchac*.

---

[a] At Populonia, an ancient Etruscan town, there was an old castle instead of a lighthouse like the famous one on the island of Pharos off Alexandria.

[b] *Cf.* in Sulpicius' letter of consolation to Cicero, *Ad Fam.* IV. v., *nos homunculi indignamur, si quis nostrum interiit* . . .

Pharos,[a] conspicuous with nightly light, has piers built there which rise into the sky; but men long ago, finding a mighty cliff to serve as a look-out where the towering hill-crest overhangs the conquered waves, laid the foundations of a castle for twin services to man—a defence on land and signal-post for sea. The memorials of an earlier age cannot be recognised; devouring time has wasted its mighty battlements away. Traces only remain now that the walls are lost: under a wide stretch of rubble lie the buried homes. Let us not chafe that human frames dissolve: from precedents we discern that towns can die.[b]

Here a joyful piece of news spreads as we listen: it was almost my decision to go back to Rome. Here do we learn that the prefecture of the Sacred City has been bestowed upon your merits, beloved friend. I'd fain include your true name in my poem; but the strict law of metre avoids certain feet.[c] Your cognomen will come in a line,[d] dearest Rufius: by that name but recently my page has sung your praise.[e] Let a day of festivity, such as years ago honoured my own home with garlands on the door, now show respect to hopes fulfilled:[f] let green

quorum vita brevior esse debet, cum uno loco tot oppidum cadavera iacent?

[c] Rufius' full name, Ceionius Rufius Vŏlūsĭanus, is inadmissible in elegiacs.

[d] The vexed line, 421, whether *Veneri* is read as dative of *Venus* or as vocative of *Venerius*, offers no sure foundation for the addition of *Venerius* to the name of Rufius. Taking *Veneri* as vocative, some editors have thought Rutilius dedicated his poem to "Venerius" Rufius.

[e] *Supra*, lines 167–178.

[f] Rufius' elevation brings back to Rutilius' mind his own prefecture: *cf.* I. 157–160.

exornent virides communia gaudia rami : 425
provecta est animae portio magna meae.[a]
sic mihi, sic potius, placeat geminata potestas :
per quem malueram, rursus honore fruor.

currere curamus velis Aquilone reverso,
cum primum roseo fulsit Eous equo. 430
incipit obscuros ostendere Corsica montes,
nubiferumque caput concolor umbra levat :
sic dubitanda[b] solet gracili vanescere cornu
defessisque oculis luna reperta latet.
haec ponti brevitas auxit mendacia famae :[c] 435
armentale ferunt quippe natasse pecus,
tempore Cyrnaeas quo primum venit in oras
forte secuta vagum femina Corsa bovem.

processu pelagi iam se Capraria tollit ;
squalet lucifugis insula plena viris. 440
ipsi se monachos Graio cognomine dicunt,
quod soli nullo vivere teste volunt.
munera Fortunae metuunt, dum damna verentur :
quisquam sponte miser, ne miser esse queat ?
quaenam perversi rabies tam stulta cerebri, 445
dum mala formides, nec bona posse pati ?

---

[a] *Cf.* I. 493, *nostrae pars maxima mentis*, and Hor. *Od.* I. iii. 8, *animae dimidium meae.*

[b] *dubitanda* = to be puzzled over, an object of uncertainty: *cf.* Virg. *Aen.* VI. 454, *aut videt aut vidisse putat per nubila lunam.*

[c] Cyrnos (Κύρνος), or Corsica, lies about 55 miles off the mainland. Itasius Lemniacus denies that it could be seen

boughs be the decoration for the joy we share: a great part of mine own life [a] has been advanced to high place. Thus, aye thus to me let this renewal of office bring pleasure: once again I enjoy dignity through the one for whom I wished it more.

When the North wind veered, we took pains to run with sails before the breeze, as soon as the Morning-star gleamed on his rosy steed. Corsica begins to show her dim mountains, and, matched in colour, the mass of shadow makes the cloud-capped crest look higher still: so 'tis the moon's way with slender horn to fade leaving us puzzled,[b] and e'en though found she yet lies hid for straining eyes. The short sea-passage here has given support to a lying legend; for folk say a herd of cattle swam across at the time when first it happened that a woman called Corsa in quest of a stray ox reached the shores of Cyrnos.[c]

As we advance at sea, Capraria now rears itself—an ill-kept isle full of men who shun the light. Their own name [d] for themselves is a Greek one, "monachoi" (monks), because they wish to dwell alone with none to see. They fear Fortune's boons, as they dread her outrages: would anyone, to escape misery, live of his own choice in misery? What silly fanaticism of a distorted brain is it to be unable to endure even [e] blessings because of your terror of

from Populonia. The story ran that a herdswoman noticed an ox used to swim the sea and return fatter. This suggested that there was a fertile island not far away.

[d] *Cognomen* is the equivalent of *nomen* in several Virgilian passages: *Aen.* III. 163; VIII. 48. It is loosely used, *supra* I. 421.

[e] *Nec* has the force of *ne . . . quidem*, as in *nec puerum*, I. 394.

sive suas repetunt factorum ergastula poenas,
  tristia seu nigro viscera felle tument,
sic nimiae bilis morbum adsignavit Homerus
  Bellerophonteis sollicitudinibus: 450
nam iuveni offenso saevi post tela doloris
  dicitur humanum displicuisse genus.

in Volaterranum, vero Vada nomine, tractum
  ingressus dubii tramitis alta lego:
despectat prorae custos clavumque sequentem 455
  dirigit et puppim voce monente regit.
incertas gemina discriminat arbore fauces
  defixasque offert limes uterque sudes:
illis proceras mos est adnectere lauros
  conspicuas ramis et fruticante coma, 460
ut praebente algam densi symplegade limi
  servet inoffensas semita clara notas.
illic me rapidus consistere Corus adegit,
  qualis silvarum frangere lustra solet.
vix tuti domibus saevos toleravimus imbres: 465
  Albini patuit proxima villa mei.

[447] fatorum (*in marg.* factorum · f ·) V.
[456] derigit *Baehrens.*
[458] limus *Baehrens.*
[461] algam RB: viam V, *Baehrens*: ulvam *Kalinka, Préchac.*
[463] rabidus *Mueller, Baehrens.*

---

[a] *Ergastula,* "prisons for slaves," prob. by metonymy here for the inmates.

ills? Whether they are like prisoners [a] who demand the appropriate penalties for their deeds, or whether their melancholy hearts are swollen with black bile, it was even so that Homer assigned the ailment of excessive bile as cause of Bellerophon's troubled soul; [b] for it was after the wounds of a cruel sorrow that men say the stricken youth conceived his loathing for human kind.

Entering on the region of Volaterra, appropriately called "The Shallows," [c] I thread my way through the deep part of the treacherous channel. At the bow the look-out watches the water beneath and gives directions to the helm behind, guiding the stern with warning shouts. A boundary on each side marks the puzzling narrows by a pair of trees, and presents a line of piles hammered in there: to these it is the custom to fix tall laurels easy to see because of their branches and bushy foliage, so that, although the shifting bank [d] of thick mud shows its mass of sea-weed, a clear passage may keep the guiding-signs unstruck. There I was driven to make a halt by a tearing North-wester of the sort that is wont to shatter the depths of the woods. Scarce safe beneath a roof did we endure the pitiless rains: the neighbouring country-seat of my own Albinus was placed at my disposal. For my

[b] Homer in reality does not explain Bellerophon's misanthropy as due to black bile (μελαγχολία), though he describes him as "eating out his heart" (ὃν θυμὸν κατέδων *Il.* VI. 202). The true reason for his grief was the loss of his three children.

[c] The name is preserved in Torre di Vada.

[d] The shifting mud-bank is compared with the fabled Symplegades of the Euxine, the floating rocks which used to clash together and rebound.

namque meus, quem Roma meo subiunxit honori,
per quem iura meae continuata togae.
non exspectatos pensavit laudibus annos;
vitae flore puer, sed gravitate senex. 470
mutua germanos iunxit reverentia mores,
et favor alternis crevit amicitiis.
praetulit ille meas, cum vincere posset, habenas;
at decessoris maior amore fuit.

subiectas villae vacat adspectare salinas; 475
namque hoc censetur nomine salsa palus,
qua mare terrenis declive canalibus intrat
multifidosque lacus parvula fossa rigat.
ast ubi flagrantes admovit Sirius ignes,
cum pallent herbae, cum sitit omnis ager, 480
tum cataractarum claustris excluditur aequor,
ut fixos latices torrida duret humus.
concipiunt acrem nativa coagula Phoebum,
et gravis aestivo crusta calore coit;
haud aliter quam cum glacie riget horridus Hister 485
grandiaque adstricto flumine plaustra vehit.
rimetur solitus naturae expendere causas
inque pari dispar fomite quaerat opus:
vincta fluenta gelu concepto sole liquescunt,
et rursus liquidae sole gelantur aquae. 490

[471] amores *Baehrens.*
[487] solitas natura VRB : solitus naturae *Castalio* : solitus naturam *Baehrens.*
[489] conspecto VRB *et vulgo* : concepto *Baehrens* (*cf.* 483).

---

[a] Albinus succeeded Rutilius as Prefect of the city in A.D. 414.

[b] *i.e.* Albinus had been appointed to high office at a singularly early age; but, if he fell short of the usual number of years, he made up for this by his merits.

own he was whom Rome linked to me as successor in office,[a] in whose person my civil jurisdiction was continued. His merit outweighed years which had not been waited for:[b] a lad in the bloom of youth, he had the worth of age. Mutual respect joined our kindred characters, and regard grew from the friendship of one for the other. He preferred that I should hold the reins of power, although he might have surpassed me: yet his affection for his predecessor has made him a greater man.

We find time to inspect the salt-pans lying near the mansion: it is on this score that value is set upon the salt marsh, where the sea-water, running down through channels in the land, makes entry, and a little trench floods the many-parted ponds. But after the Dog-star has advanced his blazing fires, when grass turns pale, when all the land is athirst, then the sea is shut out by the barrier-sluices, so that the parched ground may solidify the imprisoned waters. The natural incrustations catch the penetrating sun, and in the summer heat the heavy crust of salt cakes, just as when the wild Danube stiffens with ice and carries huge wains upon its frost-bound stream. Let him who is given to weigh natural causes examine and investigate the different effect worked in the same material:[c] frost-bound streams melt on catching the sun, and on the other hand liquid waters can be hardened[d] in the sun.

[c] *fomes* "touchwood" is here "matter," "material," or "element"; and virtually "cause" in relation to *opus* = "working," "effect." (*Cf.* note on *opus* in *Aetna*, 337, *supra* p. 391.)

[d] *i.e.* by evaporation salt can be secured from brine. Compare Lucretius' lines on the baking and the thawing action of heat, VI. 962–969.

o, quam saepe malis generatur origo bonorum![a]
tempestas dulcem fecit amara moram;
Victorinus enim, nostrae pars maxima mentis,
congressu explevit mutua vota suo.
errantem Tuscis considere compulit agris 495
et colere externos capta Tolosa Lares.[b]
nec tantum duris nituit sapientia rebus:
pectore non alio prosperiora tulit.
conscius Oceanus virtutum, conscia Thule
et quaecumque ferox arva Britannus arat, 500
qua praefectorum vicibus frenata potestas
perpetuum magni faenus amoris habet.
extremum pars illa quidem discedit in orbem,
sed tamquam media rector in urbe fuit.
plus palmae est illos inter voluisse placere, 505
inter quos minor est displicuisse pudor.
illustris nuper sacrae Comes additus aulae
contempsit summos ruris amore gradus.
hunc ego complexus ventorum adversa fefelli,
dum videor patriae iam mihi parte frui. 510

lutea protulerat sudos Aurora iugales:
antemnas tendi litoris aura iubet.

493 laus (*vel* spes) *Baehrens*. gentis *Burman*.
503 discessit VRB: discedit *Baehrens*.
504 medio . . . orbe VRB: media . . . urbe *Mueller, Baehrens*.

---

[a] Like Shakespeare's "There is some soul of goodness in things evil" (*King Henry V*. Act IV. Sc. i. l. 4).

[b] Victorinus, a Gaul like Rutilius (l. 510), had lost his home in Toulouse owing to its capture by Ataulf, King of the

How oft the fount of blessings springs from ills![a] The hateful weather produced an enjoyable delay; for Victorinus,[b] more than half my soul, by meeting me fulfilled our mutual hopes. The capture of Tolosa had forced him, a wanderer in the lands of Etruria, to settle there and dwell in a foreign home. It was not only amid distress that his wisdom shone: with heart unaltered he could face prosperity. Well did the Ocean know his merits, well did the Far North know them, and all the lands the untamed Briton ploughs, where his self-restrained authority as a Prefect's deputy[c] has earned him the lasting interest paid by strong regard. That region is parted from us far as earth's most distant bound, but he was its ruler as it might have been in the heart of Rome. A greater prize it is to have aimed at popularity with those among whom it is less discredit to be unpopular. Though attached of late to our revered Court as Right Honourable Count,[d] yet in his passion for country-life he disdained the highest grades of advancement. Embracing him I mocked the contrary winds, while I enjoyed already, methought, a part of my own native land.

Saffron Aurora had brought forward her fair-weather team: the breeze offshore tells us to haul

Visigoths, in A.D. 413 (l. 496). He had been *Vicarius* for the Praetorian Prefect of Gaul and as such had exercised authority in Britain. Though he held the distinction of *Comes Illustris*, he preferred country-life in Etruria to attendance at court.

[c] Victorinus had been *Vicarius Britanniarum*: see preceding note.

[d] The three classes of *Comites Illustres* were: (1) *in actu positi*, holding office; (2) *vacantes*, on the list for appointment; (3) *honorarii*, merely titular. Victorinus belonged to the third class.

inconcussa vehit tranquillus aplustria flatus;
mollia securo vela rudente tremunt.
adsurgit ponti medio circumflua Gorgon 515
inter Pisanum Cyrnaicumque latus.
aversor scopulos, damni monumenta recentis;
perditus hic vivo funere civis erat.
noster enim nuper iuvenis maioribus amplis,
nec censu inferior coniugiove minor, 520
impulsus furiis homines terrasque reliquit
et turpem latebram credulus exsul adit.
infelix putat illuvie caelestia pasci
seque premit laesis saevior ipse deis.
num, rogo, deterior Circaeis secta venenis? 525
tunc mutabantur corpora, nunc animi.

inde Triturritam petimus: sic villa vocatur,
quae iacet expulsis insula paene fretis.
namque manu iunctis procedit in aequora saxis,
quique domum posuit condidit ante solum. 530
contiguum stupui portum, quem fama frequentat
Pisarum emporio divitiisque maris.
mira loci facies: pelago pulsantur aperto
inque omnes ventos litora nuda patent;
non ullus tegitur per bracchia tuta recessus, 535
Aeolias possit qui prohibere minas;

518 conditus *Baehrens.*
522 agit VRB: adit *Burman*: amat *Wernsdorf.*
525 num VB: nuc (*sic*) R: non *Barth.*
528 latet VRB: iacet *Heinsius*: patet *Burman*: latere *Keene*: late *Mueller, Baehrens.*
533 pulsatur VRB: pulsantur *Barth, Baehrens.*

---

[a] This island, now Gorgona, lies about 22 miles S.W. of Leghorn. It was long occupied by monks.
[b] Homer, *Odyss.* X. 135–405.

the sail-yards up. The gentle breath of the wind carries the stern-fittings on without vibration; softly flap the sails on rigging free from any strain. There rises in the midst of the sea the wave-girt Gorgon [a] with Pisa and Corsica on either side. I shun the cliffs, which are memorials of recent disaster; here a fellow-countryman met his doom in a living death. For lately one of our youths of high descent, with wealth to match, and marriage-alliance equal to his birth, was impelled by madness to forsake mankind and the world, and made his way, a superstitious exile, to a dishonourable hiding-place. Fancying, poor wretch, that the divine can be nurtured in unwashen filth, he was himself to his own body a crueller tyrant than the offended deities. Surely, I ask, this sect is not less powerful than the drugs of Circe? [b] In her days men's bodies were transformed, now 'tis their minds.

From there we make for Triturrita: [c] that is the name of a residence, a peninsula lying in the wash of baffled waves. For it juts out into the sea on stones which man's hand has put together, and he who built the house had first to make sure building ground. I was astonished at the haven close by, which by report is thronged with Pisa's merchandise and sea-borne wealth. The place has a marvellous appearance. Its shores are buffeted by the open sea and lie exposed to all the winds: here there are not sheltering piers to protect any inner harbour-basin capable of defying the threats of Aeolus.[d]

[c] The Villa Triturrita is conjecturally placed with the neighbouring Portus Pisanus (I. 531, II. 12) between Leghorn and the mouth of the Arno, but the coast has been greatly altered owing to alluvial deposits.

[d] *Cf.* Virg. *Aen.* I. 50–91, the Cavern of the Winds.

sed procera suo praetexitur alga profundo
  molliter offensae non nocitura rati,
et tamen insanas cedendo interligat undas
  nec sinit ex alto grande volumen agi. 540

tempora navigii clarus reparaverat Eurus;
  sed mihi Protadium visere cura fuit:
quem qui forte velit certis cognoscere signis,
  virtutis specimen corde videre putet:
nec magis efficiet similem pictura colore 545
  quam quae de meritis mixta figura venit.
adspicienda procul certo prudentia vultu,
  formaque iustitiae suspicienda micat.
sit fortasse minus, si laudet Gallia civem:
  testis Roma sui praesulis esse potest. 550
substituit patriis mediocres Umbria sedes:
  virtus fortunam fecit utramque parem.
mens invicta viri pro magnis parva tuetur,
  pro parvis animo magna fuere suo.
exiguus regum victores caespes habebat, 555
  et Cincinnatos iugera pauca dabant.
haec etiam nobis non inferiora feruntur
  vomere Serrani Fabriciique foco.

539 caedendo V, *Baehrens*: cedendo B: credendo . . . unda R. interrigat VRB: interligat *Castalio*: internicat *Baehrens*.

544 speciem VRB: specimen *Castalio*. vidente VRB: vigente petat *Baehrens*: petat VB: putat R: videre putet *Heinsius*.

552 utraque V: utrãque R.

555 rectores VRB: victores *Baehrens*.

---

[a] Protadius corresponded with Symmachus, from whose letters we learn that he came from Trèves (*cf.* 549–551). A

But, fringing its own deep-water domain, the tall sea-weed is like to do no damage to a ship that strikes it without shock; and yet in giving way it entangles the furious waves and lets no huge roller surge in from the deep.

A clear South-east wind had brought again the moment for sailing; but I was eager to pay a visit to Protadius:[a] whoever perchance may wish to recognise him by sure signs should think in his heart that he is looking upon a model of goodness: no painting will ever give a truer portrait of him in colour than will the image that comes from his blended excellences. His prudence marked by steady look is evident even to a distant eye; the expression of fair-mindedness shines out, commanding respect. This tribute might perhaps be lessened were it merely that Gaul was praising a fellow-countryman; but Rome can bear witness to her former prefect. Umbria[b] replaced his ancestral home with but a humble abode: his virtue took either lot as equal. The man's unvanquished mind regards small things as great; for to his spirit great things once had been but small. A petty farm used to contain the conquerors of kings, and a few acres yielded men like Cincinnatus.[c] Such contentment in our view is deemed to fall not short of Serranus' plough and Fabricius' hearth.[d]

learned official, he was the son of an eminent rhetorician praised by Ausonius for his lectures in Constantinople, Rome and Bordeaux.

[b] Either Protadius had some property in Umbria proper, or "Umbria" here includes the part of Etruria round Pisa.

[c] For the story see Val. Max. IV. iv. 7.

[d] Rutilius here echoes Virg. *Aen.* VI. 844.

puppibus ergo meis fida in statione locatis
  ipse vehor Pisas qua solet ire pedes. 560
praebet equos, offert etiam carpenta tribunus,
  ex commilitio carus et ipse mihi,
officiis regerem cum regia tecta magister
  armigerasque pii principis excubias.
Alpheae veterem contemplor originis urbem, 565
  quam cingunt geminis Arnus et Ausur aquis;
conum pyramidis coeuntia flumina ducunt:
  intratur modico frons patefacta solo;
sed proprium retinet communi in gurgite nomen,
  et pontum solus scilicet Arnus adit. 570
ante diu quam Troiugenas fortuna Penates
  Laurentinorum regibus insereret,
Elide deductas suscepit Etruria Pisas,
  nominis indicio testificata genus.
hic oblata mihi sancti genitoris imago, 575
  Pisani proprio quam posuere foro.
laudibus amissi cogor lacrimare parentis:
  fluxerunt madidis gaudia maesta genis.
namque pater quondam Tyrrhenis praefuit arvis,
  fascibus et senis credita iura dedit. 580

559 fida VB: tuta R.
573 Elide VB: Aulide R.

---

[a] The other route would have been by sea to the mouth of the Arno and then up the river.

[b] The tribune had served in the *Scholares* or Imperial Guard, who were under the control of Rutilius when *Magister Officiorum* at the palace.

[c] Pisa was reputed to have been founded from the Pisa in Elis, near the river Alpheus (*cf.* 573–574).

So then I moor my ships in the safe anchorage, and myself drive to Pisa by the road the wayfarer goes afoot.[a] I get horses and the offer of carriages too from a tribune personally endeared to me through former comradeship,[b] when as Master of Household Duties I was controller of the palace and of the pious emperor's armed guard. I scan the ancient city of Alphean origin,[c] which the Arno and the Ausur gird with their twin waters; at their junction the rivers form the cone of a pyramid: the opening front offers access on a narrow tongue of land;[d] but 'tis the Arno that retains its own name in the united stream, and in truth the Arno alone arrives at the sea. Long time ere fortune could enrol the house of Trojan birth among Laurentum's royal line,[e] Etruria welcomed Pisa as a colony from Elis, witnessing its origin by the evidence of its name. Here was shown to me the statue of my revered father,[f] erected by the Pisans in their market-place. The honour done to my lost parent made me weep: tears of a saddened joy wet my cheeks with their flow. For my father once was governor of the land of Tuscany and administered the jurisdiction assigned to the six fasces.[g] After he had passed

[d] Those coming up-stream would face the apex of the triangle formed by the union of the two rivers, and by this tongue of land those going inland would enter on the opening "frons," the narrow strip gradually expanding into a broad front.

[e] The claim implies that Pisa was founded before Aeneas arrived in Italy.

[f] The name of Rutilius' father was Lachanius, I. 595.

[g] The *arva* are identical with the *provincia* of I. 597. Six *fasces* were the insignia of the office of *Consularis Tusciae et Umbriae*. A consul in Rome had twelve *fasces*: *cf. Laus Pisonis*, 70 (*supra*, p. 300).

narrabat, memini, multos emensus honores
  Tuscorum regimen plus placuisse sibi;
nam neque opum curam, quamvis sit magna, sacrarum
  nec ius quaesturae grata fuisse magis;
ipsam, si fas est, postponere praefecturam 585
  pronior in Tuscos non dubitabat amor.
nec fallebatur, tam carus et ipse probatis:
  aeternas grates mutua cura canit;
constantemque sibi pariter mitemque fuisse
  insinuant natis qui meminere senes. 590
ipsum me gradibus non degenerasse parentis
  gaudent, et duplici sedulitate fovent.
haec eadem, cum Flaminiae regionibus irem,
  splendoris patrii saepe reperta fides:
famam Lachanii veneratur numinis instar 595
  inter terrigenas Lydia tota suos.
grata bonis priscos retinet provincia mores
  dignaque rectores semper habere bonos,
qualis nunc Decius, Lucilli nobile pignus,
  per Coryti populos arva beata regit. 600
nec mirum, magni si redditus indole nati
  felix tam simili posteritate pater.

---

[a] Rutilius' father had been Count of the Sacred Largesses, Quaestor, and City Prefect.

[b] The *praefectura* here is that of the City Prefect, not of the Praetorian Prefect. Rutilius is apologetic (*si fas est*) over the idea of preferring any dignity to the prefecture of the august city of Rome.

[c] *Canit* here implies laudatory lines on the base of the statue rather than actual song.

[d] The regions in mind were Umbrian and Tuscan districts lying not far off the line of the great northern road from Rome.

[e] *Lydia* here means Etruria, which according to one ancient account was settled from Lydia in Asia Minor.

through many offices,[a] he used to tell, I can recall, that his governorship of Tuscany had been more to his liking than any: for neither the management of the Sacred Largesses, important though it be, nor the authority of a quaestor had brought him more pleasure. His affection, inclining more towards the Tuscans, did not hesitate to give an inferior place, if piety lets it be said, even to his prefecture in Rome.[b] Nor was he mistaken, being an equal favourite with those whom he esteemed: their mutual regard inscribes in verse undying gratitude,[c] and old men who can remember him make known to their sons how firm of purpose he was and at the same time how kindly. They are glad that I myself have not fallen off from my parent's honours, and eagerly give me a warm welcome for his sake and for my own. Often as I traversed the lands near the Flaminian Way [d] I have found the same proof of my father's renown; the whole of Lydia [e] worships Lachanius' [f] fame like some divinity among the natives of her soil. A favourite with the good, this province keeps its old-world ways and deserves always to have good governors, like Decius, the noble offspring of Lucillus,[g] who among the peoples of Corytus [h] rules o'er these happy lands. Small wonder it is that the sire, reproduced in the character of his great son, feels blest in a descendant so like

[f] The fact that the name *Lachanius* does not occur elsewhere is not enough to justify Burman's substitution of *Laecanius*.

[g] Rutilius is our sole source of information about Decius, who was *Consularis Tusciae et Umbriae* in A.D. 416, and about his father, whose satiric powers are compared to those of Juvenal and Turnus.

[h] *Corytus* or *Corythus* (now Cortona) is here used for Etruria, as being one of its ancient towns.

huius vulnificis satira ludente Camenis
  nec Turnus potior nec Iuvenalis erit.
restituit veterem censoria lima pudorem; 605
  dumque malos carpit, praecipit esse bonos.
non olim sacri iustissimus arbiter auri
  circumsistentes reppulit Harpyias?—
Harpyias, quarum discerpitur unguibus orbis,
  quae pede glutineo quod tetigere trahunt, 610
quae luscum faciunt Argum, quae Lyncea caecum,
  inter custodes publica furta volant;
sed non Lucillum Briareia praeda fefellit,
  totque simul manibus restitit una manus.

iamque Triturritam Pisaea ex urbe reversus 615
  aptabam nitido pendula vela Noto,
cum subitis tectus nimbis insorduit aether;
  sparserunt radios nubila rupta vagos.
substitimus. quis enim sub tempestate maligna
  insanituris audeat ire fretis? 620
otia vicinis terimus navalia silvis,
  sectandisque iuvat membra movere feris.
instrumenta parat venandi villicus hospes
  atque olidum doctas nosse cubile canes.
funditur insidiis et rara fraude plagarum 625
  terribilisque cadit fulmine dentis aper,

[603] livente *Baehrens*.
[612] custodes VRB (custodum ·f· *in marg.* V). volant VRB: vorant *Baehrens*.

---

[a] *Huius* applies to Lucillus, not to his son. Turnus, though a satirist, succeeded in surviving under Domitian (*vet. schol.* on Juvenal I. 20; Martial XI. x, *contulit ad saturas ingentia pectora Turnus*). Juvenal belonged to the next generation. Two lines of Turnus (one unintelligible) are given in Morel, *Fragm. Poet. Lat.* p. 134.

himself. His satire, sportive in its mordant poetry, neither Turnus nor Juvenal[a] shall surpass. The censorious file has restored old-fashioned modesty: in attacking the bad, it teaches to be good. Did not that most upright dispenser of the Sacred Largess repel in his day the Harpies who gathered round it?[b] —Harpies, whose claws rend asunder the world, their sticky talons dragging off whatever they touch; creatures who make Argus one-eyed and Lynceus blind;[c] public thieves,[d] they flit among the guardians; but their hundred-handed pillaging did not escape Lucillus, whose single hand checkmated all their hands together.

And now returning from Pisa's city to Triturrita, I was setting the hanging sails to a clear Southern wind, when the sky turned foul under a sudden pall of rain-clouds; the cloven rack scattered its vagrant lightnings. We stopped; who 'neath a spiteful storm would dare to go on seas which threatened madness? The respite from our voyage we spend in the neighbouring forests, delighted to exercise our limbs in the pursuit of game. Our innkeeper supplies the implements for the chase, and hounds trained to discover a strongly scented lair. By means of an ambush and the snare of wide-meshed nets a boar, though terrifying in the flash of his tusks, is overthrown and falls—such a one as

[b] *i.e.* as *Comes Sacrarum Largitionum*, Lucillus balked the greedy "Harpies" in their designs upon public money.

[c] Their peculations are so smart that Argus of the hundred eyes would seem to have only one eye to watch them with, while the keen-eyed Lynceus would seem to be blind.

[d] *publica furta*, abstract for concrete, means the plundering Harpies: *custodes* means the *Comites Sacrarum Largitionum*.

quem Meleagrei vereantur adire lacerti,
qui laxet nodos Amphitryoniadae.
tum responsuros persultat bucina colles,
fitque reportando carmine praeda levis. 630

interea madidis non desinit Africus alis
continuos picea nube negare dies.
iam matutinis Hyades occasibus udae:
iam latet hiberno conditus imbre Lepus,
exiguum radiis sed magnis fluctibus astrum, 635
quo madidam nullus navita linquit humum;
namque procelloso subiungitur Oarioni
aestiferumque Canem roscida praeda fugit.
vidimus excitis pontum flavescere harenis
atque eructato vertice rura tegi; 640
qualiter Oceanus mediis infunditur agris,
destituenda vago cum premit arva salo,
sive alio refluus nostro colliditur orbe
sive corusca suis sidera pascit aquis.

630 reportando V: reportanda RB: reportanti *Castalio*: reportantum *Heinsius*, *Baehrens*.
632 diem *Baehrens*.
643 alto *Baehrens*.

Meleager [a] of the strong shoulders might dread to approach, such a one as would slacken the joints of Hercules. Then mid the echoing hills leap the notes of the bugle-horn, and singing makes the booty light in carrying back.

Meanwhile the South-west wind on dripping wings fails not by means of pitch-black clouds to deny us day after day. 'Tis now the season [b] when the watery Hyades are at their morning setting, and now the Hare is buried and hidden by the winter's rain—a constellation of scanty beams but cause of mighty waves: no sailor puts out from the land which it has soaked; for it is closely linked to stormy Orion, and the dew-drenched prey flees from the heat-fraught Dog-star. We saw the sea yellowing with the disturbance of the sands and pastures covered with the scum it has belched forth, even as the Ocean pours into the midst of fields, when under errant brine it whelms the lands from which it must ebb; whether the truth be that back-flowing from another world [c] it dashes against this world of ours, or that with its own waters it feeds the twinkling stars.

[a] Meleager, son of Oeneus and Althaea (see II. 53), took part in the famous Calydonian boar-hunt.

[b] A wet and stormy period of the year coincides with the setting of the Hyades in morning twilight (late November) and with the setting of the Hare (early November). The Hare is near the left foot of Orion, and flees as a "dew-drenched prey" (638) before the burning Dog-star, Sirius.

[c] *Alio orbe* means the moon. Of the two theories here suggested regarding the cause of tides, the second refers to an ancient belief that sun and stars were fed on the waters of the ocean.

LIBER SECUNDUS

Nondum longus erat nec multa volumina passus,
  iure suo poterat longior esse liber :
taedia continuo timui incessura labori,
  sumere ne lector iuge paveret opus.
saepe cibis affert serus fastidia finis, 5
  gratior est modicis haustibus unda siti :
intervalla viae fessis praestare videtur
  qui notat inscriptus milia crebra lapis.
partimur trepidum per opuscula bina ruborem,
  quem satius fuerat sustinuisse semel. 10

tandem nimbosa maris obsidione solutis
  Pisano portu contigit alta sequi.
arridet placidum radiis crispantibus aequor,
  et sulcata levi murmurat unda sono.
incipiunt Appennini devexa videri, 15
  qua fremit aerio monte repulsa Thetis.

Italiam rerum dominam qui cingere visu
  et totam pariter cernere mente velit,
inveniet quernae similem procedere frondi,
  artatam laterum conveniente sinu. 20

[3] timuit cessura VR (censura *Mueller*: sessura *i.e.* haesura *Baehrens in not.*) : timui incessura *Purser, Keene*.

---

[a] *i.e.* the parchment had not been rolled to a great extent round its stick.

[b] One long book might prove too wearisome : hence the author thinks it advisable to begin a second book. The tone suggests that Book II either was actually or was intended to be much longer than it now is.

BOOK II

My book had not yet grown too long nor undergone many windings of its scroll; [a] in its own right it might have been longer: but I feared weariness would come upon continuous toil—feared lest my reader should shrink from handling an undivided work.[b] Ofttimes the late-delayed end of a feast brings distaste for viands: water in moderate draughts is the more welcome to thirst: the stone that by its lettering marks the many miles seems to afford the tired wayfarer some breaks upon the road. Between two booklets I divide my nervous modesty [c] which it had been better to have faced once only.

Freed at last from the stormy blockade of the sea, we had the fortune to make for the deep from Pisa's harbour. Calm smiles the surface of the waters as the sunbeams glitter: the furrowed wave whispers with gentle plash. The Apennine slopes heave in sight where Thetis [d] chafes at her repulse by a windswept promontory.

He who would embrace in his view Italy, the queen of the world, and form at once a mental picture of the whole land, will find that she extends in shape like an oak leaf,[e] contracted by the converging indentation of her sides. In length the distance

[c] *i.e.* the blushing diffidence of a modest author is spread over two books instead of one. He ought, he feels, to have boldly met his qualms of modesty and concentrated on a single book: he now has to meet them over again.

[d] Thetis, as a sea-goddess, is a metonymy for the sea. Beyond Pisa spurs of the Apennines run out into a lofty headland.

[e] *Cf.* Plin. *N.H.* III. 43, referring to Italy as *folio maxime querno adsimilata.*

milia per longum deciens centena teruntur
  a Ligurum terris ad freta Sicaniae;
in latum variis damnosa anfractibus intrat
  Tyrrheni rabies Hadriacique sali.
qua tamen est iuncti maris angustissima tellus, 25
  triginta et centum milia sola patet.
diversas medius mons obliquatur in undas,
  qua fert atque refert Phoebus uterque diem:
urget Dalmaticos eoo vertice fluctus
  caerulaque occiduis frangit Etrusca iugis. 30
si factum certa mundum ratione fatemur
  consiliumque dei machina tanta fuit,
excubiis Latiis praetexuit Appenninum
  claustraque montanis vix adeunda viis.
invidiam timuit Natura parumque putavit 35
  Arctois Alpes opposuisse minis,
sicut vallavit multis vitalia membris
  nec semel inclusit quae pretiosa tulit:
iam tum multiplici meruit munimine cingi
  sollicitosque habuit Roma futura deos. 40

quo magis est facinus diri Stilichonis acerbum,
  proditor arcani quod fuit imperii.

[34] feris *Schrader*: suis *Baehrens*: viis VRB.
[42] quod VRB: qui *vulgo*.

---

[a] A Roman mile was 143 yards less than an English mile, so that 1000 Roman miles are approximately equal to 918 English miles. This estimate of Italy's length is virtually that of Pliny, *loc. cit.* (1020 miles). But the length in a straight line from the Simplon to Cape Lucca is about 700 miles. Rutilius, as the phrase *milia teruntur* shows (*cf. terere viam*), is calculating, like Pliny, by the roads usually travelled.

[b] In Calabria, which is, however, merely the "toe" of Italy, the peninsula is only about 20 miles wide; but Rutilius follows

by road is one of a thousand miles [a] from the Ligurian territories to the Sicilian straits: on her breadth the destructive fury of the Tuscan and of the Adriatic main makes entry in varied winding curves; but where the land is narrowest between the neighbouring seas it stretches merely one hundred and thirty miles.[b] The central mountain-chain slopes towards the sundered billows where the rising and the setting Sungod brings and withdraws the day: its eastern peaks beset the Dalmatian waves, and its western spurs cleave the blue Tuscan waters. If we acknowledge that the world was made on a definite plan and if this great fabric was a god's design, then as a protective fringe for our Latin outposts he wove the Apennines, barriers scarce approachable by mountain paths. Nature feared men's jealousy (of Italy) and thought it scant defence to put the Alps in Northern invaders' way, just as she has fenced with many limbs our vital parts and placed more than one covering around the precious works she has produced. Even then the Rome that was to be deserved her encirclement of manifold bulwarks and had gods who thought anxiously for her.

Wherefore more bitter is the crime of cursed Stilicho [c] in that he was betrayer of the Empire's

Pliny's estimate of 136 miles from the Adriatic across country to Ostia (*N.H.* III. 44).

[c] For the career of Stilicho, ending with his disgrace and death in A.D. 408, see Gibbon's *Decline and Fall* and Hodgkin's *Italy and Her Invaders*. His victories over Alaric at Pollentia in 403 and over Radagaisus in 405 did not save him from charges of treasonable collusion with the barbarians. His ambition incurred relentless enmity. While the prose-writers Zosimus and Orosius take, like Rutilius, an unfavourable view of his character, Claudian is emphatic in his praises.

Romano generi dum nititur esse superstes,
  crudelis summis miscuit ima furor;
dumque timet quicquid se fecerat ipse timeri, 45
  immisit Latiae barbara tela neci:
visceribus nudis armatum condidit hostem,
  illatae † cladis liberiore dolo.
ipsa satellitibus pellitis Roma patebat
  et captiva prius quam caperetur erat. 50
nec tantum Geticis grassatus proditor armis:
  ante Sibyllinae fata cremavit opis.
odimus Althaeam consumpti funere torris;
  Nisaeum crinem flere putatur avis.
at Stilicho aeterni fatalia pignora regni 55
  et plenas voluit praecipitare colos.
omnia Tartarei cessent tormenta Neronis;
  consumat Stygias tristior umbra faces.
hic immortalem, mortalem perculit ille;
  hic mundi matrem perculit, ille suam. 60

[48] illato *Baehrens*: Iliacae cladis deteriore d. *J. S. Reid.*

---

[a] By letting Alaric enter Italy (II. 46), Stilicho had revealed the "secret" that the barbarians could invade the empire with immunity.

[b] The motive suggested for Stilicho's treachery is that he intended, by the ruin of the Roman race, to further his own interests: he counted on outliving the devastation of Italy.

[c] The implication is that, though he had made himself feared through his influence with the Goths, he is now afraid of them.

[d] The phrasing is difficult. If accepted, it seems to mean that it was safer for Stilicho to employ against Italy a secret pact with the Goths than a military invasion. But if the ablat. of comparison usually supplied with *liberiore* is dispensed with, the sense might be "with the over-bold fraud of ruin inflicted."

[e] Ovid and Claudian apply "pellitus" to the Goths.

secret.[a] As he strove to live longer than the Roman race,[b] his cruel frenzy turned the world upside down, and, while fearing that wherein he had made himself formidable,[c] he let loose the arms of the barbarians to the death of Latium: he plunged an armed foe in the naked vitals of the land, his craft being freer from risk than that of openly inflicted disaster.[d] Even Rome lay exposed to his skin-clad menials [e]—captive ere she could be captured. Nor was it only through Gothic arms that the traitor made his attack: ere this he burned the fateful books which brought the Sibyl's aid.[f] We hate Althaea for the death which came of the brand she gave to the flames;[g] birds, so the fancy runs, weep for Nisus' lock.[h] But it was Stilicho's will to hurl to ruin the eternal empire's fate-fraught pledges and distaffs still charged with destinies. Let every torment of Nero in Tartarus now halt; let an even more miserable ghost consume the Stygian torches.[i] Stilicho's victim was immortal, Nero's was mortal; the one destroyed the world's mother, the other his own.

[f] Rutilius is the sole authority for the allegation that Stilicho burned the Sibylline books which the Romans consulted in times of crisis. Their destruction thus preceded the fall of Rome by only a few years.

[g] Althaea caused the death of her son Meleager by burning the magical firebrand on which his life depended: *cf.* note on Pentadius I. (*De Fortuna*) 21–22, *supra* p. 545.

[h] Scylla caused the death of her father Nisus by depriving him of the purple lock on which his life depended: see the *Ciris* in the *Appendix Vergiliana*: *cf. crinem Nisi*, Nemes. *Cyn.* 44.

[i] *i.e.* Stilicho should suffer under the torches of the Furies even more horrible punishment than that inflicted upon the matricide Nero in Tartarus.

sed deverticulo fuimus fortasse loquaces:
  carmine propositum iam repetamus iter.
advehimur celeri candentia moenia lapsu:
  nominis est auctor Sole corusca soror.
indigenis superat ridentia lilia saxis, 65
  et levi radiat picta nitore silex.
dives marmoribus tellus, quae luce coloris
  provocat intactas luxuriosa nives.

. . . . .

[62] propositum V: preposito R: proposito B.

But in this digression we have perhaps been garrulous: let us now resume in verse the voyage we had set ourselves. On swiftly gliding course we bear towards white glittering walls: the sister who draws her radiance from the Sun is the bestower of the city's name.[a] In the colour of its native rocks it surpasses smiling lilies, and the stone flashes bedecked in polished radiance. Rich in marble, it is a land which, revelling in its white light, challenges the virgin snows.

. . . . .

[a] With this allusion to the town of Luna and the brief glance at its marble quarries, the poem, as we have it, ends abruptly.

INDEX
OF PROPER NOUNS AND ADJECTIVES

The numbers refer to pages of the Latin text: *adj.* = *adjective.*

INDEX

INDEX

INDEX

INDEX

INDEX

PRINTED IN GREAT BRITAIN BY
RICHARD CLAY AND COMPANY, LTD.,
BUNGAY, SUFFOLK.

THE LOEB CLASSICAL LIBRARY

VOLUMES ALREADY PUBLISHED

Latin Authors

AMMIANUS MARCELLINUS. Translated by J. C. Rolfe. 3 Vols.

APULEIUS: THE GOLDEN ASS (METAMORPHOSES). W. Adlington (1566). Revised by S. Gaselee.

ST. AUGUSTINE: CITY OF GOD. 7 Vols. Vol. I. G. H. McCracken. Vol. VI. W. C. Greene.

ST. AUGUSTINE, CONFESSIONS OF. W. Watts (1631). 2 Vols.

ST. AUGUSTINE, SELECT LETTERS. J. H. Baxter.

AUSONIUS. H. G. Evelyn White. 2 Vols.

BEDE. J. E. King. 2 Vols.

BOETHIUS: TRACTS and DE CONSOLATIONE PHILOSOPHIAE. Rev. H. F. Stewart and E. K. Rand.

CAESAR: ALEXANDRIAN, AFRICAN and SPANISH WARS. A. G. Way.

CAESAR: CIVIL WARS. A. G. Peskett.

CAESAR: GALLIC WAR. H. J. Edwards.

CATO: DE RE RUSTICA; VARRO: DE RE RUSTICA. H. B. Ash and W. D. Hooper.

CATULLUS. F. W. Cornish; TIBULLUS. J. B. Postgate; PERVIGILIUM VENERIS. J. W. Mackail.

CELSUS: DE MEDICINA. W. G. Spencer. 3 Vols.

CICERO: BRUTUS, and ORATOR. G. L. Hendrickson and H. M. Hubbell.

[CICERO]: AD HERENNIUM. H. Caplan.

CICERO: DE ORATORE, etc. 2 Vols. Vol. I. DE ORATORE, Books I. and II. E. W. Sutton and H. Rackham. Vol. II. DE ORATORE, Book III. De Fato; Paradoxa Stoicorum; De Partitione Oratoria. H. Rackham.

CICERO: DE FINIBUS. H. Rackham.

CICERO: DE INVENTIONE, etc. H. M. Hubbell.

CICERO: DE NATURA DEORUM and ACADEMICA. H. Rackham.

CICERO: DE OFFICIIS. Walter Miller.

CICERO: DE REPUBLICA and DE LEGIBUS; SOMNIUM SCIPIONIS. Clinton W. Keyes.

Cicero: De Senectute, De Amicitia, De Divinatione. W. A. Falconer.

Cicero: In Catilinam, Pro Flacco, Pro Murena, Pro Sulla. Louis E. Lord.

Cicero: Letters to Atticus. E. O. Winstedt. 3 Vols.

Cicero: Letters to His Friends. W. Glynn Williams. 3 Vols.

Cicero: Philippics. W. C. A. Ker.

Cicero: Pro Archia Post Reditum, De Domo, De Haruspicum Responsis, Pro Plancio. N. H. Watts.

Cicero: Pro Caecina, Pro Lege Manilia, Pro Cluentio, Pro Rabirio. H. Grose Hodge.

Cicero: Pro Caelio, De Provinciis Consularibus, Pro Balbo. R. Gardner.

Cicero: Pro Milone, In Pisonem, Pro Scauro, Pro Fonteio, Pro Rabirio Postumo, Pro Marcello, Pro Ligario, Pro Rege Deiotaro. N. H. Watts.

Cicero: Pro Quinctio, Pro Roscio Amerino, Pro Roscio Comoedo, Contra Rullum. J. H. Freese.

Cicero: Pro Sestio, In Vatinium. R. Gardner.

Cicero: Tusculan Disputations. J. E. King.

Cicero: Verrine Orations. L. H. G. Greenwood. 2 Vols.

Claudian. M. Platnauer. 2 Vols.

Columella: De Re Rustica. De Arboribus. H. B. Ash, E. S. Forster and E. Heffner. 3 Vols.

Curtius, Q.: History of Alexander. J. C. Rolfe. 2 Vols.

Florus. E. S. Forster; and Cornelius Nepos. J. C. Rolfe.

Frontinus: Stratagems and Aqueducts. C. E. Bennett and M. B. McElwain.

Fronto: Correspondence. C. R. Haines. 2 Vols.

Gellius, J. C. Rolfe. 3 Vols.

Horace: Odes and Epodes. C. E. Bennett.

Horace: Satires, Epistles, Ars Poetica. H. R. Fairclough.

Jerome: Selected Letters. F. A. Wright.

Juvenal and Persius. G. G. Ramsay.

Livy. B. O. Foster, F. G. Moore, Evan T. Sage, and A. C. Schlesinger and R. M. Geer (General Index). 14 Vols.

Lucan. J. D. Duff.

Lucretius. W. H. D. Rouse.

Martial. W. C. A. Ker. 2 Vols.

Minor Latin Poets: from Publilius Syrus to Rutilius Namatianus, including Grattius, Calpurnius Siculus, Nemesianus, Avianus, and others with "Aetna" and the "Phoenix." J. Wight Duff and Arnold M. Duff.

Ovid: The Art of Love and Other Poems. J. H. Mozley.

Ovid: Fasti. Sir James G. Frazer.

Ovid: Heroides and Amores. Grant Showerman.

Ovid: Metamorphoses. F. J. Miller. 2 Vols.

Ovid: Tristia and Ex Ponto. A. L. Wheeler.

Persius. Cf. Juvenal.

Petronius. M. Heseltine; Seneca; Apocolocyntosis. W. H. D. Rouse.

Plautus. Paul Nixon. 5 Vols.

Pliny: Letters. Melmoth's Translation revised by W. M. L. Hutchinson. 2 Vols.

Pliny: Natural History. H. Rackham and W. H. S. Jones. 10 Vols. Vols. I.–V. and IX. H. Rackham. Vols. VI. and VII. W. H. S. Jones.

Propertius. H. E. Butler.

Prudentius. H. J. Thomson. 2 Vols.

Quintilian. H. E. Butler. 4 Vols.

Remains of Old Latin. E. H. Warmington. 4 Vols. Vol. I. (Ennius and Caecilius.) Vol. II. (Livius, Naevius, Pacuvius, Accius.) Vol. III. (Lucilius and Laws of XII Tables.) (Archaic Inscriptions.)

Sallust. J. C. Rolfe.

Scriptores Historiae Augustae. D. Magie. 3 Vols.

Seneca: Apocolocyntosis. Cf. Petronius.

Seneca: Epistulae Morales. R. M. Gummere. 3 Vols.

Seneca: Moral Essays. J. W. Basore. 3 Vols.

Seneca: Tragedies. F. J. Miller. 2 Vols.

Sidonius: Poems and Letters. W. B. Anderson. 2 Vols.

Silius Italicus. J. D. Duff. 2 Vols.

Statius. J. H. Mozley. 2 Vols.

Suetonius. J. C. Rolfe. 2 Vols.

Tacitus: Dialogues. Sir Wm. Peterson. Agricola and Germania. Maurice Hutton.

Tacitus: Histories and Annals. C. H. Moore and J. Jackson. 4 Vols.

Terence. John Sargeaunt. 2 Vols.

Tertullian: Apologia and De Spectaculis. T. R. Glover. Minucius Felix. G. H. Rendall.

Valerius Flaccus. J. H. Mozley.

Varro: De Lingua Latina. R. G. Kent. 2 Vols.

Velleius Paterculus and Res Gestae Divi Augusti. F. W. Shipley.

Virgil. H. R. Fairclough. 2 Vols.

Vitruvius: De Architectura. F. Granger. 2 Vols.

Greek Authors

Achilles Tatius. S. Gaselee.

Aelian: On the Nature of Animals. A. F. Scholfield. 3 Vols.

Aeneas Tacticus, Asclepiodotus and Onasander. The Illinois Greek Club.

Aeschines. C. D. Adams.

Aeschylus. H. Weir Smyth. 2 Vols.

Alciphron, Aelian, Philostratus: Letters. A. R. Benner and F. H. Fobes.

Andocides, Antiphon, Cf. Minor Attic Orators.

Apollodorus. Sir James G. Frazer. 2 Vols.

Apollonius Rhodius. R. C. Seaton.

The Apostolic Fathers. Kirsopp Lake. 2 Vols.

Appian: Roman History. Horace White. 4 Vols.

Aratus. Cf. Callimachus.

Aristophanes. Benjamin Bickley Rogers. 3 Vols. Verse trans.

Aristotle: Art of Rhetoric. J. H. Freese.

Aristotle: Athenian Constitution, Eudemian Ethics, Vices and Virtues. H. Rackham.

Aristotle: Generation of Animals. A. L. Peck.

Aristotle: Metaphysics. H. Tredennick. 2 Vols.

Aristotle: Meterologica. H. D. P. Lee.

Aristotle: Minor Works. W. S. Hett. On Colours, On Things Heard, On Physiognomies, On Plants, On Marvellous Things Heard, Mechanical Problems, On Indivisible Lines, On Situations and Names of Winds, On Melissus, Xenophanes, and Gorgias.

Aristotle: Nicomachean Ethics. H. Rackham.

Aristotle: Oeconomica and Magna Moralia. G. C. Armstrong; (with Metaphysics, Vol. II.).

Aristotle: On the Heavens. W. K. C. Guthrie.

Aristotle: On the Soul. Parva Naturalia. On Breath. W. S. Hett.

Aristotle: Categories, On Interpretation, Prior Analytics. H. P. Cooke and H. Tredennick.

Aristotle: Posterior Analytics, Topics. H. Tredennick and E. S. Forster.

Aristotle: On Sophistical Refutations.

On Coming to be and Passing Away, On the Cosmos. E. S. Forster and D. J. Furley.

Aristotle: Parts of Animals. A. L. Peck; Motion and Progression of Animals. E. S. Forster.

ARISTOTLE: PHYSICS. Rev. P. Wicksteed and F. M. Cornford. 2 Vols.

ARISTOTLE: POETICS and LONGINUS. W. Hamilton Fyfe; DEMETRIUS ON STYLE. W. Rhys Roberts.

ARISTOTLE: POLITICS. H. Rackham.

ARISTOTLE: PROBLEMS. W. S. Hett. 2 Vols.

ARISTOTLE: RHETORICA AD ALEXANDRUM (with PROBLEMS. Vol. II.) H. Rackham.

ARRIAN: HISTORY OF ALEXANDER and INDICA. Rev. E. Iliffe Robson. 2 Vols.

ATHENAEUS: DEIPNOSOPHISTAE. C. B. GULICK. 7 Vols.

ST. BASIL: LETTERS. R. J. Deferrari. 4 Vols.

CALLIMACHUS: FRAGMENTS. C. A. Trypanis.

CALLIMACHUS, Hymns and Epigrams, and LYCOPHRON. A. W. Mair; ARATUS. G. R. MAIR.

CLEMENT of ALEXANDRIA. Rev. G. W. Butterworth.

COLLUTHUS. Cf. OPPIAN.

DAPHNIS AND CHLOE. Thornley's Translation revised by J. M. Edmonds; and PARTHENIUS. S. Gaselee.

DEMOSTHENES I.: OLYNTHIACS, PHILIPPICS and MINOR ORATIONS. I.–XVII. AND XX. J. H. Vince.

DEMOSTHENES II.: DE CORONA and DE FALSA LEGATIONE. C. A. Vince and J. H. Vince.

DEMOSTHENES III.: MEIDIAS, ANDROTION, ARISTOCRATES, TIMOCRATES and ARISTOGEITON, I. AND II. J. H. Vince.

DEMOSTHENES IV.–VI.: PRIVATE ORATIONS and IN NEAERAM. A. T. Murray.

DEMOSTHENES VII.: FUNERAL SPEECH, EROTIC ESSAY, EXORDIA and LETTERS. N. W. and N. J. DeWitt.

DIO CASSIUS: ROMAN HISTORY. E. Cary. 9 Vols.

DIO CHRYSOSTOM. J. W. Cohoon and H. Lamar Crosby. 5 Vols.

DIODORUS SICULUS. 12 Vols. Vols. I.–VI. C. H. Oldfather. Vol. VII. C. L. Sherman. Vols. IX. and X. R. M. Geer. Vol. XI. F. Walton.

DIOGENES LAERITIUS. R. D. Hicks. 2 Vols.

DIONYSIUS OF HALICARNASSUS: ROMAN ANTIQUITIES. Spelman's translation revised by E. Cary. 7 Vols.

EPICTETUS. W. A. Oldfather. 2 Vols.

EURIPIDES. A. S. Way. 4 Vols. Verse trans.

EUSEBIUS: ECCLESIASTICAL HISTORY. Kirsopp Lake and J. E. L. Oulton. 2 Vols.

GALEN: ON THE NATURAL FACULTIES. A. J. Brock.

THE GREEK ANTHOLOGY. W. R. Paton. 5 Vols.

GREEK ELEGY AND IAMBUS with the ANACREONTEA. J. M. Edmonds. 2 Vols.

The Greek Bucolic Poets (Theocritus, Bion, Moschus). J. M. Edmonds.

Greek Mathematical Works. Ivor Thomas. 2 Vols.

Herodes. Cf. Theophrastus: Characters.

Herodotus. A. D. Godley. 4 Vols.

Hesiod and The Homeric Hymns. H. G. Evelyn White.

Hippocrates and the Fragments of Heracleitus. W. H. S. Jones and E. T. Withington. 4 Vols.

Homer: Iliad. A. T. Murray. 2 Vols.

Homer: Odyssey. A. T. Murray. 2 Vols.

Isaeus. E. W. Forster.

Isocrates. George Norlin and LaRue Van Hook. 3 Vols.

St. John Damascene: Barlaam and Ioasaph. Rev. G. R. Woodward and Harold Mattingly.

Josephus. H. St. J. Thackeray and Ralph Marcus. 9 Vols. Vols. I.–VII.

Julian. Wilmer Cave Wright. 3 Vols.

Lucian. 8 Vols. Vols. I.–V. A. M. Harmon. Vol. VI. K. Kilburn.

Lycophron. Cf. Callimachus.

Lyra Graeca. J. M. Edmonds. 3 Vols.

Lysias. W. R. M. Lamb.

Manetho. W. G. Waddell: Ptolemy: Tetrabiblos. F. E. Robbins.

Marcus Aurelius. C. R. Haines.

Menander. F. G. Allinson.

Minor Attic Orators (Antiphon, Andocides, Lycurgus, Demades, Dinarchus, Hypereides). K. J. Maidment and J. O. Burrt. 2 Vols.

Nonnos: Dionysiaca. W. H. D. Rouse. 3 Vols.

Oppian, Colluthus, Tryphiodorus. A. W. Mair.

Papyri. Non-Literary Selections. A. S. Hunt and C. C. Edgar. 2 Vols. Literary Selections (Poetry). D. L. Page.

Parthenius. Cf. Daphnis and Chloe.

Pausanias: Description of Greece. W. H. S. Jones. 4 Vols. and Companion Vol. arranged by R. E. Wycherley.

Philo. 10 Vols. Vols. I.–V.; F. H. Colson and Rev. G. H. Whitaker. Vols. VI.–IX.; F. H. Colson.

Philo: two supplementary Vols. (*Translation only.*) Ralph Marcus.

Philostratus: The Life of Apollonius of Tyana. F. C. Conybeare. 2 Vols.

Philostratus: Imagines; Callistratus: Descriptions. A. Fairbanks.

Philostratus and Eunapius: Lives of the Sophists. Wilmer Cave Wright.

Pindar. Sir J. E. Sandys.

Plato: Charmides, Alcibiades, Hipparchus, The Lovers, Theages, Minos and Epinomis. W. R. M. Lamb.

Plato: Cratylus, Parmenides, Greater Hippias, Lesser Hippias. H. N. Fowler.

Plato: Euthyphro, Apology, Crito, Phaedo, Phaedrus. H. N. Fowler.

Plato: Laches, Protagoras, Meno, Euthydemus. W. R. M. Lamb.

Plato: Laws. Rev. R. G. Bury. 2 Vols.

Plato: Lysis, Symposium, Gorgias. W. R. M. Lamb.

Plato: Republic. Paul Shorey. 2 Vols.

Plato: Statesman, Philebus. H. N. Fowler; Ion. W. R. M. Lamb.

Plato: Theaetetus and Sophist. H. N. Fowler.

Plato: Timaeus, Critias, Clitopho, Menexenus, Epistulae. Rev. R. G. Bury.

Plutarch: Moralia. 15 Vols. Vols. I.–V. F. C. Babbitt. Vol. VI. W. C. Helmbold. Vol. VII. P. H. De Lacy and B. Einarson. Vol. IX. E. L. Minar, Jr., F. H. Sandbach, W. C. Helmbold. Vol. X. H. N. Fowler. Vol. XII. H. Cherniss and W. C. Helmbold.

Plutarch: The Parallel Lives. B. Perrin. 11 Vols.

Polybius. W. R. Paton. 6 Vols.

Procopius: History of the Wars. H. B. Dewing. 7 Vols.

Ptolemy: Tetrabiblos. Cf. Manetho.

Quintus Smyrnaeus. A. S. Way. Verse trans.

Sextus Empiricus. Rev. R. G. Bury. 4 Vols.

Sophocles. F. Storr. 2 Vols. Verse trans.

Strabo: Geography. Horace L. Jones. 8 Vols.

Theophrastus: Characters. J. M. Edmonds. Herodes, etc. A. D. Knox.

Theophrastus: Enquiry into Plants. Sir Arthur Hort, Bart. 2 Vols.

Thucydides. C. F. Smith. 4 Vols.

Tryphiodorus. Cf. Oppian.

Xenophon: Cyropaedia. Walter Miller. 2 Vols.

Xenophon: Hellenica, Anabasis, Apology, and Symposium. C. L. Brownson and O. J. Todd. 3 Vols.

Xenophon: Memorabilia and Oeconomicus. E. C. Marchant.

Xenophon: Scripta Minora. E. C. Marchant.

IN PREPARATION

Greek Authors

ARISTOTLE: HISTORY OF ANIMALS. A. L. Peck.
PLOTINUS: A. H. Armstrong.

Latin Authors

BABRIUS AND PHAEDRUS. Ben E. Perry.

DESCRIPTIVE PROSPECTUS ON APPLICATION

London **WILLIAM HEINEMANN LTD**
Cambridge, Mass. **HARVARD UNIVERSITY PRESS**